CLYMER

EVINRUDE/JOHNSON

OUTBOARD SHOP MANUAL
1.5-125 HP • 1956-1972

The world's finest publisher of mechanical how-to manuals

Business Directories & Books

P.O. Box 12901, Overland Park, KS 66282-2901

Copyright ©1989 PRIMEDIA Business Magazines and Media Inc.

FIRST EDITION
First Printing March, 1986
Second Printing October, 1986
Third Printing February, 1987
Fourth Printing September, 1987
Fifth Printing March, 1988
Sixth Printing June, 1988

SECOND EDITION
First Printing March, 1989
Second Printing June, 1989
Third Printing February, 1990
Fourth Printing September, 1990
Fifth Printing November, 1991
Sixth Printing September, 1992
Seventh Printing July, 1993
Eighth Printing January, 1994
Ninth Pringing November, 1994
Tenth Printing September, 1995
Eleventh Printing November, 1996
Twelfth Printing May, 1998
Thirteenth Printing June, 1999
Fourteenth Printing February, 2001
Fifteenth Printing July, 2002
Sixteenth Printing November, 2003

Printed in U.S.A.

CLYMER and colophon are registered trademarks of PRIMEDIA Business Magazines and Media Inc.

This book was printed at Von Hoffmann an ISO certified company.

ISBN: 0-89287-413-9

TOOLS AND TEST EQUIPMENT: Thorsen Tool, Dallas, Texas. and Dixson, Inc., Grand Junction, Colorado.

TECHNICAL ILLUSTRATIONS: Mitzi McCarthy, Diana Kirkland, Steve Amos and Carl Rohkar.

TECHNICAL ASSISTANCE: Certified Marine, Tujunga, California and Marine Specialties, Sun Valley, California.

COVER: Photographed by Michael Brown Photographic Productions, Los Angeles, California. Assisted by Larry Rogers. Boat courtesy of Jeff Brown and The Anchor.

All rights reserved. Reproduction or use, without express permission, of editorial or pictorial content, in any manner, is prohibited. No patent liability is assumed with respect to the use of the information contained herein. While every precaution has been taken in the preparation of this book, the publisher assumes no responsibility for errors or omissions. Neither is any liability assumed for damages resulting from use of the information contained herein. Publication of the servicing information in this manual does not imply approval of the manufacturers of the products covered.

All instructions and diagrams have been checked for accuracy and ease of application; however, success and safety in working with tools depend to a great extent upon individual accuracy, skill and caution. For this reason, the publishers are not able to guarantee the result of any procedure contained herein. Nor can they assume responsibility for any damage to property or injury to persons occasioned from the procedures. Persons engaging in the procedure do so entirely at their own risk.

General Information	1
Tools and Techniques	2
Troubleshooting	3
Lubrication, Maintenance and Tune-up	4
Engine Synchronization and Linkage Adjustments	5
Fuel System	6
Electrical Systems	7
Power Head	8
Gearcase	9
Automatic Rewind Starters	10
Power Tilt System	11
Index	12
Wiring Diagrams	13

CLYMER PUBLICATIONS
PRIMEDIA Business Magazines & Media

Chief Executive Officer Martin Maleska
Senior Vice President, Sales Operation John French
Vice President, PRIMEDIA Business Directories & Books Bob Moraczewski

EDITORIAL

Managing Editor
James Grooms

Associate Editor
Jason Beaver

Technical Writers
Ron Wright
Ed Scott
George Parise
Mark Rolling
Michael Morlan
Jay Bogart

Editorial Production Manager
Dylan Goodwin

Senior Production Editors
Greg Araujo
Shirley Renicker

Production Editors
Holly Messinger
Shara Pierceall
Darin Watson

Associate Production Editor
Susan Hartington

Technical Illustrators
Steve Amos
Errol McCarthy
Mitzi McCarthy
Bob Meyer
Mike Rose

MARKETING/SALES AND ADMINISTRATION

Publisher
Shawn Etheridge

Marketing Manager
Elda Starke

Advertising & Promotions Coordinators
Melissa Abbott
Wendy Stringfellow

Art Directors
Chris Paxton

Sales Managers
Ted Metzger, Manuals
Dutch Sadler, Marine
Matt Tusken, Motorcycles

Sales Coordinator
Marcia Jungles

Operations Manager
Patricia Kowalczewski

Customer Service Manager
Terri Cannon

Customer Service Supervisor
Ed McCarty

Customer Service Representatives
Susan Kohlmeyer
April LeBlond
Courtney Hollars
Jennifer Lassiter
Ernesto Suarez
Shawna Davis

Warehouse & Inventory Manager
Leah Hicks

The following product lines are published by PRIMEDIA Business Directories & Books.

More information available at *primediabooks.com*

CONTENTS

QUICK REFERENCE DATA IX

CHAPTER ONE
GENERAL INFORMATION 1
- Manual organization 1
- Notes, cautions and warnings................1
- Torque specifications 2
- Engine operation 2
- Fasteners..2
- Lubricants 8
- Gasket sealant 10
- Galvanic corrosion 11
- Protection from galvanic corrosion.......13
- Propellers..14

CHAPTER TWO
TOOLS AND TECHNIQUES 21
- Safety first 21
- Basic hand tools 21
- Test equipment..................................26
- Service hints.....................................28
- Special tips 30
- Mechanic's techniques 31

CHAPTER THREE
TROUBLESHOOTING..33
- Operating requirements......................34
- Starting system 34
- D.C. generator charging system 37
- Alternator charging system 39
- 20 amp charging system 41
- 6-15 amp charging systems 43
- Clipper circuit....................................45
- Shift circuit 46
- Ignition system 48
- Flywheel magneto breaker point ignition troubleshooting 49
- Battery breaker point (distributor) ignition troubleshooting 50
- CD breaker point ignition troubleshooting...................51
- CD breakerless ignition troubleshooting 59
- Fuel system 73
- Engine temperature and overheating 74
- Engine...75

CHAPTER FOUR
LUBRICATION, MAINTENANCE AND TUNE-UP 85
- Lubrication 85
- Storage...90
- Complete submersion........................96
- Anti-corrosion maintenance................97
- Engine flushing.................................97
- Tune-up..98

CHAPTER FIVE
ENGINE SYNCHRONIZATION AND LINKAGE ADJUSTMENTS 118

Engine timing 118	1- and 2-cylinder engines 120
Synchronizing 119	3- and 4-cylinder engines 128

CHAPTER SIX
FUEL SYSTEM 156

Fuel pump 156	Model E carburetor 178
Carburetors 161	Model F carburetor 182
Model A carburetor 163	Model G carburetor 188
Model B carburetor 166	Choke solenoid service 192
Model C carburetor 168	Fuel tank 193
Model D carburetor 175	Fuel line and primer bulb 196

CHAPTER SEVEN
ELECTRICAL SYSTEMS 197

Battery 197	Distributor magneto breaker point ignition 218
Battery charging system 203	Distributor battery breaker point ignition 220
Electric starting system 208	Distributor CD sensor ignition 223
Ignition systems 216	Flywheel CD sensor ignition 225
Flywheel magneto breaker point ignition 216	Flywheel CD breaker point ignition 226

CHAPTER EIGHT
POWERHEAD 229

Engine serial number 230	Breakerless distributor (flywheel CD ignition) ... 235
Fasteners and torque 230	Stator (flywheel CD ignition) 236
Gaskets and sealants 231	Power head 236
Flywheel 231	Reed block service 272
Armature plate (flywheel magneto ignition) 232	Thermostat service 273
Breaker point distributor (flywheel CD ignition) ... 234	Safety switch 274

CHAPTER NINE
GEARCASE 281

Service precautions 282	Manual shift gearcase (single housing) 302
Propeller 282	Electric shift gearcase 307
Water pump 283	Hydro-electric shift gearcase 313
Gearcase cleaning and inspection (all models) ... 289	Pressure and vacuum test 324
Manual shift gearcase (split lower housing) 294	

CHAPTER TEN
AUTOMATIC REWIND STARTERS 326

Engine cover starter 326	Flywheel mounted starter 335
Swing arm gear drive starter 329	Starter lockout adjustment 340
Side-mounted pinion gear starter 332	

CHAPTER ELEVEN
POWER TILT SYSTEM 341
- Components 341
- Operation 342
- Hydraulic pump fluid check 342
- Hydraulic pump fluid refill 342
- Preliminary check procedure 342
- Troubleshooting 343
- Electric motor test 344
- Tilt cylinder check 344
- Tilt cylinder removal/installation 345

INDEX 346

WIRING DIAGRAMS ....end of book

Quick Reference Data

TEST WHEEL PERFORMANCE

Model	Test wheel	Minimum engine rpm[1]
1.5	*	4,400
3	203229	3,850
5.5, 6	303592	4,000
7.5	203466	4,200
9.5	*	4,400
10		
1956-1957	277278	4,050
1958-1962	377455	4,050
15, 18		
1956	277278	4,500
1957-1962	376913	4,500
25, 28		
1956	375837	4,400
1957-1959	377014	4,400
1960-1962	378566	4,400
30, 33, 35	*	4,500
40	*	4,400
50 (1958-1964)	377400	4,400
75 (1958-1964)	378046	4,400
85	*	4,700

* Information not available.
1. Based on operation in test tank approximately 60 in. × 60 in. × 40 in. filled with 565 gallons of water @ 600 ft. above sea level.

SELF-DISCHARGE RATE

Temperature	Approximate allowable self-discharge per day for first 10 days (specific gravity)
100° F (37.8° C)	0.0025 points
80° F (26.7° C)	0.0010 points
50° F (10.0° C)	0.0003 points

TIGHTENING TORQUES

Standard torque values	in.-lb.	ft.-lb.
No. 6	7-10	
No. 8	15-22	
No. 10	25-35	
No. 12	35-40	
1/4 in.	60-80	5-7
5/16 in.	120-140	10-12
3/8 in.	220-240	18-20
7/16 in.	340-360	28-30

TUNE-UP SPECIFICATIONS (1- AND 2-CYLINDER) (continued)

Model year/hp	Adjustment* procedure	Adjustment* method	Wide open throttle rpm
1964			
3	3	A	4,000
5.5	3	A	4,000
9.5	3	B	4,500
18	3	A	4,500
28	5	C	4,500
40	5	D	4,500
1965			
3	3	A	4,000
5	3	A	4,000
6	3	A	4,500
9.5	3	B	4,500
18	3	A	4,500
33	5	C	4,500
40	5	D	4,500
1966			
3	3	A	4,000
5	3	A	4,000
6	3	A	4,500
9.5	3	B	4,500
18	3	A	4,500
20	3	A	4,500
33	5	C	4,500
40	5	D	4,500
1967			
3	2	A	4,000
5	2	A	4,000
6	2	A	4,500
9.5	3	B	4,500
18	4	A	4,500
20	4	A	4,500
33	5	C	4,500
40	5	D	4,500
1968			
1.5	1	A	4,000
3	1	A	4,000
5	1	A	4,000
6	1	A	4,500
9.5	3	B	4,500
18	4	A	4,500
20	4	A	4,500
33	5	C	4,500
40	5	D	4,500
1969			
1.5	1	A	4,000
4	2	A	4,500
6	2	A	4,500
9.5	3	B	4,500
18	4	D	4,500
20	4	D	4,500
25	4	D	5,500
33	5	C	4,500
40	5	D	4,500

(continued)

TUNE-UP SPECIFICATIONS (1- AND 2-CYLINDER)

Model year/hp	Adjustment* procedure	Adjustment* method	Wide open throttle rpm
1956			
3	3	A	4,000
5.5	3	A	4,000
7.5	3	A	4,000
10	3	A	4,000
15	3	A	4,000
30	5	A	4,000
1957			
3	3	A	4,000
5.5	3	A	4,000
7.5	3	A	4,000
10	3	A	4,000
18	3	A	4,500
35	5	A	4,500
1958			
3	3	A	4,000
5.5	3	A	4,000
7.5	3	A	4,000
10	3	A	4,000
18	3	A	4,500
35	5	C	4,500
1959			
3	3	A	4,000
5.5	3	A	4,000
10	3	A	4,000
18	3	A	4,500
35	5	C	4,500
1960			
3	3	A	4,000
5.5	3	A	4,000
10	3	A	4,500
18	3	A	4,500
40	5	C	4,500
1961			
3	3	A	4,000
5.5	3	A	4,000
10	3	A	4,500
18	3	A	4,500
40	5	C	4,500
1962			
3	3	A	4,000
5.5	3	A	4,000
10	3	A	4,500
18	3	A	4,500
28	5	C	4,500
40	5	C	4,500
1963			
3	3	A	4,000
5.5	3	A	4,000
10	3	A	4,500
18	3	A	4,500
28	5	C	4,500
40	5	D	4,500

(continued)

TUNE-UP SPECIFICATIONS (1- AND 2-CYLINDER) (continued)

Model year/hp	Adjustment* procedure	Adjustment* method	Wide open throttle rpm
1970			
1.5	1	A	4,000
4	2	A	4,500
6	2	A	4,500
9.5	3	B	4,500
18	4	D	4,500
20	4	D	4,500
25	4	D	5,500
33	5	C	4,500
40	5	D	4,500
1971			
2	1	A	4,500
4	2	A	4,500
6	2	A	4,500
9.5	3	B	4,500
18	4	D	4,500
20	4	D	4,500
25	4	D	5,500
40	5	C	4,500
50	3	E	5,500
1972			
2	1	A	4,500
4	2	A	4,500
6	2	A	4,500
9.5	3	B	4,500
18	4	D	4,500
20	4	D	4,500
25	4	D	5,500
40	5	C	4,500
50	3	E	5,500

*See Chapter Five.

APPROXIMATE STATE OF CHARGE

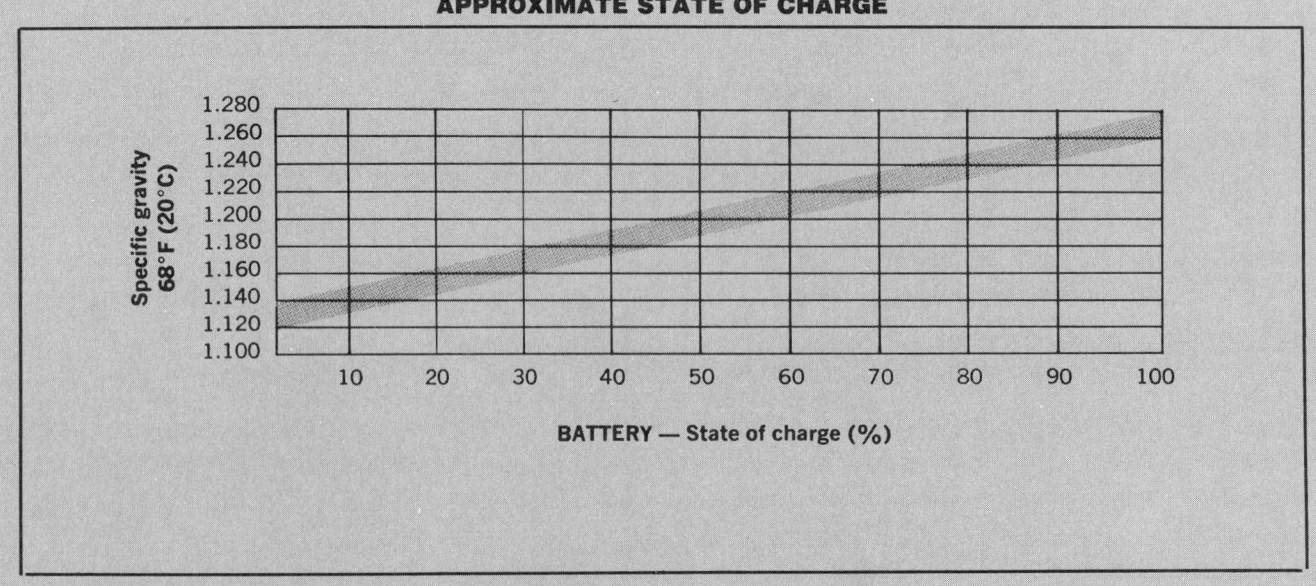

CLYMER

EVINRUDE/JOHNSON
OUTBOARD SHOP MANUAL
1.5-125 HP • 1956-1972

Introduction

This Clymer shop manual covers service and repair of all Evinrude/Johnson 1.5-125 hp engines from 1956-1972. Step-by-step instructions and hundreds of illustrations guide you through jobs ranging from simple maintenance to complete overhaul.

This manual can be used by anyone from a first time amateur to a professional mechanic. Easy to read type, detailed drawings and clear photographs give you all the information you need to do the work right.

Having a well-maintained engine will increase your enjoyment of your boat as well as assure your safety offshore. Keep this shop manual handy and use it often. It can save you hundreds of dollars in maintenance and repair bills and make yours a reliable, top-performance boat.

Chapter One

General Information

This detailed, comprehensive manual contains complete information covering maintenance, repair and overhaul. Hundreds of photos and drawings guide you throughout every procedure.

Troubleshooting, tune-up, maintenance and repair are not difficult if you know what tools and equipment to use and what to do. Anyone not afraid to get their hands dirty, of average intelligence and with some mechanical ability can perform most of the procedures in this manual. See Chapter Two for more information on tools and techniques.

A shop manual is a reference. You want to be able to find information quickly. Clymer books are designed with you in mind. All chapters are thumb tabbed and important items are indexed at the end of the manual. All procedures, tables, photos and instructions in this manual assume the reader may be working on the machine or using the manual for the first time.

Keep the manual in a handy place in your toolbox or boat. It will help you to better understand how your boat runs, lower repair and maintenance costs and generally increase your enjoyment of your boat.

MANUAL ORGANIZATION

This chapter provides general information useful to boat owners and marine mechanics.

Chapter Two discusses the tools and techniques for preventative maintenance, troubleshooting and repair.

Chapter Three provides troubleshooting and testing procedures for all systems and individual components.

Following chapters describe specific systems, providing disassembly, inspection, assembly and adjustment procedures in simple step-by-step form. Specifications concerning a specific system are included at the end of the appropriate chapter.

NOTES, CAUTIONS AND WARNINGS

The terms NOTE, CAUTION and WARNING have specific meanings in this manual. A NOTE provides additional information to make a step or procedure easier or more clear. Disregarding a NOTE could cause inconvenience, but would not cause damage or personal injury.

A CAUTION emphasizes areas where equipment damage could cause permanent mechanical damage; however, personal injury is unlikely.

A WARNING emphasizes areas where personal injury or even death could result from negligence. Mechanical damage may also occur. WARNINGS *must* be taken seriously. In some cases, serious injury or death has resulted from disregarding similar warnings.

TORQUE SPECIFICATIONS

Torque specifications throughout this manual are given in foot-pounds (ft.-lb.), inch-pounds (in.-lb.) and newton meters (N•m.). Newton meters are being adopted in place of meter-kilograms (mkg) in accordance with the International Modernized Metric System. Existing torque wrenches calibrated in meter-kilograms can be used by performing a simple conversion: move the decimal point one place to the right. For example, 4.7 mkg = 47 N•m. This conversion is accurate enough for most mechanical operations even though the exact mathematical conversion is 3.5 mkg = 34.3 N•m.

ENGINE OPERATION

All marine engines, whether two or four-stroke, gasoline or diesel, operate on the Otto cycle of intake, compression, power and exhaust phases.

Two-Stroke Cycle

A two-stroke engine requires one crankshaft revolution (two strokes of the piston) to complete the Otto cycle. All engines covered in this manual are a two-stroke design. **Figure 1** shows gasoline two-stroke engine operation.

Four-Stroke Cycle

A four-stroke engine requires two crankshaft revolutions (four strokes of the piston) to complete the Otto cycle. **Figure 2** shows gasoline four-stroke engine operation.

FASTENERS

The material and design of the various fasteners used on marine equipment are carefully thought out and designed. Fastener design determines the type of tool required to work with the fastener. Fastener material is carefully selected to decrease the possibility of physical failure or corrosion. See *Galvanic Corrosion* in this chapter for information on marine materials.

Nuts, bolts and screws are manufactured in a wide range of thread patterns. To join a nut and bolt, the diameter of the bolt and the diameter of the hole in the nut must be the same. It is just as important that the threads are compatible.

The easiest way to determine if fastener threads are compatible is to turn the nut on the bolt, or bolt into its threaded opening, using fingers only. Be sure both pieces are clean. If much force is required, check the thread condition on each fastener. If the thread condition is good but the fasteners jam, the threads are not compatible.

Four important specifications describe the thread:
1. Diameter.
2. Threads per inch.
3. Thread pattern.

GENERAL INFORMATION

TWO-STROKE OPERATING PRINCIPLES

As the piston travels downward, it uncovers the exhaust port (A) allowing the exhaust gases to leave the cylinder. A fresh air-fuel charge, which has been compressed slightly in the crankcase, enters the cylinder through the transfer port (B). Since this charge enters under pressure, it also helps to push out the exhaust gases.

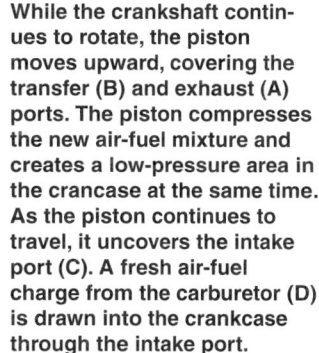

While the crankshaft continues to rotate, the piston moves upward, covering the transfer (B) and exhaust (A) ports. The piston compresses the new air-fuel mixture and creates a low-pressure area in the crancase at the same time. As the piston continues to travel, it uncovers the intake port (C). A fresh air-fuel charge from the carburetor (D) is drawn into the crankcase through the intake port.

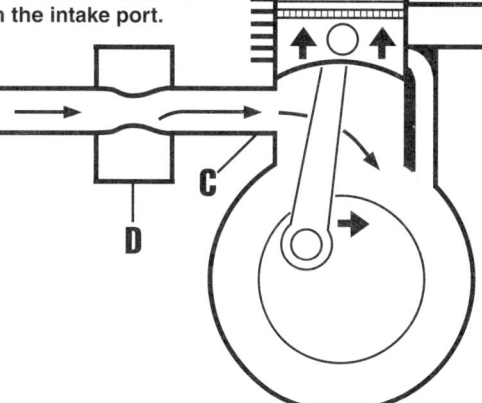

As the piston almost reaches the top of the travel, the spark plug fires, igniting the compressed air-fuel mixture. The piston continues to top dead center (TDC) and is pushed downward by the expanding gases.

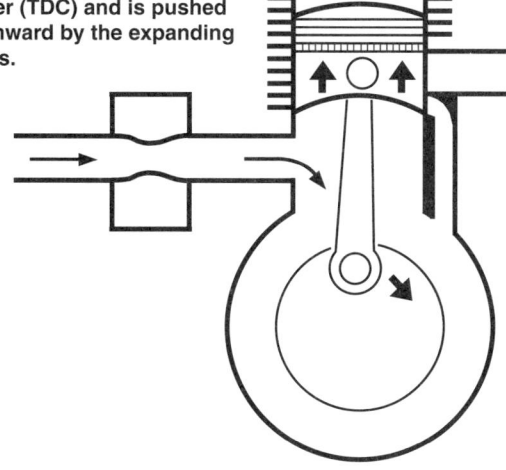

As the piston travels down, the exhaust gases leave the cylinder and the complete cycle starts all over again.

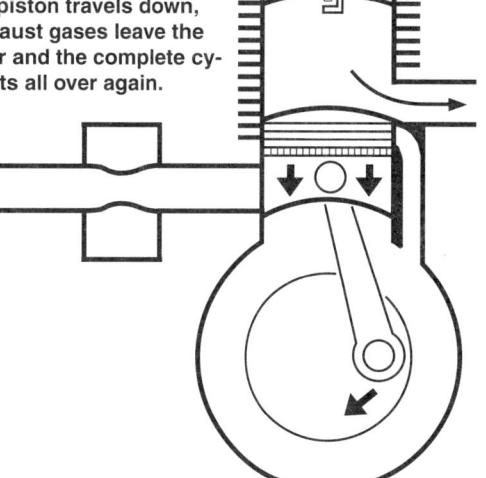

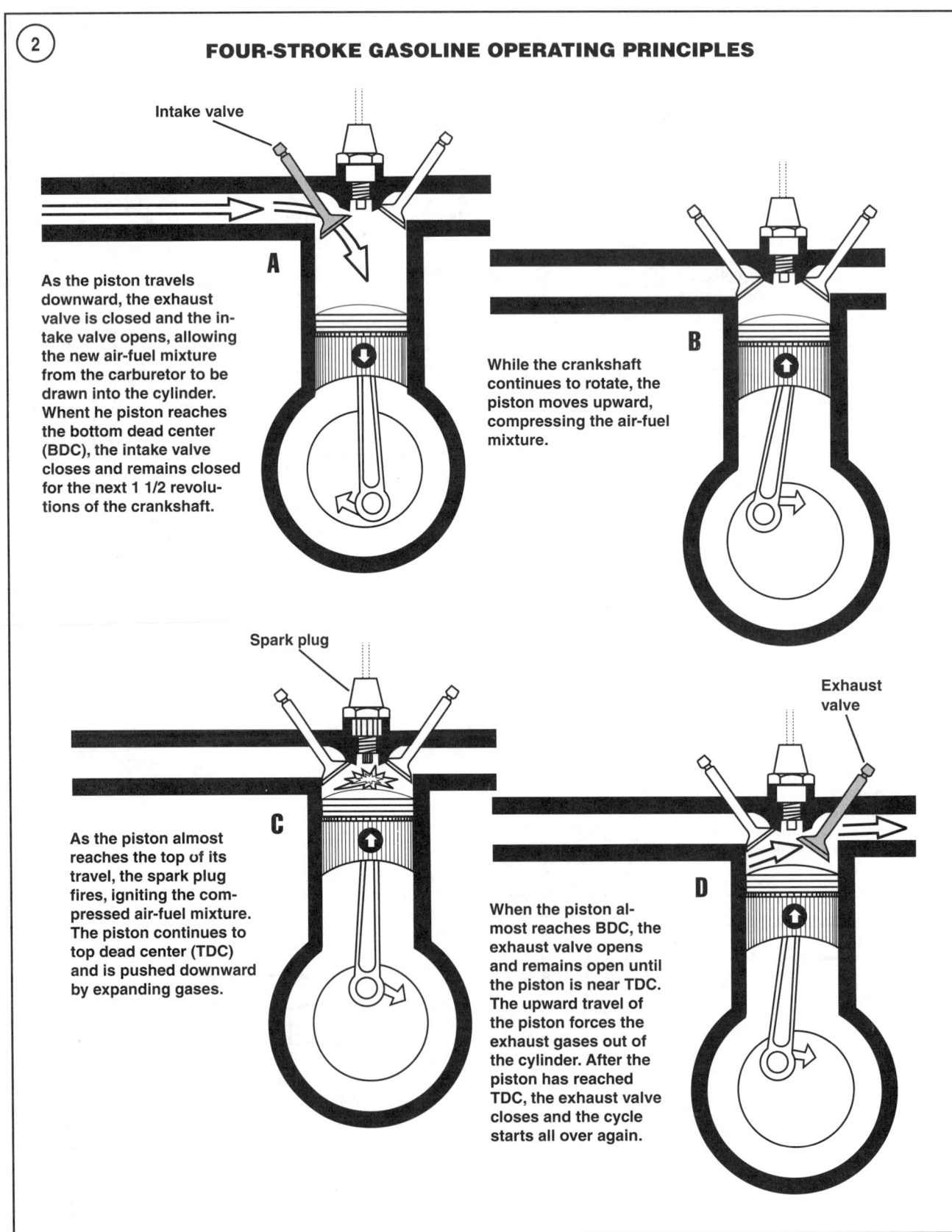

GENERAL INFORMATION

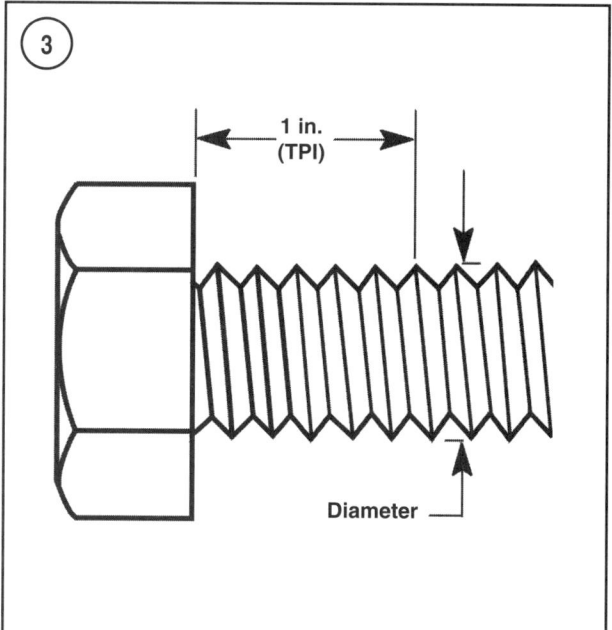

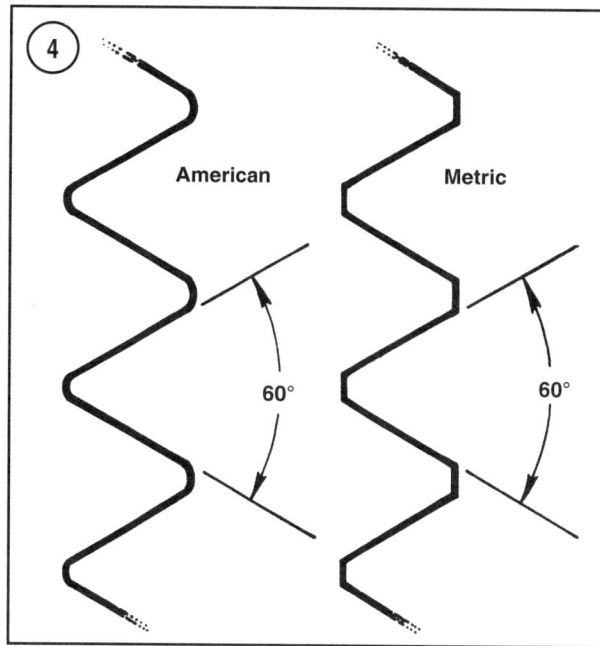

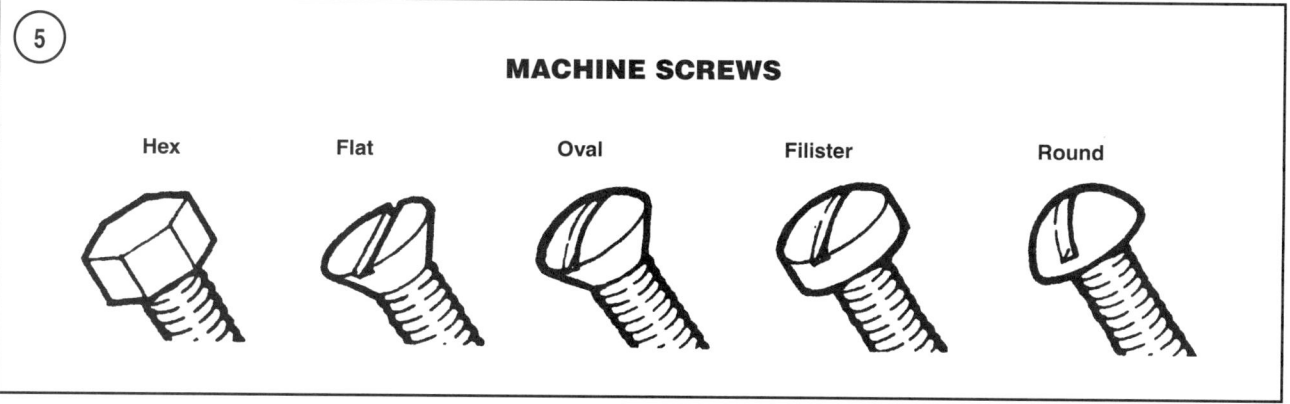

4. Thread direction

Figure 3 shows the first two specifications. Thread pattern is more subtle. Italian and British standards exist, but the most commonly used by marine equipment manufactures are American standard and metric standard. The root and top of the thread are cut differently as shown in **Figure 4**.

Most threads are cut so the fastener must be turned clockwise to tighten it. These are called right-hand threads. Some fasteners have left-hand threads; they must be turned counterclockwise to tighten. Left-hand threads are used in locations where normal rotation of the equipment would tend to loosen a right-hand threaded fastener. Assume all fasteners use right-hand threads unless the instructions specify otherwise.

Machine Screws

There are many different types of machine screws (**Figure 5**). Most are designed to protrude above the secured surface (rounded head) or be slightly recessed below the surface (flat head). In some applications the screw head is recessed well below the fastened sur-

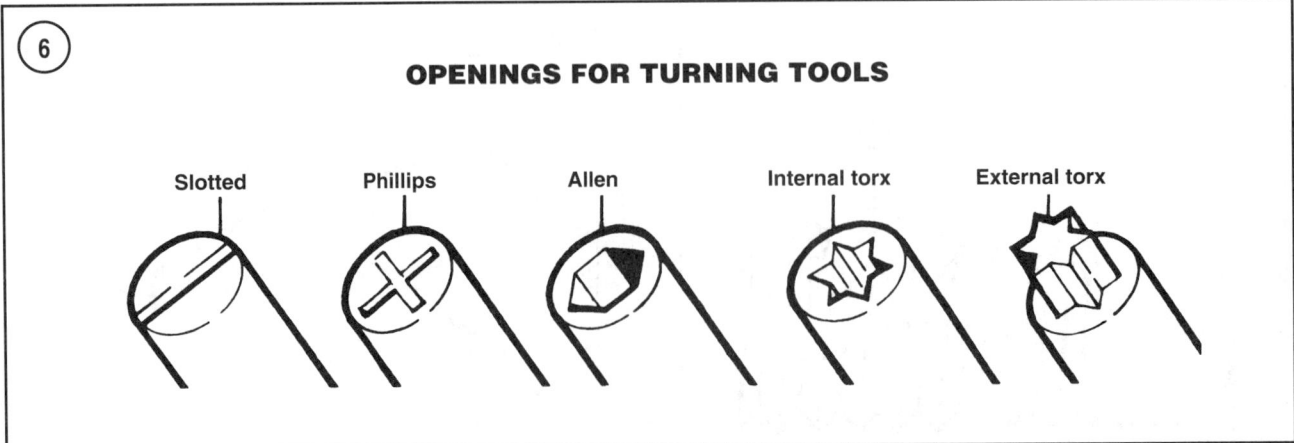

face. **Figure 6** shows a number of screw heads requiring different types of turning tools.

Bolts

Commonly called bolts, the technical name for this fastener is cap screw. They are normally described by diameter, threads per inch and length. For example, 1/4-20 × 1 indicates a bolt 1/4 in. in diameter with 20 threads per inch, 1 in. long. The measurement across two flats of the bolt head indicates the proper wrench size required to turn the bolt.

Nuts

Nuts are manufactured in a variety of types and sizes. Most are hexagonal (six-sides) and fit on bolts, screws and studs with the same diameter and threads per inch.

Figure 7 shows several types of nuts. The common nut is usually used with some type of lockwasher. Self-locking nuts have a nylon insert that helps prevent the nut from loosening; no lockwasher is required. Wing nuts are designed for fast removal by hand. Wing nuts are used for convenience in non-critical locations.

To indicate the size of a nut, manufactures specify the diameter of the opening and the threads per inch. This is similar to a bolt specifi-

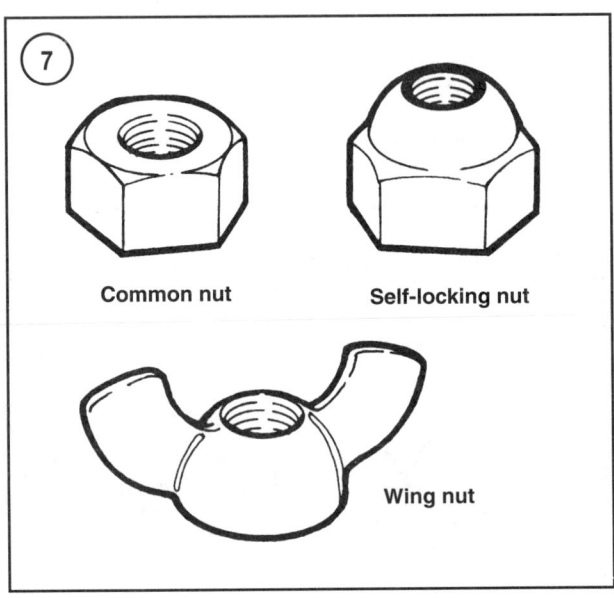

cation, but without the length dimension. The measurement across two flats of the nut indicates the wrench size required to turn the nut.

Washers

There are two basic types of washers: flat washers and lockwashers. A flat washer is a simple disc with a hole that fits the screw or bolt. Lockwashers are designed to prevent a fastener from working loose due to vibration, expansion and contraction. **Figure 8** shows several types of lockwashers. Note that flat washers are often

GENERAL INFORMATION

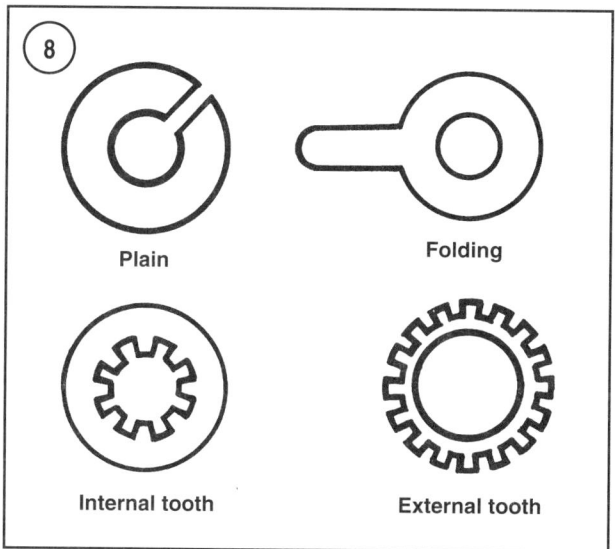

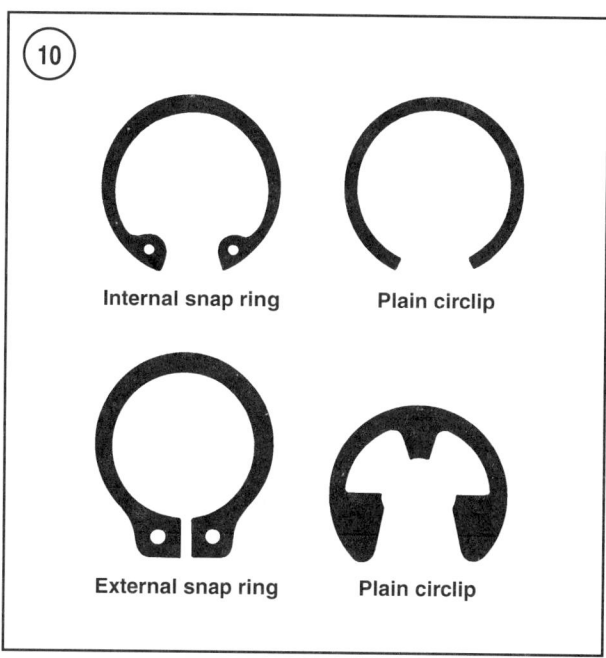

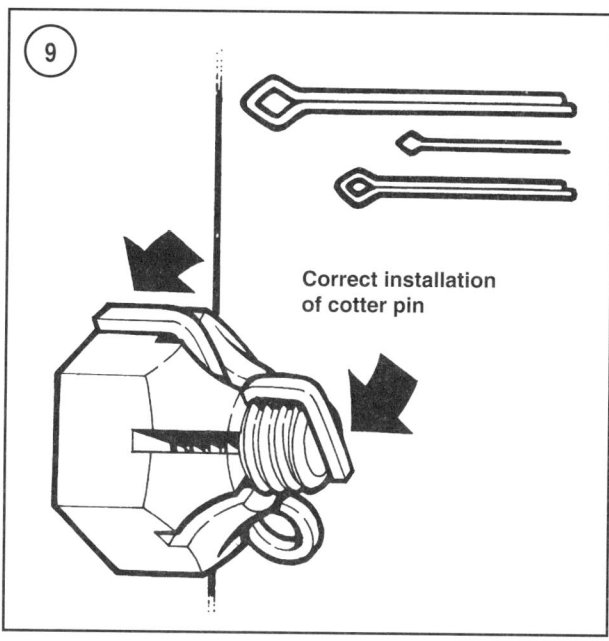

used between a lockwasher and a fastener to provide a smooth bearing surface. This allows the fastener to be turned easily with a tool.

Cotter Pins

In certain applications, a fastener must be secured so it cannot possibly loosen. The propeller nut on some marine drive systems is one such application. For this purpose, a cotter pin (**Figure 9**) and slotted or castellated nut is often used. To use a cotter pin, first make sure the pin fits snugly, but not too tight. Then, align a slot in the fastener with the hole in the bolt or axle. Insert the cotter pin through the nut and bolt or propeller shaft and bend the ends over to secure the cotter pin tightly. If the holes do not align, tighten the nut just enough to obtain the proper alignment. Unless specifically instructed to do so, never loosen the fastener to align the slot and hole. Because the cotter pin is weakened after installation and removal, never reuse a cotter pin. Cotter pins are available in several styles, lengths and diameters. Measure cotter pin length from the bottom of its head to the tip of its shortest prong.

Snap Rings

Snap rings (**Figure 10**) can be an internal or external design. They are used to retain components on shafts (external type) or inside openings (internal type). Snap rings can be reused if they are not distorted during removal. In some applications, snap rings of varying thickness (selective fit) can be selected to position or control end play of parts assemblies.

LUBRICANTS

Periodic lubrication helps ensure long service life for any type of equipment. It is especially important with marine equipment because it is exposed to salt, brackish or polluted water and other harsh environments. The type of lubricant used is just as important as the lubrication service itself, although in an emergency, the wrong type of lubricant is better than none at all. The following paragraphs describe the types of lubricants most often used on marine equipment. Be sure to follow the equipment manufacture's recommendations for the lubricant types.

Generally, all liquid lubricants are called *oil*. They may be mineral-based (including petroleum bases), natural-based (vegetable and animal bases), synthetic-based or emulsions (mixtures). *Grease* is lubricating oil that has a thickening compound added. The resulting material then usually enhanced with anticorrosion, antioxidant and extreme pressure (EP) additives. Grease is often classified by the type of thickener added; lithium and calcium soap are the most commonly used.

Two-stroke Engine Oil

Lubrication for a two-stroke engine is provided by oil mixed with the incoming air/fuel mixture. Some of the oil mist settles out in the crankcase, lubricating the crankshaft, bearings and lower end of the connecting rod. The rest of the oil enters the combustion chamber to lubricate the piston, rings and the cylinder wall. This oil is then burned along with the air/fuel mixture during the combustion process.

Engine oil must have several special qualities to work well in a two-stroke engine. It must mix easily and stay in suspension in gasoline. When burned, it cannot leave behind excessive deposits. It must also withstand the high operating temperature associated with two-stroke engines.

The National Marine Manufacturer's Association (NMMA) has set standards for oil used in two-stroke, water-cooled engines. This is the NMMA TC-W (two-cycle, water-cooled) grade. It indicates the oil's performance in the following areas:
1. Lubrication (preventing wear and scuffing).
2. Spark plug fouling.
3. Piston ring sticking.
4. Preignition.
5. Piston varnish.
6. General engine condition (including deposits).
7. Exhaust port blockage.
8. Rust prevention.
9. Mixing ability with gasoline.

In addition to oil grade, manufactures specify the ratio of gasoline and oil required during break-in and normal engine operation.

Gearcase Oil

Gearcase lubricants are assigned SAE viscosity numbers under the same system as four-stroke engine oil. Gearcase lubricant falls into the SAE 72-250 range. Some gearcase lubricants are multigrade. For example, SAE 80-90 is a common multigrade gear lubricant.

Three types of marine gearcase lubricants are generally available; SAE 90 hypoid gearcase lubricant is designed for older manual-shift units; type C gearcase lubricant contains additives designed for the electric shift mechanisms; high-viscosity gearcase lubricant is a heavier oil designed to withstand the shock loads of high performance engines or units subjected to severe duty use. Always use the gearcase lubricant specified by the manufacturer.

GENERAL INFORMATION

Grease

Greases are graded by the National Lubricating Grease Institute (NLGI). Greases are graded by number according to the consistency of the grease. These ratings range from No. 000 to No. 6, with No. 6 being the most solid. A typical multipurpose grease is NLGI No. 2. For specific applications, equipment manufactures may require grease with an additive such as molybdenum disulfide (MOS^2).

GASKET SEALANT

Gasket sealant is used instead of preformed gaskets on some applications, or as a gasket dressing on others. Three types of gasket sealant are commonly used: gasket sealing compound, room temperature vulcanizing (RTV) and anaerobic. Because these materials have different sealing properties, they cannot be used interchangeably.

Gasket Sealing Compound

This nonhardening liquid is used primarily as a gasket dressing. Gasket sealing compound is available in tubes or brush top containers. When exposed to air or heat it forms a rubber-like coating. The coating fills in small imperfections in gasket and sealing surfaces. Do not use gasket sealing compound that is old, has began to solidify or has darkened in color.

Applying Gasket Sealing Compound

Carefully scrape residual gasket material, corrosion deposits or paint from the mating surfaces. Use a blunt scraper and work carefully to avoid damaging the mating surfaces. Use quick drying solvent and a clean shop towel and wipe oil or other contaminants from the surfaces. Wipe or blow loose material or contaminants from the gasket. Brush a light coating on the mating surfaces and both sides of the gasket. Do not apply more compound than needed. Excess compound will be squeezed out as the surfaces mate and may contaminate other components. Do not allow compound into bolt or alignment pin holes

A hydraulic lock can occur as the bolt or pin compresses the compound, resulting in incorrect bolt torque.

RTV Sealant

This is a silicone gel supplied in tubes. Moisture in the air causes RTV to cure. Always place the cap on the tube as soon as possible if using RTV. RTV has a shelf life of approximately one year and will not cure properly after the shelf life expires. Check the expiration date on the tube and keep partially used tubes tightly sealed. RTV can generally fill gaps up to 1/4 in. (6.3 mm) and works well on slightly flexible surfaces.

Applying RTV Sealant

Carefully scrape all residual sealant and paint from the mating surfaces. Use a blunt scraper and work carefully to avoid damaging the mating surfaces. The mating surfaces must be absolutely free of gasket material, sealant, dirt, oil grease or other contamination. Lacquer thinner, acetone, isopropyl alcohol or similar solvents work well to clean the surfaces. Avoid using solvents with an oil, wax or petroleum base as they are not compatible with RTV compounds. Remove all sealant from bolt or alignment pin holes.

Apply RTV sealant in a continuous bead 0.08-0.12 in. (2-3 mm) thick. Circle all mounting bolt or alignment pin holes unless otherwise specified. Do not allow RTV sealant into bolt holes or other openings. A hydraulic lock can

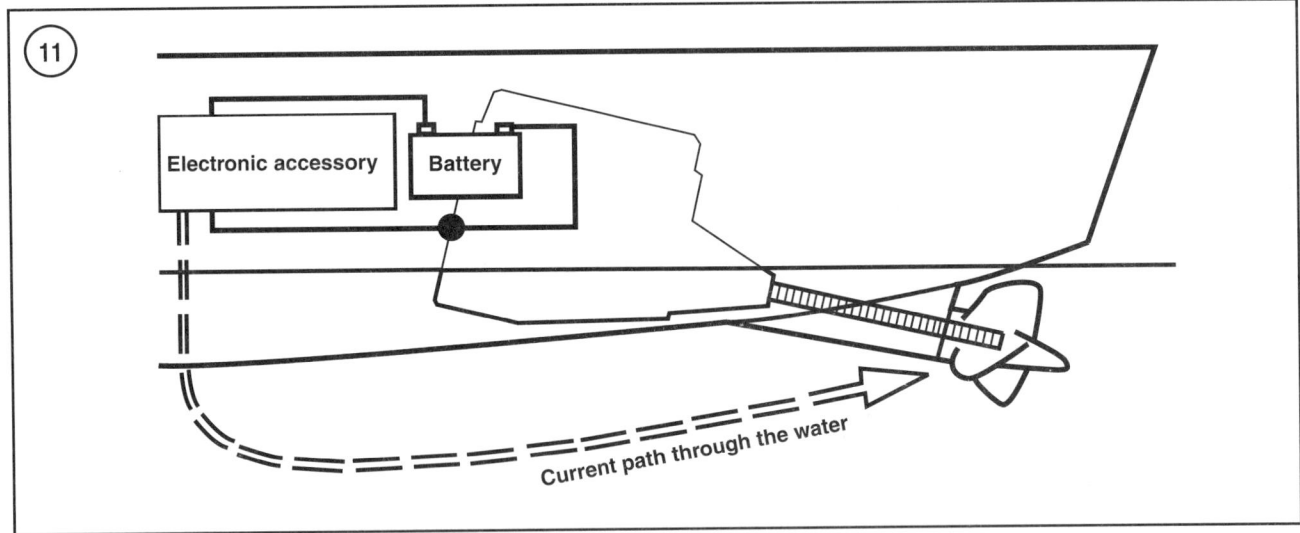

occur as the bolt or pin compresses the sealant, resulting in incorrect bolt torque. Tighten the mounting fasteners within 10 minutes after application.

Anaerobic Sealant

This is a gel supplied in tubes. It cures only in the absence of air, as when squeezed tightly between two machined mating surfaces. For this reason, it will not spoil if the cap is left off the tube. Do not use anaerobic sealant if one of the surfaces is flexible. Anaerobic sealant is able to fill gaps up to 0.030 in. (0.8 mm) and generally works best on rigid, machined flanges or surfaces.

Applying Anaerobic Sealant

Carefully scrape all residual sealant from the mating surfaces. Use a blunt scraper and work carefully to avoid damaging the mating surfaces. The mating surfaces must be absolutely free of gasket material, sealant, dirt, oil grease or other contamination. Lacquer thinner, acetone, isopropyl alcohol or similar solvents work well to clean the surfaces. Avoid using solvents with an oil, wax or petroleum base as they are not compatible with anaerobic compounds. Clean a sealant from the bolt or alignment pin holes. Apply anaerobic sealant in a 0.04 in. (1 mm) thick continuous bead onto one of the surfaces. Circle all bolt and alignment pin openings. Do not apply sealant into bolt holes or other openings. A hydraulic lock can occur as the bolt or pin compresses the sealant, resulting in incorrect bolt torque. Tighten the mounting fasteners within 10 minutes after application.

GALVANIC CORROSION

A chemical reaction occurs whenever two different types of metal are joined by an electrical conductor and immersed in an electrolytic solution such as water. Electrons transfer from one metal to the other through the electrolyte and return through the conductor.

The hardware on a boat is made of many different types of metal. The boat hull acts as a conductor between the metals. Even if the hull is wooden or fiberglass, the slightest film of water (electrolyte) on the hull provides conductivity. This combination creates a good environment for electron flow (**Figure 11**). Unfortunately, this electron flow results in galvanic corrosion

GENERAL INFORMATION

of the metal involved, causing one of the metals to be corroded or eroded away. The amount of electron flow, and therefore the amount of corrosion, depends on several factors:

1. The types of metal involved.
2. The efficiency of the conductor.
3. The strength of the electrolyte.

Metals

The chemical composition of the metal used in marine equipment has a significant effect on the amount and speed of galvanic corrosion. Certain metals are more resistant to corrosion than others. These electrically negative metals are commonly called *noble*; they act as the cathode in any reaction. Metals that are more subject to corrosion are electrically positive; they act as the anode in a reaction. The more *noble* metals include titanium, 18-8 stainless steel and nickel. Less *noble* metals include zinc, aluminum and magnesium. Galvanic corrosion becomes more severe as the difference in electrical potential between the two metals increases.

In some cases, galvanic corrosion can occur within a single piece of metal. For example, brass is a mixture of zinc and copper, and, when immersed in an electrolyte, the zinc portion of the mixture will corrode away as a galvanic reaction occurs between the zinc and copper particles.

Conductors

The hull of the boat often acts as the conductor between different types of metal. Marine equipment, such as the drive unit can act as the conductor. Large masses of metal, firmly connected together, are more efficient conductors than water. Rubber mountings and vinyl-based paint can act as insulators between pieces of metal.

Electrolyte

The water in which a boat operates acts as the electrolyte for the corrosion process. The more efficient a conductor is, the more severe and rapid the corrosion will be.

Cold, clean freshwater is the poorest electrolyte. Pollutants increase conductivity; therefore, brackish or saltwater is an efficient electrolyte. This is one of the reasons that most manufacturers recommend a freshwater flush after operating in polluted, brackish or saltwater.

Protection From Galvanic Corrosion

Because of the environment in which marine equipment must operate, it is practically impossible to totally prevent galvanic corrosion. However, there are several ways in which the process can be slowed. After taking these precautions, the next step is to *fool* the process into occurring only where you want it to occur. This is the role of sacrificial anodes and impressed current systems.

Slowing Corrosion

Some simple precautions can help reduce the amount of corrosion taking place outside the hull. These precautions are not substitutes for the corrosion protection methods discussed under *Sacrificial Anodes* and *Impressed Current Systems* in this chapter, but they can help these methods reduce corrosion.

Use fasteners made of metal more noble than the parts they secure. If corrosion occurs, the parts they secure may suffer but the fasteners are protected. The larger secured parts are more able to withstand the loss of material. Also major problems could arise if the fasteners corrode to the point of failure.

Keep all painted surfaces in good condition. If paint is scraped off and bare metal exposed, corrosion rapidly increases. Use a vinyl- or plastic-based paint, which acts as an electrical insulator.

Be careful when applying metal-based antifouling paint to the boat. Do not apply antifouling paint to metal parts of the boat or the drive unit. If applied to metal surfaces, this type of paint reacts with the metal and results in corrosion between the metal and the layer of paint. Maintain a minimum 1 in. (25 mm) border between the painted surface and any metal parts. Organic-based paints are available for use on metal surfaces.

Where a corrosion protection device is used, remember that it must be immersed in the electrolyte along with the boat to provide any protection. If you raise the gearcase out of the water with the boat docked, any anodes on the gearcase may be removed from the corrosion process rendering them ineffective. Never paint or apply any coating to anodes or other protection devices. Paint or other coatings insulate them from the corrosion process.

Any change in the boat's equipment, such as the installation of a new stainless steel propeller, changes the electrical potential and may cause increased corrosion. Always consider this when adding equipment or changing exposed materials. Install additional anodes or other protection equipment as required ensuring the corrosion protection system is up to the task. The expense to repair corrosion damage usually far exceeds that of additional corrosion protection.

Sacrificial Anodes

Sacrificial anodes are specially designed to do nothing but corrode. Properly fastening such pieces to the boat causes them to act as the anode in any galvanic reaction that occurs; any other metal in the reaction acts as the cathode and is not damaged.

Anodes are usually made or zinc, a far from a noble material. Some anodes are manufactured of an aluminum and indium alloy. This alloy is less noble than the aluminum alloy in drive system components, providing the desired sacrificial properties. The aluminum and indium alloy is more resistant to oxide coating than zinc anodes. Oxide coating occurs as the anode material reacts with oxygen in the water. An oxide coating will insulate the anode, dramatically reducing corrosion protection.

Anodes must be used properly to be effective. Simply fastening anodes to the boat in random locations will not do the job.

First determine how much anode surface is required to adequately protect the equipment's surface area. A good starting point is provided by the Military Specification MIL-A-818001, which states that one square inch of new anode protects either:
1. 800 square inches of freshly painted steel.
2. 250 square inches of bare steel or bare aluminum alloy.
3. 100 square inches of copper or copper alloy.

This rule is valid for a boat at rest. If underway, additional anode area is required to protect the same surface area.

The anode must be in good electrical contact with the metal that it protects. If possible, attach an anode to all metal surfaces requiring protection.

Good quality anodes have inserts around the fastener holes that are made of a more noble material. Otherwise, the anode could erode away around the fastener hole, allowing the anode to loosen or possibly fall off, thereby loosing needed protection.

Impressed Current System

An impressed current system can be added to any boat. The system generally consists of the anode, controller and reference electrode. The anode in this system is coated with a very noble

GENERAL INFORMATION

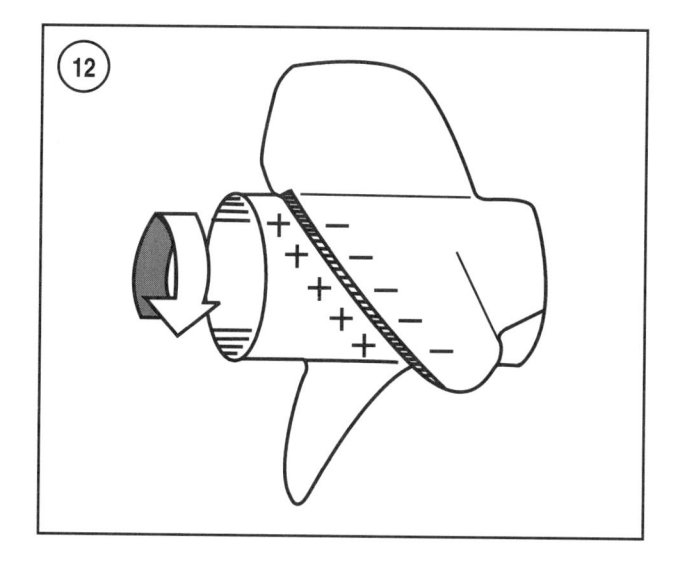

metal, such as platinum, so that it is almost corrosion-free and can last almost indefinitely. The reference electrode, under the boat's waterline, allows the control module to monitor the potential for corrosion. If the module senses that corrosion is occurring, it applies positive battery voltage to the anode. Current then flows from the anode to all other metal component, regardless of how noble or non-noble these components may be. Essentially, the electrical current from the battery counteracts the galvanic reaction to dramatically reduce corrosion damage.

Only a small amount of current is needed to counteract corrosion. Using input from the sensor, the control module provides only the amount of current needed to suppress galvanic corrosion. Most systems consume a maximum of 0.2 Ah at full demand. Under normal conditions, these systems can provide protection for 8-12 weeks without recharging the battery. Remember that this system must have constant connection to the battery. Often the battery supply to the system is connected to a battery switching device causing the operator to inadvertently shut off the system while docked.

An impressed current system is more expensive to install than sacrificial anodes but, considering its low maintenance requirements and the superior protection it provides, the long term cost may be lower.

PROPELLERS

The propeller is the final link between the boat's drive system and the water. A perfectly maintained engine and hull are useless if the propeller is the wrong type, is damaged or is deteriorated. Although propeller selection for a specific application is beyond the scope of this manual, the following provides the basic information needed to make an informed decision. The professional at a reputable marine dealership is the best source for a propeller recommendation.

How a Propeller Works

As the curved blades of a propeller rotate through the water, a high-pressure area forms on one side of the blade and a low-pressure area forms on the other side of the blade (**Figure 12**). The propeller moves toward the low-pressure area, carrying the boat with it.

Propeller Parts

Although a propeller is usually a one-piece unit, it is made of several different parts (**Figure 13**). Variations in the design of these parts make different propellers suitable for different applications.

The blade tip is the point of the blade furthest from the center of the propeller hub or propeller shaft bore. The blade tip separates the leading edge from the trailing edge.

The leading edge is the edge of the blade nearest the boat. During forward operation, this is the area of the blade that first cuts through the water.

The trailing edge is the surface of the blade furthest from the boat. During reverse operation,

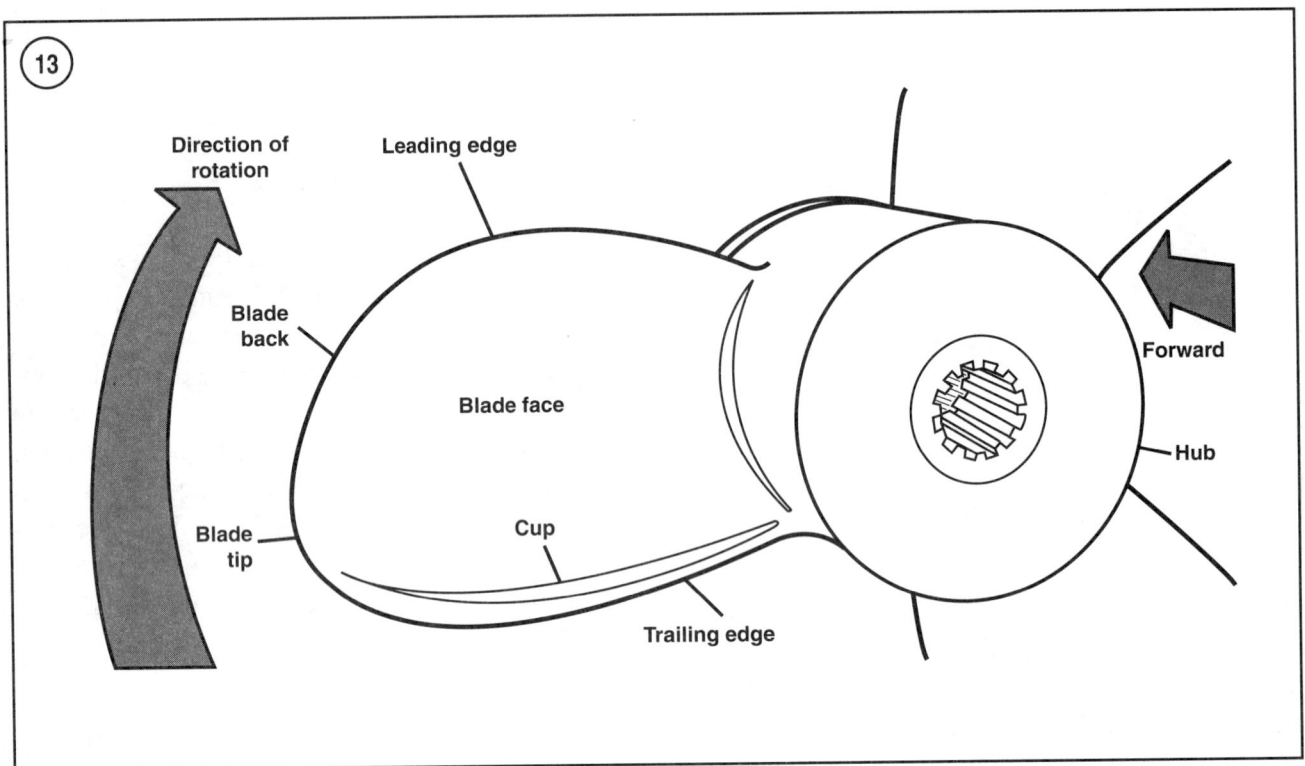

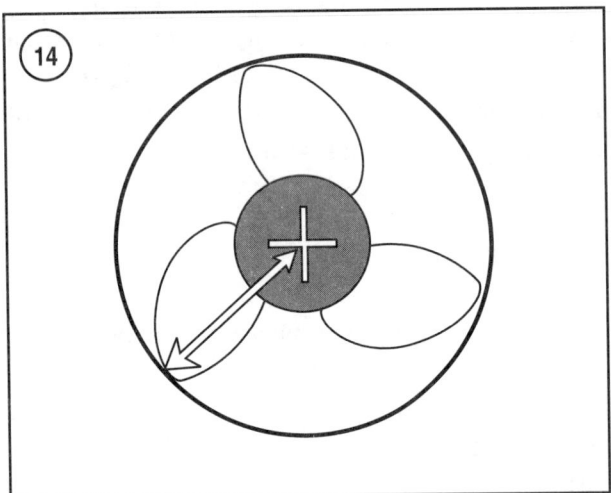

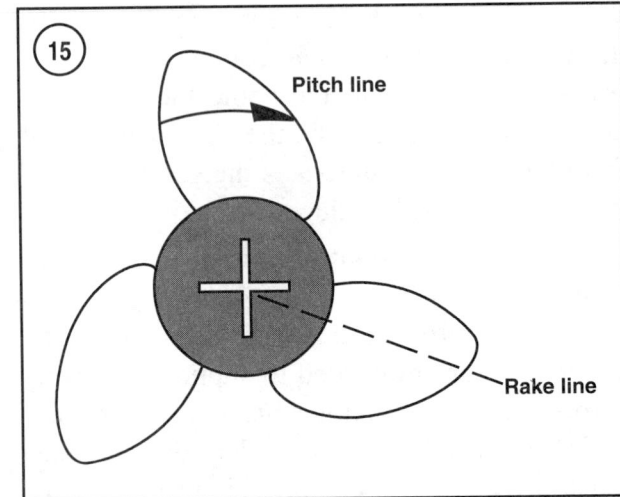

this is the area of the blade that first cuts through the water.

The blade face is the surface of the blade that faces away from the boat. During forward operation, high-pressure forms on this side of the blade.

The blade back is the surface of the blade that faces toward the boat. During forward gear operation, low-pressure forms on this side of the blade.

The cup is a small curve or lip on the trailing edge of the blade. Cupped propeller blades generally perform better than non-cupped propeller blades.

The hub is the center portion of the propeller. It connects the blades to the propeller shaft. On most drive systems, engine exhaust is routed through the hub; in this case, the hub is made up of an outer and inner portion, connected by ribs.

GENERAL INFORMATION

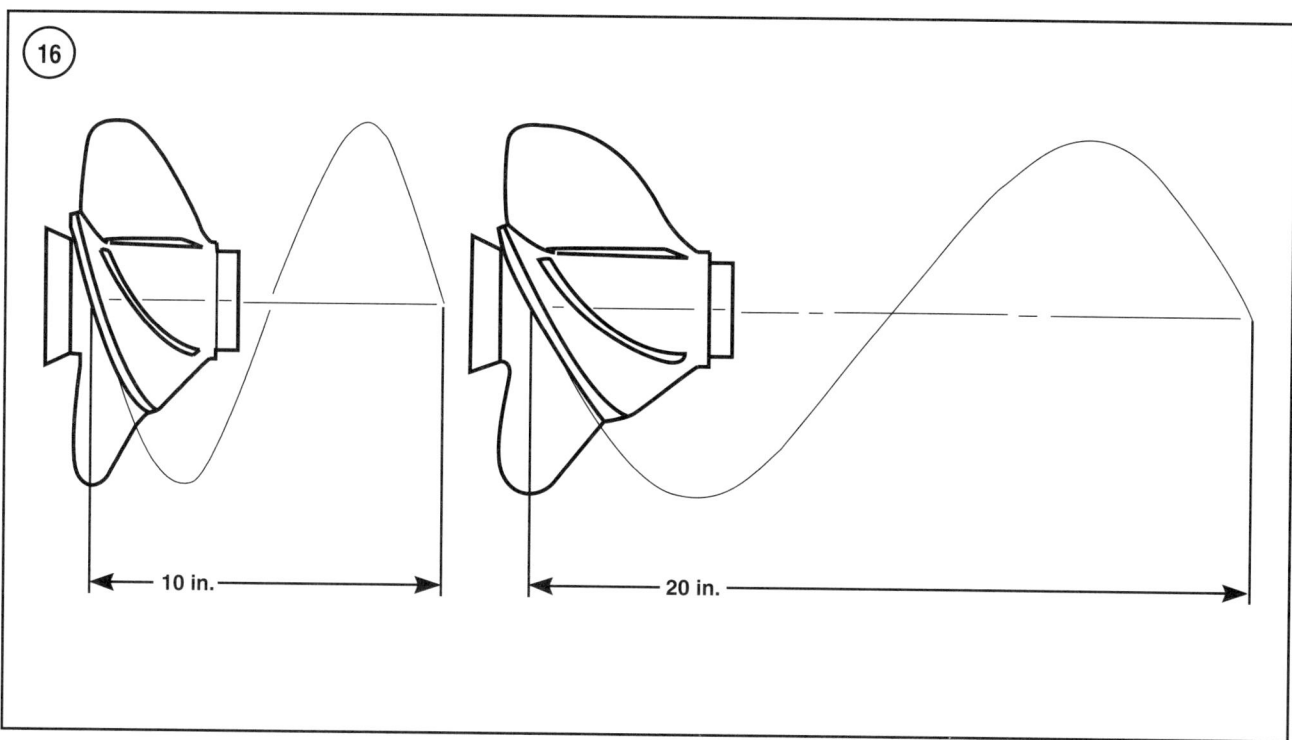

The diffuser ring is used on though-hub exhaust models to prevent exhaust gasses from entering the blade area.

Propeller Design

Changes in length, angle, thickness and material of propeller parts make different propellers suitable for different applications.

Diameter

Propeller diameter is the distance from the center of the hub to the blade tip, multiplied by two. Essentially it is the diameter of the circle formed by the blade tips during propeller rotation (**Figure 14**).

Pitch and rake

Propeller pitch and rake describe the placement of the blades in relation to the hub (**Figure 15**).

Pitch describes the theoretical distance the propeller would travel in one revolution. In A, **Figure 16**, the propeller would travel 10 inches in one revolution. In B, **Figure 16**, the propeller would travel 20 inches in one revolution. This distance is only theoretical; during operation, the propeller achieves only 75-85% of its pitch. Slip rate describes the difference in actual travel relative to the pitch. Lighter, faster boats typically achieve a lower slip rate than heavier, slower boats.

Propeller blades can be constructed with constant pitch (**Figure 17**) or progressive pitch (**Figure 18**). On a progressive propeller, the pitch starts low at the leading edge and increases toward the trailing edge. The propeller pitch specification is the average of the pitch across the entire blade. Propellers with progressive pitch usually provide better overall performance than constant pitch propellers.

Blade rake is specified in degrees and is measured along a line from the center of the hub to the blade tip. A blade that is perpendicular to the

CHAPTER ONE

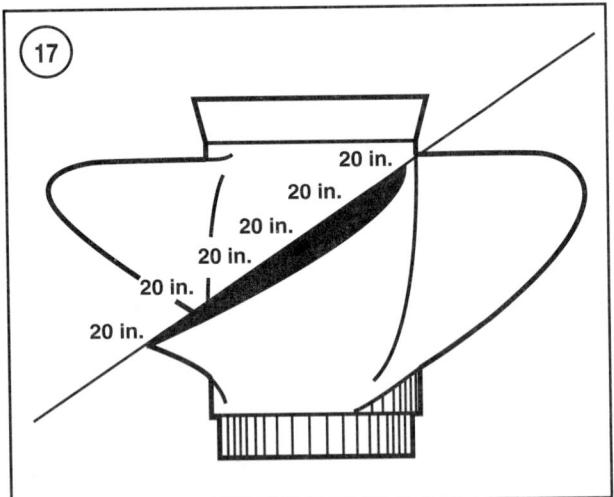

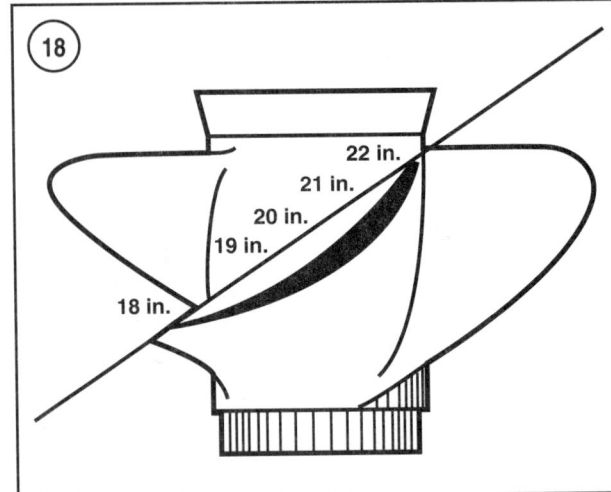

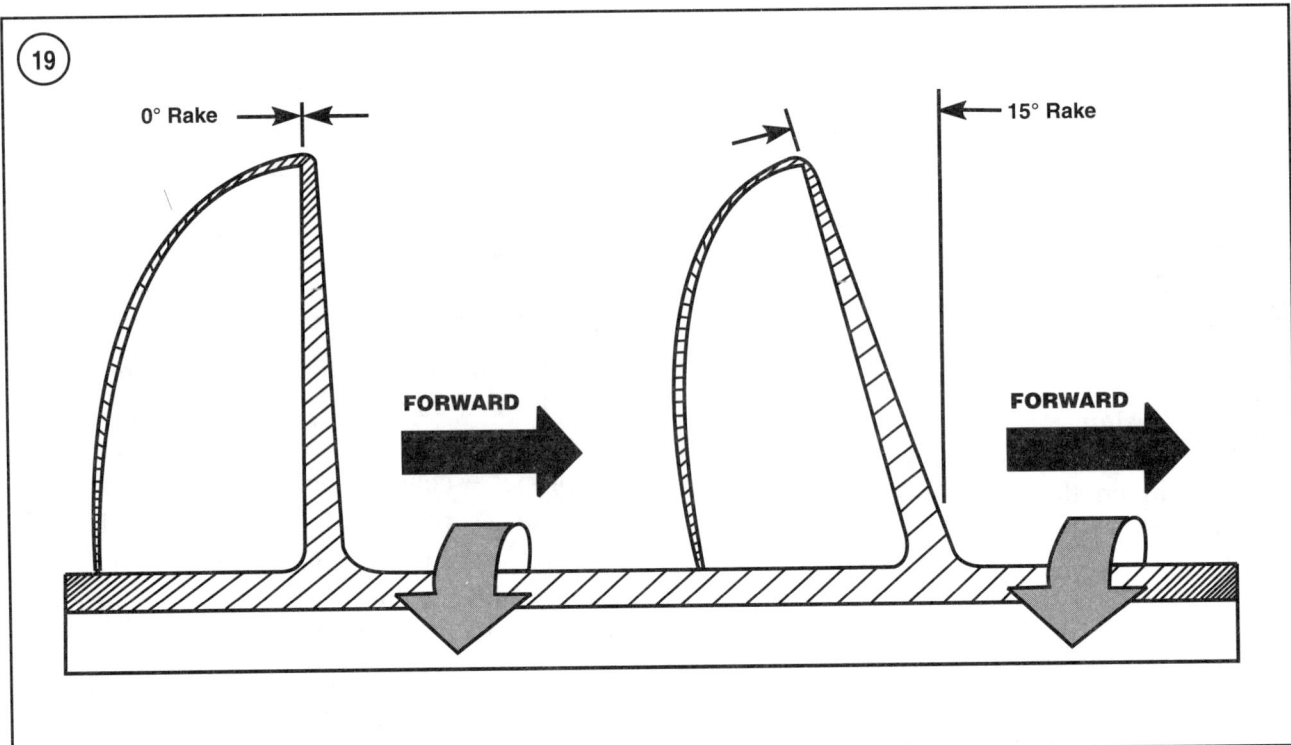

hub (**Figure 19**) has 0° rake. A blade that is angled from perpendicular (**Figure 19**) has a rake expressed by its difference from perpendicular. Most propellers have rakes ranging from 0-20°. Lighter faster boats generally perform better with propeller with a greater amount of rake. Heavier, slower boats generally perform better using a propeller with less rake.

Blade thickness

Blade thickness in not uniform at all points along the blade. For efficiency, blades are as thin a possible at all points while retaining enough strength to move the boat. Blades are thicker where they meet the hub and thinner at the blade tips (**Figure 20**). This is necessary to support the

GENERAL INFORMATION

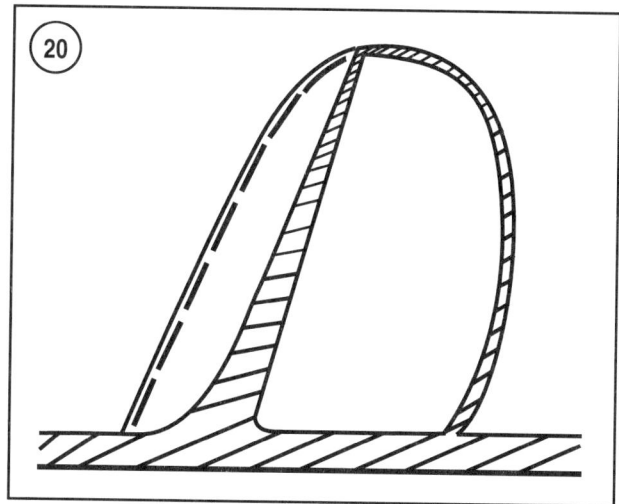

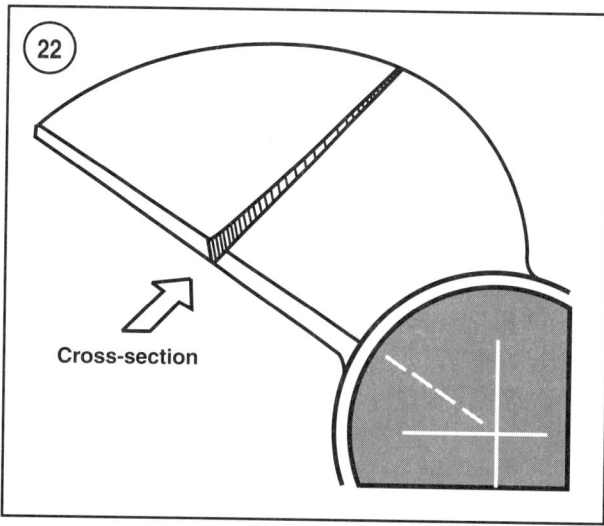

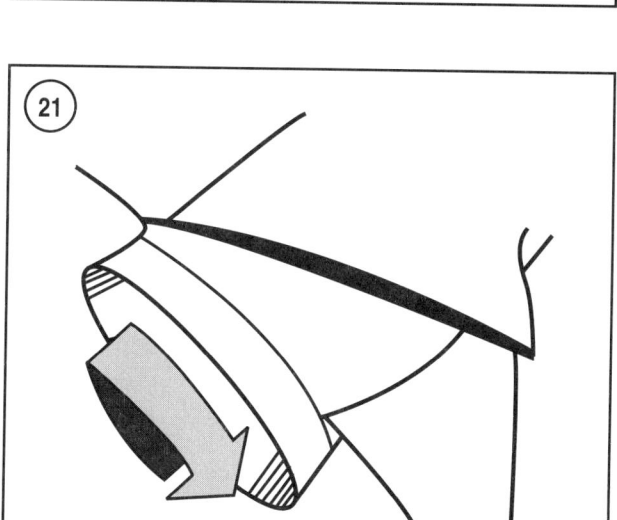

heavier loads at the hub section of the blade. Overall blade thickness is dependent on the strength of the material used.

When cut along a line from the leading edge to the trailing edge in the central portion of the blade (**Figure 21**), the propeller blade resembles and airplane wing. The blade face, where high-pressure exists during forward rotation, is almost flat. The blade back, where low-pressure exists during forward rotation, is curved, with the thinnest portions at the edges and the thickest portion at the center.

Propellers that run only partially submerged, as in racing applications, may have a wedge shaped cross-section (**Figure 22**). The leading edge is very thin and the blade thickness increases toward the trailing edge, where it is thickest. If a propeller such as this is run totally submerged, it is very inefficient.

Number of blades

The number of blades used on a propeller is a compromise between efficiency and vibration. A one-bladed propeller would the most efficient, but it would create an unacceptable amount of vibration. As blades are added, efficiency decreases, but so does vibration. Most propellers have three or four blades, representing the most practical trade-off between efficiency and vibration.

Material

Propeller materials are chosen for strength, corrosion resistance and economy. Stainless steel, aluminum, plastic and bronze are the most commonly used materials. Bronze is quite strong but rather expensive. Stainless steel is more common than bronze because of its combination of strength and lower cost. Aluminum alloy and plastic materials are the least expensive

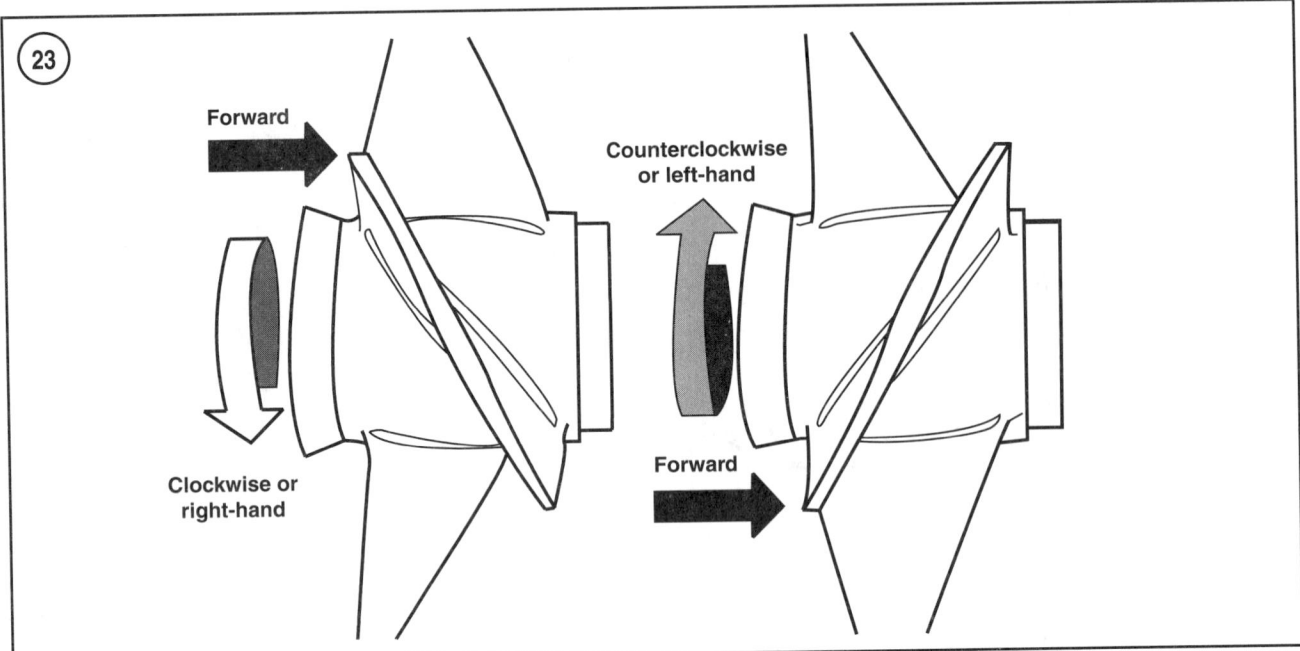

Figure 23

but usually lack the strength of stainless steel. Plastic propellers are more suited for lower horsepower applications.

Direction of rotation

Propellers are made for both right-hand and left hand rotations although right-hand is the most commonly used. As viewed from the rear of the boat while in forward gear, a right-hand propeller turns clockwise and a left-hand propeller turns counterclockwise. Off the boat, the direction of rotation is determined by observing the angle of the blades (**Figure 23**). A right-hand propeller's blade slant from the upper left to the lower right; a left-hand propeller's blades are opposite.

Cavitation and Ventilation

Cavitation and ventilation are *not* interchangeable terms; they refer to two distinct problems encountered during propeller operation.

To help understand cavitation, consider the relationship between pressure and the boiling point of water. At sea level, water boils at 212° F (100° C). As pressure increases, such as within an engine cooling system, the boiling point of the water increases—it boils at a temperature higher than 212° F (100° C). The opposite is also true. As pressure decreases, water boils at a temperature lower than 212° F (100° C). It the pressure drops low enough, water will boil at normal room temperature.

During normal propeller operation, low pressure forms on the blade back. Normally the pressure does not drop low enough for boiling to occur. However, poor propeller design, damaged blades or using the wrong propeller can cause unusually low pressure on the blade surface (**Figure 24**). If the pressure drops low enough, boiling occurs and bubbles form on the blade surfaces. As the boiling water moves to a higher pressure area of the blade, the boiling ceases and the bubbles collapse. The collapsing bubbles release energy that erodes the surface of the propeller blade.

Corroded surfaces, physical damage or even marine growth combined with high-speed operation can cause low pressure and cavitation on gearcase surfaces. In such cases, low pressure

GENERAL INFORMATION

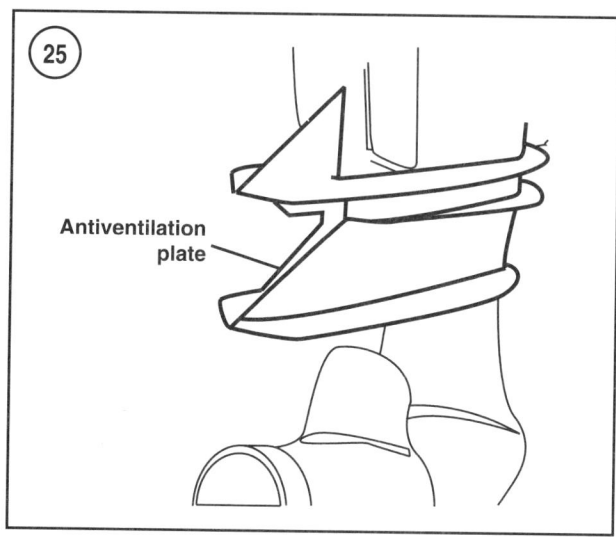

forms as water flows over a protrusion or rough surface. The boiling water forms bubbles that collapse as they move to a higher pressure area toward the rear of the surface imperfection.

This entire process of pressure drop, boiling and bubble collapse is called *cavitation*. The ensuing damage is called *cavitation burn*. Cavitation is caused by a decrease in pressure, not an increase in temperature.

Ventilation is not as complex a process as cavitation. Ventilation refers to air entering the blade area, either from above the water surface or from a though-hub exhaust system. As the blades meet the air, the propeller momentarily looses it bite with the water and subsequently loses most of its thrust. An added complication is that the propeller and engine over-rev, causing very low pressure on the blade back and massive cavitation.

Most marine drive systems have a plate (**Figure 25**) above the propeller designed to prevent surface air from entering the blade area. This plate is correctly called an *anti-ventilation plate*, although it is often incorrectly called an *anticavitation plate*.

Most propellers have a flared section at the rear of the propeller called a diffuser ring. This feature forms a barrier, and extends the exhaust passage far enough aft to prevent the exhaust gases from ventilating the propeller.

A close fit of the propeller to the gearcase is necessary to keep exhaust gasses from exiting and ventilating the propeller. Using the wrong propeller attaching hardware can position the propeller too far aft, preventing a close fit. The wrong hardware can also allow the propeller to rub heavily against the gearcase, causing rapid wear to both components. Wear or damage to these surfaces will allow the propeller to ventilate.

Chapter Two

Tools and Techniques

This chapter describes the common tools required for marine engine repair and troubleshooting. Techniques that make the work easier and more effective are also described. Some of the procedures in this book require special skills or expertise; it some cases it is better to entrust the job to a specialist or qualified dealership.

SAFETY FIRST

Professional mechanics can work for years and never suffer a serious injury. Avoiding injury is as simple as following a few rules and using common sense. Ignoring the rules can of often does lead to physical injury and/or damaged equipment.

1. Never use gasoline as a cleaning solvent.
2. Never smoke or use a torch near flammable liquids, such as cleaning solvent. Dirty or solvent soaked shop towels are extremely flammable. If working in a garage, remember that most home gas appliances have pilot lights.
3. Never smoke or use a torch in an area where a battery is being charged. Highly explosive hydrogen gas is formed during the charging process.
4. Use the proper size wrench to avoid damaged fasteners and bodily injury.
5. If loosening a tight or stuck fastener, consider what could happen if the wrench slips. Protect yourself accordingly.
6. Keep the work area clean, uncluttered and well lighted.
7. Wear safety goggles while using any type of tool. This is especially important when drilling, grinding or using a cold chisel.
8. Never use worn or damaged tools.
9. Keep a Coast Guard approved fire extinguisher handy. Ensure it is rated for gasoline (Class B) and electrical (Class C) fires.

TOOLS AND TECHNIQUES

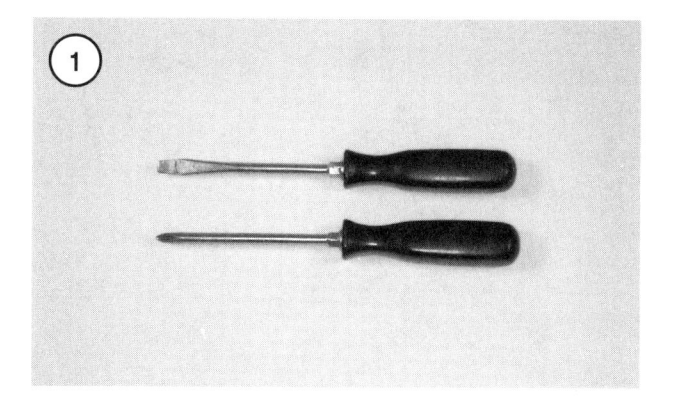

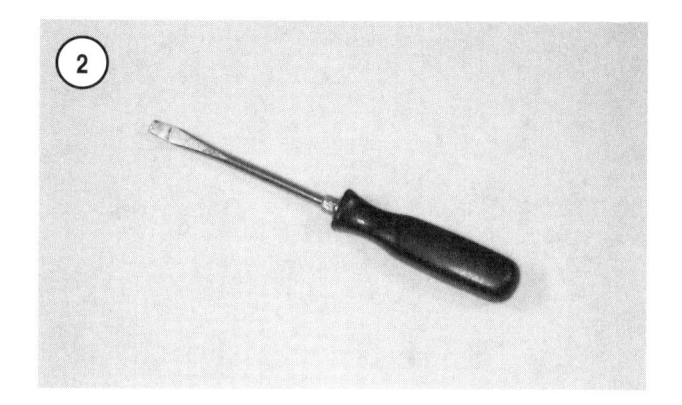

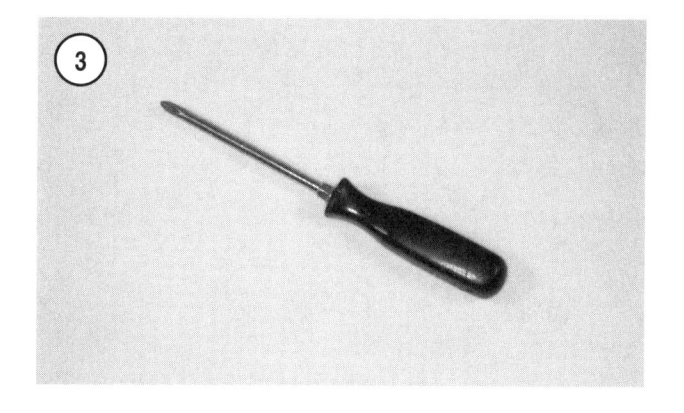

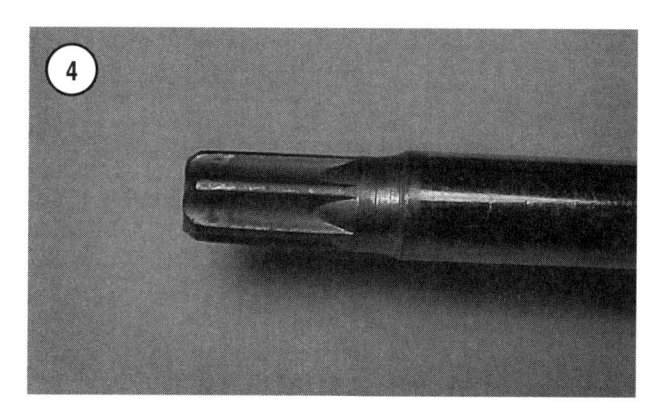

BASIC HAND TOOLS

A number of tools are required to maintain and repair a marine engine. Most of these tools are also used for home and automobile repair. Some tools are made especially for working on marine engines; these tools can be purchased from a marine dealership. Having the required tools always makes the job easier and more effective.

Keep the tools clean and in a suitable box. Keep them organized with related tools stored together. After using a tool, wipe it clean using a shop towel.

The following tools are required to perform virtually any repair job. Each tool is described and the recommended size given for starting a tool collection. Additional tools and some duplication may be added as you become more familiar with the equipment. You may need all U.S. standard tools, all metric size tools or a mixture of both.

Screwdrivers

A screwdriver (**Figure 1**) is a very basic tool, but if used improperly can do more damage than good. The slot on a screw has a definite dimension and shape. Always select a screwdriver that conforms to the shape of the screw. Use a small screwdriver for small screws and a large one for large screws or the screw head are damaged.

Three types of screwdrivers are commonly required: a slotted (flat-blade) screwdriver (**Figure 2**), Phillips screwdriver (**Figure 3**) and Torx screwdriver (**Figure 4**).

Screwdrivers are available in sets, which often include an assortment of slotted Phillips and Torx blades. If you buy them individually, buy at least the following:

a. Slotted screwdriver—5/16 × 6 in. blade.
b. Slotted screwdriver—3/8 × 12 in. blade.
c. Phillips screwdriver—No. 2 tip, 6 in. blade.

d. Phillips screwdriver—No. 3 tip, 6 in. blade.
e. Torx screwdriver—T15 tip, 6 in. blade.
f. Torx screwdriver—T20 tip, 6 in. blade.
g. Torx screwdriver—T25 tip, 6 in. blade.

Use screwdrivers only for driving screws. Never use a screwdriver for prying or chiseling. Do not attempt to remove a Phillips, Torx or Allen head screw with a slotted screwdriver; you can damage the screw head so that even the proper tool is unable to remove it.

Keep the tip of a slotted screwdriver in good condition. Carefully grind the tip to the proper size and taper if it is worn or damaged. The sides of the blade must be parallel and the blade tip must be flat. Replace a Phillips or Torx screwdriver if its tip is worn or damaged.

Pliers

Pliers come in a wide range of types and sizes. Pliers are useful for cutting, gripping, bending and crimping. Never use pliers to cut hardened objects or turn bolts or nuts. **Figure 5** shows several types of pliers.

Each type of pliers has a specialized function. General-purpose pliers are mainly used for gripping and bending. Locking pliers are used for gripping objects very tightly, like a vise. Use needlenose pliers to grip or bend small objects. Adjustable or slip-joint pliers (**Figure 6**) can be adjusted to grip various sized objects; the jaws remain parallel for gripping objects such as pipe or tubing. There are many more types of pliers. The ones described here are the most common.

Box-end and Open-end Wrenches

Box-end and open-end wrenches (**Figure 7**) are available in sets in a variety of sizes. The number stamped near the end of the wrench refers to the distance between two parallel flats on the hex head bolt or nut.

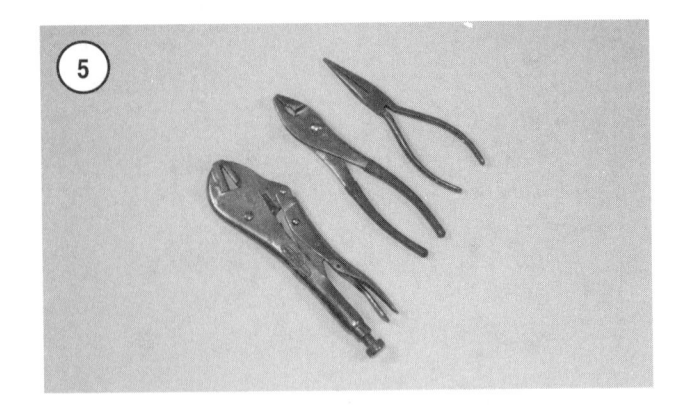

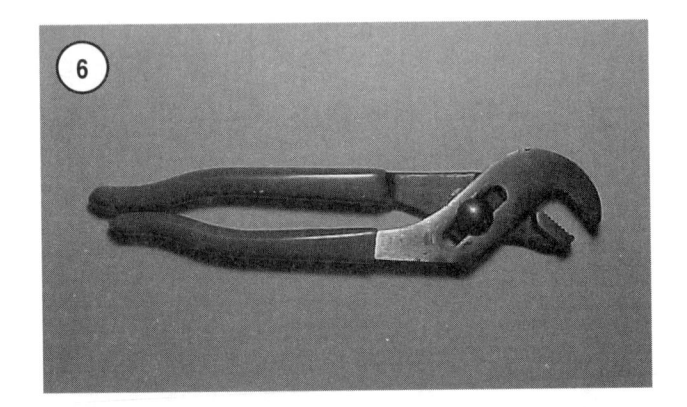

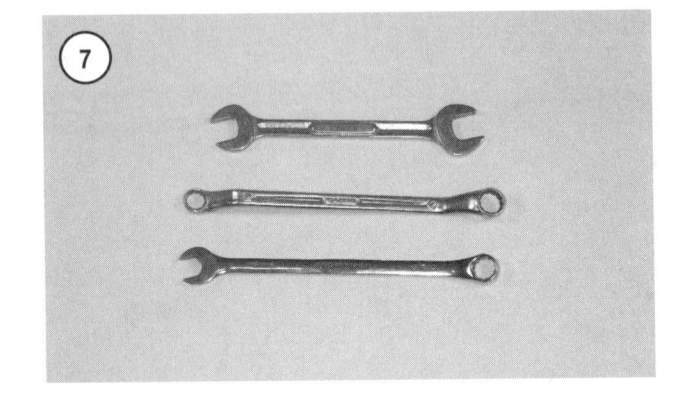

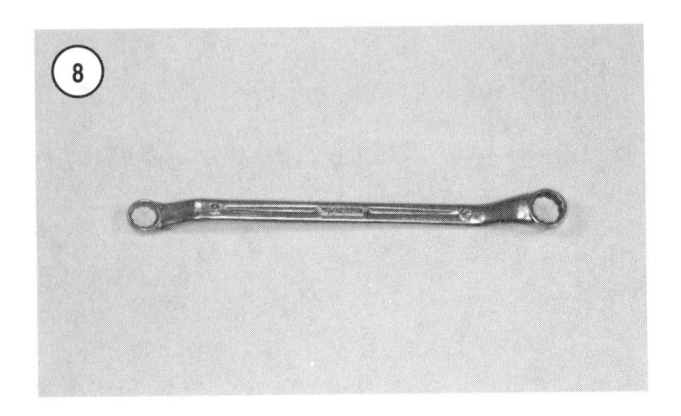

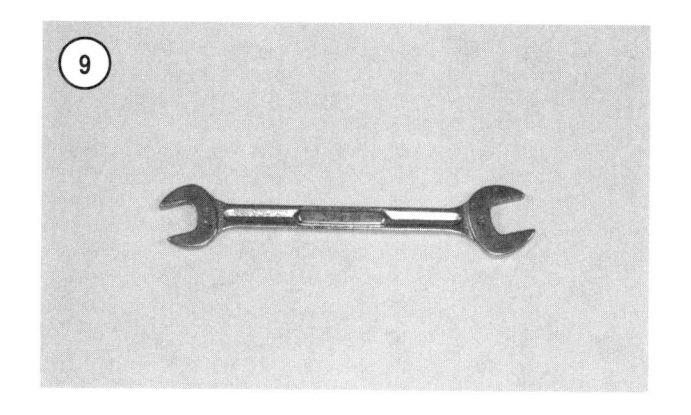

TOOLS AND TECHNIQUES

superior holding power; the 12-point allow a shorter swing if working in tight quarters.

Use an open-end wrench if a box-end wrench cannot be positioned over the nut or bolt. To prevent damage to the fastener, avoid using and open-end wrench if a large amount of tightening or loosening toque is required.

A combination wrench has both a box-end and open-end. Both ends are the same size.

Adjustable Wrenches

An adjustable wrench (**Figure 10**) can be adjusted to fit virtually any nut or bolt head. However, it can loosen and slip from the nut or bolt, causing damage to the nut and possible physical injury. Use an adjustable wrench only if a proper size open-end or box-end wrench in not available. Avoid using an adjustable wrench if a large amount of tightening or loosening torque is required.

Adjustable wrenches come in sized ranging from 4-18 in. overall length. A 6 or 8 in. size is recommended as an all-purpose wrench.

Socket Wrenches

A socket wrench (**Figure 11**) is generally faster, safer and more convenient to use than a common wrench. Sockets, which attach to a suitable handle, are available with six-point or 12-point openings and use 1/4, 3/8, and 1/2 in. drive sizes. The drive size corresponds to the square hole that mates with the ratchet or flex handle.

Torque Wrench

A torque wrench (**Figure 12**) is used with a socket to measure how tight a nut or bolt is installed. They come in a wide price range and in 1/4, 3/8, and 1/2 in. drive sizes. The drive size

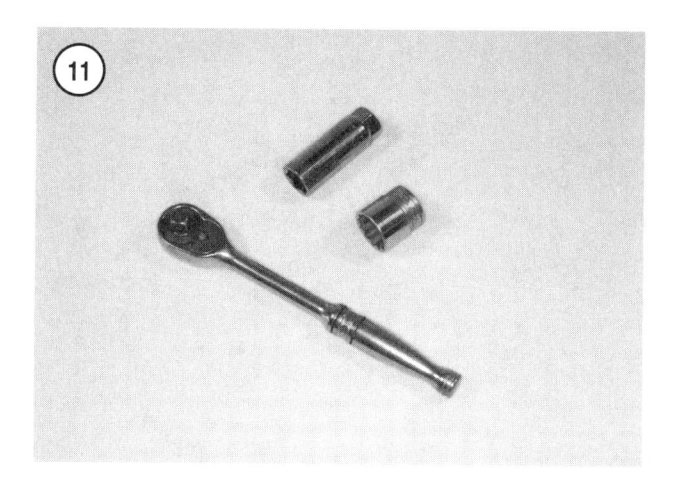

Box-end wrenches (**Figure 8**) provide a better grip on the nut and are stronger than open end wrenches. An open-end wrench (**Figure 9**) grips the nut on only two flats. Unless it fits well, it may slip and round off the points on the nut. A box-end wrench grips all six flats. Box-end wrenches are available with six-point or 12 point openings. The six-point opening provides

corresponds to the square hole that mates with the socket.

A typical 1/4 in. drive torque wrench measures in in.-lb. increments, and has a range of 20-150 in.-lb. (2.2-17 N•m). A typical 3/8 or 1/2 in. torque measures in ft.-lb. increments, and has a range of 10-150 ft.-lb. (14-203 N•m).

Impact Driver

An impact driver (**Figure 13**) makes removal of tight fasteners easy and reduces damage to bolts and screws. Interchangeable bits allow use on a variety of fasteners.

Snap Ring Pliers

Snap ring pliers are required to remove snap rings. Snap ring pliers (**Figure 14**) usually come with different size tips; many designs can be switched to handle internal or external type snap rings.

Hammers

Various types of hammers (**Figure 15**) are available to accommodate a number of applications. Use a ball-peen hammer to strike another tool, such as a punch or chisel. Use a soft-face hammer to strike a metal object without damaging it.

Never use a metal-faced hammer on engine and drive system components as severe damage will occur. You can always produce the same amount of force with a soft-faced hammer.

Always wear eye protection when using hammers. Make sure the hammer is in good condition and that the handle is not cracked. Select the correct hammer for the job and always strike the object squarely. Do not use the handle or the side of the hammer head to stroke an object.

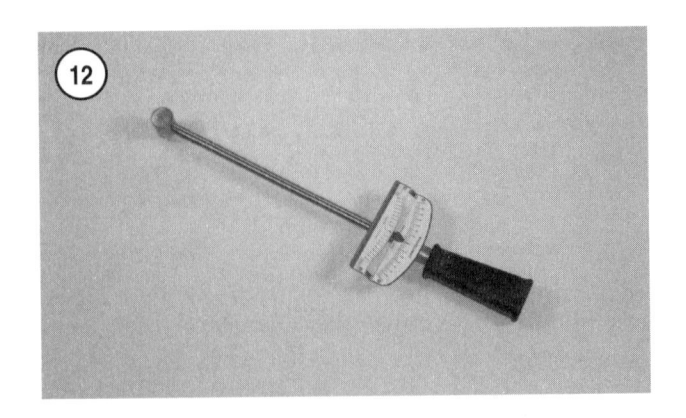

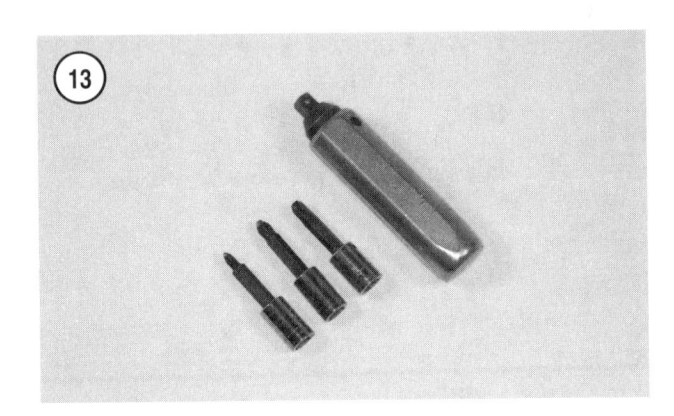

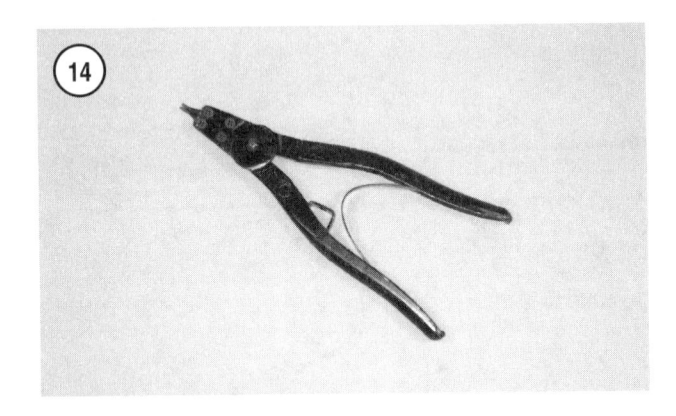

TOOLS AND TECHNIQUES

Other Special Tools

Many of the maintenance and repair procedures require special tools. Most of the necessary tools are available from a marine dealership or from tool suppliers. Instructions for their use and the manufacture's part number are included in the appropriate chapter.

Purchase the required tools from a local marine dealership or tool supplier. A qualified machinist, often at a lower price, can make some tools locally. Many marine dealerships and rental outlets will rent some of the required tools. Avoid using makeshift tools. Their use may result in damaged parts that cost far more than the recommended tool.

TEST EQUIPMENT

This section describes equipment used to perform testing, adjustments and measurements on marine engines. Most of these tools are available from a local marine dealership or automotive parts store.

Multimeter

This instrument is invaluable for electrical troubleshooting and service. It combines a voltmeter, ohmmeter and an ammeter in one unit. It is often called a VOM.

Two types of mutimeter are available, analog and digital. Analog meters (**Figure 17**) have a moving needle with marked bands on the meter face indicating the volt, ohm and amperage scales. An analog meter must be calibrated each time the scale is changed.

A digital meter (**Figure 18**) is ideally suited for electrical troubleshooting because it is easy to read and more accurate than an analog meter. Most models are auto-ranging, have automatic polarity compensation and internal overload protection circuits.

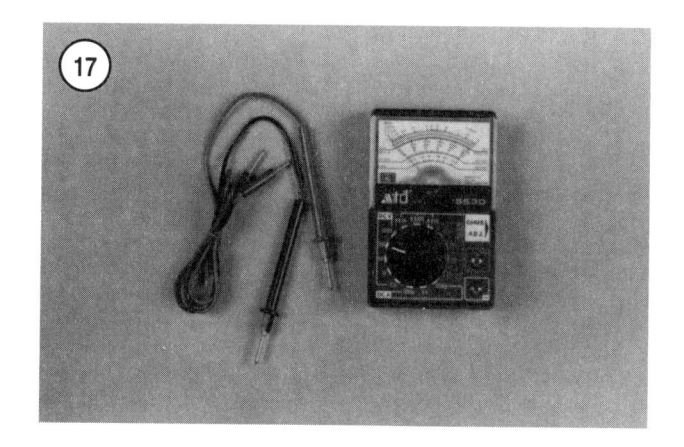

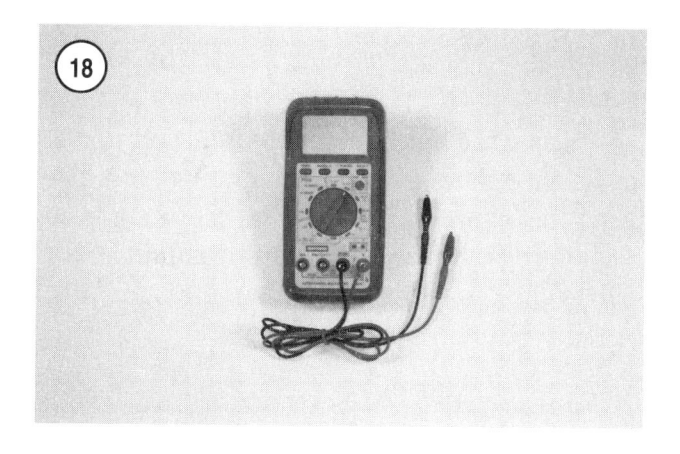

Feeler Gauges

This tool has either flat or wire measuring gauges (**Figure 16**). Use wire gauges to measure spark plug gap; use flat gauges for other measurements. A nonmagnetic (brass) gauge may be specified if working around magnetized components.

Either type of meter is suitable for most electrical testing described in this manual. An analog meter is better suited for testing pulsing voltage signals such as those produced by the ignition system. A digital meter is better suited for testing very low resistance or voltage reading (less than 1 volt or 1 ohm). The test procedure will indicate if a specific type of meter is required.

The ignition system produces electrical pulses that are too short in duration for accurate measurement with a using a conventional multimeter. Use a meter with peak-volt reading ca pability to test the ignition system. This type of meter captures the peak voltage reached during an electrical pulse.

Scale selection, meter specifications and test connections vary by the manufacturer and model of the meter. Thoroughly read the instructions supplied with the meter before performing any test. The meter and certain electrical components on the engine can be damaged if tested incorrectly. Have the test performed by a qualified professional if you are unfamiliar with the testing or general meter usage. The expense to replace damaged equipment can far exceed the cost of having the test performed by a professional.

Strobe Timing Light

This instrument is necessary for dynamic tuning (setting ignition timing while the engine is running). By flashing a light at the precise instant the spark plug fires, the position of the timing mark can be seen. The flashing light makes a moving mark appear to stand still next to a stationary mark.

Timing lights (**Figure 19**) range from inexpensive models with a neon bulb to expensive models with a xenon bulb, built in tachometer and timing advance compensator. A built in tachometer is very useful as most ignition timing specifications are based on a specific engine speed.

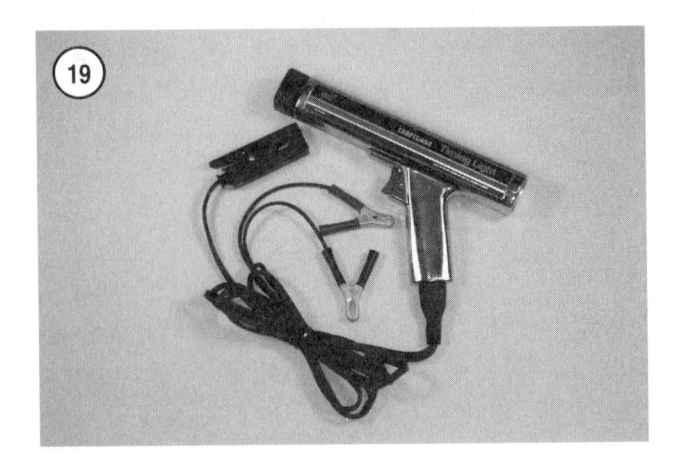

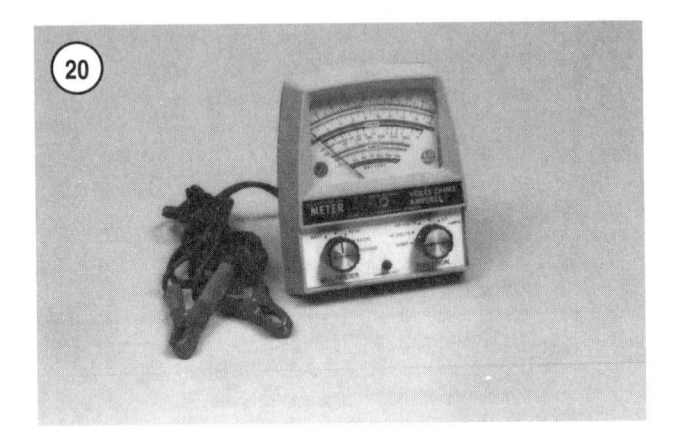

A timing advance compensator delays the strobe enough to bring the timing mark to a certain place on the scale. Although useful for troubleshooting purposes, this feature should not be used to check or adjust the base ignition timing.

Tachometer/Dwell Meter

A portable tachometer (**Figure 20**) is needed to tune and test most marine engines. Ignition timing and carburetor adjustments must be performed at a specified engine speed. Tachometers are available with either an analog or digital display.

The fuel/air mixture must be adjusted with the engine running at idle speed. If using an analog

TOOLS AND TECHNIQUES

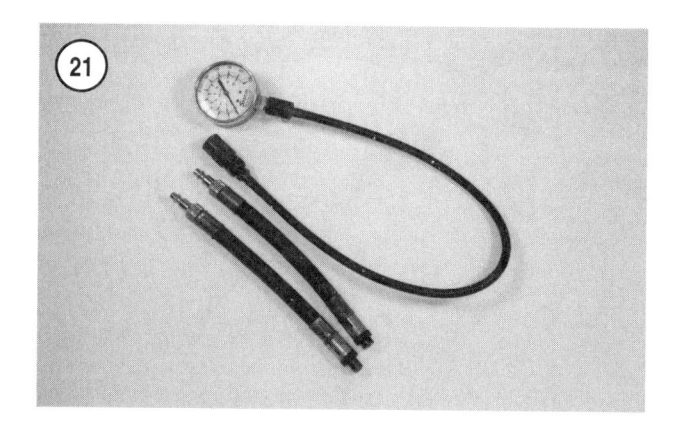

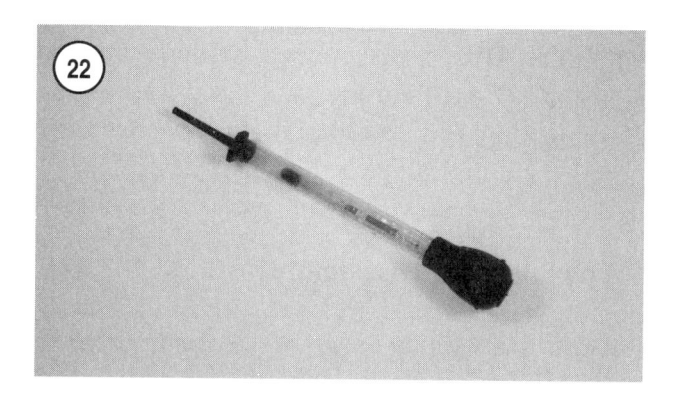

tachometer, choose one with a low range of 0-1000 rpm or 0-2000 rpm range and a high range of 0-6000 rpm. The high range setting is needed for testing purposes but lacks the accuracy needed at lower speeds. At lower speeds the meter must be capable of detecting changes of 25 rpm or less.

Digital tachometers are generally easier to use than most analog type tachometers. They provide accurate measurement at all speeds without the need to change the range or scale. Many of these use an inductive pickup to receive the signal from the ignition system.

A dwell meter is often incorporated into the tachometer to allow testing and/or adjustments to engines with a breaker point ignition system.

Compression Gauge

This tool (**Figure 21**) measures the amount of pressure created in the combustion chamber during the compression stroke. Compression indicates the general engine condition making it one of the most useful troubleshooting tools.

The easiest type to use has screw-in adapters that fit the spark plug holes. Rubber tipped, press-in type gauges are also available. This type must be held firmly in the spark plug hole to prevent leakage and inaccurate test results..

Hydrometer

Use a hydrometer to measure specific gravity in the battery. Specific gravity is the density of the battery electrolyte as compared to pure water and indicates the battery's state of charge. Choose a hydrometer (**Figure 22**) with automatic temperature compensation; otherwise the electrolyte temperature must be measured during charging to determine the actual specific gravity.

Precision Measuring Tools

Various tools are required to make precision measurements. A dial indicator (**Figure 23**), for example, is used to determine piston position in the cylinder, runout and end play of shafts and assemblies. It is also used to measure free movement between the gear teeth (backlash) in the drive unit.

Venier calipers (**Figure 24**), micrometers (**Figure 25**) and other precision tools are used to measure the size of parts, such as the piston.

Precision measuring equipment must be stored, handled and used carefully or it will not remain accurate.

SERVICE HINTS

Most of the service procedures in this manual are straightforward and can be performed by anyone reasonably handy with tools. It is suggested, however, that you consider your skills and available tools and equipment before attempting a repair involving major disassembly of the engine or drive unit.

Some operations, for example, require the use of a press. Other operations require precision measurement. Have the procedure or measurements performed by a professional if you do not have access to the correct equipment or are unfamiliar with its use.

Special Battery Precautions

Disconnecting or connecting the battery can create a spike or surge of current throughout the electrical system. This spike or surge can damage certain components of the charging system. Always verify the ignition switch is in the OFF position before connecting or disconnecting the battery or changing the selection on a battery switch.

Always disconnect both battery cables and remove the battery from the boat for charging. If the battery cables are connected, the charger may induce a damaging spike or surge of current into the electrical system. During charging, batteries produce explosive and corrosive gasses. These gases can cause corrosion in the battery compartment and creates an extremely hazardous condition.

Disconnect the cables from the battery prior to testing, adjusting or repairing many of the systems or components on the engine. This is necessary for safety, to prevent damage to test equipment and to ensure accurate testing or adjustment. Always disconnect the negative battery cable first, then the positive cable. When reconnecting the battery, always connect the positive cable first, then the negative cable.

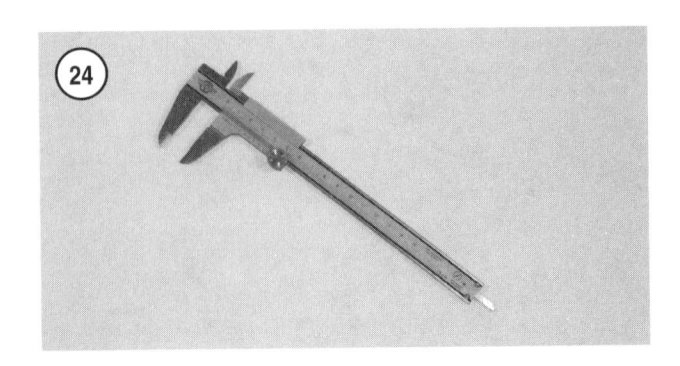

Preparation for Disassembly

Repairs go much faster if the equipment is clean before you begin work. There are special cleaners such as Gunk or Bel-Ray Degreaser, for cleaning the engine and related components. Just spray or brush on the cleaning solution, let it stand, then rinse with a garden hose.

Use pressurized water to remove marine growth and corrosion or mineral deposits from external components such as the gearcase, drive shaft housing and clamp brackets. Avoid directing pressurized water directly as seals or gaskets; pressurized water can flow past seal and gasket surfaces and contaminate lubricating fluids.

WARNING
Never use gasoline as a cleaning agent. It presents an extreme fire hazard. Always work in a well-ventilated area if using cleaning solvent. Keep a Coast Guard approved fire extinguisher, rated for gasoline fires, readily accessible in the work area.

Much of the labor charged for a job performed at a dealership is usually for removal and disas-

TOOLS AND TECHNIQUES

25

sembly of other parts to access defective parts or assemblies. It is frequently possible to perform most of the disassembly then take the defective part or assembly to the dealership for repair.

If you decide to perform the job yourself, read the appropriate section in this manual, in its entirety. Study the illustrations and text until you fully understand what is involved to complete the job. Make arrangements to purchase or rent all required special tools and equipment before starting.

Disassembly Precautions

During disassembly, keep a few general precautions in mind. Force is rarely needed to get things apart. If parts fit tightly, such as a bearing on a shaft, there is usually a tool designed to separate them. Never use a screwdriver to separate parts with a machined mating surface, such as the cylinder head or manifold. The surfaces will be damaged and leak.

Make diagrams or take instant photographs wherever similar-appearing parts are found. Often, disassembled parts are left for several days or longer before resuming work. You may not remember where everything came from, or carefully arranged parts may become disturbed.

Cover all openings after removing parts to keep contamination or other parts from entering.

Tag all similar internal parts for location and mounting direction. Reinstall all internal components in the same location and mounting direction as removed. Record the thickness and mounting location of any shims as they are removed. Place small bolts and parts in plastic sandwich bags. Seal and label the bags with masking tape.

Tag all wires, hoses and connections and make a sketch of the routing. Never rely on memory alone; it may be several days or longer before you resume work.

Protect all painted surfaces from physical damage. Never allow gasoline or cleaning solvent on these surfaces.

Assembly Precautions

No parts, except those assembled with a press fit, require unusual force during assembly. If a part is hard to remove or install, find out why before proceeding.

When assembling parts, start all fasteners, then tighten evenly in an alternating or crossing pattern unless a specific tightening sequence or procedure is given.

When assembling parts, be sure all shims, spacers and washers are installed in the same position and location as removed.

Whenever a rotating part butts against a stationary part, look for a shim or washer. Use new gaskets, seals and O-rings if there is any doubt about the conditions of the used ones. Unless otherwise specified, a thin coating of oil on gaskets may help them seal more effectively. Use heavy grease to hold small parts in place if they tend to fall out during assembly.

Use emery cloth and oil to remove high spots from piston surfaces. Use a dull screwdriver to remove carbon deposits from the cylinder head, ports and piston crown. *Do not* scratch or gouge these surfaces. Wipe the surfaces clean with a *clean* shop towel when finished.

If the carburetor must be repaired, completely disassemble it and soak all metal parts in a commercial carburetor cleaner. Never soak gaskets and rubber or plastic parts in these cleaners.

Clean rubber or plastic parts in warm soapy water. Never use a wire to clean jets and small passages because they are easily damaged. Use compressed air to blow debris from all passages in the carburetor body.

Take your time and do the job right. Break-in procedure for a newly rebuilt engine or drive is the same as for a new one. Use the recommended break-in oil and follow the instructions provided in the appropriate chapter.

SPECIAL TIPS

Because of the extreme demands placed on marine equipment, several points must be kept in mind when performing service and repair. The following are general suggestions that may improve the overall life of the machine and help avoid costly failure.

1. Unless otherwise specified, apply a threadlocking compound, such as Loctite Threadlocker, to all bolts and nuts, even if secured with a lockwasher. Use only the specified grade of threadlocking compound. A screw or bolt lost from an engine cover or bearing retainer could easily cause serious and expensive damage before the loss is noticed. When applying threadlocking compound, use only enough to lightly coat the threads. If too much is used, it can work its way down the threads and contaminate seals or bearings.

2. If self-locking fasteners are used, replace them with new ones. Do not install standard fasteners in place of self-locking ones.

3. Use caution when using air tools to remove stainless steel nuts or bolts. The heat generated during rapid spinning easily damages the threads of stainless steel fasteners. To prevent thread damage, apply penetrating oil as a cooling agent and loosen or tighten them slowly.

4. Use a wide chisel to straighten the tab of a fold-over type lockwasher. Such a tool provides a better contact surface than a screwdriver or pry bar, making straightening easier. During installation, use a new fold-over type lockwasher. If a new lockwasher is not available, fold over a tab on the washer that has not been previously used. Reusing the same tab may cause the washer to break, resulting in a loss of locking ability and a loose piece of metal adrift in the engine. When folding the tab into position, carefully pry it toward the flat on the bolt or nut. Use a pair or plies to bend the tab against the fastener. Do not use a punch and hammer to drive the tab into position. The resulting fold may be too sharp, weakening the washer and increasing its chance of failure.

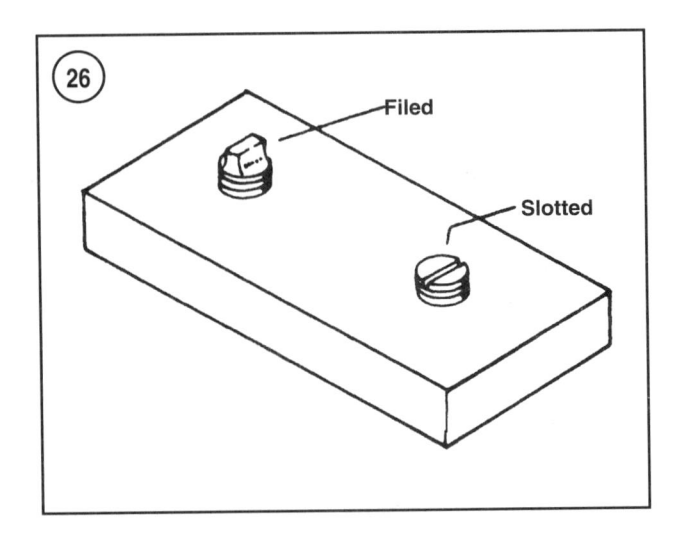

5. Use only the specified replacement parts if replacing a missing or damaged bolt, screw or nut. Many fasteners are specially hardened for the application.

6. Install only the specified gaskets. Unless specified otherwise, install them without sealant. Many gaskets are made with a material that swells when it contacts oil. Gasket sealer prevents them from swelling as intended and can result in oil leakage. Most gaskets must be a specific thickness. Installing a gasket that is too thin or too thick in a critical area could cause expensive damage.

7. Make sure all shims and washers are reinstalled in the same location and position. Whenever a rotating part contacts a stationary part, look for a shim or washer.

TOOLS AND TECHNIQUES

REMOVING BROKEN SCREWS AND BOLTS

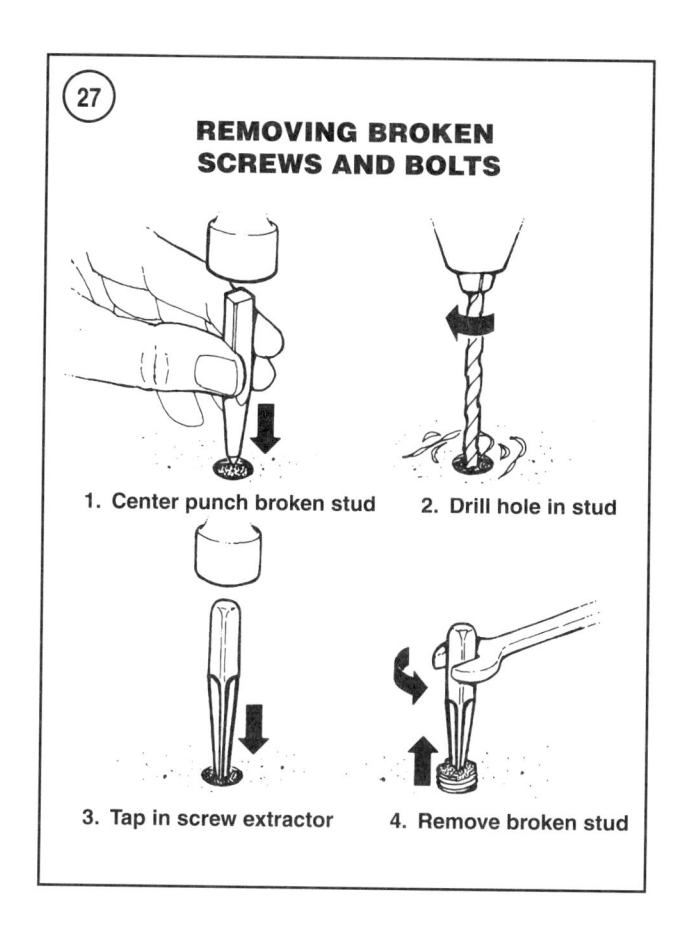

1. Center punch broken stud
2. Drill hole in stud
3. Tap in screw extractor
4. Remove broken stud

MECHANICS TECHNIQUES

Marine engines are subjected to conditions very different from most engines. They are repeatedly subjected to a corrosive environment followed by periods of non-use for weeks or longer. Such use invites corrosion damage to fasteners, causing difficulty or breakage during removal. This section provides information that is useful for removing stuck or broken fasteners and repairing damaged threads.

Removing Stuck Fasteners

When a nut or bolt corrodes and cannot be removed, several methods may be used to loosen it. First, apply penetrating oil, such as Liquid Wrench or WD-40. Apply it liberally to the threads and allow it to penetrate for 10-15 minutes. Tap the fastener several times with a small hammer; however, do not hit it hard enough to cause damage. Reapply the penetrating oil if necessary.

For stuck screws, apply penetrating oil as described, then insert a screwdriver in the slot. Tap the top of the screwdriver with a hammer. This looses the corrosion in the threads allowing it to turn. If the screw head is too damaged to use a screwdriver, grip the head with locking pliers and twist the screw from the assembly.

A Phillips, Allen or Torx screwdriver may start to slip in the screw during removal. If slippage occurs, stop immediately and apply a dab of course valve lapping compound onto the tip of the screwdriver. Valve lapping compound or a special screw removal compound is available from most hardware and automotive parts stores. Insert the driver into the screw and apply downward pressure while turning. The gritty material in the compound improves the grip on the screw, allowing more rotational force before slippage occurs. Keep the compound away from any other engine components. It is very abrasive and can cause rapid wear if applied onto moving or sliding surfaces.

Avoid applying heat unless specifically instructed because it may melt, warp or remove the temper from parts.

Removing Broken Bolts or Screws

The head of bolt or screw may unexpectedly twist off during removal. Several methods are available for removing the remaining portion of the bolt or screw.

If a large portion of the bolt or screw projects out, try gripping it with locking pliers. If the projecting portion is too small, file it to fit a wrench or cut a slot in it to fit a screwdriver (**Figure 26**). If the head breaks off flush or cannot be turned with a screwdriver or wrench, use a screw extractor (**Figure 27**). To do this, center punch the remaining portion of the screw or bolt. Select the proper size of extractor for the size of the fastener. Using the drill size specified on the extractor, drill a hole into the fastener. Do not drill deeper than the remaining fastener. Carefully tap the extractor into the hole and back the remnant out using a wrench on the extractor.

Remedying Stripped Threads

Occasionally, threads are stripped through carelessness or impact damage. Often the threads can be repaired by running a tap (for internal threads on nuts) or die (for external threads on bolts) through threads (**Figure 28**).

To clean or repair spark plug threads, use a spark plug tap. If an internal thread is damaged, it may be necessary to install a Helicoil or some other type of thread insert. Follow the manufacturer's instructions when installing their insert.

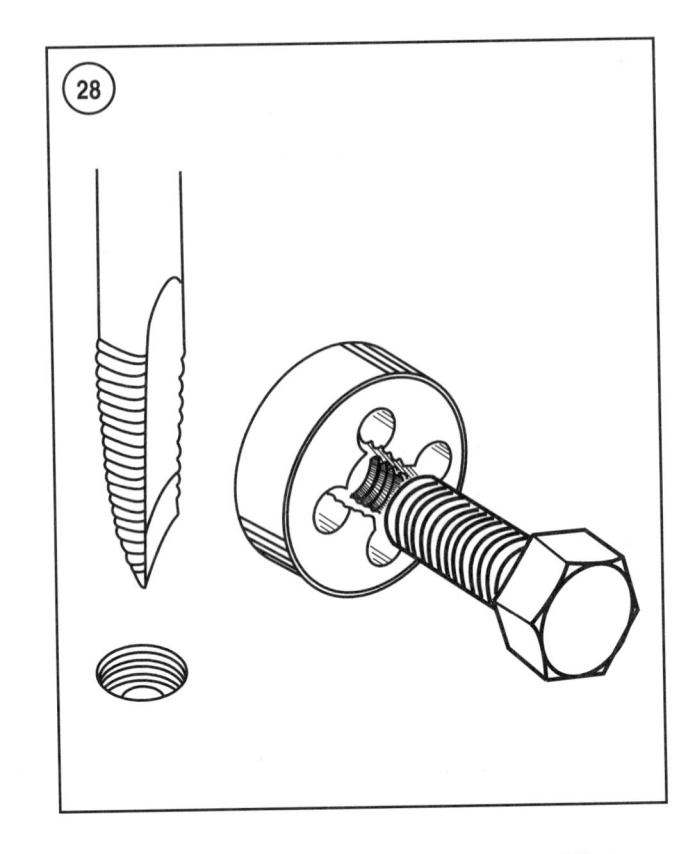

Chapter Three

Troubleshooting

Troubleshooting is a relatively simple matter when it is done logically. The first step in any troubleshooting procedure is to define the symptoms as closely as possible and then localize the problem. Subsequent steps involve testing and analyzing those areas which could cause the symptoms. A haphazard approach may eventually solve the problem, but it can be very costly in terms of wasted time and unnecessary parts replacement.

Never assume anything. Don't overlook the obvious. If the engine suddenly quits when running, check the easiest and most accessible spots first. Make sure there is gasoline in the tank, the fuel petcock is in the ON position and the spark plug wires and wiring harnesses are properly connected.

If a quick visual check of the obvious does not turn up the cause of the problem, look a little further. Learning to recognize and describe symptoms accurately will make repairs easier for you or a mechanic at the shop. Saying that "it won't run" isn't the same as saying "it quit at high speed and wouldn't start."

Gather as many symptoms together as possible to aid in diagnosis. Note whether the engine lost power gradually or all at once, what color smoke (if any) came from the exhaust and so on. Remember—the more complicated an engine is, the easier it is to troubleshoot because symptoms point to specific problems.

After the symptoms are defined, areas which could cause the problems should be tested and analyzed. You don't need fancy or complicated test equipment to determine whether repairs can be attempted at home. A few simple checks can save a large repair bill and time lost while the engine sits in a shop's service department.

On the other hand, be realistic and don't attempt repairs beyond your abilities. Service departments tend to charge heavily for putting together a disassembled engine that may have been abused. Some won't even take on such a job—so use common sense and don't get in over your head.

Proper lubrication, maintenance and periodic tune-ups as described in Chapter Four will reduce the necessity for troubleshooting. Even with the best of care, however, an outboard motor is prone to problems which will require troubleshooting. This chapter contains brief descriptions of each operating system and troubleshooting procedures to be used. **Tables 1-3** are at the end of the chapter.

OPERATING REQUIREMENTS

Every outboard motor requires 3 basic things to run properly: an uninterrupted supply of fuel and air in the correct proportions, proper ignition at the right time and adequate compression. If any of these are lacking, the motor will not run.

The electrical system is the weakest link in the chain. More problems result from electrical malfunctions than from any other source. Keep this in mind before you blame the fuel system and start making unnecessary carburetor adjustments.

If a motor has been sitting for any length of time and refuses to start, check the condition of the battery first to make sure it has an adequate charge, then look to the fuel delivery system. This includes the gas tank, fuel pump (if so equipped), fuel lines and carburetor(s). Rust may have formed in the tank, obstructing fuel flow. Gasoline deposits may have gummed up carburetor jets and air passages. Gasoline tends to lose its potency after standing for long periods. Condensation may contaminate it with water. Drain the old gas and try starting with a fresh tankful. If the carburetor is getting a satisfactory supply of good fuel, turn to the starting system.

STARTING SYSTEM

Description

Johnson/Evinrude 18 hp and larger outboard motors may be equipped with an electric starter motor (**Figure 1**). The motor is mounted vertically on the engine. When battery current is supplied to the starter motor, its pinion gear is thrust upward to engage the teeth on the engine flywheel. Once the engine starts, the pinion gear disengages from the flywheel. This is similar to the method used in cranking an automotive engine.

The electric starting system requires a fully charged battery to provide the large amount of current required to operate the starter motor. The battery may be charged externally or by a generator or alternator stator on the engine which keeps the battery charged while the engine is running.

The starting circuit on all electric-start outboards covered in this manual consists of the battery, starter motor, ignition switch, starter and choke solenoids, safety switch and connecting wiring. **Figure 2** shows a typical starting circuit.

NOTE
Some smaller engines may use a push-button ignition switch instead of the key switch discussed in this section.

Turning the ignition switch to START allows current to flow from the battery through the solenoid coil. The solenoid contacts close and allow current to flow to the starter motor.

The safety switch prevents current flow through the solenoid coil whenever the

TROUBLESHOOTING

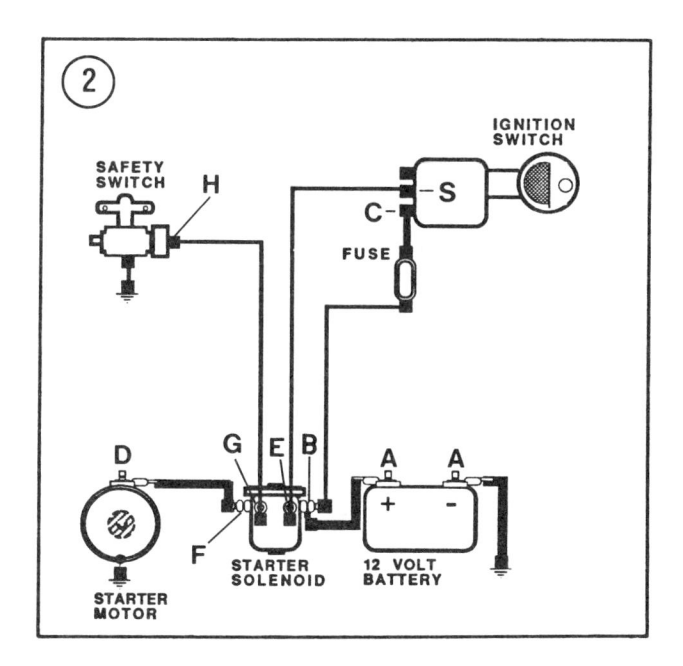

throttle lever is set beyond the START position. On models with remote control, the safety switch is located in the remote control box. On models without remote control, a plunger-operated switch rides on an armature plate shift lock cam or distributor housing cam.

The choke solenoid electrically moves the choke valve linkage to open the choke for starting.

General troubleshooting procedures are provided in **Table 1**.

Starting Difficulties With Older Engines

Many older 2-stroke engines are plagued by hard starting and generally poor running for which there seems to be no good cause. Carburetion and ignition are satisfactory and a compression test shows all is well in the engine's upper end.

What a compression test does not show is a lack of primary compression. The crankcase in a 2-stroke engine must be alternately under pressure and vacuum. After the piston closes the intake port, further downward movement of the piston causes the trapped mixture to be pressurized so it can rush quickly into the cylinder when the scavenging ports are opened. Upward piston movement creates a vacuum in the crankcase, enabling air-fuel mixture to be drawn in from the carburetor.

If the crankshaft seals or case gaskets leak, the crankcase cannot hold pressure or vacuum and proper engine operation becomes impossible. Any other source of leakage, such as defective cylinder base gaskets or porous or cracked crankcase castings, will result in the same conditions.

Older engines suffering from hard starting should be checked for pressure leaks with a small brush and soap suds solution. The following is a list of possible leakage points in the engine:

  a. Crankshaft seals.
  b. Spark plug threads.
  c. Cylinder head joint.
  d. Cylinder base joint.
  e. Carburetor mounting flange(s).
  f. Crankcase joint.

CAUTION
Do not operate an electric starter motor continuously for more than 15 seconds. Allow the motor to cool for at least 2 minutes between attempts to start the engine.

Troubleshooting Preparation (All Models)

If the following procedures do not locate the cause of the problem, refer to **Table 1** for more extensive testing. Before troubleshooting the starting circuit, make sure that:

  a. The battery is fully charged.
  b. The control lever is in NEUTRAL.
  c. Battery cables are the proper size and length. Replace cables that are undersize or relocate the battery to shorten the distance between battery and starter solenoid.

d. All electrical connections are clean and tight.
e. The wiring harness is in good condition, with no worn or frayed insulation or loose harness sockets.
f. The fuse(s) installed in the junction box or in the wiring between the ignition switch and solenoid are good, if so equipped.
g. The fuel system is filled with an adequate supply of fresh gasoline that has been properly mixed with Johnson or Evinrude 50/1 Lubricant. See Chapter Four.
h. The spark plugs are in good condition and properly gapped.
i. The ignition system is correctly timed, synchronized and adjusted. See Chapter Five.

Troubleshooting is intended only to isolate a malfunction to a certain component. If further bench testing is deemed necessary, remove the suspected component and have it tested by an authorized service center. Refer to Chapter Seven for component removal and installation procedures.

Starter motor turns slowly

1. Make sure the battery is fully charged.
2. Check for corroded or loose electrical connections. Clean and tighten as required.
3. Place an induction ampere gauge (**Figure 3**) on the cable between the starter motor terminal and solenoid to measure current draw while cranking the engine. After an initial surge, the amp gauge should read 110-140 amps. If an excessive current draw is indicated, rebuild or replace the starter motor.

Starter motor does not turn over

Refer to **Figure 2** and perform the following test sequence. Disconnect and ground the spark plug leads to prevent the engine from cranking. The starter solenoid is located in the junction box on models through 1966 and is externally mounted on the power head on 1967-1972 engines.

1. Connect a voltmeter between the battery terminals (test point A). If the voltmeter does not read 12 volts, recharge or replace the battery.
2. Connect the voltmeter between test point B and a good engine ground.
3. Turn the ignition key to the START position. If there is no voltage reading, look for corroded terminals, poor connections or defective wiring between the solenoid and battery.
4. Connect the voltmeter between test point C and a good engine ground. If there is little or no voltage shown, look for poor connections or defective wiring between the solenoid and key switch.
5. Connect the voltmeter between test point D and a good engine ground.
6. Turn the ignition key to the START position. If there is no voltage reading, proceed with Step 7. If the voltmeter reads 12 volts and the starter does not run, replace the starter.
7. Disconnect the starter cable at test point D. Connect the voltmeter between test point E and a good engine ground.
8. Turn the ignition key to the START position. If there is no voltage reading, either the key switch or the wiring between the key switch and solenoid is defective.

TROUBLESHOOTING

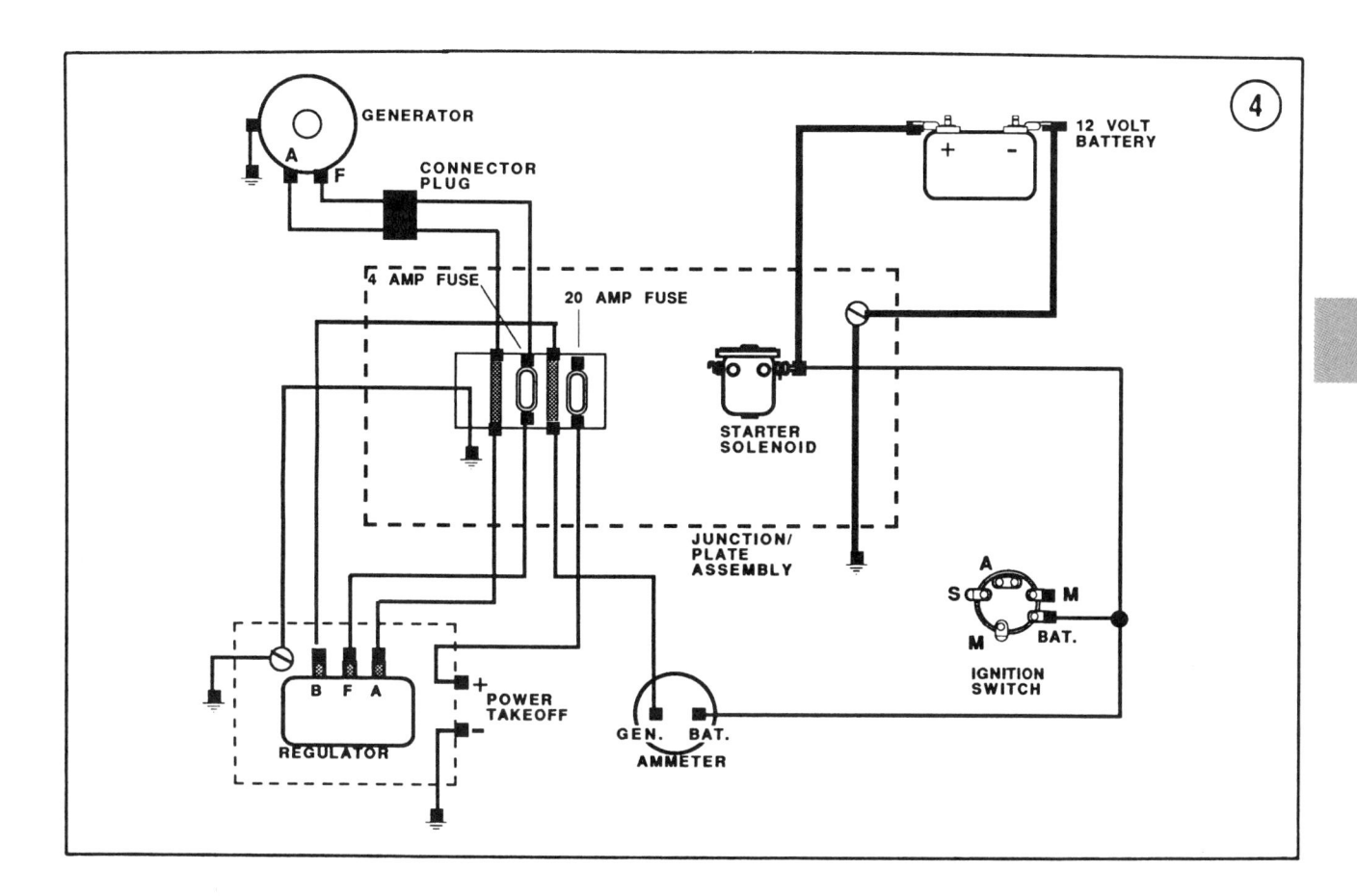

9. If the voltmeter reads 12 volts in Step 8, connect the voltmeter between test points B and F. Momentarily connect a jumper lead between the positive battery terminal and test point E. If there is a voltage reading, the solenoid is good. No reading indicates a possible defective solenoid or safety switch.

10. Leave the voltmeter connected between test points B and F. Connect a jumper lead between test point G and a good engine ground. Connect a second jumper lead between the positive battery terminal and test point E. If there is no voltage reading, replace the solenoid.

11. Disconnect the lead at test point H. Connect an ohmmeter between the switch terminal and a good engine ground. The ohmmeter should show continuity with the switch plunger depressed and no continuity when the plunger is extended. If it does not perform as stated, replace the safety switch.

12. Reconnect the starter cable at test point D.

Electric Choke Solenoid Test

1. Connect an ohmmeter between the choke solenoid terminal and a good engine ground.
2. With the meter set on the low scale, it should read approximately 3 ohms. If it does not, replace the choke solenoid.

D.C. GENERATOR CHARGING SYSTEM

Description

This charging system consists of a belt-driven generator, voltage regulator, fuse(s), ammeter, battery and connecting wiring. **Figure 4** is a schematic of the typical D.C. generator charging system.

Rotation of the generator armature past the field coils creates direct current. The generator delivers an output of 10 amps at 12 volts. The voltage regulator and fuses are enclosed in a junction box bracket-mounted to the rear of the engine.

A malfunction in the D.C. generator charging system generally causes the battery to remain undercharged. Excessive use of accessories during extended periods when the engine is operating at speeds below 1,500 rpm can also result in an undercharged battery. Since the generator is protected by its location on the power head, it is more likely that the battery, voltage regulator or connecting wiring will cause problems.

Troubleshooting Preparation

Before troubleshooting the D.C. generator charging circuit, visually check the following.
1. Determine the accessory amperage load. To do so, add up the wattage or candlepower rating of all accessories and divide by 12 (voltage). The result is the total amperage requirement of the accessories. It should not exceed 10 amps.
2. Make sure the red cable is connected to the positive battery terminal. If polarity is reversed, check for a damaged generator or voltage regulator.

NOTE
*If the battery cables are not connected to their proper terminals, the generator must be polarized after the cable connections are changed. See **Generator Removal/Installation**, Chapter Seven.*

3. Check for corroded or loose connections. Clean, tighten and insulate with OMC Black Neoprene Dip as required.
4. Check battery condition. Clean and recharge as required.
5. Check wiring harness between the generator and junction box for damaged or deteriorated insulation and corroded, loose or faulty connections. Repair or replace as required.

Generator Output Quick Check

A quick check of the generator output can be made using the ammeter installed in the boat. If the charging system is functioning properly, the ammeter needle will show a charge condition with the engine running above 2,000 rpm and all accessories off. The amount of charge will vary from only a slight needle movement (fully charged battery) to as much as 10 amps (fully discharged battery).

Troubleshooting

Refer to **Figure 4** for this procedure.
1. Disconnect the positive battery cable.
2. Remove the engine cover.
3. Disconnect all accessories from the junction box power take-off terminals.
4. Remove the junction box cover.
5. Reconnect the positive battery cable.
6. Connect a voltmeter between the junction box power take-off terminals.
   a. If the voltmeter reads 12-12.5 volts, proceed with Step 7.
   b. If the voltmeter reads less than 12-12.5 volts, check all wiring and connections. If satisfactory, recharge or replace the battery.
   c. If there is no voltmeter reading, check the 20 amp fuse in the junction box. If fuse is satisfactory, check the wiring and all connections between the battery and starter solenoid, to the ammeter terminals and back to the junction box. Pay particular attention to the 2 ground connections in the junction box and the 1 ground connection in the junction box cover. Correct any defects found.
7. With the engine mounted in a test tank or on the boat in the water, start and run at 3/4 throttle (3,500 rpm) in gear. After 15 minutes

TROUBLESHOOTING

5

RECTIFIER

FLYWHEEL   STATOR

BATTERY

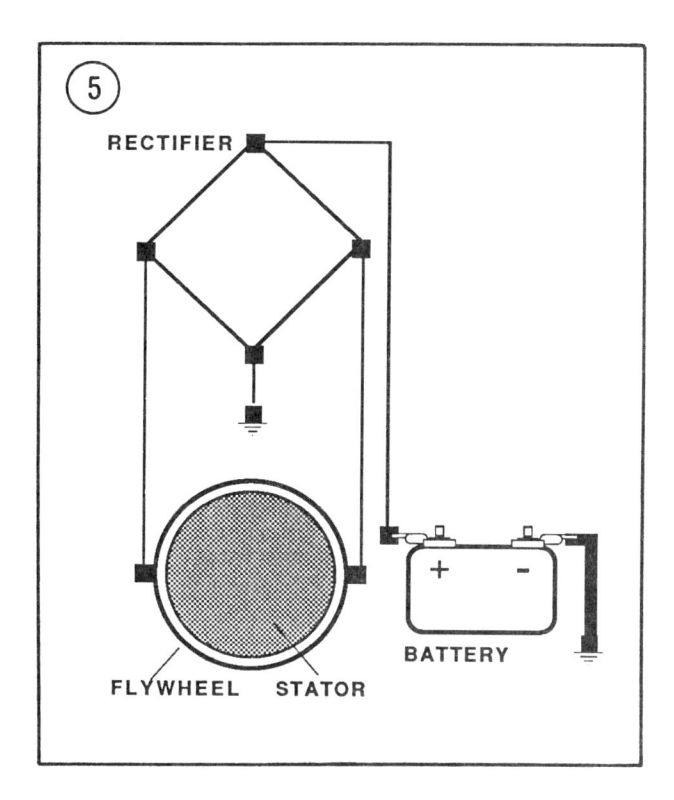

of operation, the voltmeter should read 14.5-15.2 volts with the ammeter slightly under the 10 amp mark.

8. If the voltmeter reads more than 15.2 volts with a high ammeter reading, disconnect the voltage regulator FLD lead. If the reading drops to 12.5 volts, replace the voltage regulator.

9. If the reading remains unchanged in Step 8, disconnect the field lead at the generator F terminal. If the reading still remains unchanged with the generator field lead disconnected, replace the generator.

10. If the reading drops to 12.5 volts after disconnecting the generator field lead in Step 9, there is a ground in the field lead between the generator and voltage regulator. Locate and correct, then reconnect the generator field lead and the regulator FLD lead.

11. If the voltmeter reading is correct in Step 8 but the ammeter shows a discharge condition, either the battery or ammeter leads are improperly connected. Correct as required.

12. If the voltmeter reading is correct in Step 8 but the ammeter shows no reading, disconnect the positive battery cable and remove the 4 amp fuse in the junction box. Clean the fuse clips, install a new fuse and reconnect the positive battery cable.

13. If the ammeter still shows no reading after changing the fuse in Step 12, check all wiring for correct installation and possible poor connections. Correct as required. If the wiring and connections are satisfactory, momentarily ground the regulator FLD terminal to the regulator base with a screwdriver and note the voltmeter reading.
   a. If the voltage reading is high, replace the regulator.
   b. If the voltage reading remains low, remove the voltmeter lead from the positive take-off terminal on the junction box and connect it to the regulator ARM terminal. Momentarily ground the regulator FLD terminal to the regulator base with a screwdriver and note the voltmeter reading. If the voltage increases, replace the regulator. If voltage still remains low, recheck all wiring and connections for an overlooked defect.

14. When tests have been completed, shut the engine off and remove the voltmeter. Disconnect the negative battery cable, reinstall the junction box cover and connect the electrical leads to the power take-off terminals. Reconnect the negative battery cable and install the engine cover.

ALTERNATOR CHARGING SYSTEM

A 20 amp regulated alternator charging system is used on Johnson and Evinrude outboards through 1966. The alternator charging system on 1967-1972 models may either be an unregulated 6 amp or 9 amp system, or a regulated 15 amp system.

The alternator charging system (**Figure 5**) consists of permanent magnets cast in the flywheel rim, a stator assembly containing coils wound on a laminated iron core, a rectifier to change alternating current (AC) to direct current (DC), the battery and connecting wiring. Regulated charging systems also have a voltage regulator and fuse.

A malfunction in the charging system generally causes the battery to remain undercharged. Since the stator is protected by its location underneath the flywheel, it is more likely that the battery, rectifier, regulator or connecting wiring will cause problems.

The following conditions will cause rectifier damage:
 a. Battery leads reversed.
 b. Running the engine with the battery leads disconnected.
 c. A broken wire or loose connection resulting in an open circuit.

Alternator Output Quick Check

A quick check of the alternator output can be made with an induction ammeter (**Figure 3**). Fit the ammeter over the positive battery cable and run the motor at full throttle in a test tank or on the boat in water. The induction ammeter will show the alternator output. The total electrical load on the system from the engine and accessories cannot exceed the system specification.

Alternator Output Test

Perform this test for a more accurate reading of alternator output. With the engine running in a test tank or on the boat in water, connect an AC voltmeter between a good engine ground and either of the yellow stator leads at the terminal block or quick-disconnect. See **Figure 6** (typical). If the meter does not read approximately 12 volts, check the stator and rectifier as described in this chapter.

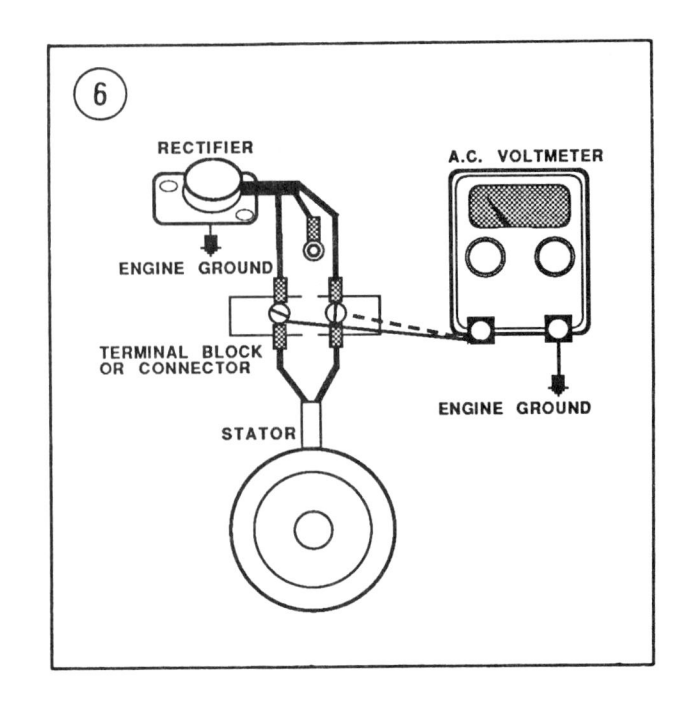

Charging System Quick Check

A quick check of the charging system can be made by turning the ignition switch ON/OFF several times with all accessories OFF.

1. Turn the switch ON. The indicator light (if so equipped) should come on, indicating that current is passing through the switch. Turn the switch ON/OFF several times to check for a dead spot in the switch.
2. Turn the switch ON while watching the ammeter needle. It should deflect slightly to the discharge side of the scale and return to center when the switch is turned OFF. Repeat this step several times.
 a. If the needle deflects considerably to the discharge side of the scale, look for a short in the ignition or electrical system.
 b. If the needle deflects to the charge side of the scale, there is reverse polarity in the system. If the battery cables are properly connected, look for incorrect connections to an accessory.
 c. If the needle does not deflect, check for defective wiring and/or poor connections in the electrical system.

TROUBLESHOOTING

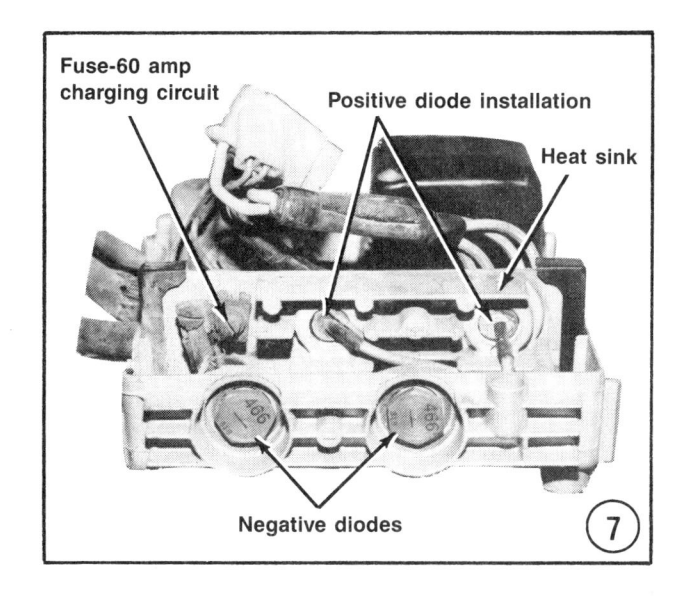

Figure 7: Fuse-60 amp charging circuit; Positive diode installation; Heat sink; Negative diodes

20 AMP CHARGING SYSTEM

Troubleshooting Preparation

Before troubleshooting the 20 amp charging circuit, visually check the following.

CAUTION
Be sure to disconnect the negative battery cable before removing the control box cover to check the diodes in Step 1 or the fuse in Step 2. A damaged diode will generally have a discolored or a burned appearance.

1. Make sure the battery cables are properly connected. If polarity is reversed, check for a damaged diode in the control box.
2A. Check the 60 amp fuse. On early models with a mechanical voltage regulator, the fuse is located in the junction box at the bottom of the positive diode heat sink (**Figure 7**). On later models with a transistorized voltage regulator, the fuse is located under the diode cover on the flywheel guard. This is not a cylindrical glass fuse; it consists of 2 pieces of metal separated by insulating material and connected by a thin metallic strip which melts when the fuse blows. If fuse replacement is required, be sure to install the ground lead between the heat sink boss and fuse.
2B. Check the 20 amp fuse installed between the ammeter and ignition switch.
3. Check for corroded or loose connections. Clean, tighten and insulate with OMC Black Neoprene Dip as required.
4. Check battery condition. Clean and recharge as required.
5. Check wiring harness between the stator and battery for damaged or deteriorated insulation and corroded, loose or faulty connections. Repair or replace as required.

Stator Test

1. Disconnect the negative battery cable.
2. Set the ohmmeter on the high ohm scale.
3. Remove the engine cover.
4. Disconnect the stator field lead connector (red and blue wires) at the engine harness.
5. Connect the red test lead to either the red or blue wire. Connect the black test lead to a good engine ground. The meter should read infinity (no continuity). If the meter shows continuity (less than 5,000 ohms), the stator field winding is grounded.
6. Set the ohmmeter on the low ohm scale.
7. Connect the ohmmeter between the disconnected red and blue wires. The meter should read between 1.69-3.14 ohms. If the reading is lower, the field winding is shorted. A higher reading indicates the winding is grounded.
8. Reconnect the field lead connector. Disconnect the stator output leads connector (2 yellow wires) at the rectifier.
9. Set the ohmmeter on the high ohm scale and repeat Step 5 to check for grounded output windings.
10. Set the ohmmeter on the low ohm scale.
11. Connect the ohmmeter between the disconnected yellow wires. The meter should read less than 1 ohm. A higher reading indicates an open or shorted output winding.
12. Replace the stator if the readings are other than specified.

Rectifier Diode Test

If a multi-meter or ohmmeter is used in place of a test lamp in this procedure, be sure that its power source is 12 volts or less.

1. Disconnect the negative battery cable.
2. Remove the engine cover.
3. Remove the junction box cover (early models) or flywheel guard diode cover (late models).
4. Disconnect the 2 positive (yellow) and 2 negative (white) diode leads (junction box diodes).
5. Connect a 12 volt test lamp between one of the positive diode terminals and the insulated heat sink (**Figure 8**), then reverse the test leads. The test lamp should light in one direction but not in the other.
6. Repeat Step 5 to check the other positive diode.
7. Connect the test lamp between one of the negative diode terminals and the junction box ground terminal (**Figure 9**), then reverse the test leads. The test lamp should light in one direction but not in the other.
8. Repeat Step 7 to check the other negative diode.
9. If the test lamp lights in both directions or does not light in either direction, replace the diode(s). See Chapter Seven.

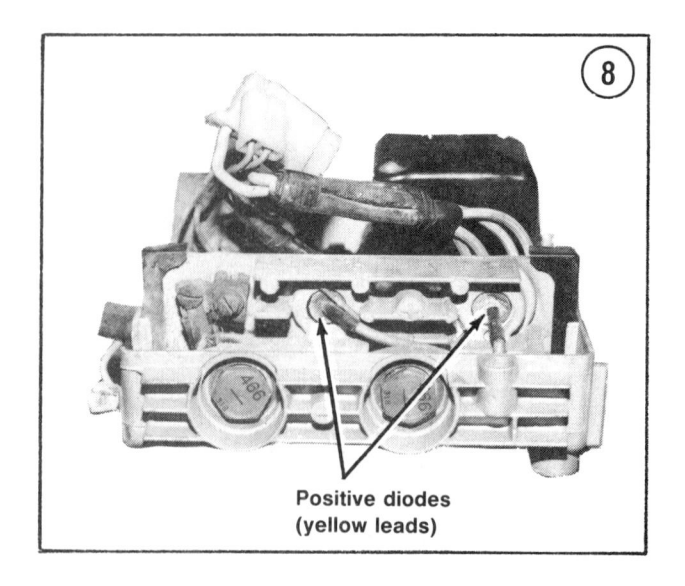

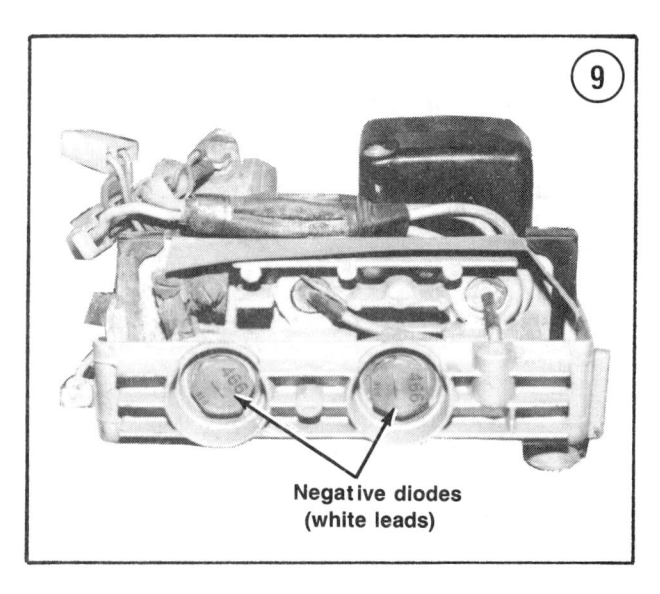

Voltage Regulator Test

Refer to **Figure 4** for this procedure.

1. Disconnect the positive battery cable.
2. Remove the engine cover.
3. Disconnect all accessories from the junction box power take-off terminals.
4. Remove the junction box cover.
5. Reconnect the positive battery cable.
6. Connect a voltmeter between the junction box power take-off terminals.
   a. If the voltmeter reads 12-12.5 volts, proceed with Step 7.
   b. If the voltmeter reads less than 12-12.5 volts, check all wiring and connections. If satisfactory, recharge or replace the battery.
   c. If there is no voltmeter reading, check the 20 amp fuse in the junction box. If fuse is satisfactory, check the wiring and all connections between the battery and starter solenoid, to the ammeter terminals and back to the junction box. Pay particular attention to the 2 ground connections in the junction box and the 1 ground connection in the junction box cover. Correct any defects found.
7. With the engine mounted in a test tank or on the boat in the water, start and run at 3/4

TROUBLESHOOTING

Figure 10

throttle (3,500 rpm) in gear. The voltmeter should indicate a higher voltage reading and the ammeter should show a charge condition.
  a. If the ammeter does not show a charge condition, it is not operating properly. Replace the ammeter.
  b. If the voltmeter does not show a higher voltage reading, shut the engine off and check the 60 amp fuse in the junction box. Replace if defective.
8. Restart the engine and run at fast idle in NEUTRAL. Carefully ground the regulator FLD terminal to the junction box ground screw (**Figure 10**). This removes the regulator from the circuit. If the voltmeter and ammeter both show an increased reading with the terminal grounded, test the transistor as described in this chapter. If the transistor passes the test, replace the regulator. If it does not pass the test, replace the regulator and transistor.

Voltage Regulator Transistor Test

1. Disconnect the positive battery cable.
2. Remove the junction box cover.
3. Reconnect the positive battery cable.
4. Connect a voltmeter between the regulator F terminal and a good ground.
5. Turn ignition switch ON, but do *not* start engine.
6. If the voltmeter reads less than 1 volt or more than 2 volts, replace the transistor. If the reading is battery voltage (12 volts), replace both the transistor and the transistor circuit resistor under the regulator. See Chapter Seven.

6-15 AMP CHARGING SYSTEMS

Troubleshooting Preparation

Before troubleshooting the charging circuit on 6, 9, 15 amp systems, visually check the following.
1. Make sure the battery cables are properly connected. If polarity is reversed, check for a damaged rectifier.

NOTE
A damaged rectifier will generally have a discolored or a burned appearance.

2. Check the 20 amp fuse installed between the ammeter and ignition switch. On regulated (15 amp) charging systems, also check the fuse installed between the voltage regulator and rectifier.
3. Check for corroded or loose connections. Clean, tighten and insulate with OMC Black Neoprene Dip as required.
4. Check battery condition. Clean and recharge as required.
5. Check wiring harness between the armature plate or stator and battery for damaged or deteriorated insulation and corroded, loose or faulty connections. Repair or replace as required.

Stator Test

Refer to **Figure 11** for this procedure.
1. Disconnect the positive battery cable.
2. Set the ohmmeter on the high ohm scale.
3. Remove the engine cover.
4. Disconnect the two yellow stator leads.
5. Connect the red test lead to either of the disconnected yellow leads. Connect the black test lead to ground. The meter should read infinity, indicating an open circuit. If any other reading is shown, the stator is shorted to ground.
6. Set the ohmmeter on the low ohm scale.
7. Connect the ohmmeter between the disconnected yellow wires. The meter should read as follows:
   a. 6 amp system—1.5 ohms ±0.5 ohms (1971-1972 50 hp) or 2 ohms ±0.2 ohms (all others).
   b. 9 amp system—0.75 ohms ±0.2 ohms.
   c. 15 amp system—0.4 ohms ±0.1 ohm (1972) or 0.5 ohms ±0.2 ohms (all others).

If the meter reads infinity, the stator windings are open.

8. Replace the stator if the readings are other than specified.

Rectifier Test

Any multi-meter or ohmmeter used in this procedure should have a power source of 12 volts or less. Refer to **Figure 12** for this procedure.
1. Disconnect the rectifier leads. Early models will use a quick-disconnect or Packard-type connector; on later models, the leads are connected to a terminal board.
2. With the ohmmeter on the high scale, connect one test lead to the yellow lead and the other test lead to ground. Note the meter reading.
3. Reverse the test leads and note the reading. The ohmmeter should read zero in one direction and infinity in the other. If the reading is the same in both directions, the diode is defective and the rectifier should be replaced. High resistance indicates an open diode; low resistance indicates a shorted diode.
4. Repeat Step 2 and Step 3 to test the other yellow or yellow/gray lead.
5. Connect one ohmmeter lead to the rectifier red lead and repeat Steps 2-4.
6. Replace the rectifier if the readings are not as specified.

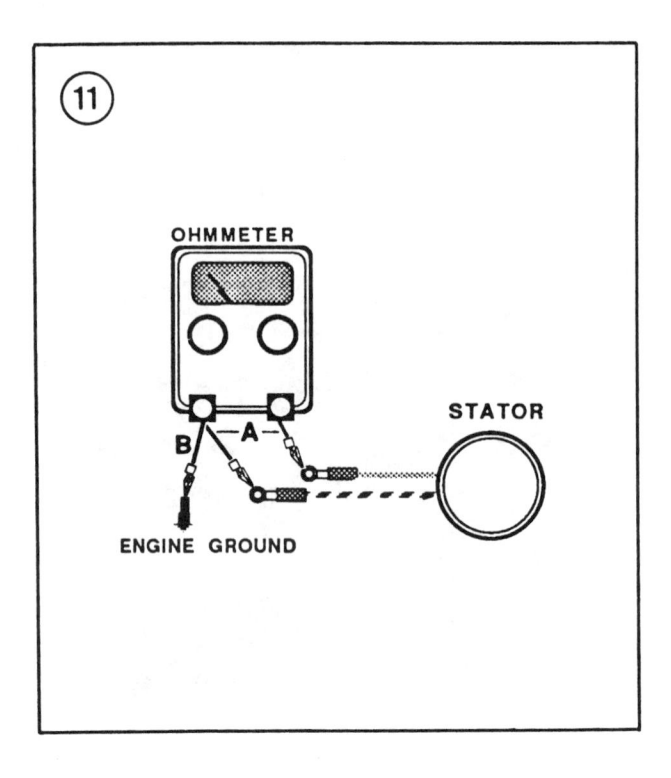

Voltage Regulator Test (15 Amp System)

Undercharged battery

1. With the engine in a test tank or on the boat in water, disconnect the voltage regulator quick-disconnect.
2. Make sure all accessories are OFF. Start engine and run at 3,000-3,600 rpm. If ammeter shows a full charge condition, replace the regulator. If there is no ammeter reading, test the stator as described in this chapter.

12

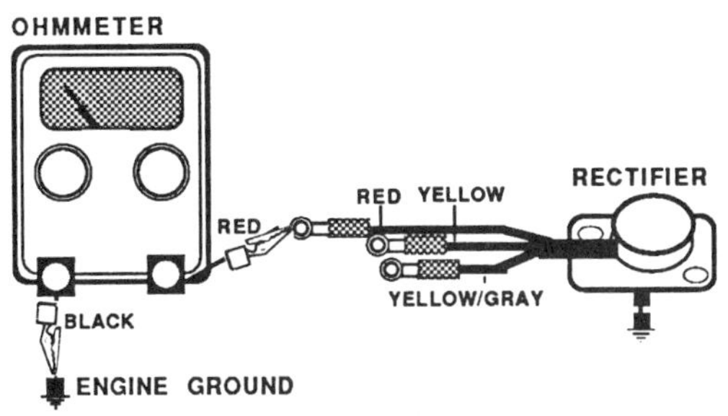

Overcharged battery

1. Run the engine in a test tank or on the boat in water for 20 minutes to stabilize the regulator.
2. Disconnect the voltage regulator quick-disconnect.
3. Make sure all accessories are OFF. With engine running at 3,000-3,600 rpm, connect a voltmeter between the connector red lead and a good engine ground. If the voltmeter reading is more than 15 volts, replace the regulator.

CLIPPER CIRCUIT

CD ignition systems are equipped with a clipper circuit for protection against intermittent battery current or a current surge from the alternator. The clipper circuit should be checked whenever one or more of the following conditions exist:

a. The battery dies suddenly or is undercharged and testing indicates the charging system is functioning properly.
b. Battery current flow is interrupted or becomes intermittent.
c. Fuses blow shortly after replacement or upon replacement.
d. The CD amplifier does not work properly.

Testing

A known-good shift diode (part No. 383840) is required to determine the correct ohmmeter test lead hook-up.

1. With the ohmmeter set on the high scale, connect one test lead to the purple/green diode lead. Connect the other test lead to the yellow diode lead.
   a. A low or zero ohms reading indicates the test lead connected to the yellow diode lead is the "case" lead.
   b. A high or infinite ohms reading indicates the test lead connected to the purple/green diode lead is the "case" lead.
2. Label or tag the "case" lead to prevent any mixup during the rest of the procedure.
3. Disconnect the clipper circuit and remove it from the engine.

NOTE

Early clipper circuits have 3 leads with a case ground; later circuits use a 4th lead (black) to provide ground.

4. Momentarily ground the purple lead to the clipper housing to discharge any remaining current.
5. Connect the ohmmeter "case" lead to ground (clipper housing or black lead). Connect the other ohmmeter lead to the yellow clipper wire. See **Figure 13**. If the meter reads less than 300 ohms, replace the clipper.
6. Repeat Step 4, then move the ohmmeter lead from the yellow to the yellow/gray clipper wire. See **Figure 14**. If the meter reads less than 300 ohms, replace the clipper.
7. Repeat Step 4, then move the ohmmeter lead from the yellow/gray to the purple clipper wire. See **Figure 15**. If the meter reads less than 300 ohms or if the needle moves

3

toward zero and then returns to an infinite position, replace the clipper.

8. Repeat Step 4, then connect the case lead to the purple clipper wire. Connect the other ohmmeter lead to ground. See **Figure 16**. The meter needle should move toward zero and then return to an infinite position. If it does not move or if it goes to zero and remains there, replace the clipper.

SHIFT CIRCUIT

Engines equipped with a hydro-electric gearcase use an electric shift circuit. The remote control shift box contains the ignition, choke and shift switches. This system incorporates two unique features:

a. A blocking diode is used at the front of the shift box to prevent current from reaching the gearcase whenever the ignition switch is OFF. If the diode fails in an open position, the engine will remain in forward gear until the stator output energizes the shift control circuit. If it fails in a closed position, the engine cannot be shut off.

b. Forward gear in the gearcase is spring-loaded for positive engagement. When the ignition switch is turned OFF, the gearcase may shift into forward gear before the engine stops. To prevent this, 2 positive shift diodes are wired into the stator circuit to function with the negative rectifier diodes in supplying current to the gearcase until flywheel rotation stops. This produces smooth shut-downs with no sudden propeller rotation.

Shift Selector Switch Test

Refer to **Figure 17** for this procedure.
1. Connect a 12 volt test lamp between test point 1 and a good engine ground. Turn the key switch on and make sure the shift lever is in NEUTRAL. The test lamp should light.

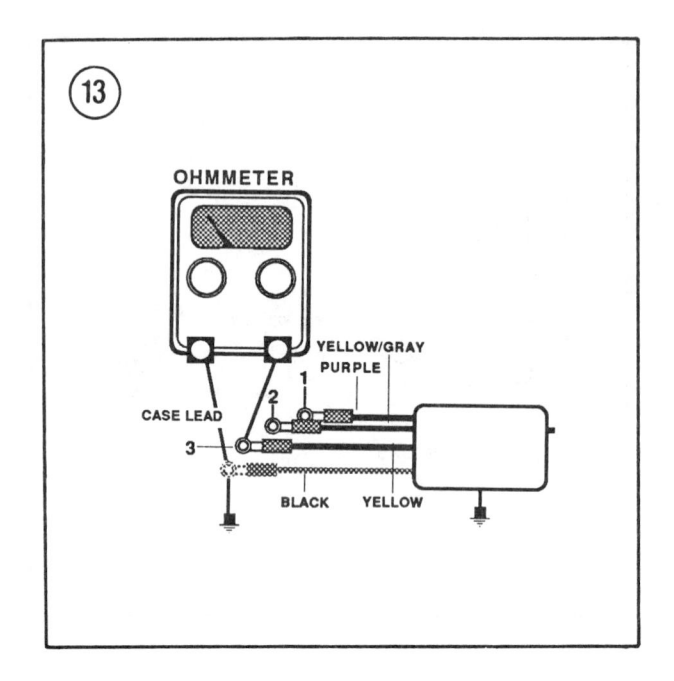

2. Place the shift lever in REVERSE and repeat Step 1 at test point 2. The test lamp should light.
3. If the test lamp does not light in Step 1 or Step 2, connect it between the purple/green lead at the terminal block and a good engine ground. If the lamp lights, replace the shift toggle switch. If the lamp does not light, check the key switch, fuse and battery condition. If these are satisfactory, test the blocking diode as described in this chapter.
4. Disconnect the white lead at test point 4. Connect the test lamp between the disconnected lead and a good engine ground. With the key switch in START, the lamp should light when the shift lever is placed in NEUTRAL.
5. If the lamp does not light in Step 4, connect it between test point 5 and a good engine ground. If the lamp lights, replace the starter solenoid.
6. If the lamp does not light in Step 5, connect it between test point 6 and a good engine ground. If the lamp lights, replace the shift toggle switch. If the lamp does not light, check the key switch, fuse and battery condition.

TROUBLESHOOTING

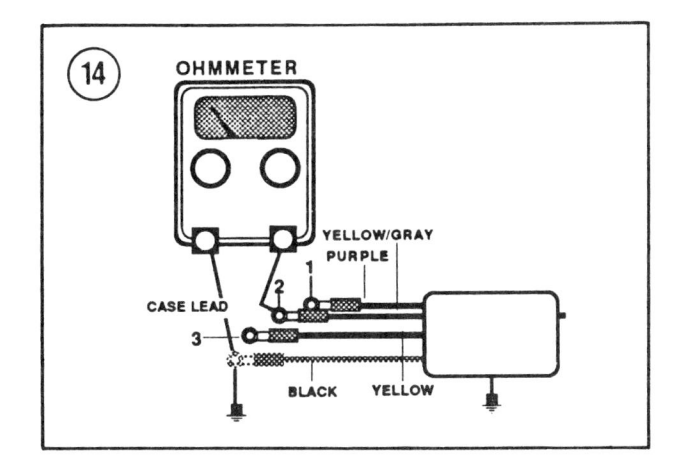

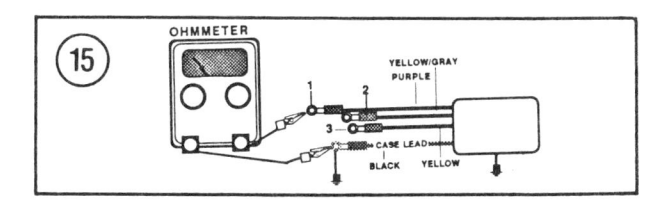

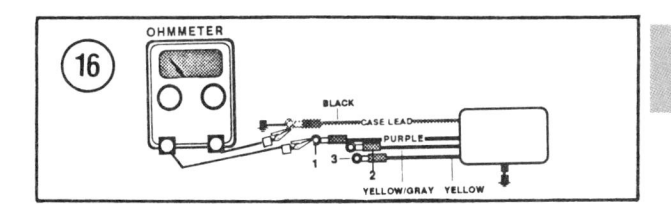

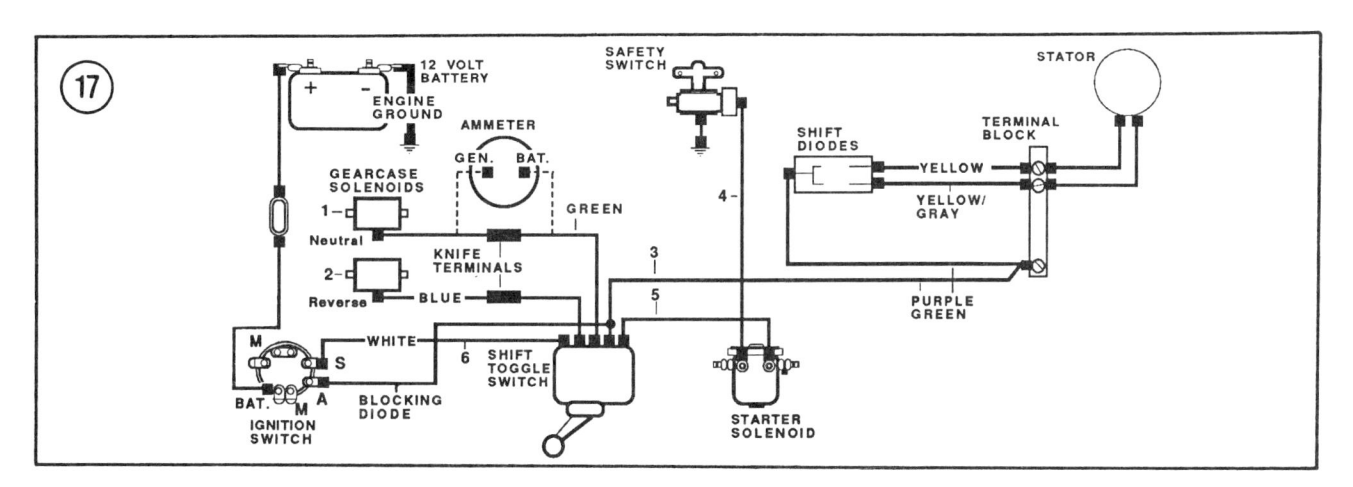

Blocking Diode Test

Refer to **Figure 17** for this procedure.

1. Disconnect the diode connection to the shift toggle switch. Connect a 12 volt test lamp between the diode lead and the key switch ignition terminal.
2. Reverse the ohmmeter connections. The test lamp should light in one direction but not in the other. If the lamp lights in both directions or does not light in either direction, replace the blocking diode.

Shift Solenoid Test

Refer to **Figure 17** for this procedure.

1. Connect a low-reading D.C. ammeter between the green leads at test point 1.
2. Place the shift lever in NEUTRAL and turn the key switch ON. The ammeter should read 1.5-2.0 amps for a period of 10 minutes. If it does not or if the reading is not within the specified range, replace the gearcase neutral shift solenoid.
3. Repeat Step 1 and Step 2 at test point 2. If the reading is not within the specified range, replace the gearcase reverse shift solenoid.

Shift Diode Test

Refer to **Figure 17** for this procedure.

1. With the key switch OFF, disconnect the shift diode leads at the terminal block.
2. Connect an ohmmeter between the purple/green and yellow diode leads. Reverse the test connections. The ohmmeter should show continuity in one direction and no continuity in the other direction.
3. Repeat Step 3 with the purple/green and yellow/gray diode leads.

4. Replace the shift diode(s) if the readings are not as specified.

IGNITION SYSTEM

The wiring harness used between the ignition switch and engine is adequate to handle the electrical needs of the outboard. It *will not* handle the electrical needs of accessories. Whenever an accessory is added, run new wiring between the battery and accessory, installing a separate fuse panel on the instrument panel.

If the ignition switch requires replacement, *never* install an automotive-type switch; it can damage the components of some ignitions. A sealed marine-type switch should always be used.

Description

Several different ignition systems have been used on the outboards covered in this book. See Chapter Seven for a full description. For the purposes of troubleshooting, the ignition systems can be divided into 4 basic types:
   a. Magneto breaker point ignition (flywheel or distributor).
   b. Battery breaker point ignition (distributor).
   c. CD breaker point ignition (flywheel).
   d. CD breakerless ignition (flywheel or distributor).

General troubleshooting procedures are provided in **Table 2**.

Troubleshooting Precautions

Several precautions should be strictly observed to avoid damage to the ignition system.
1. Do not reverse the battery connections. This reverses polarity and can damage the rectifier diodes or other components.
2. Do not "spark" the battery terminals with the battery cable connections to check polarity.
3. Do not disconnect the battery cables with the engine running.
4. Do not crank engine if the pulse pack is not grounded to engine.
5. Do not touch or disconnect any ignition components when the engine is running, while the ignition switch is ON or while the battery cables are connected.
6. If you must run an engine with a flywheel CD ignition system without the battery connected to the harness, disconnect the stator base rectifier leads and tape them separately.

Troubleshooting Preparation (All Ignition Systems)

NOTE
To test the wiring harness for poor solder connections in Step 1, bend the molded rubber connector while checking each wire for resistance.

1. Check the wiring harness and all plug-in connections to make sure that all terminals are free of corrosion, all connectors are tight and the wiring insulation is in good condition.
2. Check all electrical components that are grounded to the engine for a good ground.
3. Make sure that all ground wires are properly connected and that the connections are clean and tight.

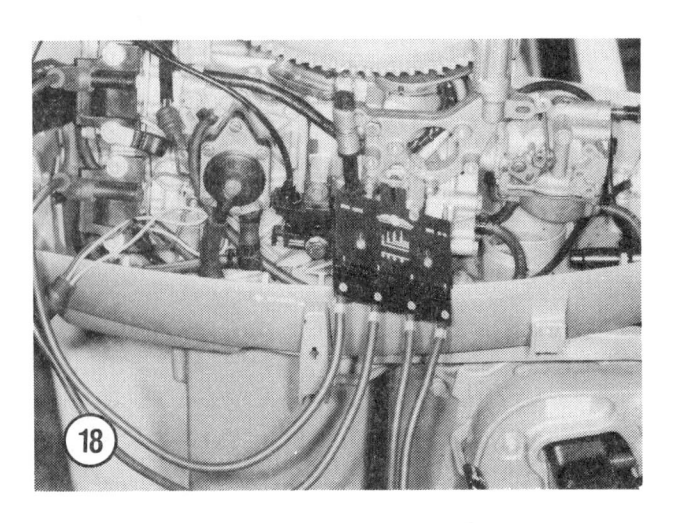

4. Check remainder of the wiring for disconnected wires and short or open circuits.
5. Make sure there is an adequate supply of fresh and properly mixed fuel available to the engine.
6. Check the battery condition on electric models. Clean terminals and recharge battery, if necessary.
7. Check spark plug cable routing. Make sure the cables are properly connected to their respective spark plugs.
8. Remove all spark plugs, keeping them in order. Check the condition of each plug. See Chapter Four.
9. Install a spark tester (**Figure 18**) and check for spark at each cylinder. If a spark tester is not available, reconnect the proper plug cable to one plug. Lay the plug against the cylinder head so its base makes a good connection and turn the engine over. If there is no spark or only a weak one, check for loose connections at the coil and battery. Repeat the check with each remaining plug. If the connections are good, the problem is most likely in the ignition system.

FLYWHEEL MAGNETO BREAKER POINT IGNITION TROUBLESHOOTING

Component Testing

An ignition analyzer must be used for accurate testing of the breaker points, condenser(s) and magneto coil(s). Check all components even if it appears you have located the problem. For example, correcting a weak condenser may increase spark output but if the magneto coil is also weak, replacing it will result in further improvement.

Johnson and Evinrude recommend the use of the a Merc-O-Tronic, Graham Model 51 or Stevens M.A.-75 tester. These can be purchased through your local Johnson or Evinrude dealer. Each analyzer includes detailed instructions for component testing as well as complete component specifications according to engine model and year of manufacture (specifications vary according to the tester used). The procedures given here are general in nature to acquaint you with component testing. Refer to the instructions provided with the particular analyzer to be used for the exact procedure.

Breaker Point Testing

1. Remove the flywheel. See Chapter Eight.
2. Disconnect the breaker point leads from the armature plate.
3. Connect one analyzer test lead to the breaker arm. Connect the other test lead to the breaker point screw terminal.
4. Set the analyzer controls according to the manufacturer's instructions.
5. If the breaker points are good, the analyzer needle will rest in the "OK" segment (Merc-O-Tronic) or green segment (Stevens).
6. If the analyzer needle does not fall within the specified segment on the scale, clean the points with electrical contact cleaner and recheck the analyzer leads to make sure the connections are tight before discarding the points. The low current used in this test makes clean points and proper connections very important.

Condenser Testing

1. Remove the flywheel. See Chapter Eight.
2. Disconnect the condenser lead from the breaker point set.
3. Connect one analyzer test lead to the condenser lead. Connect the other test lead to the breaker plate or condenser mounting clip.

WARNING
High voltage is involved in a condenser leakage test. Handle the analyzer leads carefully and turn the analyzer switch to DISCHARGE before disconnecting it from the condenser.

4. Set the analyzer controls according to manufacturer's instructions and check the

condenser for leakage, resistance and capacity.

5. Compare the results in Step 4 with the specifications provided by the analyzer manufacturer. Replace the condenser if it fails any of the 3 tests.

Magneto Coil Testing

WARNING
All coil tests should be performed on a wooden or insulated bench top to prevent shock hazards or leakage.

The magneto coil must be removed from the armature or breaker plate for testing.
1. Remove the flywheel. See Chapter Eight.
2. Remove the coil from the armature plate. See Chapter Seven.
3. Connect an ignition analyzer according to manufacturer's instructions.
4. Check the coil for continuity, power and leakage according to the manufacturer's instructions. Compare the results to the specifications provided with the analyzer. Replace the coil if it fails any of the 3 tests.

Secondary Cable Leakage Test

1. Connect the spark plug cable to a known-good coil according to the analyzer manufacturer's instructions.
2. Probe the spark plug lead insulation according to the analyzer manufacturer's instructions.
3. Replace the spark plug lead if flashover is evident or indicated.

BATTERY BREAKER POINT (DISTRIBUTOR) IGNITION TROUBLESHOOTING

Component Testing

An ignition analyzer must be used for accurate testing of the breaker points, condenser and ignition coil. Check all components even if it appears you have located the problem. For example, correcting a weak condenser may increase spark output but if the ignition coil is also weak, replacing it will result in further improvement.

Johnson and Evinrude recommend the use of the a Merc-O-Tronic, Graham Model 51 or Stevens M.A.-75 tester. These can be purchased through your local Johnson or Evinrude dealer. Each analyzer includes detailed instructions for component testing as well as complete component specifications according to engine model and year of manufacture (specifications vary according to the tester used). The procedures given here are general in nature to acquaint you with component testing. Refer to the instructions provided with the particular analyzer to be used for the exact procedure.

Breaker Point Testing

1A. Magneto ignition—Remove the distributor magneto. Remove the magneto pulley. See Chapter Eight.
1B. Battery ignition—Remove the distributor cap and rotor.
2. Disconnect the breaker point leads from the distributor breaker plate.
3. Connect one analyzer test lead to the breaker arm. Connect the other test lead to the breaker point screw terminal.
4. Set the analyzer controls according to the manufacturer's instructions.
5. If the breaker points are good, the analyzer needle will rest in the "OK" segment (Merc-O-Tronic) or green segment (Stevens).
6. If the analyzer needle does not fall within the specified segment on the scale, clean the points with electrical contact cleaner and recheck the analyzer leads to make sure the connections are tight before discarding the points. The low current used in this test makes clean points and proper connections very important.

TROUBLESHOOTING

Condenser Testing

1A. Magneto ignition—Remove the distributor magneto. Remove the magneto pulley. See Chapter Eight.

1B. Battery ignition—Remove the distributor cap and rotor.

2. Disconnect the condenser lead from the breaker point set.

3. Connect one analyzer test lead to the condenser lead. Connect the other test lead to the breaker plate or condenser mounting clip.

WARNING
High voltage is involved in a condenser leakage test. Handle the analyzer leads carefully and turn the analyzer switch to DISCHARGE before disconnecting it from the condenser.

4. Set the analyzer controls according to manufacturer's instructions and check the condenser for leakage, resistance and capacity.

5. Compare the results in Step 4 with the specifications provided by the analyzer manufacturer. Replace the condenser if it fails any of the 3 tests.

Ignition Coil Testing

WARNING
All coil tests should be performed on a wooden or insulated bench top to prevent shock hazards or leakage.

The ignition coil must be removed from the breaker plate for testing.

1A. Magneto ignition:
   a. Remove the distributor magneto. Remove the magneto pulley. See Chapter Eight.
   b. Remove the coil from the magneto housing. See Chapter Seven.

1B. Battery ignition—remove the coil.

2. Connect an ignition analyzer according to manufacturer's instructions.

3. Check the coil for continuity, power and leakage according to the manufacturer's instructions. Compare the results to the specifications provided with the analyzer. Replace the coil if it fails any of the 3 tests.

Distributor Cap Check

1. Remove the distributor or magneto housing cap.

2. Connect the distributor cap in series with the ignition coil according to analyzer manufacturer's instructions.

3. Check the cap for fractures, cracks and porosity leaks according to the manufacturer's instructions.

4. Replace the distributor cap and rotor if any defects are noted.

CD BREAKER POINT IGNITION TROUBLESHOOTING

1968 55, 65 and 85 HP; 1969 HP

A CD test meter and S-80 or M-80 neon tester (available from your Johnson or Evinrude dealer) are required for these procedures. Make sure the battery is fully charged. Disconnect and ground the spark plug leads to prevent the engine from starting while cranking.

Input voltage test

Refer to **Figure 19** for test points.

1. Set CD tester selector switch to the 50 volt scale. Set the other switch to the plus (+) setting.

2. Connect the black tester lead to a good engine ground. Insert the red tester lead probe in the red wire terminal of the amplifier connector.

3. Turn the ignition switch ON. The tester should indicate battery voltage (12 volts).

4. Crank the engine and note the tester scale. It should read 9.5 volts or more. If the reading is less than specified and the battery

CHAPTER THREE

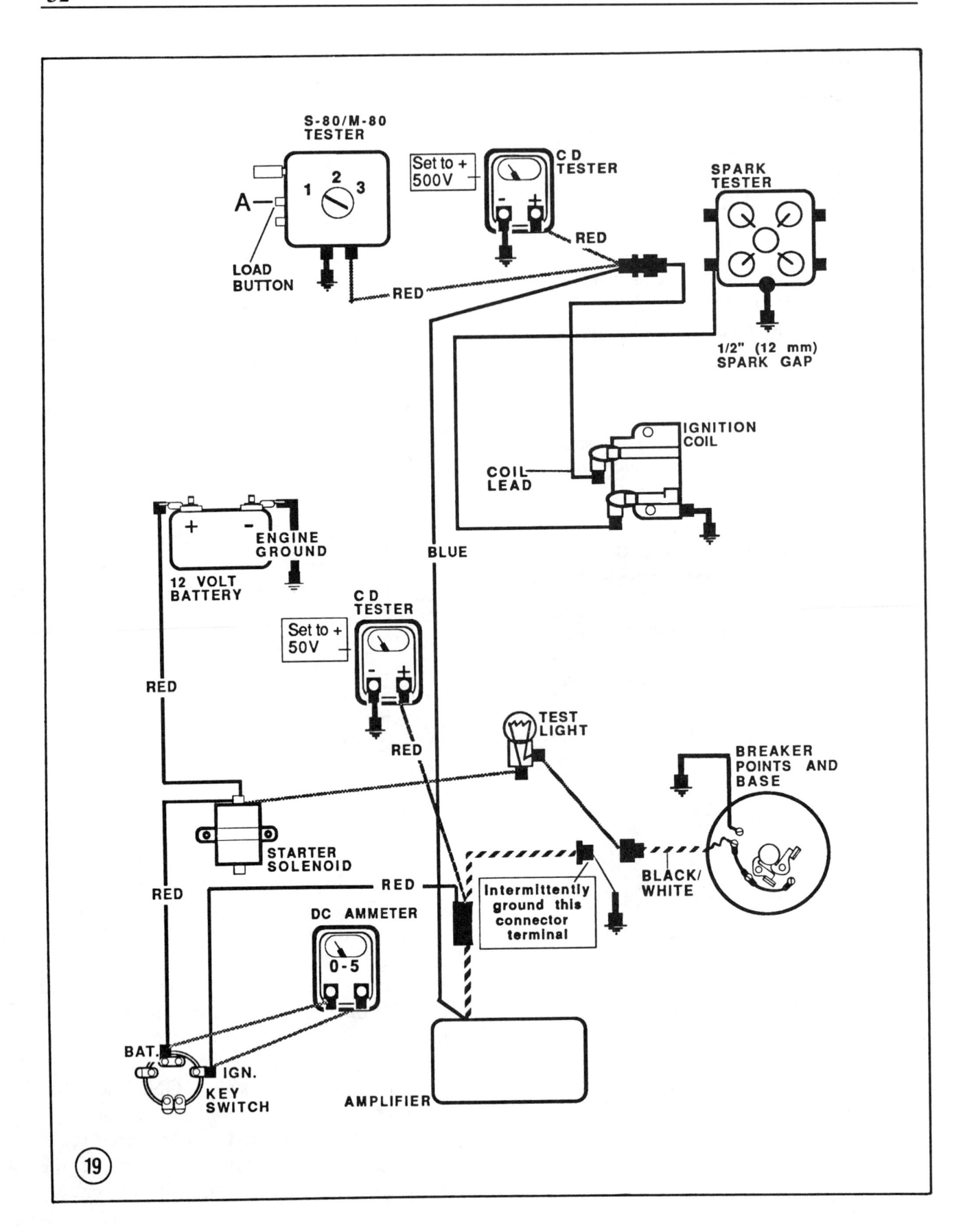

⑲

TROUBLESHOOTING

was fully charged before starting the test, remove the starter and have its current draw checked by a dealer or qualified marine electrical specialist.

Amplifier output test

Refer to **Figure 19** for test points.
1. Set CD tester selector switch to the 500 volt scale. Set the other switch to the plus (+) setting.
2. Connect the black tester lead to a good engine ground. Insert the red tester lead probe in the blue wire terminal of the amplifier-to-coil connector.
3. Crank the engine and note the tester scale. It should read 250 volts or more.
4. If there is no reading in Step 3, disconnect the coil from the circuit. Connect the S-80 or M-80 tester between the blue wire terminal of the amplifier-to-coil connector and a good engine ground. Set the tester on position 1. Depress load button A and crank the engine with the ignition switch while watching the tester neon light.
  a. If the light glows steadily, the amplifier is good. Replace the coil.
  b. If the light does not glow, disconnect the wire between the amplifier and breaker points. With the ignition switch ON, intermittently touch the amplifier connector to ground. If the neon light does not glow intermittently with the making and breaking of the ground connection, replace the amplifier.

Coil output test

Refer to **Figure 19** for test points.
1. Connect the coil high tension lead to a spark tester with its gap set at 1/2 in.
2. Crank the engine. If strong, steady sparks jump the tester gap, the coil is good. If the sparks are weak or erratic, replace the coil.

Breaker point test
(except 1968-1969 55 hp)

Perform this test if the engine will not start. Refer to **Figure 19** for test points.
1. Disconnect the breaker point-to-amplifier lead.
2. Connect a 12 volt test lamp between the breaker point lead and the battery side of the starter solenoid.
3. With ignition switch OFF and distributor positioned at full advance, rotate the flywheel clockwise. The test lamp should light when the flywheel timing mark aligns with the lifting ring pointer, indicating that the points have opened.
4. If either set of breaker points fails to open at the correct time, remove the flywheel and adjust the points to 0.010 in. (old) or 0.012 in. (new). See Chapter Four.
5. If breaker points are adjusted, check engine timing. See Chapter Five.

Breaker point test
(1968-1969 55 hp)

Perform this test if the engine will not start. The breaker points are wired in delayed parallel and both sets affect each cylinder. To check both sets of points, locate the flywheel timing mark. Measure 1 3/8 in. counterclockwise from the existing mark on the outer edge of the flywheel and scribe a second timing mark. See **Figure 20**. Refer to **Figure 19** for test points.
1. Disconnect the breaker point-to-amplifier lead.
2. Connect a 12 volt test lamp between the breaker point lead and the battery side of the starter solenoid.
3. With ignition switch OFF and distributor positioned at full advance, rotate the flywheel clockwise. The test lamp should go out when the existing flywheel timing mark aligns with the ring gear guard boss, indicating that one set of points has opened.

4. Continue to rotate the flywheel clockwise until the second timing mark aligns with the ring gear guard boss, indicating that the second set of points has closed.
5. If the test lamp fails to indicate light as the timing marks align, adjust the points to 0.010 in. (old) or 0.012 in. (new). See Chapter Four.
6. If breaker point adjustment is required, run engine and check timing after setting the points. See Chapter Five.

Amplifier intermittent miss test

This test should be performed with the engine in a test tank or on the boat in the water. Refer to **Figure 19** for test points.
1. Set CD tester selector switch to the 500 volt scale. Set the other switch to the plus (+) setting.
2. Connect the black tester lead to a good engine ground. Insert the red tester lead probe in the blue wire terminal of the amplifier-to-coil connector.
3. Reconnect the spark plug leads.
4. Start the engine and note the tester scale. It should read 250 volts or more. If tester needle wavers or the reading is less than specified, check battery condition. If battery is satisfactory, perform the *Coil Output Test* above.

5. If the engine misses but the tester reading is stable in Step 4, connect a 0-5 amp ammeter in series between the key switch and amplifier. With the engine running at idle, the ammeter should read less than one amp.
6. Increase engine speed to the rpm where the miss occurs and note the ammeter reading. If the needle wavers, check for a loose connection in the amplifier connector leading to the battery. If connections are good, replace the amplifier.

1970-1971 60 HP

A CD test meter and S-80 or M-80 neon tester (available from your Johnson or Evinrude dealer) are required for these procedures. Make sure the battery is fully charged. Disconnect and ground the spark plug leads to prevent the engine from starting while cranking.

Input voltage test

Refer to **Figure 21** for test points.
1. Set CD tester selector switch to the 50 volt scale. Set the other switch to the plus (+) setting.
2. Connect the black tester lead to a good engine ground. Connect the red tester lead to terminal 6 on the terminal block.

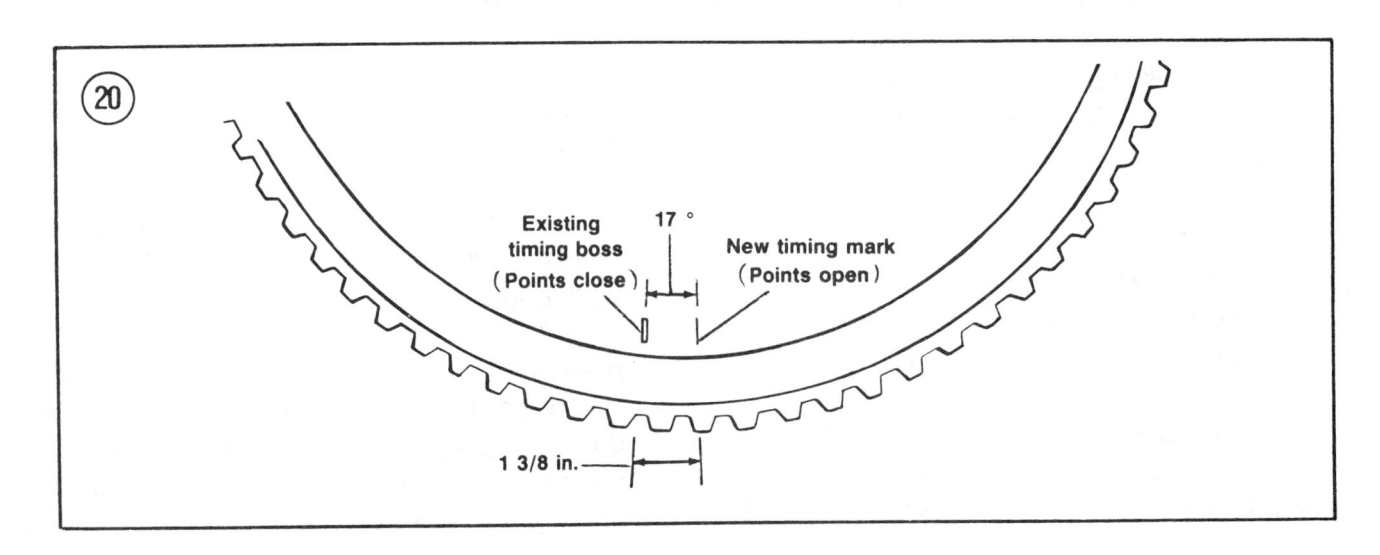

20

Existing timing boss (Points close) — 17° — New timing mark (Points open)

1 3/8 in.

TROUBLESHOOTING

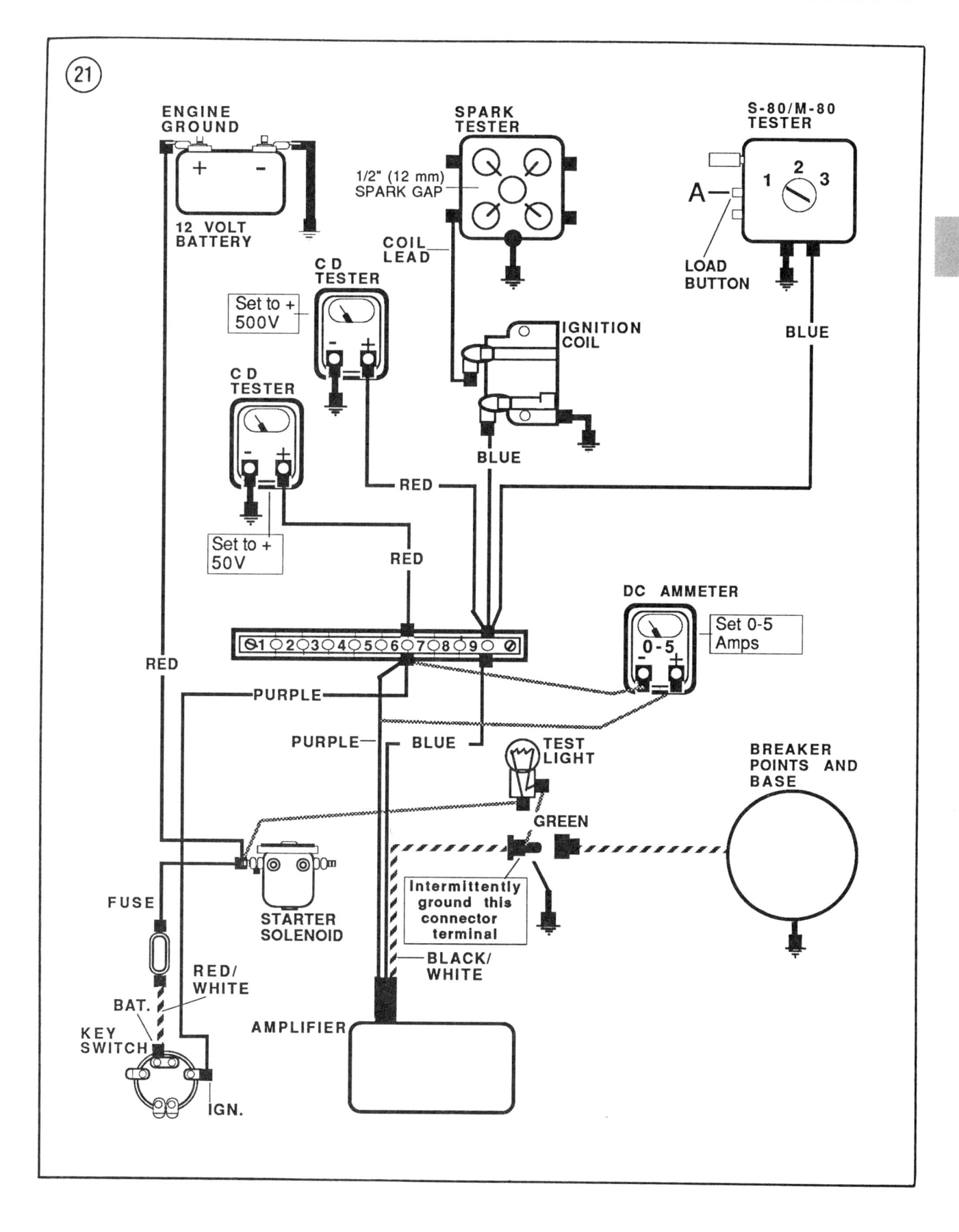

3. Turn the ignition switch ON. The tester should indicate battery voltage (12 volts).
4. Crank the engine and note the tester scale. It should read 9.5 volts or more. If the reading is less than specified and the battery was fully charged before starting the test, remove the starter and have its current draw checked by a dealer or qualified marine electrical specialist.

Amplifier output test

Refer to **Figure 21** for test points.
1. Set CD tester selector switch to the 500 volt scale. Set the other switch to the plus (+) setting.
2. Connect the black tester lead to a good engine ground. Connect the red tester lead to terminal 9 on the terminal block.
3. Crank the engine and note the tester scale. It should read 250 volts or more.
4. If there is no reading in Step 3, disconnect the wire between the amplifier and breaker points. With the ignition switch ON, intermittently touch the amplifier connector to ground. The tester should read 250 volts or more each time the connector is grounded.
5. If there is no reading in Step 5, disconnect the amplifier blue lead at terminal 9 of the terminal block connection. Connect the S-80 or M-80 tester between the amplifier blue wire and a good engine ground. Set the tester on position 1. Depress load button A and touch amplifier breaker point lead to ground while watching the tester neon light.
   a. If the light glows steadily, the amplifier is good. Replace the coil.
   b. If the light does not glow, replace the amplifier.

Coil output test

Refer to **Figure 21** for test points.
1. Connect the coil high tension lead to a spark tester with its gap set at 1/2 in.

2. Crank the engine. If strong, steady sparks jump the tester gap, the coil is good. If the sparks are weak or erratic, replace the coil.

Breaker point test

Perform this test if the engine will not start. The breaker points are wired in delayed parallel and both sets affect each cylinder. To check both sets of points, locate the flywheel timing mark. Measure 1 3/8 in. counterclockwise from the existing mark on the outer edge of the flywheel and scribe a second timing mark. See **Figure 20**. Refer to **Figure 21** for test points.
1. Disconnect the breaker point-to-amplifier lead.
2. Connect a 12 volt test lamp between the breaker point lead and the battery side of the starter solenoid.
3. With ignition switch OFF and distributor positioned at full advance, rotate the flywheel clockwise. The test lamp should go out when the existing flywheel timing mark aligns with the ring gear guard boss, indicating that one set of points has opened.
4. Continue to rotate the flywheel clockwise until the second timing mark aligns with the ring gear guard boss, indicating that the second set of points has closed.
5. If the test lamp fails to indicate light as the timing marks align, adjust the points to 0.010 in. (old) or 0.012 in. (new). See Chapter Four.
6. If breaker point adjustment is required, run engine and check timing after setting the points. See Chapter Five.

Amplifier intermittent miss test

This test should be performed with the engine in a test tank or on the boat in the water. Refer to **Figure 21** for test points.
1. Set CD tester selector switch to the 500 volt scale. Set the other switch to the plus (+) setting.

TROUBLESHOOTING

2. Connect the black tester lead to a good engine ground. Insert the red tester lead probe in terminal 9 on the terminal block.
3. Connect a 0-5 amp ammeter in series with terminal 6 and the purple amplifier lead.
4. Reconnect the spark plug leads.
5. Start the engine. Increase engine speed to the rpm where the miss occurs and note the scale on both testers. If either tester needle wavers, replace the amplifier.

1969-1972 85 HP; 1971 100 HP

A CD test meter and S-80 or M-80 neon tester (available from your Johnson or Evinrude dealer) are required for these procedures. Make sure the battery is fully charged. Disconnect and ground the spark plug leads to prevent the engine from starting while cranking.

Input voltage test

Refer to **Figure 22** for test points.
1. Set CD tester selector switch to the 50 volt scale. Set the other switch to the plus (+) setting.
2. Connect the black tester lead to a good engine ground. Connect the red tester lead to terminal 8 or 9 of the terminal block.
3. Turn the ignition switch ON. The tester should indicate battery voltage (12 volts). If it does not, check the wiring between the ignition switch and the battery.
4. Crank the engine and note the tester scale. It should read 9.5 volts or more. If the reading is less than specified and the battery was fully charged before starting the test, remove the starter and have its current draw checked by a dealer or qualified marine electrical specialist.

Amplifier output test

Refer to **Figure 22** for test points.

1. Set CD tester selector switch to the 500 volt scale. Set the other switch to the plus (+) setting.
2. Connect the black tester lead to a good engine ground. Connect the red tester lead to terminal 5 of the terminal block.
3. Crank the engine and note the tester scale. It should read 250 volts or more.

CAUTION
Perform Step 4 with the engine in a test tank or on the boat in the water.

4. If the engine will run, connect the spark plug leads. Start and run the engine at a speed where it begins to misfire and note the tester scale. It should indicate almost 300 volts with a steady needle position.
5. If there is no reading in Step 3, disconnect the coil from the circuit. Connect the S-80 or M-80 tester between the blue wire terminal of the amplifier-to-coil connector and a good engine ground. Set the tester on position 1. Depress load button A and crank the engine with the ignition switch while watching the tester neon light.
   a. If the light glows steadily, the amplifier is good. Replace the coil.
   b. If the light does not glow, disconnect the wire between the amplifier and breaker points. With the ignition switch ON, intermittently touch the amplifier connector to ground. If the neon light glows each time the ground connection is made, check point gap and adjust as required. See Chapter Four. If the neon light does not glow when the ground connection is made, replace the amplifier.

Coil output test

Refer to **Figure 22** for test points.
1. Connect the coil high tension lead to a spark tester with its gap set at 1/2 in.

CHAPTER THREE

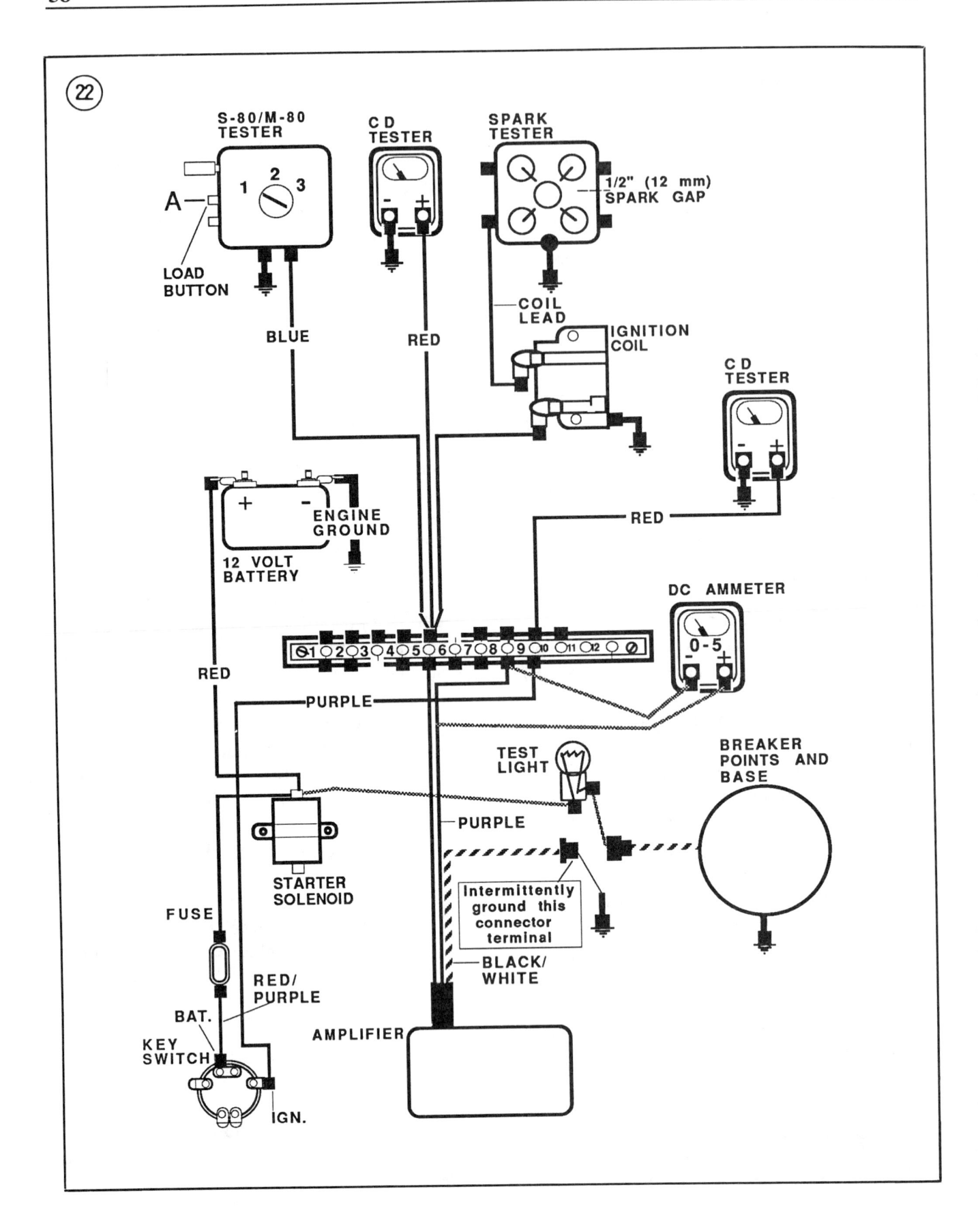

TROUBLESHOOTING

2. Crank the engine. If strong, steady sparks jump the tester gap, the coil is good. If the sparks are weak or erratic, replace the coil.

Breaker point test

Perform this test if the engine will not start. Refer to **Figure 22** for test points.
1. Disconnect the breaker point-to-amplifier lead.
2. Connect a 12 volt test lamp between the breaker point lead and the battery side of the starter solenoid.
3. With ignition switch OFF and distributor positioned at full advance, rotate the flywheel clockwise. The test lamp should go out when the flywheel timing mark aligns with the timing pointer.
4. If the test lamp fails to go out at the proper time, remove the flywheel and adjust the breaker points. See Chapter Four.

Amplifier intermittent miss test

This test should be performed with the engine in a test tank or on the boat in the water. Refer to **Figure 22** for test points.
1. Set CD tester selector switch to the 500 volt scale. Set the other switch to the plus (+) setting.
2. Connect the black tester lead to a good engine ground. Connect the red tester lead to terminal 5 on the terminal block.
3. Connect a 0-5 amp ammeter in series between the amplifier and terminal 8 or 9 on the terminal block.
4. Reconnect the spark plug leads.
5. Start the engine. Increase engine speed to the rpm where the miss occurs and note the scale on both testers. If either tester needle wavers, check for loose wiring connections. If connections are satisfactory, replace the amplifier.

CD BREAKERLESS IGNITION TROUBLESHOOTING

1967-1968 100 HP

A CD test meter and S-80 or M-80 neon tester (available from your Johnson or Evinrude dealer) are required for these procedures. Make sure the battery is fully charged. Disconnect and ground the spark plug leads to prevent the engine from starting while cranking.

Replacement pulse packs are designated as Phase II packs. When replacing an original pack with a Phase II pack, remove and discard the original rotor and voltage suppressor. Install the new rotor furnished with the Phase II pack. Check timing and set to specifications. See Chapter Five.

Pulse pack input test

Refer to **Figure 23** for test points.
1. Set CD tester selector switch to the 50 volt scale. Set the other switch to the plus (+) setting.
2. Connect the black tester lead to a good engine ground. Insert the red tester lead probe in the red wire connector between the voltage suppressor and ignition switch.
3. Turn the ignition switch ON. If the tester does not indicate battery voltage (12 volts), check the ignition switch.
4. Remove the red tester lead probe and insert it in the red wire connector between the voltage suppressor and pulse pack.
5. Turn the ignition switch ON. If the tester does not indicate battery voltage (12 volts), check the voltage suppressor.
6. With tester leads connected as in Step 4, crank the engine and note the tester scale. It should read 9.5 volts or more. If the reading is less than specified and the battery was fully charged before starting the test, remove the starter and have its current draw checked by a dealer or qualified marine electrical specialist.

Pulse pack output test

Refer to **Figure 23** for test points.

1. Set CD tester selector switch to the 500 volt scale. Set the other switch to the plus (+) setting.
2. Connect the black tester lead to a good engine ground. Connect the red tester lead probe to the green wire terminal of the coil.
3. Crank the engine and note the tester scale. It should read 250 volts or more.

CAUTION
Perform Step 4 with the engine in a test tank or on the boat in the water.

4. If the engine will run, connect the spark plug leads. Start and run the engine at a speed where it begins to misfire and note the tester scale. It should indicate almost 300 volts with a steady needle position.
5. If there is no reading in Step 4, remove the flywheel and distributor cap. Bypass the vacuum switch on 1968 100 hp engines with a jumper lead. Insert a flat feeler gauge between the rotor and sensor. With the ignition switch on, the tester should read 250 volts or more. Reinstall distributor cap and flywheel. Remove vacuum switch bypass, if installed.
6. If there is no reading in Step 3, disconnect the coil from the circuit. Connect the S-80 or M-80 tester between the green pulse pack wire and a good engine ground. Set the tester on position 1. Depress load button A and crank the engine with the ignition switch while watching the tester neon light. If the light glows steadily, the amplifier is good. Replace the coil.

Coil output test

Refer to **Figure 23** for test points.

1. Connect the coil high tension lead to a spark tester with its gap set at 1/2 in.
2. Crank the engine. If strong, steady sparks jump the tester gap, the coil is good. If the sparks are weak or erratic, replace the coil.

Sensor circuit test

Refer to **Figure 23** for test points.

1. With the flywheel and distributor cap removed, disconnect the blue leads at the sensor.
2. Connect an ohmmeter (low scale) between the disconnected sensor leads. If meter does not read 4-6 ohms, replace the sensor.
3. If sensor reading is satisfactory, remove the sensor and visually check for cracks across the sensor eye. If no cracks are found, reinstall sensor and set air gap to 0.028 in. See Chapter Four.

NOTE
It is possible that the sensor will give a good ohmmeter reading, yet ground out in operation. If this problem is suspected, remove the sensor and perform a condenser leakage test with an ignition analyzer, applying approximately 500 volts to the sensor. Replace the sensor if it fails the leakage test.

Amperage input to pulse pack test

This test should be performed with the engine in a test tank or on the boat in the water. Refer to **Figure 23** for test points.

1. Connect a 0-5 amp ammeter in series between the ignition switch and pulse pack.
2. Reconnect the spark plug leads.
3. Start and run the engine at idle. The ammeter should indicate 0.4-0.6 amps. Increase engine speed to full throttle. The ammeter reading should not exceed 2.75 amps. If the readings are not as specified, replace the pulse pack.

TROUBLESHOOTING

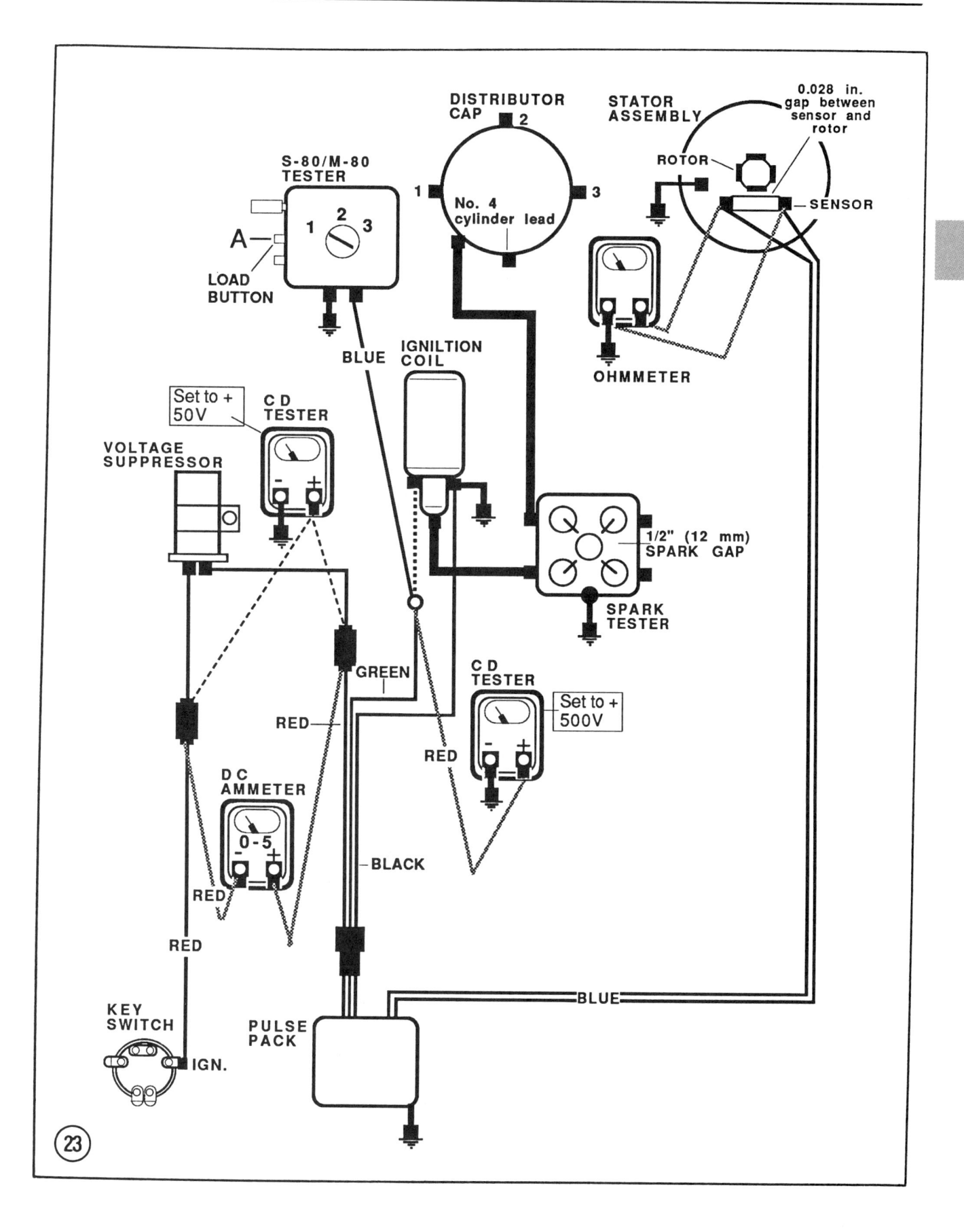

1969-1970 115 HP

A CD test meter and S-80 or M-80 neon tester (available from your Johnson or Evinrude dealer) are required for these procedures. Make sure the battery is fully charged. Disconnect and ground the spark plug leads to prevent the engine from starting while cranking.

Ignition safety circuit test

Refer to **Figure 24** for test points.
1. Set CD tester selector switch to the 50 volt scale. Set the other switch to the plus (+) setting.
2. Connect the black tester lead to a good engine ground. Connect the red tester lead to terminal 8 or 9 on the terminal board.
3. Turn the ignition switch ON. If the tester does not indicate battery voltage (12 volts), check the ignition switch.
4. Move the red tester lead to terminal 7 on the terminal block. Crank the engine. The tester should show 9.5 volts.
5. If there is no reading in Step 4, remove the red tester lead from terminal 7. Crank the engine while alternately touching the red tester lead to terminals 1, 2, 3 and 4.
   a. If there is no reading, check the alternator stator, shift diodes and rectifier as described in this chapter.
   b. If there is a reading, replace the safety switch.

Safety circuit leakage test

Refer to **Figure 24** for test points.
1. Turn ignition switch ON. Remove safety switch lead from terminal 7 on the terminal block and connect it to a test lamp.
2. If the test lamp glows in Step 1, remove the yellow and yellow/gray leads from terminals 1, 2, 3 and 4 on the terminal block.
   a. If the test lamp does not go out, replace the safety switch.
   b. If the test lamp goes out, check the shift diode and rectifier as described in this chapter.

Pulse pack output test

Refer to **Figure 24** for test points.
1. Set CD tester selector switch to the 500 volt scale. Set the other switch to the plus (+) setting.
2. Connect the black tester lead to a good engine ground. Connect the red tester lead probe to terminal 5 on the terminal block.

> *CAUTION*
> *Perform Step 3 with the engine in a test tank or on the boat in the water.*

3. Start and run the engine. The tester scale should read 250 volts or more.
4. If there is no reading in Step 3, disconnect the lead at terminal 5. Connect an S-80 or M-80 tester between the disconnected lead and a good engine ground. Crank the engine and depress load button A. The tester scale should read 250 volts or more.
5. If there is no reading in Step 4, connect the test sensor into the pulse pack sensor plug. Connect terminals 7 and 8 with a jumper lead. With the S-80 or M-80 tester connected as in Step 4, activate the test sensor. If the tester gives a reading, perform the *Sensor Circuit Test* in this chapter. If no reading is given, replace the pulse pack.

Sensor circuit test

Refer to **Figure 24** for this procedure.
1. Disconnect sensor-to-pulse pack connector. Connect an ohmmeter (low scale) between the connector terminals. If the meter does not read 4-6 ohms, replace the sensor.
2. Set the ohmmeter on the high scale and connect it between one sensor lead and ground. Open and close the throttle to activate the anti-reverse spring. The meter

TROUBLESHOOTING

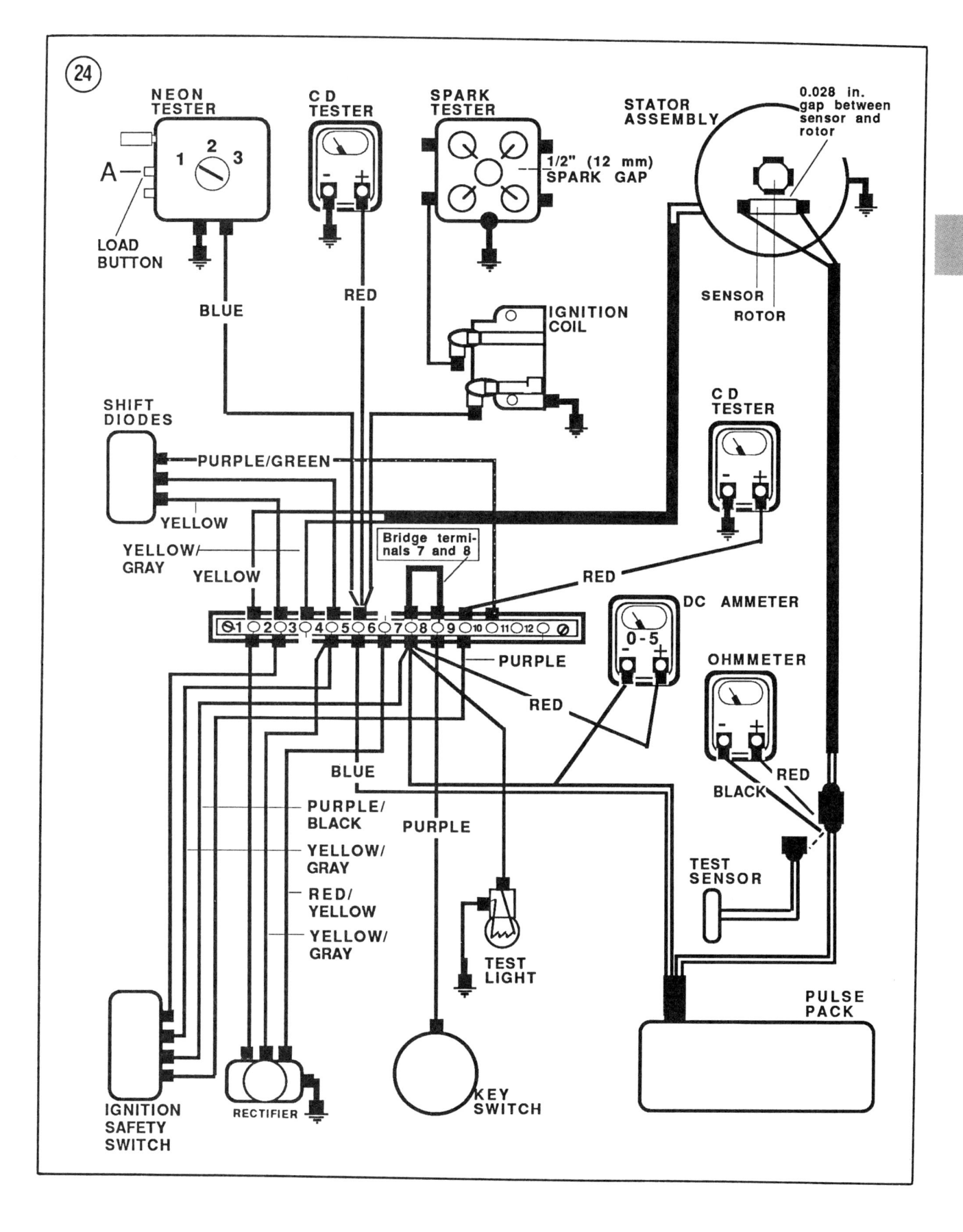

should read at least 100,000 ohms. Move the wires back and forth while watching the meter scale for indications of a ground condition (a reading of less than 100,000 ohms indicates a ground condition).

3. If sensor reading is satisfactory, remove the flywheel and distributor cap.

   a. Check the distributor cap and rotor for carbon tracks, corrosion or cracks. Correct as required.
   b. Remove the sensor and visually check for cracks across the sensor eye. If no cracks are found, reinstall sensor and set air gap to 0.028 in. See Chapter Four.

NOTE
It is possible that the sensor will give a good ohmmeter reading, yet ground out in operation. If this problem is suspected, remove the sensor and perform a condenser leakage test with an ignition analyzer, applying approximately 500 volts to the sensor. Replace the sensor if it fails the leakage test.

Coil output test

Refer to **Figure 24** for test points.
1. Connect the coil high tension lead to a spark tester with its gap set at 1/2 in.
2. Crank the engine. If strong, steady sparks jump the tester gap, the coil is good. If the sparks are weak or erratic, replace the coil.

Intermittent miss test

This test should be performed with the engine in a test tank or on the boat in the water. Refer to **Figure 24** for test points.
1. Set CD tester selector switch to the 500 volt scale. Set the other switch to the plus (+) setting.
2. Connect a 0-5 amp ammeter in series between terminal 7 on the terminal board and the pulse pack.
3. Reconnect the spark plug leads.

4. Start and run the engine at idle. Connect the black tester lead to a good engine ground and the red tester lead to terminal 5 on the terminal board. The tester should read 250 volts or more and the ammeter should show a steady 2.75 amp reading. If the readings are not as specified, replace the pulse pack.

1971-1972 115 HP; 1972 100 HP

A CD test meter and S-80 or M-80 neon tester (available from your Johnson or Evinrude dealer) are required for these procedures. Make sure the battery is fully charged. Disconnect and ground the spark plug leads to prevent the engine from starting while cranking.

Pulse pack input test

Refer to **Figure 25** for test points.
1. Set CD tester selector switch to the 50 volt scale. Set the other switch to the plus (+) setting.
2. Connect the black tester lead to a good engine ground. Connect the red tester lead to terminal 8 or 9 on the terminal board.
3. Turn the ignition switch ON. The tester should indicate battery voltage (12 volts). If it does not, check the ignition switch.
4. Crank the engine. The tester should show 9.5 volts. If it does not and the battery is fully charged, remove the starter motor and have its current draw tested by a dealer or qualified marine electrical shop.

Pulse pack output test

Refer to **Figure 25** for test points.
1. Set CD tester selector switch to the 500 volt scale. Set the other switch to the plus (+) setting.
2. Connect the black tester lead to a good engine ground. Connect the red tester lead probe to terminal 5 on the terminal block.

TROUBLESHOOTING

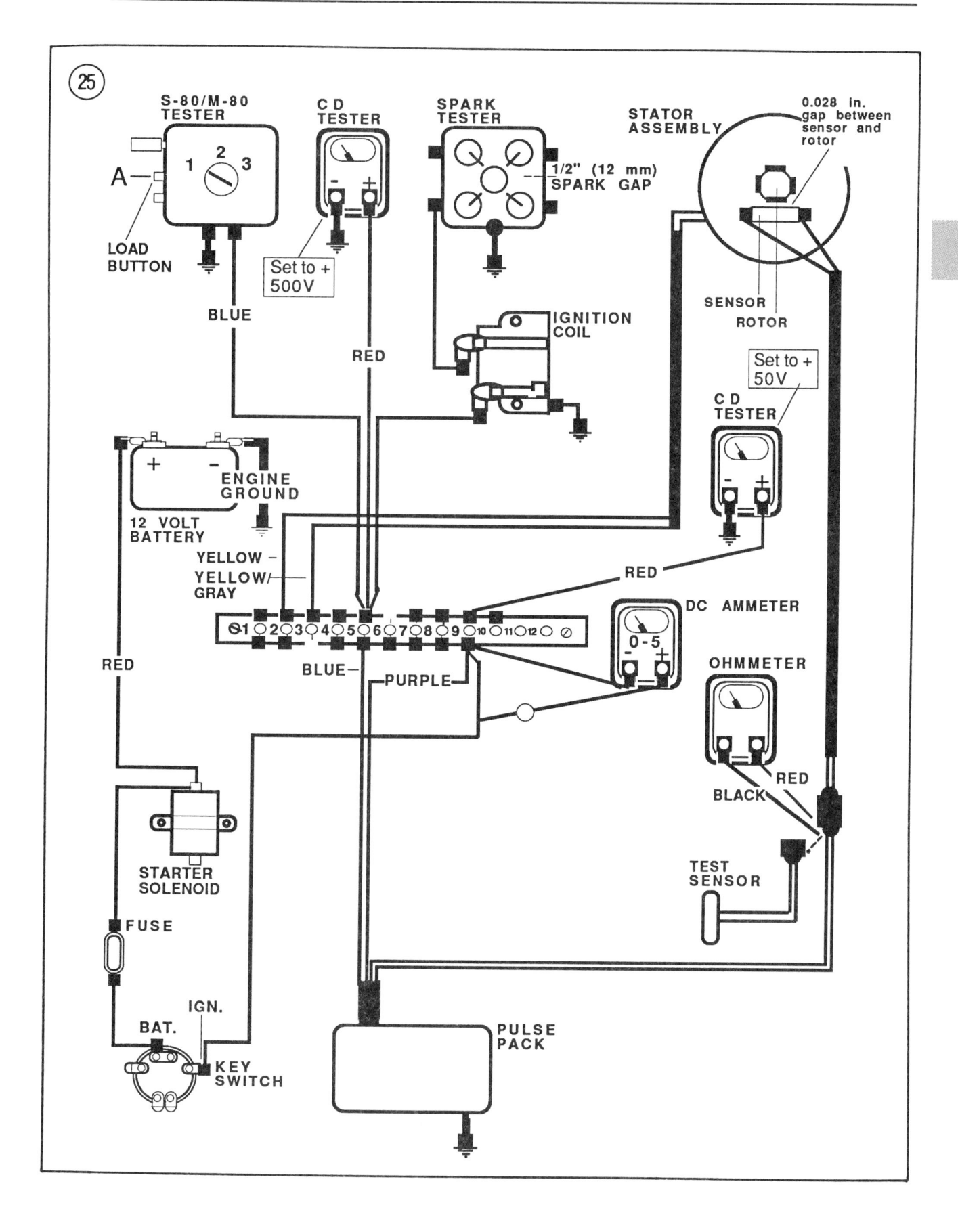

3. Crank the engine. The tester scale should read 250 volts or more.

4. If there is no reading in Step 3, disconnect the sensor plug. Connect a known-good sensor to the pulse pack connector. Activate the test sensor; the tester should read 250 volts or more.

5. If there is no reading in Step 4, disconnect the coil primary lead at terminal 5. Connect an S-80 or M-80 tester between the disconnected lead and a good engine ground. If the tester reads 250 volts or more when the test sensor is activated, perform the *Coil Output Test* and *Sensor Circuit Test* as described in this chapter. If there is still no reading, replace the pulse pack.

Coil output test

Refer to **Figure 25** for test points.

1. Connect the coil high tension lead to a spark tester with its gap set at 1/2 in.

2. Crank the engine. If strong, steady sparks jump the tester gap, the coil is good. If the sparks are weak or erratic, replace the coil.

Sensor circuit test

Refer to **Figure 25** for this procedure.

1. Disconnect sensor-to-pulse pack connector. Connect an ohmmeter (low scale) between the connector terminals. If the meter does not read 4-6 ohms, check for a shorted lead on the base connections.

2. Set the ohmmeter on the high scale and connect it between one sensor lead and ground. Open and close the throttle to activate the anti-reverse spring. The meter should read at least 100,000 ohms. Move the wires back and forth while watching the meter scale for indications of a ground condition.

3. If sensor reading is satisfactory, remove the flywheel and distributor cap.
   a. Check the distributor cap and rotor for carbon tracks, corrosion or cracks. Correct as required.
   b. Remove the sensor and visually check for cracks across the sensor eye. If no cracks are found, reinstall sensor and set air gap to 0.028 in. See Chapter Four.

Intermittent miss test

This test should be performed with the engine in a test tank or on the boat in the water. Refer to **Figure 25** for test points.

1. Set CD tester selector switch to the 500 volt scale. Set the other switch to the plus (+) setting.

2. Connect the black tester lead to a good engine ground. Connect the red tester lead to terminal 5.

3. Connect a 0-5 amp ammeter in series between terminal 8 or 9 on the terminal board and the pulse pack purple wire.

4. Reconnect the spark plug leads.

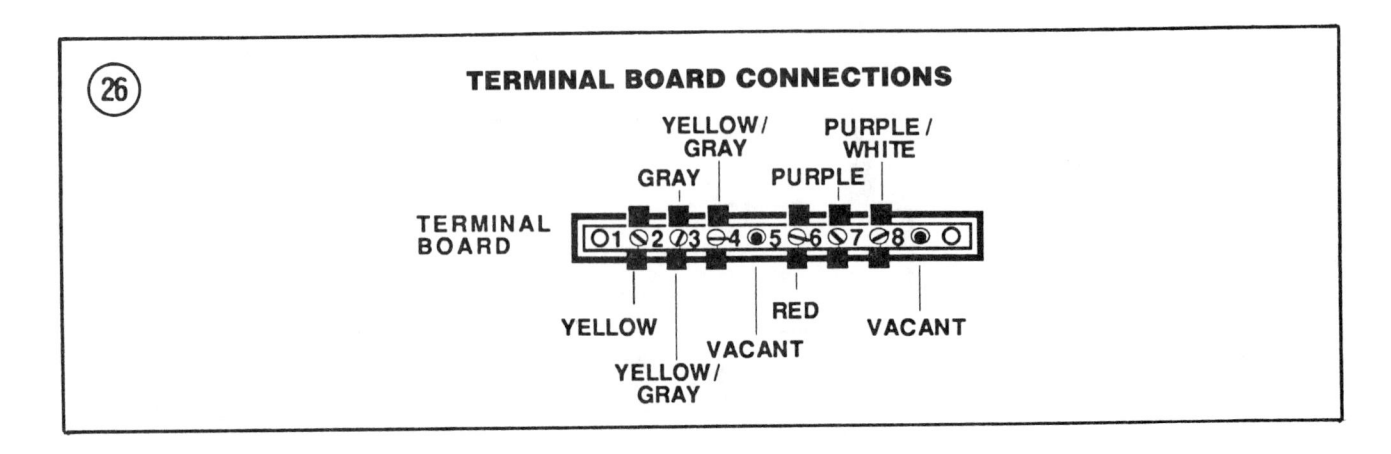

(26) TERMINAL BOARD CONNECTIONS

TROUBLESHOOTING

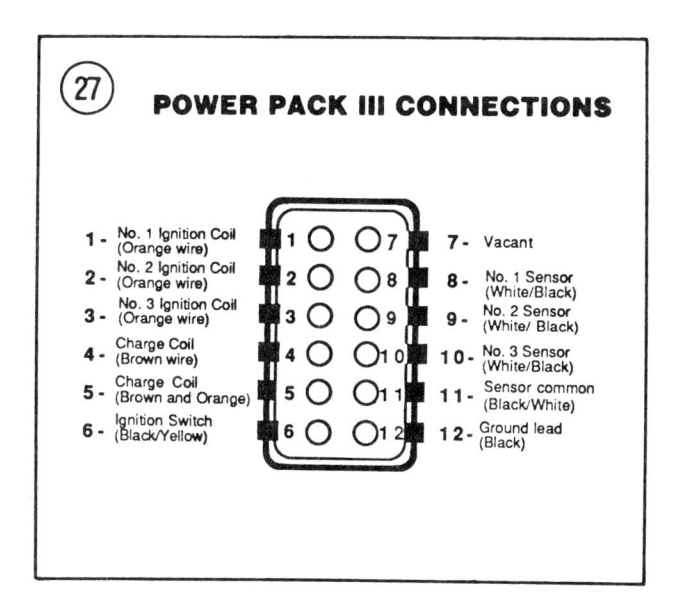

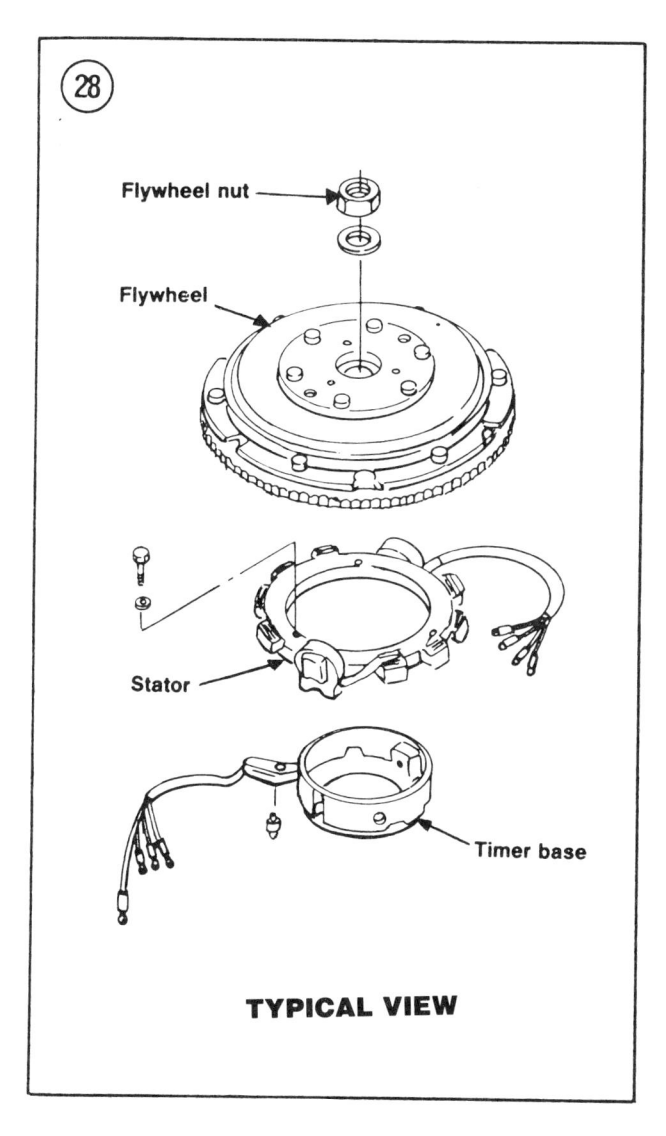

27 POWER PACK III CONNECTIONS

1 - No. 1 Ignition Coil (Orange wire)
2 - No. 2 Ignition Coil (Orange wire)
3 - No. 3 Ignition Coil (Orange wire)
4 - Charge Coil (Brown wire)
5 - Charge Coil (Brown and Orange)
6 - Ignition Switch (Black/Yellow)
7 - Vacant
8 - No. 1 Sensor (White/Black)
9 - No. 2 Sensor (White/Black)
10 - No. 3 Sensor (White/Black)
11 - Sensor common (Black/White)
12 - Ground lead (Black)

28

- Flywheel nut
- Flywheel
- Stator
- Timer base

TYPICAL VIEW

5. Start the engine. Increase engine speed to the point where the miss occurs. Note the needle position on both meters. If either needle wavers or if the ammmeter reading is more than 1.8 amps, replace the pulse pack.

1972 65 HP

Figure 26 shows the terminal board connections. Although many terminal boards have the wire colors embossed either on the board itself or on the cover (if used), not all models will use all of the wires and connections shown. Double check your connections if necessary by referring to **Figure 26**.

Figure 27 shows the power pack terminals. Refer to the diagram when reconnecting power pack leads to avoid any misconnections that can cause damage to the power pack or ignition.

The 3 sensor coils are potted in the timer base (**Figure 28**) and are replaced as an assembly. The charge coils are located in the potted stator assembly. If defective, replace the charge coils and stator as an assembly.

Coat all electrical terminal connections (except ground stud, nut and terminal motor cable-to-bypass cover) with OMC Black Neoprene Dip after reconnecting the leads to the terminal board or power pack.

An S-80 or M-80 neon tester (available from your Johnson or Evinrude dealer) is required for these procedures. Make sure the battery is fully charged. Disconnect and ground the spark plug leads to prevent the engine from starting while cranking.

Ignition output test

Refer to **Figure 29** for this procedure.
1. Connect a spark tester as shown in **Figure 29**. Set the tester air gap to 1/2 in.
2. Crank the engine with the ignition switch while watching the spark tester. If strong,

29

IGNITION SPARK TEST

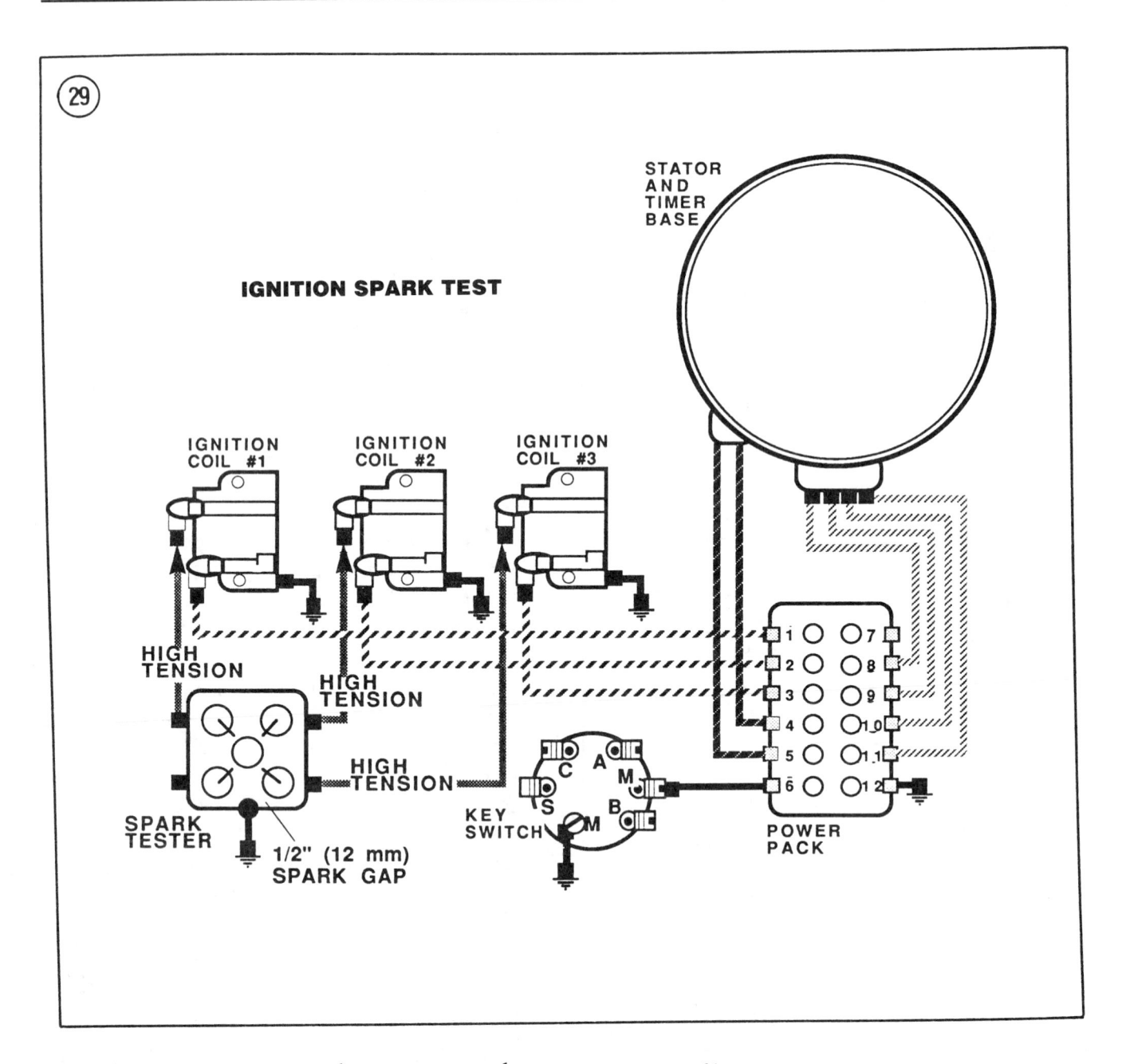

steady and alternate sparks appear at the spark tester, the ignition coil output is good.
3. If the sparks at 1 or 2 tester gaps are weak or erratic or if there is no spark at 1 or 2 gaps, perform the *Sensor Coil Output Test* in this chapter.
4. If the sparks are weak or erratic at all 3 tester gaps, perform the *Charge Coil Output Test* in this chapter.
5. If there is no spark from any of the coils, perform the *Key Switch Test* in this chapter.

Sensor coil output test

Refer to **Figure 30** for this procedure.
1. With the spark tester installed as shown in **Figure 30**, disconnect the sensor leads at terminals 8, 9, 10 and 11 of the power pack.
2. Mark cylinder number on each ignition coil lead and disconnect at terminals 2 and 3.
3. Connect the black test lead to terminal 8 and the blue test lead to terminal 11. Set neon light switch on position 3.

TROUBLESHOOTING

SENSOR COIL TEST

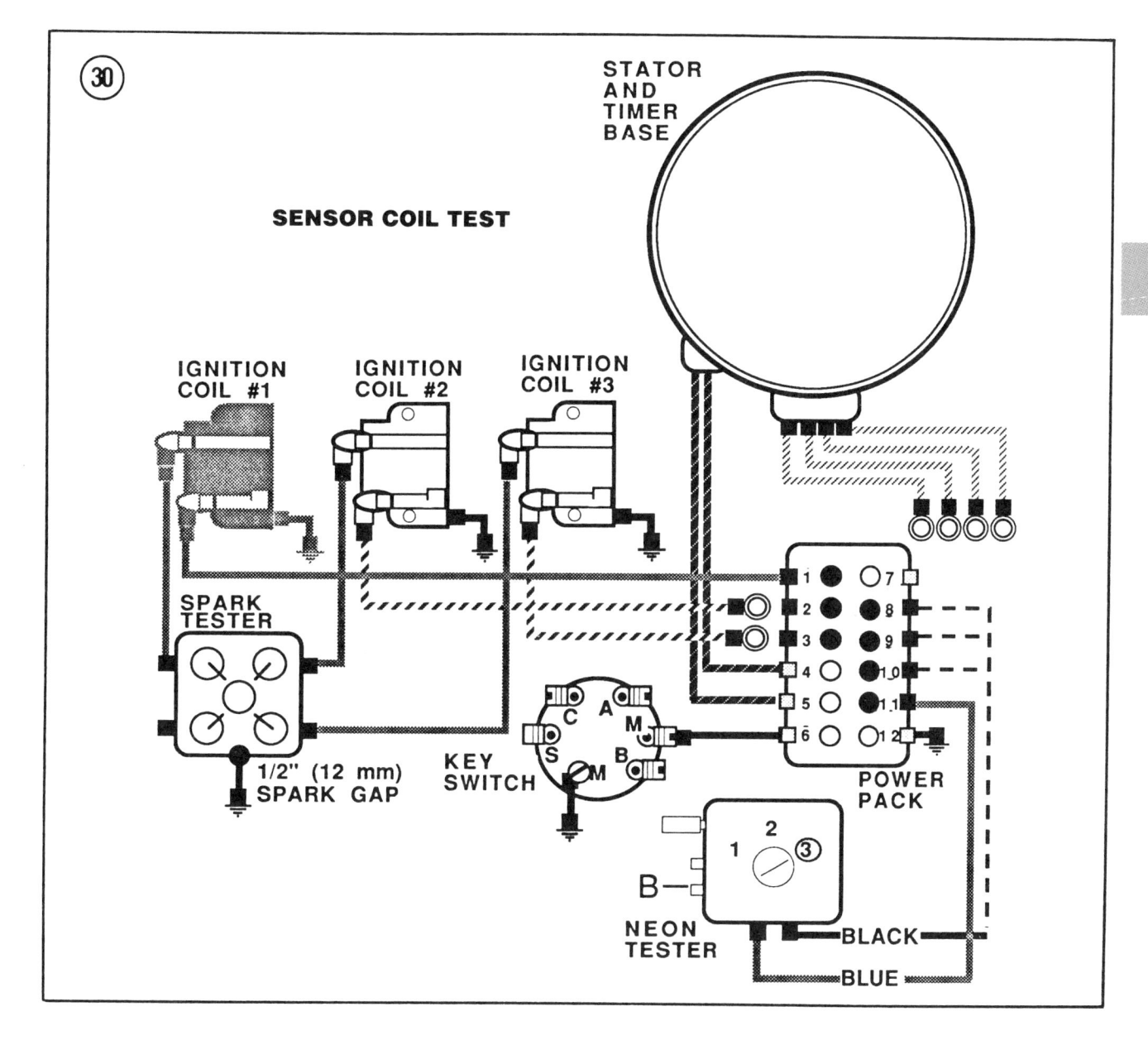

4. Crank the engine with the ignition switch while watching the spark tester and rapidly tapping tester load button B:
   a. If there is a spark on the ignition coil output, check the sensor coil resistance as described in this chapter.
   b. If there is no spark, perform the *Power Pack Output Test* in this chapter.
5. Reconnect the coil lead at terminal 2 and disconnect the coil lead at terminal 1. Move the black test lead to terminal 9 and repeat Step 4.
6. Reconnect the coil lead at terminal 3 and disconnect the coil lead at terminal 1. Move the black test lead to terminal 10 and repeat Step 4.

Charge coil output test

Refer to **Figure 31** for this procedure.
1. Disconnect the charge coil leads at power pack terminals 4 and 5.
2. Connect the neon tester leads between the 2 disconnected charge coil leads.

CHAPTER THREE

CHARGE COIL TEST

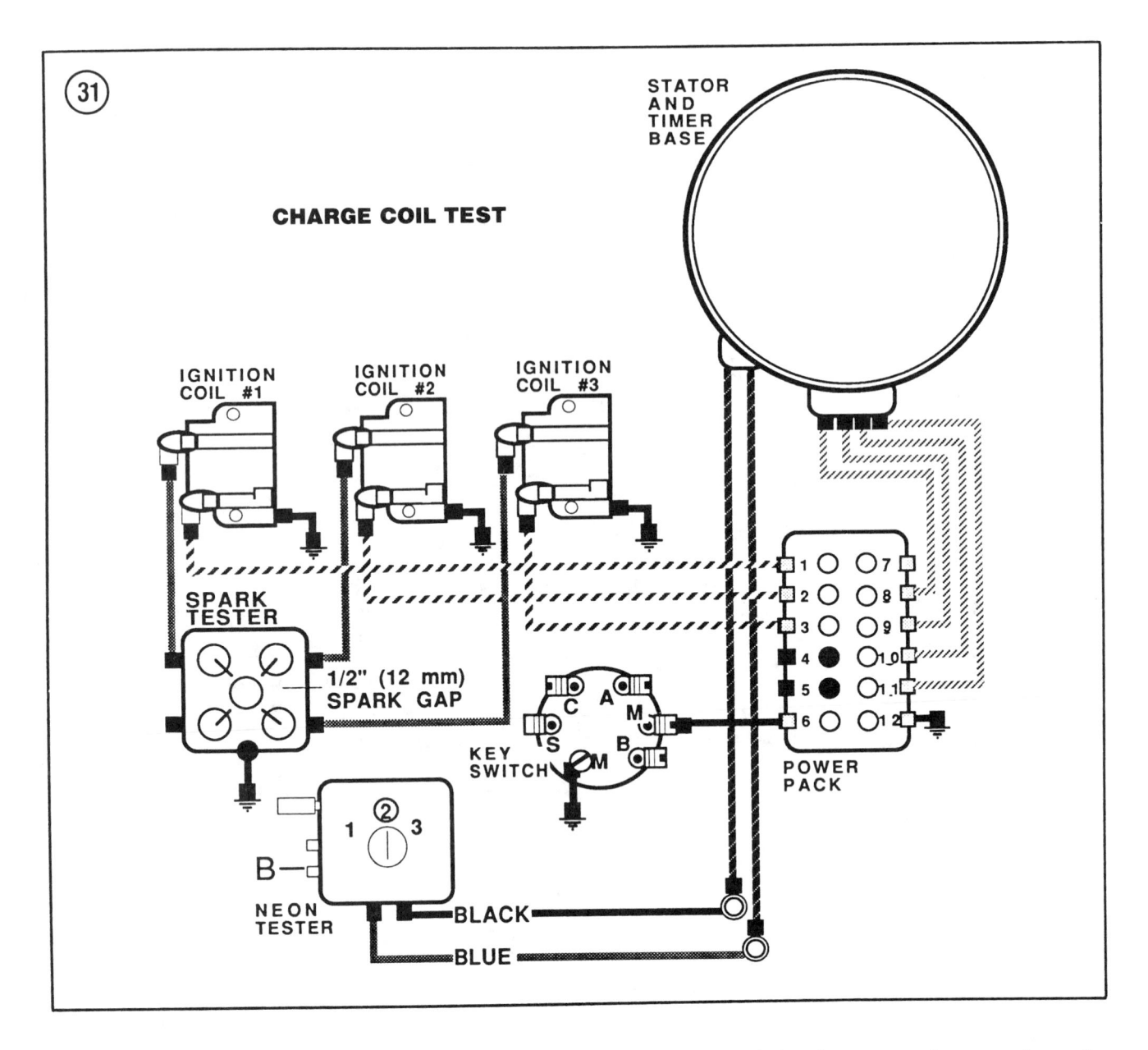

3. Set neon light switch on position 2. Depress load button B and crank the engine with the ignition switch while watching the tester neon light:
 a. If the light glows steadily, perform the *Sensor Coil Output Test* in this chapter.
 b. If the light glows intermittently, check the charge coil output leads for an open or a short to ground and make sure the power pack ground lead (terminal 12) is good. If leads are good, replace the charge coil and stator assembly.
 c. If the light does not glow, replace the charge coil and stator assembly.
4. Reconnect the charge coil leads at the power pack.

Power pack output test

Refer to **Figure 32** for this procedure.
1. Mark each ignition coil primary lead with the cylinder number, then disconnect from terminals 1, 2 and 3 of the power pack.

TROUBLESHOOTING

POWER PACK OUTPUT TEST

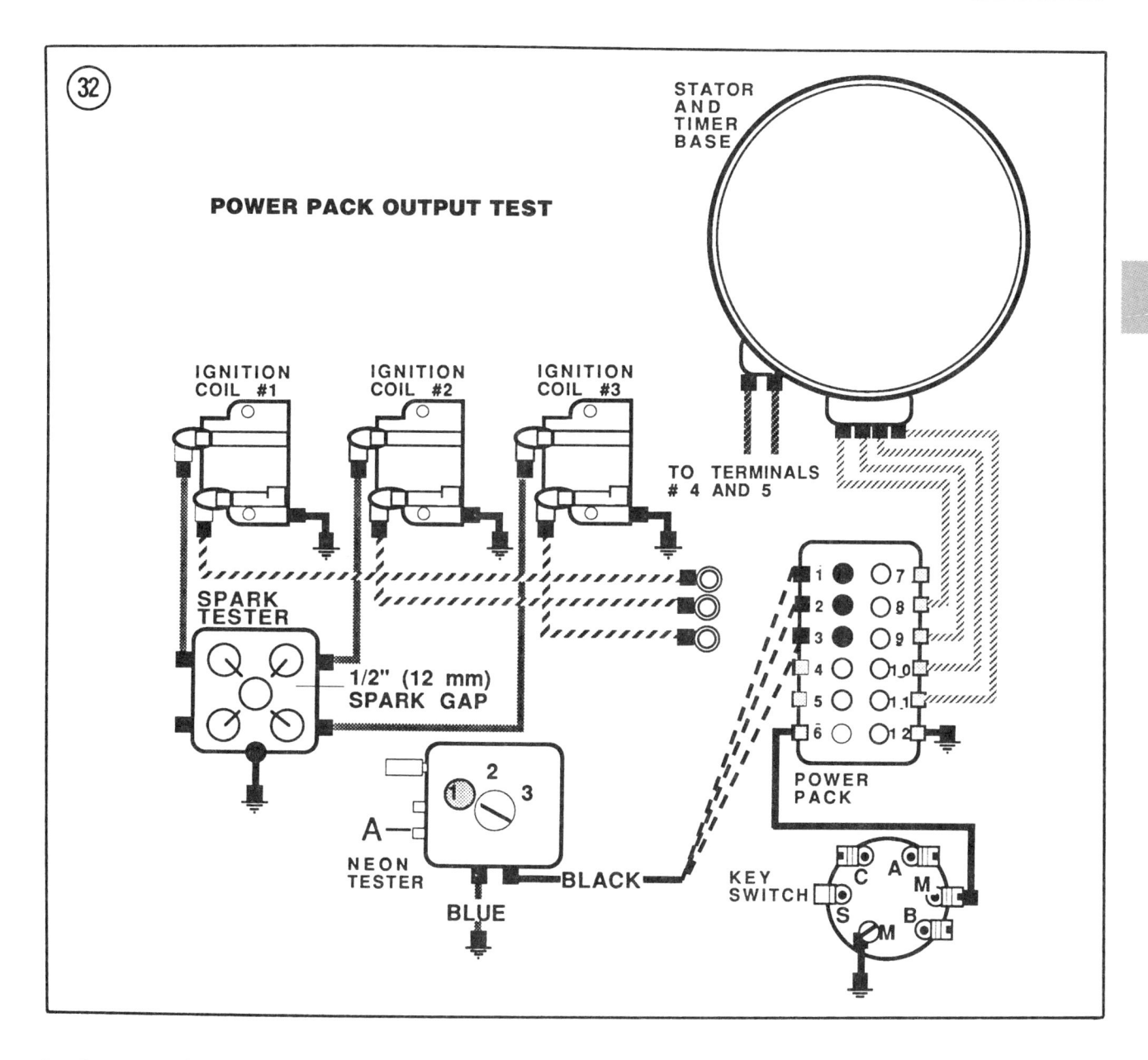

2. Connect the black test lead to terminal 1 and the blue test lead to a good engine ground.

3. Set neon light switch on position 1 and depress load button A. Crank the engine with the ignition switch while watching the tester neon light.

4. Move the black test lead to terminal 2 and repeat Step 3. Then move the black test lead to terminal 3 and repeat Step 3:
   a. If the test light emits a steady glow on all outputs, replace the ignition coils.
   b. If the test light is steady, dim or intermittent on 1 or 2 outputs, replace the power pack.
   c. If there is no light on any output, check the power pack ground at terminal 12. If the ground is good, perform the *Key Switch Test* in this chapter. If the switch is good, replace the power pack.

5. Reconnect the coil leads at the power pack.

(33)

KEY SWITCH TEST

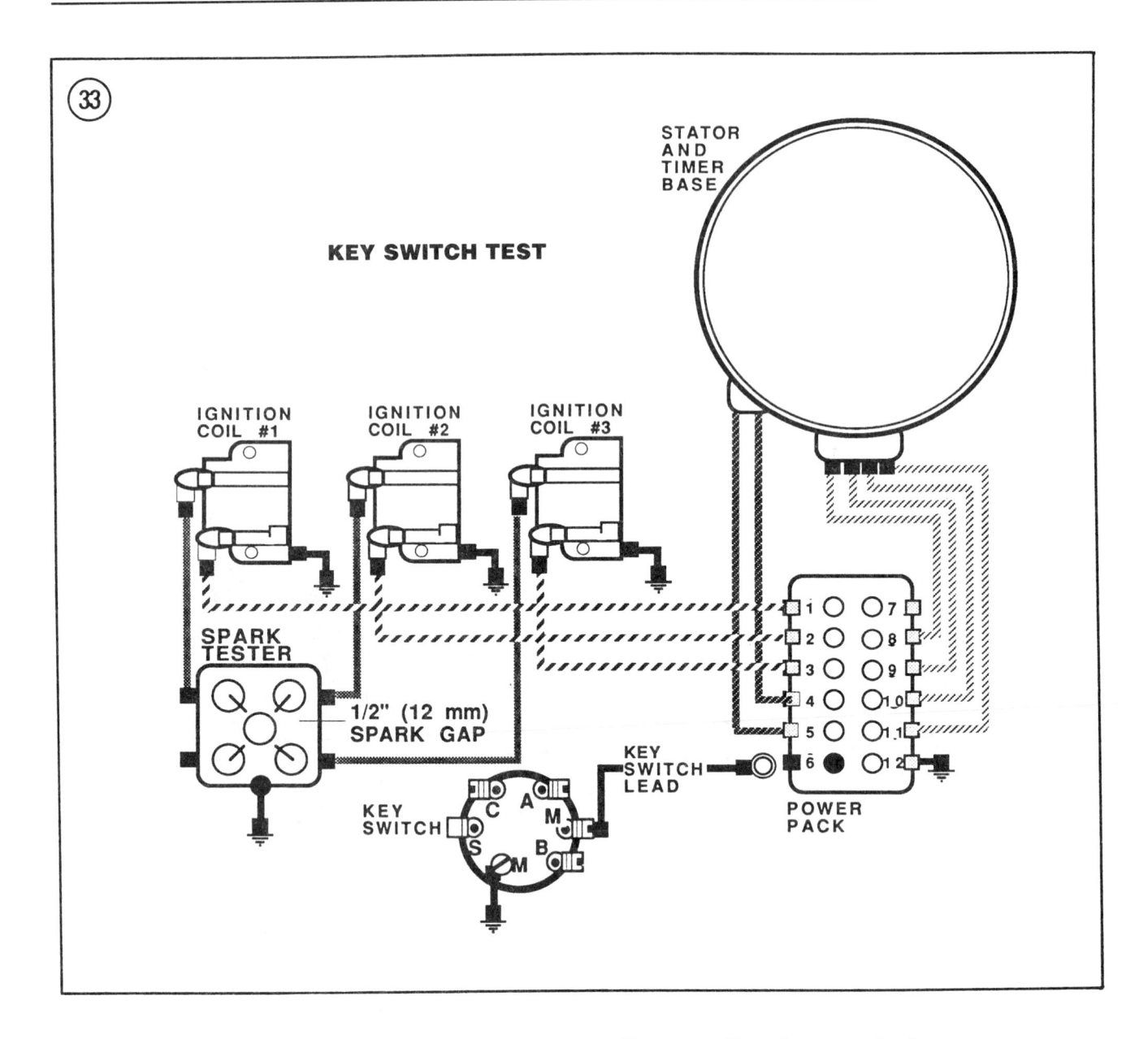

Key switch test

Refer to **Figure 33** for this procedure.

1. With the spark tester installed as shown in **Figure 33**, disconnect the key switch lead at power pack terminal 6.

2. Crank the engine and watch the spark tester. If there is no spark or a spark at only one test gap, the key switch is good. If there is a spark at all gaps, check the key switch lead for defects. If the lead is good, replace the key switch.

Sensor coil resistance check

1. Disconnect the sensor leads from power pack terminals 8, 9, 10 and 11.

2. Connect one ohmmeter test lead to the disconnected black/white lead. Alternately connect the other ohmmeter test lead to the white/black wires and note the reading. If it is not 7.5-9.5 ohms at room temperature (70° F), replace the sensor coil and timer base assembly.

3. Set the ohmmeter on the high scale. Connect the black test lead to a good engine

TROUBLESHOOTING

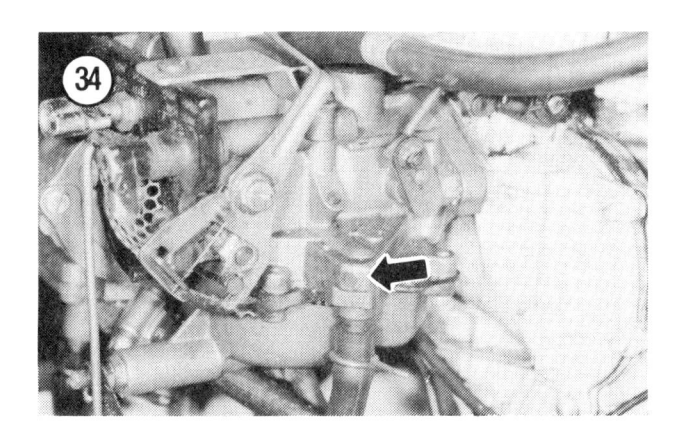

ground and the red test lead alternately to the disconnected sensor leads. The ohmmeter should read infinity at each connection. If it does not, a sensor coil is grounded. Replace the sensor coil and timer base assembly.

Charge coil resistance check

1. Disconnect the charge coil leads at power pack terminals 4 and 5.
2. Set the ohmmeter on the high scale and connect the test leads between the disconnected charge coil leads.
3. If the ohmmeter reading is not 870-930 ohms at room temperature (70° F), replace the charge coil and stator assembly.

FUEL SYSTEM

Many outboard owners automatically assume that the carburetor is at fault when the engine does not run properly. While fuel system problems are not uncommon, carburetor adjustment is seldom the answer. In many cases, adjusting the carburetor only compounds the problem by making the engine run worse.

Fuel system troubleshooting should start at the gas tank and work through the system, reserving the carburetor(s) as the final point. Most fuel system problems result from an empty fuel tank, sour fuel, a plugged fuel filter or a malfunctioning fuel pump. **Table 3** provides a series of symptoms and causes that can be useful in localizing fuel system problems.

Troubleshooting

As a first step, check the fuel flow. Remove the fuel tank cap and look into the tank. If there is fuel present, disconnect and ground the spark plug lead(s) as a safety precaution. Disconnect the fuel line at the carburetor (**Figure 34**, typical) and place it in a suitable container to catch any discharged fuel. See if gas flows freely from the line when the primer bulb is squeezed. If there is no fuel flow from the line:
 a. The fuel petcock may be shut off or blocked by rust or foreign matter.
 b. The fuel line may be stopped up or kinked.
 c. A primer bulb check valve may be defective.
 d. The anti-siphon valve (if so equipped) may be malfunctioning.
 e. The fuel pump may be defective.

If a good fuel flow is present, crank the engine 10-12 times to check fuel pump operation. A pump that is operating satisfactorily will deliver a good, constant flow of fuel from the line. If the amount of flow varies from pulse to pulse, the fuel pump is probably failing.

In accordance with industry safety standards, late-model boats with a built-in fuel tank will have some form of anti-siphon device installed between the tank outlet and engine fuel inlet. This device is designed to shut the fuel supply off in case the boat capsizes or is involved in an accident. When an older motor is installed on a newer boat, it is not unusual for an anti-siphon device malfunction to be mistaken for a defective fuel pump.

Anti-siphon devices can malfunction in one of the following ways:

Anti-siphon valve

1. Orifice in valve is too small or clogs easily.
2. Valve sticks in closed or partially closed position.
3. Valve fluctuates between open and closed position.
4. Thread sealer, metal filing or dirt/debris clogs orifice or lodges in the relief spring.

Solenoid-operated fuel shut-off valve

1. Solenoid fails with valve in closed position.
2. Solenoid malfunctions, leaving valve in partially closed position.

Manually-operated fuel shut-off valve

1. Valve is left in completely closed position.
2. Valve is not fully opened.

The easiest way to determine if the anti-siphon valve is defective is to bypass it by operating the engine with a remote fuel supply such as an outboard fuel tank.

Carburetor chokes can also present problems. A choke that sticks open will show up as a hard starting problem; one that sticks closed will result in a flooding condition.

During a hot engine shut-down, the fuel bowl temperature can rise above 200°, causing the fuel inside to boil. While marine carburetors are vented to atmosphere to prevent this problem, there is a possibility that some fuel will percolate over the high-speed nozzle.

A leaking inlet needle and seat or a defective float will allow an excessive amount of fuel into the intake manifold. Pressure in the fuel line after the engine is shut down forces fuel past the leaking needle and seat. This raises the fuel bowl level, allowing fuel to overflow into the manifold.

Excessive fuel consumption may not necessarily mean an engine or fuel system problem. Marine growth on the boat's hull, a bent or otherwise damaged propeller or a fuel line leak can cause an increase in fuel consumption. These areas should all be checked *before* blaming the carburetor.

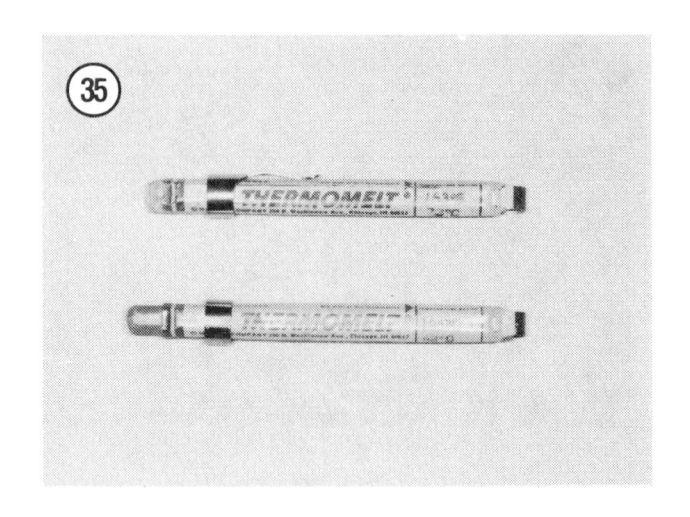

ENGINE TEMPERATURE AND OVERHEATING

Proper engine temperature is critical to good engine operation. An engine that runs too hot will be damaged internally. One that operates too cool will not run smoothly or efficiently.

A variety of problems can cause engine overheating. Some of the most commonly encountered are a defective thermostat, a low-output or defective water pump, damaged or mispositioned water passage restrictors or even engine flashing (excess casting material) in the cylinder head casting water discharge passage that was not removed during manufacture.

Troubleshooting

Engine temperature can be checked with the use of Markal thermomelt sticks available at your local marine dealer. This heat-sensitive stick looks like a large crayon (**Figure 35**) and will melt on contact with a metal surface at a specific temperature. Two thermomelt sticks are required to properly check a Johnson or

TROUBLESHOOTING

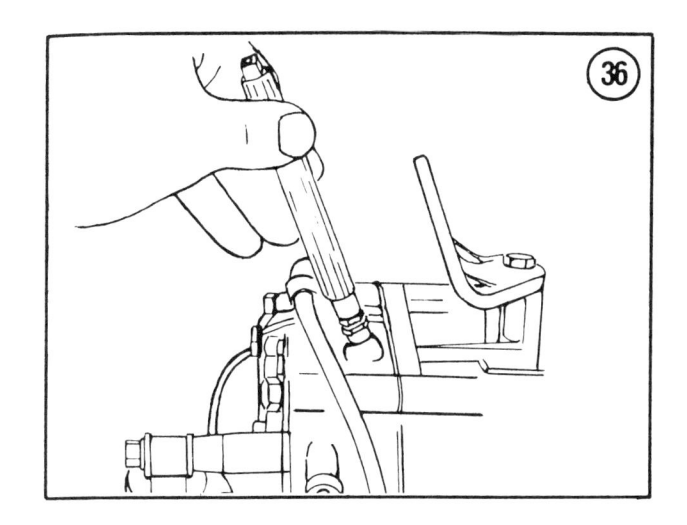

Evinrude outboard: a 125° F (52° C) stick and a 163° F (73° C) stick. The stick should not be applied to the center of the cylinder head, as this area may normally run hotter than 163° F.

The test is most efficient when carried out on a motor operating on a boat in the water. If necessary to perform the test using a test tank, run the engine at 3,000 rpm for a minimum of 5 minutes to assure that it is at operating temperature. Make sure inlet water temperature is below 80° F (26° C) and perform the test as follows:

1. Mark the cylinder water jacket with each stick (**Figure 36**). The mark will appear similar to a chalk mark. Make sure sufficient material is applied to the metal surface.
2. With the engine at operating temperature and running at idle in FORWARD gear, the 125° F stick mark should melt. If it does not melt on thermostat-equipped models, the thermostat is stuck open and the engine is running cold.
3. With the engine at operating temperature and running at full throttle in FORWARD gear, the 163° F stick mark should not melt. If it does, the power head is overheating. Look for a defective water pump, clogged or leaking cooling system. On thermostat-equipped models, the thermostat may be stuck closed.

ENGINE

Engine problems are generally symptoms of something wrong in another system, such as ignition, fuel or starting. If properly maintained and serviced, the engine should experience no problems other than those caused by age and wear.

Overheating and Lack of Lubrication

Overheating and lack of lubrication cause most engine mechanical problems. Outboard motors create a great deal of heat and are not designed to operate at a standstill for any length of time. Using a spark plug of the wrong heat range can burn a piston. Incorrect ignition timing, a defective water pump or thermostat, a propeller that is too large (over-propping) or an excessively lean fuel mixture can also cause the engine to overheat.

Preignition

Preignition is the premature burning of fuel and is caused by hot spots in the combustion chamber (**Figure 37**). The fuel actually ignites before it is supposed to. Glowing deposits in the combustion chamber, inadequate cooling or overheated spark plugs can all cause preignition. This is first noticed in the form of a power loss but will eventually result in extensive damage to the internal parts of the engine because of higher combustion chamber temperatures.

Detonation

Commonly called "spark knock" or "fuel knock," detonation is the violent explosion of fuel in the combustion chamber prior to the proper time of combustion (**Figure 38**). Severe damage can result. Use of low octane gasoline is a common cause of detonation.

Even when high octane gasoline is used, detonation can still occur if the engine is improperly timed. Other causes are over-advanced ignition timing, lean fuel mixture at or near full throttle, inadequate engine cooling, cross-firing of spark plugs, excessive accumulation of deposits on piston and combustion chamber or the use of a prop that is too large (over-propping).

Since outboard motors are noisy, engine knock or detonation is likely to go unnoticed by owners, especially at high engine rpm when wind noise is also present. Such inaudible detonation, as it is called, is usually the cause when engine damage occurs for no apparent reason.

Poor Idling

A poor idle can be caused by improper carburetor adjustment, incorrect timing or ignition system malfunctions. Check the gas cap vent (if so equipped) for an obstruction.

Misfiring

Misfiring can result from a weak spark or a dirty spark plug. Check for fuel contamination. If misfiring occurs only under heavy load, as when accelerating, it is usually caused by a defective spark plug. Run the motor at night to check for spark leaks along the plug wire and under spark plug cap or use a spark leak tester.

WARNING
Do not run engine in a dark garage to check for spark leak. There is considerable danger of carbon monoxide poisoning.

Water Leakage in Cylinder

The fastest and easiest way to check for water leakage in a cylinder is to check the spark plugs. Water will clean a spark plug. If one of the plugs on a multi-cylinder engine is clean and the others are dirty, there is most likely a water leak in the cylinder with the clean plug.

To remove all doubt, install a dirty plug in each cylinder. Run the engine in a test tank or on the boat in water for 5-10 minutes. Shut the engine off and remove the plugs. If one plug is clean and the others are dirty (or if all plugs are clean), a water leak in the cylinder(s) is the problem.

Flat Spots

If the engine seems to die momentarily when the throttle is opened and then recovers, check for a dirty main jet in the

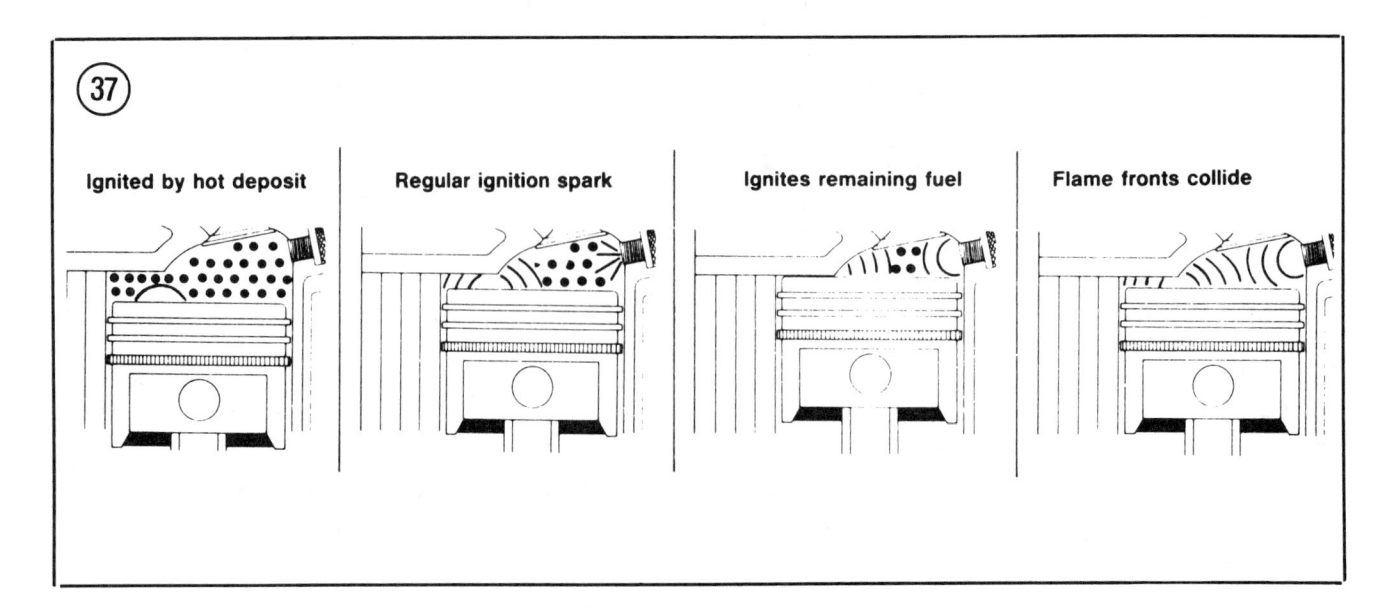

---

(37)

| Ignited by hot deposit | Regular ignition spark | Ignites remaining fuel | Flame fronts collide |

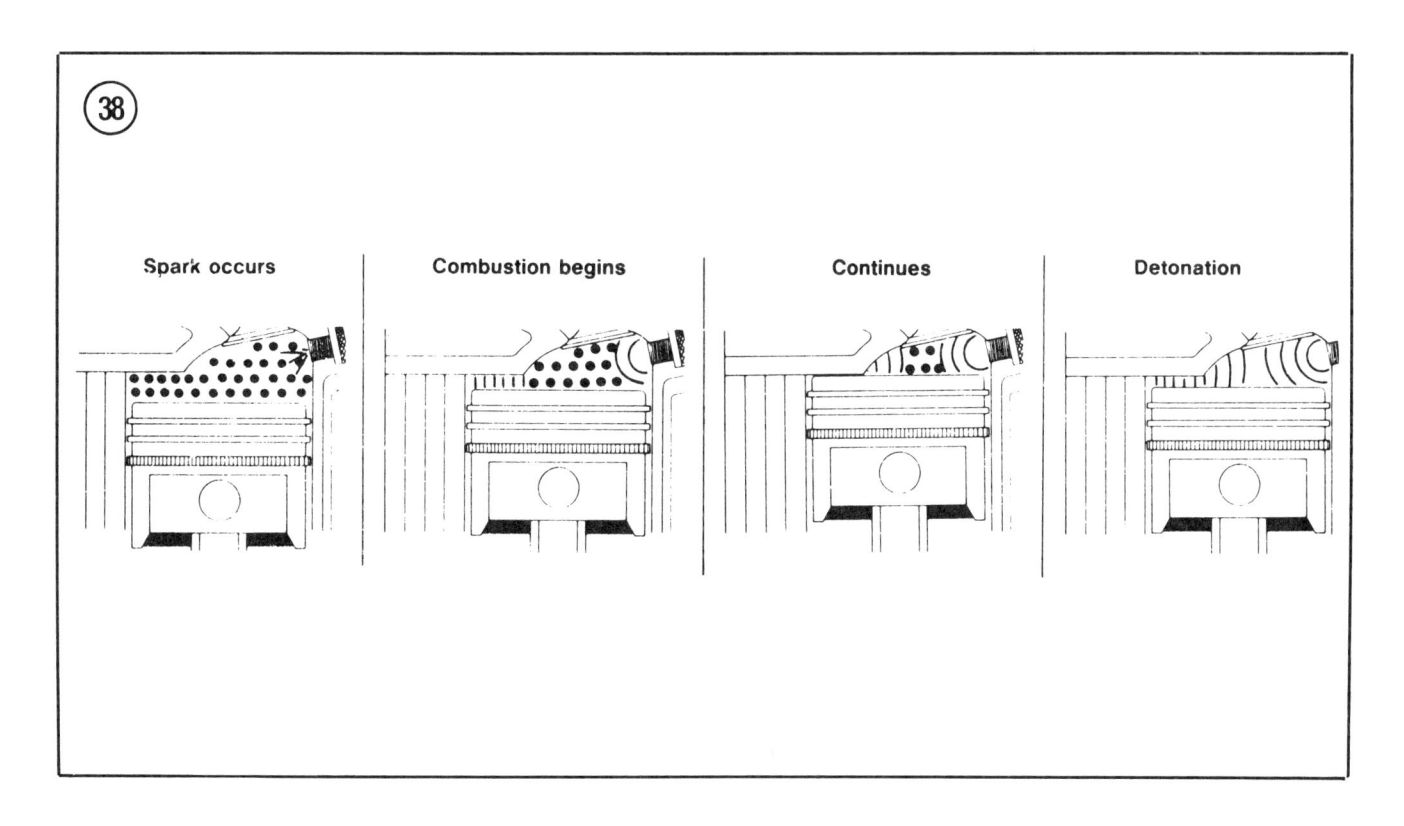

TROUBLESHOOTING

carburetor, water in the fuel or an excessively lean mixture.

Power Loss

Several factors can cause a lack of power and speed. Look for air leaks in the fuel line or fuel pump, a clogged fuel filter or a choke/throttle valve that does not operate properly. Check ignition timing.

A piston or cylinder that is galling, incorrect piston clearance or a worn/sticky piston ring may be responsible. Look for loose bolts, defective gaskets or leaking machined mating surfaces on the cylinder head, cylinder or crankcase. Also check the crankcase oil seal; if worn, it can allow gas to leak between cylinders.

Piston Seizure

This is caused by one or more pistons with incorrect bore clearances, piston rings with an improper end gap, the use of an oil/fuel mixture containing less than 1 part oil to 50 parts of gasoline or an oil of poor quality, a spark plug of the wrong heat range or incorrect ignition timing. Overheating from any cause may result in piston seizure.

Excessive Vibration

Excessive vibration may be caused by loose motor mounts, worn bearings or a generally poor running motor.

Engine Noises

Experience is needed to diagnose accurately in this area. Noises are difficult to differentiate and even harder to describe. Deep knocking noises usually mean main bearing failure. A slapping noise generally comes from a loose piston. A light knocking noise during acceleration may be a bad connecting rod bearing. Pinging should be corrected immediately or damage to the piston will result. A compression leak at the head-to-cylinder joint will sound like a rapid on-off squeal.

(38)

| Spark occurs | Combustion begins | Continues | Detonation |

Table 1 STARTER TROUBLESHOOTING

Trouble	Cause	Remedy
Pinion does not move when starter is turned on	Blown fuse	Replace fuse.
	Pinion rusted to armature shaft	Remove, clean or replace as required.
	Series coil or shunt broken or shorted	Replace coil or shunt.
	Loose switch connections	Tighten connections.
	Rusted or dirty plunger	Clean plunger.
Pinion meshes with ring gear but starter does not run	Worn brushes or brush springs touching armature	Replace brushes or brush springs.
	Dirty or burned commutator	Clean or replace as required.
	Defective armature field coil	Replace armature.
	Worn or rusted armature shaft bearing	Replace bearing.
Starter motor runs at full speed before pinion meshes with ring gear	Worn pinion sleeve	Replace sleeve.
	Pinion does not stop in correct position	Replace pinion.
Pinion meshes with gear and motor starts but engine does not crank	Defective overrunning clutch	Replace overrunning clutch.
Starter motor does not stop when turned off after engine has started	Rusted or dirty plunger	Clean or replace plunger.

(continued)

TROUBLESHOOTING

Table 1 STARTER TROUBLESHOOTING (continued)

Trouble	Cause	Remedy
Starter motor speed low and high-current draw	Armature may be dragging on pole shoes from bent shaft, worn bearings or loose pole shoes	Replace shaft or bearings and/or tighten pole shoes.
	Tight or dirty bearings	Loosen or clean bearings.
High current draw with no armature rotation	A direct ground switch, at terminal or at brushes or field connections	Replace defective parts.
	Frozen shaft bearings which prevent armature from rotating	Loosen, clean or replace bearings.
Starter motor has grounded armature or field winding	Field and/or armature is burned or lead is thrown out of commutator due to excess leakage	Raise grounded brushes from commutator and insulate them with cardboard. Use an ignition analyzer and test points to check between insulated terminal or starter motor and starter motor frame (remove ground connection of shunt coils on motors with this feature). If analyzer shows resistance (meter needle moves to right), there is a ground. Raise other brushes from armature and check armature and fields separately to locate ground.
Starter motor has grounded armature or field winding	Current passes through armature first, then to ground field windings	Disconnect grounded leads, then locate any abnormal grounds in starter motor.
Starter motor fails to operate and draws no current and/or high resistance	Open circuit in fields or armature, at connections or brushes or between brushes and commutator	Repair or adjust broken or weak brush springs, worn brushes, high insulation between commutator bars or a dirty, gummy or oily commutator.

(continued)

Table 1 STARTER TROUBLESHOOTING (continued)

Trouble	Cause	Remedy
High resistance in starter motor	Low no-load speed and a low current draw and low developed torque	Closed "open" field winding on unit which has 2 or 3 circuits in starter motor (unit in which current divides as it enters, taking 2 or 3 parallel paths).
High free speed and high current draw	Shorted fields in starter motor	Install new fields and check for improved performance. (Fields normally have very low resistance, thus it is difficult to detect shorted fields, since difference in current draw between normal starter motor field windings would not be very great.)
Excessive voltage drop	Cables too small	Install larger cables to accomodate high current draw.
High circuit resistance	Dirty connections	Clean connections.
Starter does not operate	Run-down battery	Check battery with hydrometer. If reading is below 1.230, recharge or replace battery.
	Poor contact at terminals	Remove terminal clamps. Scrape terminals and clamps clean and tighten bolts securely.
	Wiring or key switch corroded	Install new switch or wiring. Coat with sealer to protect against further corrosion.
	Starter solenoid	Check for resistance between: (a) positive (+) terminal of battery and large input terminal of starter solenoid, (b) large wire at top of starter motor and negative (−) terminal of battery, and (c) small terminal of starter solenoid and positive battery terminal. Key switch must be in START position. Repair all defective parts.
	Starter motor	With a fully charged battery, connect a negative (−) jumper wire to upper terminal on side of starter motor and a positive jumper to large lower terminal of starter motor. If motor still does not operate, remove for overhaul or replacement.

(continued)

TROUBLESHOOTING

Table 1 STARTER TROUBLESHOOTING (continued)

Trouble	Cause	Remedy
Starter turns over too slowly	Low battery or poor contact at battery terminal	See "Starter does not operate".
	Poor contact at starter solenoid or starter motor	Check all terminals for looseness and tighten all nuts securely.
	Starter mechanism	Disconnect positive (+) battery terminal. Rotate pinion gear in disengaged position. Pinion gear and motor should run freely by hand. If motor does not turn over easily, clean starter and replace all defective parts.
Starter spins freely but does not engage engine	Low battery or poor contact at battery terminal	See "Starter does not operate."
	Poor contact at starter solenoid or starter motor	See "Starter does not operate."
	Dirty or corroded pinion drive	Clean thoroughly and lubricate the spline underneath the pinion with Lubriplate 777
Starter does not engage freely	Pinion or flywheel gear	Inspect mating gears for excessive wear. Replace all defective parts.
	Small anti-drift spring	If drive pinion interferes with flywheel gear after engine has started, inspect anti-drift spring located under pinion gear. Replace all defective parts. NOTE: If drive pinion tends to stay engaged in flywheel gear when starter motor is in idle position, start motor @ 1/4 throttle to allow starter pinion gear to release flywheel ring gear instantly.
Starter keeps on spinning after key is turned ON	Key not fully returned	Check that key has returned to normal ON position from START position. Replace switch if key constantly stays in START position.
	Starter solenoid	Inspect starter solenoid to see if contacts have become stuck in closed position. If starter does not stop running with small yellow lead disconnected from starter solenoid, replace starter solenoid.

(continued)

Table 1 STARTER TROUBLESHOOTING (continued)

Trouble	Cause	Remedy
Wiring or key switch	Inspect all wires for defects	Open remote control box and inspect wiring @ switches. Repair or replace all defective parts.
Wires overheat	Battery terminals improperly connected	Check that negative marking on harness matches that of battery. If battery is connected improperly, red wire to rectifier will overheat.
	Short circuit in system	Inspect all wiring connections and wires for looseness or defects. Open remote control box and inspect wiring @ switches.
	Short circuit in choke solenoid	Repair or replace all defective parts. Check for high resistance. If blue choke wire heats rapidly when choke is used, choke solenoid may have internal short. Replace if defective.
	Short circuit in starter solenoid	If yellow starter solenoid lead overheats, there may be internal short (resistance) in starter solenoid. Replace if defective.
	Low battery voltage	Battery voltage is checked with an ampere-volt tester when battery is under a starting load. Battery must be recharged if it registers under 9.5 volts. If battery is below specified hydrometer reading of 1.230, it will not turn engine fast enough to start it.

Table 2 IGNITION TROUBLESHOOTING

Symptom	Probable cause
Engine won't start, but fuel and spark are good	Defective or dirty spark plugs. Spark plug gap set too wide. Improper spark timing. Shorted stop button. Air leaks into fuel pump. Broken piston ring(s). Cylinder head, crankcase or cylinder sealing faulty. Worn crankcase oil seal.

(continued)

TROUBLESHOOTING

Table 2 IGNITION TROUBLESHOOTING (continued)

Symptom	Probable cause
Engine misfires @ idle	Incorrect spark plug gap. Defective, dirty or loose spark plugs. Spark plugs of incorrect heat range. Leaking or broken high tension wires. Weak armature magnets. Defective coil or condenser. Defective ignition switch. Spark timing out of adjustment.
Engine misfires @ high speed	See "Engine misfires @ idle." Coil breaks down. Coil shorts through insulation. Spark plug gap too wide. Wrong type spark plugs. Too much spark advance.
Engine backfires	Cracked spark plug insulator. Improper timing. Crossed spark plug wires. Improper ignition timing.
Engine preignition	Spark advanced too far. Incorrect type spark plug. Burned spark plug electrodes.
Engine noises (knocking at power head)	Spark advanced too far.
Ignition coil fails	Extremely high voltage. Moisture formation. Excessive heat from engine.
Spark plugs burn and foul	Incorrect type plug. Fuel mixture too rich. Inferior grade of gasoline. Overheated engine. Excessive carbon in combustion chambers.
Ignition causing high fuel consumption	Incorrect spark timing. Leaking high tension wires. Incorrect spark plug gap. Fouled spark plugs. Incorrect spark advance. Weak ignition coil. Preignition.

Table 3 FUEL SYSTEM TROUBLESHOOTING

Symptom	Probable cause
No fuel @ carburetor	No gas in tank. Air vent in gas cap not open. Air vent in gas cap clogged. Fuel tank sitting on fuel line. Fuel line fittings not properly connected to engine or fuel tank.

(continued)

Table 3 FUEL SYSTEM TROUBLESHOOTING (continued)

Symptom	Probable cause
No fuel at carburetor (continued)	Air leak @ fuel connection. Fuel pickup clogged. Defective fuel pump.
Flooding @ carburetor	Choke out of adjustment. High float level. Float stuck. Excessive fuel pump pressure. Float saturated beyond buoyancy.
Rough operation	Dirt or water in fuel. Reed valve open or broken. Incorrect fuel level in carburetor bowl. Carburetor loose @ mounting flange. Throttle shutter not closing completely. Throttle shutter valve installed incorrectly.
Carburetor spit-back at idle	Chipped or broken reed valve(s).
Engine misfires @ high speed	Dirty carburetor. Lean carburetor adjustment. Restriction in fuel system. Low fuel pump pressure.
Engine backfires	Poor quality fuel. Air-fuel mixture too rich or too lean. Improperly adjusted carburetor.
Engine preignition	Excessive oil in fuel. Inferior grade of gasoline. Lean carburetor mixture.
Spark plugs burn and foul	Fuel mixture too rich. Inferior grade of gasoline.
High gas consumption: Flooding or leaking	Cracked carburetor casting. Leaks @ line connections. Defective carburetor bowl gasket. High float level. Plugged vent hole in cover. Loose needle and seat. Defective needle valve seat gasket. Worn needle valve and seat. Foreign matter clogging needle valve. Worn float pin or bracket. Float binding in bowl. High fuel pump pressure.
Overrich mixture	Choke lever stuck. High float level. High fuel pump pressure.
Abnormal speeds	Carburetor out of adjustment. Too much oil in fuel.

Chapter Four

Lubrication, Maintenance and Tune-up

The modern outboard motor delivers more power and performance than ever before, with higher compression ratios, new and improved electrical systems and other design advances. Proper lubrication, maintenance and tune-ups have thus become increasingly important as ways in which you can maintain a high level of performance, extend engine life and extract the maximum economy of operation.

You can do your own lubrication, maintenance and tune-ups if you follow the correct procedures and use common sense. The following information is based on recommendations from Johnson and Evinrude that will help you keep your outboard motor operating at its peak performance level.

Tables 1-3 are at the end of the chapter.

LUBRICATION

Proper Fuel Selection

Two-stroke engines are lubricated by mixing oil with the fuel. The various components of the engine are thus lubricated as the fuel-oil mixture passes through the crankcase and cylinders. Since two-stroke fuel serves the dual function of producing ignition and distributing the lubrication, the use of low octane marine white gasolines should be avoided. Such gasolines also have a tendency to cause ring sticking and port plugging.

All Johnson and Evinrude outboards will use any gasoline with a minimum posted pump octane rating of 86 that works satisfactorily in an automotive engine. However, obtaining regular unleaded gasoline with an octane rating that high is becoming extremely difficult. Premium lead-free gasoline is preferable to leaded gasoline, as it offers longer spark plug life.

Sour Fuel

Fuel should not be stored for more than 60 days (under ideal conditions). Gasoline forms gum and varnish deposits as it ages. Such fuel will cause starting problems. OMC 2+4 Fuel

Conditioner (part No. 173549) may be used to prevent gum and varnish formation during storage or prolonged periods of non-use but it is always better to drain the tank in such cases. Always use fresh gasoline when mixing fuel for your outboard.

Gasohol

Some gasolines sold for marine use now contain alcohol, although this fact may not be advertised. A mixture of 10 percent ethyl alcohol and 90 percent unleaded gasoline is called blended gasoline or gasohol. This is considered suitable for use in Johnson and Evinrude outboards. Some gasolines, however, contain methyl alcohol or methanol. This is *not* recommended for use.

Fuels with an alcohol content tend to slowly absorb moisture from the air. When the moisture content of the fuel reaches approximately one percent, it combines with the alcohol and separates from the fuel. This separation does not normally occur when gasohol is used in an automobile, as the tank is generally emptied within a few days after filling it.

The problem does occur in marine use, however, because boats often remain idle between start-ups for days or even weeks. This length of time permits separation to take place. The alcohol-water mixture settles at the bottom of the fuel tank. Since outboard motors will not run on this mixture, it is necessary to drain the fuel tank, flush out the fuel system with clean gasoline and then remove, clean and reinstall the spark plugs before the engine can be started.

Continued use of fuels containing alcohol can cause deterioration of fuel system components. The major danger of using gasohol in an outboard motor is that a shot of the water-alcohol mix may be picked up and sent to one of the carburetors of a multicylinder engine. Since this mixture contains no oil, it will wash oil off the bore of any cylinder it enters. The other carburetor(s) receiving good fuel-oil mixture will keep the engine running while the cylinder receiving the water-alcohol mixture can suffer internal damage.

The problem of unlabeled and improperly blended gasohol has become so prevalent around the United States that Miller Tools (32615 Park Lane, Garden City, MI 48135) now offers an Alcohol Detection Kit (part No. C-4846) so that owners and mechanics can determine the quality of fuel being used.

The kit cannot differentiate between types of alcohol (ethanol, methanol, etc.) nor is it considered to be absolutely accurate from a scientific standpoint, but it is accurate enough to determine whether or not there is sufficient alcohol in the fuel to cause the user to take precautions.

Recommended Fuel Mixture

Use the gasoline specified for your Johnson or Evinrude outboard and mix wth Johnson or Evinrude 50/1 Lubricant in the following ratios:

CAUTION
Do not, under any circumstances, use multigrade or other high detergent automotive oils, or oils containing metallic additives. Such oils are harmful to 2-stroke engines. Since they do not mix properly with gasoline, do not burn as 2-stroke oils do and leave an ash residue, their use may result in piston scoring, bearing failure or other engine damage.

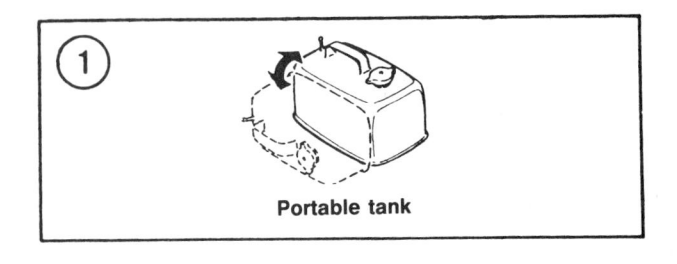

①
Portable tank

LUBRICATION, MAINTENANCE AND TUNE-UP

1956-1963

a. Thoroughly mix one quart of Johnson or Evinrude 50/1 Lubricant with each 6 gallons of gasoline in your fuel tank. This provides the recommended 24:1 mixture.

b. Operation in Canada requires mixing one U.S. quart of Johnson or Evinrude 50/1 Lubricant to each 5 imperial gallons of gasoline in the fuel tank.

CAUTION
Whenever a power head is rebuilt, it should be treated as a new engine. Use a double strength (twice the normal amount of oil) mixture of gasoline and Johnson or Evinrude 50/1 lubricant during the 10 hour break-in period and keep maximum engine speed under 3/4 throttle during this time.

1964-1972

a. Thoroughly mix one pint of Johnson or Evinrude 50/1 Lubricant with each 6 gallons of gasoline in your fuel tank. This provides the recommended 50:1 mixture.

b. Operation in Canada requires mixing one U.S. pint of Johnson or Evinrude 50/1 Lubricant to each 5 imperial gallons of gasoline in the fuel tank.

CAUTION
*There are a number of oil products on the market which specify use at 100:1. They are **not** BIA-TC-W approved and should not be used.*

If Johnson or Evinrude 50/1 Lubricant is not available, any high-quality 2-stroke oil intended for outboard use may be substituted, provided the oil meets BIA rating TC-W and specifies so on the container. Follow the manufacturer's mixing instructions on the container but do not exceed a 24:1 (1956-1963) or 50:1 (1964-1972) ratio.

Correct Fuel Mixing

Mix the fuel and oil outdoors or in a well-ventilated indoor location. Mix the fuel directly in the remote tank.

WARNING
Gasoline is an extreme fire hazard. Never use gasoline near heat, sparks or flame. Do not smoke while mixing fuel.

Using less than the specified amount of oil can result in insufficient lubrication and serious engine damage. Using more oil than specified causes spark plug fouling, erratic carburetion, excessive smoking and rapid carbon accumulation which can cause preignition.

Cleanliness is of prime importance. Even a very small particle of dirt can cause carburetion problems. Always use fresh gasoline. Gum and varnish deposits tend to form in gasoline stored in a tank for any length of time. Use of sour fuel can result in carburetor problems and spark plug fouling.

Above 32° F (10° C)

Measure the required amounts of gasoline and 50/1 Lubricant accurately. Pour the specified amount of oil into the portable tank and add one-half of the gasoline to be mixed. Replace the tank filler cap and mix the fuel by tipping the tank on its side and back to an upright position several times. See **Figure 1**. Remove the tank cap and add the balance of the gasoline, then mix again.

If a built-in tank is used, insert a large metal filter funnel in the tank filler neck. Slowly pour the 50/1 Lubricant into the funnel at the same time the tank is being filled with gasoline. See **Figure 2**.

Below 32° F (0° C)

Measure the required amounts of gasoline and 50/1 Lubricant accurately. Pour about one gallon of gasoline in the tank and then add the required amount of oil. Replace the tank filler cap and shake the tank to thoroughly mix the fuel and oil. Remove the cap and add the balance of the gasoline.

If a built-in tank is used, insert a large metal filter funnel in the tank filler neck. Mix the required amount of 50/1 Lubricant with one gallon of gasoline in a separate container. Slowly pour the mixture into the funnel at the same time the tank is being filled with gasoline.

Consistent Fuel Mixtures

The carburetor idle adjustment is sensitive to fuel mixture variations which result from the use of different oils and gasolines or from inaccurate measuring and mixing. This may require readjustment of the idle needle. To prevent the necessity for constant readjustment of the carburetor from one batch of fuel to the next, always be consistent. Prepare each batch of fuel exactly the same as previous ones.

Pre-mixed fuels sold at some marinas are not recommended for use in Johnson or Evinrude outboards, since the quality and consistency of pre-mixed fuels can vary greatly. The possibility of engine damage resulting from use of an incorrect fuel mixture outweighs the convenience offered by pre-mixed fuel.

Lower Drive Unit Lubrication

Change the lower drive lubricant after the first 10 hours of operation. Check the lubricant level every 30 days. Replace lubricant at 50 hour intervals or at least once per season. Use OMC Premium Blend Gearcase Lubricant (part No. 172820).

CAUTION
Do not use regular automotive grease in the lower drive. Its expansion and foam characteristics are not suitable for marine use.

1.5 and 3 hp models

1. Place a suitable container under the gearcase.
2. Remove the drain/fill plug from the starboard side of the gearcase.
3. Position the gearcase with the starboard side facing down and let the lubricant drain completely. If necessary, use a small suction pump to remove the lubricant.
4. Reposition gearcase with drain/fill hole facing up. Slowly fill with OMC Premium Blend Gearcase Lubricant until it appears at the hole.

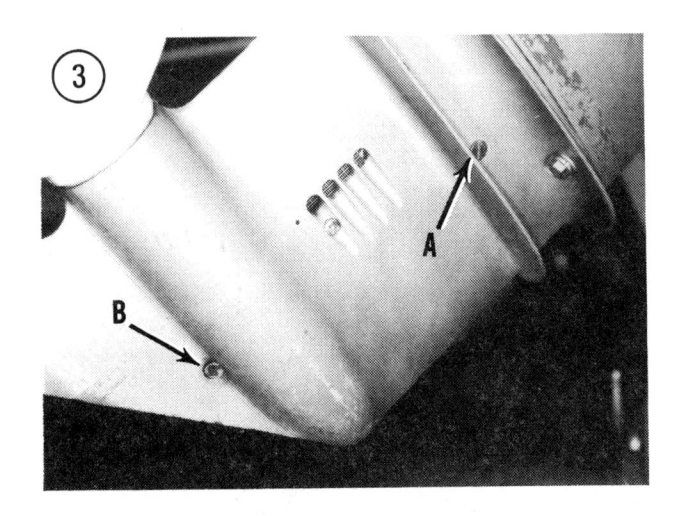

LUBRICATION, MAINTENANCE AND TUNE-UP

5. Install the drain/fill plug and tighten to 60-80 in.-lb. (7-9 N•m).

4-125 hp models

1. Place a suitable container under the gearcase.

NOTE
If the lubricant is white or creamy in color or metallic particles are found in Step 5, remove and disassemble the gearcase to determine and correct the cause of the problem.

2. Locate and remove the oil level plug and washer. See A, **Figure 3** (typical).

CAUTION
*The gearcase on models with a shift capability will have a Phillips head screw located beside the slotted drain/fill plug (**Figure 4**). The Phillips head screw secures the shift rod in place—do not remove it by mistake or it will be necessary to disassemble the gearcase to properly realign the components and reinstall the screw.*

3. Locate and remove the drain/fill plug and washer. See B, **Figure 3** (typical).
4. Allow the lubricant to completely drain. If necessary, use a small suction pump to remove the lubricant.

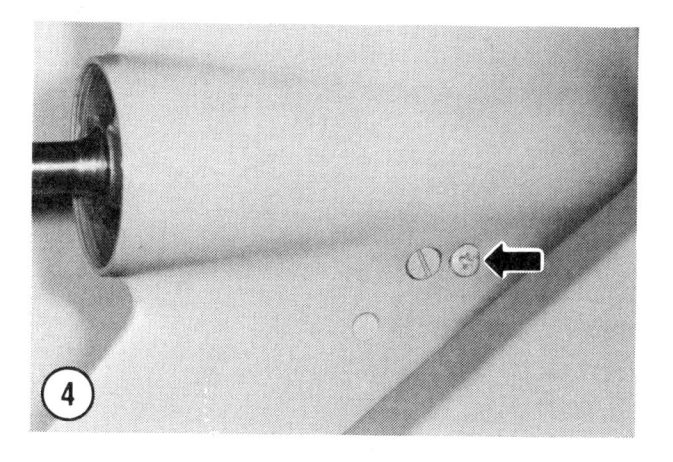

NOTE
If the lubricant is creamy in color or metallic particles are found in Step 5, remove and disassemble the gearcase to determine and correct the cause of the problem.

5. Wipe a small amount of lubricant on a finger and rub the finger and thumb together. Check for the presence of metallic particles in the lubricant. Note the color of the lubricant. A white or creamy color indicates water in the lubricant. Check the drain container for signs of water separation from the lubricant.
6. Inject OMC Premium Blend Gearcase Lubricant into the drain/fill plug hole until excess fluid flows out the oil level plug hole.
7. Drain about one fluid ounce of fluid to allow for lubricant expansion.
8. Install the oil level plug. Remove the lubricant tube or nozzle from the drain/fill hole and install the drain/fill plug. Be sure the washers are in good condition and properly positioned under the head of each plug so water will not leak past the threads into the housing. Tighten both plugs to 60-80 in.-lb. (7-9 N•m).
9. Wipe any excess lubricant off the lower drive exterior.

Other Lubrication Points

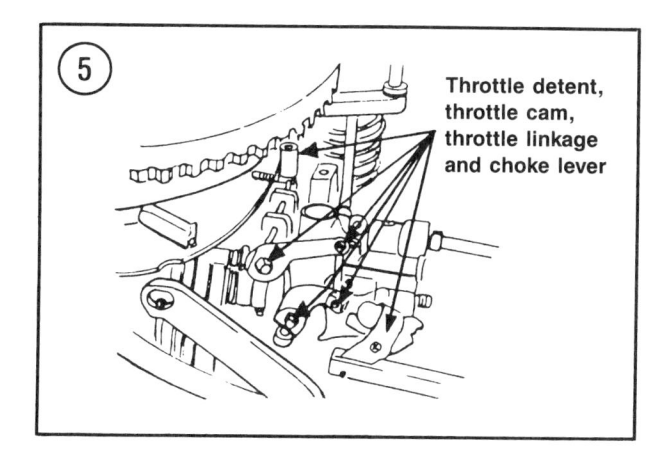

Refer to **Figures 5-12** (inline) or **Figures 13-24** (V4) and **Table 1** for other lubricant points, frequency of lubrication and lubricant to be used.

In addition to these lubrication points, some motors may also have grease fittings provided at critical points where bearing surfaces are not externally exposed. These fittings should be lubricated at least each once season with an automotive type grease gun and OMC Triple-Guard Grease (part No. 173655).

CAUTION
When lubricating the steering cable on models so equipped, make sure its core is fully retracted into the cable housing. Lubricating the cable while extended can cause a hydraulic lock to occur.

Salt Water Corrosion of Gearcase Bearing Carrier/Nut

Salt water corrosion that is allowed to build up unchecked can eventually split the gearcase and destroy the lower unit. If the motor is used in salt water, remove the propeller assembly and bearing housing at least once a year after the initial 20-hour inspection. Clean all corrosive deposits and dried-up lubricant from each end of the housing. See **Figure 25** (typical). Clean the gearcase internal threads and cover nut external threads. Install new O-rings on housing (if so equipped). Apply a liberal amount of OMC Gasket Sealing Compound to each end of the housing and to the gearcase and cover nut threads. Make sure the Gasket Sealing Compound does not get into the bearings. Install the bearing housing and tighten screws to specifications (Chapter Nine). Lubricate the propeller shaft splines with OMC Triple-Guard Grease and reinstall the propeller (Chapter Nine).

STORAGE

The major consideration in preparing an outboard motor for storage is to protect it

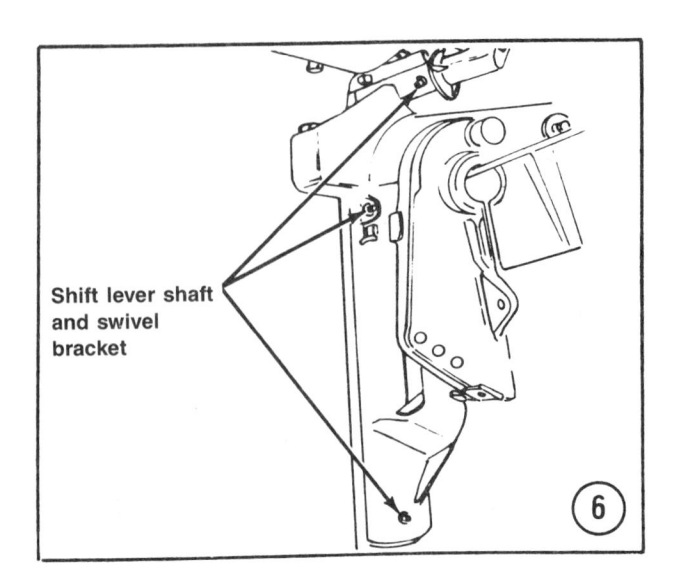

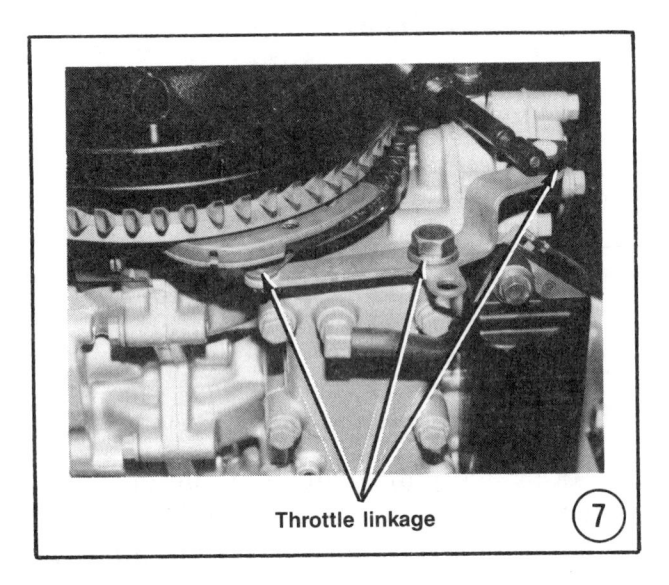

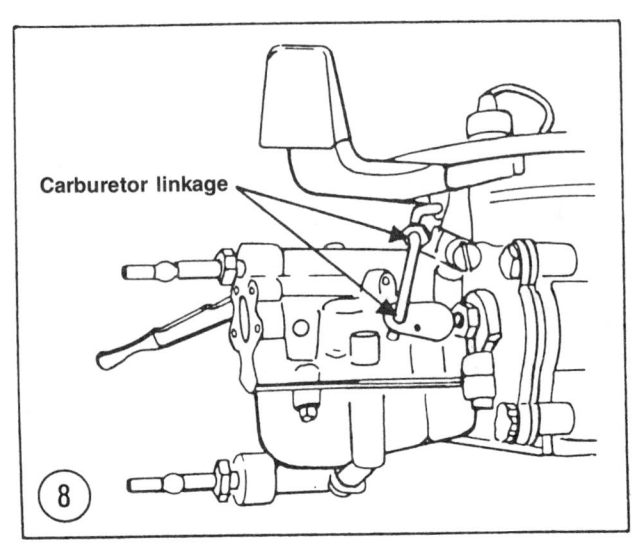

LUBRICATION, MAINTENANCE AND TUNE-UP

Magneto and throttle linkage

Swivel bracket, shift lever shaft and clamp screws

Starter motor pinion shaft

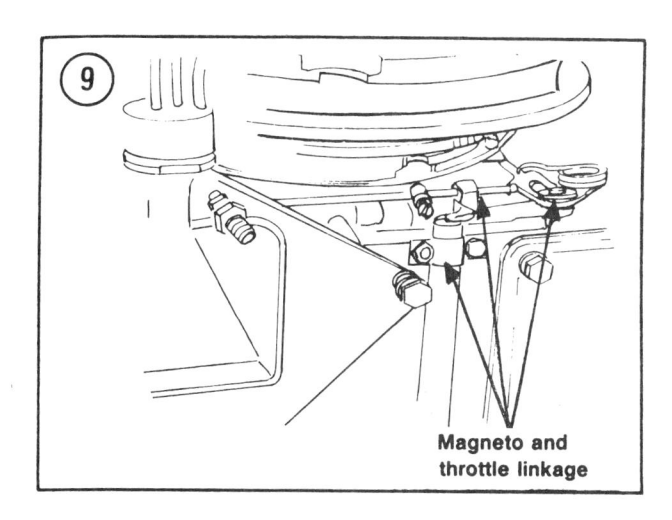

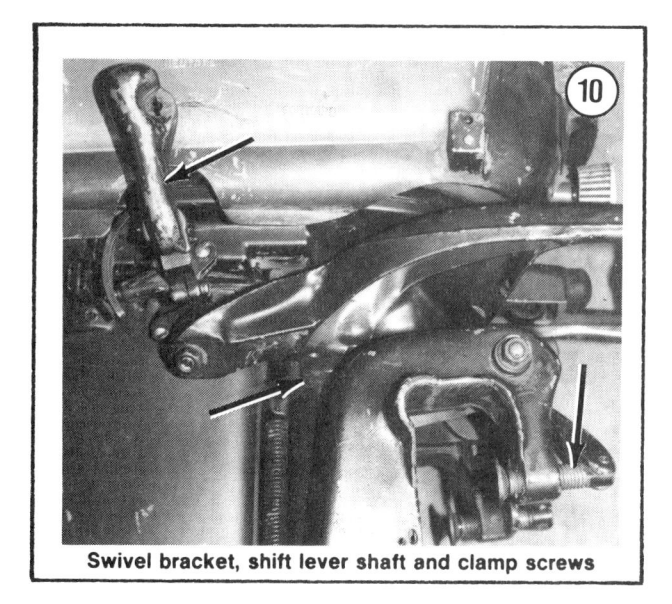

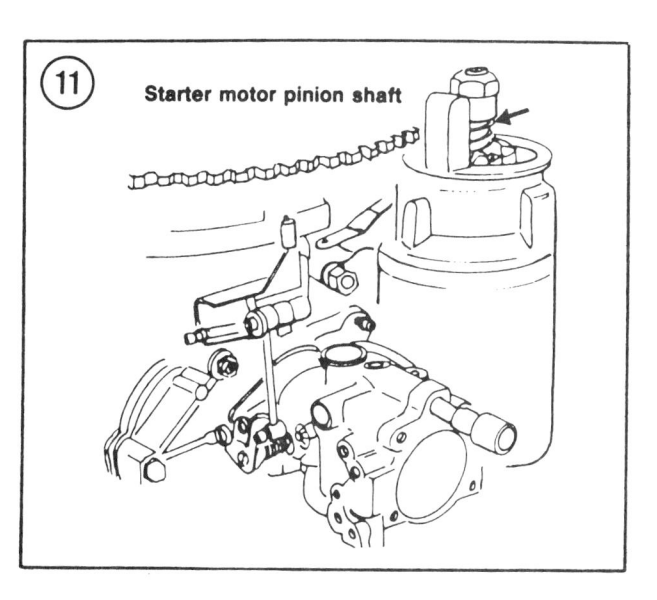

Vertical throttle shaft and gears

from rust, corrosion and dirt. Johnson and Evinrude recommend the following procedure.

1. Remove the engine cover or cowling. Remove the air silencer front cover, if so equipped.
2. Operate the motor in a test tank with the proper test wheel (**Table 2**) or on the boat in the water. Start the engine and let it warm up.
3. Disconnect the fuel line and let engine run at low rpm while pouring OMC Rust Preventive Oil or OMC Storage Fogging Oil into each carburetor throat until the engine smokes excessively.
4. Shut the engine off. Reinstall air silencer front cover, if so equipped.
5. Remove the spark plug(s) as described in this chapter. Clean and regap or replace plugs. Leave spark plug leads disconnected.
6. Retard throttle and rotate flywheel several times to drain any water from the water pump.
7. Clean and lubricate starter motor drive mechanism, if so equipped.
8. Drain carburetor float chamber. Remove and replace the fuel filter.
9. Service the portable fuel tank as follows:
   a. Disconnect the fuel line from the tank and remove the screws holding the

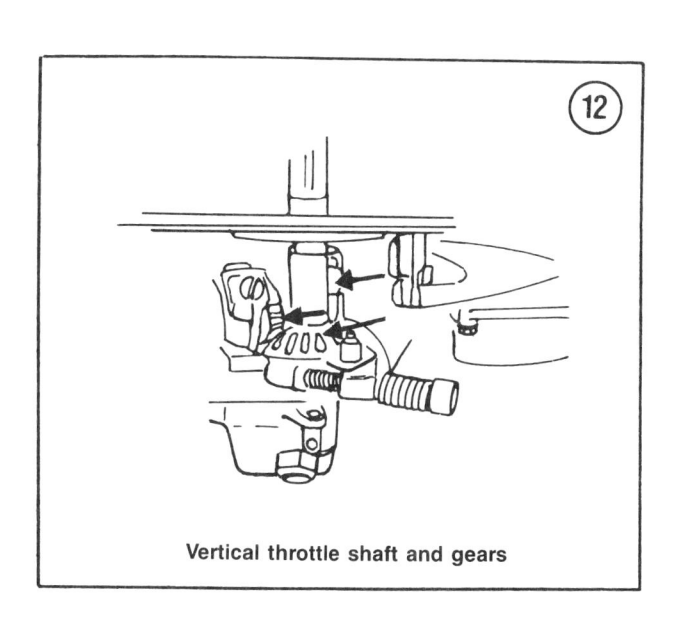

cover in the tank. Remove the cover with fuel outlet tube and filter assembly.

b. Clean the fine wire mesh filter at the bottom of the outlet tube by rinsing it in clean benzine.

c. Reinstall filter assembly, outlet tube and cover in fuel tank.

d. Store tank in a well-ventilated area away from heat or open flame.

10. Drain and refill the gearcase as described in this chapter. Check condition of level and drain/fill plug gaskets. Replace as required.

11. Refer to **Figures 5-12** (inline) or **Figures 13-24** (V4) and **Table 1** as appropriate. Lubricate motor at all specified points.

12. Remove and check propeller condition. Remove any burring from drive pin hole and

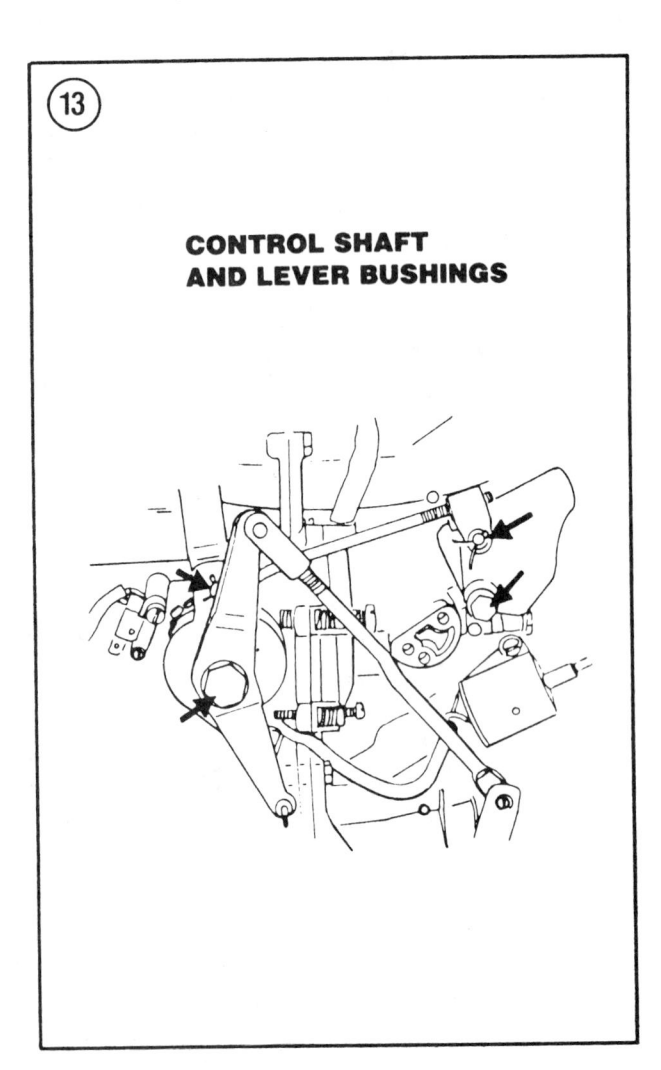

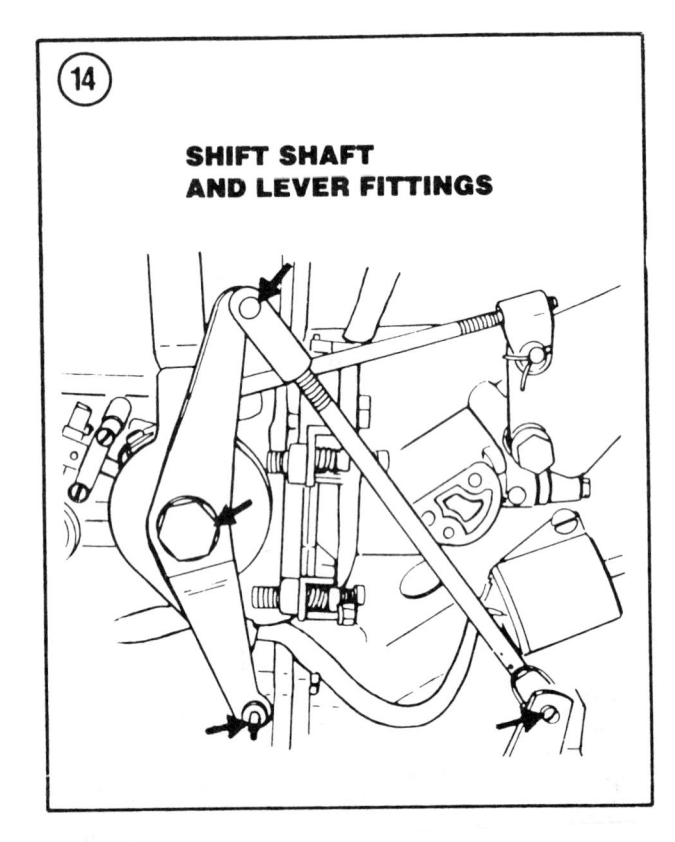

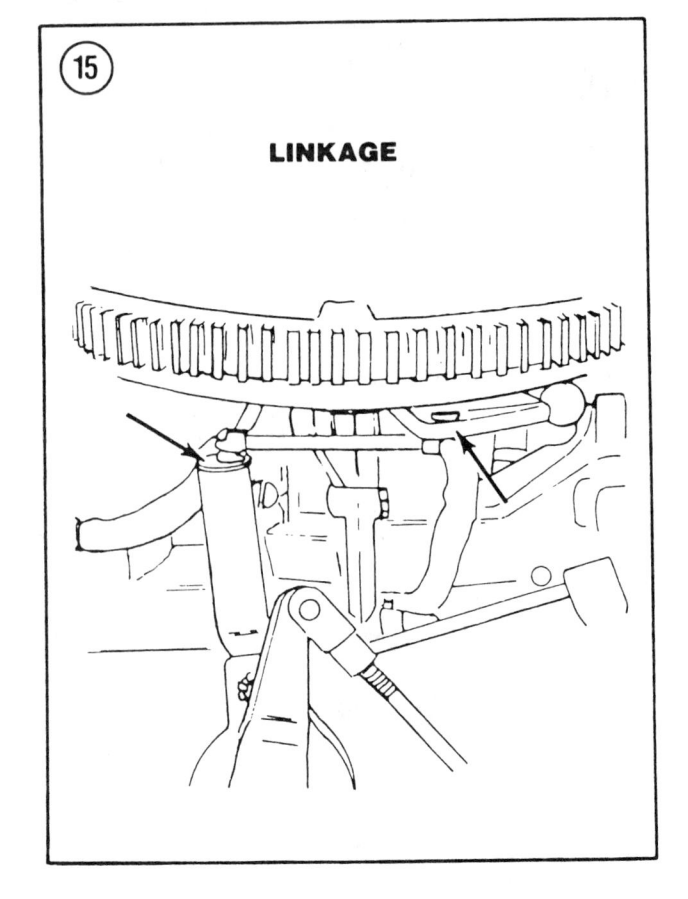

⑭ SHIFT SHAFT AND LEVER FITTINGS

⑬ CONTROL SHAFT AND LEVER BUSHINGS

⑮ LINKAGE

LUBRICATION, MAINTENANCE AND TUNE-UP

93

⑰

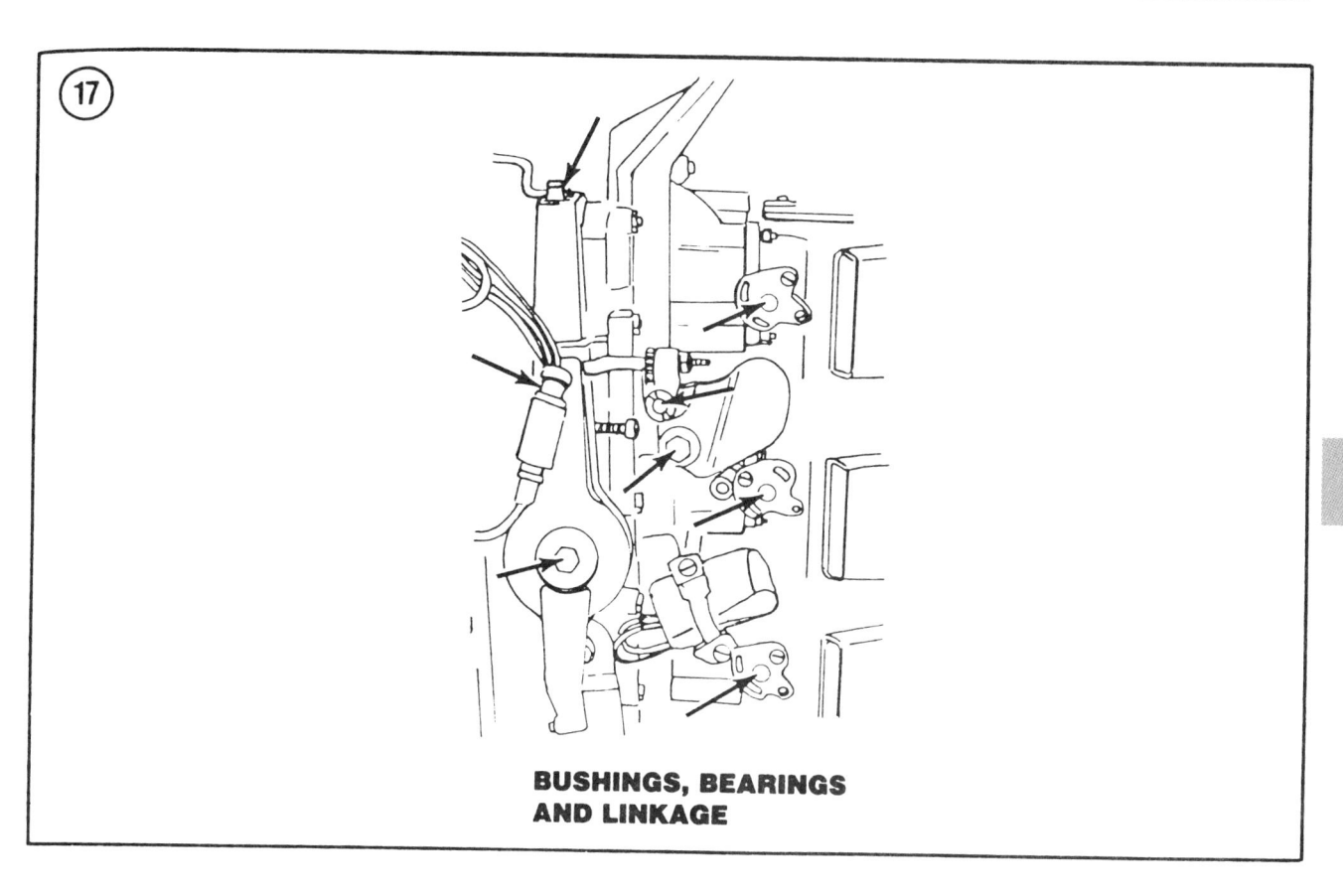

BUSHINGS, BEARINGS AND LINKAGE

⑯

CARBURETOR, CAM AND THROTTLE LINKAGE

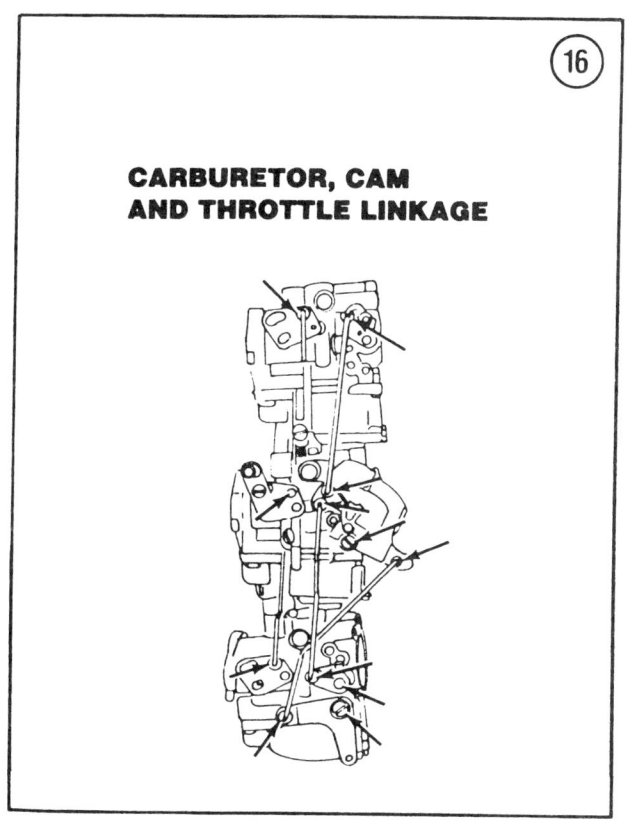

⑱

SHIFT SHAFT AND LEVER FITTING

CHAPTER FOUR

19 TILT TUBE SHAFT

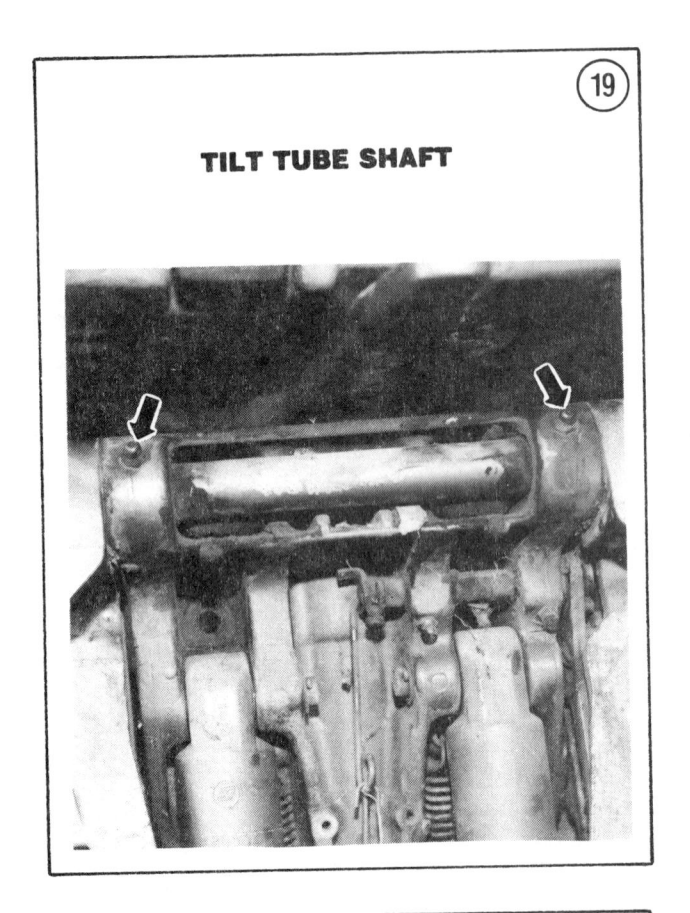

20 SWIVEL BRACKET, TILT LEVER AND SHAFT

21 MOTOR COVER LEVER SHAFTS

22 POWER TRIM/TILT RESERVOIR

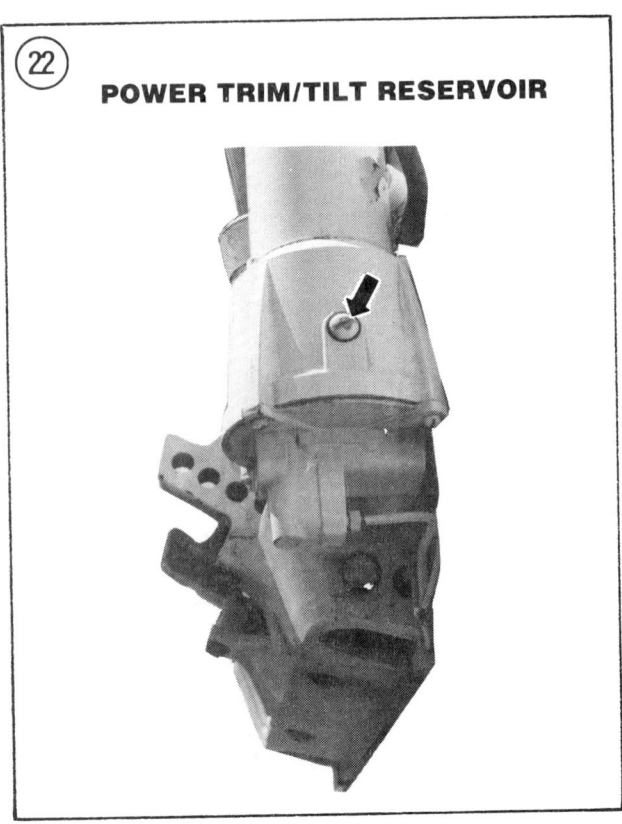

LUBRICATION, MAINTENANCE AND TUNE-UP

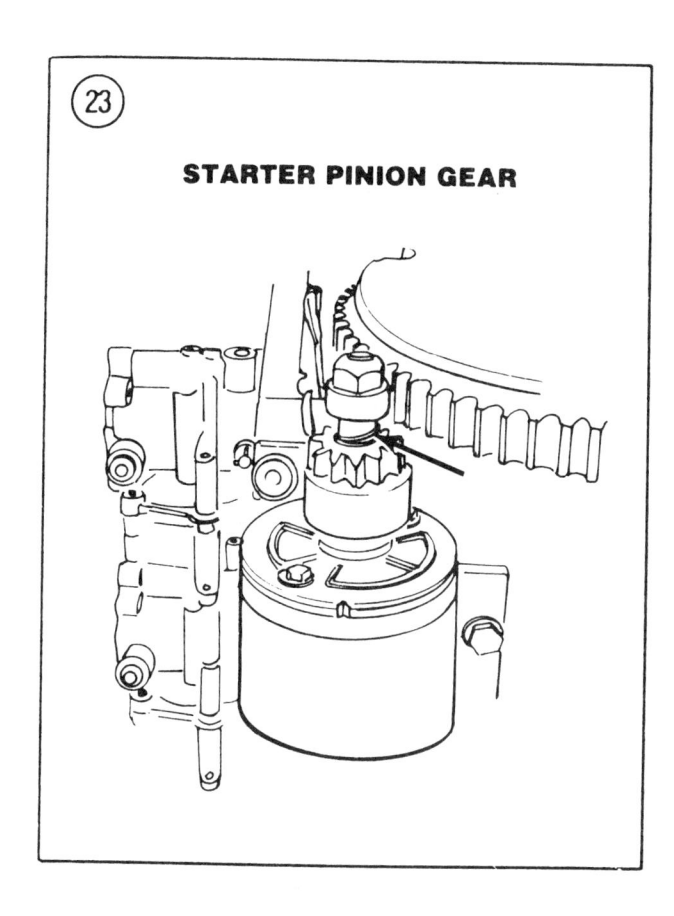

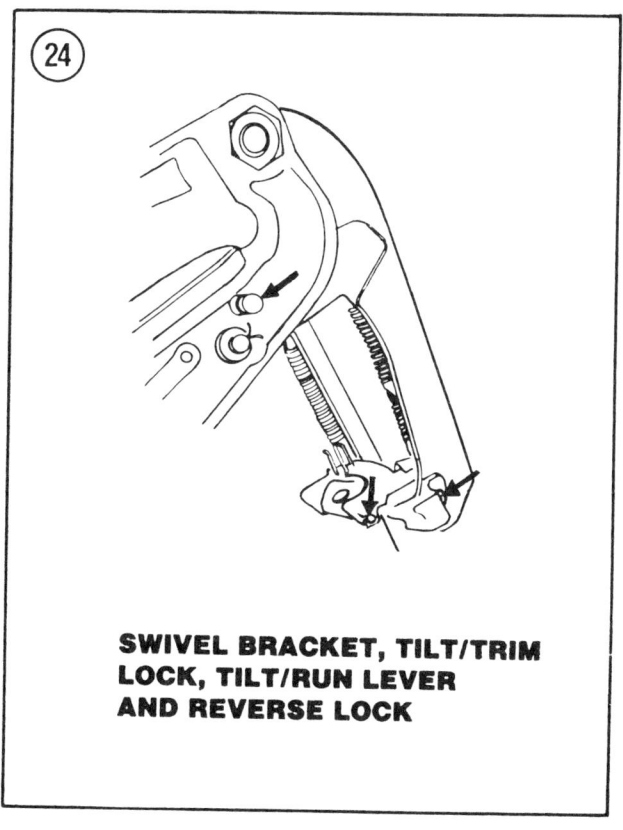

Figure 23 — STARTER PINION GEAR

Figure 24 — SWIVEL BRACKET, TILT/TRIM LOCK, TILT/RUN LEVER AND REVERSE LOCK

13. Clean the motor, including all accessible power head parts. Remove all dirt, grease and scum with OMC All-Purpose Marine Cleaner and apply OMC Boat Polish. Install the cowling or engine cover.

CAUTION
Make certain that all water drain holes in the lower drive are free and open to allow water to drain out. Water expands as it freezes and can crack the gearcase or water pump.

14. Store the motor upright in a dry and well-ventilated area.
15. Service the battery (if so equipped) as follows:
    a. Disconnect the negative battery cable, then the positive battery cable.
    b. Remove all grease, corrosion and dirt from the battery surface.
    c. Check the electrolyte level in each battery cell and top up with distilled water, if necessary. Fluid level in each cell should not be higher than 3/16 in. above the perforated baffles.
    d. Lubricate the terminal bolts with petroleum jelly.

CAUTION
A discharged battery can be damaged by freezing.

   e. With the battery in a fully-charged condition (specific gravity 1.260-1.275), store in a dry place where the temperature will not drop below freezing. Do not store on a concrete surface.
   f. Recharge the battery every 45 days or whenever the specific gravity drops below 1.230. Before charging, cover the plates with distilled water, but not more than 3/16 in. above the perforated baffles. The charge rate should not exceed 6 amps. Discontinue charging

when the specific gravity reaches 1.260 at 80° F (27° C).

g. Before placing the battery back into service after storage, remove the excess petroleum jelly from the terminals, leaving a small amount on. Install battery in a fully-charged state.

COMPLETE SUBMERSION

An outboard motor which has been lost overboard should be recovered as quickly as possible. If the motor was running when submerged, disassemble and clean it immediately—any delay will result in rust and corrosion of internal components once it has been removed from the water. If the motor was not running and appears to be undamaged mechanically with no abrasive dirt or silt inside, take the following emergency steps immediately.

1. Wash the outside of the motor with clean water to remove weeds, mud and other debris.
2. Remove the engine cover or cowling.
3. If recovered from salt water, flush motor completely with fresh water.
4. Remove the spark plug(s) as described in this chapter.
5. Remove the carburetor float bowl cover(s). See Chapter Six.
6. Disconnect the charge coil connectors.

CAUTION
Do not force the motor if it does not turn over freely by hand in Step 7. This may be an indication of internal damage such as a bent connecting rod or broken piston.

7. Drain as much water as possible from the power head by placing the motor in a horizontal position. Manually rotate the flywheel with the spark plug hole(s) facing downward.
8. Pour alcohol into the carburetor throat(s) to displace water. Manually rotate the flywheel at least a full turn, then position the motor so you can pour alcohol into the spark plug hole(s). Manually rotate the flywheel another full turn.
9. Repeat Step 8 using OMC Engine Tuner (part No. 172650).
10. Reinstall spark plug(s) and carburetor float bowl cover(s).

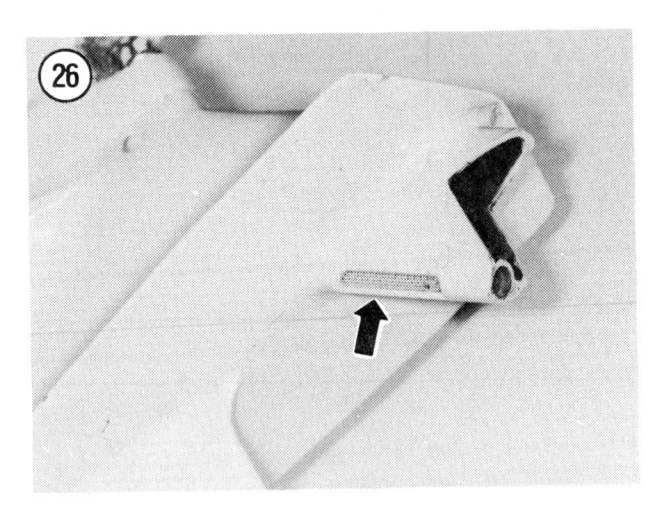

CAUTION
If there is a possibility that sand may have entered the power head, do not try to start the motor or severe internal damage may occur.

11. Try starting the motor with a fresh fuel source. If motor will start, let it run at least

LUBRICATION, MAINTENANCE AND TUNE-UP

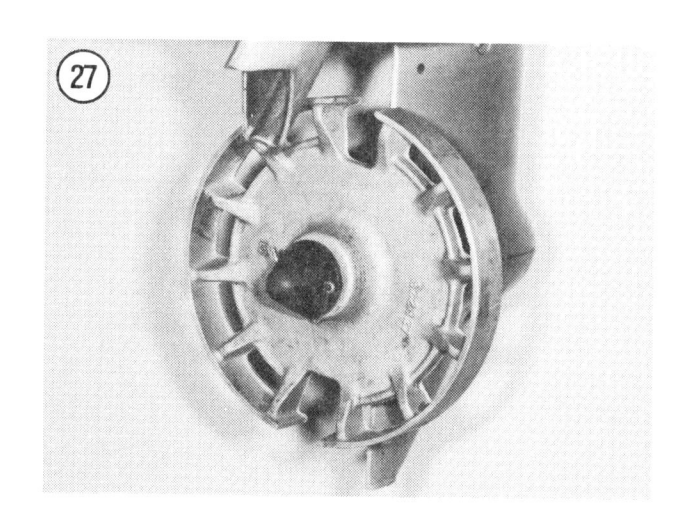

one hour to eliminate any water remaining inside.

CAUTION
If it is not possible to disassemble and clean the motor immediately in Step 12, resubmerge the power head in water to prevent rust and corrosion formation until such time as it can be properly serviced.

12. If the motor will not start in Step 11, try to diagnose the cause as fuel, electrical or mechanical and correct. If the engine cannot be started within 2 hours, disassemble, clean and oil all parts thoroughly as soon as possible.

ANTI-CORROSION MAINTENANCE

1. Flush the cooling system with fresh water as described in this chapter after each time the motor is used in salt water. Wash exterior with fresh water.
2. Dry exterior of motor and apply a good primer coat over any paint nicks and scratches. Let primer flash off, then apply the appropriate color of OMC Spray Paint Engine Finish. If OMC paints are not available, use a suitable tin anti-fouling paint; do not use paints containing mercury or copper. Do not paint sacrificial anodes or trim tab.
3. Lubricate power head with OMC Triple-Guard Grease. Apply OMC Black Neoprene Dip to all electrical connections as required.
4. Check condition of sacrificial anodes and trim tab. Replace any that are less than half their original size.
5. Lubricate more frequently than specified in **Table 1**. If used consistently in salt water, lubricate twice as often as specified.

ENGINE FLUSHING

Periodic engine flushing will prevent salt or silt deposits from accumulating in the water passageways. This procedure should also be performed whenever an outboard motor is operated in salt water or polluted water.

Keep the engine in an upright position during and after flushing. This prevents water from passing into the power head through the drive shaft housing and exhaust ports during the flushing procedure. It also eliminates the possibility of residual water being trapped in the drive shaft housing or other passageways.

Some Johnson and Evinrude outboards have the water intake located on the exhaust port (**Figure 26**). These models require the use of flushing devices other than a flush-test unit. See your Johnson or Evinrude dealer for the proper flushing device. Johnson and Evinrude recommend the outboard be run with a test wheel instead of the propeller when operated in a test tank or with a flush-test device. See **Figure 27** (typical). Test wheel recommendations provided by Johnson and Evinrude are given in **Table 2**.

1. Remove the propeller and install the correct test wheel.
2. Attach a flushing device from the front of the lower drive according to manufacturer's instructions. See **Figure 28** (typical).
3. Connect a garden hose between a water tap and the flushing device.

4. Open the water tap partially—do not use full pressure.

5. Shift into NEUTRAL, then start motor. Keep engine speed at idle speed (below 1,000 rpm).

6. Adjust water flow so that there is a slight loss of water around the rubber cups of the flushing device.

7. Check the motor to make sure that water is being discharged from the "tell-tale" nozzle. If it is not, stop the engine immediately and determine the cause of the problem.

NOTE
Flush the motor for at least 5 minutes if used in salt water.

8. Flush motor until discharged water is clear. Stop the motor.

9. Close water tap and remove flushing device from lower drive.

10. Remove test wheel and reinstall propeller.

TUNE-UP

A tune-up consists of a series of inspections, adjustments and parts replacements to compensate for normal wear and deterioration of outboard engine components. Regular tune-ups are important for power, performance and economy. Johnson and Evinrude recommend that their outboards be serviced every 6 months or 50 hours of operation, whichever comes first. If subjected to limited use, the engine should be tuned at least once a year.

Since proper outboard motor operation depends upon a number of interrelated system functions, a tune-up consisting of only one or two corrections will seldom give lasting results. For best results, a thorough and systematic procedure of analysis and correction is necessary.

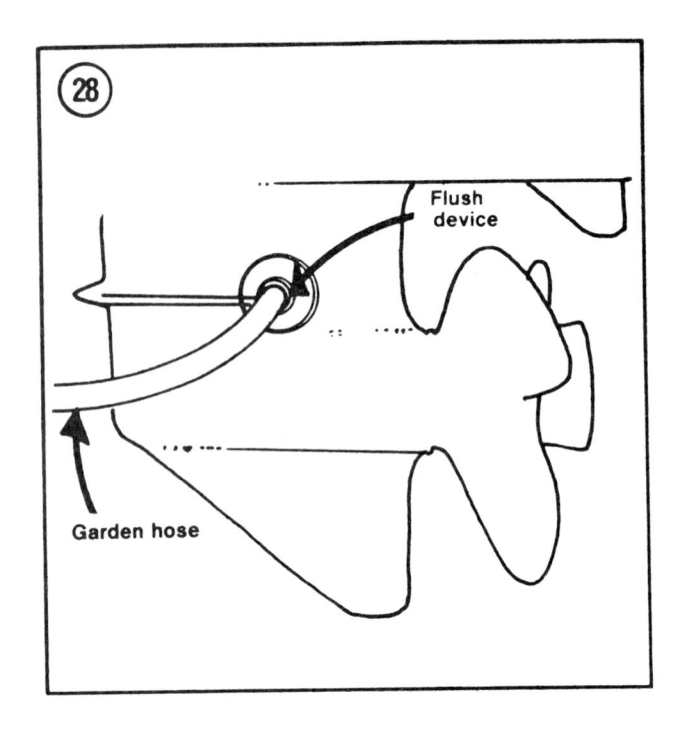

Prior to performing a tune-up, it is a good idea to flush the engine as described in this chapter and check for satisfactory water pump operation.

The tune-up sequence recommended by Johnson and Evinrude includes the following:
   a. Compression check.
   b. Spark plug service.
   c. Gearcase and water pump check.
   d. Fuel system service.
   e. Ignition system service.
   f. Battery, starter motor and solenoid check (if so equipped).
   g. Wiring harness check.
   h. Engine synchronization and adjustment (Chapter Five).
   i. Performance test (on boat).

Anytime the fuel or ignition systems are adjusted or defective parts replaced, the engine timing, synchronization and adjustment *must* be checked. These procedures have been separated from the tune-up sequence and are found in Chapter Five. Perform the timing, synchronization and adjustment procedure for your engine *before* running the performance test.

LUBRICATION, MAINTENANCE AND TUNE-UP

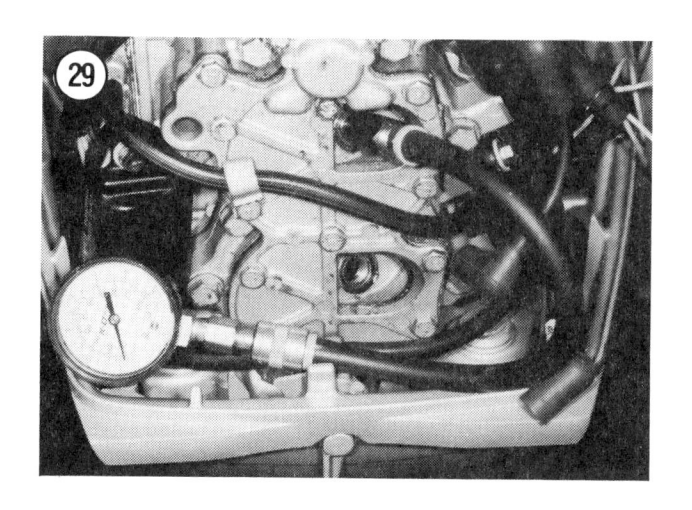

Compression Check

An accurate cylinder compression check gives a good idea of the condition of the basic working parts of the engine. It is also an important first step in any tune-up, as an engine with low or unequal compression between cylinders *cannot* be satisfactorily tuned. Any compression problem discovered during this check must be corrected before continuing with the tune-up procedure.

1. With the engine warm, disconnect the spark plug wire(s) and remove the plug(s) as described in this chapter.
2. Ground the spark plug wire(s) to the engine to disable the ignition system.

NOTE
The No. 1 cylinder is the top (inline) or starboard top (V4) cylinder.

3. Connect the compression tester to the No. 1 spark plug hole according to manufacturer's instructions. See **Figure 29** (typical).
4. Make sure the throttle is set to the wide open position, then crank the engine through at least 4 compression strokes. Record the gauge reading.
5. Repeat Step 3 and Step 4 on each cylinder of multicylinder engines.

While the minimum cylinder compression should not be less than 100 psi, the actual readings are not as important as the differences in readings when interpreting the results. A variation of more than 15 psi between 2 cylinders indicates a problem with the lower reading cylinder, such as worn or sticking piston rings and/or scored pistons or cylinders. In such cases, pour a tablespoon of engine oil into the suspect cylinder and repeat Step 3 and Step 4. If the compression is raised significantly (by 10 psi in an older engine) the rings are worn and should be replaced.

Many outboard owners are plagued by hard starting and generally poor running for which there seems to be no good cause. Carburetion and ignition check out satisfactorily and a compression test may show that everything is well in the engine's upper end. With everything apparently pointing to a sound engine, they focus on the propeller as the cause of the problem and start swapping props, often with disastrous results.

What a compression test does *not* show is lack of primary compression. In a 2-stroke engine, the crankcase must be alternately under high pressure and low pressure. After the piston closes the intake port, further downward movement of the piston causes the entrapped mixture to be pressurized so that it can rush quickly into the cylinder when the scavenging ports are opened. Upward piston movement creates a lower pressure in the crankcase, enabling fuel/air mixture to pass in from the carburetor.

When the crankshaft seals or case gaskets leak, the crankcase cannot hold pressure and proper engine operation becomes impossible. Any other source of leakage, such as defective cylinder base gaskets or a porous or cracked crankcase casting will result in the same conditions.

If the power head shows signs of overheating (discolored or scorched paint) but the compression test turns up nothing abnormal, check the cylinder(s) visually through the transfer ports for possible scoring. A cylinder can be slightly scored and still deliver a relatively good compression reading. In such a case, it is also a good idea to double-check the water pump operation as a possible cause for overheating.

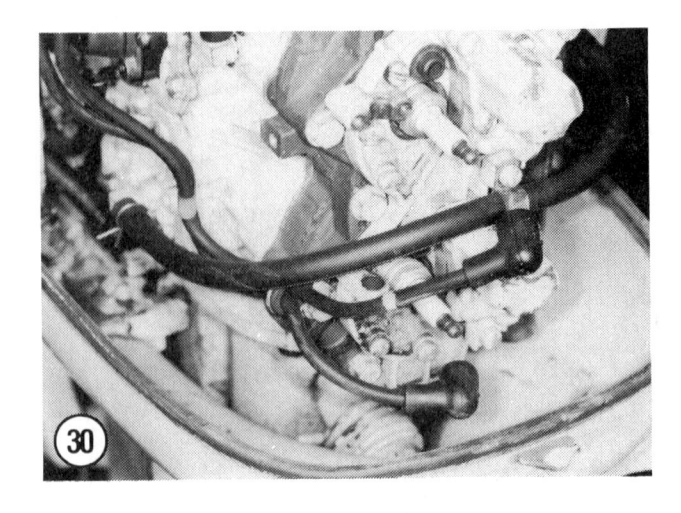

Spark Plugs

Johnson and Evinrude outboards are equipped with spark plugs selected for average use conditions. Under adverse use conditions, the recommended spark plug may foul or overheat. In such cases, check the ignition and carburetion systems to make sure they are operating correctly. If no defect is found, replace the spark plug with one of a hotter or colder heat range as required. **Table 3** contains the recommended spark plugs for all models covered in this book.

Spark Plug Removal

CAUTION
Whenever the spark plugs are removed, dirt around them can fall into the plug holes. This can cause engine damage that is expensive to repair.

1. Blow out any foreign matter from around the spark plugs with compressed air. Use a compressor if you have one. If you do not, use a can of compressed inert gas, available from photo stores.
2. Disconnect the spark plug wires (**Figure 30**, typical) by twisting the wire boot back and forth on the plug insulator while pulling outward. Pulling on the wire instead of the boot may cause internal damage to the wire.
3. Remove the plugs with an appropriate size spark plug socket or box end wrench. Keep the plugs in order so you know which cylinder they came from.
4. Examine each spark plug. See **Figure 31** for conventional gap plugs and **Figure 32** for surface gap plugs. Compare plug condition with **Figure 33** (conventional gap) or **Figure 34** (surface gap). Spark plug condition indicates engine condition and can warn of developing trouble.
5. Check each plug for make and heat range. All should be of the same make and number or heat range.
6. Discard the plugs. Although they could be cleaned and reused if in good condition, they seldom last very long. New plugs are inexpensive and far more reliable.

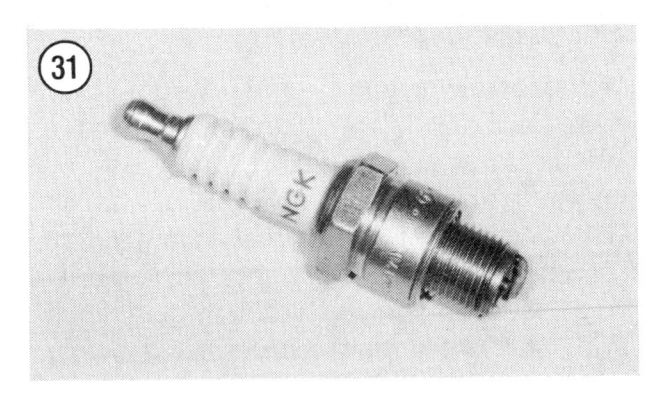

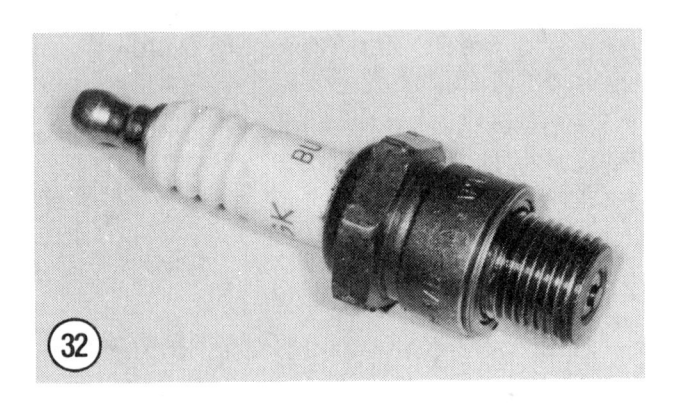

LUBRICATION, MAINTENANCE AND TUNE-UP

**SPARK PLUG ANALYSIS
(CONVENTIONAL GAP SPARK PLUGS)**

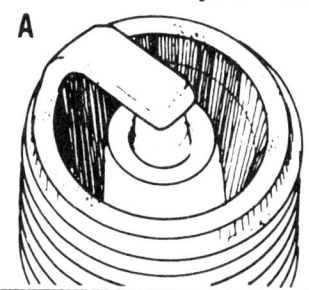

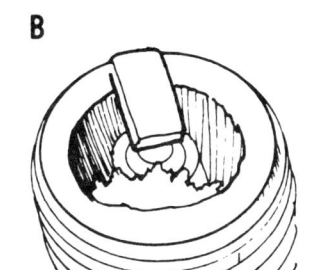

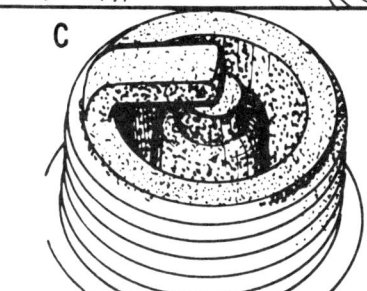

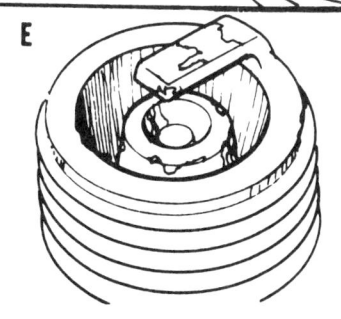

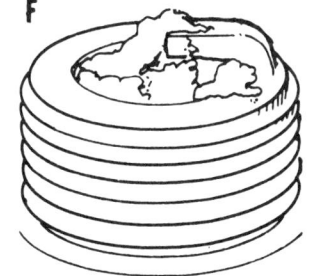

A.

B.

C.

D.

E.

F.

A. Normal—Light tan to gray color of insulator indicates correct heat range. Few deposits are present and the electrodes are not burned.
B. Core bridging—These defects are caused by excessive combustion chamber deposits striking and adhering to the firing end of the plug. In this case, they wedge or fuse between the electrode and core nose. They originate from the piston and cylinder head surfaces. Deposits are formed by one or more of the following:
  a. Excessive carbon in cylinder.
  b. Use of non-recommended oils.
  c. Immediate high-speed operation after prolonged trolling.
  d. Improper fuel-oil ratio.
C. Wet fouling—Damp or wet, black carbon coating over entire firing end of plug. Forms sludge in some engines. Caused by one or more of the following:
  a. Spark plug heat range too cold.
  b. Prolonged trolling.
  c. Low-speed carburetor adjustment too rich.
  d. Improper fuel-oil ratio.
  e. Induction manifold bleed-off passage obstructed.
  f. Worn or defective breaker points.
D. Gap bridging—Similar to core bridging, except the combustion particles are wedged or fused between the electrodes. Causes are the same.
E. Overheating—Badly worn electrodes and premature gap wear are indicative of this problem, along with a gray or white "blistered" appearance on the insulator. Caused by one or more of the following:
  a. Spark plug heat range too hot.
  b. Incorrect propeller usage, causing engine to lug.
  c. Worn or defective water pump.
  d. Restricted water intake or restriction somewhere in the cooling system.
F. Ash deposits or lead fouling—Ash deposits are light brown to white in color and result from use of fuel or oil additives. Lead fouling produces a yellowish brown discoloration and can be avoided by using unleaded fuels.

102

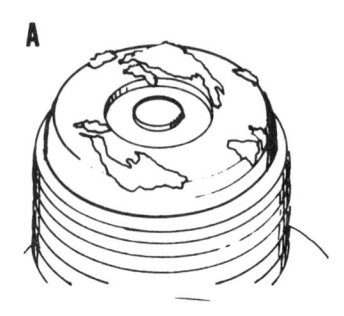

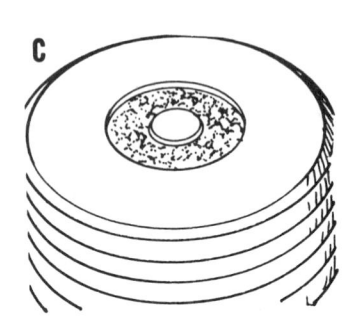

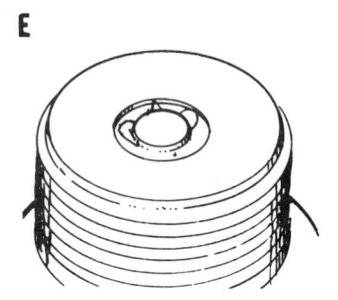

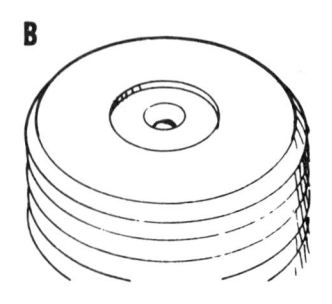

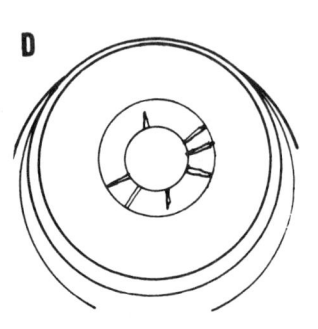

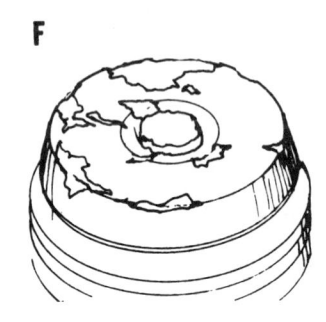

CHAPTER FOUR

**SURFACE GAP
SPARK PLUG ANALYSIS**

A. Normal—Light tan or gray colored deposits indicate that the engine/ignition system condition is good. Electrode wear indicates normal spark rotation.
B. Worn out—Excessive electrode wear can cause hard starting or a misfire during acceleration.
C. Cold fouled—Wet oil-fuel deposits are caused by "drowning" the plug with raw fuel mix during cranking, overrich carburetion or an improper fuel-oil ratio. Weak ignition will also contribute to this condition.

D. Carbon tracking—Electrically conductive deposits on the firing end provide a low—resistance path for the voltage. Carbon tracks form and can cause misfires.
E. Concentrated arc—Multi-colored appearance is normal. It is caused by electricity consistently following the same firing path. Arc path changes with deposit conductivity and gap erosion.
F. Aluminum throw-off—Caused by preignition. This is not a plug problem but the result of engine damage. Check engine to determine cause and extent of damage.

LUBRICATION, MAINTENANCE AND TUNE-UP

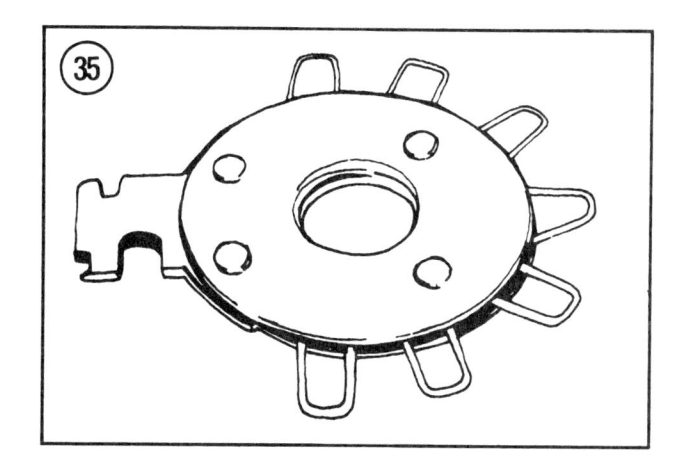

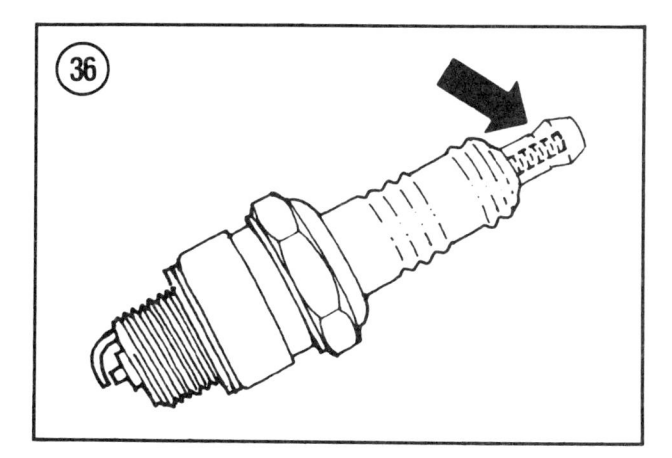

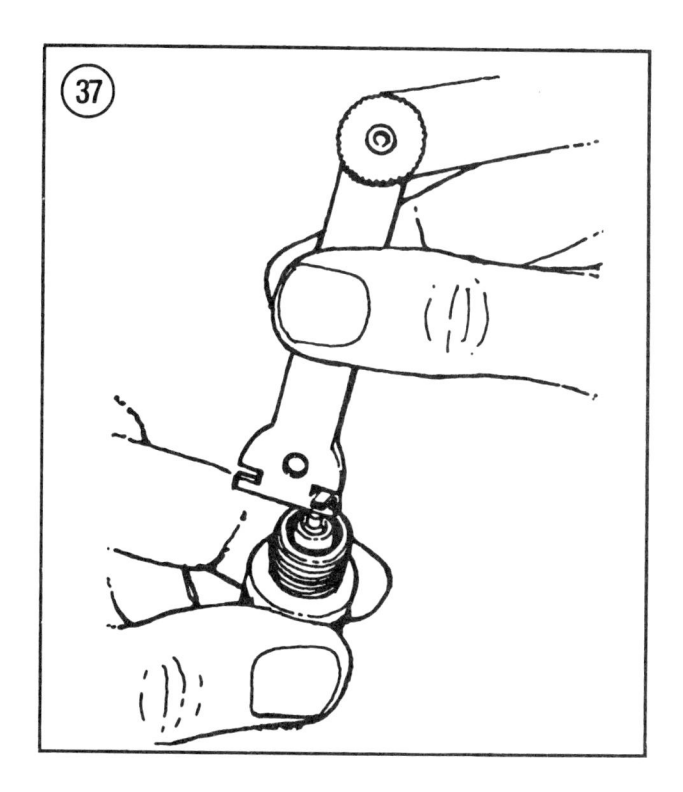

Gapping Plugs
(Conventional Gap Only)

New plugs should be carefully gapped to ensure a reliable, consistent spark. Use a special spark plug tool with a wire gauge. See **Figure 35** for one common type.

1. Remove the plugs and gaskets from the boxes. Install the gaskets.

NOTE
Some plug brands may have small end pieces that must be screwed on (Figure 36) before the plugs can be used.

2. Insert the appropriate size wire gauge (**Table 3**) between the electrodes. If the gap is correct, there will be a slight drag as the wire is pulled through. If there is no drag, or if the wire will not pull through, bend the side electrode with the gapping tool (**Figure 37**) to change the gap. Remeasure with the wire gauge.

CAUTION
Never try to close the electrode gap by tapping the spark plug on a solid surface. This can damage the plug internally. Always use the gapping and adjusting tool to open or close the gap.

Spark Plug Installation

Improper installation of spark plugs is one of the most common causes of poor spark plug performance in outboard engines. The gasket on the plug must be fully compressed against a clean plug seat in order for heat transfer to take place effectively. This requires close attention to proper tightening during installation.

1. Inspect the spark plug hole threads and clean them with a thread chaser (**Figure 38**). Wipe cylinder head seats clean before installing the new plugs.
2. Screw each plug in by hand until it seats. Very little effort is required. If force is

necessary, the plug is cross-threaded. Unscrew it and try again.

3. Tighten the spark plugs. If you have a torque wrench, tighten to 17-20 ft.-lb. (24-27 N•m). If not, seat the plug finger-tight on the gasket, then tighten an additional 1/4 turn with a wrench.

4. Inspect each spark plug wire before reconnecting it to its cylinder. If insulation is damaged or deteriorated, install a new plug wire. Push wire boot onto plug terminal and make sure it seats fully.

Gearcase and Water Pump Check

A faulty water pump or one that performs below specifications can result in extensive engine damage. Thus, it is a good idea to replace the water pump impeller, seals and gaskets once a year or whenever the lower drive is removed for service. See Chapter Nine.

Fuel System Service

The clearance between the carburetor and choke shutter should not be greater than 0.015 in. when the choke is closed or a hard starting condition will result. When changing from one brand of gasoline to another, it may be necessary to readjust the carburetor idle mixture needle slightly (1/4 turn) to accommodate the variations in volatility.

Fuel Lines

1. Visually check all fuel lines for kinks, leaks, deterioration or other damage.
2. Disconnect fuel lines and blow out with compressed air to dislodge any contamination or foreign material.
3. Coat fuel line fittings sparingly with OMC Gasket Sealing Compound and reconnect the lines.

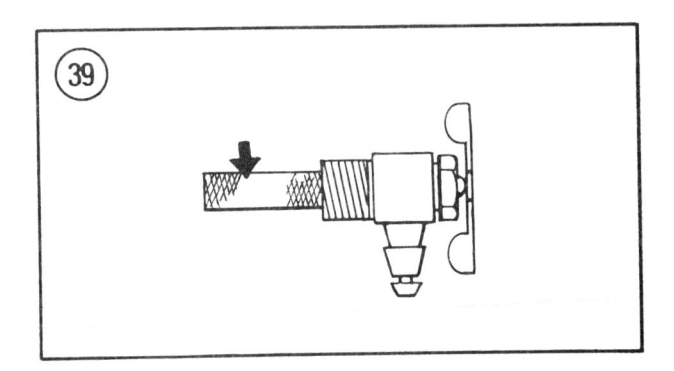

Engine Fuel Filter Service

Three types of engine fuel filters are used: a petcock filter screen installed in the fuel shut-off valve between the fuel tank and carburetor on 1.5 and 3 hp models, a fuel pump filter screen or a sediment bowl filter element. The sediment bowl is located in the carburetor float bowl (1956-1959) or on the fuel pump (1960-on).

Petcock Filter Screen (1.5 and 3 hp)

Refer to **Figure 39** for this procedure.
1. Unscrew and remove the fuel shut-off valve.
2. Remove the filter from the filter cup.
3. Clean filter in OMC Engine Tuner. Blow dry with compressed air.
4. Installation is the reverse of removal. Use a drop of OMC Gasoila on the shut-off valve threads before installing valve in fuel tank.

LUBRICATION, MAINTENANCE AND TUNE-UP

Sediment Bowl Filter

Refer to **Figure 41** for this procedure.
1. Loosen the sediment bowl yoke screw. Swing the yoke over the bowl. Remove the bowl.
2A. Fuel pump—Remove the filter element.
2B. Carburetor—Unscrew the flat milled washer and remove the gasket and filter element.
3. Discard the filter element and gasket.
4. Wash the bowl thoroughly in clean solvent and blow dry with compressed air.
5. Installation is the reverse of removal. Tighten the yoke screw securely. Start the engine and check for leaks.

Fuel Pump Filter Screen

Refer to **Figure 40** for this procedure.
1. Remove the screw holding the filter cover to the fuel pump.
2. Remove the filter screen from the pump housing or filter cover.
3. Clean the screen in OMC Engine Tuner. If screen is excessively dirty or plugged, discard it and install a new one.
4. Install the filter screen in the filter cover.
5. Reinstall the filter cover to the fuel pump and tighten the screw securely.
6. Check filter assembly for leakage by priming the fuel system with the fuel line primer bulb.

Fuel Pump

The fuel pump does not generally require service during a tune-up. Fuel pump diaphragms are fragile and one that is defective often produces symptoms that are diagnosed as an ignition system problem. A common malfunction results from a tiny pinhole or crack in the diaphragm caused by an engine backfire. This defect allows gasoline to enter the crankcase and wet-foul the spark plug at idle speed, causing hard starting and engine stall at low rpm. The problem disappears at higher speeds, as fuel quantity is limited. Since the plug is not fouled by excess fuel at higher speeds, it fires normally.

Fuel Pump Pressure Test (Inline Engines)

Perform this test with the engine running in a test tank or on the boat in the water.
1. Momentarily loosen the fuel tank cap to release any pressure. Make sure fuel tank is not more than 24 in. below the fuel pump.

2. Tee a pressure gauge between the carburetor and fuel pump. See **Figure 42** (typical).
3. Connect a tachometer according to manufacturer's specifications.
4. Start the engine and note the pressure gauge. The pump pressure must be at least 1 psi at 600 rpm, 1.5 psi at 2,500-3,000 rpm and 2.5 psi at 4,500 rpm. If not, rebuild the fuel pump with a new diaphragm, check valves and gasket. See Chapter Six.

Fuel Pump Pressure Test (V4)

Perform this test with the engine running in a test tank or on the boat in the water.
1. Momentarily loosen the fuel tank cap to release any pressure. Make sure the fuel tank is not more than 24 in. below the fuel pump.
2. Tee a pressure gauge between the carburetor and fuel pump. See **Figure 43** (typical).
3. Connect a tachometer according to manufacturer's instructions.
4. Remove the fuel pump filter cover. Make sure the filter is clean, then reinstall the cover.
5. Start the engine and run at full throttle for one minute to stabilize pump pressure. The pressure should be between 2 1/2-6 psi.
6A. If the pressure is less than 2 1/2 psi, stop the engine and pressurize the fuel system with the primer bulb. Hold the pressure and inspect the pump, lines and fittings for leaks. If there are no leaks, replace the fuel pump.
6B. If the pressure is 2 1/2-3 1/2 psi with a portable fuel tank and the fuel pump filter is new or clean, replace the pump. It will cause problems as the filter screen gradually gets dirty.
6C. If the pressure is less than 2 1/2 psi and the boat has a built-in fuel tank, connect the

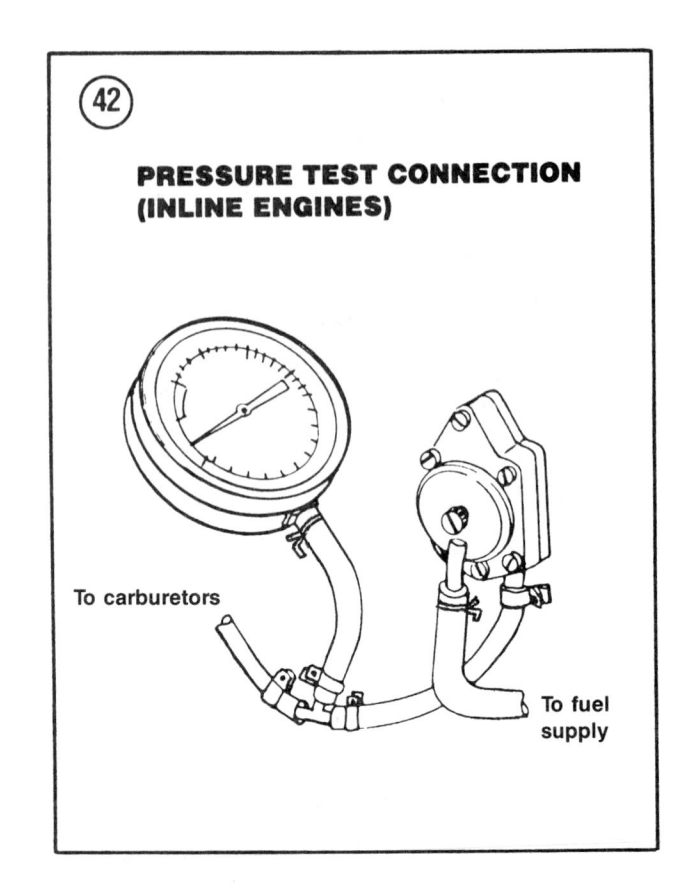

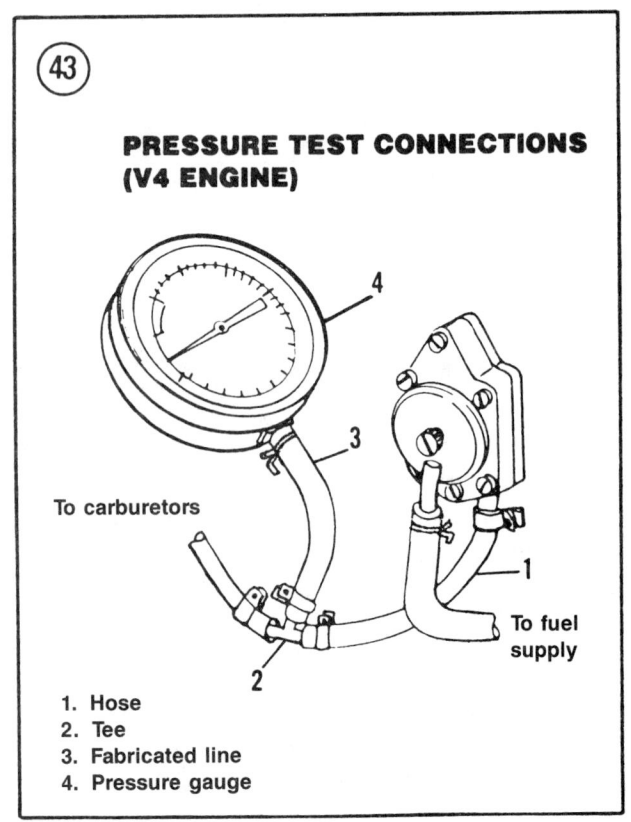

LUBRICATION, MAINTENANCE AND TUNE-UP

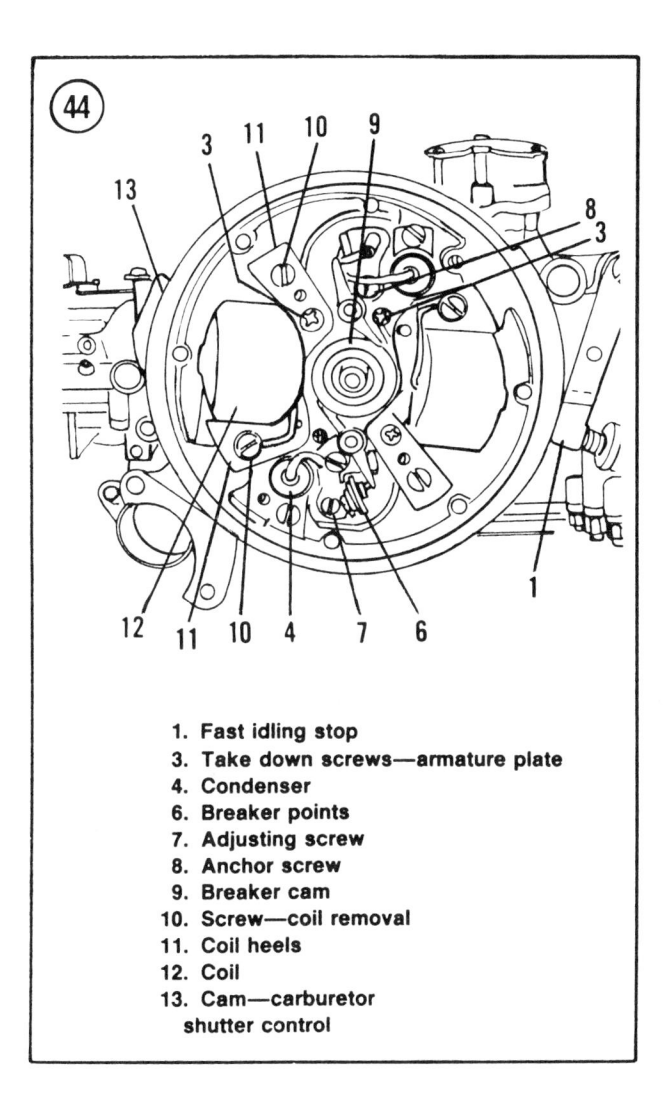

Figure 44

1. Fast idling stop
3. Take down screws—armature plate
4. Condenser
6. Breaker points
7. Adjusting screw
8. Anchor screw
9. Breaker cam
10. Screw—coil removal
11. Coil heels
12. Coil
13. Cam—carburetor shutter control

engine to a portable fuel tank and repeat the test. If the pressure increases when the engine is connected to the portable tank, there is a restriction somewhere in the built-in tank system. If the pressure remains the same, replace the fuel pump.

Breaker Point Ignition System Service

The condition and gap of the breaker points will greatly affect engine operation. Burned or badly oxidized points will allow little or no current to pass. A gap that is too narrow will not allow the coil to build up sufficient voltage and will result in a weak spark. An excessive point gap will allow the points to open before the primary current reaches its maximum.

While slightly pitted points can be dressed with a file, this should be done only as a temporary measure, as the points may arc after filing. Oxidized, dirty or oily points can be cleaned with alcohol but new points are inexpensive and always preferable for efficient engine operation.

The condenser absorbs the surge of high voltage from the coil and prevents current from arcing across the points when they open. Condensers can be tested with a condenser tester but are also inexpensive and should be replaced as a matter of course whenever new breaker points are installed.

An ignition analyzer must be used for an accurate check of the breaker points. Johnson and Evinrude recommend the use of the Merc-O-Tronic, Graham Model 51 or Stevens M.A.-75 tester. These can be purchased through your local Johnson or Evinrude dealer.

Check the breaker points as described in *Breaker Point Testing*, Chapter Three. If they fail to perform as specified, clean the points with an electrical contact cleaner—do not file. If they still do not deliver a satisfactory reading, replace the points as described in this chapter.

NOTE
Breaker points must be adjusted correctly. An error in gap of 0.0015 in. will change engine timing by as much as one degree.

Breaker Point Replacement (Flywheel Magneto Ignition)

Refer to **Figure 44** for this procedure.
1. Remove the flywheel. See Chapter Eight.
2. Move the armature plate to the full advance position.
3. Disconnect all breaker point and condenser leads.

4. Remove the hairpin clip at the top of each breaker point pivot post with needlenose pliers.

5. Loosen the adjusting and locking screws. Remove the retainer holding each breaker point set together.

6. Remove the movable half of each breaker point set, then remove the locking screw and washer holding the remaining half to the armature plate. Remove the point set(s).

7. Remove the condenser attaching screws. Remove each condenser.

8. Check the cam oiler wick. If wick is dry, apply 2-3 drops of light engine oil. Do not overlubricate the wick.

9. Install the non-movable side of a new breaker point set on the armature plate pivot post and secure in place with the washer and locking screw.

10. Slide the movable side of the new breaker point set over the pivot post and fit into position. The movable arm spring should rest on the inside of the flat post.

11. Reinstall the retainer to hold the point set together. **Figure 45** shows the assembled point set.

12. Repeat Steps 8-10 to install the second point set.

13. Install the hairpin clip in each breaker point pivot post groove.

CAUTION
Do not rotate the crankshaft counterclockwise in Step 14 or Step 16 or the water pump impeller may be damaged.

14. Temporarily reinstall the flywheel nut and use a wrench to rotate the crankshaft clockwise until the breaker arm rubbing block is positioned on the high point of the cam.

15. Turn the adjusting screw to obtain a gap of 0.020 in. Measure gap with a flat feeler gauge. The gap is correct when the feeler gauge offers a slight drag as it is slipped between the points. When the gap is correct, tighten the locking screw securely and recheck the point gap. **Figure 46** shows the screw location.

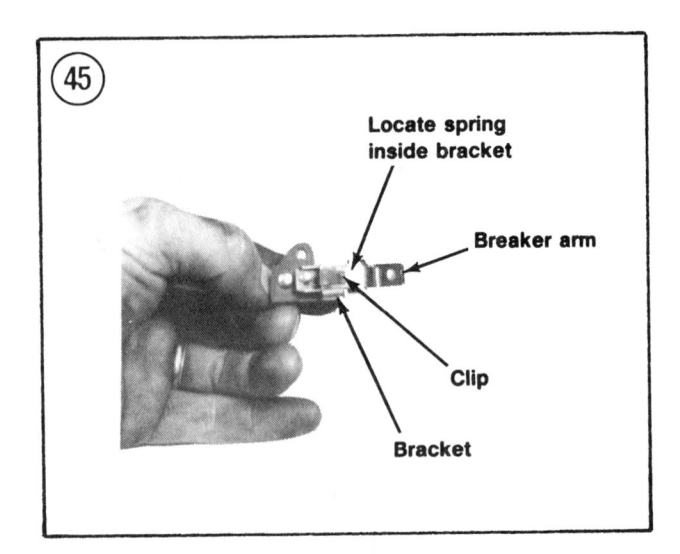

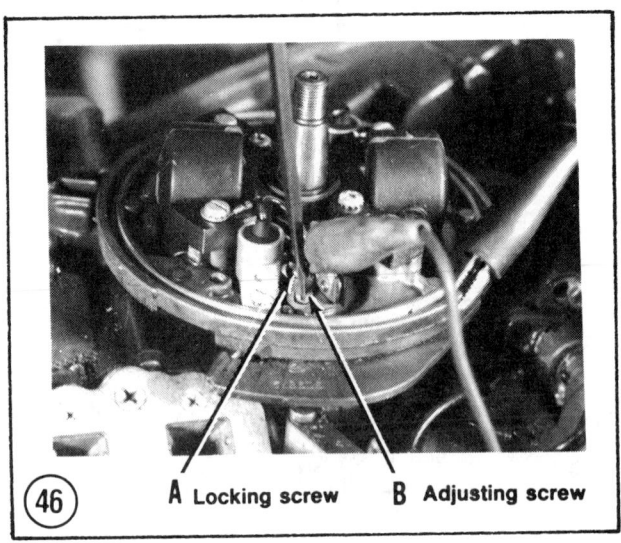

16. Rotate the crankshaft clockwise to position the second point set rubbing block on the high point of the cam.

17. Repeat Step 15.

18. Install each new condenser and tighten its attaching screw securely.

19. Connect the breaker point and condenser leads.

20. Remove the flywheel nut and reinstall the flywheel.

LUBRICATION, MAINTENANCE AND TUNE-UP

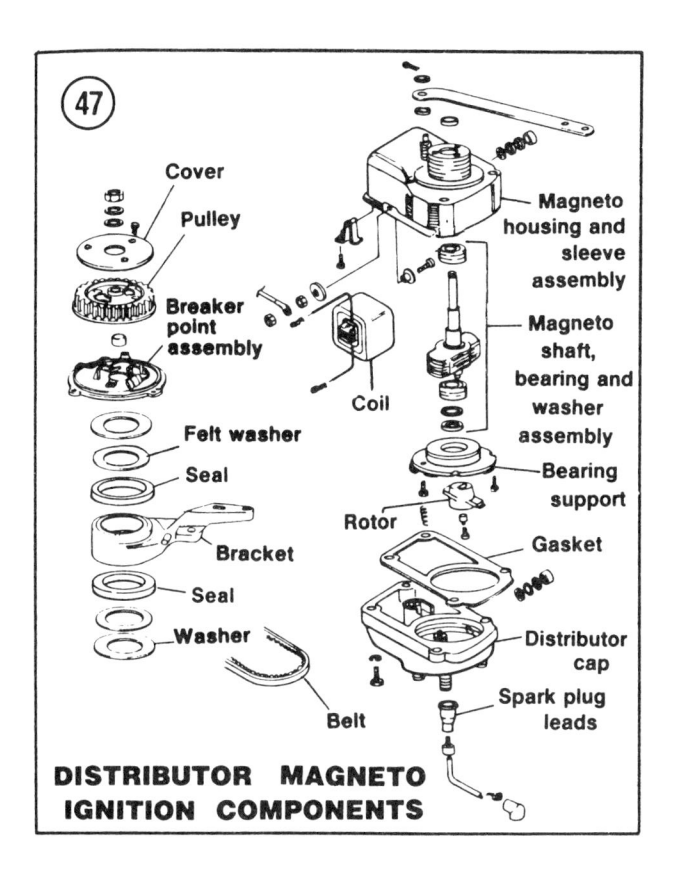

DISTRIBUTOR MAGNETO IGNITION COMPONENTS (Figure 47): Cover, Pulley, Breaker point assembly, Felt washer, Seal, Bracket, Seal, Washer, Belt, Coil, Rotor, Magneto housing and sleeve assembly, Magneto shaft, bearing and washer assembly, Bearing support, Gasket, Distributor cap, Spark plug leads.

Breaker Point Replacement (Distributor Magneto Ignition)

Refer to **Figure 47** for this procedure.

1. Remove the distributor magneto. See Chapter Eight. Remove the pulley from the magneto housing.
2. Carefully study the wire routing inside the housing or make a diagram for reinstallation reference.
3. Disconnect all breaker point and condenser leads.
4. Remove the hairpin clip at the top of each breaker point pivot post with needlenose pliers.
5. Remove the adjusting and locking screws. Remove the screws and wave washers. Remove the breaker point sets. Save the jumper lead installed between the point sets.
6. Remove the condenser attaching screw. Remove the condenser.
7. Remove and discard the cam oiler wick. Install a new wick.
8. Install a new condenser. Tighten the attaching screw securely.
9. Install the non-movable side of a new breaker point set on the distributor base pivot post and secure in place with the washer and locking screw.
10. Slide the movable side of the new breaker point set over the pivot post and fit into position. The movable arm spring should rest on the inside of the flat post.
11. Reinstall the retainer to hold the point set together. **Figure 45** shows the assembled point set.
12. Repeat Steps 9-11 to install the second point set.
13. Install the hairpin clip in each breaker point pivot post groove.
14. Attach the condenser lead, primary lead and one end of the jumper lead to the point set nearest the condenser. Connect the other end of the jumper lead and the "stop" or "kill" switch lead (if so equipped) to the other point set.
15. Make sure all leads are properly positioned and will not rub against any moving parts. If a drawing was made in Step 2, refer to it for proper wire positioning.
16. Position the rubbing block of one point set on the high point of the cam.
17. Turn the adjusting screw to obtain a gap of 0.022 in. (0.020 in. for used points). Measure gap with a flat feeler gauge. The gap is correct when the feeler gauge offers a slight drag as it is slipped between the points. When the gap is correct, tighten the locking screw securely and recheck the point gap. See **Figure 46**.
18. Position the second point set rubbing block on the high point of the cam.
19. Repeat Step 17.
20. Reinstall the distributor magneto pulley. Reinstall the magneto housing. See Chapter Eight.
21. Check and adjust timing. See Chapter Five.

Breaker Point Replacement (Distributor Battery Ignition)

Refer to **Figure 48** for this procedure.

1. Remove the distributor cap from the distributor housing. Remove the distributor rotor. See Chapter Eight.
2. Carefully study the wire routing inside the housing or make a diagram for reinstallation reference.
3. Disconnect all breaker point and condenser leads.
4. Remove the hairpin clip at the top of each breaker point pivot post with needlenose pliers.
5. Remove the adjusting and locking screws. Remove the screws and wave washers. Remove the breaker point sets. Save the jumper lead installed between the point sets.
6. Remove the condenser attaching screw. Remove the condenser.
7. Remove and discard the cam oiler wick. Install a new wick.
8. Install a new condenser. Tighten the attaching screw securely.
9. Install the non-movable side of a new breaker point set on the distributor base pivot post and secure in place with the washer and locking screw.
10. Slide the movable side of the new breaker point set over the pivot post and fit into position. The movable arm spring should rest on the inside of the flat post.
11. Reinstall the retainer to hold the point set together. **Figure 45** shows the assembled point set.
12. Repeat Steps 9-11 to install the second point set.
13. Install the hairpin clip in each breaker point pivot post groove.
14. Attach the condenser lead and one end of the jumper lead to the point set nearest the condenser. Connect the other end of the jumper lead and the primary lead to the other point set.
15. Make sure all leads are properly positioned and will not rub against any moving parts. If a drawing was made in Step 2, refer to it for proper wire positioning.

CAUTION
Do not rotate the crankshaft counterclockwise in Step 16 or Step 18 or the water pump impeller may be damaged.

16. Rotate the flywheel clockwise to position the rubbing block of one point set on the high point of the cam.
17. Turn the adjusting screw to obtain a gap of 0.020 in. Measure gap with a flat feeler gauge. The gap is correct when the feeler gauge offers a slight drag as it is slipped between the points. When the gap is correct,

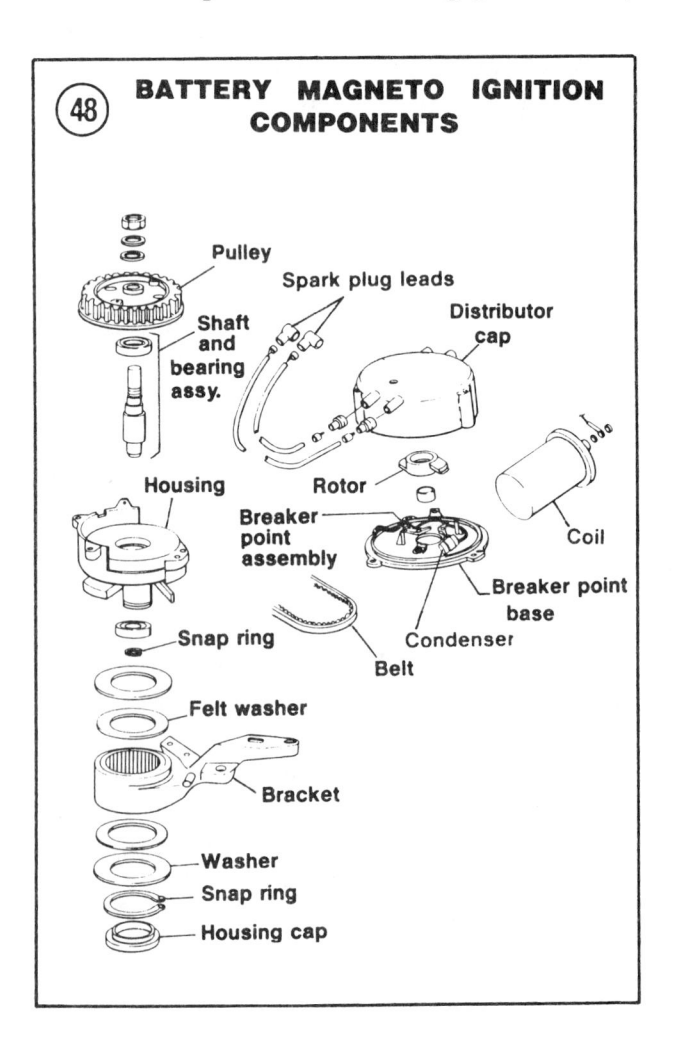

48 BATTERY MAGNETO IGNITION COMPONENTS

- Pulley
- Shaft and bearing assy.
- Spark plug leads
- Distributor cap
- Housing
- Rotor
- Breaker point assembly
- Coil
- Breaker point base
- Condenser
- Belt
- Snap ring
- Felt washer
- Bracket
- Washer
- Snap ring
- Housing cap

LUBRICATION, MAINTENANCE AND TUNE-UP

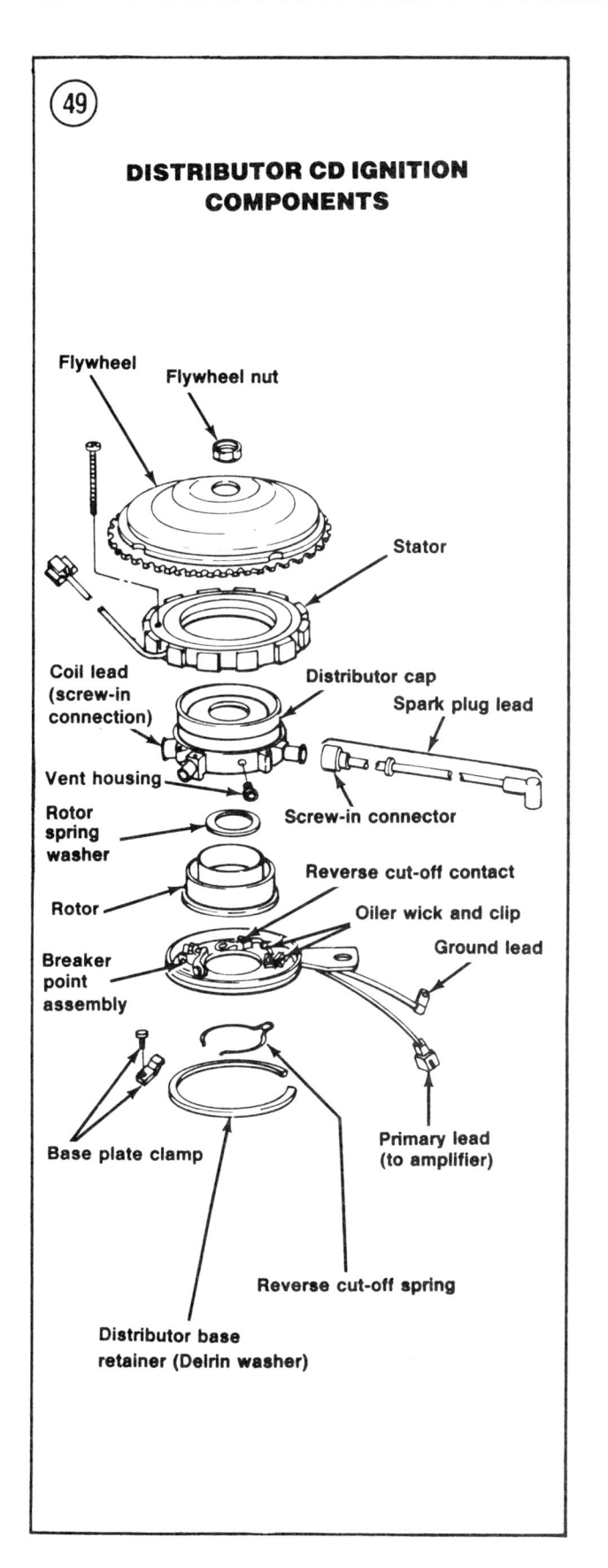

tighten the locking screw securely and recheck the point gap. See **Figure 46**.
18. Repeat Step 15 to position the second point set rubbing block on the high point of the cam.
19. Repeat Step 17.
20. Reinstall the distributor rotor and cap.
21. Check and adjust timing. See Chapter Five.

Breaker Point Replacement (Distributor CD Ignition)

Refer to **Figure 49** for this procedure.
1. Remove the flywheel. See Chapter Eight.
2. Disconnect the yellow stator leads, remove the stator attaching screws and remove the stator from the distributor cap.
3. Disconnect the coil and spark plug leads at the distributor cap.
4. Remove the distributor cap assembly from the base plate.
5. Remove the wave washer from inside the distributor rotor. Remove the rotor.
6. Remove and discard the reverse cut-out spring (**Figure 50**).

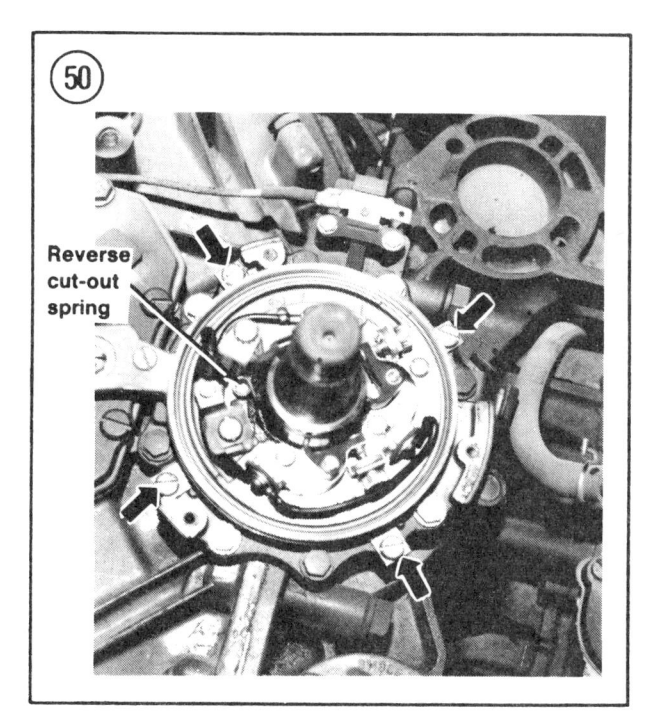

7. Disconnect the distributor base ground lead and the primary lead to the amplifier.

NOTE
Base plate removal is not required to replace the breaker points. However, a breaker point lead passes under the plate and is held in place with a retainer. If the lead is damaged, it can ground the points.

8. Remove the retaining clips and screws holding the base plate in position on the power head. See arrows, **Figure 50**. Remove and invert the base plate to check the condition of the lead. Repair or replace as required.
9. Carefully study the wire routing inside the base plate or make a diagram for reinstallation reference.
10. Remove the screws holding the point sets in position. Disconnect each point set lead at the terminal block, then remove the point sets.
11. Reposition the base plate on the power head. Lubricate the nylon base plate retainer ring with Shell EP-2 grease (or equivalent). Compress the ring and work it into the power head upper bearing recess as the base plate is seated. Install the base plate retaining clips and screws. See arrows, **Figure 50**.

NOTE
Do not forget to install the anti-reverse spring in Step 12. This acts as an ignition system ground to prevent the engine from running backwards after a backfire.

12. Install a new anti-reverse spring. Lightly lubricate the area on the crankshaft where the spring rides with OMC Extreme Pressure Grease (part No. 173652).
13. Reconnect the distributor base ground lead and primary lead to amplifier.
14. Install new breaker point sets to the base plate and tighten the attaching screws.

15. Make sure all leads are properly positioned and will not rub against any moving parts. If a drawing was made in Step 9, refer to it for proper wire positioning.

CAUTION
Do not rotate the crankshaft counterclockwise in Step 16 or Step 18 or the water pump impeller may be damaged.

16. Temporarily reinstall the flywheel nut and use a wrench to rotate the flywheel clockwise until the rubbing block of one point set is positioned on the high point of the cam.
17. Turn the adjusting screw to obtain a gap of 0.012 in. (0.010 for used points). Measure gap with a flat feeler gauge. See **Figure 51**. The gap is correct when the feeler gauge offers a slight drag as it is slipped between the points.
18. Rotate the flywheel clockwise to position the rubbing block of the second point set on the high point of the cam.
19. Repeat Step 16.
20. Remove the flywheel nut.
21. Install the distributor rotor, indexing its tab with the crankshaft recess. Make sure rotor is properly seated, then install the wave washer.

LUBRICATION, MAINTENANCE AND TUNE-UP

22. Install the distributor cap and seat it on the upper bearing housing.
23. Reconnect the coil and spark plug leads to the distributor cap.
24. Reinstall the stator. Wipe the stator screw threads with Loctite and tighten to 48-60 in.-lb. Connect the stator leads.
25. Reinstall the flywheel. See Chapter Eight.
26. Check and adjust timing. See Chapter Five.

Sensor Gap Check and Adjustment (Breakerless Distributor CD Ignition)

This adjustment should be necessary only when the distributor has been removed from the power head.

1. Align one trigger wheel or rotor lobe with the sensor.
2. Turn the ignition switch ON.
3. Disconnect pulse transformer lead and hold it about 3/8 in. from power head with insulated pliers.
4. Depress vacuum switch diaphragm to close ignition circuit and bridge the rotor/sensor gap with a flat feeler gauge. The pulse transformer lead should spark each time the gap is bridged, indicating a good sensor. If it does not, replace the sensor.
5. Turn the ignition switch OFF and reconnect the pulse transformer lead.
6. Measure the gap between the sensor and trigger wheel or rotor lobe with a flat feeler gauge. If it is not 0.028 in., loosen the sensor adjusting screws and move the sensor as required to obtain the specified gap with a slight drag on the feeler gauge when passed through the gap.

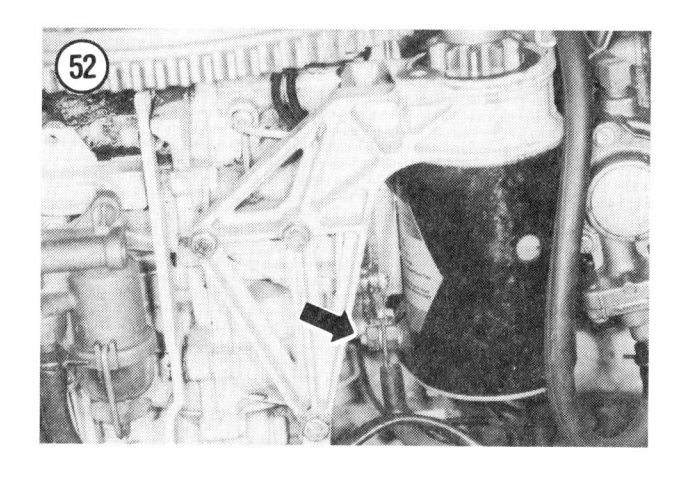

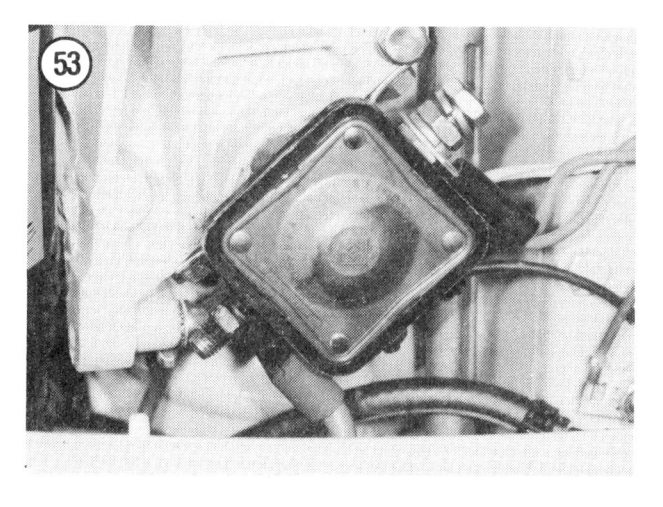

Battery and Starter Motor Check (Electric Start Models Only)

1. Check the battery's state of charge. See Chapter Seven.
2. Connect a voltmeter between the starter motor positive terminal (**Figure 52**) and ground.
3. Turn ignition switch to START and check voltmeter scale.
   a. If voltage exceeds 9.5 volts and the starter motor does not operate, replace the motor.
   b. If voltage is less than 9.5 volts, recheck battery and connections. Charge battery, if necessary, and repeat procedure.

Solenoid Check (Electric Start Models Only)

Any good volt/ohm/ammeter (VOA) can be used for this test.

1. Disconnect all leads from the starter solenoid. See **Figure 53** (typical).

2. Connect the VOA meter leads to the soldered solenoid terminals (1 and 2, **Figure 54**).

3. Set the meter to the R×1 scale. The meter should indicate continuity. If not, replace the solenoid.

4. Set the meter to the R×1K scale. Connect the meter leads between the threaded terminals (3 and 4, **Figure 54**).

5. Connect a 12-volt battery between the soldered solenoid terminals (1 and 2, **Figure 54**). The solenoid should click and the VOA meter should read zero ohms. If not, replace the solenoid.

Internal Wiring Harness Check

1. Check the wiring harness for signs of frayed or chafed insulation.
2. Check for loose connections between the wires and terminal ends.
3. Check harness connector for bent electrical pins.
4. Check harness connector and pin sockets for signs of corrosion. Clean as required.
5. If harness is suspected of contributing to electrical malfunctions, check all wires for continuity and resistance between harness connection and terminal end. Repair or replace as required.

Engine Synchronization and Adjustment

See Chapter Five.

Performance Test (On Boat)

Before performance testing the engine, make sure that the boat bottom is cleaned of all marine growth and that there is no evidence of a "hook" or "rocker" (**Figure 55**) on the bottom. Any of these conditions will reduce performance considerably.

The boat should be performance tested with an average load and with the motor tilted at an angle that will allow the boat to ride on an even keel. If equipped with an adjustable trim tab, it should be properly adjusted to allow the boat to steer in either direction with equal ease.

Check engine rpm at full throttle. If not within the maximum rpm range for the motor as specified in Chapter Five, check the propeller pitch. A high pitch propeller will reduce rpm while a lower pitch prop will increase it.

Readjust the idle mixture and speed under actual operating conditions as required to obtain the best low-speed engine performance.

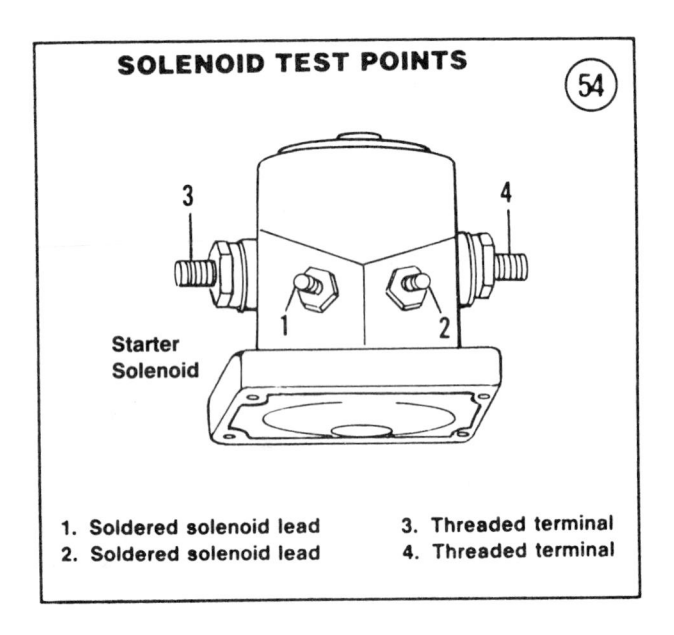

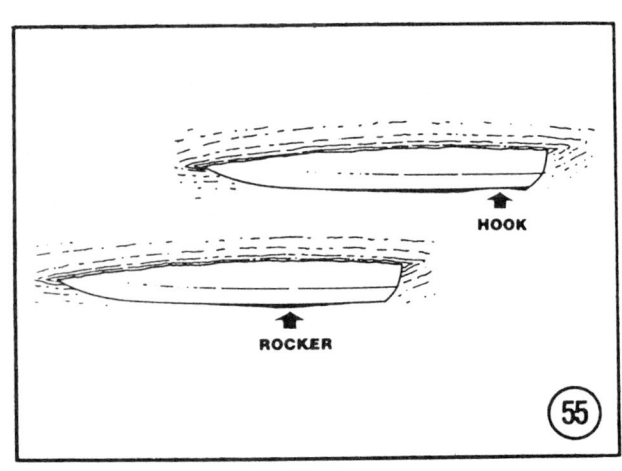

SOLENOID TEST POINTS (54)

Starter Solenoid

1. Soldered solenoid lead
2. Soldered solenoid lead
3. Threaded terminal
4. Threaded terminal

(55) HOOK / ROCKER

LUBRICATION, MAINTENANCE AND TUNE-UP

Table 1 LUBRICATION & MAINTENANCE[1]

Lubrication points	Figure No.
1.5-40 HP	
Clamp screws, steering handle pivot and tilt/run lever	10
Throttle detent, cam, linkage and choke lever	5
Magneto and throttle linkage	7, 9
Shift lever fitting, reverse lock and swivel bracket	6
Fuel shut-off/choke shaft (integral tank)	—
Choke shaft (remote tank)	—
Choke linkage	8
Rear motor cover latch	—
Starter motor pinion gear shaft	11[2]
Vertical throttle shaft and gears	12
50 AND 60 HP	
Control shaft and control lever bushings	13
Shift shaft fittings and lever	17
Swivel bracket, tilt lock lever, tilt lever link and shaft	20
Tilt tube shaft	19
Starter motor pinion gear shaft	23[2]
Trailering lock	—
Carburetor and choke linkage	—
Engine cover latches	—
55 HP	
Carburetor and choke linkage	15
Swivel bracket, tilt lever and shaft	20
Tilt tube shaft	19
Shift shaft fitting and lever	14
Trailering lock	—
Tiller steering joint	—
Engine cover latches	—
65 AND 75 HP	
Shift, throttle, carburetor, choke linkages and springs; throttle cam, roller shaft, shift lever shaft and cover latch	15
Tilt tube shaft	19
Swivel bracket, tilt lock lever and reverse lock	24
Starter motor pinion gear shaft	23[2]
Power trim/tilt reservoir	22[3]
Engine cover latches	—

(continued)

Table 1 LUBRICATION & MAINTENANCE[1] (continued)

Lubrication points	Figure No.
V4	
Control shaft bushings, bearings and shift linkage	17
Carburetor, cam and throttle linkage	16
Tilt tube shaft	19
Swivel bracket fitting, tilt/trim lock, tilt/run lever and reverse lock (manual models)	24
Starter motor pinion gear shaft	23[2]
Power trim/tilt reservoir	22

1. Lubricate with OMC Triple-Guard Grease every 60 days (fresh water) or 30 days (salt water) as required. Figures are representative of the models. Grease fitting locations may differ according to year and manual/power trim models.
2. Use Lubriplate 777.
3. Use OMC Power Trim and Tilt Fluid.

Table 2 TEST WHEEL PERFORMANCE

Model	Test wheel	Minimum engine rpm[1]
1.5	*	4,400
3	203229	3,850
5.5, 6	303592	4,000
7.5	203466	4,200
9.5	*	4,400
10		
1956-1957	277278	4,050
1958-1962	377455	4,050
15, 18		
1956	277278	4,500
1957-1962	376913	4,500
25, 28		
1956	375837	4,400
1957-1959	377014	4,400
1960-1962	378566	4,400
30, 33, 35	*	4,500
40	*	4,400
50 (1958-1964)	377400	4,400
75 (1958-1964)	378046	4,400
85	*	4,700

* Information not available.
1. Based on operation in test tank approximately 60 in. × 60 in. × 40 in. filled with 565 gallons of water @ 600 ft. above sea level.

LUBRICATION, MAINTENANCE AND TUNE-UP

Table 3 RECOMMENDED SPARK PLUGS

Model/hp	Champion plug type	Gap (in.)
1- and 2-cylinder		
All 1956	J6J[1]	0.030
1971-1972 50 hp		
50	UL77V	(see note 2)
50ES, 50R	L77J4	0.040
All others	J4J[1]	0.030
3- and 4-cylinder		
50 hp	J4J[1]	0.030
55 hp	L76V*	(see note 2)
60 hp		
ES	L76V*	(see note 2)
VX (Std. ignition)	J4J[1]	0.030
VXH (CD ignition)	L76V*	(see note 2)
65 hp		
ES	L77J4	0.040
VX (Std. ignition)	J4J[1]	0.030
VXH (CD ignition)	L76V*	(see note 2)
75 and 80 hp	J4J[1]	0.030
85 hp		
1968	J4J[1]	0.030
1969-1972	L76V*	(see note 2)
90 hp	J4J[1]	0.030
100 hp		
1966	J4J[1]	0.030
1967-1968	L77J4	0.040
1971-1972	L76V*	(see note 2)
115 and 125 hp	L76V*	(see note 2)

1. Champion J4J and J6J plugs are superseded by J6C.
2. Not adjustable.
* Sustained low-speed operation; Use L77J4 gapped @ 0.040 in.

Chapter Five

Engine Synchronization and Linkage Adjustments

If an engine is to deliver its maximum efficiency and peak performance, the ignition system must be timed and carburetor operation synchronized with the ignition. This procedure is the final step of a tune-up. It must also be performed whenever the fuel or ignition systems are serviced or adjusted.

Procedures for engine synchronization and adjustment on Johnson and Evinrude outboards differ according to model and ignition system. Because of the large number of models and model years covered in this manual, this chapter is divided into self-contained sections according to synchronization and adjustment procedures rather than individual models. Each section specifies the appropriate procedure, sequence and method to be followed. Read the general information at the beginning of the chapter, then refer to **Table 1** (1- and 2-cylinder) to determine the appropriate procedure or **Table 2** (3- and 4-cylinder) for the specifications to be used with your outboard.

Table 1 and **Table 2** are at the end of the chapter.

ENGINE TIMING

As engine rpm increases, the ignition system must fire the spark plug(s) more rapidly. Proper ignition timing synchronizes spark plug firing with engine speed.

Timing is not adjustable on engines with a breaker point ignition. Ignition timing with this system depends upon correct initial

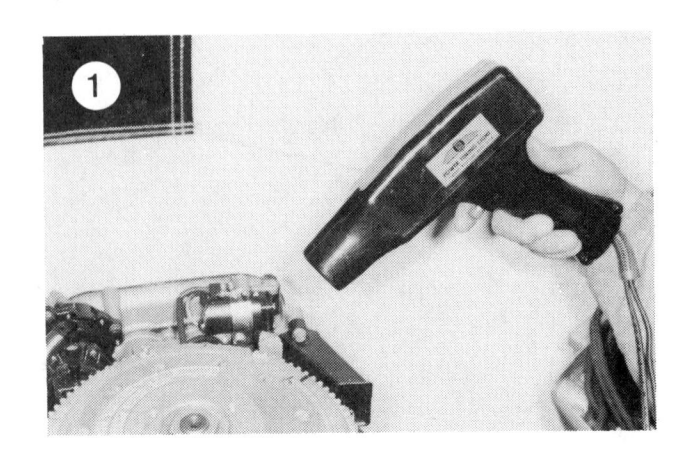

ENGINE SYCHRONIZATION AND LINKAGE ADJUSTMENTS

setting of the breaker point gap. All engines equipped with a flywheel CD breaker point ignition require a point setting of 0.012 in. (new) or 0.010 in. (used). All other engines equipped with breaker point ignitions use a point setting of 0.022 in. (new) or 0.020 in. (used).

Timing can be checked with a timing light (**Figure 1**) on engines equipped with timing marks. If the timing marks on the flywheel and armature plate or timing pointer do not align properly, the breaker point gap must be reset.

If the procedure for your engine specifies that the engine be running while setting the timing, the engine must be run at full throttle in forward gear unless otherwise stated. This requires the use of a test tank and test wheel, as timing an engine while speeding across open water is neither easy nor safe.

SYNCHRONIZING

As engine speed increases, spark timing must increase to fire the spark plugs at a more rapid rate. This means that the carburetor must provide an increased amount of fuel for combustion. Synchronizing is the process of timing the carburetor operation to the ignition (and thereby the engine speed).

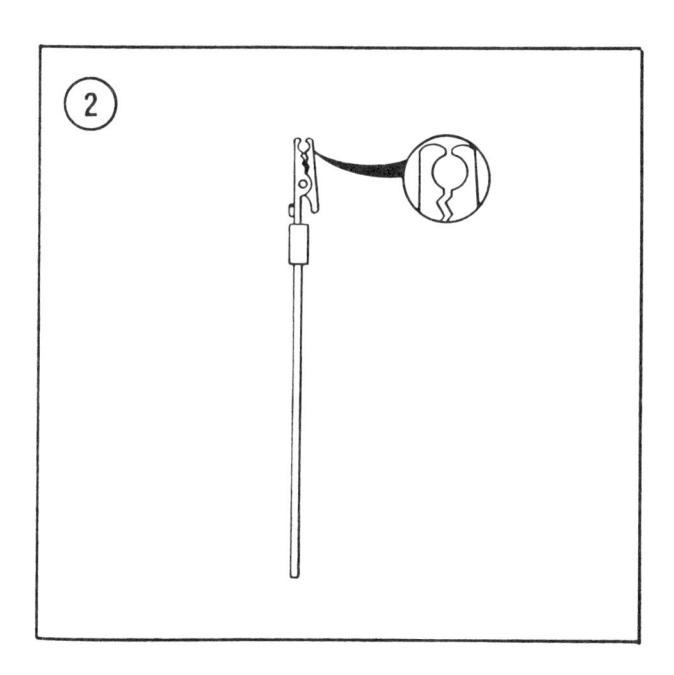

Required Equipment

Static timing of an engine with a breaker point ignition is set by adjusting the breaker point gap with a flat feeler gauge. A timing light can then be used to check timing mark alignment on engines so equipped.

Dynamic engine timing uses a stroboscopic timing light connected to the No. 1 spark plug wire. See **Figure 1**. As the engine is cranked or operated, the light flashes each time the spark plug fires. When the light is pointed at the moving flywheel, the mark on the flywheel appears to stand still. The flywheel mark should align with the stationary timing pointer on the engine.

A tachometer connected to the engine is used to determine engine speed during idle and high-speed adjustments.

To properly synchronize an engine, you must know what to look for. The decisive moment in proper synchronization is when the cam follower causes the carburetor throttle shaft to start to move (this should not be confused with the initial contact between the cam follower and cam).

Since there is a good deal of play in the linkage between the cam follower and throttle shaft, the use of a simple tool called a throttle shaft amplifier is recommended. This tool can be made with an alligator clip and a length of stiff wire (a paper clip will do). Properly used, the tool will exaggerate the movement of the carburetor throttle shaft and tell you that it's moving. The tool is especially useful on engines where the throttle cam and cam follower are partially hidden by the flywheel.

To make the tool, enlarge the alligator clip's gripping surface by grinding out the front teeth on one side and secure the wire to the end of the clip. See **Figure 2**.

CAUTION
Never operate the engine without water circulating through the gearcase to the engine. This will damage the water pump and the gearcase and can cause engine damage.

Some form of water supply is required whenever the engine must be operated during the procedure. Using a test tank is the most convenient method, although the procedures may be carried out with the boat in the water.

CAUTION
Do not use a flushing device to provide water during synchronization and linkage adjustment. Without the exhaust backpressure of a submerged gearcase, the engine will run lean. The proper propeller or test wheel must be used to put a load on the propeller shaft or engine damage can result from excessive rpm.

1- AND 2-CYLINDER ENGINES

Refer to **Table 1** to select the adjustment procedure pertaining to your outboard. For example, suppose you have a 1964 40 hp. **Table 1** tells you to use procedure 5 and adjustment method D. With a 1968 6 hp engine, you would use procedure 1 and adjustment method A.

Procedure 1

Engines adjusted with this procedure have their primary pickup located on the port side of the throttle cam mark.

Throttle cam adjustment

1. Remove the engine cover.
2. Set the throttle grip to the STOP position.
3. Install the tool shown in **Figure 2** to the end of the throttle shaft opposite the cam follower linkage. Bend the tool wire 90° upward for easier viewing. See **Figure 3**.
4. Slowly rotate the throttle grip toward the ADVANCE position until the cam follower starts to open the throttle. The timing mark on the throttle cam should align with the flat port edge of the cam follower. See **Figure 4**.
5. If the roller and throttle cam marks do not align in Step 4, use adjustment method A and loosen the throttle cam mounting screws. Adjust the cam position until the throttle valve is closed and there is no play in the linkage. The throttle cam mark must align with the starboard edge (2 hp) or the flat port side (all others) of the cam follower as the two make contact. Retighten the cam screws.

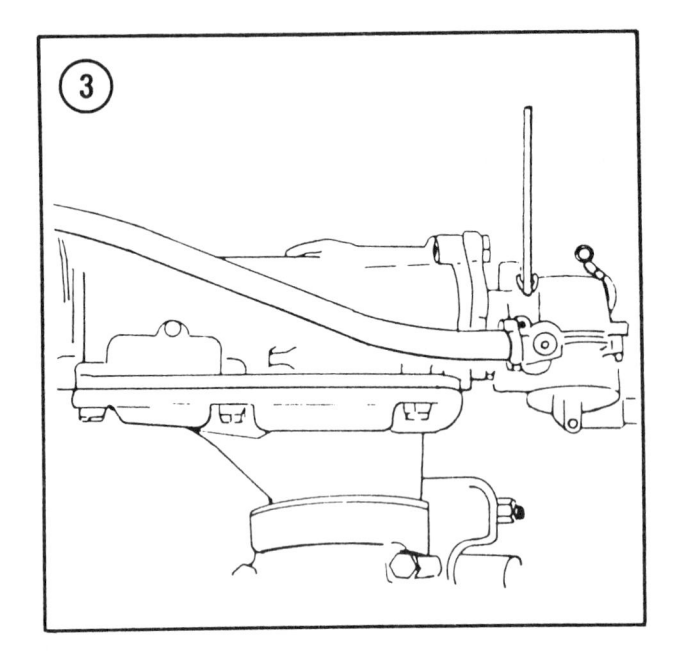

Needle valve adjustment (1.5, 2 and 3 hp)

1. Install the engine in a test tank with the proper test wheel or on the boat in the water with the correct propeller.
2. Turn the carburetor high- and low-speed needles inward until they barely seat.
3. Back the high-speed needle out 1/2 turn (1.5 and 2 hp) or 3/4 turn (3 hp). Back the low-speed needle out 1 1/4 turns.
4. Remove the knob from each needle.
5. Start the engine and run at half throttle until the engine reaches operating temperature.

ENGINE SYCHRONIZATION AND LINKAGE ADJUSTMENTS

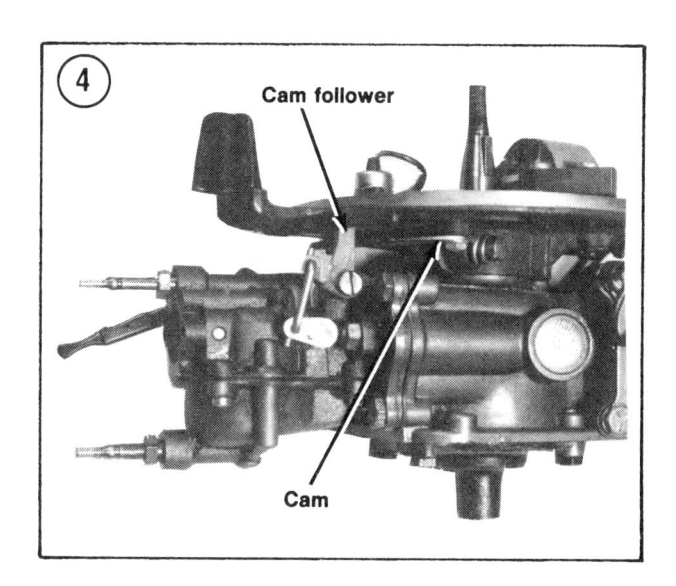

4 Cam follower

Cam

6. Connect a tachometer according to manufacturer's instructions. Run engine at full throttle and adjust the high-speed needle until the best high speed setting is obtained.

NOTE
The engine requires approximately 15 seconds to respond to adjustment in Step 7.

7. Bring engine speed back to 700-750 rpm and adjust the low-speed needle to produce the highest rpm and smoothest operation.
8. Repeat Step 6 after the final low-speed adjustment has been made in Step 7.
9. Reinstall each adjustment knob on its needle without disturbing the needle valve setting.
10. Run the engine in gear at idle and note the tachometer. If throttle cam and needle valve adjustments are correct, the engine should idle at 550 rpm in gear.
11. Shut the engine off; remove the test equipment and install the engine cover.

Needle valve adjustment (5 and 6 hp)

1. Install the engine in a test tank with the proper test wheel or on the boat in the water with the correct propeller.

2. Turn the carburetor low-speed needle inward until it barely seats.
3. Back the low-speed needle out 1 1/4 turns (5 hp) or 1/2 turn (6 hp).
4. Remove the knob from the needle.
5. Start the engine and run at half throttle until the engine reaches operating temperature.
6. Connect a tachometer according to manufacturer's instructions.

NOTE
The engine requires approximately 15 seconds to respond to adjustment in Step 7.

7. Bring engine speed back to 700-750 rpm and adjust low-speed needle to produce the highest rpm and smoothest operation.
8. Reinstall the adjustment knob on its needle without disturbing the needle valve setting.
9. Run the engine in gear at idle and note the tachometer. If throttle cam and needle valve adjustments are correct, the engine should idle at 550 rpm in gear.
10. Shut the engine off; remove the test equipment and install the engine cover.

Procedure 2

Engines adjusted with this procedure have their primary pickup located on the starboard side of the throttle cam mark.

Throttle cam adjustment

1. Remove the engine cover.
2. Set the throttle grip to the STOP position.
3. Install the tool shown in **Figure 2** to the end of the throttle shaft opposite the cam follower linkage. Bend the tool wire 90° upward for easier viewing. See **Figure 3**.
4. Slowly rotate the throttle grip toward the ADVANCE position until the starboard edge of the cam follower aligns with the timing mark on the throttle cam.

5. If the throttle valve is not closed when the marks are aligned in Step 4, use adjustment method A and loosen the throttle cam mounting screws (**Figure 5**). Adjust the cam position until the throttle valve is closed and there is no play in the linkage. The throttle valve should now start to open when the rounded starboard edge of the cam follower aligns with the throttle cam mark (4 hp) or when the flat port side of the cam follower passes the mark on the cam (6 hp). Retighten the cam screws.

Needle valve adjustment (4 hp)

1. Install the engine in a test tank with the proper test wheel or on the boat in the water with the correct propeller.
2. Turn the carburetor high- and low-speed needles inward until they barely seat.
3. Back the high-speed needle out 3/4 turn; back the low-speed needle out 1 3/4 turns.
4. Remove the knob from each needle.
5. Start the engine and run at half throttle until the engine reaches operating temperature.
6. Connect a tachometer according to manufacturer's instructions. Run engine at full throttle and adjust the high-speed needle until the best high speed setting is obtained.

NOTE

The engine requires approximately 15 seconds to respond to adjustment in Step 7.

7. Bring engine speed back to 700-750 rpm and adjust low-speed needle to produce the highest rpm and smoothest operation.
8. Repeat Step 6 after the final low-speed adjustment has been made in Step 7.
9. Reinstall each adjustment knob on its needle without disturbing the needle valve setting.

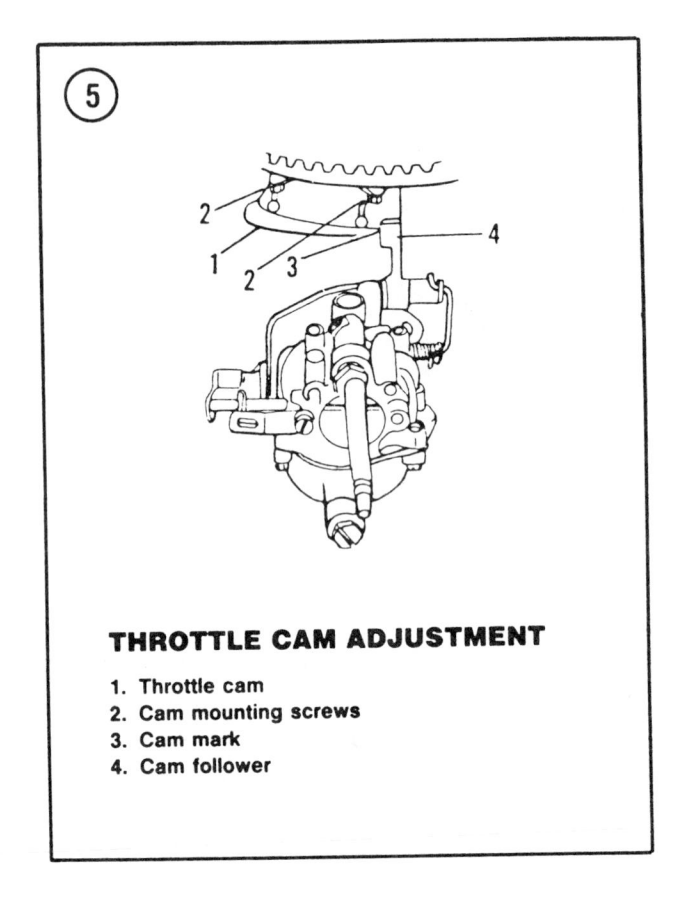

THROTTLE CAM ADJUSTMENT
1. Throttle cam
2. Cam mounting screws
3. Cam mark
4. Cam follower

10. Run the engine in gear at idle and note the tachometer. If throttle cam and needle valve adjustments are correct, the engine should idle at 550-600 rpm in gear.
11. Shut the engine off; remove the test equipment and install the engine cover.

Needle valve adjustment (6 hp)

1. Install the engine in a test tank with the proper test wheel or on the boat in the water with the correct propeller.
2. Turn the carburetor low-speed needle inward until it barely seats.
3. Back the low-speed needle out 3/4 turn.
4. Remove the knob from the needle.
5. Start the engine and run at half throttle until the engine reaches operating temperature.
6. Connect a tachometer according to manufacturer's instructions.

ENGINE SYCHRONIZATION AND LINKAGE ADJUSTMENTS

6

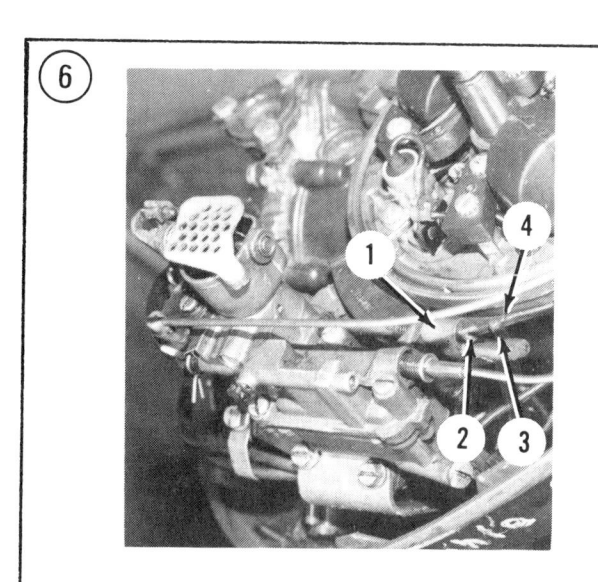

1. Throttle lever
2. Cam follower adjustment screw
3. Cam follower
4. Timing mark

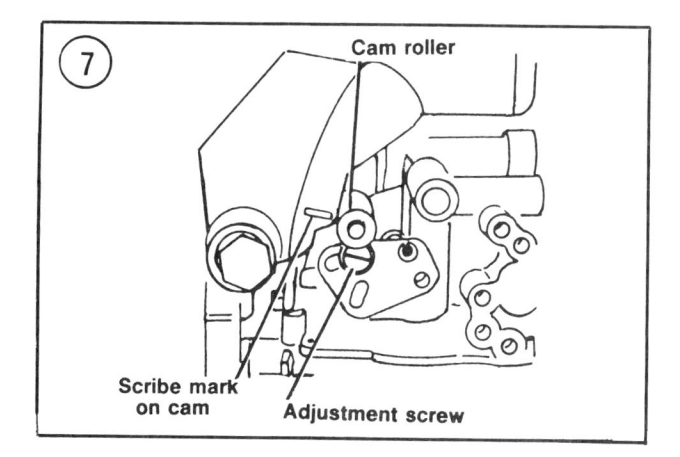

7

Cam roller
Scribe mark on cam
Adjustment screw

NOTE
The engine requires approximately 15 seconds to respond to adjustment in Step 7.

7. Bring engine speed back to 700-750 rpm and adjust low-speed needle to produce the highest rpm and smoothest operation.
8. Reinstall the adjustment knob on its needle without disturbing the needle valve setting.
9. Run the engine in gear at idle and note the tachometer. If throttle cam and needle valve adjustments are correct, the engine should idle at 550 rpm in gear.

10. Shut the engine off; remove the test equipment and install the engine cover.

Procedure 3

Engines adjusted with this procedure have their primary pickup located at the center of the throttle cam mark.

Throttle cam adjustment

1. Remove the engine cover.
2. Set the throttle grip to the STOP position.
3. Install the tool shown in **Figure 2** to the end of the throttle shaft opposite the cam follower linkage. Bend the tool wire 90° upward for easier viewing. See **Figure 3**.
4. Slowly rotate the throttle grip toward the ADVANCE position until the throttle cam mark intersects the throttle cam roller on the throttle cam. See **Figure 6** or **Figure 7** (typical).
5. If the throttle valve is not closed when the roller and mark align in Step 4, use the adjustment method specified in **Table 1** as required:
   a. Method A—Loosen the throttle cam mounting screws. Adjust the cam position until the throttle valve is closed and there is no play in the linkage. Make sure the throttle valve is closed and the cam mark and cam follower intersect, then tighten the cam screws. See **Figure 5** for typical cam screw location.
   b. Method B—Loosen the cam follower screw on the throttle lever. Move the cam follower until it just touches the throttle cam. Rotate the throttle grip until the cam follower aligns with the center of the cam mark. Make sure throttle valve is closed, then move throttle lever roller against the cam follower and tighten the screw. See **Figure 6** (typical).

c. Method E—Align the throttle cam scribe mark with the center of the cam follower roller and loosen the throttle arm screw. See **Figure 7** (typical). Move the throttle arm as required to close the throttle valves, then tighten the screw. Move the throttle lever to its wide-open position. If there is more than 0.020 in. clearance between the cam and roller (**Figure 8**), adjust the full throttle screw (**Figure 9**) as required to bring the clearance to 0.020 in. or less.

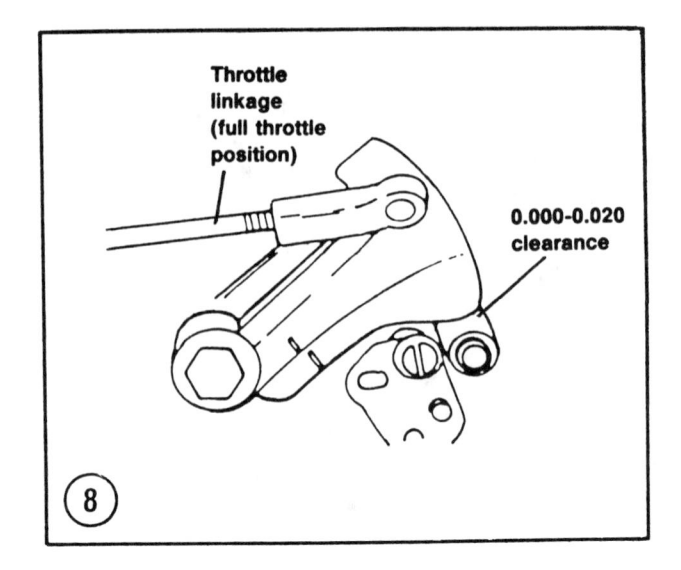

Needle valve adjustment

1. Install the engine in a test tank with the proper test wheel or on the boat in the water with the correct propeller.
2. Remove the air silencer cover and gasket, if so equipped.
3. Turn the carburetor low-speed needle(s) inward until they barely seat.
4. Back the low-speed needle(s) out 5/8 turn (multiple carburetors), 3/4 turn (9.5 hp) or one full turn (all others).
5. Single carburetor—Remove the knob or low-speed valve arm from the needle.
6. Multiple carburetors—Disconnect the linkage.
7. Start the engine and run at half throttle until the engine reaches operating temperature.
8. Connect a tachometer according to manufacturer's instructions.

NOTE
The engine requires approximately 15 seconds to respond to adjustment in Step 8.

9. Single carburetor—Bring engine speed back to 700-750 rpm and adjust low-speed needle to produce the highest rpm and smoothest operation.
10. Multiple carburetors—Bring engine speed back to 750-800 rpm and adjust the needles one at a time to produce the highest rpm and smoothest operation.
11. Single carburetor—Reinstall the adjustment knob or low-speed valve arm on its needle without disturbing the needle valve setting.
12. Multiple carburetors—Reconnect the linkage without disturbing the needle valve setting.
13. Run the engine in gear at idle and note the tachometer. If throttle cam and needle valve adjustments are correct, the engine should idle at 550 rpm (9.5 hp) or 650 rpm (all others) in gear.

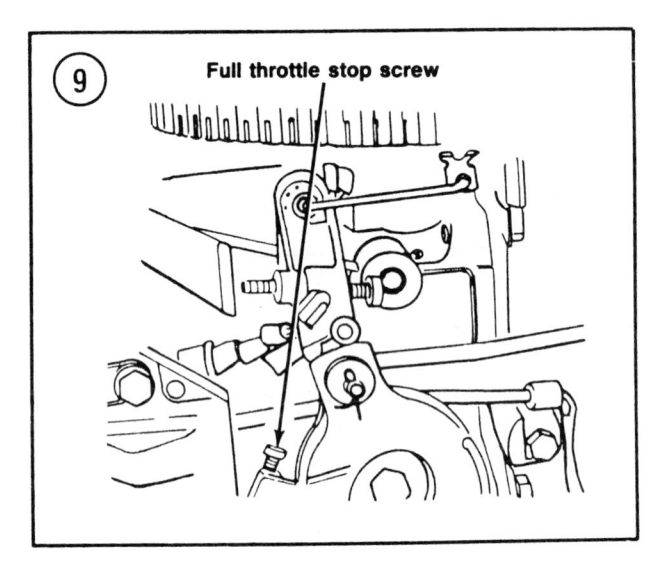

ENGINE SYCHRONIZATION AND LINKAGE ADJUSTMENTS

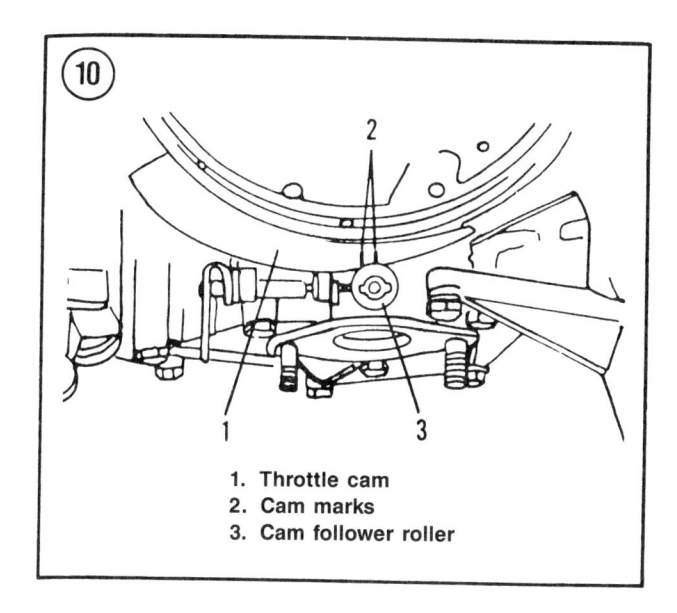

Figure 10
1. Throttle cam
2. Cam marks
3. Cam follower roller

Figure 11
- Throttle shaft arm
- Throttle shaft arm screw

3. Install the tool shown in **Figure 2** to the end of the throttle shaft opposite the cam follower linkage. Bend the tool wire 90° upward for easier viewing. See **Figure 3**.
4. Slowly rotate the throttle grip toward the ADVANCE position until the cam follower roller is centered between the 2 marks on the throttle cam. See **Figure 10** (typical).
5. If the throttle valve is not closed when the roller is centered between the cam marks in Step 4, use the adjustment method specified in **Table 1** as required:
   a. Method A—Loosen the throttle cam mounting screws. Adjust the cam position until the throttle valve is closed and there is no play in the linkage, then tighten the cam screws. The throttle valve should start to open after the edge of the roller passes the second cam mark. See **Figure 5** for typical cam screw location.
   b. Method D—Center the cam follower roller between the throttle cam marks. Loosen the throttle shaft arm screw. See **Figure 11** (typical). Hold the cam follower tightly against the cam and tighten the screw. The throttle valve should start to open as the edge of the roller passes the second cam mark.

Needle valve adjustment

1. Install the engine in a test tank with the proper test wheel or on the boat in the water with the correct propeller.
2. Turn the carburetor low-speed needle inward until it barely seats.
3. Back the low-speed needle out 1-2 turns.
4. Disconnect the low-speed valve arm from the needle.
5. Start the engine and run at half throttle until the engine reaches operating temperature.
6. Connect a tachometer according to manufacturer's instructions.

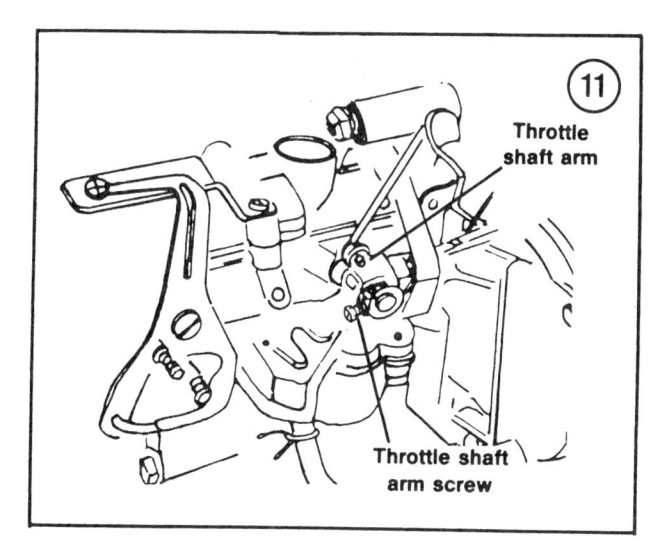

14. Shut the engine off; remove the test equipment and install the air silencer gasket and cover (if so equipped) and the engine cover.

Procedure 4

Engines adjusted with this procedure have their primary pickup located between the 2 throttle cam marks.

Throttle cam adjustment

1. Remove the engine cover.
2. Set the throttle grip to the STOP position.

NOTE
The engine requires approximately 15 seconds to respond to adjustment in Step 7.

7. Bring engine speed back to 700-750 rpm and adjust low-speed needle to produce the highest rpm and smoothest operation.
8. Reinstall the low-speed valve arm on the needle without disturbing the needle valve setting.
9. Run the engine in gear at idle and note the tachometer. Adjust the idle adjustment screw until the engine idles at 550-650 rpm in gear.
10. Shut the engine off; remove the test equipment and install the engine cover.

Procedure 5

Engines adjusted with this procedure have a fixed pointer on the intake manifold that must align with the throttle cam mark.

Throttle cam adjustment

1. Remove the engine cover.
2. Set the throttle grip to the STOP position.
3. Install the tool shown in **Figure 2** to the end of the throttle shaft opposite the cam follower linkage. Bend the tool wire 90° upward for easier viewing. See **Figure 3**.
4. Slowly rotate the throttle grip toward the ADVANCE position until the throttle cam mark aligns with the intake manifold projection. See **Figure 12** (typical).
5. If the throttle valve is not closed with the cam follower roller touching the cam when the cam mark is aligned with the manifold projection in Step 4, use the adjustment method specified in **Table 1** as required:
   a. Method A—Loosen the throttle cam mounting screws. Adjust the cam position until the throttle valve is closed and there is no play in the linkage, then tighten the cam screws. The throttle valve should start to open after the edge of the roller passes the manifold projection. See **Figure 5** for typical cam screw location.
   b. Method C—Loosen the throttle arm clamp screw. See **Figure 13** (typical). Align the cam mark with the manifold projection and make sure the throttle valve is closed. Turn the throttle shaft eccentric screw until the cam follower roller touches the cam, then tighten the clamp screw.
   b. Method D—Align the cam mark with the manifold projection and make sure the throttle valve is closed. Loosen the throttle shaft arm screw. See **Figure 14**

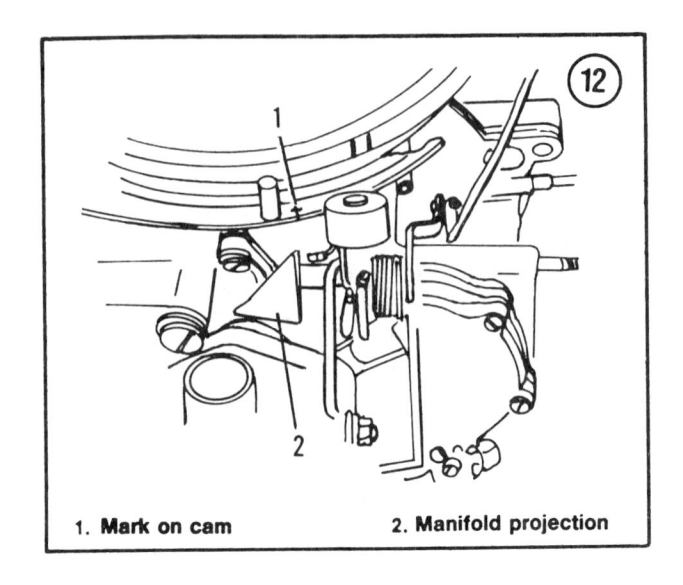

⑫
1. Mark on cam   2. Manifold projection

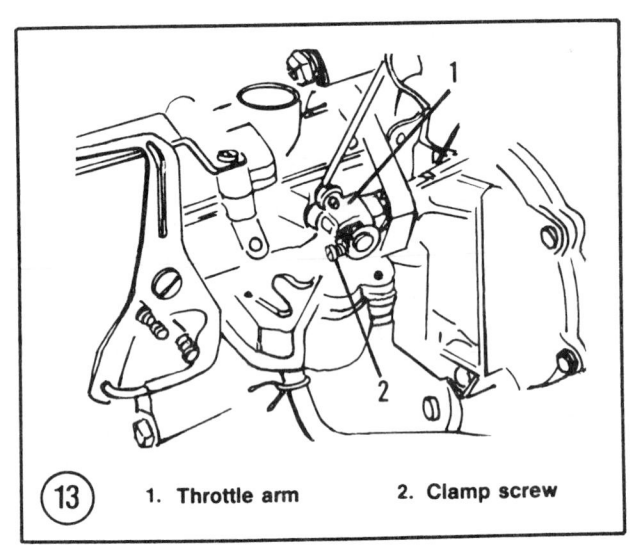

⑬
1. Throttle arm   2. Clamp screw

ENGINE SYCHRONIZATION AND LINKAGE ADJUSTMENTS

1. Cam adjustment screws
2. Cam mark
3. Cam follower roller

2. Turn the carburetor high- and low-speed needles inward until they barely seat.
3. Back the high-speed needle out 3/8 turn. Back the low-speed needle out 1 1/4 turns.
4. Remove the knob from each needle.
5. Start the engine and run at half throttle until the engine reaches operating temperature.
6. Connect a tachometer according to manufacturer's instructions. Run engine at full throttle and adjust the high-speed needle until the best high speed setting is obtained.

NOTE
The engine requires approximately 15 seconds to respond to adjustment in Step 7.

7. Bring engine speed back to 700-750 rpm and adjust low-speed needle to produce the highest rpm and smoothest operation.
8. Repeat Step 6 after the final low-speed adjustment has been made in Step 7.
9. Reinstall each adjustment knob on its needle without disturbing the needle valve setting.
10. Run the engine in gear at idle and note the tachometer. Adjust the idle screw until the engine idles at 650 rpm in gear.
11. Shut the engine off; remove the test equipment and install the engine cover.

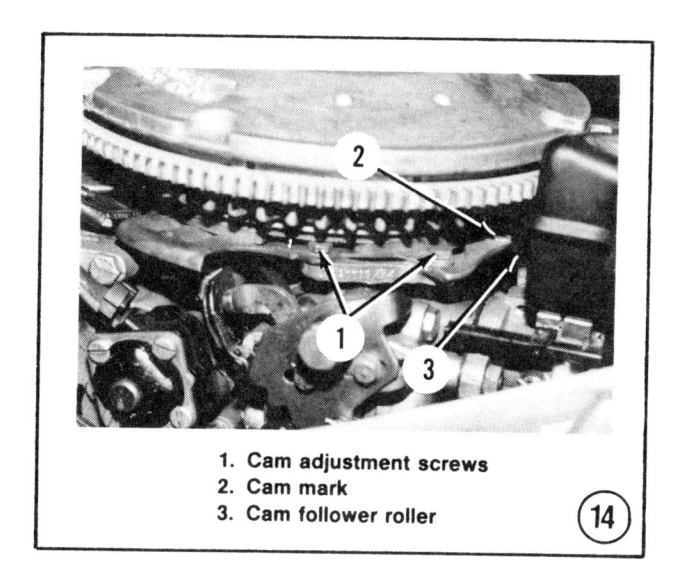

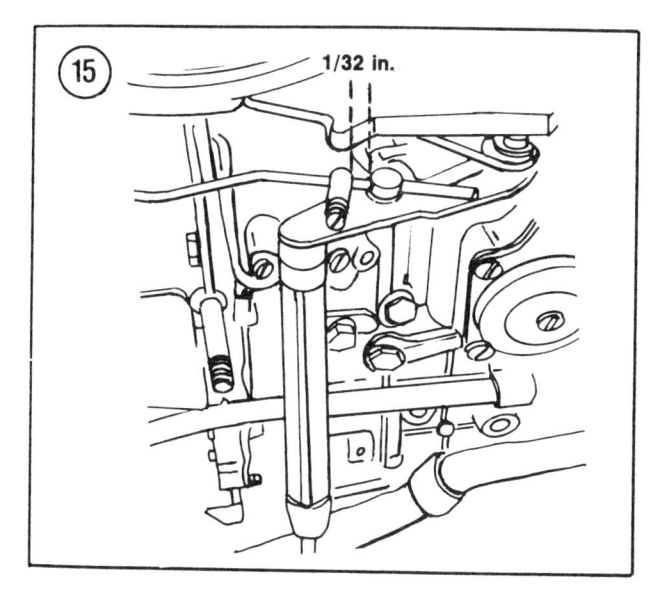

(typical). Position the cam follower roller against the cam and tighten the screw.

6. Manually rotate the armature base to its full spark position. Adjust the control rod collar to provide 1/32 in. clearance from the pivot pin. See **Figure 15** (typical).

Needle valve adjustment
(high- and low-speed needles)

1. Install the engine in a test tank with the proper test wheel or on the boat in the water with the correct propeller.

Needle valve adjustment
(low-speed needle only)

1. Install the engine in a test tank with the proper test wheel or on the boat in the water with the correct propeller.
2. Loosen the screw in the center of the low-speed needle adjusting knob. Pull the knob out until it will rotate past the stop at the left of the knob.
3. Turn the carburetor low-speed needle inward until it barely seats.
4. Back the low-speed needle out 7/8 turn.

5. Start the engine and run at half throttle until the engine reaches operating temperature.

6. Connect a tachometer according to manufacturer's instructions.

NOTE
The engine requires approximately 15 seconds to respond to adjustment in Step 7.

7. Bring engine speed back to 700-750 rpm in gear and adjust low-speed needle to produce the highest rpm and smoothest operation.

8. Reinstall the adjustment knob on its needle without disturbing the needle valve setting.

9. Run the engine in gear at idle and note the tachometer. Adjust the idle screw until the engine idles at 650 rpm in gear.

10. Shut the engine off; remove the test equipment and install the engine cover.

3- AND 4-CYLINDER ENGINES

Refer to **Table 2** at the end of the chapter for the appropriate tune-up data for your engine.

1958-1959 50 HP V4

Cam follower and linkage adjustment

1. Remove the engine cover.
2. Remove the spark plugs and ground the spark plug leads to prevent the engine from accidentally starting.
3. Rotate the flywheel clockwise until the timing marks on the rewind starter housing, flywheel and crankcase align. See A, **Figure 16** (typical).
4. Turn the speed control lever or grip until the timing marks on the distributor pulley, distributor housing and magneto support bracket align. See B, **Figure 16** (typical).
5. When all timing marks are properly aligned, loosen the spark link adjusting screw on the throttle cam (**Figure 17**). Disconnect the link from the cam.
6. Slowly rotate the throttle cam. As the throttle cam mark aligns with the center of the nylon cam roller, the cam roller should just start to open the throttle valve.
7. If the cam roller does not start to open the throttle valve in Step 6, loosen the adjustment screw under the cam roller enough to properly position the roller, then tighten the screw. See **Figure 18**.
8. Shift the engine into FORWARD gear while rotating the propeller to assure that it engages properly.

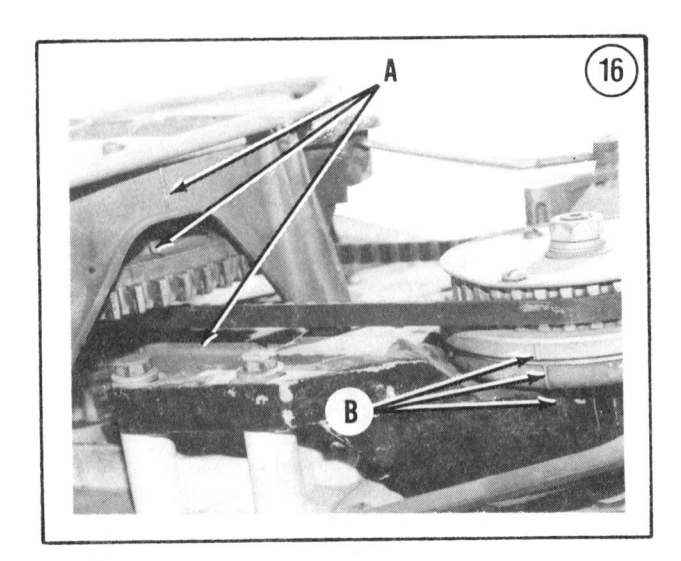

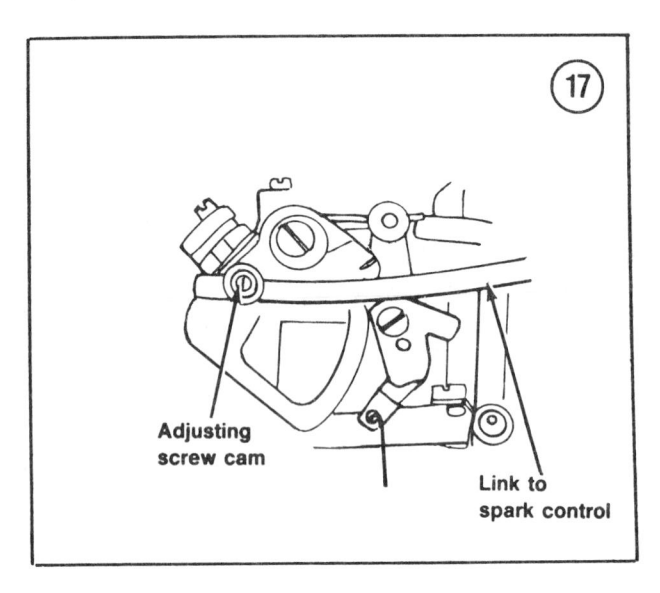

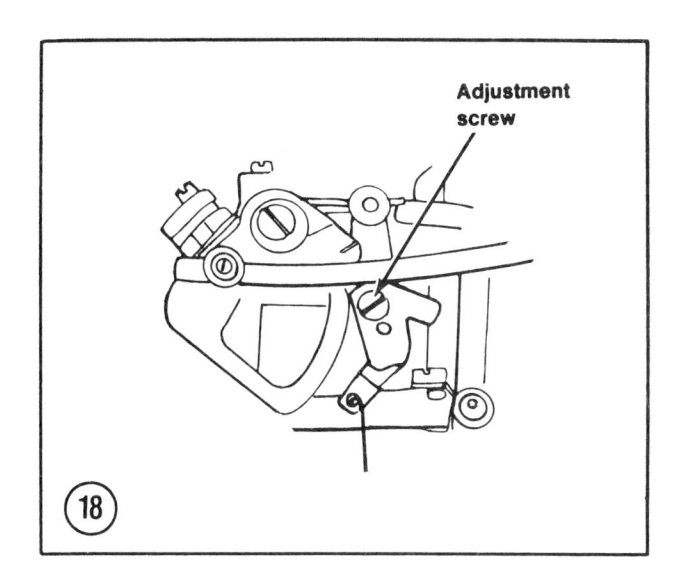

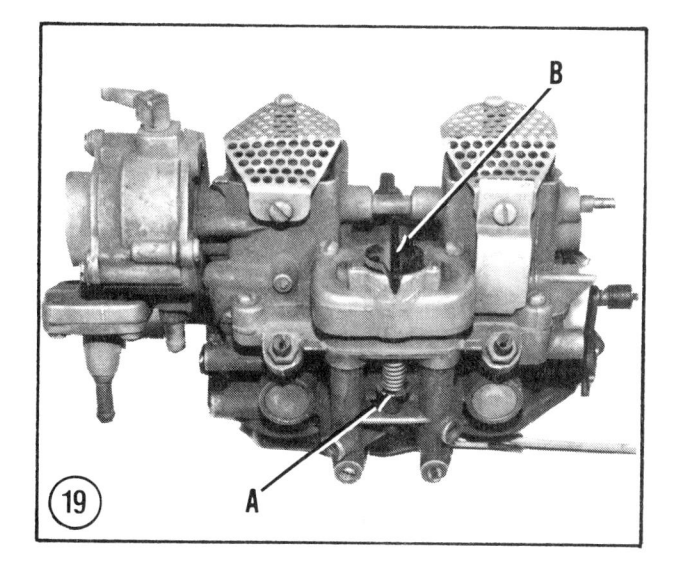

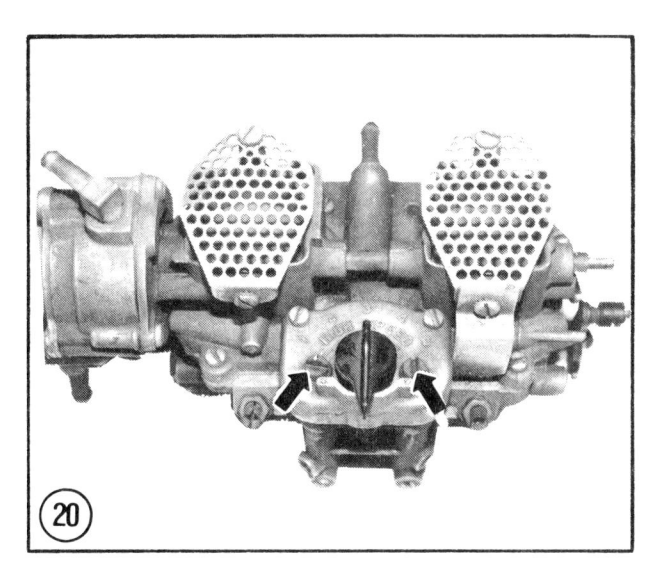

ENGINE SYCHRONIZATION AND LINKAGE ADJUSTMENTS

9. Rotate the magneto housing to its full advance position. Use a large rubber band or other appropriate device to hold the magneto in this position if an assistant is not available.
10. Measure the clearance between the throttle shaft arm and its stop with a flat feeler gauge. It should be 0.020 in. if adjustments are correctly made to this point.
11. Reinstall the spark control link to the throttle cam. Move the cam to its wide-open throttle position and tighten the adjusting screw.
12. Release the magneto housing and return it to the idle position.
13. Use the arm at the bottom of the tower shaft to rotate the shaft to a full advance position. Hold the tower shaft in this position.
14. If adjustments have been made correctly, the throttle cam, tower shaft arm and distributor should all rest against their respective stops. If not, repeat the procedure.

Carburetor adjustment

1. Install the engine in a test tank with the proper test wheel.
2. Lift the synchronizing lever (A, **Figure 19**) off its seat far enough to rotate the adjustment knob (B, **Figure 19**) 180°, disengaging the high-speed needle valve synchronizing gears.
3. Slowly turn each carburetor high-speed needle inwards until it lightly seats. See **Figure 20**.
4. Back each high-speed needle out approximately 5/8 turn.
5. Depress and hold the low-speed limiter cap while seating the needle valve as in Step 3, then back the needle valve out approximately 1 1/2 turns. See **Figure 21**. Repeat this step with the other low-speed limiter cap and needle valve.
6. Start the engine and run at half throttle until the engine reaches operating temperature (the tell-tale water stream will

increase noticeably when the thermostat opens).

7. Connect a tachometer according to manufacturer's instructions. Run engine at full throttle and alternately adjust the high-speed needles until the best high speed setting is obtained.

8. Bring engine speed back to a low idle rpm and alternately adjust the low-speed needles to produce the smoothest operation.

9. When low-speed needle balance is obtained, run engine at full throttle and repeat the adjustment in Step 7 to further balance the high-speed needles.

10. Set the throttle at its slow-running position and repeat the adjustment in Step 8 to further balance the low-speed needles.

11. Repeat the sequence in Steps 7-10 as often as necessary until maximum performance is obtained throughout the range from slow to high speed without hesitation.

12. Once the adjustments are completed, shut the engine off. Lift the synchronizing lever, rotate the adjustment knob 180° and re-engage the synchronizing gears. The lever index or pointer end should fall at a midpoint (position No. 3) between the adjustment limits. See **Figure 22**.

13. Reposition each low-speed needle limiter cap so that its pointer falls at the midpoint between the adjustment limits.

14. Remove the test equipment. Reinstall the engine cover.

1960-1966 60-100 HP V4; 1967 60 and 80 HP V4

This section covers both magneto and battery ignition models during a transitional period when both types of ignitions were used in some model years. Although the adjustment procedures are virtually identical for both ignition systems, the changeover from magneto to battery ignition required design modifications that resulted in the relocation of some timing marks. Where confusion might exist, such changes are noted.

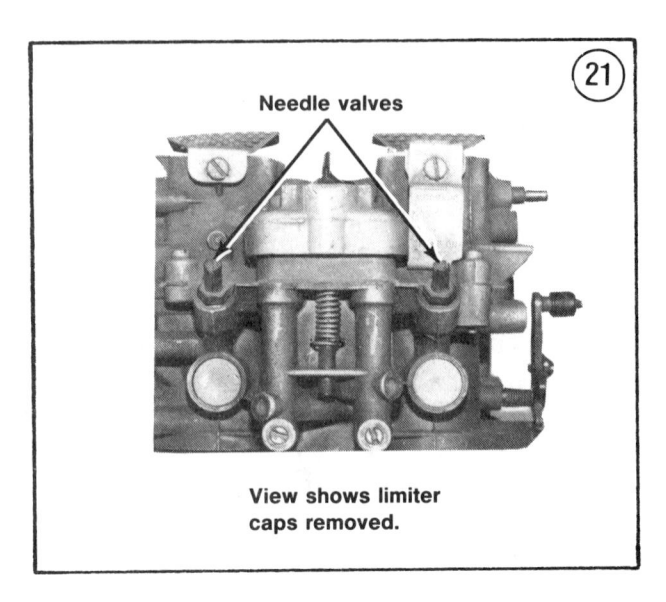

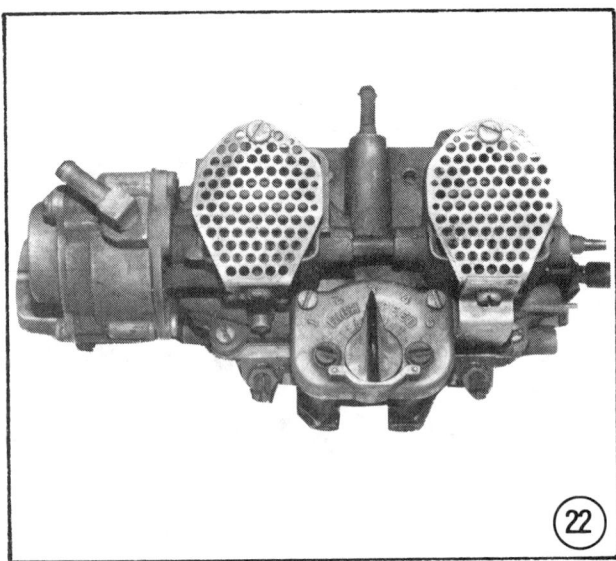

Belt timing (magneto ignition)

1. Remove the engine cover.
2. Remove the spark plugs and ground the spark plug leads to prevent the engine from accidentally starting.
3. Rotate the flywheel clockwise until the timing marks on the rewind starter housing, flywheel and crankcase align. See A, **Figure**

ENGINE SYCHRONIZATION AND LINKAGE ADJUSTMENT

Belt timing (battery ignition)

1. Remove the engine cover.
2. Remove the spark plugs and ground the spark plug leads to prevent the engine from accidentally starting.
3. Rotate the flywheel clockwise until the timing mark on the flywheel rim aligns with the embossed belt timing mark on the water jacket cover.
4. Loosen all distributor bracket bolts. Move bracket toward crankshaft and tighten one bolt. This reduces drive belt tension.
5. Rotate the distributor pulley until its timing mark aligns with the distributor bracket timing mark.
6. Hold the pulley and bracket timing marks in alignment. Loosen the bracket bolt and adjust distributor position to provide proper belt tension. The belt should deflect 5/16-3/8 in. under approximately one pound of pressure.
7. Tighten bracket bolts securely.

Cam follower and linkage synchronization

1. Remove the engine cover.
2. Remove the spark plugs and ground the spark plug leads to prevent the engine from accidentally starting.
3. Shift the engine into FORWARD gear while rotating the propeller to assure that it engages properly.
4. Disconnect the remote control cable, if so equipped at the engine.
5. Rotate the magneto or distributor housing to its full advance position until it rests against the stop. Use a large rubber band or other appropriate device to hold the magneto or distributor in this position if an assistant is not available.
6. Viewed from the top, the triangular boss cast in the cylinder block should align with the inside of the control linkage. **Figure 25** shows the alignment points in a rest position

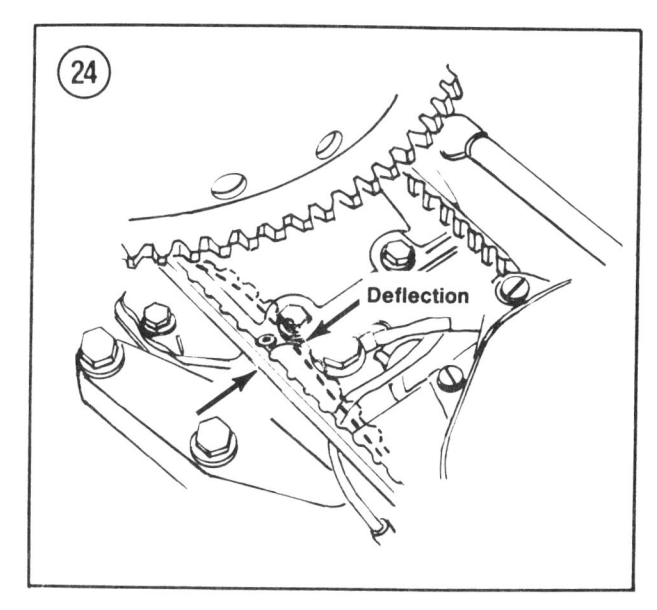

16 (typical). At this point, the magneto pulley timing marks should align with the safety switch plunger. See **Figure 23** (typical).
4. If the marks do not align, loosen the magneto bracket screws and release the belt tension, then rotate the pulley until the marks align as specified.
5. Adjust bracket position to provide proper belt tension. The belt should deflect 5/16-3/8 in. under approximately one pound of pressure. See **Figure 24**.
6. Tighten bracket screws securely.

for identification purposes; **Figure 26** shows their proper alignment.

7. If the linkage and triangular boss do not align when the magneto or distributor housing are held in the position described in Step 5, loosen the 2 linkage screws. See **Figure 27** (typical). Adjust the linkage length as required to obtain proper alignment as shown in **Figure 26**, then tighten the screws securely.

NOTE
The throttle control rod may be attached in different ways. Some engines use a single setscrew; others use inner/outer locking setscrews. The outer setscrew is removed completely, then the inner one is loosened enough to remove the rod. Other engines use a nylon yoke and link pin to hold the rod to the throttle cam.

8. Disconnect the throttle control rod at the throttle cam. See **Figure 28** (typical).

NOTE
The throttle cam is located on top of 90 hp engines and on the port side of all others.

9. Slowly rotate the throttle cam to align its mark with the center of the nylon cam roller. Loosen the clamp screw under the cam roller and move the throttle arm as required to close the throttle valves with the roller touching the cam. Retighten the screw. See **Figure 28** (port location) or **Figure 29** (top location).

10. Reinstall the throttle rod to the throttle cam but do not tighten setscrew(s) or install link pin.

NOTE
Step 11 and Step 12 apply only to 60, 75 and 80 hp engines.

11. Move the throttle lever to its wide-open position and insert a 0.020 in. flat feeler gauge

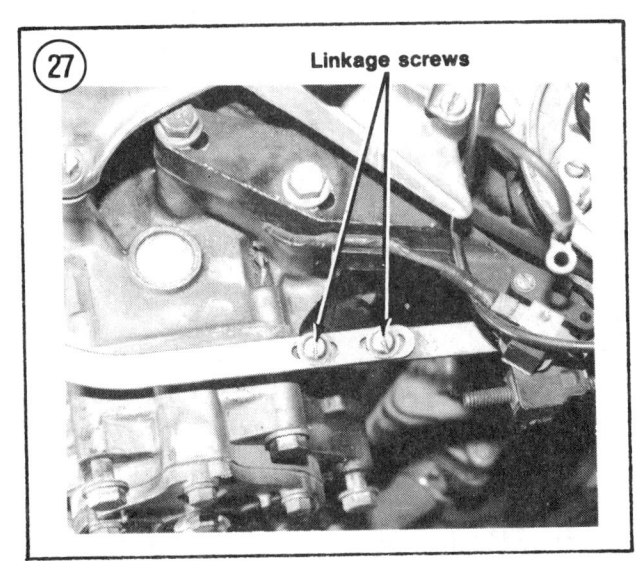

ENGINE SYCHRONIZATION AND LINKAGE ADJUSTMENT

Figure 28 — Set and lock screws; Clamp screw

Figure 29 — Adjustment screw

Figure 30 — Throttle shaft arm; Stop

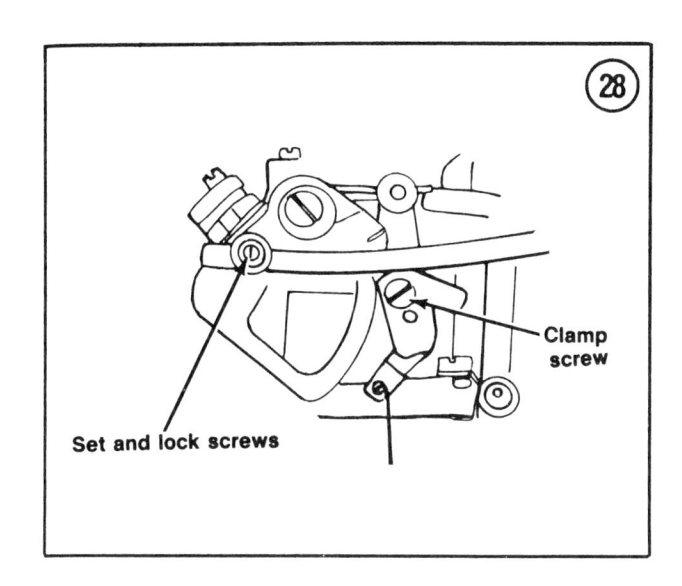

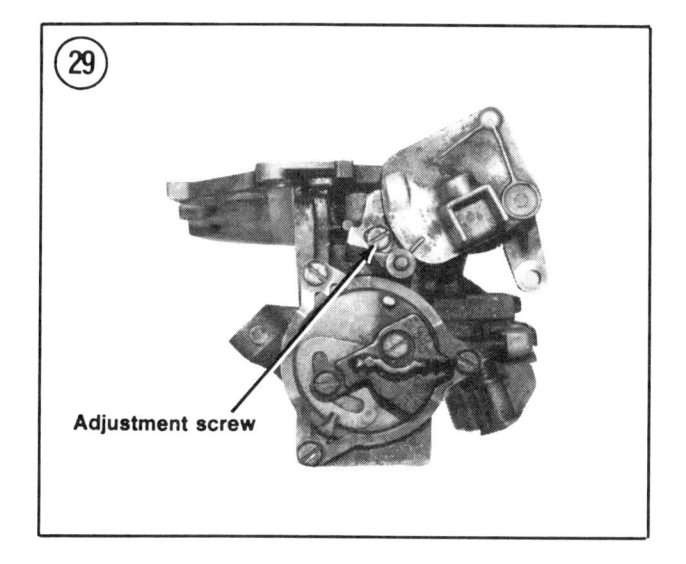

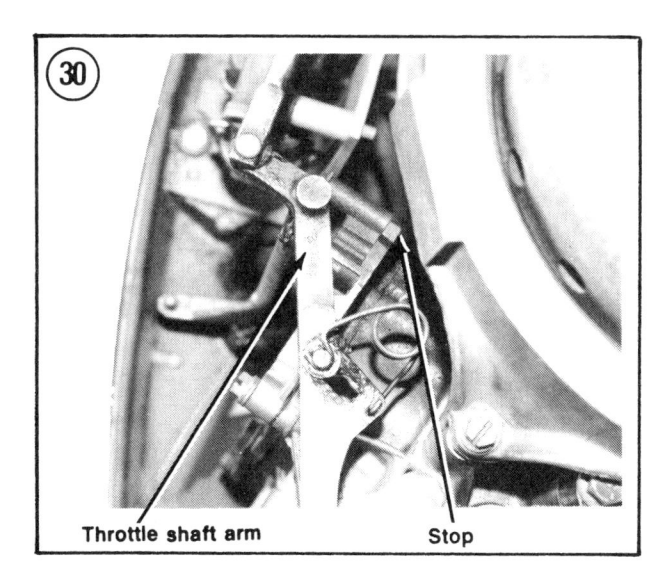

between the throttle shaft arm and its stop. See **Figure 30**.

12. Move the throttle cam to its wide-open throttle position and tighten the setscrew(s) or install the link pin. Remove the feeler gauge.
13. Release the magneto or distributor housing and return it to the idle position.
14. Use the arm at the bottom of the tower shaft to rotate the shaft to a full advance position. Hold the tower shaft in this position.
15. If adjustments have been made correctly, the throttle cam, tower shaft arm and magneto or distributor housing should all rest against their respective stops.

Carburetor Adjustment
(1964-1965 60 HP)

See *1958-1959 50 HP V4* in this chapter.

Carburetor Adjustment
(1966-1967 60 HP, 1960-1965 75 HP and 1966-1967 80 HP)

Some carburetors installed on these engines may be equipped with fixed high-speed jets instead of adjustable needle valves. Omit the high-speed adjustment steps if your carburetors do not have adjustable needle valves. Refer to **Figure 31** for this procedure.

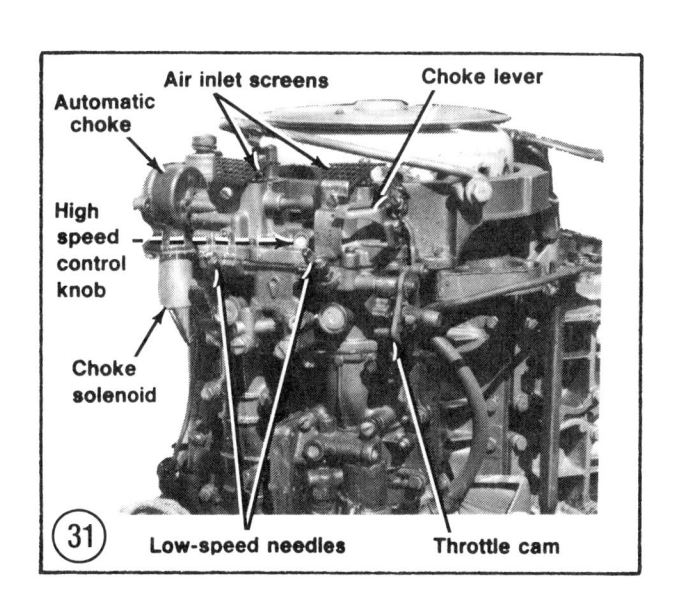

Figure 31 — Automatic choke; Air inlet screens; Choke lever; High speed control knob; Choke solenoid; Low-speed needles; Throttle cam

1. Install the engine in a test tank with the proper test wheel.
2. Remove the low-speed adjusting knob from each needle. Reinstall knobs upside-down on needles to clear adjustment stops. Gently seat each needle valve, then back out approximately 1 1/4 turns.
3. Lift the high-speed control knob and rotate 180° until pointer rests on control gear cover.
4. Turn each high-speed needle valve inwards until it barely seats, then back each one out approximately 3/4 turn.
5. Start the engine and run at half throttle until the engine reaches operating temperature (the tell-tale water stream will increase noticeably when the thermostat opens).
6. Connect a tachometer according to manufacturer's instructions. Run engine at full throttle and turn one high-speed needle clockwise until the engine starts to slow down, then rotate the needle counterclockwise 2 notches. Repeat this step to adjust the other high-speed needle valve.
7. Bring engine speed back to a fast idle (800 rpm) and turn one low-speed needle clockwise until the engine spits or hesitates slightly, then rotate the needle counterclockwise until the highest rpm and smoothest performance are obtained. Repeat this step to adjust the other low-speed needle valve.
8. When low-speed needle balance is obtained, run engine at full throttle and repeat the adjustment in Step 6 to further balance the high-speed needles.
9. Set the throttle at its fast idle position and repeat the adjustment in Step 7 to further balance the low-speed needles.
10. Repeat the sequence in Steps 6-9 as often as necessary until maximum performance is obtained throughout the range from slow to high speed without hesitation. Final adjustments should always be made with the high-speed needles.
11. Adjust the idle speed screws to obtain an idle speed of 600-650 rpm in gear.
12. Once the adjustments are completed, shut the engine off. Return the high-speed control knob to its original position.
13. Reinstall each low-speed needle knob correctly without disturbing the needle valve adjustment.
14. Remove the test equipment. Reinstall the engine cover.

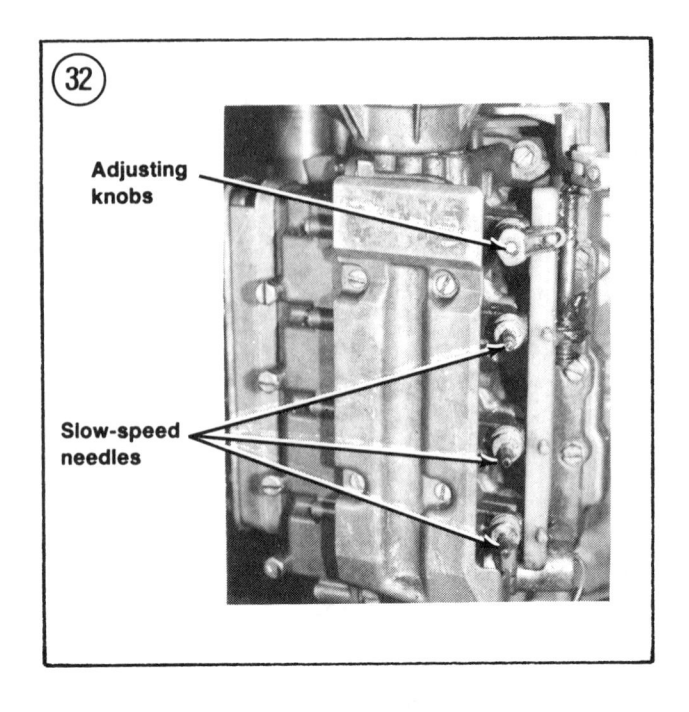

Carburetor Adjustment
(1963-1964 90 HP and 1966-1967 100 HP)

Refer to **Figure 32** for this procedure.
1. Install the engine in a test tank with the proper test wheel.
2. Move the low-speed control knob link arm to its leanest (lowest) position. Remove all 4 nylon knobs.
3. Gently seat each needle valve, then back it out approximately 3/4 turn.
4. Start the engine and run at half throttle in gear until the engine reaches operating temperature (the tell-tale water stream will

ENGINE SYCHRONIZATION AND LINKAGE ADJUSTMENT

7. When low-speed needle balance is obtained, engine speed should be approximately 2,000-2,200 rpm. Increase engine speed to 3,500-4,000 rpm to clear the crankcase and cylinders, then return it to 1,500 rpm and repeat Step 6.

8. Repeat the sequence in Step 6 and Step 7 as often as necessary until the highest rpm is obtained.

9. Make sure the link arm is in its extreme downward (leanest) position and install the nylon knobs on each needle without disturbing the setting of any needle valve.

10. Once the knobs are installed, lift the bar until all knobs are horizontal. This will enrich the needle valve setting by approximately 1/8 turn.

11. Adjust the idle speed screw to obtain an idle speed of 650 rpm in gear.

12. Once the adjustments are completed, shut the engine off. Remove the test equipment. Reinstall the engine cover.

1967 100 HP V4

This model uses a breakerless distributor CD ignition.

Belt timing

1. Remove the engine cover.
2. Remove the spark plugs and ground the spark plug leads to prevent the engine from accidentally starting.
3. Rotate the flywheel clockwise until the timing mark on the flywheel rim aligns with the embossed belt timing mark on the ring gear cover (**Figure 33**) or cylinder block (**Figure 34**).
4. Loosen all distributor bracket bolts. Move bracket toward crankshaft and tighten one bolt. This reduces drive belt tension.
5. Rotate the distributor pulley until its timing mark aligns with the distributor bracket timing mark (**Figure 35**).

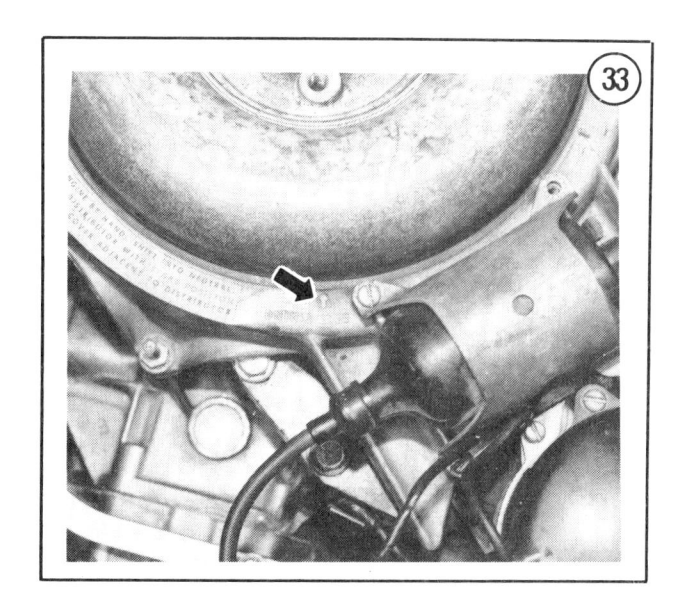

increase noticeably when the thermostat opens).

5. Connect a tachometer according to manufacturer's instructions. Increase engine speed to full throttle to clear the crankcase and cylinders, then return it to 1,500 rpm in gear.

6. Turn the top low-speed needle counterclockwise until the highest rpm is obtained. Repeat this step to adjust the other needle valves from top to bottom, waiting approximately 15 seconds between adjustments for the engine to respond.

6. Hold the pulley and bracket timing marks in alignment. Loosen the bracket bolt and adjust distributor position to provide proper belt tension. The belt should deflect 1/4-3/8 in. under approximately one pound of pressure. See **Figure 36**.
7. Tighten bracket bolts securely.

Cam follower and linkage synchronization

See *1960-1966 60-100 HP V4; 1967 60 and 80 HP V4* in this chapter.

Engine timing

Engine timing should not change under normal operating conditions. It should be checked, however, when the electronic pack has been replaced or when the adjustment screw seal is broken.

1. Install the engine in a test tank with the proper test wheel.
2. Connect a tachometer and timing light according to manufacturer's instructions.
3. Start the engine and run at half throttle until the engine reaches operating temperature (the tell-tale water stream will increase noticeably when the thermostat opens).
4. Bring engine speed back to 500 rpm. Point the timing light at the distributor housing. The timing marks on the housing and distributor pulley must align. There is no adjustment possible.
5. If the timing marks do not align in Step 4, shut the engine off and locate the problem. It is most likely a missing or damaged Woodruff key allowing the pulley or trigger wheel to move. It might also be an improperly mounted sensor. Correct the problem before proceeding.
6. With the engine running at 4,500 rpm in gear, point the timing light at the ring gear timing mark. If the engine has 2 ring gear timing marks (front and rear) as shown in **Figure 37**, use the rear timing mark with the

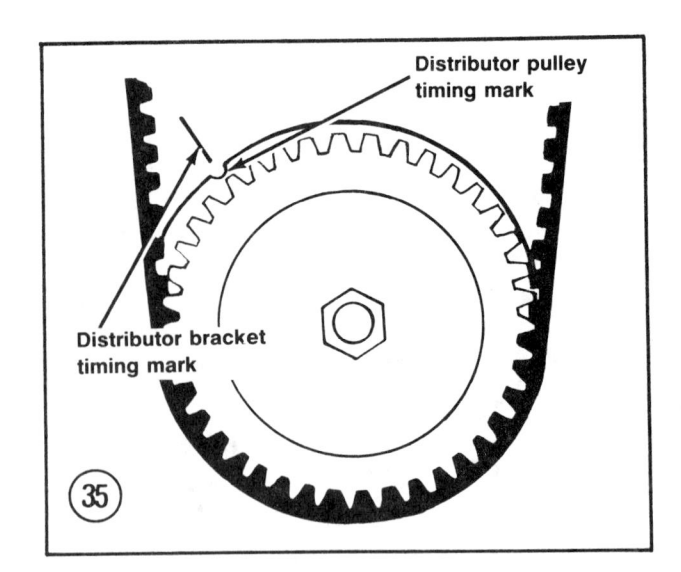

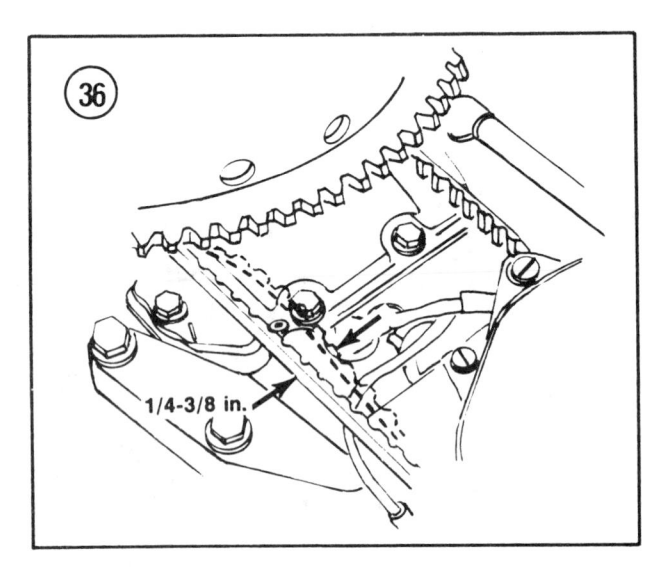

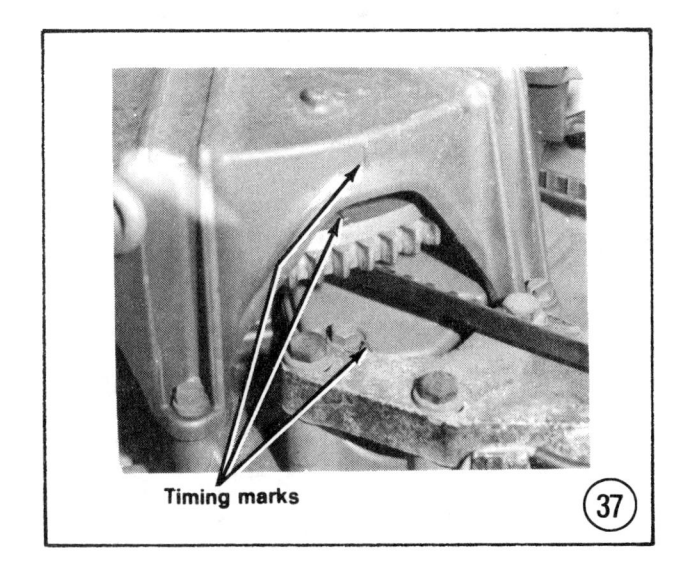

ENGINE SYCHRONIZATION AND LINKAGE ADJUSTMENT

(38) Sealed adjustment screw

(39) UPPER CARBURETOR LINKAGE ADJUSTMENT

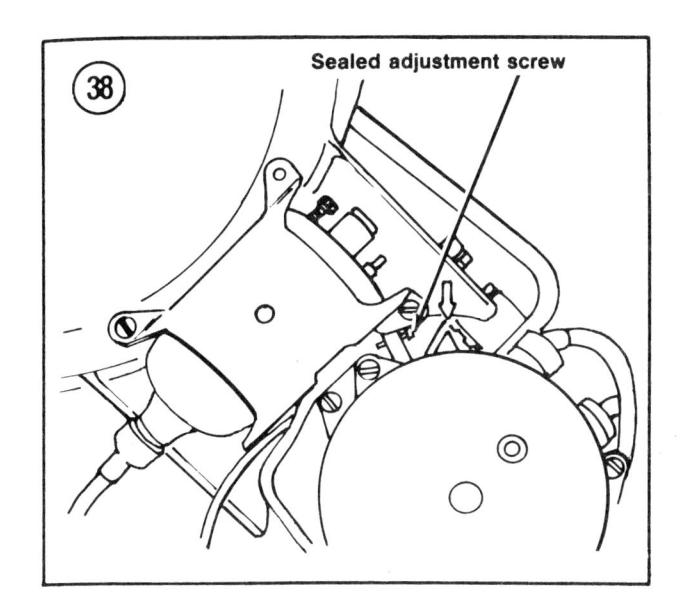

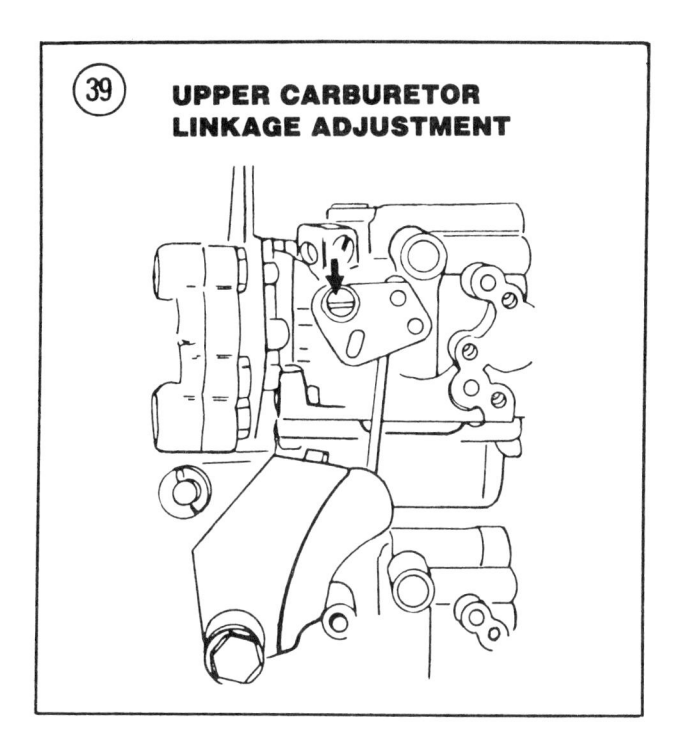

timing light connected to the No. 1 cylinder (to use the front timing mark, the light must be connected to the No. 3 cylinder).
7. If the timing marks do not align, loosen the sealed adjustment screw locknut and adjust the screw (**Figure 38**) as required to bring the marks into alignment.
8. Shut the engine off and remove the test equipment.

Carburetor adjustment

See *Carburetor Adjustment (1966-1967 60 HP, 1960-1965 75 HP and 1966-1967 80 HP)* in this chapter.

1968-1969 55 HP; 1970-1971 60 HP

Throttle valve synchronization

1. Remove the engine cover.
2. Remove the spark plugs and ground the spark plug leads to prevent accidental starting of the engine.
3. Remove the low-speed adjustment lever. Remove the air silencer cover.
4. Retard the throttle lever to a point where the throttle cam roller does not touch the cam.
5. Loosen the upper carburetor lever adjustment screw (**Figure 39**).
6. Rotate the throttle shaft partially open, then let it snap back to the closed position. Apply finger pressure to the lever (**Figure 39**) and tighten the adjustment screw.
7. Move the cam follower while watching the throttle valves. If the throttle valves do not start to move at the same time, repeat Steps 4-6.

Choke valve synchronization

1. Loosen the choke link fastener screw.
2. Close the chokes by applying finger pressure on the upper and lower choke shaft levers, then tighten the choke link screw.
3. Make sure manual choke lever is in the OFF position.
4. Loosen the choke solenoid bracket screws. Move the solenoid as required to obtain 1/4 in. clearance as shown in **Figure 40**, then tighten the bracket screws.

Throttle cam adjustment

1. Connect a throttle shaft amplifier tool (**Figure 2**) to the top carburetor throttle shaft.

2. Watching the amplifier tool, slowly rotate the throttle cam. As the end of the tool starts to move, check the cam and cam follower alignment. The embossed or scribed mark on the cam should align with the center of the cam follower roller. See **Figure 41**.

3. If the roller and cam mark do not align in Step 2, loosen the center carburetor throttle arm screw (**Figure 41**). Align the throttle cam mark with the center of the roller. Move the carburetor throttle arm until the throttle valves are closed. Depress the cam follower lever to maintain the alignment and tighten the throttle arm screw.

4. Repeat Step 2 to check the adjustment. If incorrect, repeat Step 3, then repeat Step 2 as required.

Linkage synchronization

If the engine is being reassembled and the yoke has been removed from the throttle control rod, reinstall yoke on rod and adjust it to provide a distance of 4 31/32 in. from the end of the rod to the face of the yoke.

NOTE
Steps 1-3 apply to models with timing grid on ring gear guard.

1. Move the distributor base and throttle lever against their full throttle stops.

2. If the carburetor throttle shaft does not rest against its full throttle stop, disconnect the throttle cam yoke, loosen the throttle control rod locknut and adjust the yoke position on the control rod as required to properly position the throttle shaft. See **Figure 42** (typical).

3. Reconnect the throttle cam yoke and tighten the locknut securely. Repeat Step 1 and recheck throttle shaft and stop relation.

NOTE
Steps 4-9 apply to models with timing grid on flywheel.

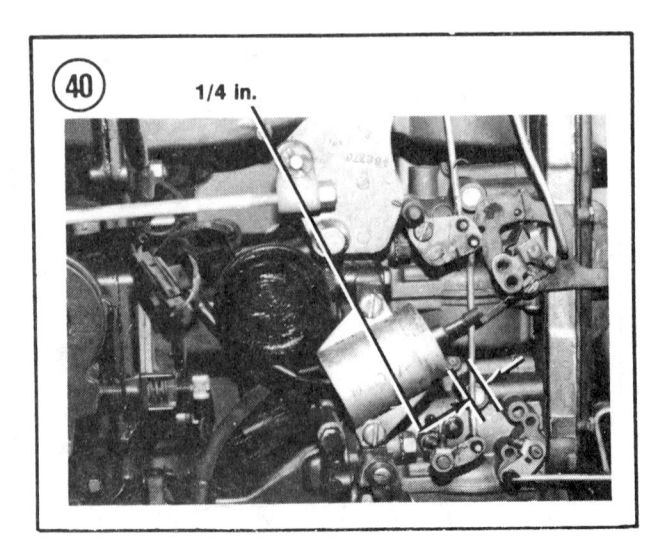

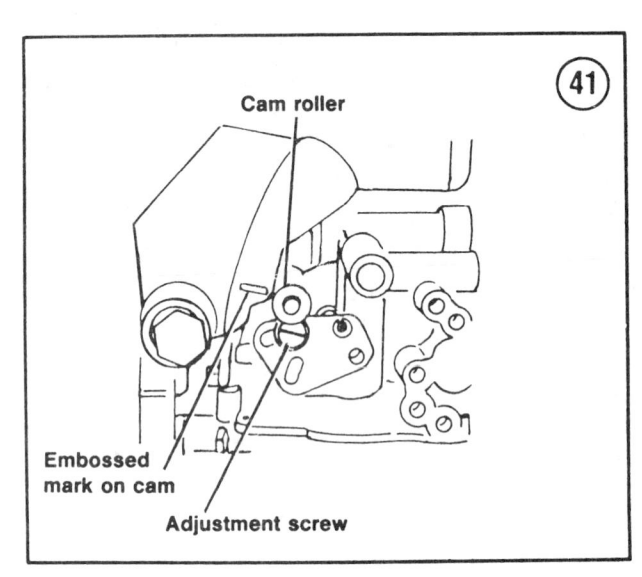

4. Connect a timing light to the No. 1 cylinder according to manufacturer's instructions.

5. Start the engine and adjust the idle speed screw (**Figure 43**) until the 2° ATDC mark on the flywheel aligns with the timing pointer.

6. Shut the engine off. Hold the throttle lever against the idle stop screw. The embossed mark on the throttle cam should align with the center of the cam follower roller.

7. If the roller and cam mark do not align in Step 3, disconnect the throttle cam yoke, loosen the throttle control rod locknut and adjust the yoke position on the control rod as

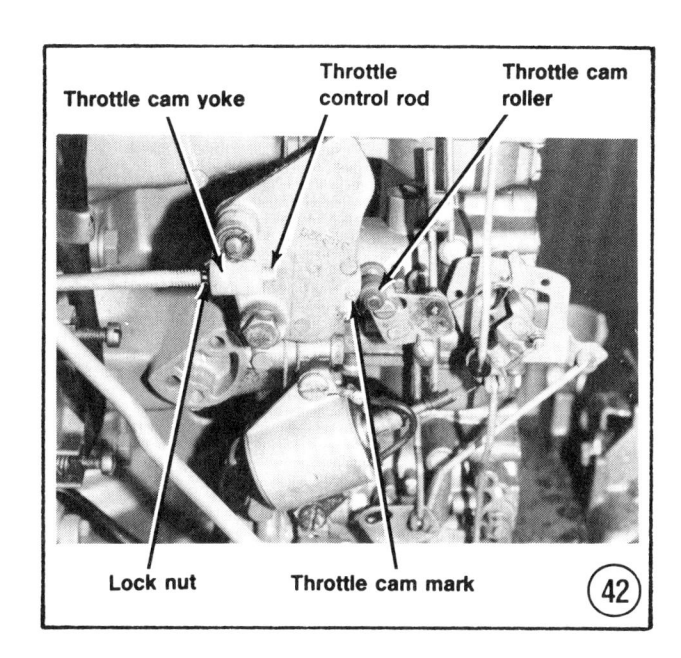

ENGINE SYCHRONIZATION AND LINKAGE ADJUSTMENT

Figure 42: Throttle cam yoke, Throttle control rod, Throttle cam roller, Lock nut, Throttle cam mark

Figure 43: Wide open throttle adjustment screw, Cam, Cam mark, Throttle cam yoke, Idle speed adjustment screw

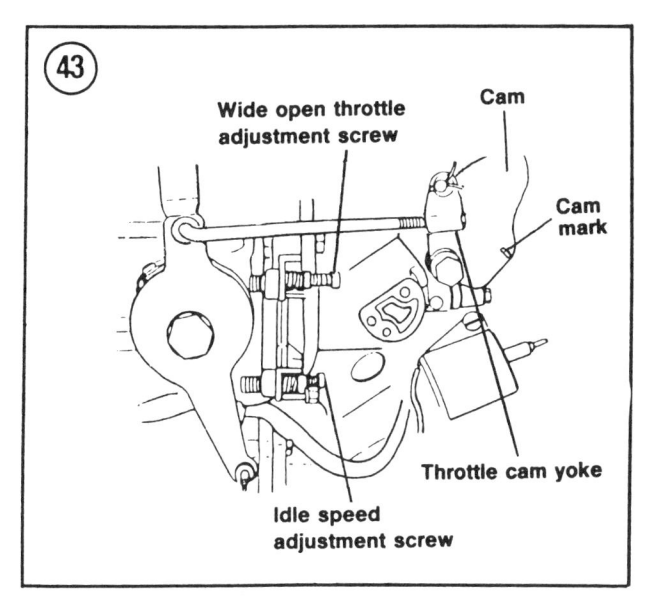

required to properly align the roller and mark. See **Figure 42** (typical).

8. Reconnect the throttle cam yoke and tighten the locknut securely.

9. Move the throttle lever to its full advance position. If the throttle valves are not fully open, adjust the wide open throttle stop screw as required.

10. Start the engine and adjust the idle speed screw as required to obtain an engine speed of 650 rpm in gear.

Maximum spark advance

CAUTION
This procedure should be performed in a test tank with the proper test wheel installed on the engine. The use of the propeller and/or a flushing device can result in an incorrect setting and possible engine damage.

1. Install the engine in a test tank with the proper test wheel.
2. Connect a timing light and tachometer according to manufacturer's instructions.
3. Start the engine and run at 500-600 rpm until the engine reaches operating temperature (the tell-tale water stream will increase noticeably when the thermostat opens).

NOTE
On some engines, the timing marks are reversed, with the timing mark on the flywheel and the timing grid on the ring gear guard.

4. Increase engine speed to 4,500 rpm. Check the timing mark position with the timing light. The specified mark on the flywheel grid should align with the timing mark on the ring gear guard.

WARNING
Do not attempt to adjust the spark advance with the engine running in Step 5. The adjustment screw is located close to or under the moving flywheel and vibrates slightly when the engine is running. If the screwdriver slips out of the screw, serious personal injury can result.

5. If the timing marks do not align as specified, shut the engine off and loosen the adjusting screw locknut (**Figure 44**). Adjust the screw clockwise to retard or counterclockwise to advance timing as required, then tighten the locknut. One full turn in either direction changes timing approximately one degree.

6. Restart the engine and repeat Step 4. If timing mark alignment is still incorrect, repeat Step 5, then Step 3 and Step 4 as required.

Carburetor adjustment

1. Install the engine in a test tank with the proper test wheel.
2. With the low-speed lever and air silencer cover removed, disconnect the low-speed needle valve linkage and remove the needle valve adjustment levers.
3. Turn each low-speed needle valve inwards until it barely seats, then back each one out approximately 5/8 turn (55 HP) or 3/4 turn (60 HP).
4. Start the engine and run at half throttle until the engine reaches operating temperature (the tell-tale water stream will increase noticeably when the thermostat opens).
5. Connect a tachometer according to manufacturer's instructions.
6A. 55 HP—Run engine at 700-750 rpm and alternately adjust the low-speed needles to obtain the highest rpm and smoothest performance, waiting approximately 15 seconds between adjustments for the engine to respond.
6B. 60 HP—Run engine at 650-700 rpm and alternately adjust the No. 2 and No. 3 carburetors to obtain the highest rpm and smoothest performance, waiting approximately 15 seconds between adjustments for the engine to respond. Increase engine speed to 1,000-1,200 rpm and adjust the No. 1 carburetor.
7. Reinstall the needle valve adjustment levers pointing to the starboard side of the engine without disturbing the needle valve setting. Reconnect the linkage to the levers.
8. Adjust the idle speed screw to obtain an engine speed of 600-650 rpm (55 HP) or 650 rpm (60 HP) in gear.

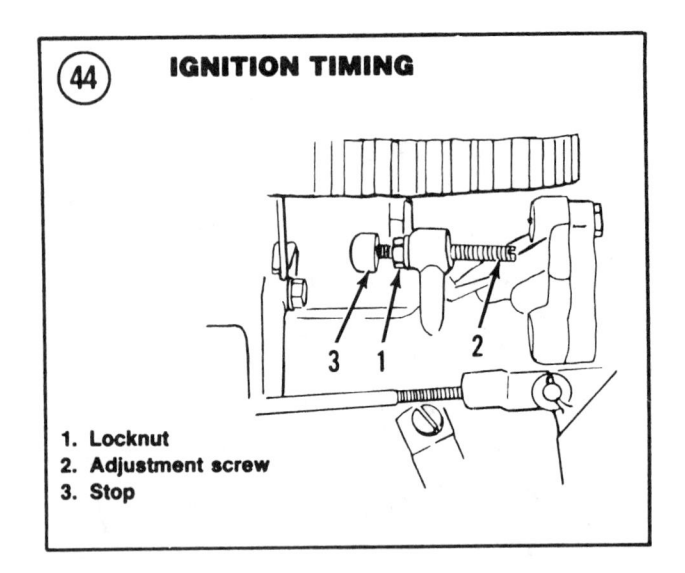

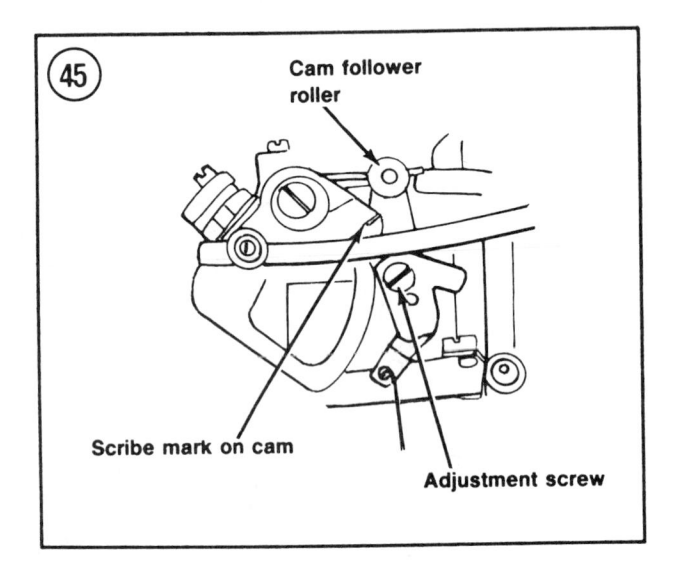

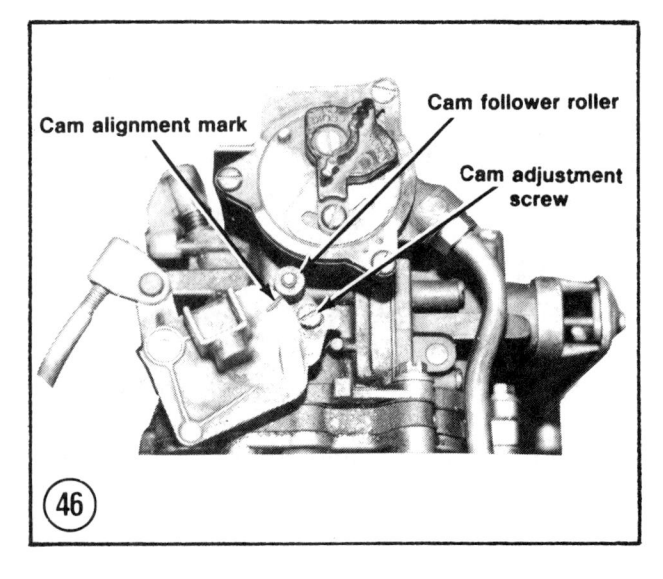

44 IGNITION TIMING

1. Locknut
2. Adjustment screw
3. Stop

45

Cam follower roller
Scribe mark on cam
Adjustment screw

46

Cam alignment mark
Cam follower roller
Cam adjustment screw

ENGINE SYCHRONIZATION AND LINKAGE ADJUSTMENT

47 Control shaft — Full throttle stop

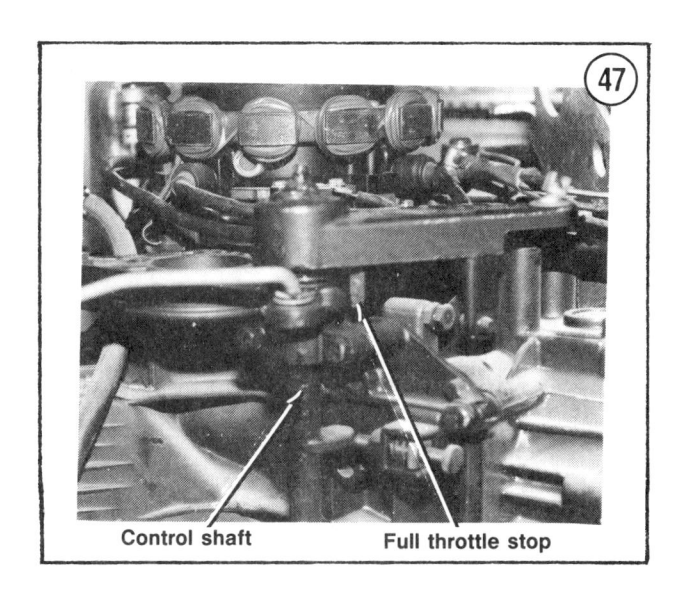

48 Timing marks

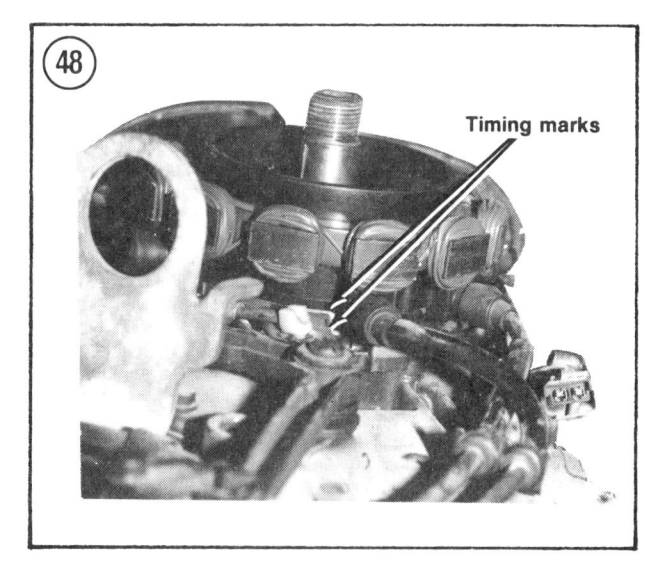

49 Throttle cam follower, Throttle cam yoke, Throttle shaft arm stop, Throttle cam, Throttle shaft arm

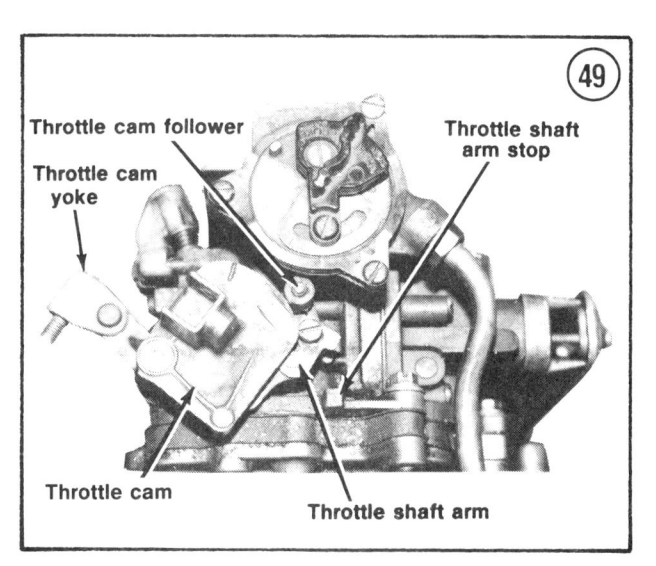

1968 65, 85 and 100 HP

Throttle cam adjustment

1. Connect a throttle shaft amplifier tool (**Figure 2**) to the top carburetor throttle shaft.
2. Watching the amplifier tool, slowly rotate the throttle cam. As the end of the tool starts to move, check the cam and cam follower alignment. The embossed or scribed mark on the cam should align with the center of the cam follower roller. See **Figure 45** (65 and 85 hp) or **Figure 46** (100 hp).
3. If the roller and cam mark do not align in Step 2, loosen the adjustment screw (**Figure 45** or **Figure 46**). Align the throttle cam mark with the center of the roller. Move the carburetor throttle arm until the throttle valves are closed. Depress the cam follower lever to maintain the alignment and tighten the throttle arm screw.
4. Repeat Step 2 to check the adjustment. If incorrect, repeat Step 3, then repeat Step 2 as required.

Linkage synchronization

If the engine is being reassembled and the yoke has been removed from the throttle control rod, reinstall yoke on rod and adjust it until the throttle shaft arm rests against its stop when the control shaft is in its full throttle position. See **Figure 47** (typical).

1. Move the distributor base against its full throttle stop to align the base plate arm and distributor cap marks. See **Figure 48** (typical). The throttle cam mark should intersect the center of the cam follower roller just as the roller contacts the cam.
2. Move the control shaft to its full throttle position (against its stop). The carburetor throttle shaft arm should also rest against its full throttle stop. See **Figure 49** (typical). If it does not, disconnect the throttle cam yoke, loosen the throttle control rod locknut and adjust the yoke position on the control rod as

required to properly position the throttle shaft. See **Figure 45** (65 and 85 hp) or **Figure 49** (100 hp).
3. Reconnect the throttle cam yoke and tighten the locknut securely. Repeat Step 1 and recheck throttle shaft and stop relation.

Maximum spark advance

CAUTION
This procedure should be performed in a test tank with the proper test wheel installed on the engine. The use of the propeller and/or a flushing device can result in an incorrect setting and possible engine damage.

1. Install the engine in a test tank with the proper test wheel.
2. Connect a timing light and tachometer according to manufacturer's instructions.
3. Start the engine and run at half-throttle in gear until the engine reaches operating temperature (the tell-tale water stream will increase noticeably when the thermostat opens).

NOTE
The flywheel has 2 timing marks. Use the straight mark for Step 4.

4. Increase engine speed to full throttle. Check the timing mark position with the timing light. The specified mark on the flywheel should align with the square timing mark on the lift bracket.

WARNING
Do not attempt to adjust the spark advance with the engine running in Step 5. The adjustment screw is located close to or under the moving flywheel and vibrates slightly when the engine is running. If the screwdriver slips out of the screw, serious personal injury can result.

5. If the timing marks do not align as specified, shut the engine off and loosen the adjusting screw locknut (**Figure 50**). Adjust the screw clockwise to retard or counterclockwise to advance timing as required, then tighten the locknut. One full turn in either direction changes timing approximately one degree.
6. Restart the engine and repeat Step 4. If timing mark alignment is still incorrect, repeat Step 5, then Step 3 and Step 4 as required.

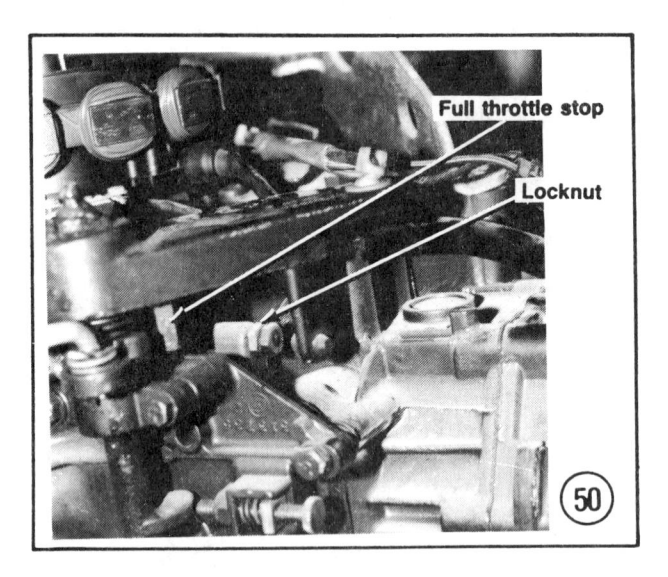

Carburetor adjustment

1. Install the engine in a test tank with the proper test wheel.
2A. 65 and 85 hp—Carefully remove the low-speed adjusting knobs and reinstall upside down on the low-speed needle valves so they will clear the carburetor stops.
2B. 100 hp—With the low-speed lever and air silencer cover removed, center the low-speed control knob link and remove the needle valve adjustment knobs.
3. Turn each low-speed needle valve inward until it barely seats, then back each one out approximately 5/8 turn.
4. 100 hp—Reinstall the 4 knobs without disturbing the needle valve adjustment.
5. Start the engine and run at half throttle until the engine reaches operating

ENGINE SYCHRONIZATION AND LINKAGE ADJUSTMENT

Figure 51 — Throttle linkage with labels: Top scribe mark on cam, Throttle arm, Cam follower adjustment screw, Cam roller, Idle adjustment screw.

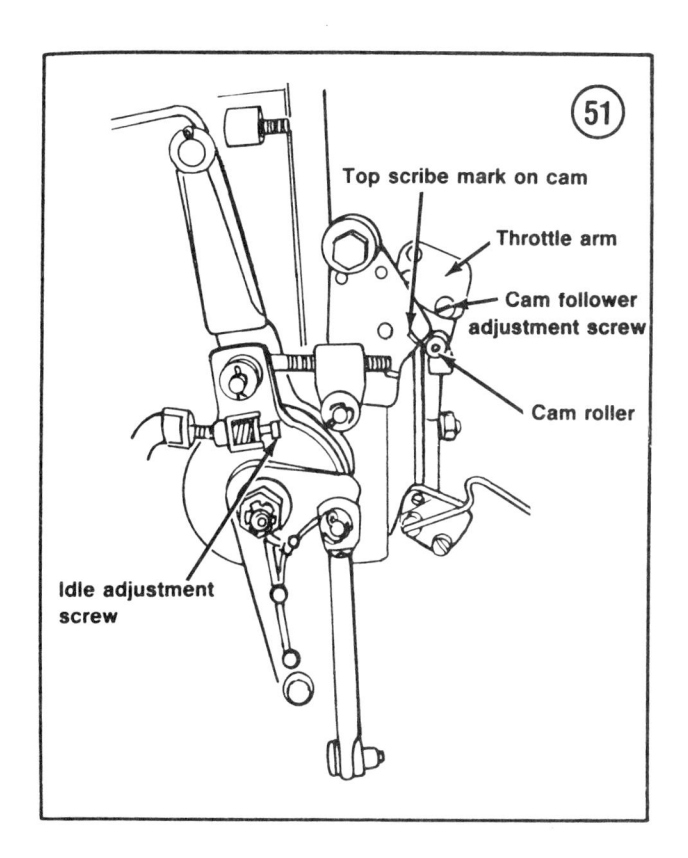

temperature (the tell-tale water stream will increase noticeably when the thermostat opens).

6. Connect a tachometer according to manufacturer's instructions.

7A. 65 and 85 hp—Run engine at 700-750 rpm in gear. Adjust one low-speed needle clockwise until the engine hesitates, then turn the needle counterclockwise until the engine reaches its highest rpm and smoothest operation. Repeat this adjustment with the other low-speed needle. Quickly open the throttle. If the engine hesitates, repeat the adjustment. When adjustment is correct, the engine should respond without hesitation.

7B. 100 HP—Run engine at 650 rpm in gear. Adjust control link up or down as required (moving the link up enriches the mixture; moving it down leans the mixture out). Wait approximately 15 seconds between adjustments for the engine to respond. Increase engine speed to 3,500-4,000 rpm to clear the crankcase and cylinders. Bring engine speed back to 650 rpm and repeat adjustment if necessary.

8. 65 and 85 hp—Carefully remove needle valve adjusting knobs and reinstall in their correct position without disturbing the setting.

9. Adjust the idle speed screw to obtain an engine speed of 650 rpm in gear.

1969-1970 85 and 115 HP

Throttle cam adjustment

1. Connect a throttle shaft amplifier tool (**Figure 2**) to the top carburetor throttle shaft.
2. Watching the amplifier tool, slowly rotate the throttle cam. As the end of the tool starts to move, check the cam and cam follower alignment. The upper embossed mark on the cam should align with the center of the cam follower roller. See **Figure 51**.
3. If the roller and cam mark do not align in Step 2, loosen the cam follower adjustment screw (**Figure 51**). Align the upper throttle cam mark with the center of the roller. Move the carburetor throttle arm until the throttle valves are closed. Depress the cam follower lever to maintain the alignment and tighten the throttle arm screw.
4. Repeat Step 2 to check the adjustment. If incorrect, repeat Step 3, then repeat Step 2 as required.

Linkage synchronization

If the engine is being reassembled and the yoke has been removed from the throttle control rod, reinstall yoke on rod and adjust it until the throttle shaft arm rests against its stop when the control shaft is in its full throttle position. See **Figure 52** (typical).

1. Move the distributor base against its full throttle stop to align the base plate arm and distributor cap timing marks. See **Figure 53** (typical). If necessary, adjust the spark advance stop screw to provide timing mark alignment.

2. With the distributor base and cap marks aligned, the lower throttle cam mark should intersect the center of the cam follower roller just as the roller contacts the cam (**Figure 52**). If it does not, disconnect the throttle cam yoke, loosen the throttle control rod locknut and adjust the yoke position on the control rod as required to properly align the marks.

3. Reconnect the throttle cam yoke and tighten the locknut securely. Repeat Step 1 and recheck cam mark and roller relation.

Maximum spark advance

CAUTION
This procedure should be performed in a test tank with the proper test wheel installed on the engine. The use of the propeller and/or a flushing device can result in an incorrect setting and possible engine damage.

1. Install the engine in a test tank with the proper test wheel.
2. Connect a timing light and tachometer according to manufacturer's instructions.
3. Start the engine and run at half-throttle in gear until the engine reaches operating temperature (the tell-tale water stream will increase noticeably when the thermostat opens).

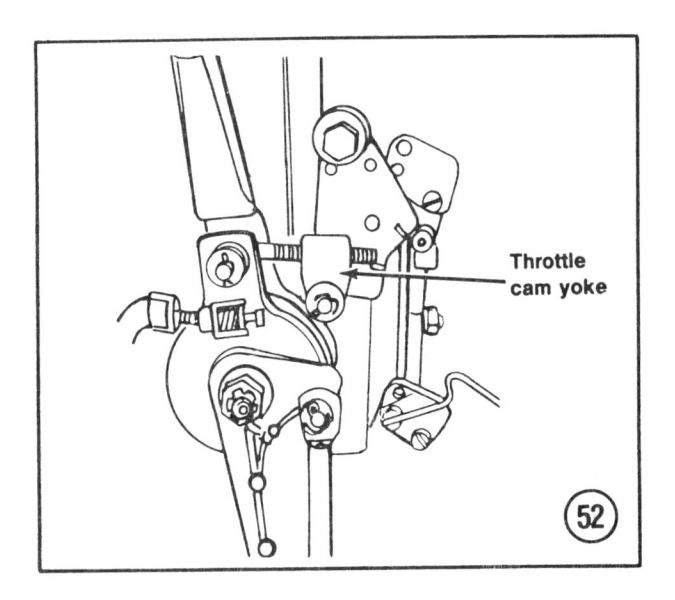

NOTE
The flywheel has 2 timing marks. Use the straight mark for Step 4.

4. Increase engine speed to 4,500 rpm. Check the timing mark position with the timing light. The flywheel timing mark should align with the lift bracket timing indicator. See **Figure 54**.

WARNING
Do not attempt to adjust the spark advance with the engine running in Step 5. The adjustment screw is located close to or under the moving flywheel and vibrates slightly when the engine is running. If the screwdriver slips out of the screw, serious personal injury can result.

5. If the timing marks do not align as specified, shut the engine off and loosen the adjustment screw locknut (**Figure 55**). Adjust the screw clockwise to retard or counterclockwise to advance timing as required, then tighten the locknut. One full turn in either direction changes timing approximately one degree.

6. Restart the engine and repeat Step 4. If timing mark alignment is still incorrect, repeat Step 5, then Step 3 and Step 4 as required.

ENGINE SYCHRONIZATION AND LINKAGE ADJUSTMENT

Carburetor adjustment

1. Install the engine in a test tank with the proper test wheel.
2. With the outer low-speed lever and air silencer cover removed, center the low-speed control knob link and remove the needle valve adjustment knobs. See **Figure 56** (typical).
3. Turn each low-speed needle valve inward until it barely seats, then back each one out approximately 7/8 turn.
4. Start the engine and run at half throttle until the engine reaches operating temperature (the tell-tale water stream will increase noticeably when the thermostat opens).
5. Connect a tachometer according to manufacturer's instructions.
6. Run engine at 700-750 rpm in gear. Adjust one low-speed needle clockwise until the engine hesitates, then turn the needle counterclockwise until the engine reaches its highest rpm and smoothest operation. Repeat this adjustment with each remaining low-speed needle. Quickly open the throttle. If the engine hesitates, repeat the adjustment. When adjustment is correct, the engine should respond without hesitation.
7. Reinstall the 4 knobs without disturbing the needle valve adjustment.
8. Adjust the idle speed screw (**Figure 51**) to obtain an engine speed of 650 rpm in gear.

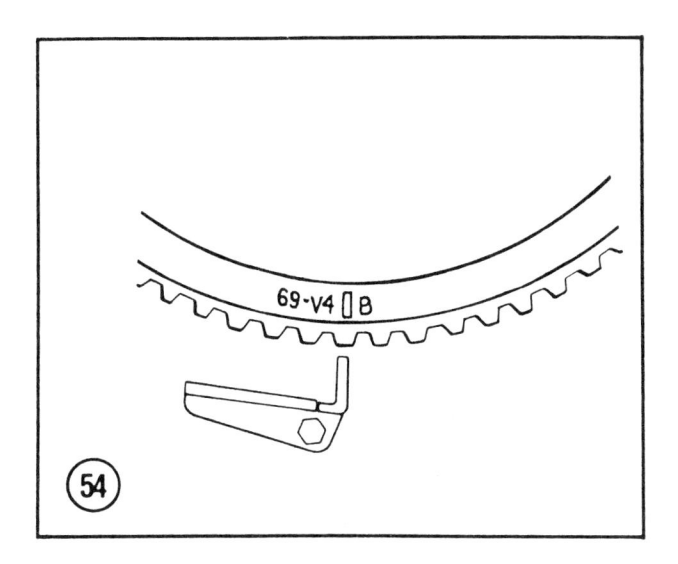

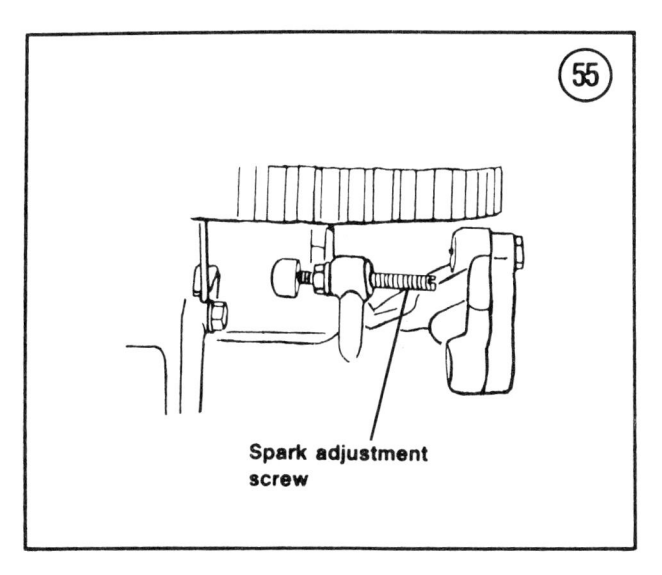

1971-1972 85, 100 and 125 HP

Throttle and choke linkage adjustment

1. Remove the engine cover.
2. Remove the air silencer cover.
3. Retard the throttle lever to a point where the throttle cam does not touch the cam follower roller.

4. Loosen the throttle linkage adjustment screw (**Figure 57**). The throttle shaft return spring should close the throttle valve.

5. Rotate the throttle shafts partially open, then let them snap back to the closed position. Apply a slight upward pressure on the adjusting link tab to remove any backlash and tighten the adjustment screw.

6. Move the cam follower while watching the throttle valves. If the throttle valves do not start to move at the same time, repeat Steps 3-5.

7. Repeat Step 3 and loosen the choke linkage adjustment screw (**Figure 57**).

8. Manually close the choke valves, then apply a slight upward pressure on the adjusting link tab to remove any backlash and tighten the adjustment screw.

Throttle cam adjustment

1. Connect a throttle shaft amplifier tool (**Figure 2**) to the top carburetor throttle shaft.
2. Watching the amplifier tool, slowly rotate the throttle cam. As the end of the tool starts to move, check the cam and cam follower alignment. The upper embossed mark on the cam should align with the center of the cam follower roller. See **Figure 58**.
3. If the roller and cam mark do not align in Step 2, loosen the cam follower adjustment screw (**Figure 51**). Align the upper throttle cam mark with the center of the roller. Move the carburetor throttle arm until the throttle valves are closed. Depress the cam follower lever to maintain the alignment and tighten the throttle arm screw.
4. Repeat Step 2 to check the adjustment. If incorrect, repeat Step 3, then repeat Step 2 as required.

Linkage synchronization

If the engine is being reassembled and the yoke has been removed from the throttle

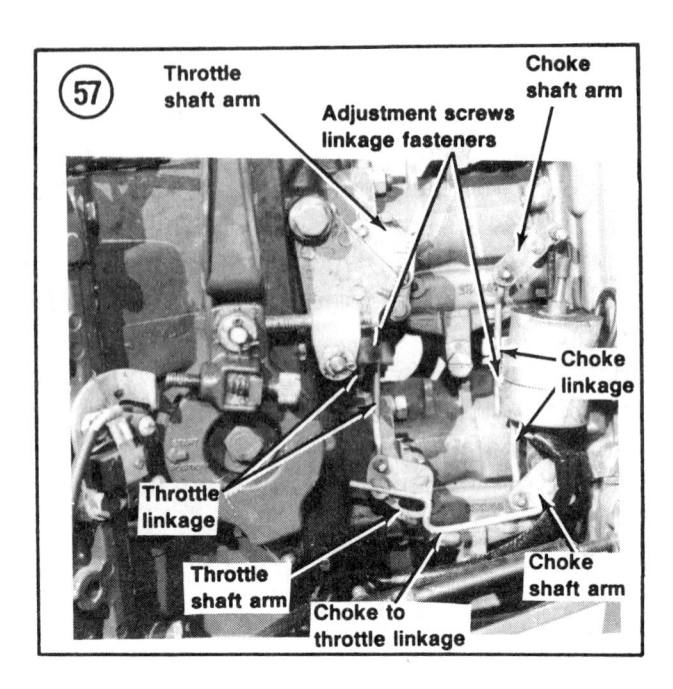

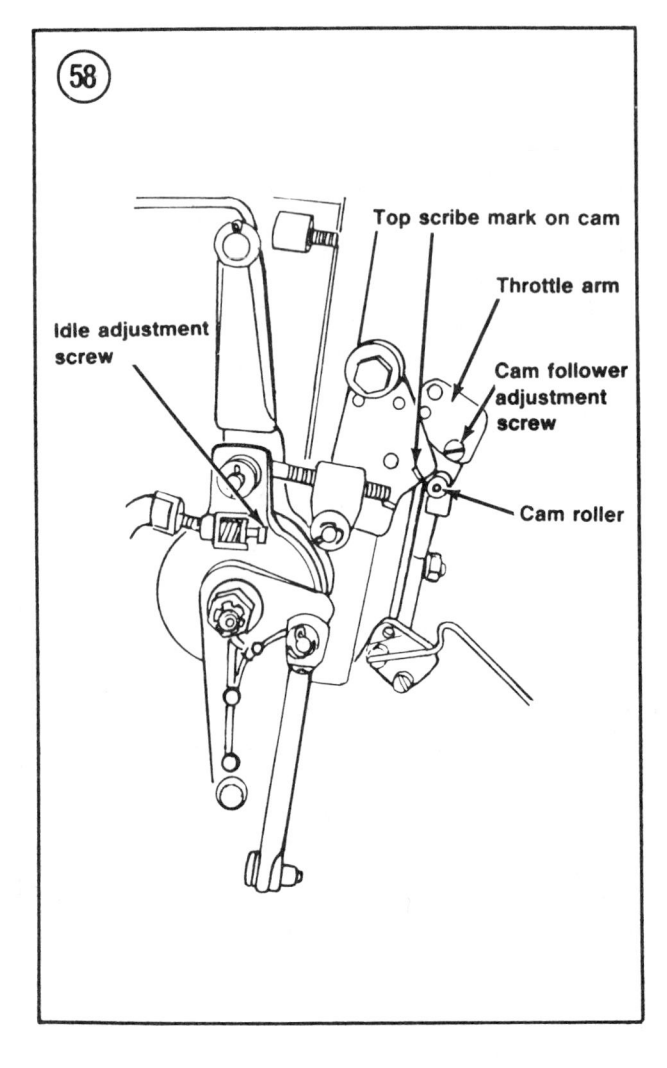

ENGINE SYCHRONIZATION AND LINKAGE ADJUSTMENT

Figure 59 — Full throttle adjustment screw; Idle speed adjustment screw

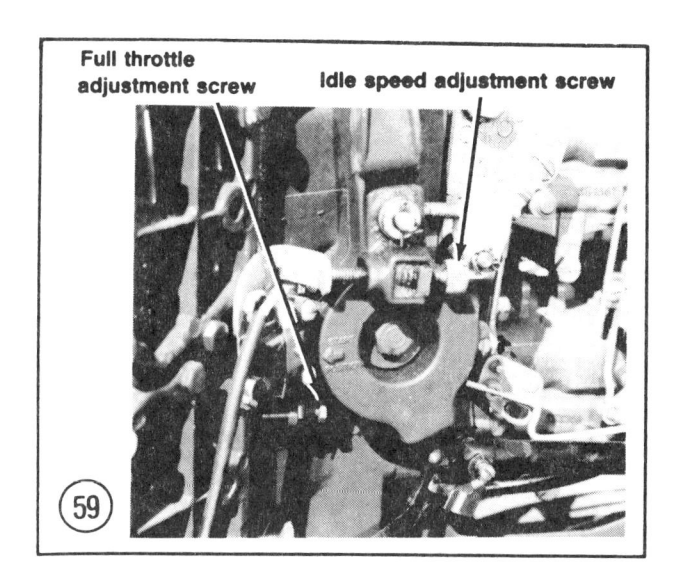

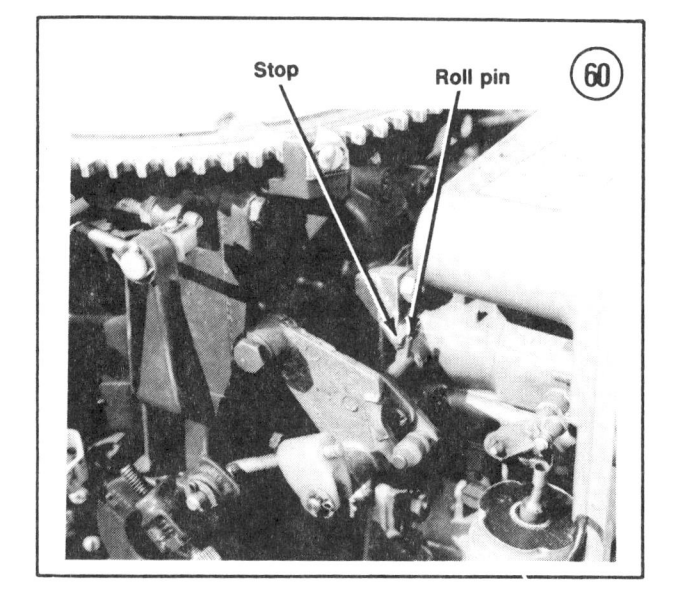

Figure 60 — Stop; Roll pin

control rod, reinstall yoke on rod and adjust it until the throttle shaft arm rests against its stop when the control shaft is in its full throttle position.

1. Install the engine in a test tank with the proper test wheel.
2. Connect a timing light according to manufacturer's instructions.
3. Start the engine and check the spark advance with the timing light, adjusting the idle speed screw (**Figure 59**) as required to align the 5° advance mark on the flywheel with the timing pointer.

4. Shut the engine off and make sure the upper embossed mark on the throttle cam aligns with the center of the cam follower roller. If it does not, disconnect the throttle cam yoke (**Figure 51**), loosen the throttle control rod locknut and adjust the yoke position on the control rod as required to properly align the marks.
5. Reconnect the throttle cam yoke and tighten the locknut securely. Repeat Step 3 and recheck cam mark and roller relation.
6. Open the throttle to the full throttle position. The upper carburetor roll pin should contact its stop. See **Figure 60**. Hold the throttle lever in that position.
7. Loosen the full throttle adjustment screw locknut and adjust the screw (**Figure 59**) to allow the throttle valves to open fully without loading the throttle shaft. Tighten the locknut.
8. Insert a strip of tracing paper between the roll pin and throttle stop. There should be a slight drag (0.003 in. clearance) on the paper when it is removed if the adjustment is correct.

Maximum spark advance

CAUTION
This procedure should be performed in a test tank with the proper test wheel installed on the engine. The use of the propeller and/or a flushing device can result in an incorrect setting and possible engine damage.

1. Install the engine in a test tank with the proper test wheel.
2. Connect a timing light and tachometer according to manufacturer's instructions.
3. Start the engine and run at half-throttle in gear until the engine reaches operating temperature (the tell-tale water stream will increase noticeably when the thermostat opens).

NOTE
If the flywheel has 2 timing grids, use the grid marked V4 for Step 4.

4. Increase engine speed to 4,500 rpm. Check the timing mark position with the timing light. The specified flywheel timing mark should align with the timing indicator.

WARNING
Do not attempt to adjust the spark advance with the engine running in Step 5. The adjustment screw is located close to or under the moving flywheel and vibrates slightly when the engine is running. If the screwdriver slips out of the screw, serious personal injury can result.

5. If the timing marks do not align as specified, shut the engine off and loosen the adjustment screw locknut (**Figure 61**). Adjust the screw clockwise to retard or counterclockwise to advance timing as required, then tighten the locknut. One full turn in either direction changes timing approximately one degree.

6. Restart the engine and repeat Step 4. If timing mark alignment is still incorrect, repeat Step 5, then Step 3 and Step 4 as required.

Carburetor adjustment (1971 models)

1. Install the engine in a test tank with the proper test wheel.

2. With the outer low-speed lever and air silencer cover removed, center the low-speed control knob link and remove the needle valve adjustment knobs. See **Figure 62** (typical).

3. Turn each low-speed needle valve inwards until it barely seats, then back each one out approximately 7/8 turn.

4. Start the engine and run at half throttle until the engine reaches operating temperature (the tell-tale water stream will increase noticeably when the thermostat opens).

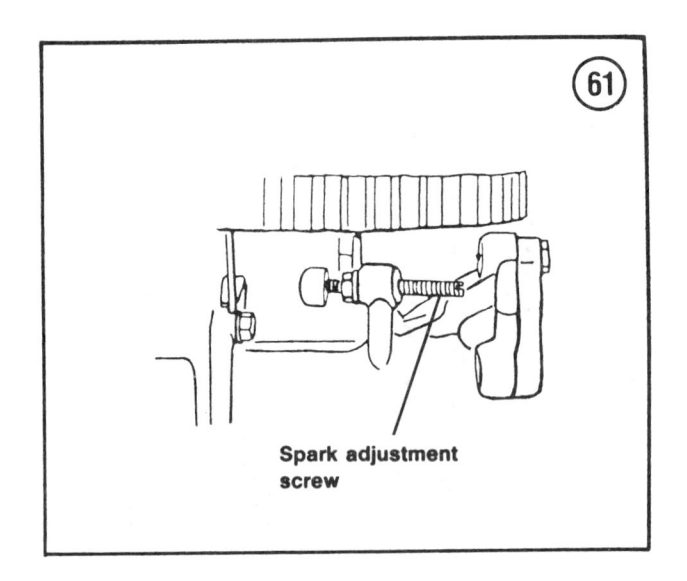

5. Connect a tachometer according to manufacturer's instructions.

6. Run engine at 700-750 rpm in gear. Adjust one low-speed needle clockwise until the engine hesitates, then turn the needle counterclockwise until the engine reaches its highest rpm and smoothest operation. Repeat this adjustment with each remaining low-speed needle. Quickly open the throttle. If the engine hesitates, repeat the adjustment. When adjustment is correct, the engine should respond without hesitation (final

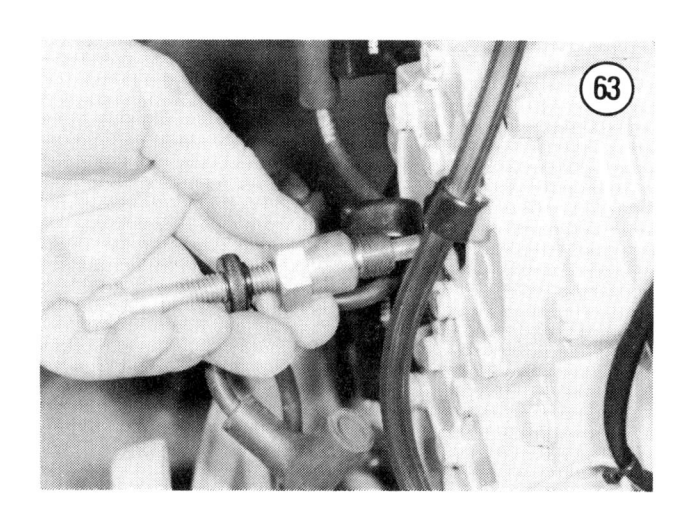

ENGINE SYCHRONIZATION AND LINKAGE ADJUSTMENT

adjustment should be within 3/4-1 turn open).

7. Reinstall the 4 knobs without disturbing the needle valve adjustment.
8. Adjust the idle speed screw (**Figure 58**) to obtain an engine speed of 600-650 rpm in gear.

Carburetor adjustment (1972 models)

Carburetors used on these engines have fixed high- and low-speed jets. Only an idle adjustment is required.

1. Install the engine in a test tank with the proper test wheel.
2. Connect a tachometer according to manufacturer's instructions.
3. Start the engine and run at half throttle until the engine reaches operating temperature (the tell-tale water stream will increase noticeably when the thermostat opens).
4. Adjust the idle speed screw (**Figure 58**) to obtain an engine speed of 650 rpm in gear.

1972 65 HP

Timing pointer alignment

1. Disconnect the spark plug leads. Remove the spark plugs.
2. Install piston stop tool No. 384887 in the No. 1 spark plug hole. See **Figure 63**.
3. Rotate the flywheel clockwise until the piston contacts the piston stop tool. This should be at approximately the 26° BTDC mark on the flywheel.
4. Mark the flywheel rim directly across from the timing pointer.
5. Rotate the flywheel counterclockwise until the piston contacts the piston stop tool again and repeat Step 4.
6. Remove the piston stop tool and measure the distance between the marks made in Step 4 and Step 5. The mid-point between the 2 marks should fall directly on the TDC mark cast into the flywheel if timing pointer alignment is correct.
7. If the mid-point does not fall on the flywheel TDC mark, the pointer is out of alignment. Rotate the flywheel to align the mid-point with the pointer. Hold the flywheel in this position and loosen the pointer screws. Move the pointer to align with the TDC mark cast into the flywheel and tighten the pointer screws.

Throttle and choke linkage adjustment

1. Remove the engine cover.
2. Remove the air silencer cover.
3. Retard the throttle lever to a point where the throttle cam does not touch the cam follower roller.
4. Loosen the upper and lower carburetor throttle arm retaining screws. The throttle shaft return spring should close the throttle valve. Tighten the screws.
5. Repeat Step 3 and loosen the choke linkage adjustment screws.
6. Manually close the choke valves and tighten the adjustment screws.

Throttle cam adjustment

1. Connect a throttle shaft amplifier tool (**Figure 2**) to the top carburetor throttle shaft.

Figure 64: Cam roller, Embossed mark on cam, Adjustment screw

Figure 65: Throttle lever, Rod, Yoke, Retaining pin & washer, Throttle stop screw, Idle adjustment screw

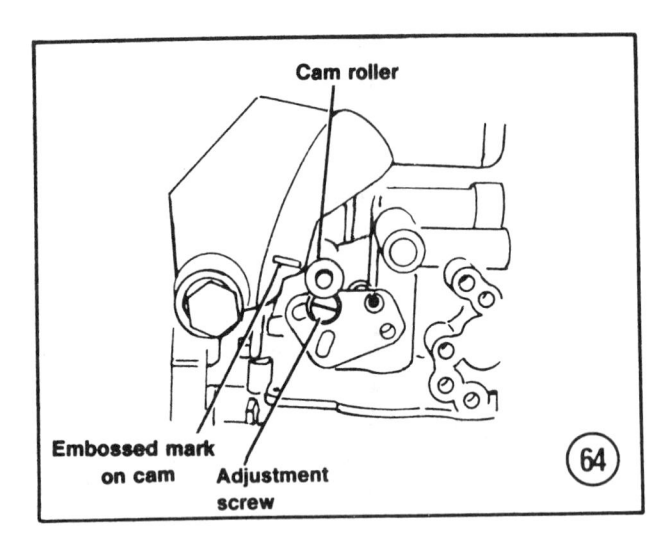

2. Watching the amplifier tool, slowly rotate the throttle cam. As the end of the tool starts to move, check the cam and cam follower alignment. The embossed or scribed mark on the cam should align with the center of the cam follower roller. See **Figure 64**.

3. If the roller and cam mark do not align in Step 2, loosen the center carburetor throttle arm screw (**Figure 65**). Align the throttle cam mark with the center of the roller. Move the carburetor throttle arm until the throttle valves are closed. Depress the cam follower lever to maintain the alignment and tighten the throttle arm screw.

4. Repeat Step 2 to check the adjustment. If incorrect, repeat Step 3, then repeat Step 2 as required.

Linkage synchronization

If the engine is being reassembled and the yoke has been removed from the throttle control rod, reinstall yoke on rod and adjust it to provide a distance of 4 31/32 in. from the end of the rod to the face of the yoke.

1. Connect a timing light to the No. 1 cylinder according to manufacturer's instructions.

2. Start the engine and adjust the idle speed screw (**Figure 65**) until the 8° mark on the flywheel grid aligns with the timing pointer.

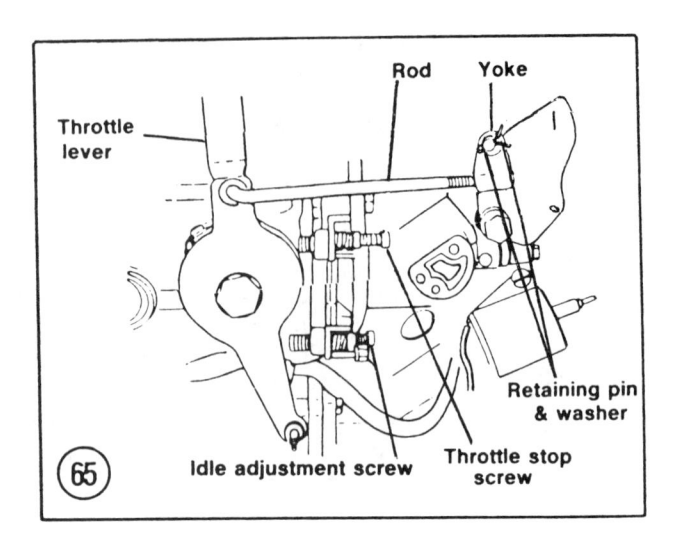

3. Shut the engine off. Hold the throttle lever against the idle stop screw. The embossed mark on the throttle cam should align with the center of the cam follower roller.

4. If the roller and cam mark do not align in Step 3, disconnect the throttle cam yoke, loosen the throttle control rod locknut and adjust the yoke position on the control rod as required to properly align the roller and mark. See **Figure 65** (typical).

5. Reconnect the throttle cam yoke and tighten the locknut securely.

6. Move the throttle lever to its full advance position. If the throttle valves are not fully open, adjust the wide open throttle stop screw as required.

7. Start the engine and adjust the idle speed screw as required to obtain an engine speed of 650 rpm in gear.

Maximum spark advance

CAUTION
This procedure should be performed in a test tank with the proper test wheel installed on the engine. The use of the propeller and/or a flushing device can result in an incorrect setting and possible engine damage.

1. Install the engine in a test tank with the proper test wheel.

ENGINE SYCHRONIZATION AND LINKAGE ADJUSTMENT

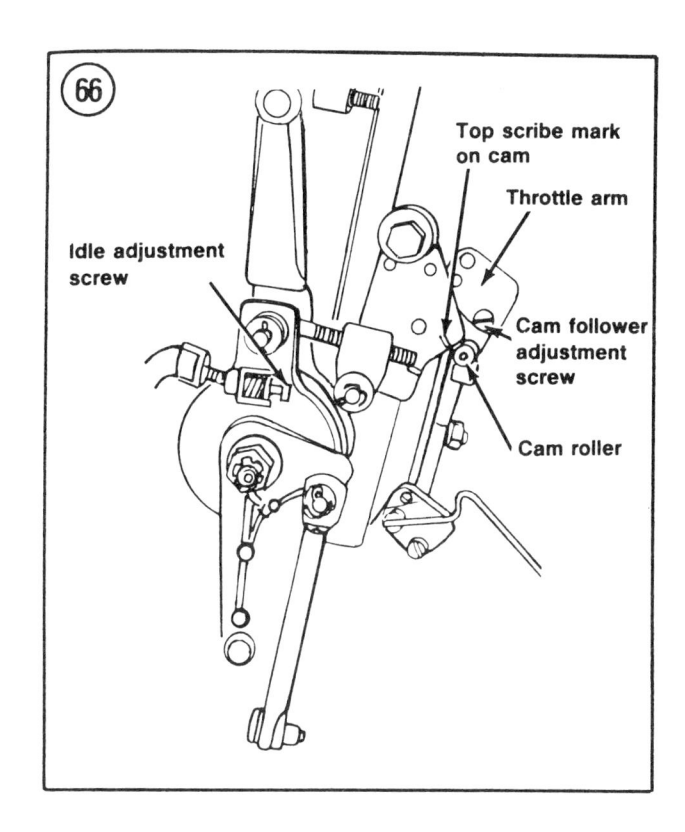

66 Top scribe mark on cam
Throttle arm
Idle adjustment screw
Cam follower adjustment screw
Cam roller

2. Connect a timing light and tachometer according to manufacturer's instructions.
3. Start the engine and run at half-throttle until the engine reaches operating temperature (the tell-tale water stream will increase noticeably when the thermostat opens).
4. Increase engine speed to 4,300-4,600 rpm. Check the timing mark position with the timing light. The specified mark on the flywheel grid should align with the timing pointer.

WARNING
Do not attempt to adjust the spark advance with the engine running in Step 5. The adjustment screw is located close to or under the moving flywheel and vibrates slightly when the engine is running. If the screwdriver slips out of the screw, serious personal injury can result.

5. If the timing marks do not align as specified, shut the engine off and loosen the adjusting screw locknut (**Figure 66**). Adjust the screw clockwise to retard or counterclockwise to advance timing as required, then tighten the locknut. One full turn in either direction changes timing approximately one degree.
6. Restart the engine and repeat Step 4. If timing mark alignment is still incorrect, repeat Step 5, then Step 3 and Step 4 as required.

Carburetor adjustment

1. Install the engine in a test tank with the proper test wheel.
2. With the low-speed lever and air silencer cover removed, disconnect the low-speed needle valve linkage and remove the needle valve adjustment levers.
3. Turn each low-speed needle valve inward until it barely seats, then back each one out approximately 5/8 turn.
4. Start the engine and run at half-throttle in gear until the engine reaches operating temperature (the tell-tale water stream will increase noticeably when the thermostat opens).
5. Connect a tachometer according to manufacturer's instructions.
6. Run engine at 650 rpm and alternately adjust the No. 2 and No. 3 carburetors to obtain the highest rpm and smoothest performance, waiting approximately 15 seconds between adjustments for the engine to respond. Increase engine speed to 1,000-1,200 rpm and adjust the No. 1 carburetor.
7. Reinstall the needle valve adjustment levers pointing to the starboard side of the engine without disturbing the needle valve setting. Reconnect the linkage to the levers.
8. Adjust the idle speed screw to obtain an engine speed of 1,000-1,100 rpm in neutral.

Table 1 TUNE-UP SPECIFICATIONS (1- AND 2-CYLINDER)

Model year/hp	Adjustment procedure	Adjustment method	Wide open throttle rpm
1956			
3	3	A	4,000
5.5	3	A	4,000
7.5	3	A	4,000
10	3	A	4,000
15	3	A	4,000
30	5	A	4,000
1957			
3	3	A	4,000
5.5	3	A	4,000
7.5	3	A	4,000
10	3	A	4,000
18	3	A	4,500
35	5	A	4,500
1958			
3	3	A	4,000
5.5	3	A	4,000
7.5	3	A	4,000
10	3	A	4,000
18	3	A	4,500
35	5	C	4,500
1959			
3	3	A	4,000
5.5	3	A	4,000
10	3	A	4,000
18	3	A	4,500
35	5	C	4,500
1960			
3	3	A	4,000
5.5	3	A	4,000
10	3	A	4,500
18	3	A	4,500
40	5	C	4,500
1961			
3	3	A	4,000
5.5	3	A	4,000
10	3	A	4,500
18	3	A	4,500
40	5	C	4,500
1962			
3	3	A	4,000
5.5	3	A	4,000
10	3	A	4,500
18	3	A	4,500
28	5	C	4,500
40	5	C	4,500

(continued)

ENGINE SYCHRONIZATION AND LINKAGE ADJUSTMENTS

Table 1 TUNE-UP SPECIFICATIONS (1- AND 2-CYLINDER) (continued)

Model year/hp	Adjustment procedure	Adjustment method	Wide open throttle rpm
1963			
3	3	A	4,000
5.5	3	A	4,000
10	3	A	4,500
18	3	A	4,500
28	5	C	4,500
40	5	D	4,500
1964			
3	3	A	4,000
5.5	3	A	4,000
9.5	3	B	4,000
18	3	A	4,500
28	5	C	4,500
40	5	D	4,500
1965			
3	3	A	4,000
5	3	A	4,000
6	3	A	4,500
9.5	3	B	4,500
18	3	A	4,500
33	5	C	4,500
40	5	D	4,500
1966			
3	3	A	4,000
5	3	A	4,000
6	3	A	4,500
9.5	3	B	4,500
18	3	A	4,500
20	3	A	4,500
33	5	C	4,500
40	5	D	4,500
1967			
3	2	A	4,000
5	2	A	4,000
6	2	A	4,500
9.5	3	B	4,500
18	4	A	4,500
20	4	A	4,500
33	5	C	4,500
40	5	D	4,500
1968			
1.5	1	A	4,000
3	1	A	4,000
5	1	A	4,000
6	1	A	4,500
9.5	3	B	4,500
18	4	A	4,500
20	4	A	4,500
33	5	C	4,500
40	5	D	4,500

(continued)

Table 1 TUNE-UP SPECIFICATIONS (1- AND 2-CYLINDER) (continued)

Model year/hp	Adjustment procedure	Adjustment method	Wide open throttle rpm
1969			
1.5	1	A	4,000
4	2	A	4,500
6	2	A	4,500
9.5	3	B	4,500
18	4	D	4,500
20	4	D	4,500
25	4	D	5,500
33	5	C	4,500
40	5	D	4,500
1970			
1.5	1	A	4,000
4	2	A	4,500
6	2	A	4,500
9.5	3	B	4,500
18	4	D	4,500
20	4	D	4,500
25	4	D	5,500
33	5	C	4,500
40	5	D	4,500
1971			
2	1	A	4,500
4	2	A	4,500
6	2	A	4,500
9.5	3	B	4,500
18	4	D	4,500
20	4	D	4,500
25	4	D	5,500
40	5	C	4,500
50	3	E	5,500
1972			
2	1	A	4,500
4	2	A	4,500
6	2	A	4,500
9.5	3	B	4,500
18	4	D	4,500
20	4	D	4,500
25	4	D	5,500
40	5	C	4,500
50	3	E	5,500

ENGINE SYCHRONIZATION AND LINKAGE ADJUSTMENTS

Table 2 TUNE-UP SPECIFICATIONS (3- AND 4-CYLINDER)

Model year/hp	Timing (rpm @ mark or degrees)	Wide open throttle rpm
50	—	4,000
55	4,500 @ mark	5,000
60		
1964-1967	—	4,500
1970-1971	4,500 @ 22	5,000
65	4,500 @ mark	5,000
75	—	4,500
80	—	4,500
85		
1969-1970	4,500 @ mark	5,000
1971-1972	4,500 @ 28	5,000
90	—	4,500
100		
1966	—	4,500
1967-1968	4,500 @ mark	5,000
1971-1972	4,500 @ 28	5,000
115	4,500 @ mark	5,000
125	4,500 @ 26	5,000

Chapter Six

Fuel System

This chapter contains removal, overhaul, installation and adjustment procedures for fuel pumps, carburetors, remote fuel tanks and connecting lines used with the Johnson and Evinrude outboards covered in this book. **Figure 1** shows the components of a typical Johnson and Evinrude fuel system.

Table 1 is at the end of the chapter.

FUEL PUMP

Johnson and Evinrude engines manufactured from 1956-1959 were designed with a pressurized fuel system which did not require a fuel pump. A hand primer pump located in the fuel tank is used to supply fuel to the engine for starting. Once the engine starts, pressure from one cylinder is transferred to the tank by a line. This pressurizes the tank, which supplies a steady flow of fuel through a second line as long as the engine is running. A relief valve built into the tank is designed to prevent tank pressure from exceeding safe levels.

The diaphragm-type fuel pump used on 1960 and later outboard engines is operated by crankcase pressure. Since this type of fuel pump cannot create sufficient pressure to draw fuel from the tank during cranking, fuel is transferred to the carburetor for starting by operating the primer bulb installed in the fuel line between the tank and carburetor.

Pressure pulsations created by movement of the pistons reach the fuel pump through a

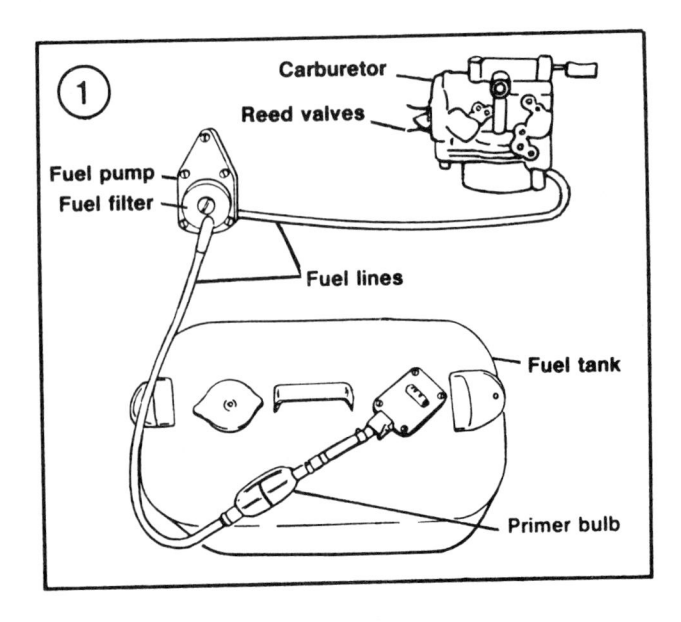

FUEL SYSTEM

passageway between the crankcase and the pump.

Upward piston motion creates a low pressure on the pump diaphragm. This low pressure opens the inlet check valve in the pump, drawing fuel from the line into the pump. At the same time, the low pressure draws the air-fuel mixture from the carburetor into the crankcase.

Downward piston motion creates a high pressure on the pump diaphragm. This pressure closes the inlet check valve and opens the outlet check valve, forcing the fuel into the carburetor and drawing the air-fuel mixture from the crankcase into the cylinder for combustion. **Figure 2** shows the operational sequence of a typical outboard fuel pump.

Johnson and Evinrude fuel pumps are self-contained, remote assemblies. Fuel pump shape, size and location vary according to engine size and model year. Older engines use a sediment bowl and filter arrangement (**Figure 3**). The sediment bowl and filter may be attached directly to the pump or remotely mounted between the pump and carburetor. Later engines use a pump with integral filter screen. See **Figure 4** (typical).

Outboard fuel pumps are extremely simple in design and reliable in operation. Diaphragm failures are the most common problem, although the use of dirty or

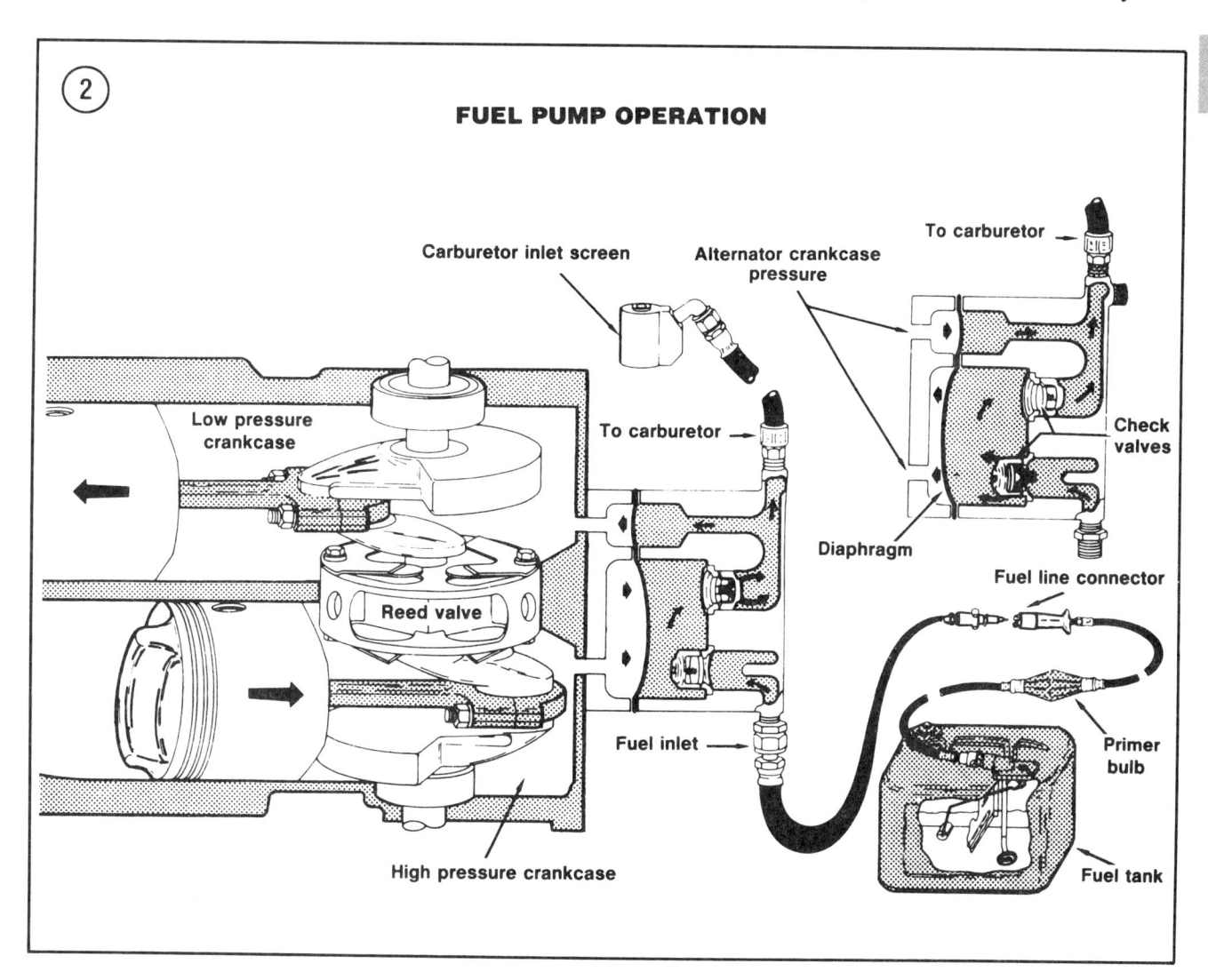

② FUEL PUMP OPERATION

improper fuel-oil mixtures can cause check valve problems. Johnson and Evinrude fuel pumps equipped with a sediment bowl filter can be disassembled and rebuilt; those using a filter screen are non-serviceable and must be replaced if defective.

Removal/Installation

1. Remove the screw holding the filter screen cap on pumps so equipped. See **Figure 5**. Remove the cap and screen.
2. Identify and disconnect all lines connected to the fuel pump.

NOTE
Only the bottom outer screws which hold the filter screen type pump to the powerhead must be removed in Step 3. The remaining visible screws hold the pump components together.

3. Remove the screws holding the pump assembly to the engine. See **Figure 6** (sediment bowl) or **Figure 7** (filter screen).
4. Remove the pump from the engine and discard the gasket.
5. Installation is the reverse of removal. Use a new gasket.

Disassembly/Assembly
(Sediment Bowl Pump)

Refer to **Figure 8** for this procedure.
1. Secure the pump housing by its mounting ears in a vise with protective jaws.

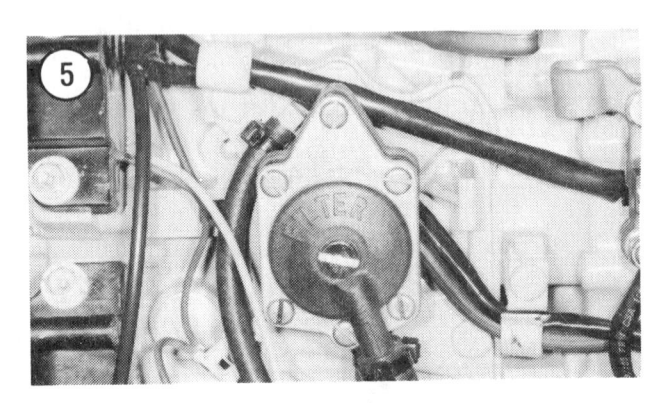

FUEL SYSTEM

⑧

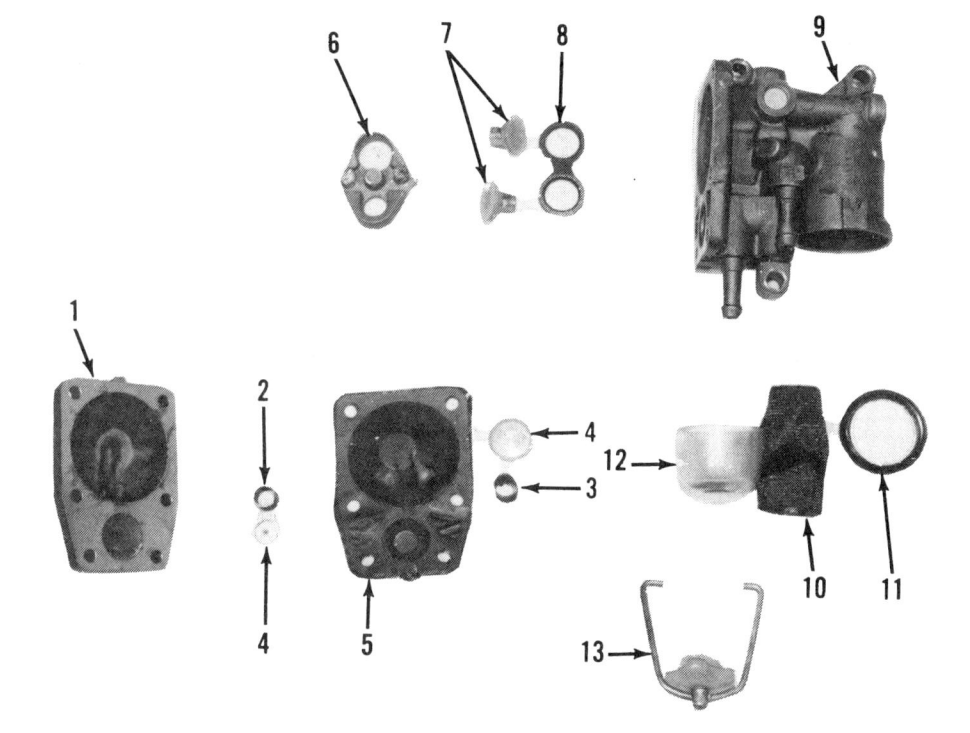

1. Fuel pump cover
2. Short spring
3. Long spring
4. Cap
5. Diaphragm
6. Retainer
7. Check valve
8. Gasket
9. Fuel pump body
10. Filter element
11. Gasket
12. Fuel bowl
13. Bowl yoke

2. Loosen the sediment bowl yoke screw. Swing the yoke over the bowl. Remove the bowl and filter element. Discard the bowl gasket and filter element.

3. Reposition the pump housing in the vise to provide access to the cover screws at the rear of the pump.

4. Remove the cover screws and cover.

5. Remove the spring, plastic cap and pump diaphragm.

6. Remove the plastic cap and spring installed in the housing under the diaphragm.

7. Remove the screws holding the check valve retainer. Remove the retainer.

8. Note the positioning of the check valves for reinstallation reference. Remove the check valves and gasket. Discard the gasket.

9. Clean and inspect the pump components as described in this chapter.

10. Secure the pump housing in a vise with protective jaws.

11. Install a new check valve through the valve gasket. Fit the gasket into the pump housing with the check valve facing towards the bottom of the pump.

12. Place the other new check valve on top of the gasket and install the retainer. The retainer alignment tab must fit into the housing recess (**Figure 9**).

13. Install a new long diaphragm spring on the retainer boss, then fit the large nylon cap on the spring with its smooth surface facing upwards. See **Figure 10**.

NOTE
The spring installed in Step 13 will exert upward pressure on the diaphragm and attempting to complete Step 14 and Step 15 without working carefully and with patience can result in mispositioning of one or both springs or caps and the diaphragm.

14. Place the new pump diaphragm over the housing. Position the cap and short spring over the support recess (**Figure 11**).

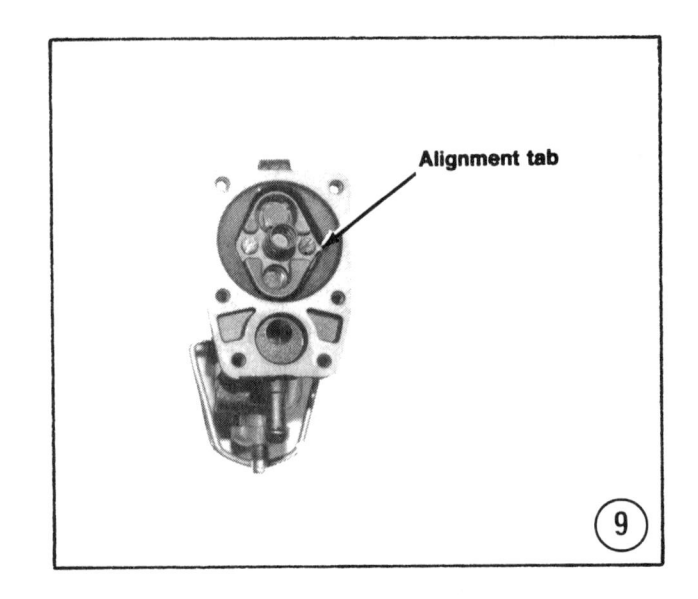

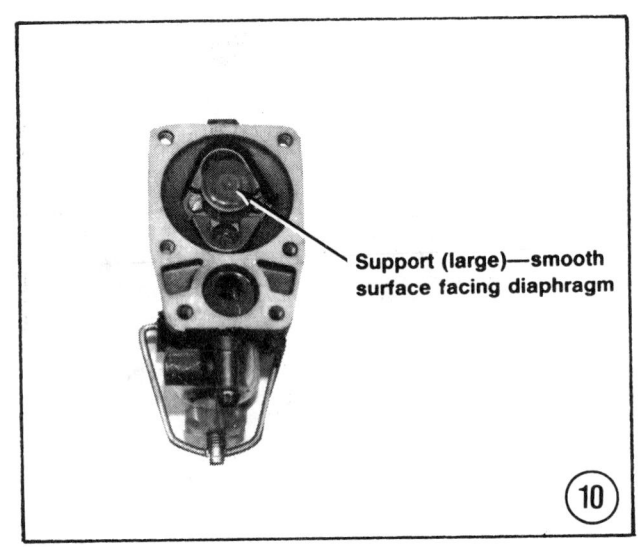

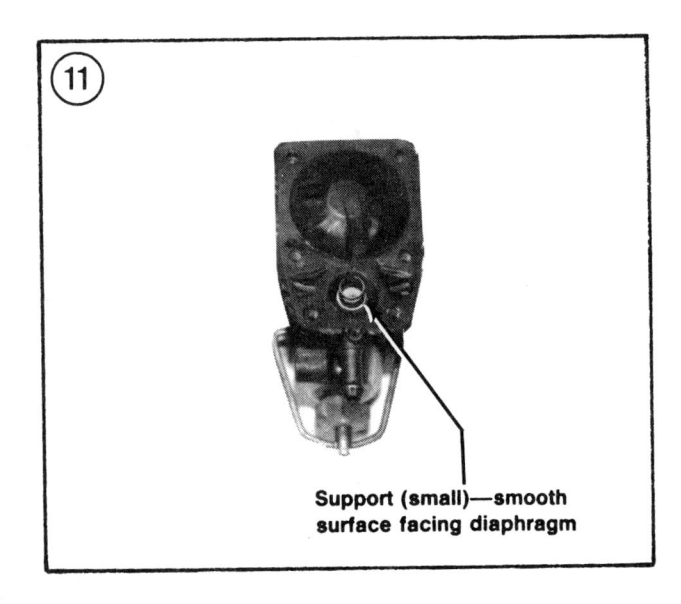

FUEL SYSTEM

12

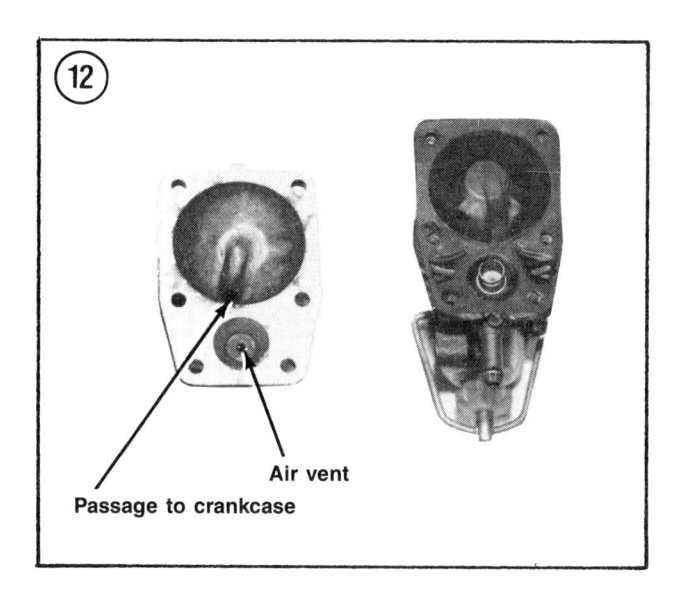

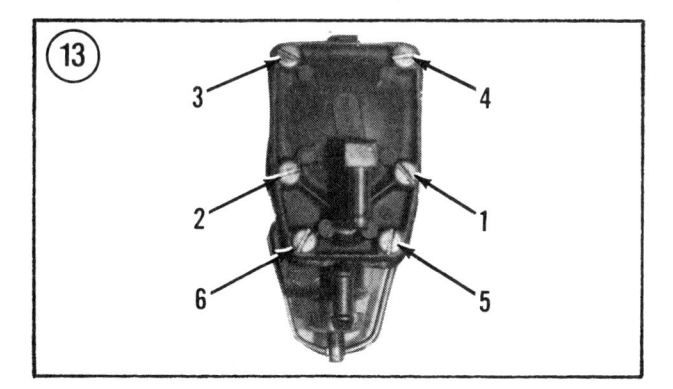

Air vent
Passage to crankcase

13

3, 4, 2, 1, 6, 5

15. Carefully fit the cover over the diaphragm and gently press it into position to avoid upsetting the springs or supports. See **Figure 12**.

16. Hold the cover in this position and make sure the cover, gasket and housing holes all align, then thread each cover screw into place. Tighten all screws securely following the sequence shown in **Figure 13**.

17. Install a new filter element and seat on the index leg inside the housing.

18. Install a new gasket. Fit the sediment bowl in place over the gasket.

19. Swing the yoke over the bowl. Press bowl against pump and tighten yoke screw securely.

20. Install the pump to the engine as described in this chapter.

Cleaning and Inspection

1. Clean housing in gasoline and dry with compressed air.
2. Check housing condition. Make sure the check valve seats provide a flat contact area for the check valves. Replace the housing if cracks or rough gasket mating surfaces are found.
3. Check the housing fittings. If loose or damaged, tighten or replace as required.

CARBURETORS

A wide variety of carburetors has been used on the engines covered in this book. For ease in providing service information, they have been divided into 7 major groups and labeled A to G. Refer to **Table 1** to determine which carburetor group is used with your engine.

Variations exist within each model group. Early carburetors have a high-speed needle valve; later ones use a fixed high-speed orifice in the float bowl. Depending upon engine application and model year, the carburetor may have one of several choke designs: manual, electric, hot air/electric, or hot water.

An exploded drawing is included with service instructions for each model group. Since the drawing is typical of all carburetors within the group, it may have more or less external parts than the one you are servicing. The essential components, however, remain the same from one carburetor to another, as do the basic service procedures.

When removing and installing a carburetor, make sure that the mounting nuts are securely tightened. A loose carburetor will cause a lean-running condition.

Cleaning and Inspection

Before removing and disassembling any carburetor, be sure you have the proper overhaul kit, the proper tools and a sufficient quantity of fresh cleaning solvent. Work slowly and carefully, follow the disassembly procedures, refer to the exploded drawing of the carburetor when necessary and do not apply excessive force at any time.

It is not necessary to disassemble the carburetor linkage or remove the throttle cam or other external components. Choke housings should not be disassembled beyond the steps provided nor removed from the carburetor body. Wipe the carburetor casting and linkage with a cloth moistened in solvent to remove any contamination and operating film. Clean the carburetor castings with an aerosol type solvent and a brush. Do not submerge them in a hot tank or carburetor cleaner. A sealing compound is used around the metering tubes and on the casting to eliminate porosity problems. A hot tank or submersion in carburetor cleaner will remove this sealing compound and can affect carburetor operation. It will also destroy choke shaft bushings.

Spray the cleaner on the casting and scrub off any gum or varnish with a small bristle brush. Spray the cleaner through the casting metering passages. Never clean passages with a wire or drill, as you may enlarge the passage and change the carburetor calibration.

Blow castings dry with low pressure (25 psi or less) compressed air. The use of higher pressures can damage the sealing compound.

Check the float for fuel absorption. Check the float arm for wear in the hinge pin and needle valve contact areas. Replace as required.

Check the needle valve tip for grooving, nicks or scratches. **Figure 14** shows a good valve tip (1), a valve tip damaged from excessive pressure when seating (2) and one with wear on one side caused by vibration resulting from the use of a damaged propeller (3).

Check the throttle and choke shafts for excessive wear or play. The throttle and choke valves must move freely without binding. Replace the carburetor if any of these defects are noted.

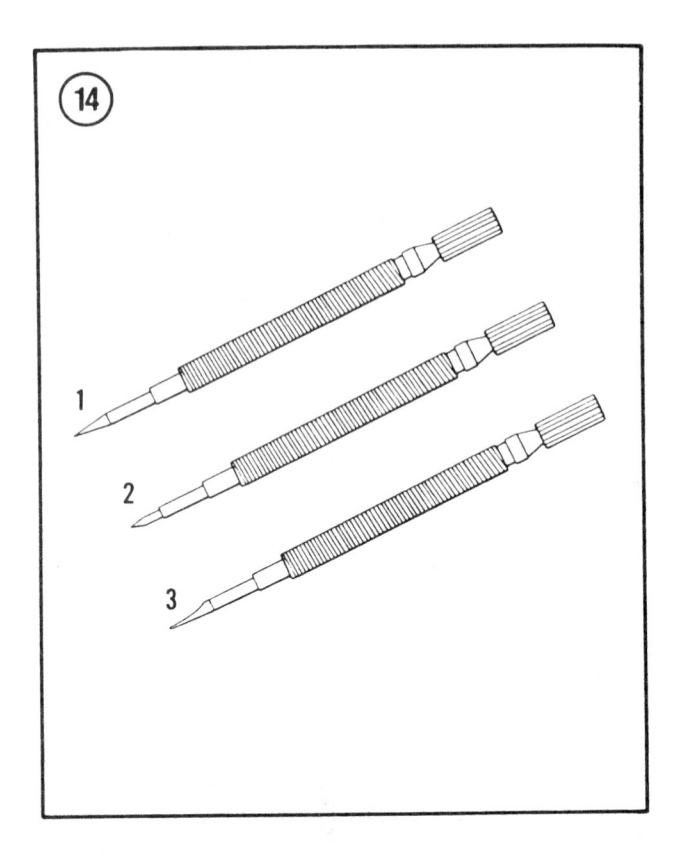

Clean all gasket residue from mating surfaces and remove any nicks, scratches or slight distortion with a surface plate and emery cloth.

Core Plugs and Lead Shot

Certain openings in the carburetor casting are covered with a core plug or have a lead shot installed. These usually require service only if the openings are leaking. **Figure 15** shows a carburetor with the core plug over the low-speed orifices removed (A) and a typical lead shot installed (B).

Core Plug Service

1. If leakage is noted, secure the carburetor in a vise with protective jaws.
2. Hold a flat-end punch in the center of the core plug and tap sharply with a hammer to

FUEL SYSTEM

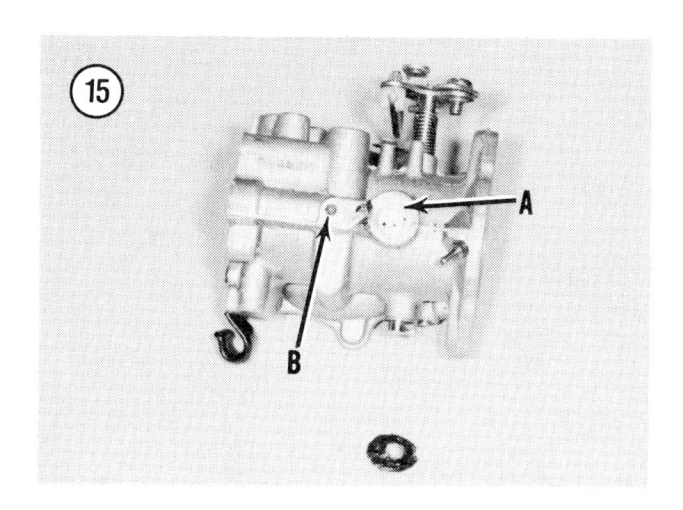

15

flatten the plug. Cover the plug area with OMC Adhesive M.

CAUTION
Do not drill more than 1/16 in. below the core plug in Step 3 or the casting will be damaged.

3. If this does not solve the leakage problem or if the low-speed orifices are completely plugged, carefully drill a 1/8 in. hole through the center of the plug and pry it from the casting with a punch.
4A. Clean all residue from the core plug hole in the casting. If the hole is out-of-round, replace the casting.
4B. If the low-speed orifices are plugged, clean with a brush and carburetor cleaner.
5. Coat the outer edge of a new core plug with OMC Adhesive M and position it in the casting opening with its convex side facing up.
6. Hold a flat end punch in the center of the core plug and tap sharply with a hammer to flatten the plug.
7. Coat the core plug with engine oil and blow compressed air (25 psi or less) through the casting passage to check for leakage.
8. Wipe the oil from the core plug and coat with OMC Adhesive M.

Lead Shot Service

1. If leakage is noted, secure the carburetor in a vise with protective jaws.
2. Tap the center of the lead shot sharply with a small hammer and appropriate size punch.
3. If leakage remains, carefully pry the lead shot from its opening with a suitable knife, awl or other sharp instrument.
4. Clean any residue from the lead shot opening in the casting.
5. Install a new lead shot in the opening and flatten out with a hammer and appropriate size punch.
6. Coat the core plug with engine oil and blow compressed air (25 psi or less) through the casting passages to check for leakage.
7. Clean the oil from the casting after pressure testing.

MODEL A CARBURETOR

Removal/Installation

1. Electric start—Disconnect the negative battery cable.
2. Disconnect the fuel line at the engine or fuel tank quick-disconnect.
3. Remove the engine cover.
4. Remove the air silencer, if so equipped.
5. Disconnect the throttle and choke linkage at the carburetor.
6. Remove the knob(s) from the needle valve(s).
7A. Integral fuel tank—With the fuel shut-off valve closed, disconnect both ends of the fuel line between the valve and carburetor. Remove the line.
7B. Remote fuel tank—Disconnect the fuel line at the carburetor.
8. Loosen the carburetor mounting nuts with an open-end wrench. If clearance is a problem, pull the carburetor against the nuts while continuing to loosen them. Remove the mounting nuts and lockwashers.

CHAPTER SIX

MODEL A CARBURETOR COMPONENTS PART I

1. Body
2. Inlet needle valve assembly
3. High-speed nozzle/gasket
4. Float
5. Gasket
6. Fuel filter assembly
7. High-speed needle valve
8. Low-speed needle valve
9. Packing nut
10. Packing
11. Throttle shaft
12. Choke shaft

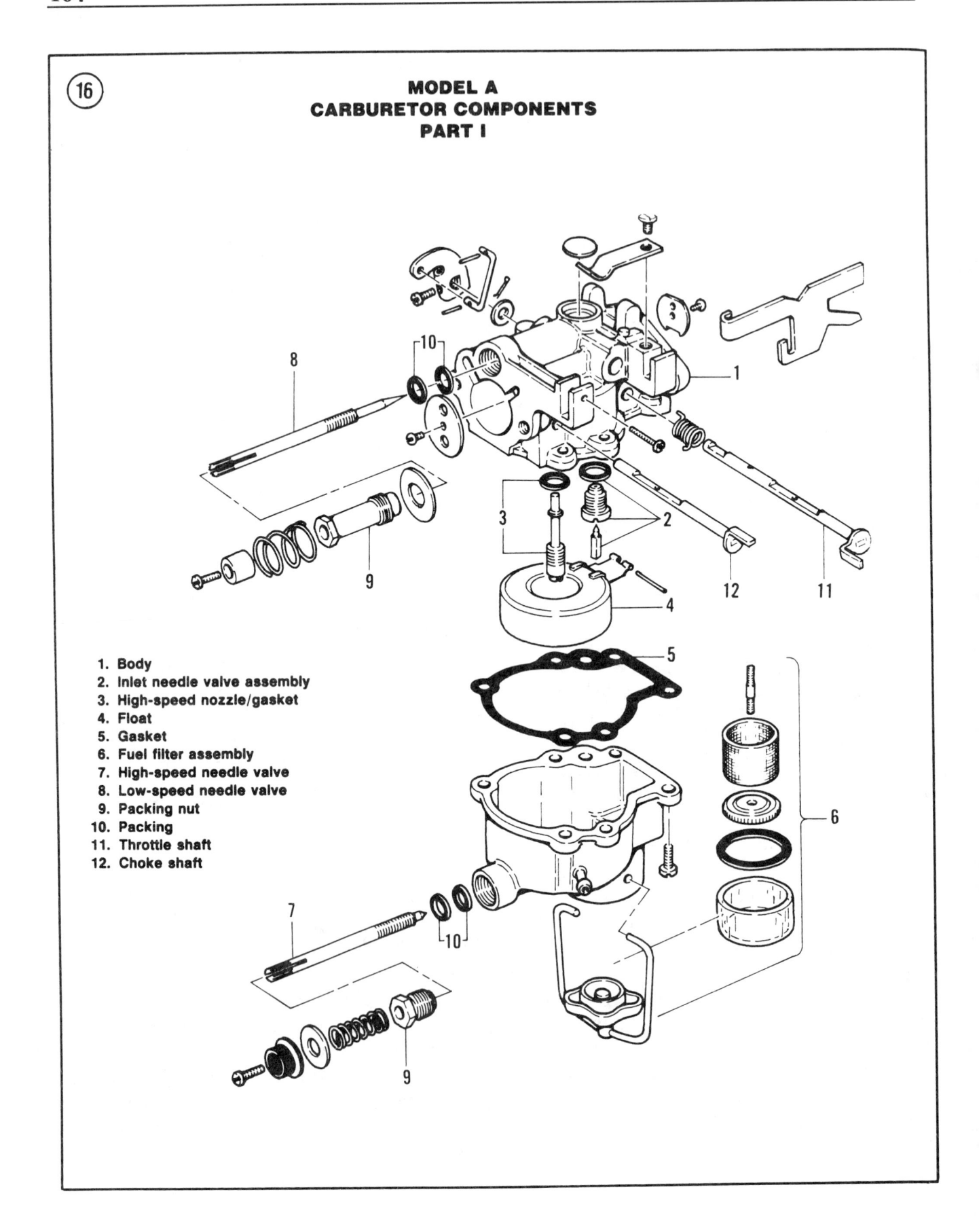

FUEL SYSTEM

MODEL A CARBURETOR COMPONENTS PART III (17)

- Low-speed needle valve
- Packing nut
- High-speed nozzle
- Boss gasket
- Lead shot
- Packing
- Core plug
- Gasket
- Cam follower
- Needle valve assembly
- Needle valve spring
- Packing nut
- Float assembly
- Gasket
- Float chamber
- Lead shot
- Packing
- High-speed needle valve

MODEL A CARBURETOR COMPONENTS PART II (18)

1. Carburetor body
2. Needle valve bushing
3. Packing
4. Packing nut
5. Needle valve
6. High-speed nozzle
7. Inlet needle, valve seat and gasket
8. Gasket
9. Float hinge pin
10. Float assembly
11. Float chamber
12. Orifice
13. Washer
14. Screw plug

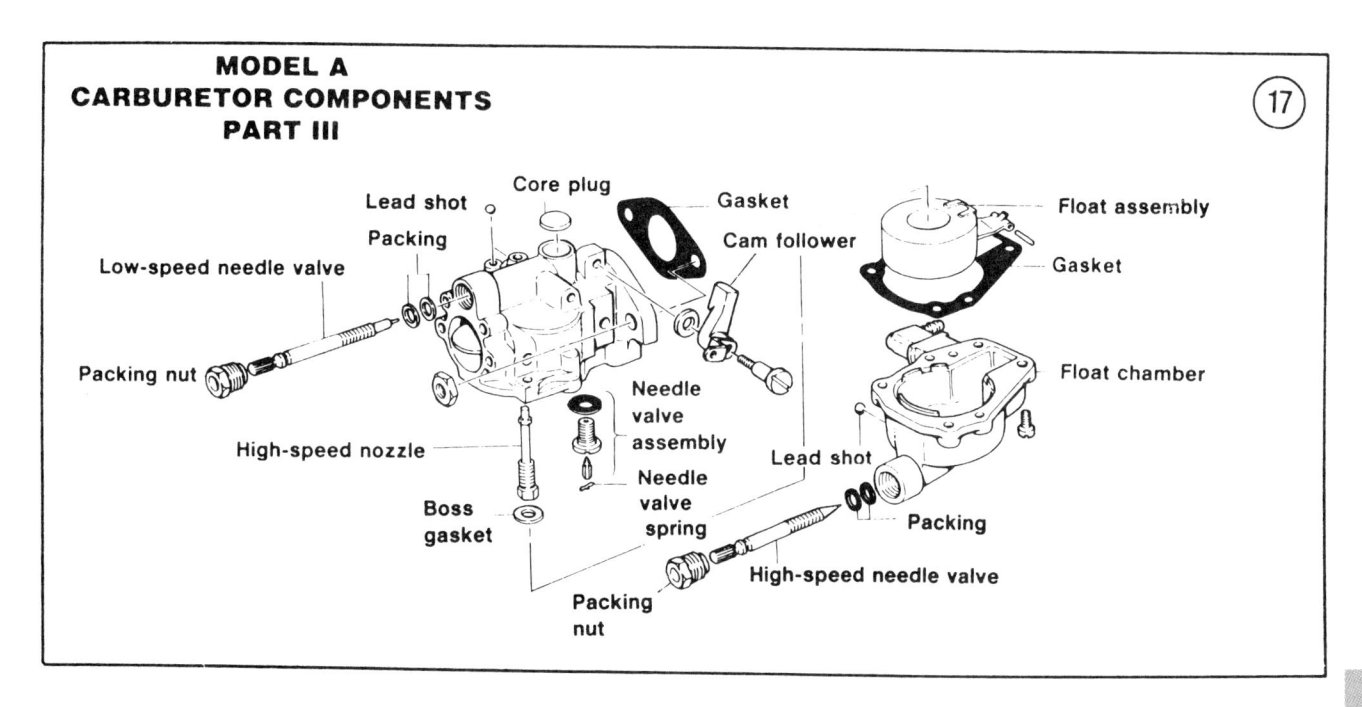

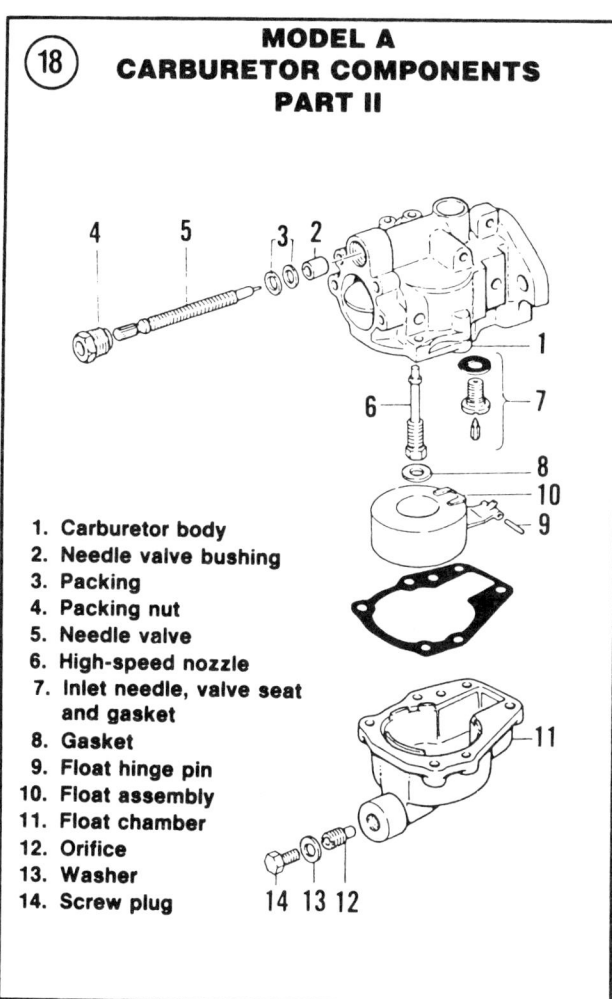

9. Remove the carburetor and gasket from the intake manifold. Discard the gasket.
10. Clean all gasket residue from the manifold mounting surface.
11. Installation is the reverse of removal. Use a new mounting gasket. Tighten mounting nuts alternately to avoid carburetor warpage. Adjust the carburetor (Chapter Five).

Disassembly/Assembly

Refer to **Figures 16-18** (typical) for this procedure.

1. Remove the packing sleeve or nut from each needle valve with a suitable box-end wrench.
2. Remove the needle valve(s). Remove and discard the needle valve packings/washers.
3. If carburetor is fitted with only one needle valve, remove the screw plug and washer from the float chamber. Drain the fuel from the chamber into a suitable container and remove the high-speed orifice with a fixed jet driver (part No. 379664) or equivalent tool.
4. If carburetor has an attached filter bowl:
   a. Loosen the bowl yoke screw. Swing the yoke over the bowl. Remove the bowl.

b. Unscrew the flat milled washer, then remove the gasket and filter element. Discard the bowl gasket and filter element.

5. Remove the screws holding the float chamber to the carburetor body. Remove the float chamber and discard the gasket.

6. Remove the float assembly hinge pin. Lift the float and needle valve from the float chamber.

7. Remove the fuel inlet needle valve seat with a wide-blade screwdriver. Discard the seat gasket.

8. Remove the high-speed nozzle. Remove and discard the nozzle gasket.

9. Assembly is the reverse of disassembly, plus the following:
   a. Compare new gaskets to the old ones to make sure all holes are properly punched. Remove any loose gasket fibers or stamping crumbs adhering to the new gaskets.
   b. Start the packing sleeve/nut into the carburetor, then install and lightly seat the needle valve. Back needle valve out 3/4 turn (high-speed) or 1 1/4 turns (low-speed), then tighten the sleeve/nut just enough to put a drag on the needle valve when it is turned.
   c. Adjust the float as described in this chapter.
   d. Install on engine and adjust carburetor (Chapter Five).

Float Adjustment

1. Invert the carburetor body with its gasket surface horizontal, allowing the float weight to close the needle valve.

2. If the float is not parallel with the casting face (**Figure 19**), bend the metal float arm carefully (to avoid forcing the needle valve into its seat) as necessary to position the float parallel with the float bowl mating surface.

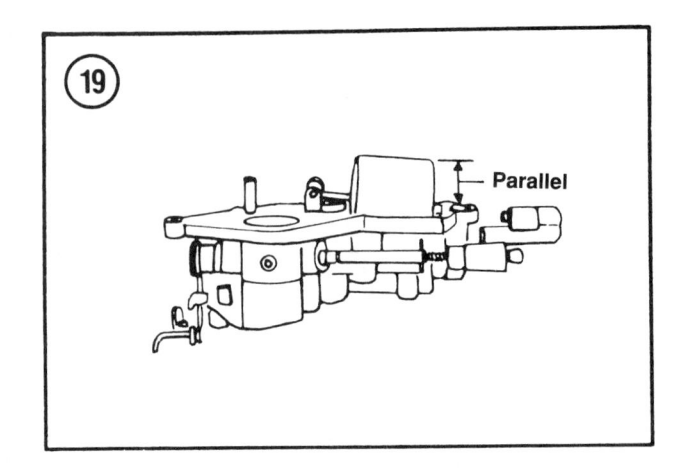

MODEL B CARBURETOR

Removal/Installation

1. Disconnect the fuel line at the engine or fuel tank quick-disconnect.
2. Remove the engine cover.
3. Disconnect the fuel line at the carburetor. Plug the line to prevent leakage.
4A. Cable control model—Remove the low-speed needle valve knob and turn the cable counterclockwise to remove the needle valve from the carburetor. Save the washer and spring installed between the needle valve retaining clip and carburetor. Discard the O-ring.
4B. Linkage control model—Disconnect the linkage. Remove the low-speed needle valve knob and linkage.
5. Remove the 5 screws holding the carburetor to the intake manifold. Remove the carburetor and gasket. Discard the gasket.
6. Clean all gasket residue from the manifold mounting surface.
7. Installation is the reverse of removal. Use a new gasket. Tighten the flat head attaching screw first to prevent carburetor distortion. Back the cable control model needle valve out 1 1/2 turns after lightly seating it. Adjust the carburetor (Chapter Five).

Disassembly/Assembly

Refer to **Figure 20** for this procedure.

FUEL SYSTEM

⑳

**MODEL B
CARBURETOR COMPONENTS**

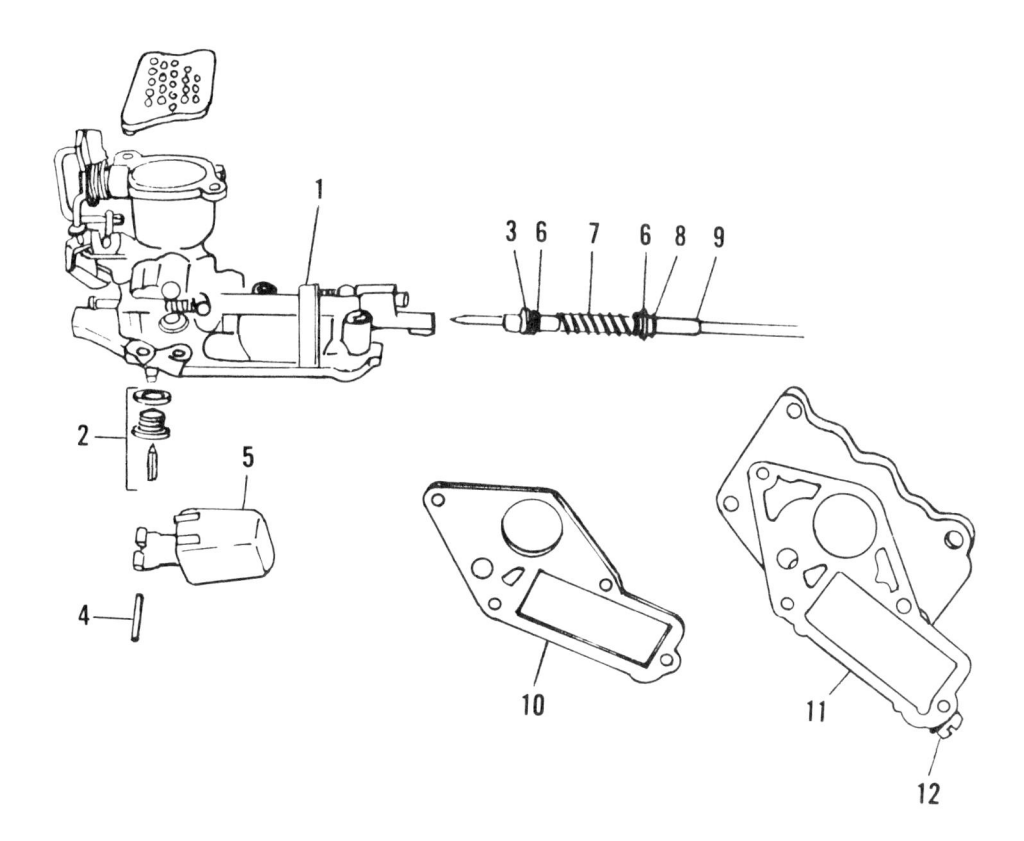

1. Carburetor body
2. Float valve assembly
3. "O ring"
4. Hinge pin
5. Float assembly
6. Washer
7. Slow-speed spring
8. Retaining ring
9. Slow-speed needle valve
10. Gasket
11. Float chamber
12. Plug & gasket

1. Remove the screw plug at the base of the float chamber (if so equipped) and drain the fuel in the chamber into a suitable container.
2. Remove the 4 screws holding the carburetor body to the float chamber. Separate the body and float chamber. Discard the gasket.
3. Note the positioning of the washers and spring on the low-speed needle valve. Loosen the packing nut (turn counterclockwise). Remove the needle valve, washers and spring. Save the washers and spring. Discard the O-ring.
4. Remove the float assembly hinge pin. Lift the float and inlet needle from the float chamber.
5. Remove the inlet needle valve seat with a wide-blade screwdriver. Discard the seat gasket.
6. Remove the high-speed jet from the float chamber with a fixed jet screwdriver (part No. 317002) or equivalent. See **Figure 21**.
7. Assembly is the reverse of disassembly, plus the following:
   a. Compare new gaskets to the old ones to make sure all holes are properly punched. Remove any loose gasket fibers or stamping crumbs adhering to the new gaskets.
   b. Linkage control model—Start the packing nut into the carburetor, then install and lightly seat the needle valve. Back needle valve out 3/4 turn, then tighten the nut just enough to put a drag on the needle valve when it is turned.
   c. Adjust the float as described in this chapter.
   d. Install on engine and adjust carburetor (Chapter Five).

Float Adjustment

1. Invert the carburetor body with its gasket surface horizontal, allowing the float weight to close the needle valve.

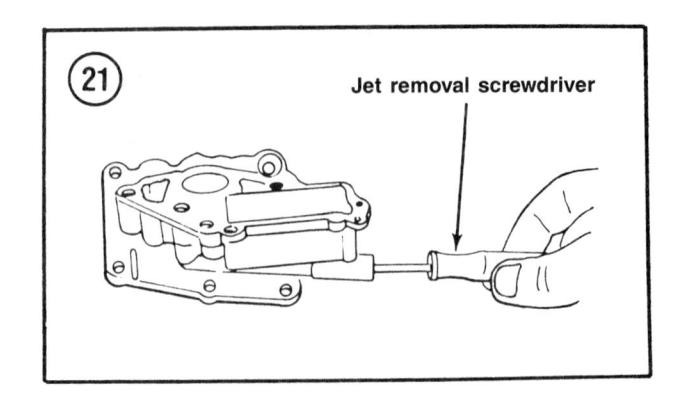

Jet removal screwdriver

2. If the float is not parallel with the casting face (**Figure 19**), bend the metal float arm carefully (to avoid forcing the needle valve into its seat) and bring the float within specifications. Make sure the float is centered in the float bowl after adjustment.
3. Return the carburetor body to its normal running position and check float drop. The distance between the carburetor body and the float as shown in **Figure 22** should be 1 7/16 in. ± 1/16 in.
4. If the float drop is incorrect, carefully bend the float tang until the drop is within specifications.

MODEL C CARBURETOR

Removal/Installation

1. Electric start—Disconnect the negative battery cable.
2. Disconnect the fuel line at the engine or fuel tank quick-disconnect.
3. Remove the engine cover.
4. Remove the air silencer, if so equipped.
5. Disconnect the fuel line at the carburetor. Plug the line to prevent leakage.
6. Hot air/electric choke—Remove the heat tube shield. Loosen the compression nut located under the plate holding the heat tube at the exhaust manifold. Loosen the compression nut holding the heat tube to the carburetor. Unscrew the nuts and remove the tube. Disconnect the choke solenoid electrical lead.

FUEL SYSTEM

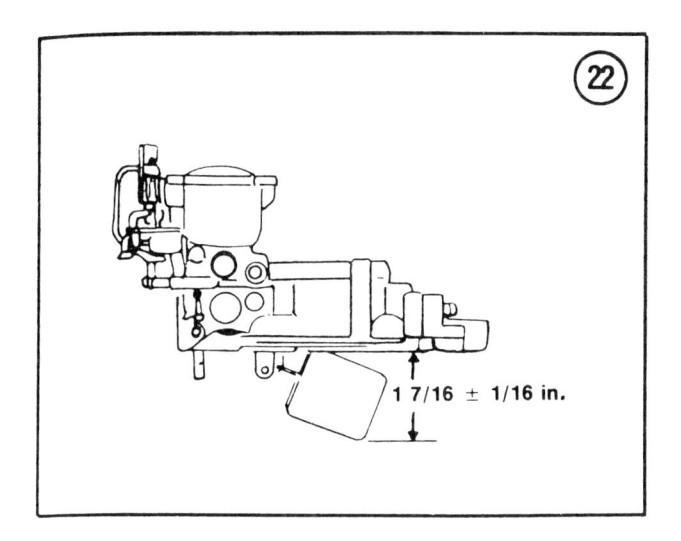

�22

1 7/16 ± 1/16 in.

7. Electric start—Remove the starter and generator.
8. Electric choke—Disconnect the choke solenoid electrical lead.
9. Water choke—Disconnect the water inlet line at the top of the choke. Disconnect the water outlet and vacuum lines at the bottom of the choke.
10. Loosen the carburetor mounting nuts with an open-end wrench. If clearance is a problem, pull the carburetor against the nuts while continuing to loosen them. Remove the mounting nuts and lockwashers.
11. Remove the carburetor and gasket from the intake manifold. Discard the gasket.
12. Clean all gasket residue from the manifold mounting surface.
13. Installation is the reverse of removal. Use a new mounting gasket. Tighten mounting nuts alternately to avoid carburetor warpage. Adjust the carburetor (Chapter Five).

Disassembly/Assembly (Electric Choke Solenoid)

Refer to **Figure 23** (typical) for this procedure.
1. Remove the carburetor as described in this chapter.
2. Scribe a mark on the solenoid and clamp for reinstallation reference.
3. Remove the cotter pin from the solenoid plunger link. Remove the washers and link.
4. Remove the solenoid clamp. Remove the solenoid.
5. Remove the cotter pin at each end of the choke rod. Remove the choke rod from the upper and lower body linkage.
6. Hold the low-speed needle valve knob and remove the screw in the center of the knob. Remove the knob from the needle valve.
7. Remove the screw(s) holding the front shield to the carburetor, if so equipped. Remove the shield and repeat this step to remove the cover screen.
8. Loosen the low-speed needle valve packing nut. Back the needle valve out, then remove the packing nut.
9. Thread an old needle valve into the low-speed needle valve position. Secure the end of the needle valve in a vise and gently tap on the carburetor body until the needle valve comes free with the sleeve and packing.
10A. High-speed needle valve—Repeat Step 8 to remove the high-speed needle valve, then use a small screwdriver to pry the packing from the carburetor.
10B. Fixed high-speed jet—Remove the screw plug and washer from the float chamber. Drain the fuel from the chamber into a suitable container and remove the fixed orifice with a suitable jet remover.
11. Remove the screws holding the float chamber to the carburetor body. Remove the float chamber and discard the gasket.
12. If carburetor has an attached filter bowl:
   a. Loosen the bowl yoke screw. Swing the yoke over the bowl. Remove the bowl.
   b. Unscrew the flat milled washer, then remove the gasket and filter element. Discard the bowl gasket and filter element.
13. Remove the float assembly hinge pin. Lift the float and needle valve from the float chamber.

CHAPTER SIX

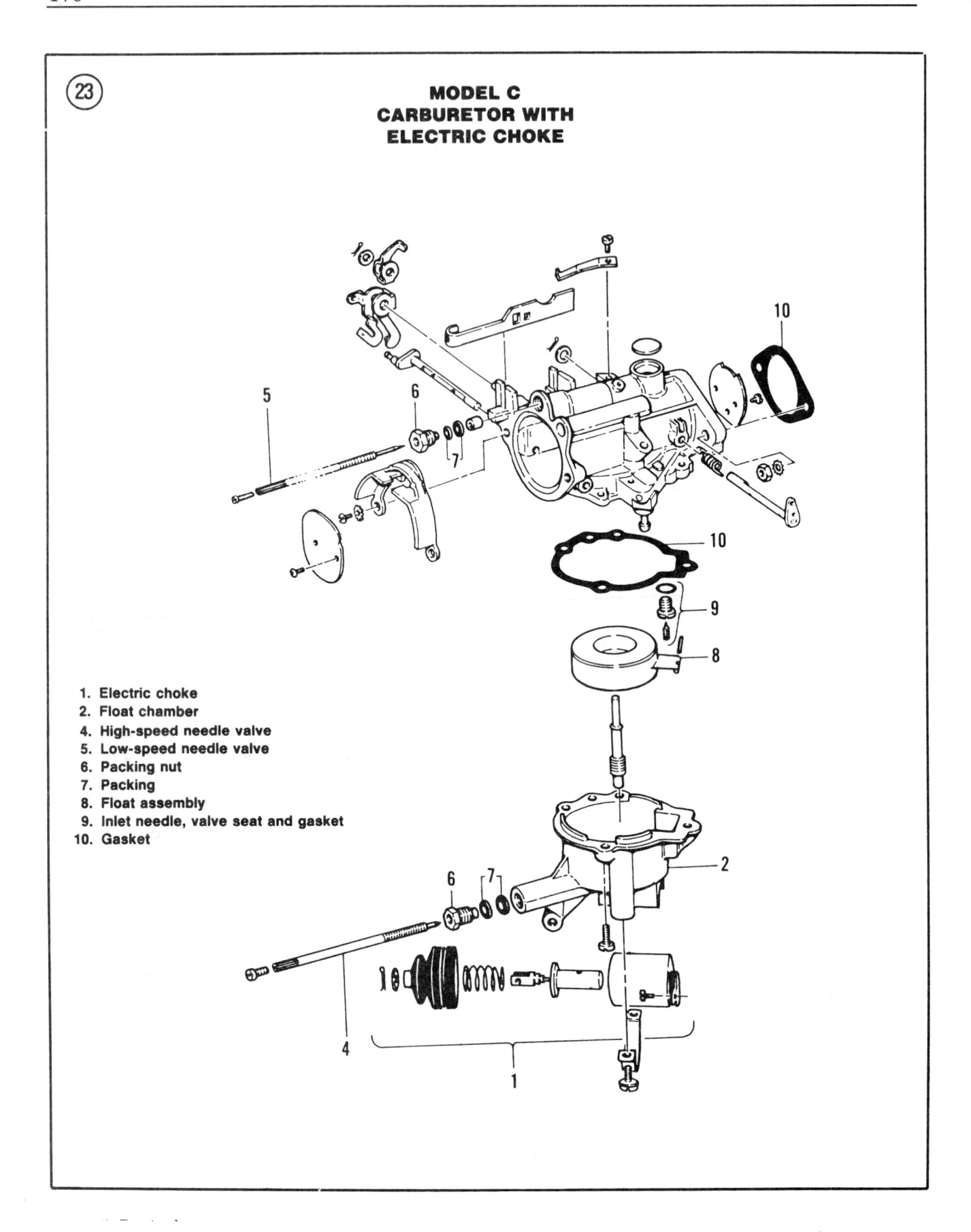

MODEL C CARBURETOR WITH ELECTRIC CHOKE

1. Electric choke
2. Float chamber
4. High-speed needle valve
5. Low-speed needle valve
6. Packing nut
7. Packing
8. Float assembly
9. Inlet needle, valve seat and gasket
10. Gasket

FUEL SYSTEM

14. Remove the fuel inlet needle valve seat with a wide-bladed screwdriver. Discard the seat gasket.
15. Remove the high-speed nozzle. Remove and discard the nozzle gasket.
16. Assembly is the reverse of disassembly, plus the following:
   a. Compare new gaskets to the old ones to make sure all holes are properly punched. Remove any loose gasket fibers or stamping crumbs adhering to the new gaskets.
   b. Install the low-speed bushing and washers, then start the packing nut into the carburetor. Install and lightly seat the needle valve. Back needle valve out 1 1/2 turns, then tighten the nut just enough to put a drag on the needle valve when it is turned. Repeat this step if carburetor is equipped with a high-speed needle valve, backing it out 3/4 turn.
   c Adjust the float as described in this chapter.
   d. Install on engine and adjust carburetor (Chapter Five).

Float Adjustment

1. Invert the carburetor body with its gasket surface horizontal, allowing the float weight to close the needle valve.
2. If the float is not parallel with the casting face (**Figure 19**), bend the metal float arm carefully (to avoid forcing the needle valve into its seat) and bring the float within specifications. Make sure the float is centered in the float bowl after adjustment.

**Disassembly/Assembly
(Hot Water Choke)**

Refer to **Figure 24** (typical) for this procedure.

1. Remove the carburetor as described in this chapter.
2. Scribe a mark on the choke cap and base for reinstallation reference. See **Figure 25**.
3. Remove the 3 cap screws (**Figure 26**). Remove the cap from the choke housing.
4. Remove the diaphragm housing screws. Remove the housing. Remove the spring, valve and support from the diaphragm housing. Remove the diaphragm from the choke housing.
5. Hold the low-speed needle valve knob and remove the screw in the center of the knob. Remove the knob from the needle valve.
6. Remove the screw(s) holding the front shield to the carburetor, if so equipped. Remove the shield and repeat this step to remove the cover screen.
7. Loosen the low-speed needle valve packing nut. Back the needle valve out, then remove the packing nut.
8. Thread an old needle valve into the low-speed needle valve position. Secure the end of the needle valve in a vise and gently tap on the carburetor body until the needle valve comes free with the sleeve and packing.
9A. High-speed needle valve—Repeat Step 7 to remove the high-speed needle valve, then use a small screwdriver to pry the packing from the carburetor.
9B. Fixed high-speed jet—Remove the screw plug and washer from the float chamber. Drain the fuel from the chamber into a suitable container and remove the fixed orifice with a suitable jet remover.
10. Remove the screws holding the float chamber to the carburetor body. Remove the float chamber and discard the gasket.
11. If carburetor has an attached filter bowl:
   a. Loosen the bowl yoke screw. Swing the yoke over the bowl. Remove the bowl.
   b. Unscrew the flat milled washer, then remove the gasket and filter element. Discard the bowl gasket and filter element.

CHAPTER SIX

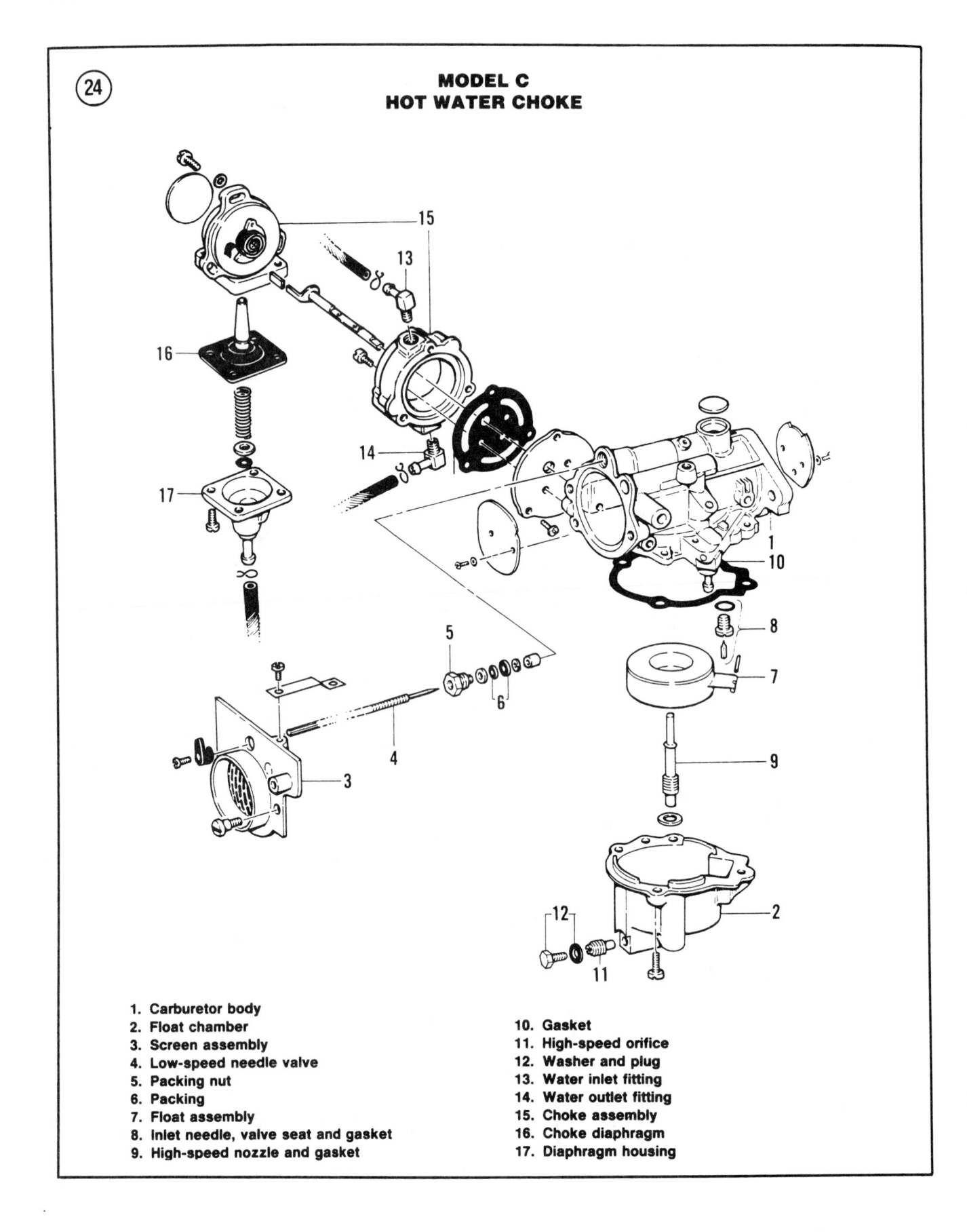

MODEL C HOT WATER CHOKE

1. Carburetor body
2. Float chamber
3. Screen assembly
4. Low-speed needle valve
5. Packing nut
6. Packing
7. Float assembly
8. Inlet needle, valve seat and gasket
9. High-speed nozzle and gasket
10. Gasket
11. High-speed orifice
12. Washer and plug
13. Water inlet fitting
14. Water outlet fitting
15. Choke assembly
16. Choke diaphragm
17. Diaphragm housing

FUEL SYSTEM

fibers or stamping crumbs adhering to the new gaskets.
b. Install the low-speed bushing and washers, then start the packing nut into the carburetor. Install and lightly seat the needle valve. Back needle valve out 1 1/2 turns, then tighten the nut just enough to put a drag on the needle valve when it is turned. Repeat this step if carburetor is equipped with a high-speed needle valve, backing it out 3/4 turn.
c. Adjust the float as described in this chapter.
d. Install carburetor on engine and adjust as described in Chapter Five.

Float Adjustment

1. Invert the carburetor body with its gasket surface horizontal, allowing the float weight to close the needle valve.
2. If the float is not parallel with the casting face (**Figure 19**), bend the metal float arm carefully (to avoid forcing the needle valve into its seat) and bring the float within specifications. Make sure the float is centered in the float bowl after adjustment.

Disassembly/Assembly (Hot Air/Electric Choke)

Refer to **Figure 27** (typical) for this procedure.
1. Remove the carburetor as described in this chapter.
2. Note the relationship of the choke cap and housing marks for reinstallation reference.
3. Remove the 3 cap screws. Remove the cap and gasket from the choke housing. Discard the gasket.
4. Remove the screws holding the solenoid to the carburetor. Remove the solenoid assembly and gasket from the choke housing. Discard the gasket.

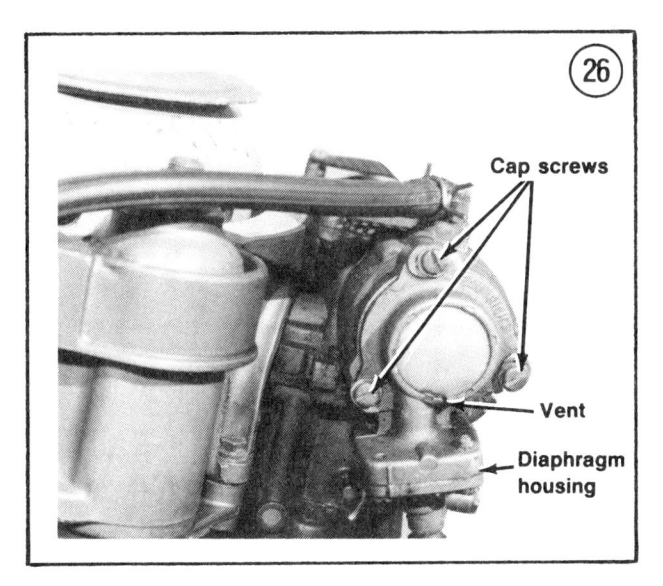

12. Remove the float assembly hinge pin. Lift the float and needle valve from the float chamber.
13. Remove the fuel inlet needle valve seat with a wide-bladed screwdriver. Discard the seat gasket.
14. Remove the high-speed nozzle. Remove and discard the nozzle gasket.
15. Assembly is the reverse of disassembly, plus the following:
  a. Compare new gaskets to the old ones to make sure all holes are properly punched. Remove any loose gasket

CHAPTER SIX

(27) MODEL C CARBURETOR WITH HOT AIR/ELECTRIC CHOKE

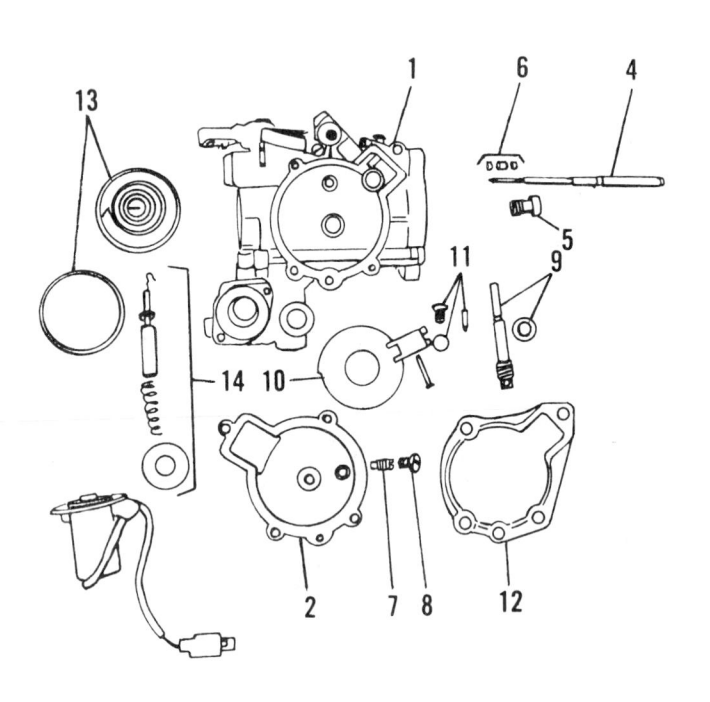

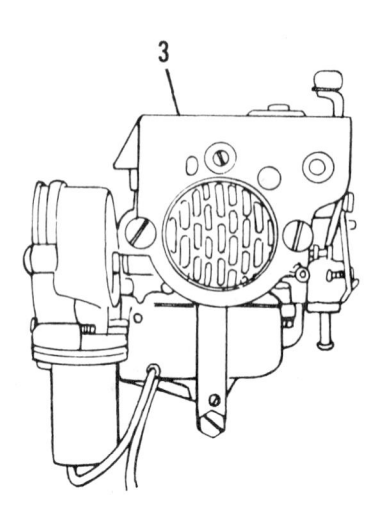

1. Carburetor body
2. Float chamber
3. Screen assembly
4. Low-speed needle valve
5. Packing nut
6. Packing
7. High-speed orifice
8. Washer and plug
9. High-speed nozzle and gasket
10. Float assembly
11. Inlet needle, valve seat and gasket
12. Gasket
13. Choke assembly
14. Choke solenoid assembly

FUEL SYSTEM

5. Disconnect the choke housing spring from the choke lever with needlenose pliers. Remove the spring and plunger.
6. Hold the low-speed needle valve knob and remove the screw in the center of the knob. Remove the knob from the needle valve.
7. Remove the screw(s) holding the front shield (if so equipped) to the carburetor. Remove the shield and repeat this step to remove the cover screen.
8. Loosen the low-speed needle valve packing nut. Back the needle valve out, then remove the packing nut.
9. Thread an old needle valve into the low-speed needle valve position. Secure the end of the needle valve in a vise and gently tap on the carburetor body until the needle valve comes free with the sleeve and packing.
10A. High-speed needle valve—Repeat Step 8 to remove the high-speed needle valve, then use a small screwdriver to pry the packing from the carburetor.
10B. Fixed high-speed jet—Remove the screw plug and washer from the float chamber. Drain the fuel from the chamber into a suitable container and remove the fixed orifice with a suitable jet remover.
11. Remove the screws holding the float chamber to the carburetor body. Remove the float chamber and discard the gasket.
12. If carburetor has an attached filter bowl:
    a. Loosen the bowl yoke screw. Swing the yoke over the bowl. Remove the bowl.
    b. Unscrew the flat milled washer, then remove the gasket and filter element. Discard the bowl gasket and filter element.
13. Remove the float assembly hinge pin. Lift the float and needle valve from the float chamber.
14. Remove the fuel inlet needle valve seat with a wide-bladed screwdriver. Discard the seat gasket.
15. Remove the high-speed nozzle. Remove and discard the nozzle gasket.
16. Assembly is the reverse of disassembly, plus the following:
    a. Compare new gaskets to the old ones to make sure all holes are properly punched. Remove any loose gasket fibers or stamping crumbs adhering to the new gaskets.
    b. Install the low-speed bushing and washers, then start the packing nut into the carburetor. Install and lightly seat the needle valve. Back needle valve out 1 1/2 turns, then tighten the nut just enough to put a drag on the needle valve when it is turned. Repeat this step if carburetor is equipped with a high-speed needle valve, backing it out 3/4 turn.
    c. Adjust the float as described in this chapter.
    d. Install on engine and adjust carburetor (Chapter Five).

Float Adjustment

1. Invert the carburetor body with its gasket surface horizontal, allowing the float weight to close the needle valve.
2. If the float is not parallel with the casting face (**Figure 19**), bend the metal float arm carefully (to avoid forcing the needle valve into its seat) and bring the float within specifications. Make sure the float is centered in the float bowl after adjustment.

MODEL D CARBURETOR

Removal/Installation

1. Electric start—Disconnect the negative battery cable.
2. Disconnect the fuel line at the engine or fuel tank quick-disconnect.
3. Remove the engine cover.
4. Disconnect all fuel lines at the fuel pump.

CHAPTER SIX

CARBURETOR (EARLY 50-70 HP)

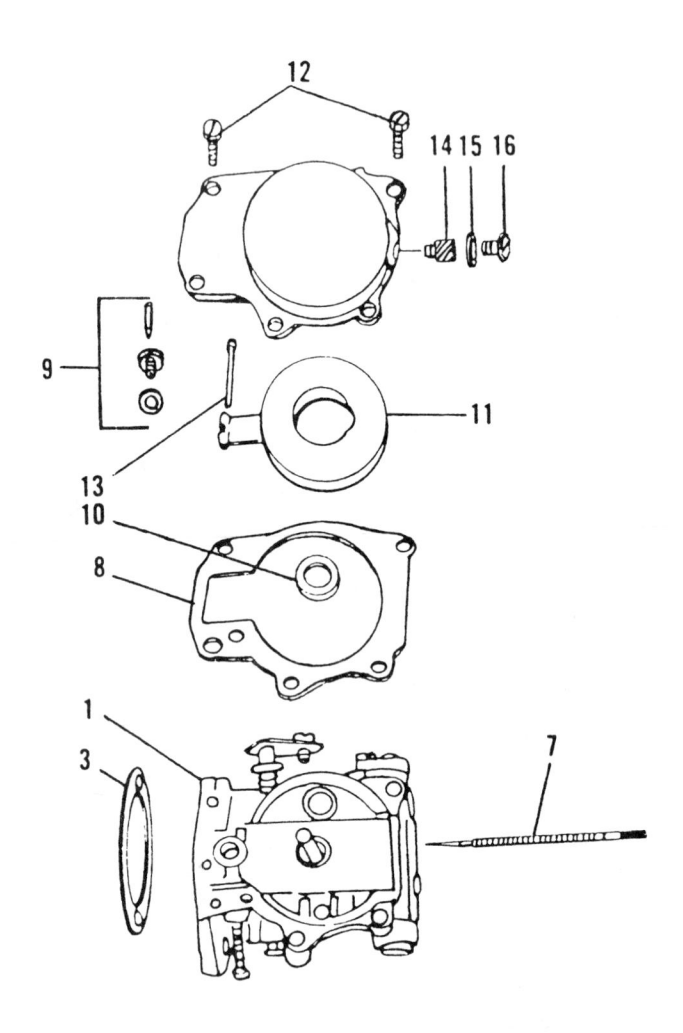

1. Body
3. Mounting gasket
7. Low-speed needle valve
8. Fuel bowl gasket
9. Needle valve and seat assembly
10. Nozzle gasket
11. Float assembly
12. Float bowl screws
13. Float pin
14. High-speed orifice plug
15. Washer
16. Screw plug

FUEL SYSTEM

8. Remove the air silencer and fuel pump as an assembly.
9. Disconnect the choke solenoid spring.
10. Remove the ring gear guard.
11. Disconnect the fuel lines between the carburetor(s) to be removed.
12. Loosen the carburetor mounting nuts with an open-end wrench. If clearance is a problem, pull the carburetor against the nuts while continuing to loosen them. Remove the mounting nuts and lockwashers. Repeat this step if more than one carburetor is being removed.
13. Remove the carburetor and gasket from the intake manifold. Discard the gasket.
14. Clean all gasket residue from the manifold mounting surface.
15. Installation is the reverse of removal. Use a new mounting gasket. Tighten mounting nuts alternately to avoid carburetor warpage. Adjust the choke linkage, throttle linkage and carburetor (Chapter Five) before reinstalling the air silencer cover.

Disassembly/Assembly

Refer to **Figure 28** for this procedure.
1. Remove the float chamber drain or fuel line plug and washer. Drain any fuel remaining in the carburetor into a suitable container.
2. Remove the fixed high-speed orifice from the float bowl with jet remover part No. 379664 or a suitable equivalent. **Figure 29** shows the plug and orifice removed.
3. Temporarily reinstall the low-speed needle valve knob and remove the needle valve (**Figure 30**) from the carburetor.
4. Insert a length of wire with a hooked end in the needle valve keyhole slot and remove the Delrin retainer.
5. Remove the float chamber screws. Separate the float chamber from the main body (**Figure 31**). Discard the float chamber gasket.

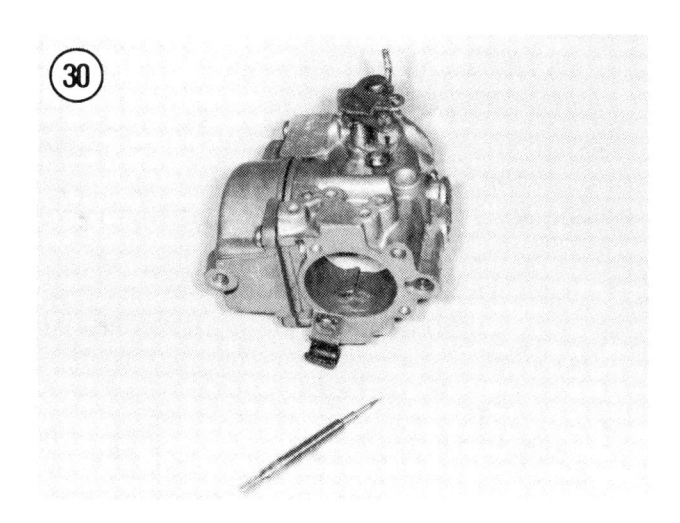

5. Remove the low-speed adjustment lever screw. Remove the lever from the air silencer cover.
6. Remove the air silencer cover and gasket. Disconnect the drain hose.
7. Pull the throttle, choke and low-speed needle valve linkages from the top and bottom carburetor lever retainers.

6. Remove the float hinge pin. Remove the float and inlet needle valve from the float chamber. See **Figure 32**.
7. Remove the inlet needle valve seat (**Figure 33**) with a wide-blade screwdriver. Discard the seat gasket.
8. Remove and discard all gaskets, O-rings or sealing washers in the carburetor body casting.
9. Assembly is the reverse of disassembly, plus the following:
  a. Compare new gaskets to the old ones to make sure all holes are properly punched. Remove any loose gasket fibers or stamping crumbs adhering to the new gaskets.
  b. Install the Delrin retainer in the carburetor, then install and lightly seat the needle valve. Back needle valve out 5/8 turn.
  c. Adjust the float as described in this chapter.
  d. Install on engine and adjust the choke linkage, throttle linkage and carburetor (Chapter Five).

Float Adjustment

1. Invert the carburetor body with its gasket surface horizontal, allowing the float weight to close the needle valve.
2. If the float is not parallel with the casting face (**Figure 19**), bend the metal float arm carefully (to avoid forcing the needle valve into its seat) and bring the float within specifications. Make sure the float is centered in the float bowl after adjustment.

MODEL E CARBURETOR

Removal/Installation

1. Electric start—Disconnect the negative battery cable.
2. Disconnect the fuel line at the engine or fuel tank quick-disconnect.
3. Remove the engine cover.
4. Disconnect the throttle control rod at the throttle cam. Some engines use a single screw; others have an outer and inner setscrew that must be removed. Remove the return spring.
5. Hot air/electric choke—Remove the heat tube shield. Loosen the compression nut located under the plate holding the heat tube at the exhaust manifold. Loosen the compression nut holding the heat tube to the carburetor. Unscrew the nuts and remove the tube. Disconnect the choke solenoid electrical lead.
6. Electric choke—Disconnect the choke solenoid electrical lead.
7. Water choke—Disconnect the water inlet line at the top of the choke. Disconnect the water outlet and vacuum lines at the bottom of the choke.
8. Remove the 3 bolts holding the carburetor to the intake manifold. Remove the

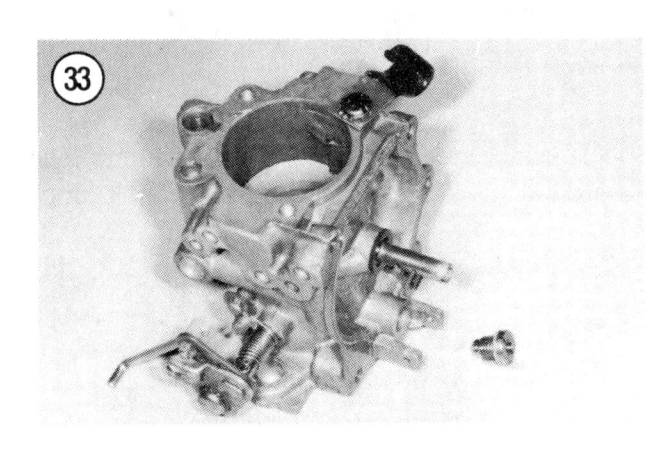

FUEL SYSTEM

carburetor from the manifold and disconnect the fuel line at its rear. Remove and discard the gasket.

9. Clean all gasket residue from the manifold mounting surface.

10. Installation is the reverse of removal. Use a new mounting gasket. Tighten mounting bolts alternately to avoid carburetor warpage. Adjust the choke linkage, throttle linkage and carburetor (Chapter Five).

Disassembly/Assembly

Refer to **Figure 34** or **Figure 35** (typical) for this procedure.

1A. If equipped with an electric choke solenoid:
   a. Scribe a mark on the solenoid and clamp for reinstallation reference.
   b. Remove the cotter pin from the solenoid plunger link. Remove the washers and link.

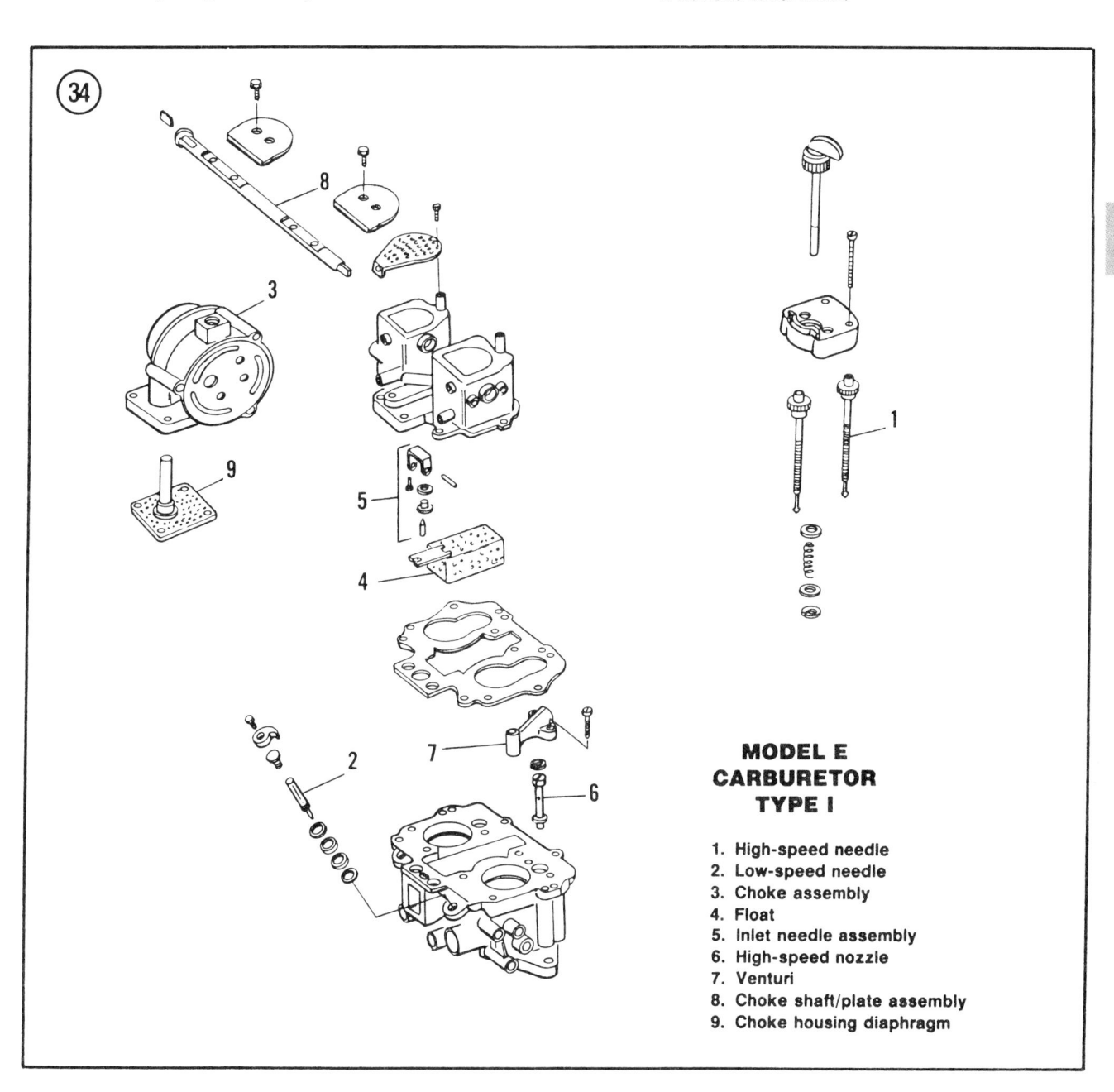

MODEL E CARBURETOR TYPE I

1. High-speed needle
2. Low-speed needle
3. Choke assembly
4. Float
5. Inlet needle assembly
6. High-speed nozzle
7. Venturi
8. Choke shaft/plate assembly
9. Choke housing diaphragm

c. Remove the solenoid clamp. Remove the solenoid.
d. Remove the cotter pin at each end of the choke rod. Remove the choke rod from the upper and lower body linkage.

1B. If equipped with a hot water choke:
a. Scribe a mark on the choke cap and base for reinstallation reference. See **Figure 25**.
b. Remove the 3 cap screws (**Figure 26**). Remove the cap from the choke housing.
c. Remove the diaphragm housing screws. Remove the housing. Remove the spring, valve and support from the diaphragm housing. Remove the diaphragm from the choke housing.

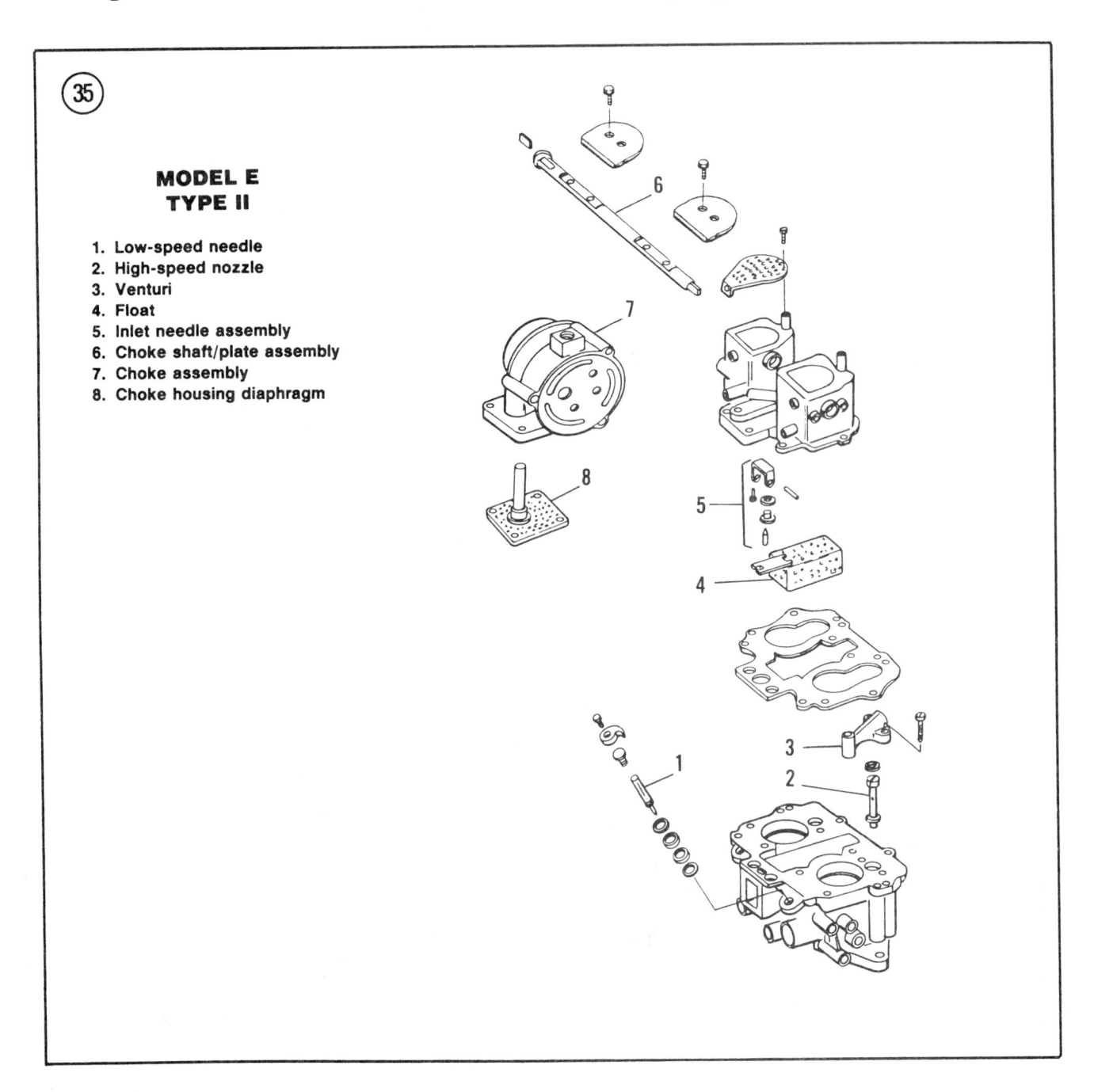

㉟

MODEL E TYPE II

1. Low-speed needle
2. High-speed nozzle
3. Venturi
4. Float
5. Inlet needle assembly
6. Choke shaft/plate assembly
7. Choke assembly
8. Choke housing diaphragm

FUEL SYSTEM

1C. If equipped with a hot air/electric choke:
   a. Note the relationship of the choke cap and housing marks for reinstallation reference.
   b. Remove the 3 cap screws. Remove the cap and gasket from the choke housing. Discard the gasket.
   c. Remove the screws holding the solenoid to the carburetor. Remove the solenoid assembly and gasket from the choke housing. Discard the gasket.
   d. Disconnect the choke housing spring from the choke lever with needlenose pliers. Remove the spring and plunger.
2. Remove all screws from the top of the carburetor. If there is a clip under one screw, be sure to note its position for reassembly reference.
3. High-speed needle valve—Disconnect the rod between the low- and high-speed needle valves. Remove the rod, washers and spring. Back out both high-speed needle valves.
4. Separate the air horn from the carburetor body.
5. Invert the air horn and remove the float hinge pin. Remove the float and inlet needle valve from the float chamber.
6. Remove the inlet needle valve seat with a wide-bladed screwdriver. Discard the seat gasket.
7A. If the carburetor is not equipped with a high-speed needle valve, remove the low-speed needle valve, venturis and high-speed tubes as follows:
   a. Hold the low-speed adjusting knob and remove the screw from the knob. Pull the knob off the needle valve.
   b. Loosen the packing nut and back the low-speed needle valve out of the carburetor.
   c. Remove the packing nut and packing.
   d. Remove the venturi screws. Remove the venturis.
   e. Remove the O-ring from each high-speed tube.
   f. Turn the high-speed tube counterclockwise with a suitable screwdriver and remove from the carburetor. Repeat this step with the second high-speed tube.
7B. If the carburetor is equipped with a high-speed needle valve, remove the low-speed needle valve, venturis and high-speed tubes as follows:
   a. Remove the low-speed needle adjusting knob and back the needle out of the carburetor.
   b. Remove and discard the needle valve O-ring.
   c. Remove the venturi screws. Remove the venturis and high-speed tubes as an assembly.
8. Remove the drain plugs from the bottom of the carburetor and drain any fuel remaining in the carburetor into a suitable container.

NOTE
Some carburetors which use a high-speed needle valve also use a high-speed orifice.

9. Remove the fixed high-speed orifices from the carburetor with jet remover part No. 317001 or a suitable equivalent.
10. Assembly is the reverse of disassembly, plus the following:
   a. Compare new gaskets to the old ones to make sure all holes are properly punched. Remove any loose gasket fibers or stamping crumbs adhering to the new gaskets.
   b. If equipped with high-speed needle valves, install the venturi screws lightly and center each venturi in the carburetor throat with OMC tool part No. 379242, then tighten the venturi screws.
   c. Install and lightly seat the needle valves. Back each low-speed needle valve out

1 1/2 turns. Back high-speed needle valves out 3/4 turn.

d. Adjust the float as described in this chapter.
e. Install carburetor on engine and adjust the choke linkage, throttle linkage and carburetor (Chapter Five).

Float Adjustment

1. Invert the carburetor body with its gasket surface horizontal, allowing the float weight to close the needle valve.
2. If the float is not parallel with the casting face (**Figure 19**), bend the metal float arm carefully (to avoid forcing the needle valve into its seat) and bring the float within specifications. Make sure the float is centered in the float bowl after adjustment.

MODEL F CARBURETOR

This carburetor differs considerably from other Johnson and Evinrude designs. The heavy (and expensive) 4-bbl. carburetor housing functions as 4 individual carburetors, each containing a float and all other basic circuits. Fuel level is extremely critical, requiring that all 4 floats be properly adjusted to provide a sufficient and balanced amount of fuel to each cylinder. For proper operation, carburetor adjustments must be balanced and exactly on specification.

Early models use a hot air choke on the top of the carburetor with an electric solenoid at the bottom; later models are equipped with an automatic choke and top-mounted solenoid. The automatic choke may be manually operated. When in automatic, a thermal switch installed in the cylinder block energizes the 2-stage solenoid to place the choke in a "warm-up" mode when engine temperature is 75° F or less. A manual override switch on the control box allows the user to energize the choke at any temperature. **Figure 36** shows the automatic choke components and operation.

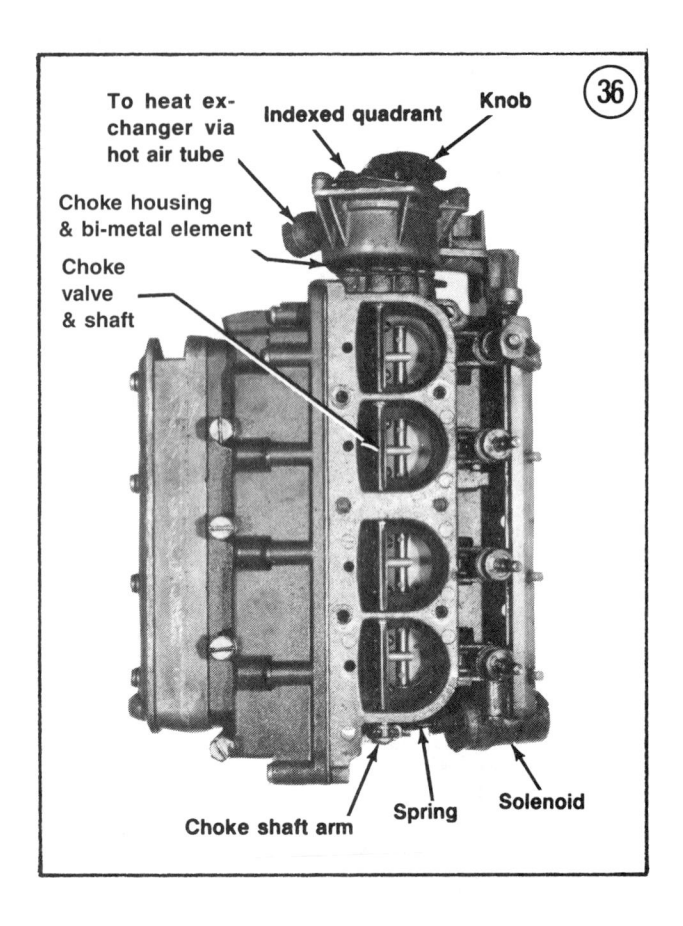

Removal/Installation

1. Electric start—Disconnect the negative battery cable.
2. Disconnect the fuel line at the engine or fuel tank quick-disconnect.
3. Remove the engine cover.
4. Unscrew the heat exchanger tube gland nuts at the choke housing and heat exchanger. Move the tube back to one side to permit carburetor removal.
5. Disconnect the fuel line at the carburetor. See A, **Figure 37**.
6. Disconnect the choke solenoid at the connector. See B, **Figure 37** (bottom-mounted choke).
7. Remove the cotter pin and disconnect the throttle control rod at the throttle cam assembly. See A, **Figure 38**.

FUEL SYSTEM

183

forward to provide clearance. Note that a ground lead is connected to the long bolt.

11. When all bolts are removed, remove the carburetor and gasket. Discard the gasket.

12. Installation is the reverse of removal. Use a new mounting gasket. Tighten mounting bolts alternately to avoid carburetor warpage. Be sure to reinstall ground lead under the appropriate bolt. Adjust the choke linkage, throttle linkage and carburetor (Chapter Five).

Disassembly/Assembly

Refer to **Figure 39** for this procedure.

1. Remove the choke lead clamp screw and move the clamp away from the carburetor body.

2. Remove the bracket holding the choke solenoid to the carburetor body. Remove the solenoid.

3. Remove the adjustment knob from each needle valve. Remove the screws holding the vertical or gang bar to the carburetor. Remove the vertical bar with adjustment knobs attached.

4. Remove each of the high-speed jet passage plugs (**Figure 40**) and drain the carburetor float bowls into a suitable container.

5. Remove the 4 screws holding the float chamber cover plate. Remove the cover plate.

6. Remove the float chamber screws (**Figure 41**). Holding the carburetor body and float chamber together, carefully invert the assembly to position the float chamber on the workbench. This will prevent the floats and inlet needles from falling out when the two units are separated.

7. Lift the carburetor body up and off the float chamber.

8. Carefully remove each of the floats with needlenose pliers. Position in order of removal for proper reinstallation.

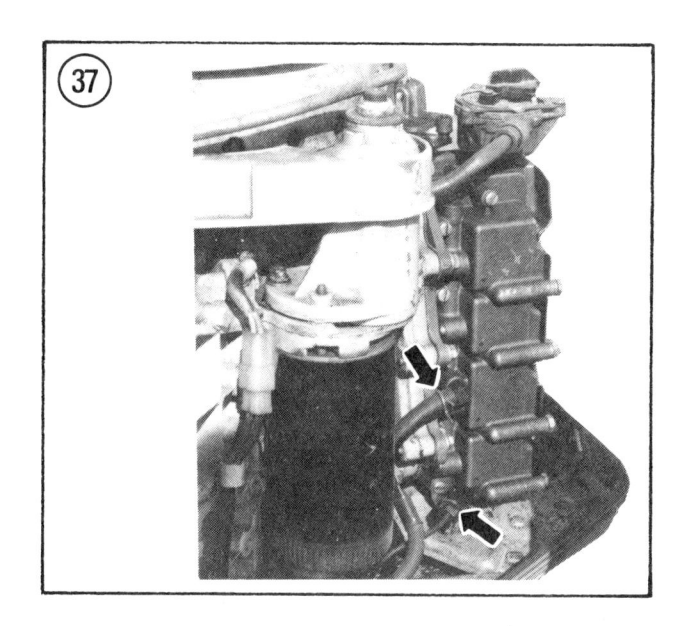

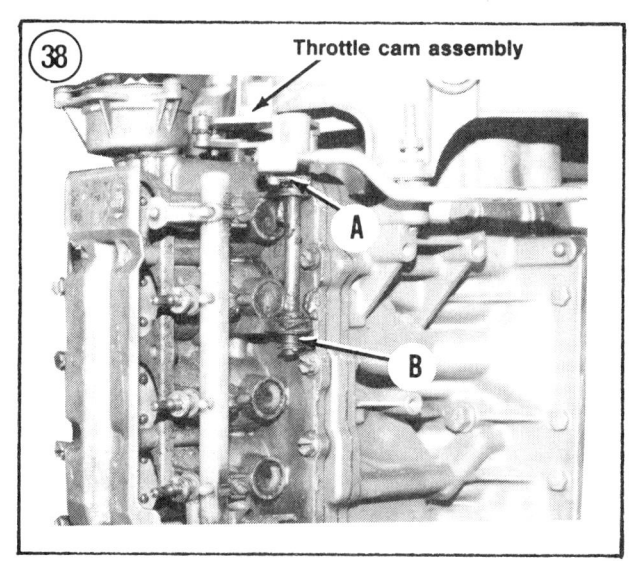

8. Remove the cotter pin from the bottom of the throttle cam assembly (B, **Figure 38**). Disconnect the throttle cam assembly from the carburetor. Make sure to retain the washers and spring.

9. Disconnect the hose at the bottom of the shield on the front of the carburetor. Remove the screws holding the shield. Remove the shield.

10. Use a 3/8 in. flexible socket and extension to remove the 10 bolts holding the carburetor to the intake manifold. Loosen the bolts alternately, pulling the carburetor

CHAPTER SIX

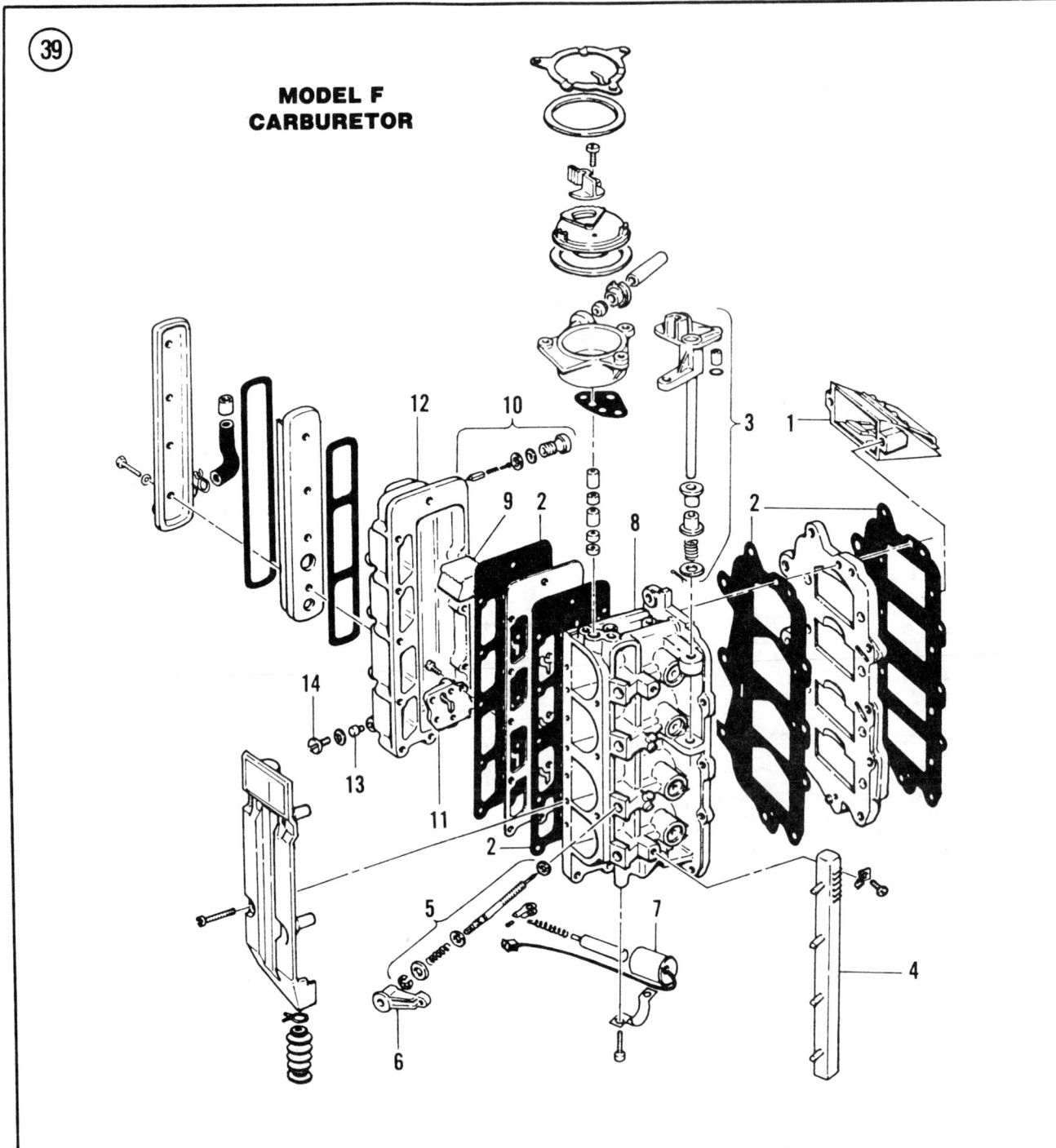

MODEL F CARBURETOR

1. Reed block
2. Gasket
3. Heated choke assembly
4. Adjusting link
5. Needle valve assembly
6. Knob
7. Choke solenoid
8. Carburetor body
9. Float
10. Inlet needle and seat assembly
11. High-speed tube
12. Float chamber
13. Jet plug
14. Screw

FUEL SYSTEM

40
Float chamber, Float, Gasket, Spring & Pin, Seat, Needle, O-ring, Hinge pin, Screw plug & Washer, Orifice plug

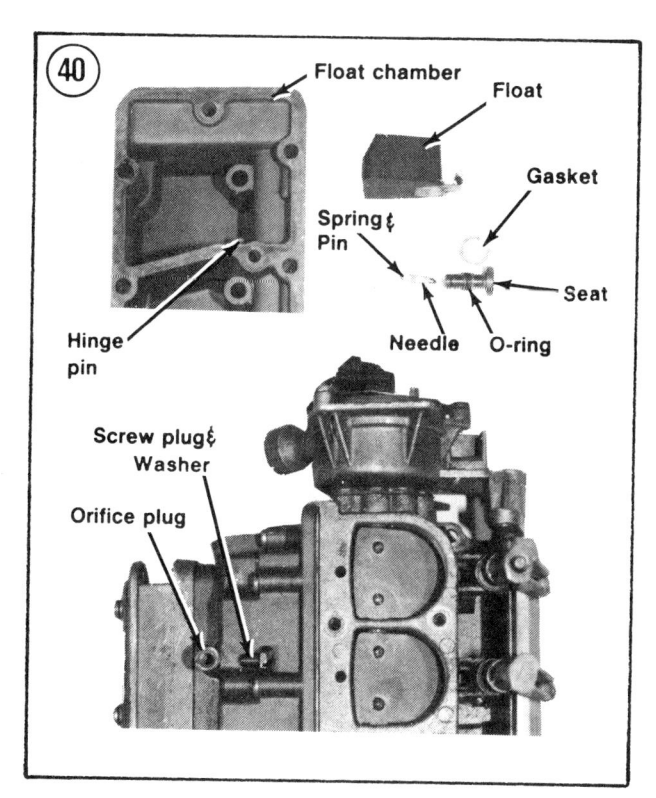

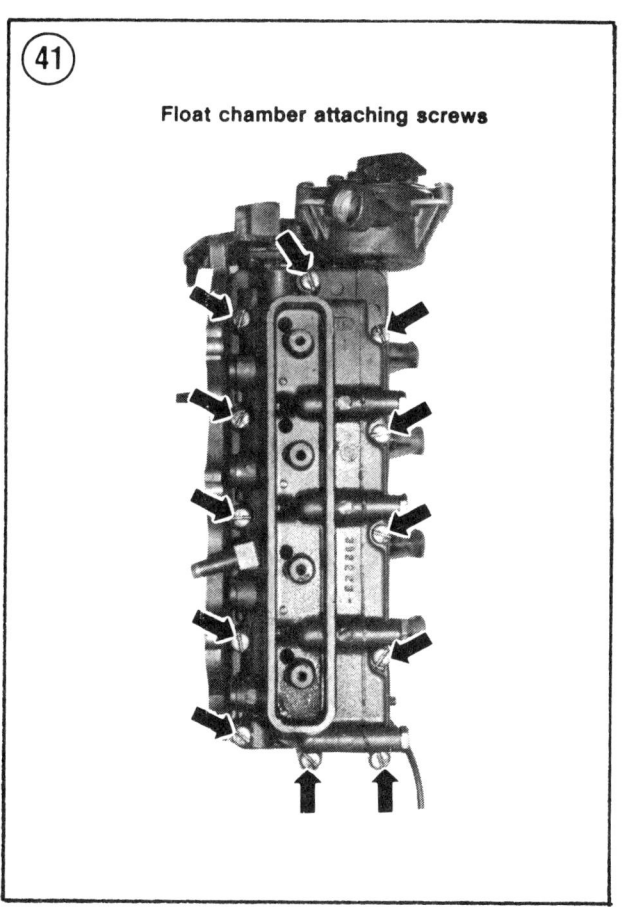

41 Float chamber attaching screws

42 O-ring, Washer, Spring, Washer, Needle valve, Retaining ring

NOTE
Each inlet needle valve contains a spring, pin and needle. Do not lose these components if the same inlet needle valves are to be reinstalled.

9. Remove one inlet needle, needle seat and gasket (**Figure 40**). Discard the gasket and place the inlet needle and seat with its float. Repeat this step for each remaining chamber.

10. Remove the 4 high-speed orifices (**Figure 40**) from the carburetor body with jet remover part No. 379664 or part No. 317002.

11. Remove each of the low-speed needle valves from the carburetor body (**Figure 42**). Be sure to retain the washers and spring used with each needle valve. Pry the O-ring from each low-speed needle opening with a small screwdriver or hooked awl. Discard the O-rings.

12. Remove each of the 4 high-speed tube assemblies (**Figure 43**) from the float chamber side of the carburetor.

13. If equipped with a heated choke, remove the choke cap retainer screws. Remove the retainer, washer and choke housing.

14. This completes disassembly of the carburetor for normal cleaning purposes. Do *not* immerse the carburetor in cleaning solvent as it will destroy the choke shaft bushings. The choke and throttle shafts

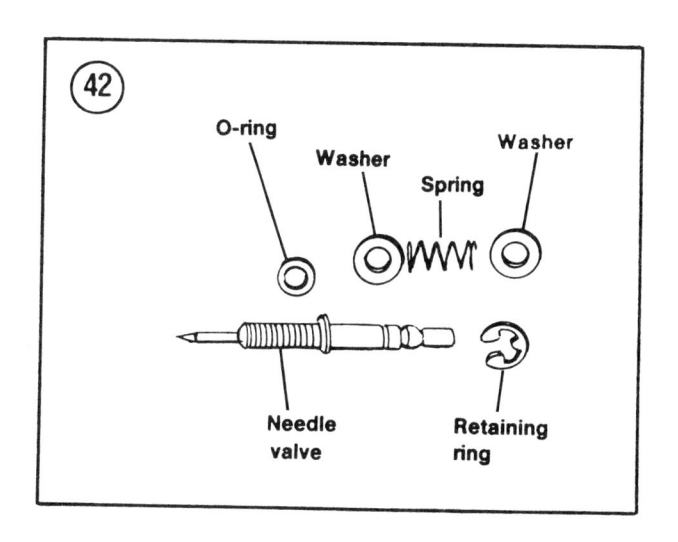

should be removed only if they are bent or otherwise damaged. This service requires experience in shaft and throttle valve alignment and should be performed by a Johnson or Evinrude dealer.

15. After cleaning, apply low-pressure (25 psi or less) compressed air to each of the lettered passages shown in **Figure 44**. If they are clean, air should be felt at the corresponding lettered passage shown in **Figure 44**. If a passage has more than one outlet, alternately place a finger over each passage to make sure air is felt at all.

16. Assembly is the reverse of disassembly, plus the following:
   a. Compare new gaskets to the old ones to make sure all holes are properly punched. Remove any loose gasket fibers or stamping crumbs adhering to the new gaskets.
   b. Sandwich each low-speed needle valve spring between its corresponding washers. Install assembly on needle valve. Install and lightly seat the needle valves. Back each needle valve out 1/2 turn.
   c. Make sure the inlet needle valves are properly assembled. If installing new ones from an overhaul kit, assemble them to match the old ones removed.
   d. Install the inlet needle valves finger-tight, then install the floats to retain the needles in the valve seats and tighten the seats securely.
   e. Adjust each float as described in this chapter.
   f. Lower carburetor body onto float chamber. Hold assembly together and invert to position carburetor body on workbench, then install attaching screws.
   g. Position the bottom-mounted choke solenoid so its base is 1/2 in. from bottom of carburetor base and tighten the bracket. See **Figure 45**.

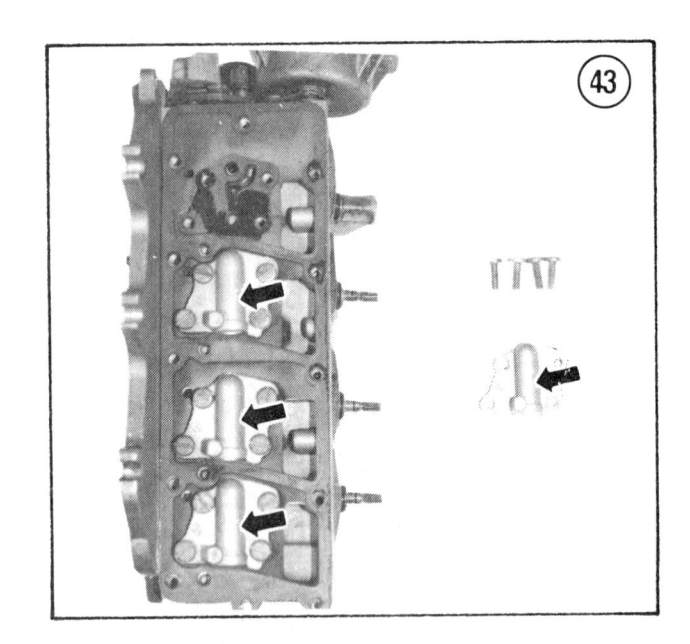

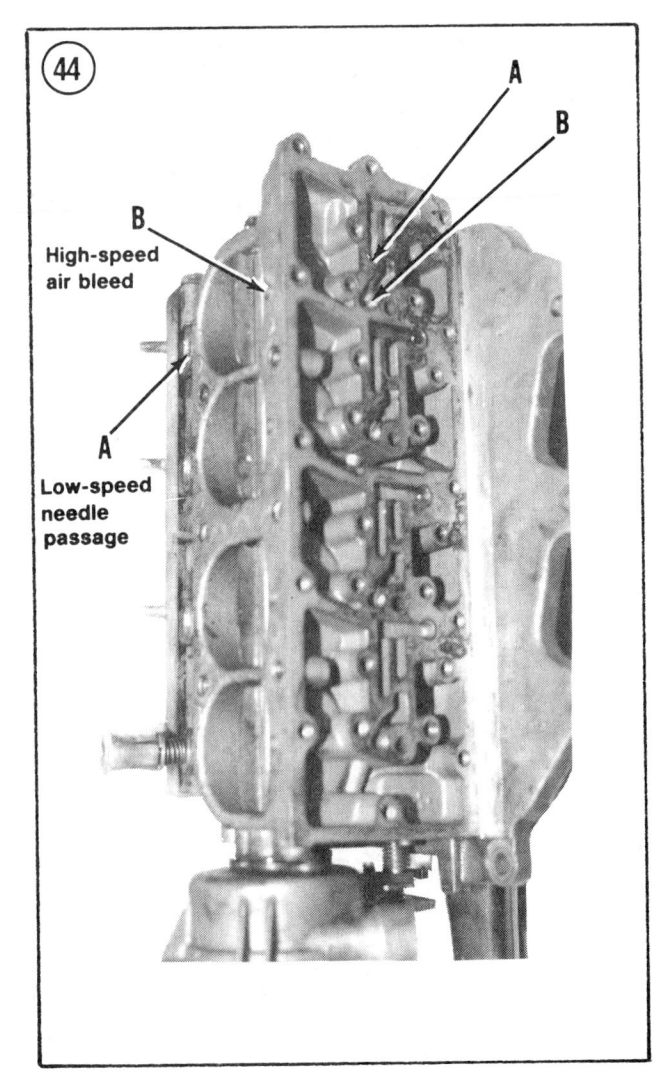

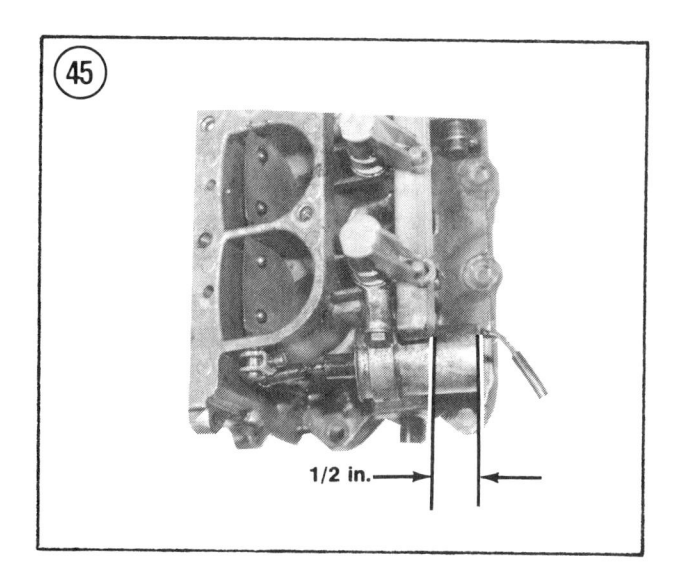

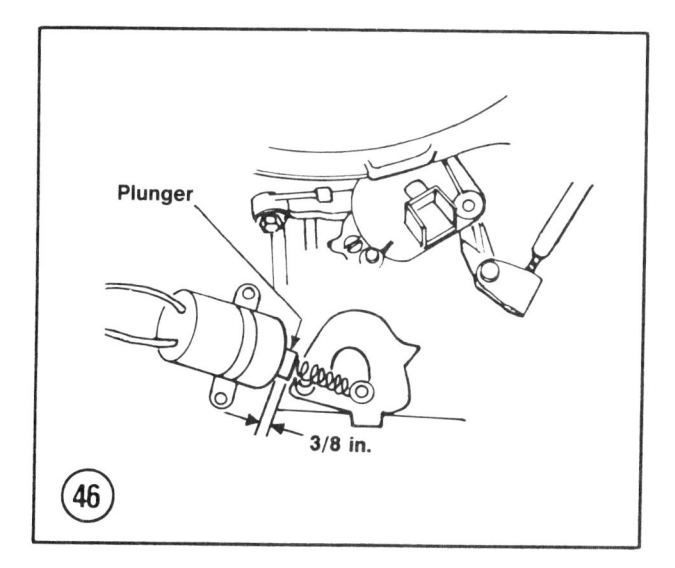

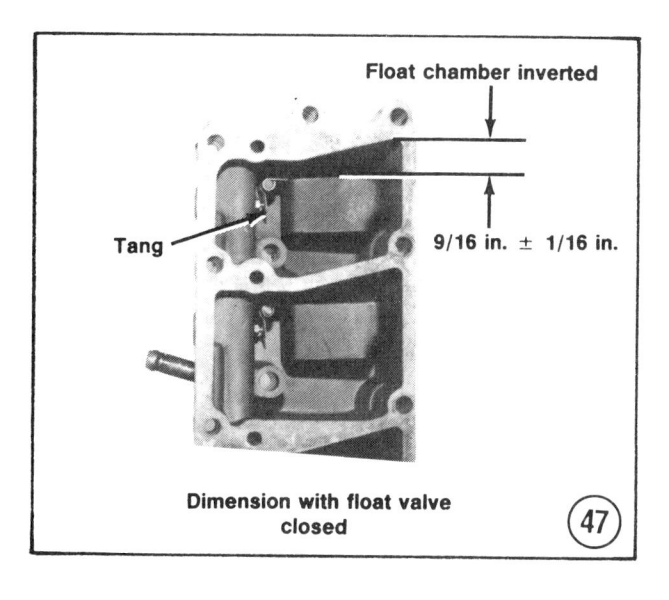

FUEL SYSTEM

h. Position top-mounted solenoid so its plunger extends 3/8 in. from front of solenoid case. See **Figure 46**.

i. Install carburetor on engine and adjust the choke linkage, throttle linkage and carburetor (Chapter Five).

Float Adjustment

Proper float adjustment requires the use of OMC float gauge part No. 380546. All 4 floats must be adjusted to the same height; if 1 float is slightly above or below the others, the corresponding engine cylinder will receive an incorrect air/fuel mixture, resulting in a poor running engine.

1. Position the carburetor body so the floats hang down, allowing the weight of each float to close its respective inlet needle valve.

2. Insert the float gauge in the float chamber with its tang resting on the machined surface and its edges flush against the top of the float and the float chamber. If the distance between the top of the float and the top of the float chamber is correct (9/16 in. ± 1/64 in.), the gauge will fit properly. See **Figure 47**.

3. If a float requires adjustment, fit the slotted end of the gauge over the metal float tang and bend carefully (to avoid forcing the needle valve into its seat) until the float is within specifications. Make sure the float is centered in the float bowl after adjustment.

4. Stand the float chamber right side up and measure float drop with the gauge. The drop should be 17/64 in. ± 1/64 in. when measured at the points shown in **Figure 48**.

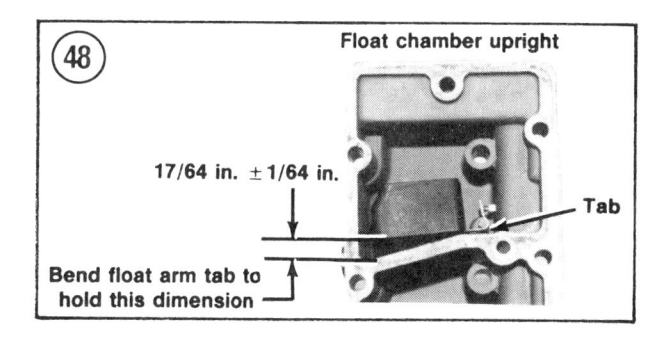

5. If float drop adjustment is required, fit the slotted end of the gauge over the float tab and bend until the float is within specifications. Make sure the float is centered in the float bowl after adjustment.

MODEL G CARBURETOR

Removal/Installation

Refer to **Figure 49** for this procedure.
1. Electric start—Disconnect the negative battery cable.
2. Disconnect the fuel line at the engine or fuel tank quick-disconnect.
3. Remove the engine cover.
4. Remove the fuel pump from the base of the air silencer.
5. Remove the screw holding the low-speed adjustment arm (if so equipped) and remove the arm.
6. Remove the 3 screws holding the air silencer cover. Remove the cover.
7. If equipped with a low-speed adjustment arm, remove the low-speed arms, linkage and bellcrank assembly.
8. Disconnect the hose between the air silencer and intake manifold.
9. Disconnect the retaining ring and choke solenoid spring from the upper choke arm.
10. Remove the 4 screws holding the air silencer body. Remove the air silencer.
11. Disconnect the fuel lines between the carburetors.
12. Disconnect the throttle and choke linkage at the carburetors.
13. Remove the 2 nuts holding the carburetor to the intake manifold. Loosen the nuts alternately, pulling the carburetor forward to provide clearance. Remove the carburetor and gasket from the intake manifold. Discard the gasket.
14. Installation is the reverse of removal. Use a new mounting gasket. Tighten mounting nuts alternately to avoid carburetor warpage. Adjust the choke linkage, throttle linkage and carburetor (Chapter Five).

Disassembly/Assembly

Refer to **Figure 50** (low-speed needle valves) or **Figure 51** (low-speed orifices) for this procedure.
1. Invert carburetor over a suitable container and tip the front down to drain any remaining fuel out of the bowl vent.

NOTE
If the orifice plugs have not been removed before, they may be difficult to loosen in Step 2. To prevent stripping the plug slot, support the float chamber on a solid surface and tap the plug gently with a small mallet. This should loosen the screw sufficiently for easy removal with a screwdriver.

2. Remove the drain plugs and O-rings from the float chamber. Discard the O-rings.
3. Remove the high-speed orifice from each plug hole with jet remover part No. 317002 or equivalent and record the number stamped on it for correct reassembly reference. **Figure 52** (dual plug design) shows the drain plugs and orifices on one side. **Figure 53** (single plug design) shows the drain plugs and orifices on both sides.
4A. If equipped with low-speed needle valves, back the needle valves out and remove from the carburetor. Insert a length of wire with a hooked end in the needle valve key slot and remove the Delrin retainer and bushing. Note that a black retainer is installed on the port side and a white retainer on the starboard side.
4B. If equipped with low-speed orifices, remove the low-speed cover plugs. Remove the orifices from the float chamber with jet remover part No. 317002 or equivalent. See **Figure 54**.

FUEL SYSTEM

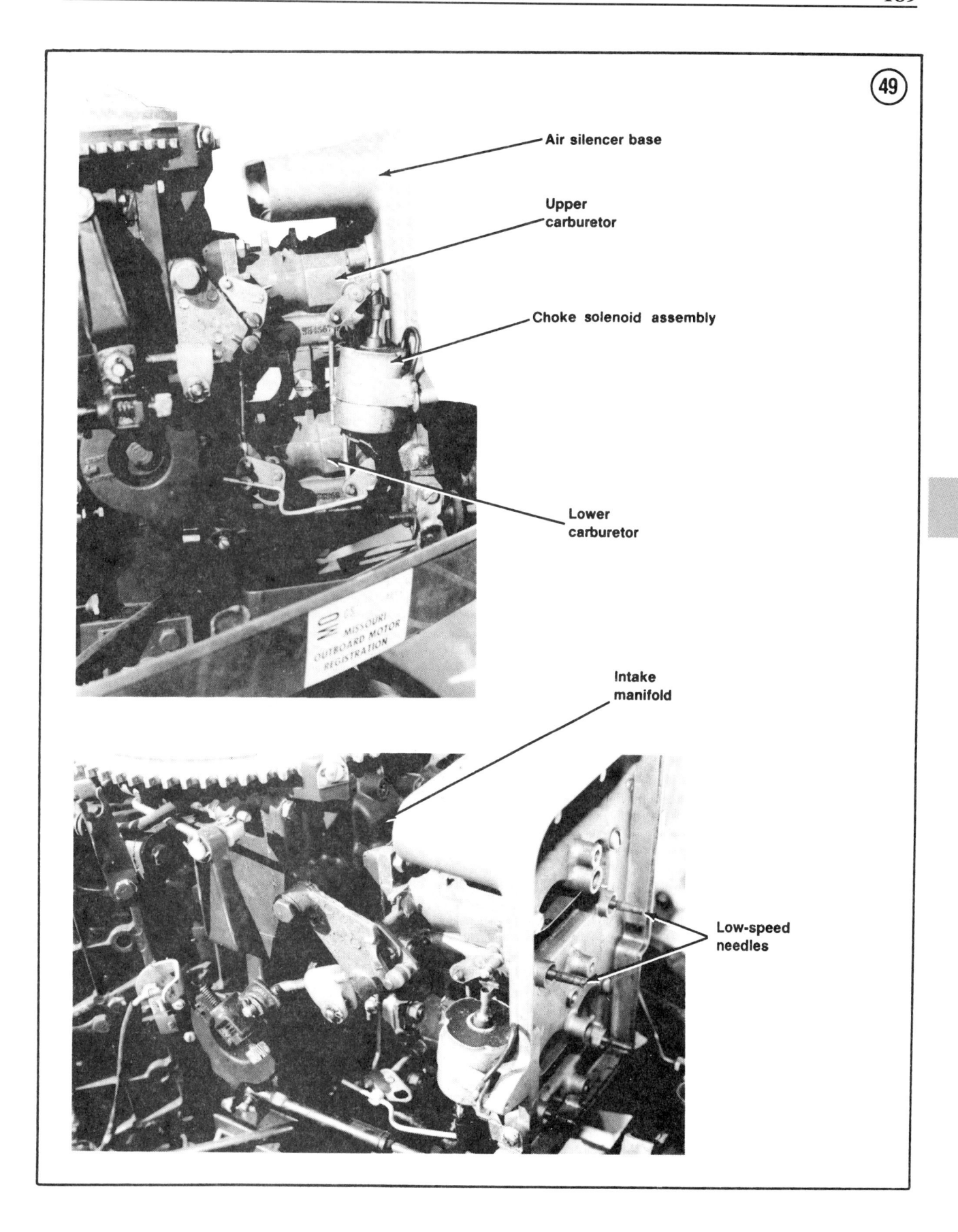

49

- Air silencer base
- Upper carburetor
- Choke solenoid assembly
- Lower carburetor
- Intake manifold
- Low-speed needles

CHAPTER SIX

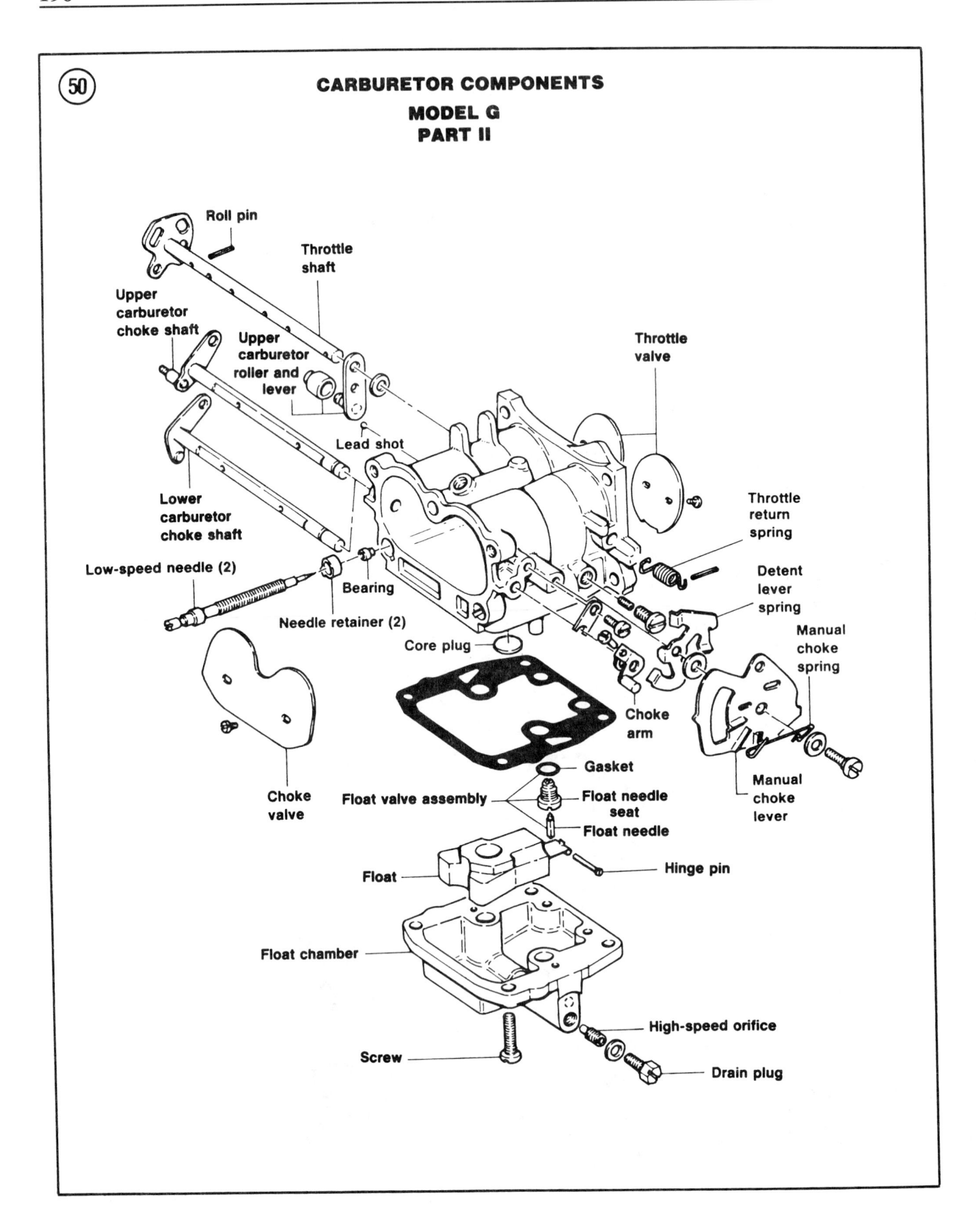

CARBURETOR COMPONENTS
MODEL G
PART II

- Roll pin
- Throttle shaft
- Upper carburetor choke shaft
- Upper carburetor roller and lever
- Throttle valve
- Lead shot
- Lower carburetor choke shaft
- Throttle return spring
- Low-speed needle (2)
- Bearing
- Needle retainer (2)
- Detent lever spring
- Core plug
- Manual choke spring
- Choke arm
- Choke valve
- Gasket
- Float valve assembly
- Float needle seat
- Float needle
- Manual choke lever
- Float
- Hinge pin
- Float chamber
- High-speed orifice
- Screw
- Drain plug

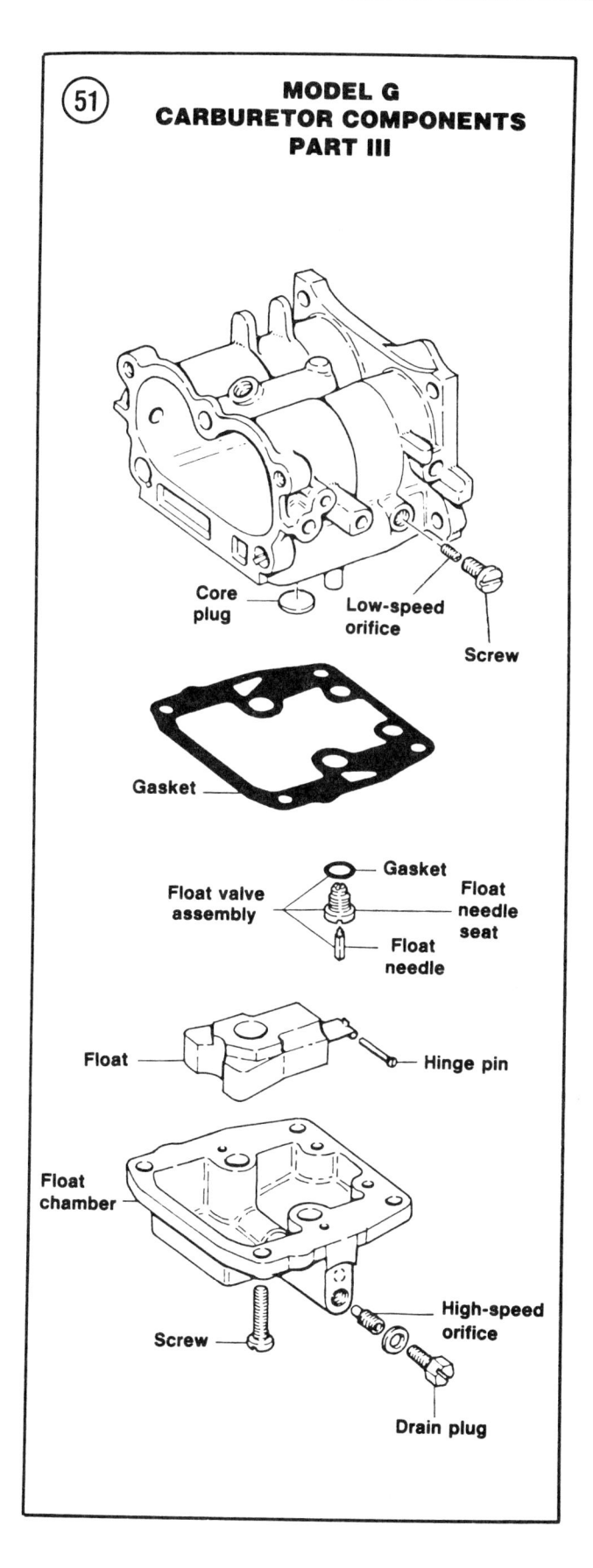

FUEL SYSTEM

51 MODEL G CARBURETOR COMPONENTS PART III

- Core plug
- Low-speed orifice
- Screw
- Gasket
- Float valve assembly
- Gasket
- Float needle seat
- Float needle
- Float
- Hinge pin
- Float chamber
- Screw
- High-speed orifice
- Drain plug

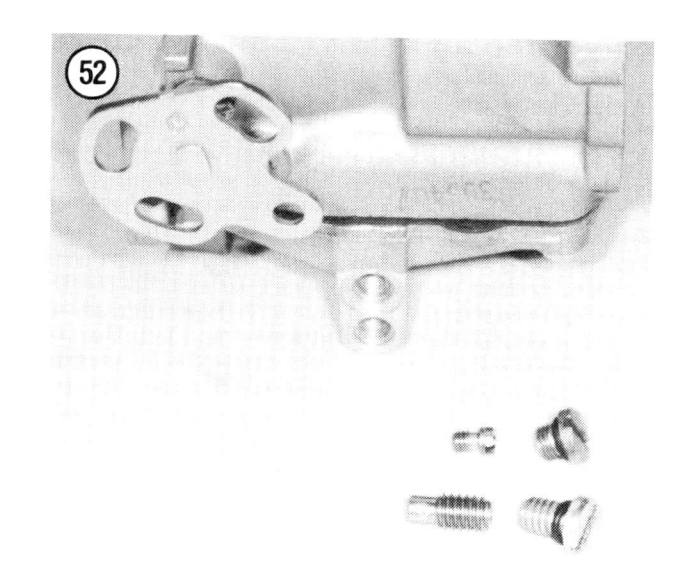

52

53

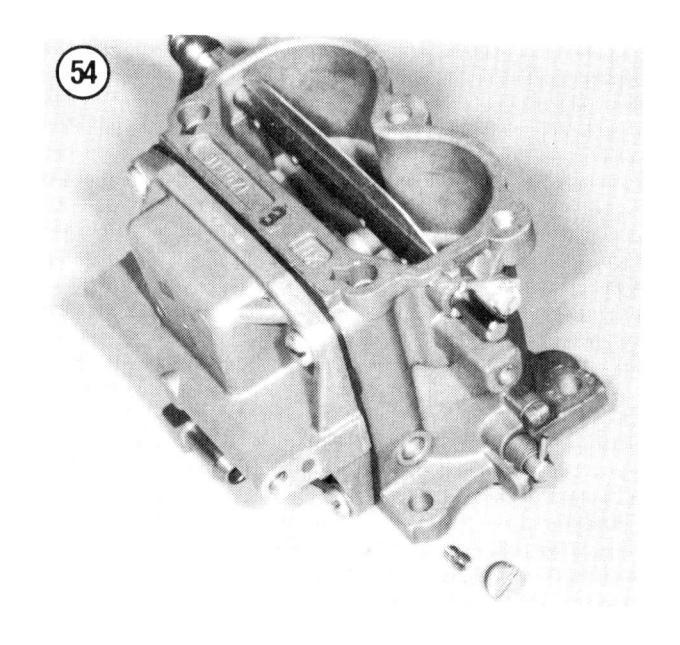

54

5. Remove the float chamber screws. Separate the float chamber from the main body casting (**Figure 55**). Discard the gasket.
6. Remove the nylon float hinge pin. Remove the float (**Figure 56**).
7. Remove the inlet needle from the valve, then remove the valve seat with a wide-blade screwdriver. See **Figure 57**. Discard the seat gasket.
8. Assembly is the reverse of disassembly, plus the following:

   a. Compare new gaskets to the old ones to make sure all holes are properly punched. Remove any loose gasket fibers or stamping crumbs adhering to the new gaskets.

   b. If equipped with low-speed needle valves, install retainer (black on port side; white on starboard side) in carburetor. Slip nylon bearings on needle valve ends, thread needle valves into the carburetor and lightly seat. Back each low-speed needle valve out 7/8 turn.

   c. Adjust the float as described in this chapter.

   d. Install on engine and adjust the choke linkage, throttle linkage and carburetor (Chapter Five).

Float Adjustment

1. Invert the carburetor body with its gasket surface horizontal, allowing the float weight to close the needle valve.

2. If the float is not parallel with the casting face (**Figure 58**), bend the metal float arm carefully (to avoid forcing the needle valve into its seat) and bring the float within specifications. Make sure the float is centered in the float bowl after adjustment.

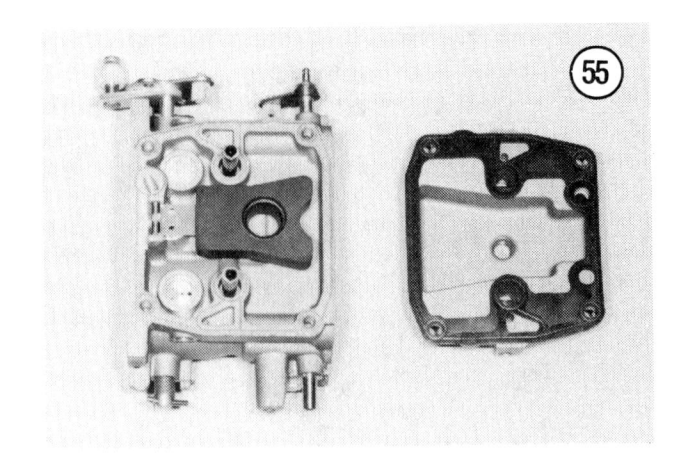

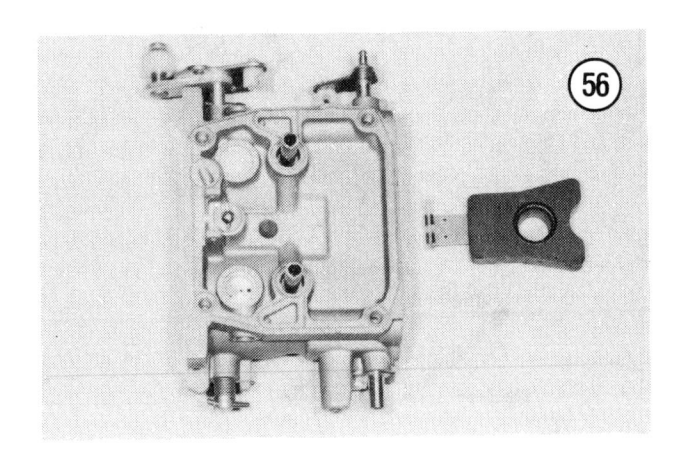

CHOKE SOLENOID SERVICE

Removal/Installation

1. Disconnect the solenoid link and retaining ring from the upper choke arm.

2. Disconnect the solenoid electrical lead(s). Remove the leads from the wire routing clamp.

NOTE
Some solenoids are installed with a ground lead under one of the bracket screws. If not equipped with a ground lead, the solenoid ground is through the case.

3. Remove the solenoid bracket screws. See **Figure 59** (typical). Remove the solenoid.
4. Installation is the reverse of removal. Coat the solenoid lead connections with OMC Black Neoprene Dip, if necessary.

FUEL SYSTEM

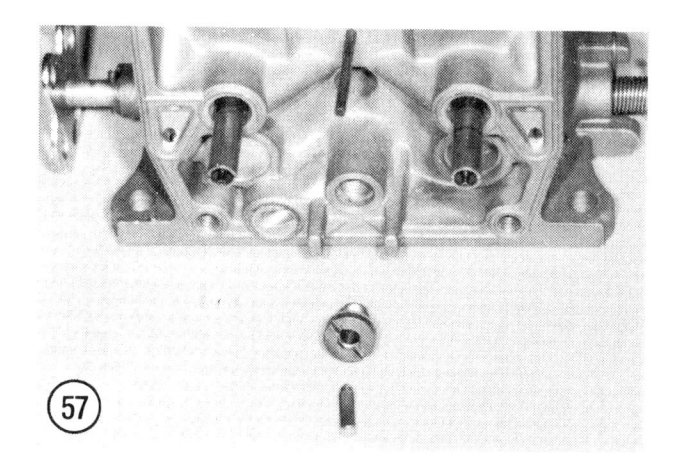

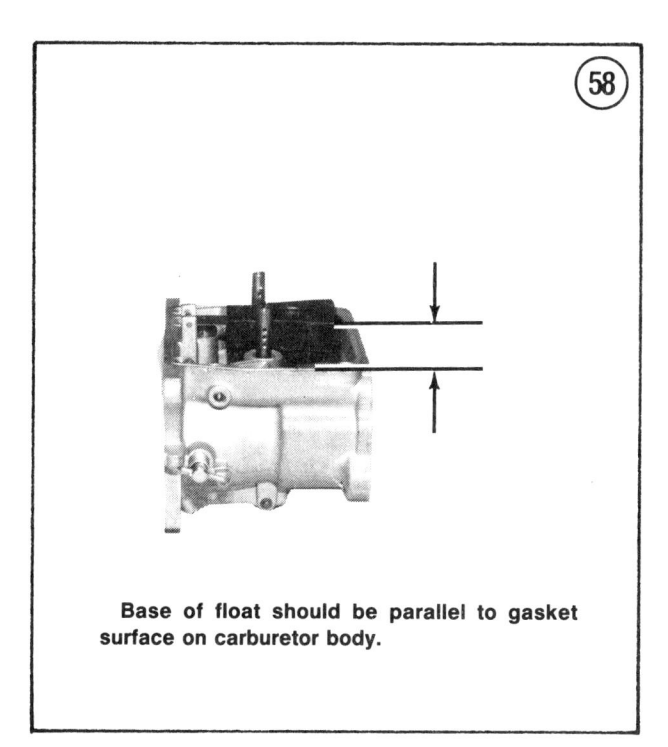

⑤⑦

⑤⑧

Base of float should be parallel to gasket surface on carburetor body.

⑤⑨

Choke Solenoid Test

1. Make sure the solenoid plunger is clean, dry and free of all corrosion.
2. Connect an ohmmeter between the solenoid case (ground) or ground lead and the purple/yellow lead. The solenoid should read 7-8.5 ohms.
3. Connect the ohmmeter between the solenoid case or ground lead and the purple/white lead. The ohmmeter should read 3-5 ohms.
4. If the ohmmeter readings are not as specified, replace the choke solenoid.

FUEL TANK

Johnson and Evinrude 1.5, 2 and 3 hp models have an integral fuel tank. All other models must be connected to a portable tank or one that is built into the boat.

Figure 60 shows the components of a pressurized portable fuel tank used with 1956-1959 models. **Figure 61** shows the components of the non-pressurized portable fuel tank used with 1960 and later models.

When some oils are mixed with gasoline and stored in a warm place, a bacterial substance will form. This substance is clear and covers the fuel pickup, restricting flow through the fuel system. Bacterial formation can be prevented by using OMC 2+4 Fuel Conditioner (part No. 173549) on a regular basis. If bacterial substance is present, it can be removed with OMC Engine Tuner (part No. 172650).

To remove any dirt or water that may have entered the tank during refilling, clean the inside of the tank once each season by flushing with clean lead-free gasoline or kerosene.

Check the inside and outside of the tank for signs of rust, leakage or corrosion. Replace as required. Do not attempt to patch the tank with automotive fuel tank repair materials. Portable marine fuel tanks are subject to

194　　　　　　　　　　　　　　　　　　　　　　　　　　　　　　　CHAPTER SIX

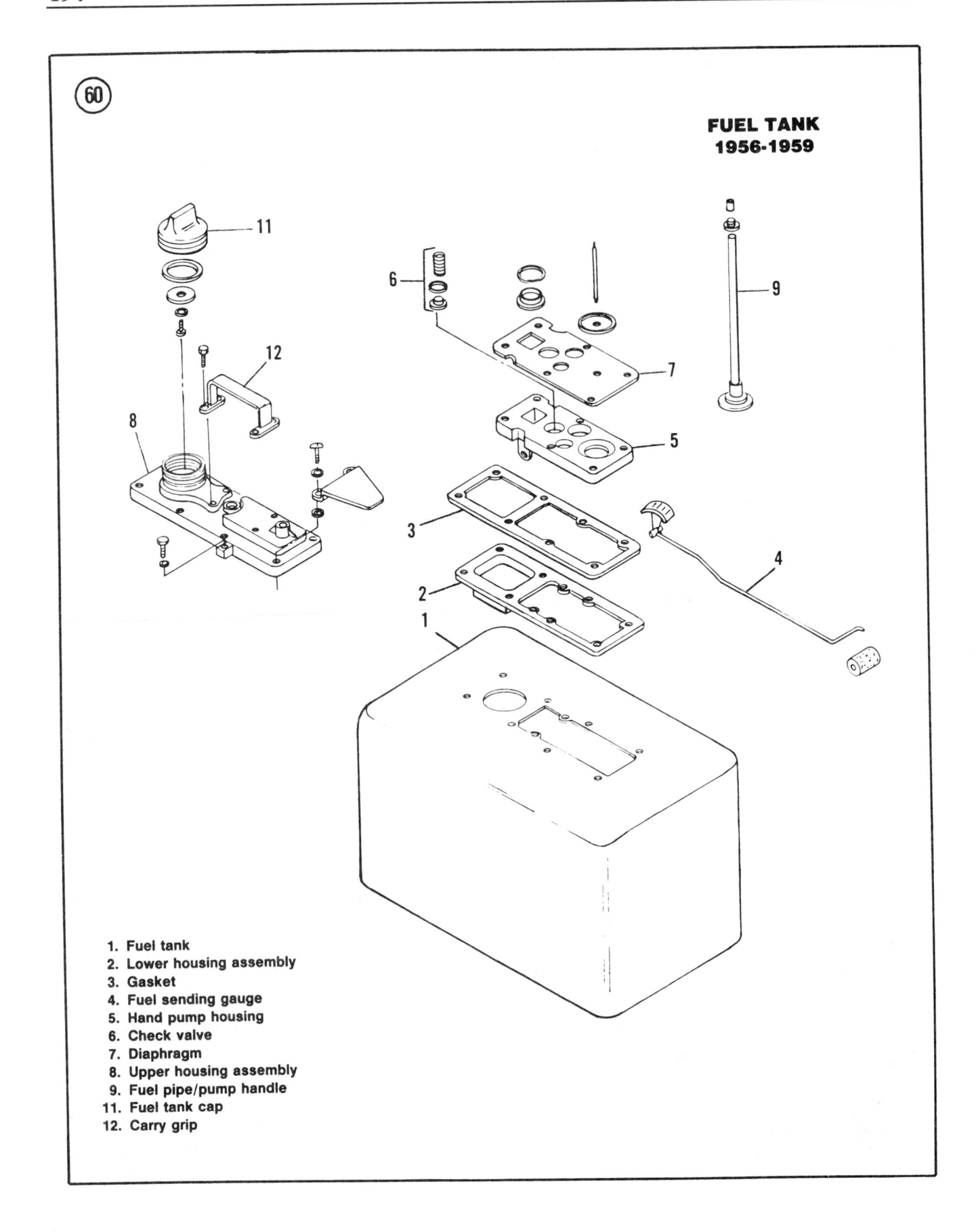

FUEL TANK 1956-1959

⑥⓪

1. Fuel tank
2. Lower housing assembly
3. Gasket
4. Fuel sending gauge
5. Hand pump housing
6. Check valve
7. Diaphragm
8. Upper housing assembly
9. Fuel pipe/pump handle
11. Fuel tank cap
12. Carry grip

FUEL SYSTEM

FUEL TANK
1960-ON

(Models Without Indicator Assembly)

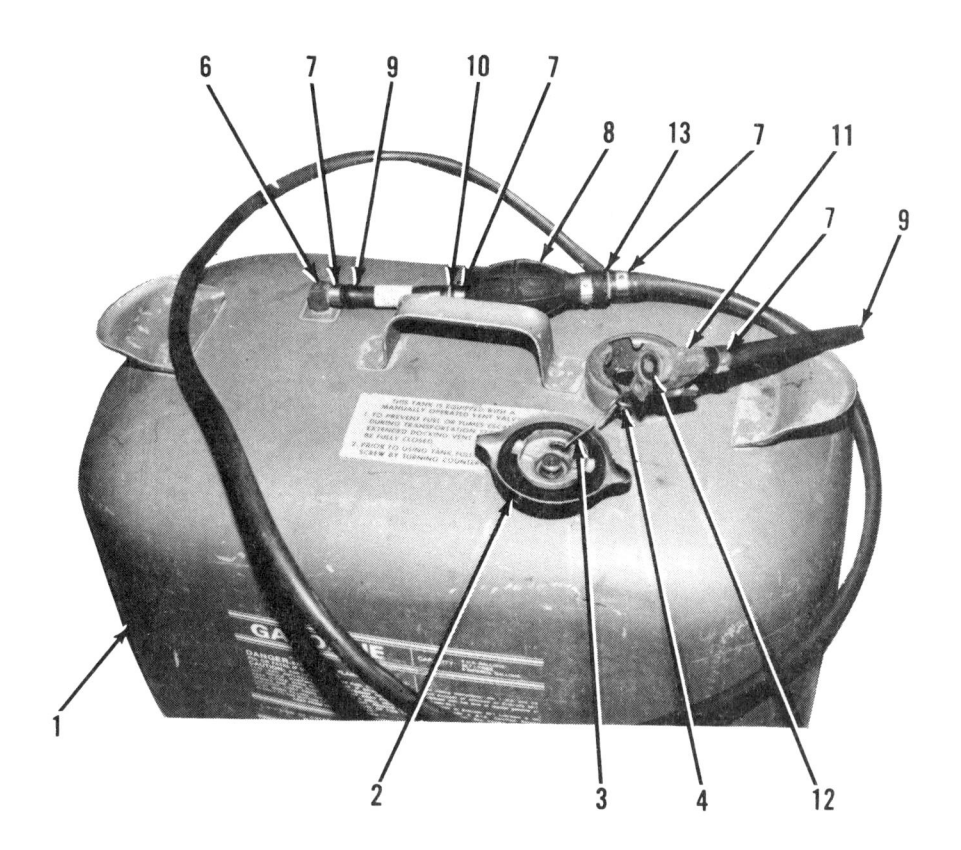

⑥₁

1. Fuel tank
2. Cap
3. Anchor link
4. Cap anchor
6. Elbow/fuel line
7. Clamp
8. Primer bulb
9. Short hose
10. Nipple and valve assembly
11. Fuel line connector
12. O-ring
13. Nipple and valve assembly

much greater pressure and vacuum conditions.

The pressurized tank uses an integral hand pump and relief valve assembly. The hand pump contains check valves and a diaphragm much like the fuel pump on 1960 and later engines. Maintaining this type of fuel tank in good working order is not difficult, provided the required parts can be obtained. The combination pump/sending unit/filter can be removed to rebuild the pump or to clean the filter screen or tank.

To check the fuel tank filter for possible restrictions, disconnect the fuel line and remove the upper housing assembly from the tank. The filter on the end of the pickup tube can be cleaned with OMC Engine Tuner.

Alcohol blended with gasoline may cause a gradual deterioration of the indicator lens in portable fuel tanks. The use of a tank with an alcohol-resistant lens is recommended if blended fuels are used with any frequency.

FUEL LINE AND PRIMER BULB

When priming the engine, the primer bulb should gradually become firm. If it does not become firm or if it stays firm even when disconnected, a check valve inside the primer bulb is malfunctioning.

The line should be checked periodically for cracks, breaks, restrictions and chafing. The bulb should be checked periodically for proper operation. Make sure all fuel line connections are tight and securely clamped.

Table 1 CARBURETOR USAGE

Model/hp	Type
Inline	
1.5-28	A
9.5	B
30-40	C
55, 60, 65	D
V4	
50, 60, 65, 80, 1968 85	E
90 and 1966-1968 100	F
1969-1972 85, 1971-1972 100, 115, 125	G

Chapter Seven

Electrical Systems

This chapter provides service procedures for the battery, starter motor (electric start models) and each ignition system used on Johnson and Evinrude outboard motors during the years covered by this manual. Wiring diagrams are included at the end of the book. **Tables 1-4** are at the end of the chapter.

BATTERY

Since batteries used in marine applications endure far more rigorous treatment than those used in an automotive charging system, they are constructed differently. Marine batteries have a thicker exterior case to cushion the plates inside during tight turns and rough weather. Thicker plates are also used, with each one individually fastened within the case to prevent premature failure. Spill-proof caps on the battery cells prevent electrolyte from spilling into the bilges.

Automotive batteries are not designed to be run down and recharged repeatedly. For this reason, they should *only* be used in an emergency situation when a suitable marine battery is not available.

Johnson and Evinrude recommend that any battery used with an outboard motor have a minimum cold cranking amperage of 350 amps and a reserve capacity of at least 100 minutes.

Some of the outboards covered in this manual are equipped with a 6-volt electrical system. Be sure to install the correct battery for your system.

CAUTION
*Sealed or maintenance-free batteries are **not** recommended for use with the unregulated charging systems used on Johnson or Evinrude outboards. Excessive charging during continued high-speed operation will cause the electrolyte to boil, resulting in its loss. Since water cannot be added to such batteries, such overcharging will ruin the battery.*

Separate batteries may be used to provide power for any accessories such as lighting, fish finders, depth finder, etc. To determine the required capacity of such batteries, calculate the average discharge rate of the accessories and refer to **Table 1**.

Batteries may be wired in parallel to double the ampere hour capacity while maintaining a 12-volt system. See **Figure 1**. For accessories which require 24 volts, batteries may be wired in series (**Figure 2**) but only accessories specifically requiring 24 volts should be connected into the system. Whether wired in parallel or in series, charge the batteries individually.

Battery Installation in Aluminum Boats

If a battery is not properly secured and grounded when installed in an aluminum boat, it may contact the hull and short to ground. This will burn out remote control cables, tiller handle cables or wiring harnesses.

The following preventive steps should be taken when installing a battery in a metal boat:

1. Choose a location as far as practical from the fuel tank while providing access for maintenance.
2. Install the battery in a plastic battery box with cover and tie-down strap (**Figure 3**).
3. If a covered container is not used, cover the positive battery terminal with a non-conductive shield or boot (**Figure 4**).
4. Make sure the battery is secured inside the battery box and that the box is fastened in position with the tie-down strap.

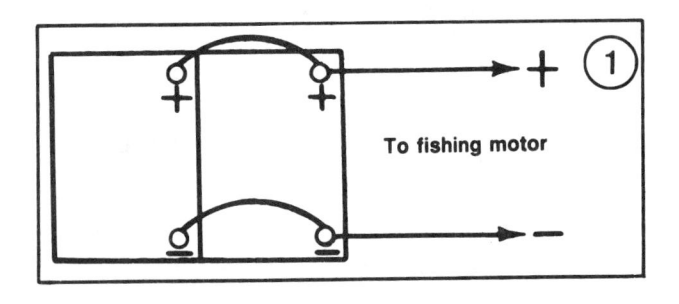

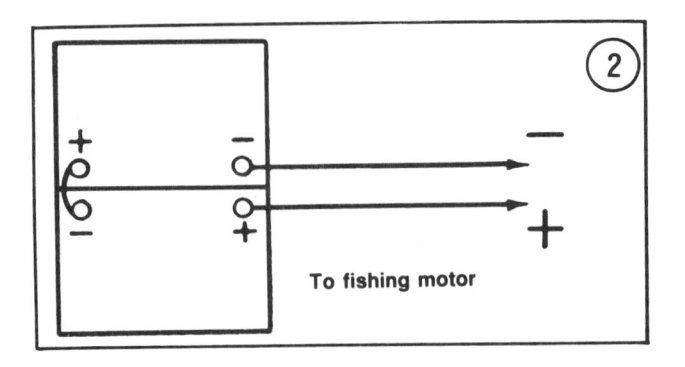

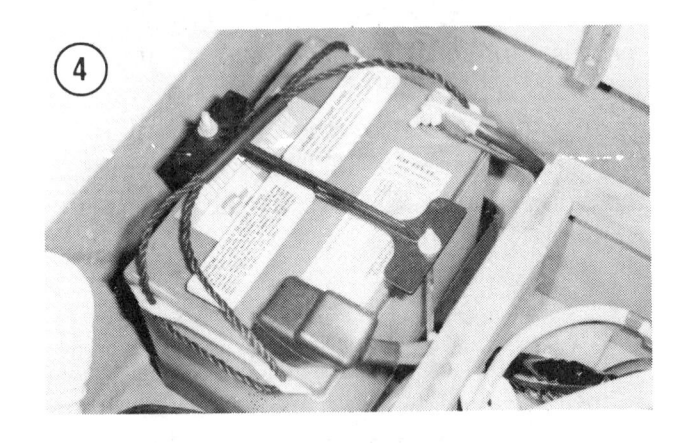

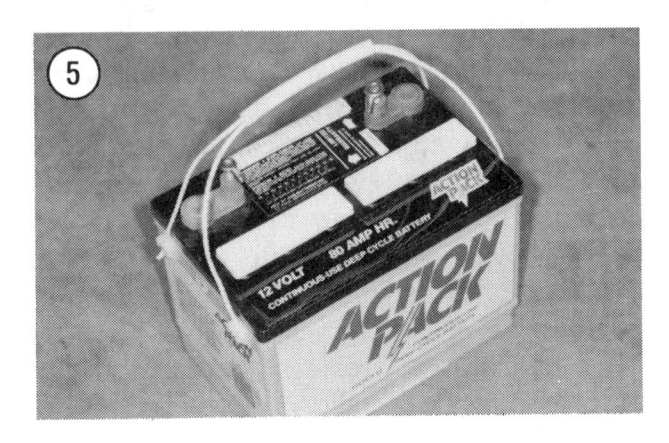

ELECTRICAL SYSTEMS

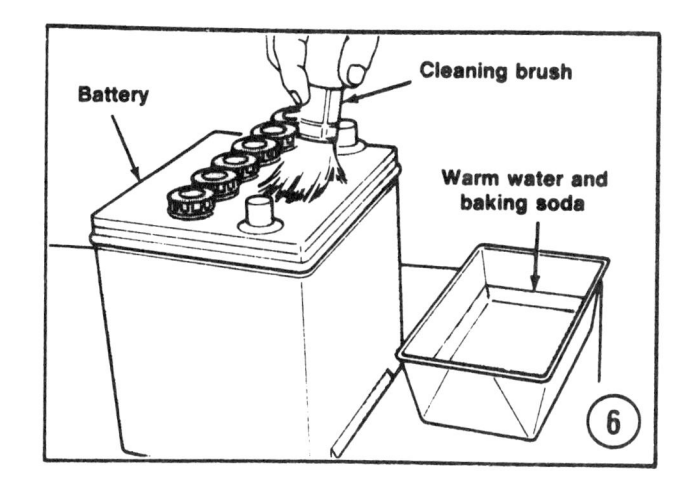

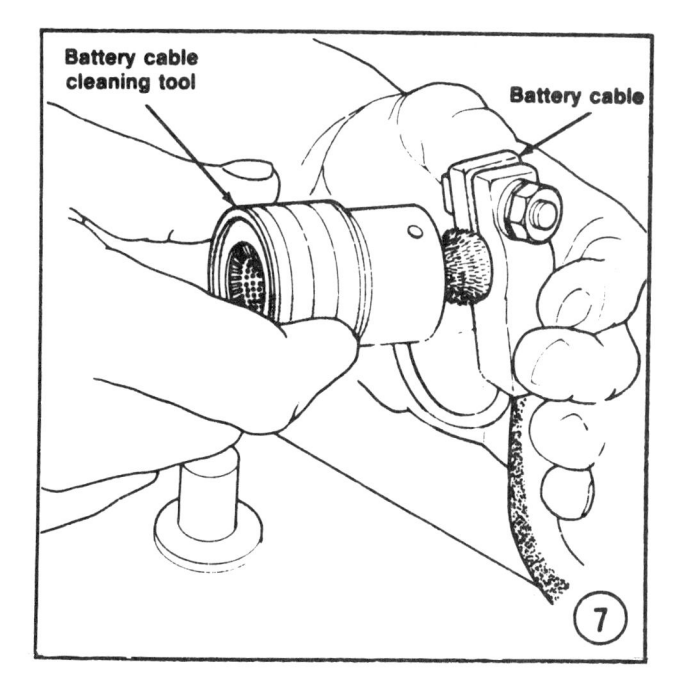

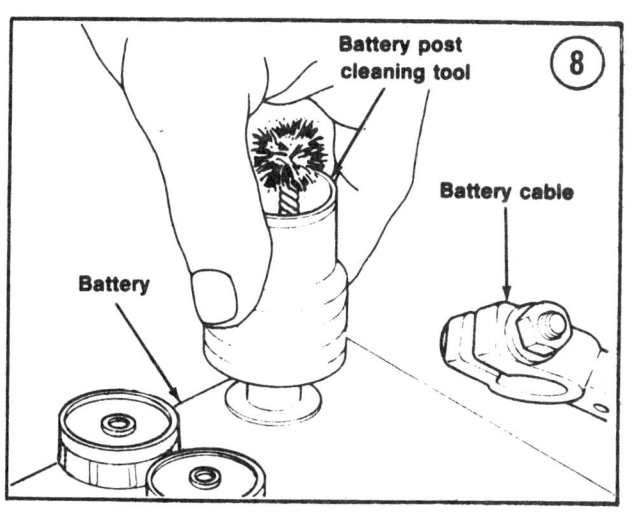

Care and Inspection

1. Remove the battery container cover (**Figure 3**) or hold-down (**Figure 4**).
2. Disconnect the negative battery cable. Disconnect the positive battery cable.

*Some batteries have a built-in carry strap (**Figure 5**) for use in Step 3.*

3. Attach a battery carry strap to the terminal posts. Remove the battery from the battery tray or container.
4. Check the entire battery case for cracks.
5. Inspect the battery tray or container for corrosion and clean if necessary with a solution of baking soda and water.

NOTE
Keep cleaning solution out of the battery cells in Step 6 or the electrolyte will be seriously weakened.

6. Clean the top of the battery with a stiff bristle brush using the baking soda and water solution (**Figure 6**). Rinse the battery case with clear water and wipe dry with a clean cloth or paper towel.
7. Position the battery in the battery tray or container.
8. Clean the battery cable clamps with a stiff wire brush or one of the many tools made for this purpose (**Figure 7**). The same tool is used for cleaning the battery posts. See **Figure 8**.
9. Reconnect the positive battery cable, then the negative cable.

CAUTION
Be sure the battery cables are connected to their proper terminals. Connecting the battery backwards will reverse the polarity and damage the rectifier, voltage regulator and generator, if so equipped.

10. Tighten the battery connections and coat with a petroleum jelly such as Vaseline or a light mineral grease.

NOTE
Do not overfill the battery cells in Step 11. The electrolyte expands due to heat from charging and will overflow if the level is more than 3/16 in. above the battery plates.

11. Remove the filler caps and check the electrolyte level. Add distilled water, if necessary, to bring the level up to 3/16 in. above the plates in the battery case. See **Figure 9**.

Testing

Hydrometer testing is the best way to check battery condition. Use a hydrometer with numbered graduations from 1.100-1.300 rather than one with just color-coded bands. To use the hydrometer, squeeze the rubber ball, insert the tip in a cell and release the ball (**Figure 10**).

NOTE
Do not attempt to test a battery with a hydrometer immediately after adding water to the cells. Charge the battery for 15-20 minutes at a rate high enough to cause vigorous gassing and allow the water and electrolyte to mix thoroughly.

Draw enough electrolyte to float the weighted float inside the hydrometer. When using a temperature-compensated hydrometer, release the electrolyte and repeat this process several times to make sure the thermometer has adjusted to the electrolyte temperature before taking the reading.

Hold the hydrometer vertically and note the number in line with the surface of the electrolyte (**Figure 11**). This is the specific gravity for the cell. Return the electrolyte to the cell from which it came.

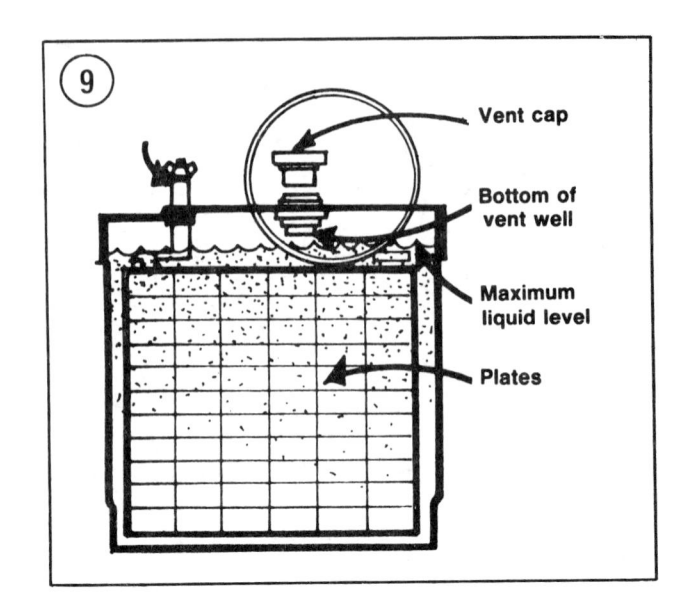

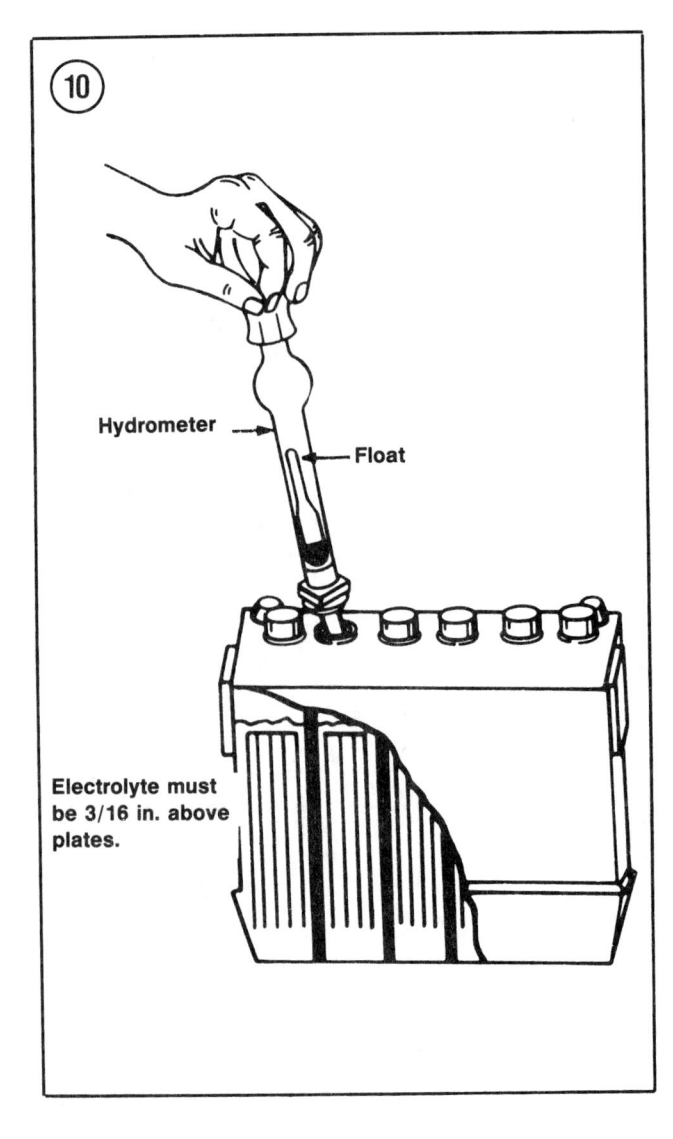

ELECTRICAL SYSTEMS

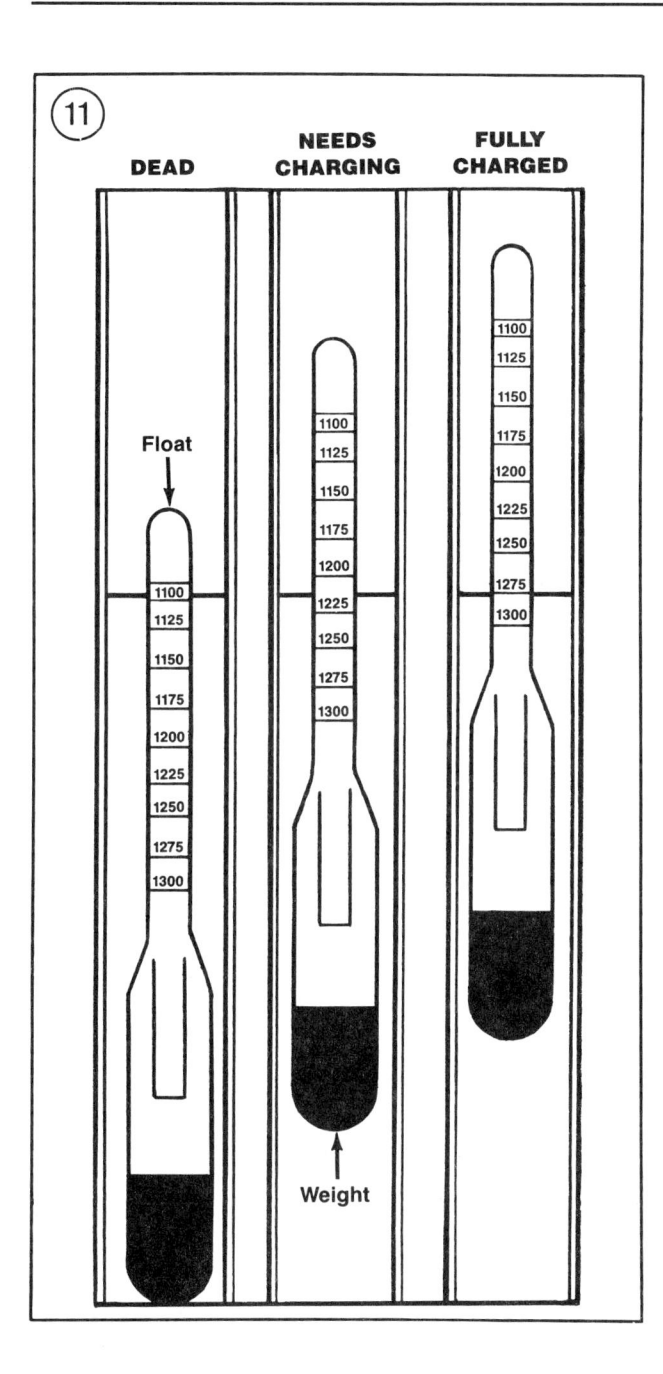

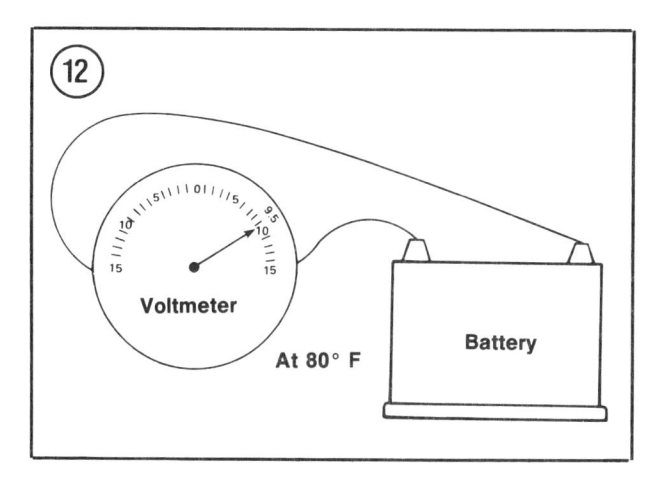

The specific gravity of the electrolyte in each battery cell is an excellent indicator of that cell's condition. A fully charged cell will read 1.260 or more at 68° F (20° C). A cell that is 75 percent charged will read from 1.220-1.230 while one with a 50 percent charge reads from 1.170-1.180. If the cell tests below 1.120, the battery must be recharged and one that reads 1.100 or below is dead. Charging is also necessary if the specific gravity varies more than 0.050 from cell to cell.

NOTE
If a temperature-compensated hydrometer is not used, add 0.004 to the specific gravity reading for every 10° above 80° F (25° C). For every 10° below 80° F (25° C), subtract 0.004.

Battery Storage

Wet cell batteries discharge slowly when stored. They discharge faster when warm than when cold. See **Table 2**. Before storing a battery for the season, clean the case with a solution of baking soda and water. Rinse with clear water and wipe dry. The battery should be fully charged (no change in specific gravity when 3 readings are taken 1 hour apart) and then stored in as cool and dry a place as possible.

Charging

A good state of charge should be maintained in batteries used for starting. Check the battery with a voltmeter as shown in **Figure 12**. Any battery that cannot deliver at least 9.6 volts (12-volt battery) or 4.8 volts (6-volt battery) under a starting load should be recharged. If recharging does not hold the charge, replace the battery.

The battery does not have to be removed from the boat for charging, but it is a recommended safety procedure since a charging battery gives off highly explosive hydrogen gas. In many boats, the area around the battery is not well ventilated and the gas may remain in the area for hours after the charging process has been completed. Sparks or flames occuring near the battery can cause it to explode, spraying battery acid over a wide area.

For this reason, it is important that you observe the following precautions:
a. Do not smoke around batteries that are charging or have been recently charged.
b. Do not break a live circuit at the battery terminals and cause an electrical arc that can ignite the hydrogen gas.
c. Disconnect the battery from the engine to prevent damage to the rectifier diodes. Disconnect the negative battery cable first, then the positive cable. Make sure the electrolyte is fully topped up.

Connect the charger to the battery—negative to negative, positive to positive. If the charger output is variable, select a 4 amp setting. Set the voltage regulator to 6 or 12 volts as required and plug the charger in. If the battery is severely discharged, allow it to charge for at least 8 hours. Batteries that are not as badly discharged require less charging time. **Table 3** gives approximate state of charge according to specific gravity reading. Check the charging progress with the hydrometer.

Jump Starting

If the battery becomes severely discharged, it is possible to start and run an engine by jump starting it from another battery. If the proper procedure is not followed, however, jump starting can be dangerous. Check the electrolyte level before jump starting any battery. If it is not visible or if it appears to be frozen, do not attempt to jump start the battery.

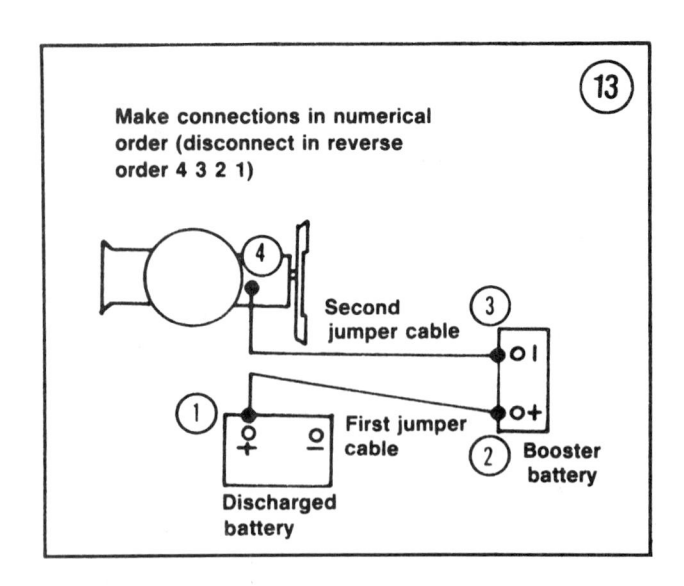

WARNING
Use extreme caution when connecting a booster battery to one that is discharged to avoid personal injury or damage to the system.

1. Connect the jumper cables in the order and sequence shown in **Figure 13**.

WARNING
An electrical arc may occur when the final connection is made. This could cause an explosion if it occurs near the battery. For this reason, the final connection should be made to a good ground away from the battery and not to the battery itself.

2. Check that all jumper cables are out of the way of moving engine parts.
3. Start the engine. Once it starts, run it at a moderate speed.

CAUTION
Running the engine at wide-open throttle may damage the electrical system.

4. Remove the jumper cables in the exact reverse order shown in **Figure 13**. Remove the cables at point 4, then 3, 2 and 1.

ELECTRICAL SYSTEMS

BATTERY CHARGING SYSTEM

Two types of battery charging system are used on the Johnson and Evinrude outboards covered in this manual: a D.C. generator system and an A.C. alternator system.

A malfunction in the battery charging system will result in an undercharged battery. Perform the following visual inspection to determine the cause of the problem. If the visual inspection proves satisfactory, test the generator or stator and rectifier. See Chapter Three.

1. Check the junction box fuses (D.C. generator system) or the fuse in the line between the rectifier and battery (A.C. alternator system), as equipped.
2. Make sure that the battery cables are connected properly. The red cable must be connected to the positive battery terminal. If polarity is reversed, check for a damaged rectifier and/or voltage regulator.
3. Inspect the battery terminals for loose or corroded connections. Tighten or clean as required.
4. Inspect the physical condition of the battery. Look for bulges or cracks in the case, leaking electrolyte or corrosion build-up.
5. Carefully check the condition of the wiring between the D.C. generator or A.C. stator and battery for signs of chafing, deterioration or other damage.
6. Check the remaining circuit wiring for corroded, loose or disconnected connections. Clean, tighten or connect as required.
7. Determine if the electrical load on the battery from accessories is greater than the battery capacity.

D.C. Generator System

The D.C. generator system consists of a belt-driven generator, voltage regulator, fuse(s), ammeter, battery and connecting wiring. Rotation of the generator armature past the field coils creates direct current. This current is passed through a voltage regulator, which limits the generator output to protect the battery and accessories from excessive voltage. The voltage regulator and fuses are enclosed in a protective junction box mounted at the rear of the engine. **Figure 14** is a schematic of the typical Johnson and Evinrude generator charging system.

The generator is rated at 10 amps at 12 volts. If the electrical accessory load exceeds 10 amps or if several accessories are in use while the engine runs at speeds under 1,500 rpm for lengthy intervals, the battery will not receive sufficient current to maintain its charge. Such usage may in fact result in the battery losing part or all of its charge.

If a twin outboard installation is used, only one engine should be equipped with a generator charging system. This is sufficient to maintain a proper battery charge.

Generator Removal/Installation

1. Disconnect the positive battery cable.
2. Remove the engine cover.
3. Remove the manual starter assembly, if so equipped. See Chapter Ten.
4. Hold the generator shaft from rotating with an open-end wrench placed on the collar under the pulley. Remove the nut and lockwasher holding the generator pulley cover with a second wrench. See **Figure 15**. Remove the cover.
5. Loosen the generator through-bolt nuts and release the belt tension.
6. Remove the drive belt from the pulley.
7. Remove the nuts holding the bracket to the power head. Remove the bracket and generator.
8. Disconnect the armature and field leads from the generator. Remove the screw holding the generator strap to the bracket.
9. To reinstall, reconnect the armature and field leads to the generator. Install the

204   CHAPTER SEVEN

14

GENERATOR

VOLTAGE REGULATOR

BATTERY

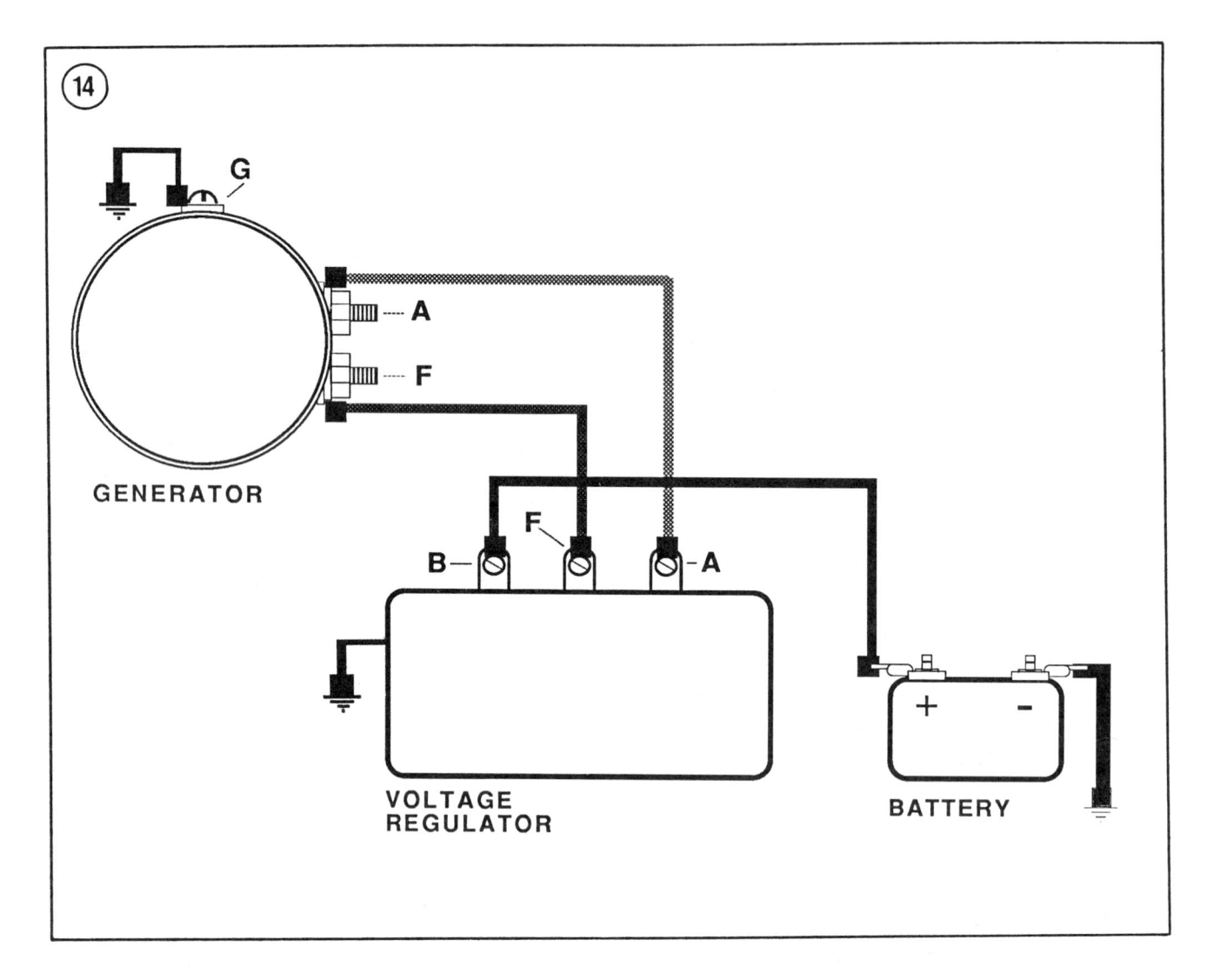

generator strap but do not tighten the screw at this point.

10A. 2-cylinder—Position generator and bracket assembly, pushing the bracket rearward until its stops contact the machined pads on the cylinder head. Install attaching bolts and tighten to specifications (**Table 4**).

10B. V4—Position generator and bracket assembly on power head. Install attaching bolts and tighten to specifications (**Table 4**).

11. Make sure the Woodruff key is installed in the generator shaft. Index the generator pulley slot with the shaft key and install the pulley.

12. Slip the drive belt over the pulley. Install the pulley cover, lockwasher and nut. Hold

15

ELECTRICAL SYSTEMS

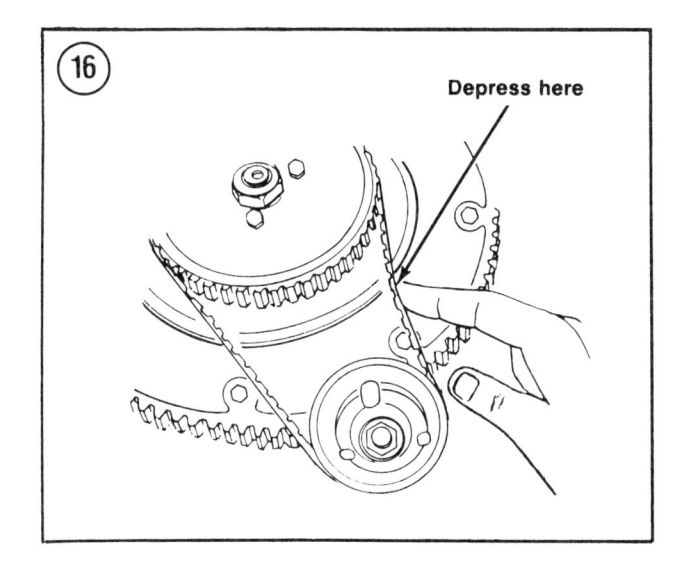

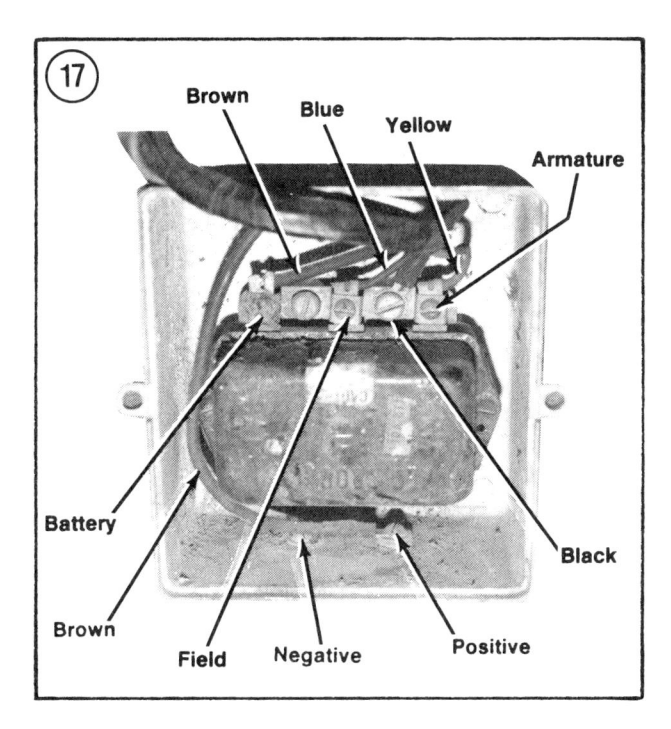

Figure 16 — Depress here

Figure 17 — Brown, Blue, Yellow, Armature, Black, Positive, Negative, Field, Brown, Battery

the pulley collar with an open-end wrench and tighten cover nut securely.

CAUTION
Correct belt tension is important in Step 13. Insufficient tension will lead to undercharging; excessive tension will cause premature generator bearing wear.

13. Pivot generator in bracket to adjust belt tension to 1/4-3/8 in. (2-cylinder) or 1/8-3/16 in. (V4) when depressed at the point shown in **Figure 16**. When tension is correct, tighten through-bolt nuts to 70-80 in.-lb. Tighten generator strap screw. Recheck belt tension.
14. Reconnect the positive battery cable.

CAUTION
*Do **not** neglect to polarize the generator in Step 15. Failure to do so will cause serious damage to the electrical system components.*

15. Momentarily connect a jumper wire between the regulator ARM and BAT terminals. Do this carefully to avoid touching the FLD terminal.
16. Disconnect the positive battery cable.
17. Reverse Steps 1-3 to complete installation.

Voltage Regulator Removal/Installation

The voltage regulator is located in the cover of the junction box at the rear of the engine.

1. Disconnect the positive battery cable.
2. Remove the junction box cover.
3. Label and disconnect the electrical leads at the voltage regulator terminals. See **Figure 17**.
4. Remove the screws holding the voltage regulator to the cover. Remove the regulator.
5. Install the new regulator in the cover. Tighten attaching screws securely.
6. Connect the electrical leads to the new regulator terminals.
7. Reconnect the positive battery cable.
8. Momentarily connect a jumper wire between the regulator ARM and BAT terminals. Do this carefully to avoid touching the FLD terminal.
9. Disconnect the positive battery cable.
10. Install the junction box cover, then reconnect the positive battery cable.

A.C. Alternator System

The alternator charging system can provide more electrical current at lower engine operating speeds than a D.C. generator system. It consists of a stator containing a number of coils (**Figure 18**), a rotor of permanent magnets located in the flywheel rim (**Figure 18**), a rectifier, fuse(s), battery and connecting wiring. A voltage regulator is used to maintain the voltage at a safe level on models through 1967 and those 1968-1972 models equipped with a 15 amp charging system.

Rotation of the rotor magnets past the stator coils creates alternating current. This current is sent to the rectifier where it is converted into direct current. The current passes through the voltage regulator, which maintains a controlled output, and is then supplied to charge the battery or operate electrical accessories. **Figure 19** is a schematic of the typical Johnson and Evinrude alternator charging system through 1966; **Figure 20** is a schematic of typical 1967-1972 alternator charging systems.

The mechanical voltage regulator and rectifier diodes are enclosed in a protective junction box mounted at the rear of the engine on models through 1966 (some 1965-1966 V4 engines use a transistorized voltage regulator in the junction box). A transistorized voltage regulator (15 amp system only) and rectifier are used on 1967-1972 models and are mounted externally on the engine. Exact location varies with model year and horsepower rating. **Figure 21** shows the rectifier used with 1967-1972 models. The voltage regulator will be found close to this type of rectifier if the outboard is equipped with a 15 amp charging system.

Stator Removal/Installation

See Chapter Eight.

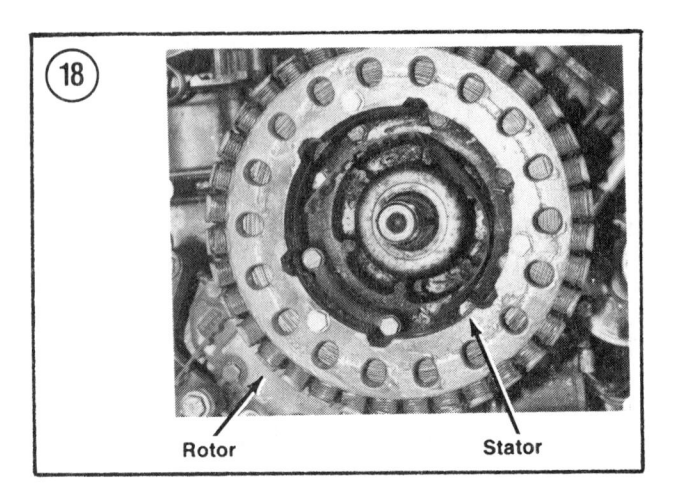

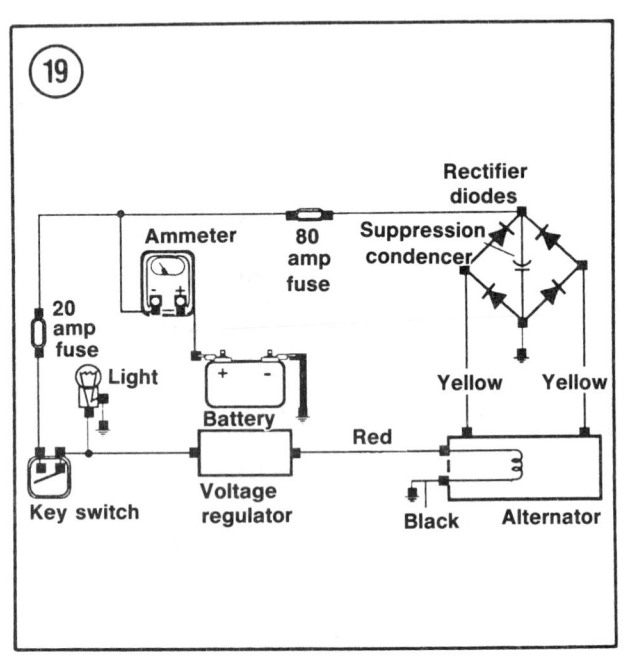

Junction Box Voltage Regulator/Transistor Removal/Installation

Refer to **Figure 22** for this procedure.
1. Disconnect the positive battery cable.
2. Remove the junction box cover.
3. Label and disconnect the electrical leads at the voltage regulator terminals.
4. Remove the screws holding the voltage regulator to the junction box. Remove the regulator.
5. If just the transistor is to be replaced, unsolder its leads from the regulator and

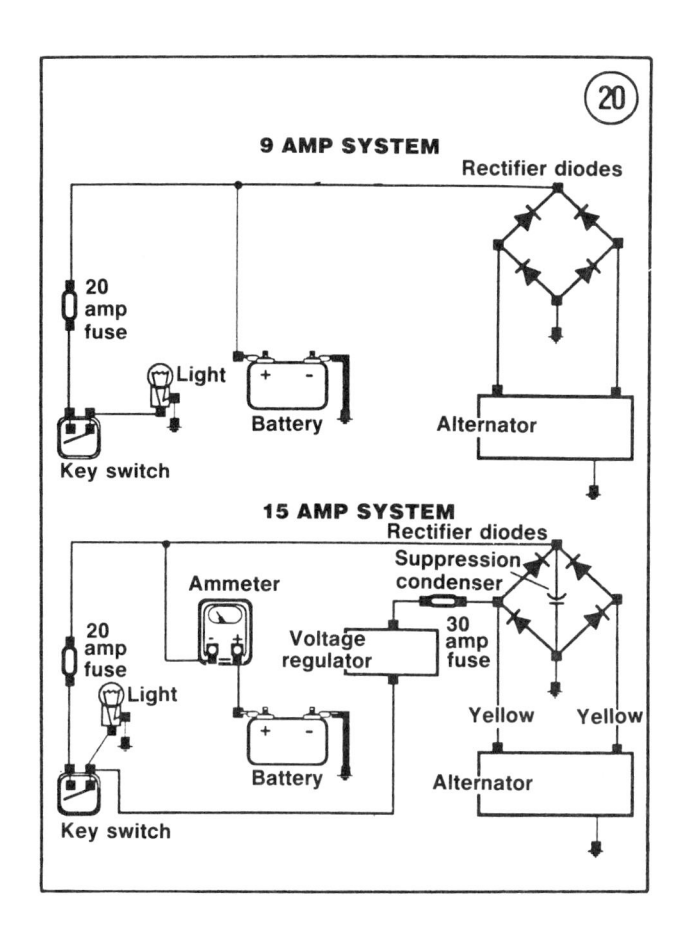

ELECTRICAL SYSTEMS

⑳

9 AMP SYSTEM

15 AMP SYSTEM

㉒

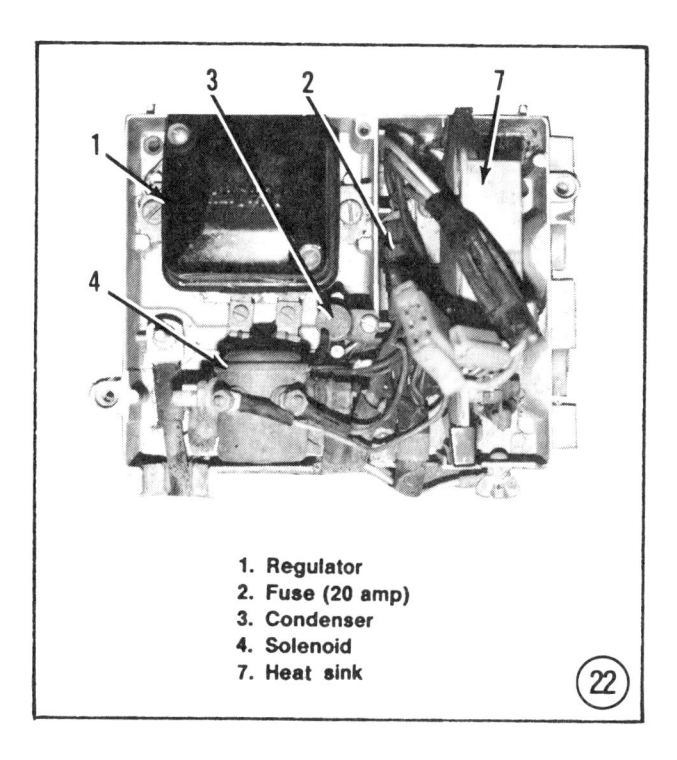

1. Regulator
2. Fuse (20 amp)
3. Condenser
4. Solenoid
7. Heat sink

to position the connector so that it will not interfere with regulator movement or the regulator will function erratically.

7. Connect the electrical leads to the new regulator terminals.
8. Install the junction box cover, then reconnect the positive battery cable.

External Voltage Regulator Removal/Installation

1. Disconnect the positive battery cable.
2. Disconnect the electrical connector at the voltage regulator.

NOTE
Depending upon the particular installation, it may be necessary to reposition wires or temporarily remove other components to provide clear access to the regulator screws for removal in Step 3.

3. Remove the screws holding the voltage regulator to the power head. Remove the regulator.

㉑

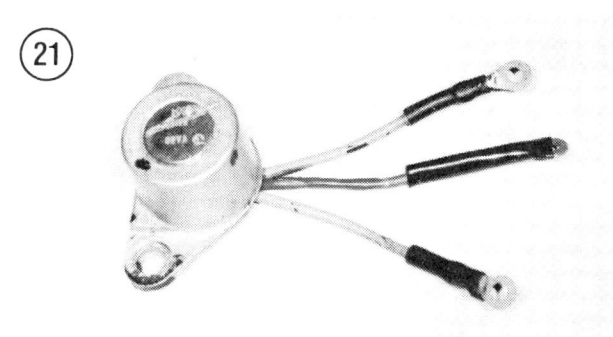

remove from the control box. To install a new transistor, solder its red lead to the regulator F terminal and its black lead to the resistor under the regulator. Use rosin core solder.

6. Install the new regulator in the junction box. Tighten attaching screws securely.

NOTE
The voltage regulator is mounted on a rubber base to absorb vibration. Be sure

4. Installation is the reverse of removal.

Junction Box Rectifier Diodes
Removal/Installation

Refer to **Figure 22** for this procedure.
1. Disconnect the positive battery cable.
2. Remove the junction box cover.
3. Disconnect the positive diode electrical leads.
4. Unbolt and remove the heat sink containing the positive diodes. See **Figure 23**.
5. Disconnect the negative diode electrical leads.
6. Remove the negative diodes with an appropriate socket and ratchet.
7. Installation is the reverse of removal. Wipe negative diode threads with light oil and tighten to 15 ft.-lb.

External Rectifier
Removal/Installation

1. Disconnect the positive battery cable.
2. Disconnect the rectifier lead connectors.

NOTE
Depending upon the particular installation, it may be necessary to reposition wires or temporarily remove other components to provide clear access to the rectifier screws for removal in Step 3.

3. Remove the screws holding the rectifier to the power head or bracket. Remove the rectifier assembly.
4. Installation is the reverse of removal.

ELECTRIC STARTING SYSTEM

Outboards covered in this manual may use a rope-operated mechanical (rewind) starting system or an electric (starter motor) starting system. The electric starting circuit consists of the battery, an ignition switch, safety switch, the starter motor, starter solenoid and connecting wiring. **Figure 24** shows a typical electric start schematic.

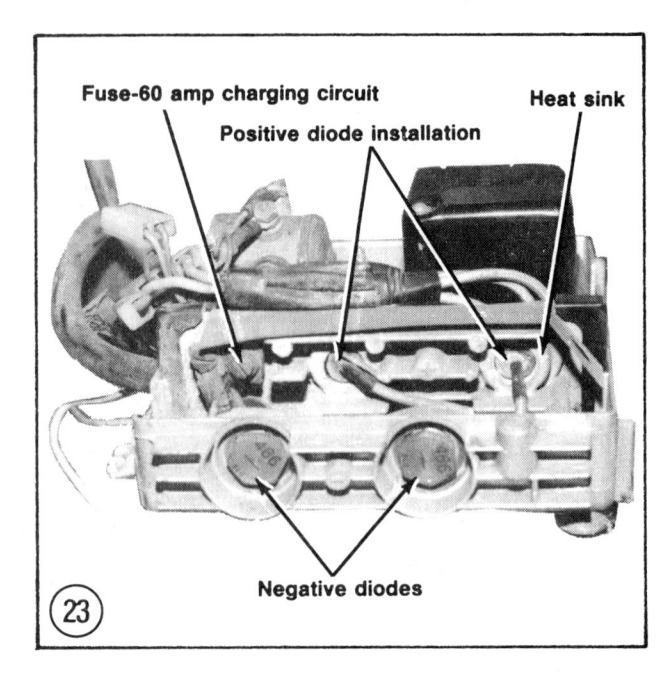

Starting system operation and troubleshooting is described in Chapter Three.

Starter Motor

Marine starter motors are very similar in design and operation to those found on automotive engines. Johnson and Evinrude outboards may be equipped with an Autolite, Bosch, Delco-Remy or Prestolite starter motor. All use an inertia-type drive in which external spiral splines on the armature shaft mate with internal splines on the drive assembly.

The starter motor produces a very high torque but only for a brief period of time, due to heat buildup. Never operate the starter motor continuously for more than 15 seconds. Let the motor cool for at least 2 minutes before operating it again.

If the starter motor does not turn over, check the battery and all connecting wiring for loose or corroded connections. If this does not solve the problem, refer to Chapter Three. Except for brush replacement, service

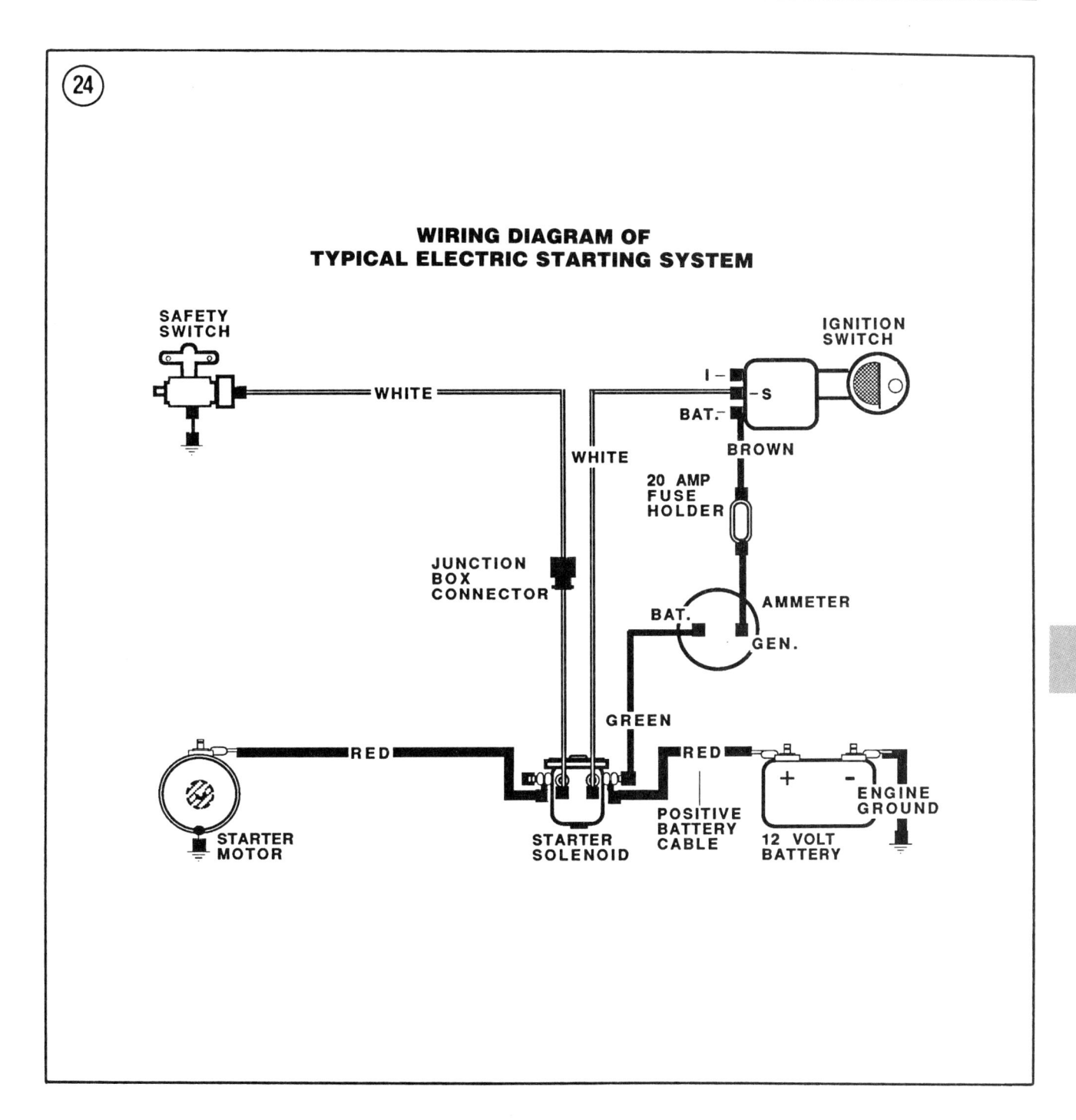

ELECTRICAL SYSTEMS

24

WIRING DIAGRAM OF TYPICAL ELECTRIC STARTING SYSTEM

to the starter motor by the amateur mechanic is limited to replacement with a new or rebuilt unit.

Some of the outboards covered in this manual are equipped with a 6 volt electrical system. Be sure to install the correct starter for your system.

Starter Motor
Removal/Installation
(2-cylinder)

1. Disconnect the negative battery cable.
2. Remove the engine cover.
3. Remove the air silencer, if it interferes with starter removal.

4. Disconnect the starter cables from their terminals.
5. Remove the ring gear guard nut (A, **Figure 25**).
6. Remove the bracket mounting bolts (B, **Figure 25**).
7. Remove the starter motor and bracket as an assembly.
8. Installation is the reverse of removal. Tighten mounting bolts to specifications (**Table 4**).

Starter Motor
Removal/Installation
(All Others)

1. Disconnect the negative battery cable.
2. Remove the engine cover.
3. Disconnect the starter cables from their terminals.
4A. If starter is installed on port side of engine, remove the air silencer if it interferes with starter removal. Remove the 3 bracket attaching bolts. Remove the starter/bracket assembly.
4B. If starter is installed on starboard side of engine, remove the 2 through-bolts and the single bracket bolt. See **Figure 26** (typical). Remove the U-shaped bracket assembly, then carefully remove the starter motor to prevent the end caps from separating from the frame. Once removed, temporarily reinstall the through-bolts.
5. Installation is the reverse of removal. Be sure to install small rubber sleeve on the outer through-bolt between the starter and mounting flange, if used. See **Figure 26**. Tighten mounting bolts to specifications (**Table 4**).

Brush Replacement
(Autolite)

Alway replace brushes in complete sets.
1. Remove the starter as described in this chapter.

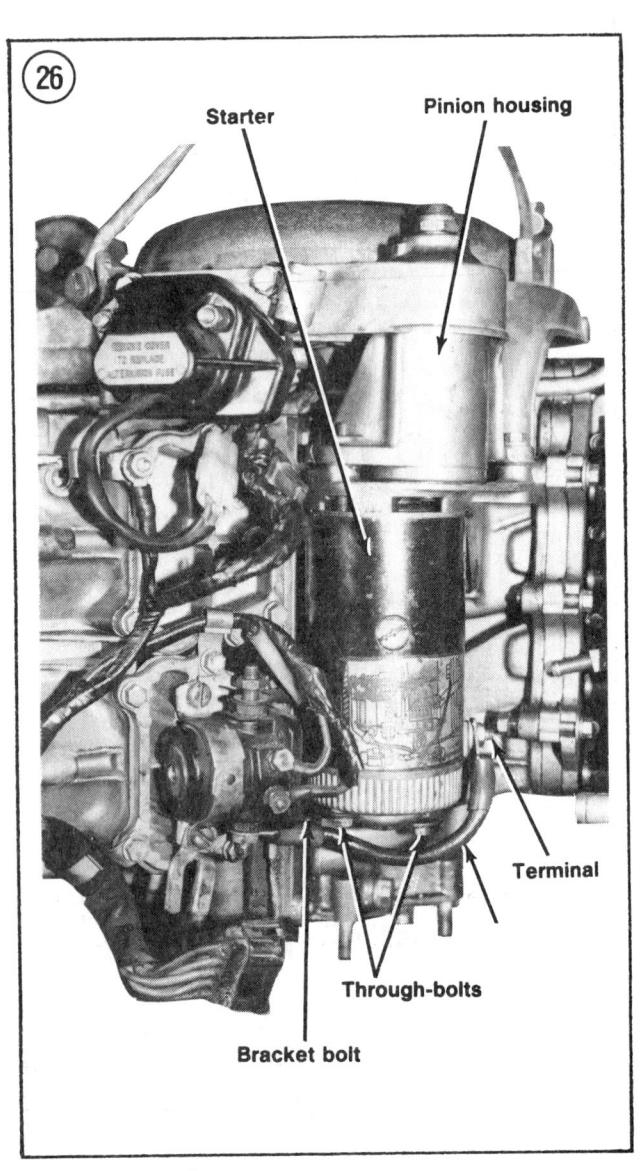

ELECTRICAL SYSTEMS

BOSCH STARTER COMPONENTS

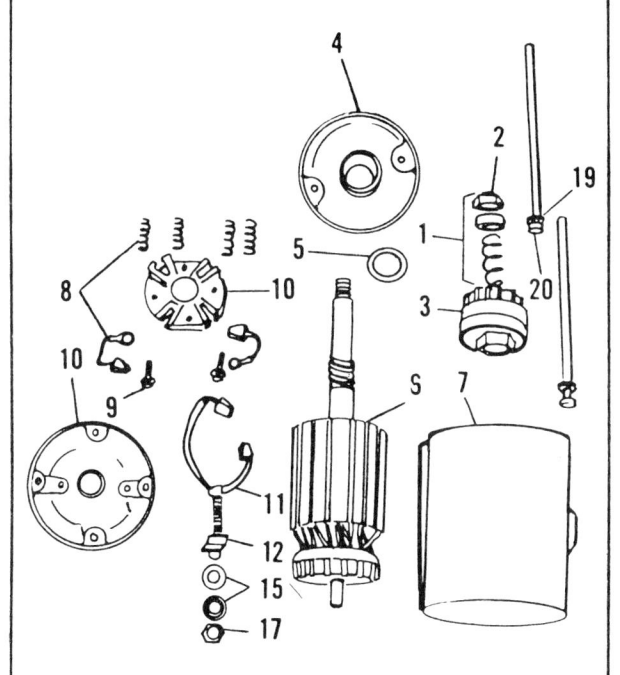

1. Pinion nut and spring assembly
2. Pinion nut
3. Pinion gear
4. End cap
5. Armature shaft washer
6. Armature
7. Starter frame
8. Negative brush and spring assembly
9. Screw
10. End cap and brush holder assembly
11. Positive brush assembly
12. Insulation bushing
15. Washer
17. Input stud nut
19. Washer
20. Center bolt

2. Remove the end band and through-bolts.
3. Remove the brush end plate, bushing and insulator plate.
4. Remove the armature.
5. Note position of brushes in the brush holder. Pull back and hold the brush retaining clip with a wire hook, then remove the brush. Repeat this step to remove remaining brushes.
6. Note location of brush holder with respect to end terminal and remove the brush holder.
7. Inspect the brushes. Replace all brushes if any are worn to 3/8 in. or less.
8. Check the brush holder for cracks or broken mounting pads.
9. To replace ground brushes, remove the brush lead attaching screws from the starter frame. Take out the brushes and install new ones.
10. To replace field coil brushes, cut the insulated brush leads as close as possible to the field coils. Attach new brush leads with the clips provided in the brush replacement kit. Solder the connections together with rosin core solder and a 300-watt soldering iron.
11. Install the armature.
12. Install the brush holder. Insert brushes in the holder and install the brush springs.

NOTE
Position brush leads in their correct brush hole slots to prevent a potential ground.

13. Install brush insulator, bushing and end plate.
14. Install and tighten through-bolts.
15. Install end band and tighten screw securely.

Brush Replacement (Bosch)

Always replace brushes in complete sets. Refer to **Figure 27** for this procedure.

1. Remove the starter as described in this chapter. Separate it from the mounting bracket, unless bracket is welded to motor housing.
2. Remove the 2 through-bolts and carefully tap commutator end cap from the starter frame. Do not lose the end cap brush springs.
3. Inspect the brushes in the brush holder on the commutator end of the armature. Replace all brushes if any are oil-soaked or worn to 3/8 in. or less.
4. Remove brush and springs from brush holder. Remove brush holder from commutator end.
5. Check brush holder straightness. If brushes do not show full-face contact with commutator, holder is probably bent.
6. Install the insulated brush and terminal set in the commutator end cap as shown in **Figure 28**.
7. Install the brush holder in the commutator end cap. Install the brush springs in the holder. Insert the brushes and tighten the brush lead screws to the holder.
8. Fit the insulated brushes in the holder slots. **Figure 29** shows the reassembled brush holder and commutator end cap assembly.
9. Align the commutator and drive end cap marks. Hold the brushes in place and assemble the end cap to the frame. A putty knife with a 1×1/2 in. slot cut in its end makes a suitable tool for keeping the brushes in place during this step.
10. Wipe the through bolt threads with engine oil. Install and tighten bolts to specifications (**Table 4**). Apply OMC Black Neoprene Dip around the end cap and frame joints.
11. Reinstall the mounting bracket, if removed.

Brush Replacement (Delco-Remy)

Two sizes of Delco-Remy starters are used. The smaller one has 1 negative and 1 positive brush; the larger one uses 2 of each. Always replace brushes in complete sets.

1. Remove the starter as described in this chapter.
2. Scribe identifying marks on the frame and end caps for reassembly reference.
3. Remove the 2 through-bolts and carefully tap the commutator end cap to separate it from the starter frame.
4. Remove the washers from the end of the armature shaft, noting the quantity and sequence of installation for reassembly. Remove the armature and drive end cap from the front of the starter frame.
5. Remove the brushes from their holders. Remove the brush springs.
6. Inspect the brushes. Replace all brushes if any are worn to 3/8 in. or less.
7. Drill out the rivets holding the negative brush holders to the starter motor frame. Remove the brush holders and brushes.

Figure 28
1. Long lead
2. Commutator end cap
3. Slot
4. Insulated terminal

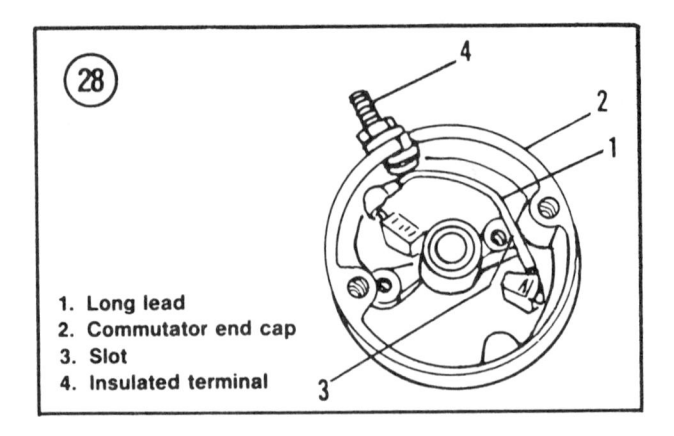

Figure 29
1. Insulated brush
2. Ground brush
3. Insulated terminal

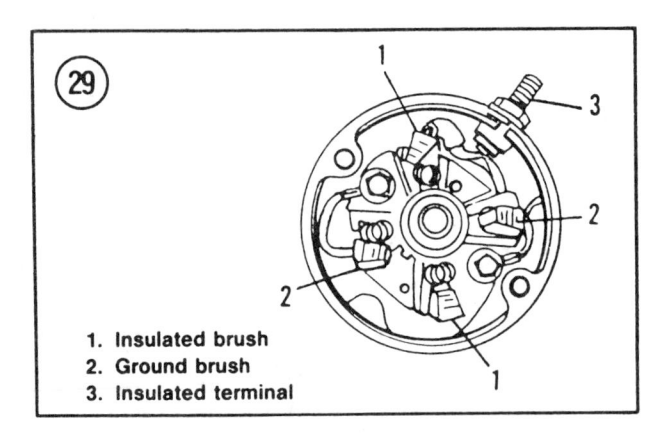

ELECTRICAL SYSTEMS

30

a. Positive brushes
b. Negative brushes

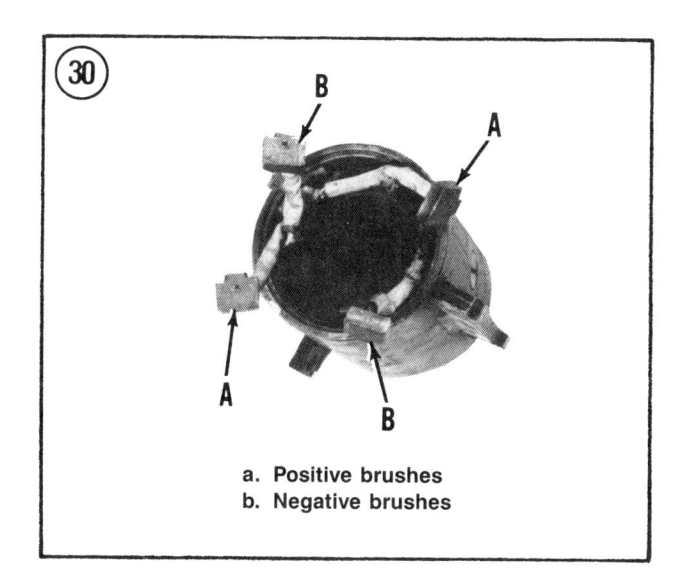

8. Cut the positive brush leads at the point where they are attached to the field coils.
9. File or grind off solder from ends of field coil leads where old brushes were connected.
10. Use rosin soldering flux and solder the new brush leads to the field coils, making sure that they are in the right position to reach the brush holders.

NOTE
The leads should be soldered to the back side of the coils so that excessive solder will not rub the armature. Do not overheat the leads, as the solder will run onto the leads and they will no longer be flexible.

11. Install the new negative brushes and holders to the frame with the screws, washers and nuts provided.
12. Install the armature in the starter frame, aligning the drive end plate mark with the starter frame mark. Hold the brushes in place and assemble the end cap to the frame. A putty knife with a 1 × 1/2 in. slot cut in its end makes a suitable tool for keeping the brushes in place during this step.
13. Reinstall the washers on the armature shaft in the same order as removed.
14. Install the end cap with the scribed marks on cap and starter frame aligned.

15. Wipe the through-bolt threads with engine oil. Install and tighten through-bolts to specifications (**Table 4**). Apply OMC Black Neoprene Dip around the end cap and frame joints.

Brush Replacement (Prestolite)

Always replace brushes in complete sets.
1. Remove the starter as described in this chapter.
2. Remove the 2 through-bolts and carefully tap the commutator end cap to separate it from the starter frame.
3. Remove the washers from the end of the armature shaft, noting the quantity and sequence of installation for reassembly. Remove the armature and drive end cap from the front of the starter frame.
4. Remove the positive terminal and brush from the starter frame. See **Figure 30**.
5. Inspect the brushes. Replace all brushes if any are worn to 3/8 in. or less.
6. Cut the negative brush lead at the point where it is attached to the field coil. See **Figure 30**.
7. File or grind off solder from end of field coil lead where old brush was connected.
8. Use rosin soldering flux and solder the new brush lead to the field coil, making sure that it is in the right position to reach the brush holder.

NOTE
The lead should be soldered to the back side of the coil so that excessive solder will not rub the armature. Do not overheat the lead, as the solder will run onto the lead and it will no longer be flexible.

9. Install a new brush and insulated terminal assembly (**Figure 30**).
10. Install the brush plate with the notch facing the positive terminal. Route the brush leads over the plate as shown in **Figure 31**.

11. Install one brush spring and brush in the holder. Secure in place with a brush retaining tool or tie in place with a length of thread. Repeat this step for the other brush. See **Figure 31**.
12. Install the armature in the starter frame, aligning the drive end plate tab with the starter frame slot.
13. Remove the brush retaining tools from the brushes.
14. Reinstall the washers on the armature shaft in the same order as removed.
15. Install the end cap with the raised lines facing the positive terminal.
16. Wipe the through-bolt threads with engine oil. Install and tighten through-bolts to specifications (**Table 4**). Apply OMC Black Neoprene Dip around the end cap and frame joints.

Safety Switch

A safety switch is incorporated in the starting circuit of electric start models to prevent starter motor engagement if the throttle lever is moved beyond the START position. The switch is also used on models equipped with a vacuum cut-out switch to prevent the cut-out switch from operating at full throttle. See Chapter Eight for switch operation and adjustment.

Starter Solenoid

The solenoid (**Figure 32**) acts as a switch connecting the battery and starter motor. Although it appears identical to a common automotive-type solenoid, it is wired differently internally. If an automotive solenoid is used instead of the proper marine-type, the current could be sent to ground, burning the connecting wires and destroying the vacuum-operated cut-out switch. *Always* use a marine-type replacement solenoid.

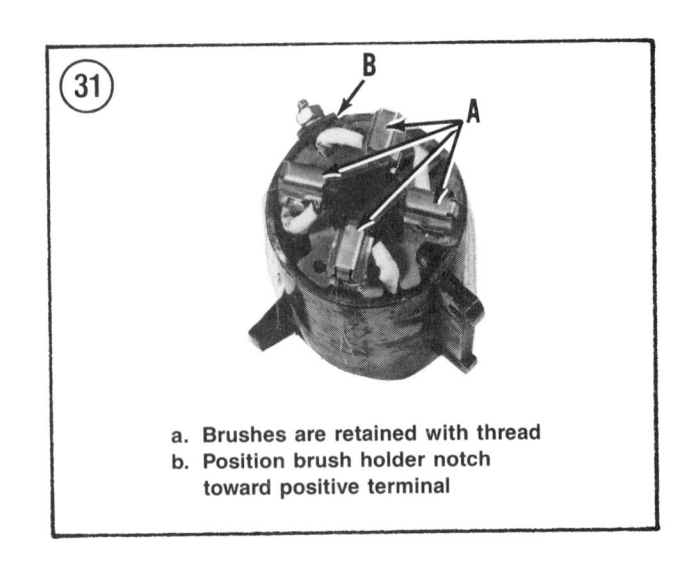

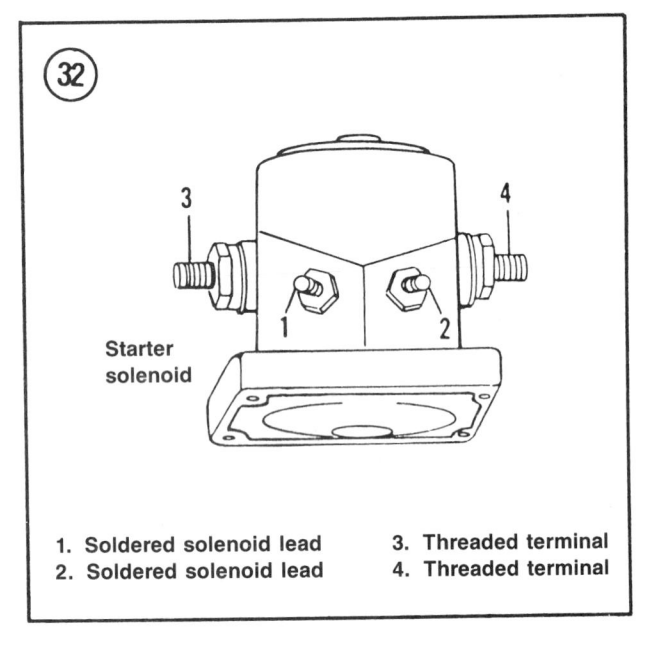

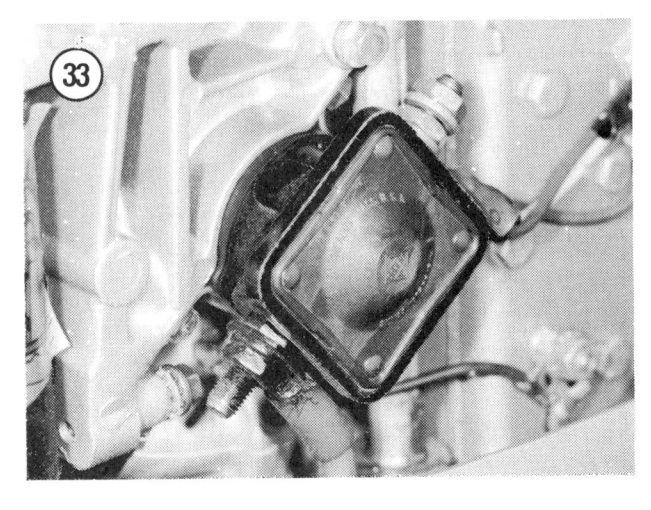

ELECTRICAL SYSTEMS

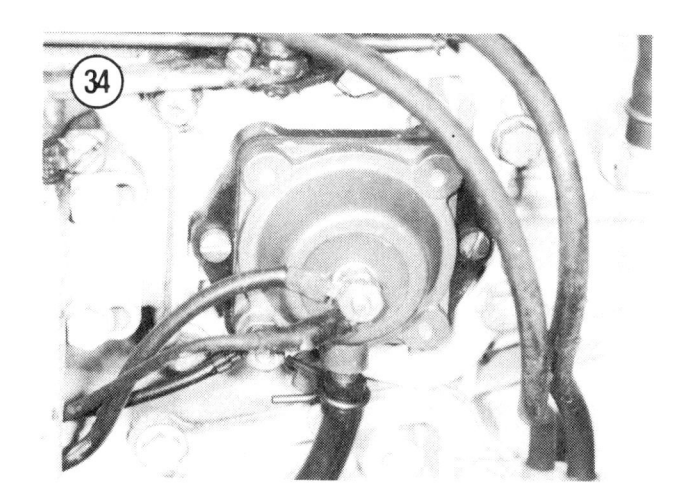

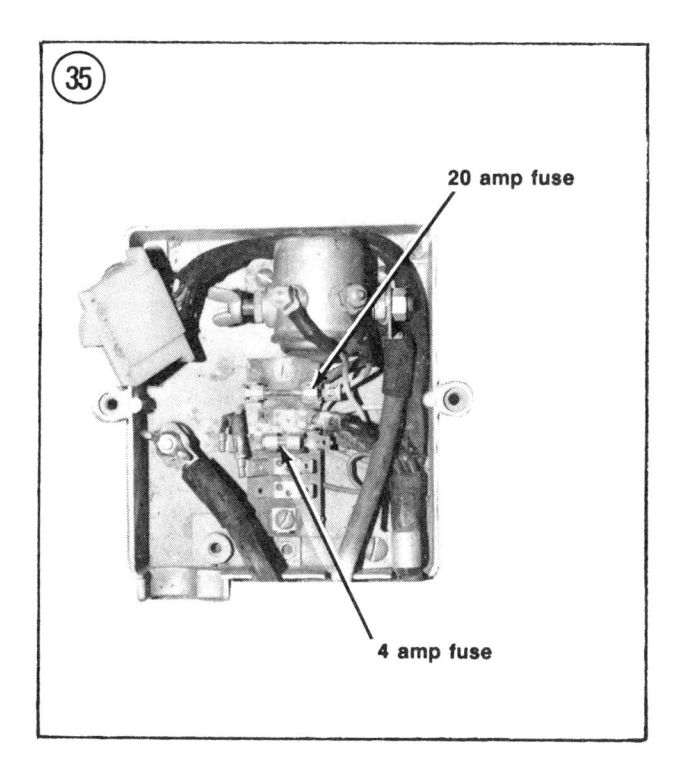

Figure 34

Figure 35
- 20 amp fuse
- 4 amp fuse

The starter solenoid is enclosed in the junction box at the rear of the engine on models through 1966. The solenoid used on 1967-1972 models is mounted externally on the engine. Exact location varies with model year and horsepower rating. Some starter solenoids are very similar in appearance to the vacuum-operated cut-out switch. See **Figure 33** (solenoid) and **Figure 34** (cut-out switch). The cut-out switch can be identified by its vacuum lines.

Removal/Installation (Junction Box Mounting)

Refer to **Figure 35** for this procedure.
1. Disconnect the negative battery cable.
2. Remove the junction box cover.
3. Label and disconnect the electrical leads at the solenoid terminals.
4. Remove the screws holding the solenoid. Remove the regulator.
5. Install the new solenoid in the box. Tighten attaching screws securely.
6. Connect the electrical leads to the new solenoid terminals.
7. Install the junction box cover, then reconnect the positive battery cable.

Removal/Installation (External Mounting)

1. Disconnect the positive battery cable.
2. Disconnect the wires from the solenoid terminals.
3. Remove the screws holding the solenoid. Remove the solenoid.
4. Installation is the reverse of removal.

Vacuum-operated Cut-out Switch

If the throttle is suddenly closed while the engine is running at a fast idle in NEUTRAL, crankcase vacuum increases rapidly. This can cause erratic cylinder firing, increasing engine rpm sharply even through the throttle is closed. To prevent this problem, a vacuum cut-out switch (**Figure 34**) momentarily shorts out the lower cylinder breaker point when crankcase vacuum is high. The starting circuit safety switch is also incorporated in this circuit to prevent the cut-out switch from operating at full throttle.

The vacuum switch housing contains a spring-loaded vacuum diaphragm with a center button grounded to the housing. A center contact in the switch is connected to the lower cylinder breaker point in the magneto. The inner chamber of the housing is connected to manifold vacuum. As vacuum increases, the diaphragm is drawn to the center contact. When the diaphragm button and center contact touch, the lower breaker point set is grounded out.

Removal/Installation

1. Disconnect the vacuum line and electrical leads at the switch.
2. Remove the adapter mounting screws. Remove the switch and adapter from the power head.
3. Installation is the reverse of removal.

IGNITION SYSTEMS

The outboards covered in this manual use one of the following ignition systems:
   a. Flywheel magneto breaker point ignition.
   b. Distributor magneto breaker point ignition.
   c. Distributor battery breaker point ignition.
   d. Distributor CD sensor ignition.
   e. Flywheel CD sensor ignition.
   f. Flywheel CD breaker point ignition.

Refer to Chapter Three for troubleshooting and test procedures.

FLYWHEEL MAGNETO BREAKER POINT IGNITION

This ignition system uses a coil and laminated core, condenser and breaker point set for each cylinder. The components are mounted on an armature plate under the flywheel which revolves with the crankshaft. A cam on the crankshaft opens and closes the breaker points to produce ignition at the correct time. The system is self-energizing and does not require the use of a battery to provide electrical current. **Figure 36** shows the system components. Troubleshooting and test procedures are given in Chapter Three.

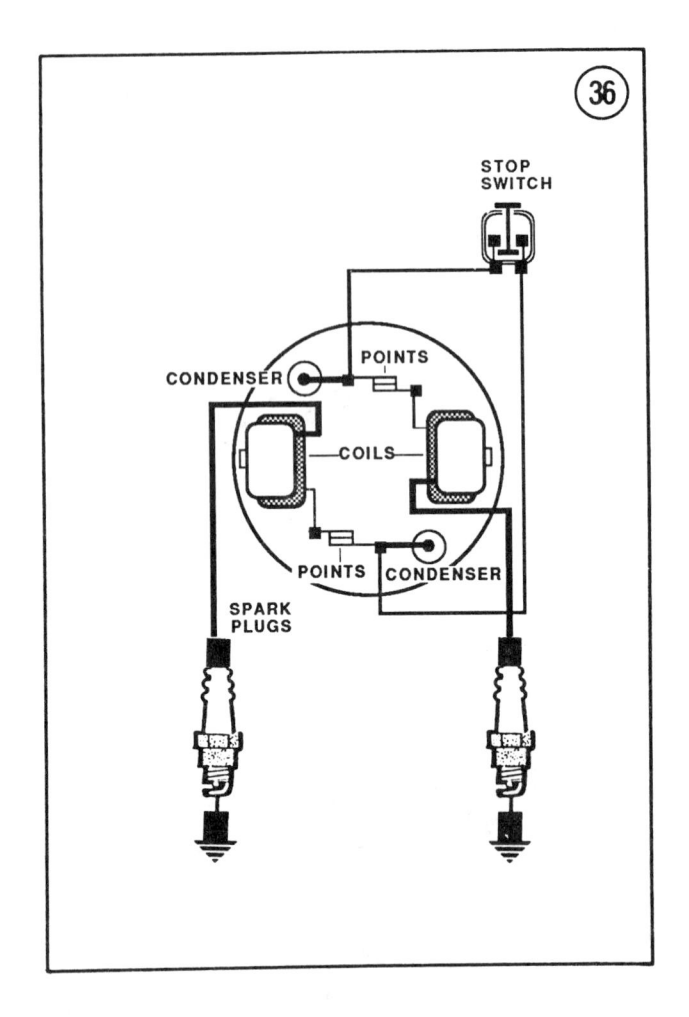

The key or ignition switch used in this system closes the circuit between the magneto and ground in the OFF position. In some models, it grounds the breaker points. This is just the opposite of how an automotive-type ignition switch operates. If switch replacement is necessary, do *not* use an automotive-type replacement switch or damage may result to the magneto system.

The wiring harness installed between the key or ignition switch and the engine is not capable of carrying an accessory load. Whenever accessories are installed, they should *not* be connected through the switch. Always install separate wiring with its own fuse. Failure to do so can damage the magneto system.

ELECTRICAL SYSTEMS

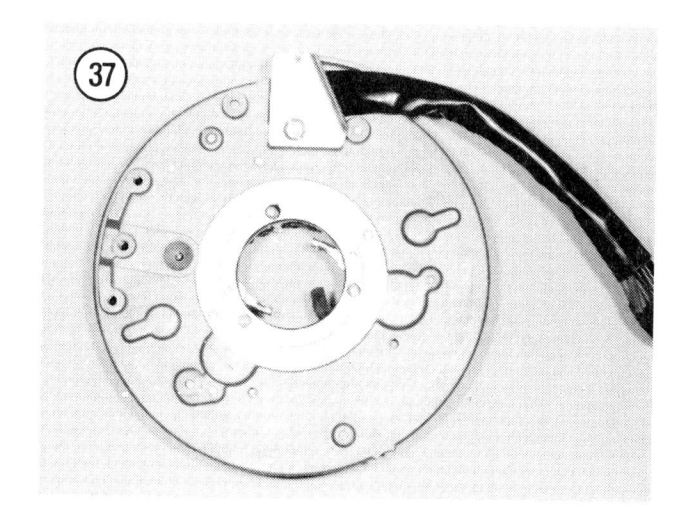

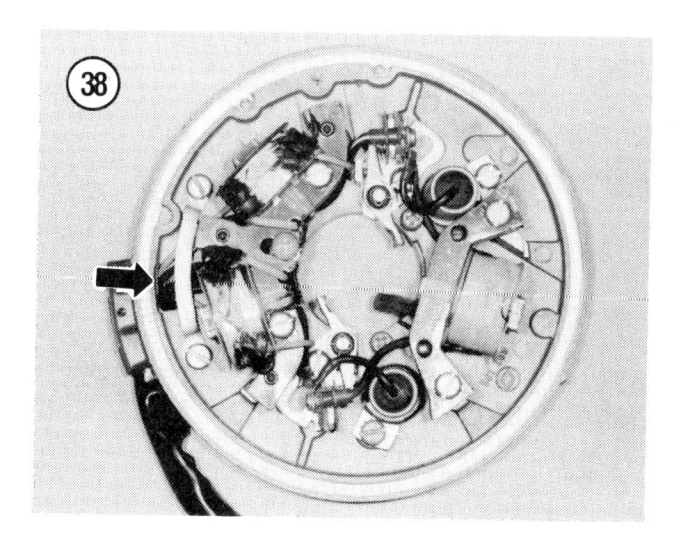

37

38

Operation

As the flywheel rotates, magnets around its outer diameter create a current that flows through the closed breaker points. This flow of current through the coil primary winding builds a strong magnetic field in the coil primary winding. When the cam opens the No. 1 point set, the magnetic field collapses, inducing a high voltage (approximately 18,000 volts) in the coil secondary winding that is sent to the No. 1 spark plug. The condenser absorbs any residual current remaining in the primary windings. This eliminates arcing at the points and produces a stronger spark at the plug. The breaker points close and the flywheel continues to rotate, duplicating the sequence in 2-cylinder engines for the No. 2 point set and ignition coil to fire the No. 2 spark plug.

Armature Plate
Removal/Installation

See Chapter Eight.

Breaker Point and
Condenser Replacement

See *Tune-up*, Chapter Four.

Ignition Coil
Removal/Installation

The primary and secondary ignition coils are a combined assembly mounted on the armature plate.

1. Remove the armature plate. See Chapter Eight.
2. Disconnect the coil lead wires at the breaker point set and ground.
3. Turn the armature plate over and remove the cover plate, if used. See **Figure 37** (typical).
4. Remove the 2 screws holding the wiring lead strap in place, if used. See **Figure 38**.
5. Remove the 3 screws holding the coil to the armature plate.
6. Remove the coil and lead from the armature plate.
7. Disconnect the high tension lead from the coil.
8. Installation is the reverse of removal. Make sure the coil is properly aligned when reinstalled. The heels on the laminated core should be flush with the armature plate machined surfaces. The use of a coil locating ring (part No. 317001) which is machined to fit over the armature plate bosses is recommended. See **Figure 39**. Position all leads carefully so they will not rub against the flywheel. Coat all electrical connections with OMC Black Neoprene Dip.

DISTRIBUTOR MAGNETO BREAKER POINT IGNITION

This ignition system uses a single coil, condenser, 2 breaker point sets and a rotor. The components are mounted in a magneto housing containing 2 permanent magnets and bracket-mounted to the power head. The pulley-driven rotor and 2-lobe cam produce 4 sparks during each revolution of the rotor.

The system is self-energizing and does not require the use of a battery to provide electrical current. **Figure 40** shows the distributor magneto system components. Troubleshooting and test procedures are given in Chapter Three.

Operation

The rotor is driven at crankshaft speed by the timing belt. Each time a cam lobe opens the breaker point set, the magnetic field collapses, inducing a high voltage (approximately 18,000 volts) in the coil secondary winding that is sent to the appropriate spark plug. The condenser absorbs any residual current remaining in the primary windings. This eliminates arcing at the points and produces a stronger spark at the plug.

Distributor Magneto Removal/Installation

1. Disconnect the positive battery cable.
2. Remove the engine cover.
3. Disconnect the safety switch and ignition key switch leads.
4. Twist spark plug leads counterclockwise and remove from distributor cap.
5. Remove the head bolts which hold the spark plug lead retainers to the power head.
6. Remove the 2 linkage screws and disconnect the linkage.
7. Remove the 3 bracket mounting screws. Slide magneto bracket forward and remove the drive belt from the pulley.
8. Remove the magneto and bracket assembly.
9. Installation is the reverse of removal. Adjust belt tension and check linkage adjustment and carburetor synchronization. See Chapter Five.

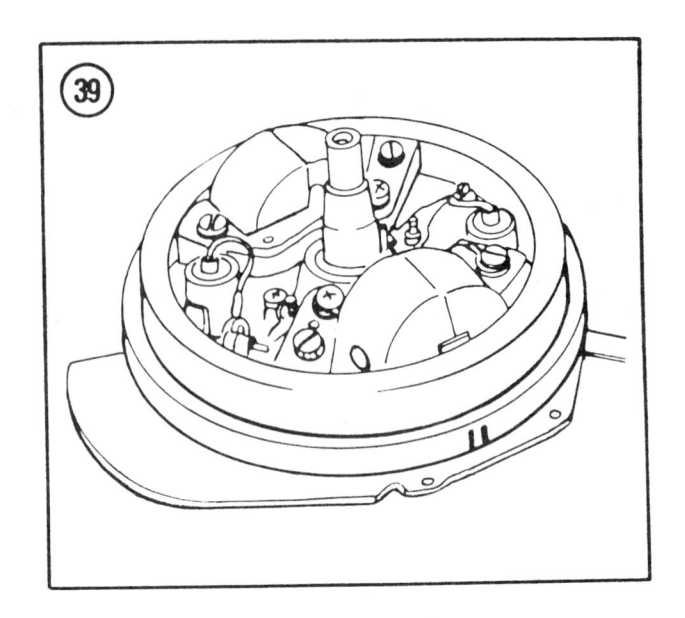

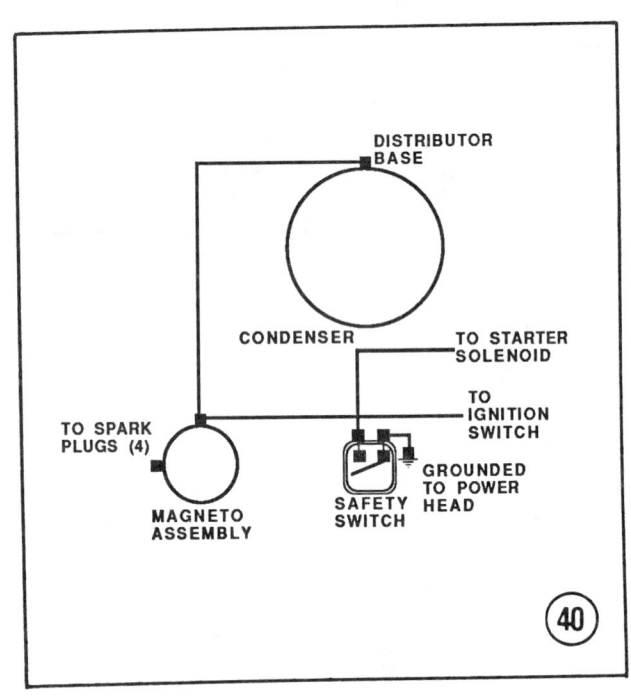

Magneto Housing Disassembly

Refer to **Figure 41** for this procedure.

ELECTRICAL SYSTEMS

Figure 41

DISTRIBUTOR MAGNETO IGNITION COMPONENTS

Components shown: Cover, Pulley, Breaker point assembly, Felt washer, Seal, Bracket, Seal, Washer, Belt, Coil, Rotor, Magneto housing and sleeve assembly, Magneto shaft, bearing and washer assembly, Bearing support, Gasket, Distributor cap, Spark plug leads.

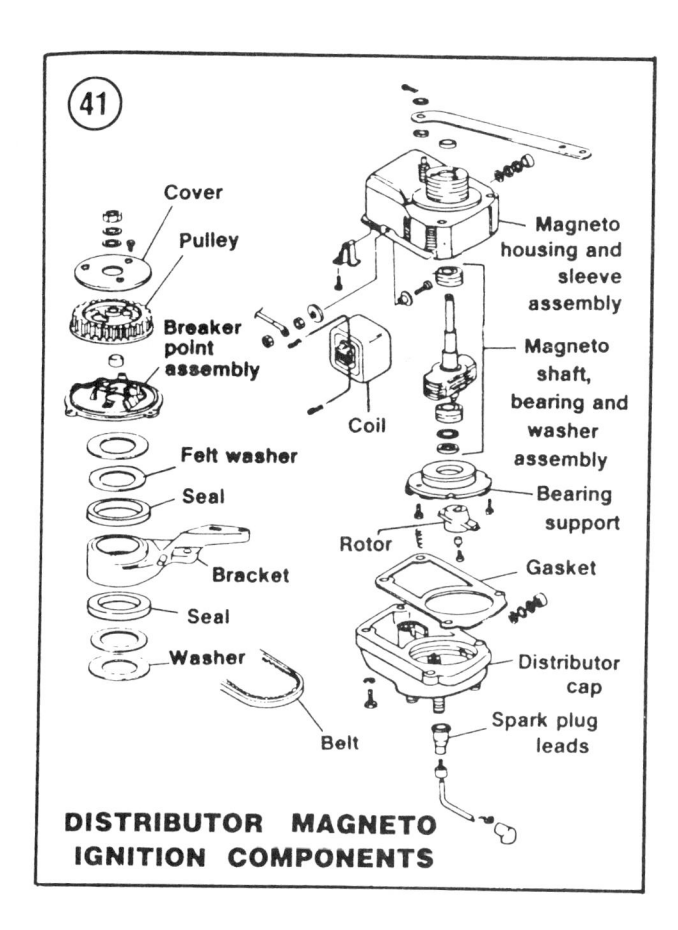

1. Remove the magneto pulley, cam and shaft key.
2. Remove the breaker plate assembly.
3. Separate the bearing bracket from the magneto housing. Be sure to note positioning of the washers.
4. Remove the distributor cap and rotor.
5. If spark plug leads were not removed from the distributor cap, unscrew in a counterclockwise direction.
6. Disconnect the coil primary and ground leads. Remove the coil from the housing.

NOTE
This completes normal disassembly. Magneto shaft removal will damage the shaft bearings. The shaft should not be removed unless bearing replacement is definitely indicated.

7. If magneto shaft bearing replacement is required, remove the bearing support screws from the housing and remove the shaft and bearing assembly with an arbor press.

Cleaning and Inspection

1. Check the distributor cap carbon brush and spring. Make sure the brush moves freely in its socket with ample spring tension to contact the rotor. Replace the brush and spring if worn excessively or spring tension is weak.
2. Wipe the inside of the distributor cap with a clean cloth. Check cap for signs of burning, pitting, cracking or corrosion. Scrape any deposits off the terminals.
3. Check the rotor for signs of burning, pitting or corrosion. Scrape or file the rotor tip clean as required. Fit rotor on distributor shaft and check for wobble. If noted, replace the spring clip on the rotor.
4. Check the distributor cap and magneto housing vents. Make sure they are securely in place and clean. Replace the vents if loose or dirty.
5. Hold housing in one hand and slowly rotate the shaft with the other hand, noting any roughness. Move the shaft up-and-down and side-to-side to check for end or side play. If shaft does not rotate smoothly without play, replace the bearings.

Magneto Housing Assembly

Refer to **Figure 41** for this procedure.
1. If shaft was removed for bearing replacement, install new bearings on the shaft. Support the housing and press the shaft and upper bearing in place.
2. Install bearing washer and felt washer in bearing support recess, then press support in place over the lower bearing. Install the bearing support screws.
3. Install ignition coil. Reconnect primary and ground leads.

4. Install rotor on shaft. Fit carbon brush and spring in distributor cap. Install cap to housing.
5. Install bearing bracket to housing. Make sure to install the washers in the same positions as noted during disassembly.
6. Install breaker plate assembly to magneto housing. Install key and cam on shaft.
7. Install magneto pulley and tighten the attaching nut to 19-21 ft.-lb.
8. If spark plug leads were removed, reinstall and turn clockwise to tighten.
9. Install magneto housing as described in this chapter.
10. Adjust belt tension and check linkage adjustment and carburetor synchronization. See Chapter Five.

Magneto Timing Belt Replacement

1. Remove the rewind starter assembly. See Chapter Ten.
2. Remove the magneto pulley cover plate.
3. Remove the old belt from the engine.
4. Carefully slip a new belt over the flywheel and thread it between the flywheel and power head components. Make sure the belt engages the pulley under the flywheel, then install on magneto pulley.
5. Reinstall magneto pulley cover plate and rewind starter.
6. Remove the spark plugs and ground the spark plug leads.
7. Rotate the flywheel clockwise to align the timing marks on the flywheel, rewind starter housing and bypass cover plate. The timing mark should now align with the safety switch plunger (**Figure 42**). If not, loosen the magneto bracket screws and rotate the pulley to align the marks.
8. Adjust magneto bracket to provide 5/16-3/8 in. belt deflection when depressed at the point shown in **Figure 43**. When deflection is correct, tighten bracket screws.

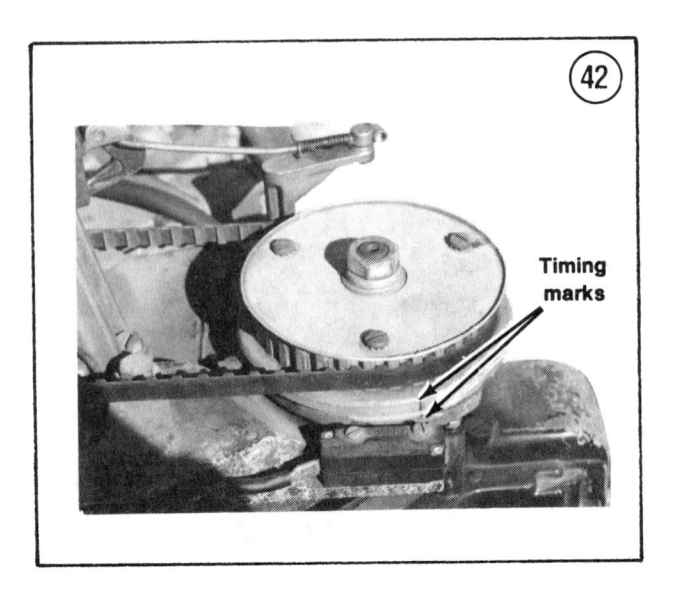

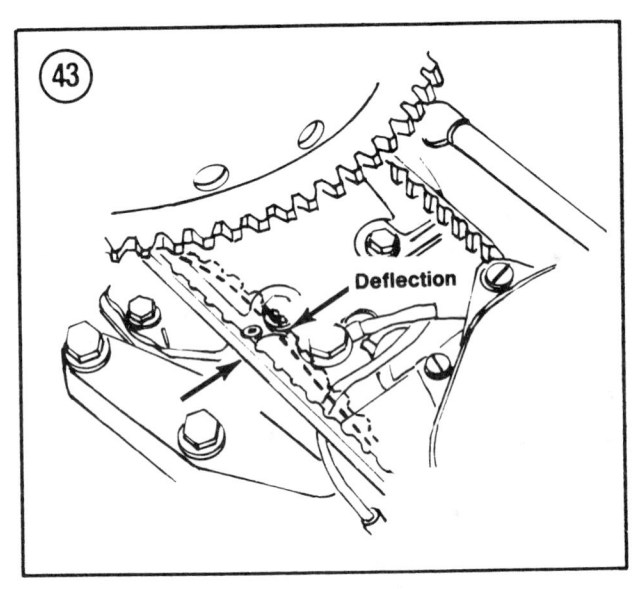

9. Check magneto linkage and carburetor synchronization. See Chapter Five.

DISTRIBUTOR BATTERY BREAKER POINT IGNITION

This ignition system is similar to the the distributor magneto breaker point ignition, but uses a battery to provide operating current instead of having current induced in the coil by magneto magnets. The ignition coil is a separate unit and mounted on the power head. The primary coil circuit incorporates a lead with a one-ohm resistance

ELECTRICAL SYSTEMS

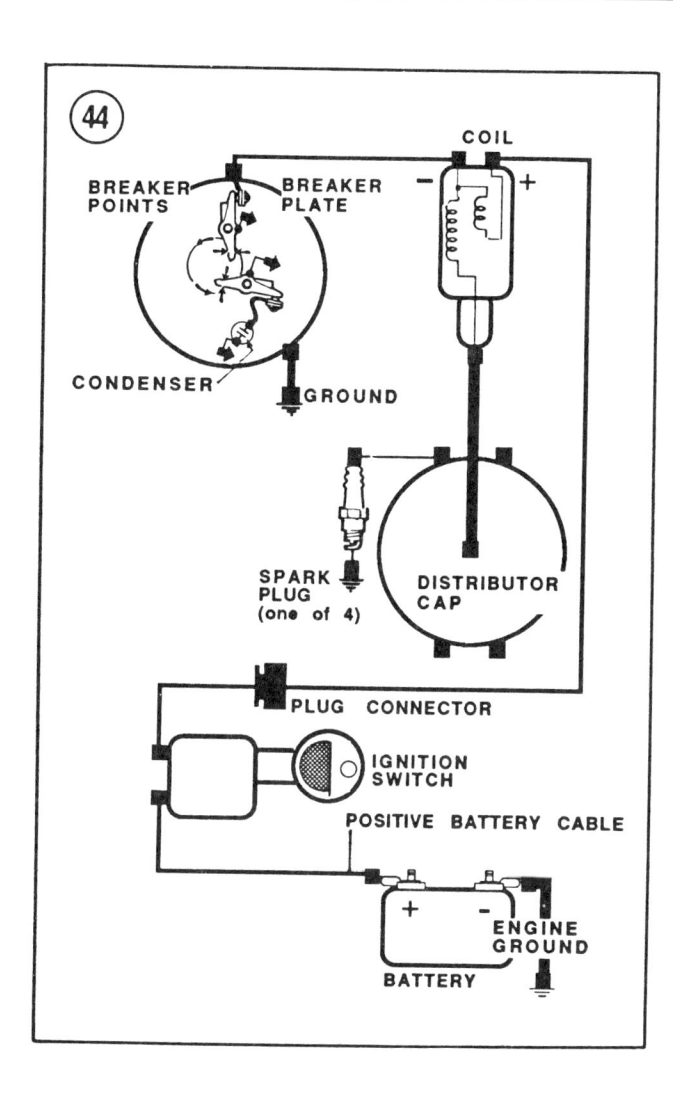

44

BREAKER POINTS
BREAKER PLATE
COIL
CONDENSER
GROUND
SPARK PLUG (one of 4)
DISTRIBUTOR CAP
PLUG CONNECTOR
IGNITION SWITCH
POSITIVE BATTERY CABLE
ENGINE GROUND
BATTERY

as part of the wiring harness. **Figure 44** shows the distributor magneto system components.

Troubleshooting and test procedures are given in Chapter Three.

Operation

The rotor is driven at crankshaft speed by the timing belt. Each time a cam lobe opens the breaker point set, the magnetic field collapses, inducing a high voltage (approximately 18,000 volts) in the coil secondary winding that is sent to the appropriate spark plug. The condenser absorbs any residual current remaining in the primary windings. This eliminates arcing at the points and produces a stronger spark at the plug.

Distributor Removal/Installation

1. Disconnect the positive battery cable.
2. Remove the engine cover.
3. Twist the spark plug and coil leads counterclockwise and remove from the distributor cap.
4. Disconnect the safety switch lead.
5. Remove the 2 linkage screws and disconnect the linkage.
6. Remove the distributor cap and rotor.
7. Disconnect the breaker point lead at the coil.
8. Remove the ignition coil and ring gear cover.
9. Remove the 3 bracket mounting screws. Slide distributor bracket forward and remove the drive belt from the pulley.
10. Remove the distributor and bracket assembly.
11. Installation is the reverse of removal. Adjust belt tension and check linkage adjustment and engine synchronization. See Chapter Five.

Distributor Disassembly

Refer to **Figure 45** for this procedure.
1. Remove the distributor cam, shaft key and spring.
2. Remove the pulley nut, lockwasher and flat washer. Remove the pulley.
3. Remove the cap at the bottom of the housing. Remove the large snap ring with snap ring pliers.
4. Remove the housing and washers from the bracket.
5. If distributor shaft or shaft bearings require replacement, separate the shaft and upper bearing from the housing with an arbor press. Press the upper bearing off the shaft and the lower bearing from the housing.

Cleaning and Inspection

1. Check the distributor cap carbon brush and spring. Make sure the brush moves freely in its socket with ample spring tension to contact the rotor. Replace the brush and spring if worn excessively or spring tension is weak.
2. Wipe the inside of the distributor cap with a clean cloth. Check cap for signs of burning, pitting, cracking or corrosion. Scrape any deposits off the terminals.
3. Check the rotor for signs of burning, pitting or corrosion. Scrape or file the rotor tip clean as required. Fit rotor on distributor shaft and check for wobble. If noted, replace the spring clip on the rotor.
4. Check the distributor cap and distributor housing vents. Make sure they are securely in place and clean. Replace the vents if loose or dirty.
5. Hold housing in one hand and slowly rotate the shaft with the other hand, noting any roughness. Move the shaft up-and-down and side-to-side to check for end or side play. If shaft does not rotate smoothly without play, replace the bearings.

Distributor Assembly

Refer to **Figure 45** for this procedure.
1. If distributor shaft was removed from the housing, press a new lower shaft bearing into the housing. Install a new upper bearing on the shaft with an arbor press, applying pressure against the inner race. Press the shaft and upper bearing into the housing, applying pressure against the outer race.
2. Reinstall pulley on distributor shaft. Install a new flat washer, lockwasher and the pulley nut. Hold pulley from moving with a spanner wrench and tighten pulley nut to 19-21 ft.-lb. with a 3/4 in. deep-wall socket.
3. Install distributor shaft key and detent spring. Long end of spring should face shaft

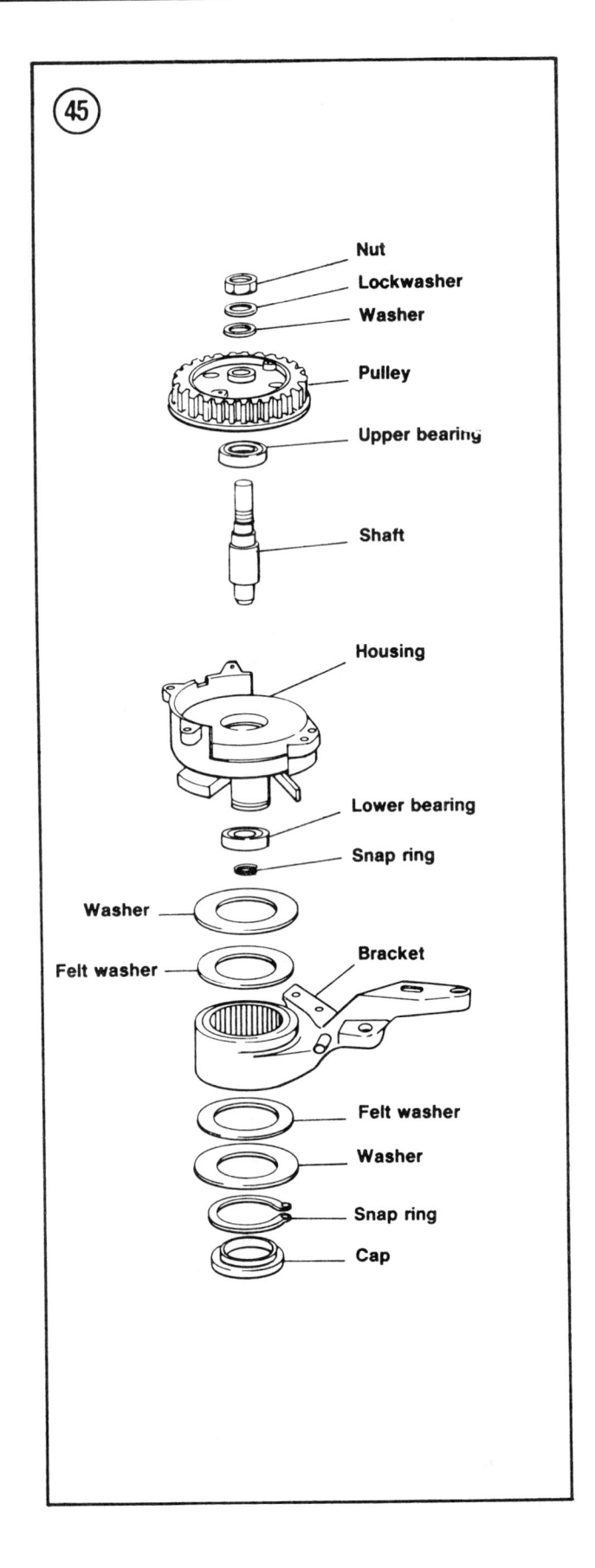

ELECTRICAL SYSTEMS

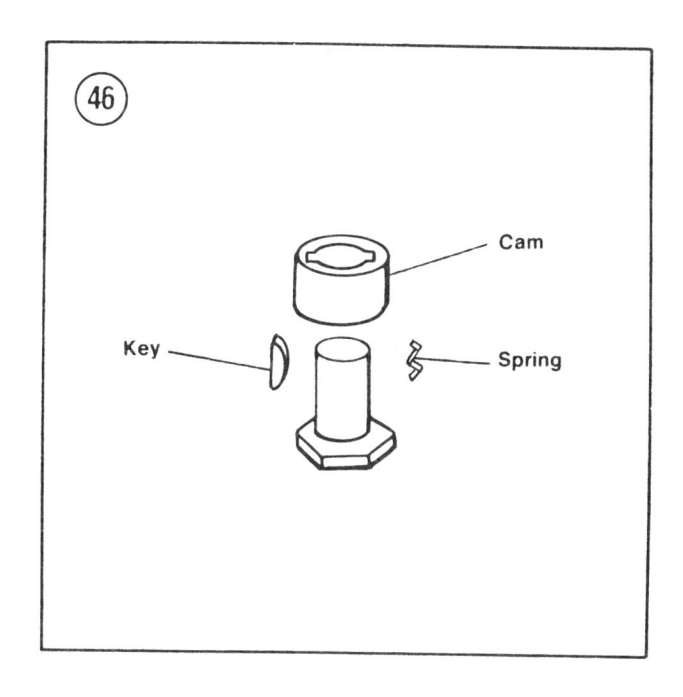

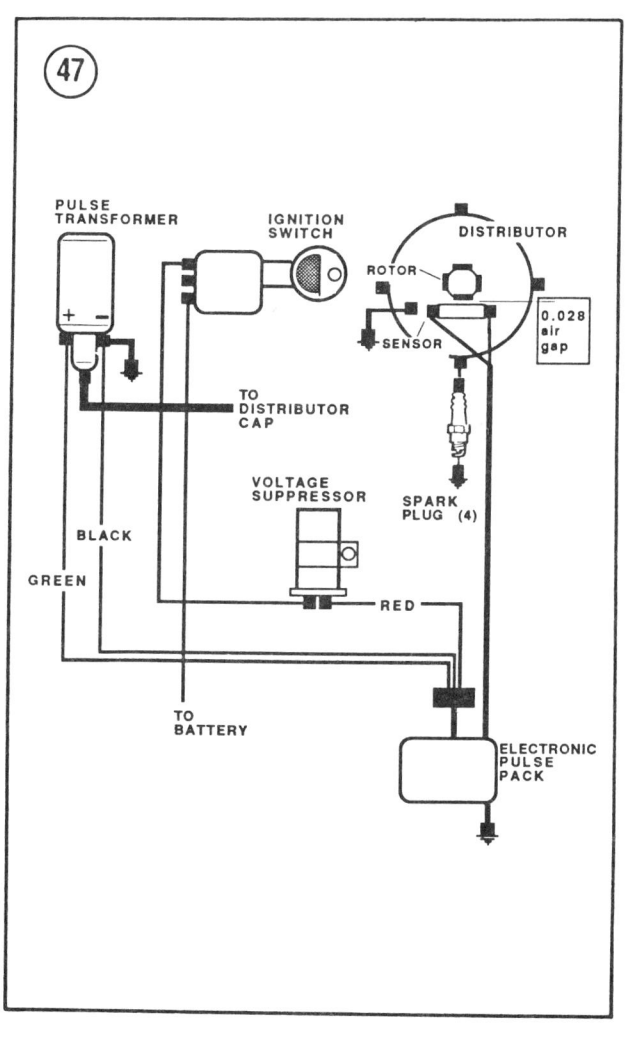

nut. Align cam with key and spring, then install cam against shaft nut. See **Figure 46**.

4. Install snap ring on bottom of distributor shaft. Fit shaft into bracket with metal and felt washers, then install felt and metal washers on bottom of housing.
5. Install large snap ring on housing and reinstall cap.
6. Install distributor as described in this chapter.
7. Check timing and belt tension. See Chapter Five.
8. Install breaker point and plate assembly (Chapter Four).
9. Check distributor linkage and carburetor synchronization. See Chapter Five.

DISTRIBUTOR CD SENSOR IGNITION

This ignition system is used only on the 1967 100 hp engine. It consists of a distributor with trigger wheel and sensor assembly, a pulse transformer and an electronic pulse pack containing a transformer, capacitor and electronic switch. The pulse pack is sealed in epoxy and bracket-mounted on the lower rear motor cover. **Figure 47** is a schematic of the system. Troubleshooting and test procedures are given in Chapter Three.

Operation

Current provided by the battery is stepped up to 300 volts by a transistorized converter and stored in a capacitor in the pulse pack. When a trigger wheel leg aligns with the sensor in the distributor, the electronic switch is closed. This sends the capacitor voltage to the pulse transformer, where it is stepped up to 25,000 volts and sent to the spark plugs. As soon as the spark plug fires, the electronic switch opens again and the capacitor is recharged.

Distributor Removal/Installation

1. Disconnect the negative battery cable.
2. Remove the engine cover.
3. Disconnect the safety switch lead.
4. Twist spark plug and coil leads counterclockwise and remove from distributor cap.
5. Remove distributor cap from breaker plate assembly.
6. Remove the 2 linkage screws and disconnect the control shaft linkage.
7. Remove the distributor rotor.
8. Disconnect the ignition coil leads.
9. Remove the ring gear cover.
10. Remove the 3 bracket mounting screws. Slide distributor bracket forward and remove the drive belt from the pulley.
11. Remove the distributor and bracket assembly.
12. Installation is the reverse of removal. Adjust belt tension and check linkage adjustment and engine synchronization. See Chapter Five.

Distributor Disassembly

Refer to **Figure 48** for this procedure.
1. Carefully pry the trigger wheel off the distributor shaft with 2 screwdrivers.
2. Remove the distributor shaft key.
3. Remove the 2 screws holding the sensor unit plate to the distributor pulley.
4. If sensor is to be replaced, remove the attaching screws and remove the sensor.
5. Remove the pulley nut, lockwasher and flat washer. Remove the pulley.
6. Remove the cap at the bottom of the housing. Remove the large snap ring with snap ring pliers.
7. Remove the housing and washers from the bracket.

NOTE
This completes normal disassembly. Distributor shaft removal will damage

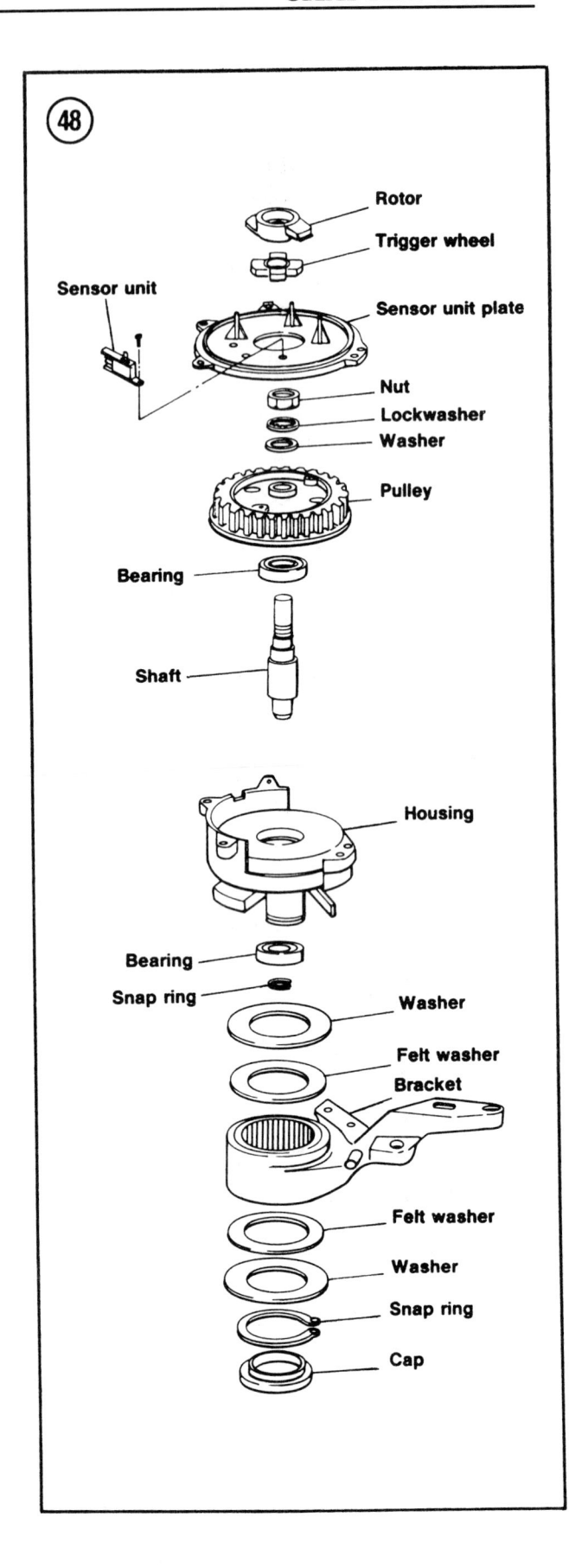

ELECTRICAL SYSTEMS

the shaft bearings. The shaft should not be removed unless bearing replacement is definitely indicated.

8. If distributor shaft or shaft bearings require replacement, separate the shaft and upper bearing from the housing with an arbor press. Press the upper bearing off the shaft and the lower bearing from the housing.

Cleaning and Inspection

1. Check the distributor cap carbon brush and spring. Make sure the brush moves freely in its socket with ample spring tension to contact the rotor. Replace the brush and spring if worn excessively or spring tension is weak.
2. Wipe the inside of the distributor cap with a clean cloth. Check cap for signs of burning, pitting, cracking or corrosion. Scrape any deposits off the terminals.
3. Check the rotor for signs of burning, pitting or corrosion. Scrape or file the rotor tip clean as required. Fit rotor on distributor shaft and check for wobble. If noted, replace the spring clip on the rotor.
4. Check the distributor cap and drive pulley vents. Make sure they are securely in place and clean. Replace the vents if loose or dirty.
5. Hold housing in one hand and slowly rotate the shaft with the other hand, noting any roughness. Move the shaft up-and-down and side-to-side to check for end or side play. If shaft does not rotate smoothly without play, replace the bearings.

Distributor Assembly

Refer to **Figure 48** for this procedure.
1. If distributor shaft was removed from the housing, install a new upper bearing on the shaft with an arbor press, applying pressure against the inner race. Press the shaft and upper bearing into the housing, applying pressure against the outer race. Press a new bottom bearing in place, applying pressure equally to the inner and outer races of top and bottom bearings.
2. Reinstall pulley on distributor shaft. Install a new flat washer, lockwasher and the pulley nut. Tighten pulley nut to 19-21 ft.-lb.
3. Fit cam over shaft and ball assembly, then install shaft key and press trigger wheel in place over the key using a 9/16 in. deep-wall socket.
4. Install snap ring on bottom of distributor shaft. Fit shaft into bracket with metal and felt washers, then install felt and metal washers on bottom of housing.
5. Install large snap ring on housing and reinstall cap.
6. Install distributor as described in this chapter.
7. Check timing and belt tension. See Chapter Five.
8. Install distributor plate assembly and check sensor gap adjustment (Chapter Four).
9. Check distributor linkage and carburetor synchronization. See Chapter Five.

FLYWHEEL CD SENSOR IGNITION

This ignition system is essentially the same as the distributor CD ignition used on the 1967 100 hp engine. It consists of a distributor housing (located under the flywheel) with a sensor rotor and sensor assembly, a pulse transformer and an electronic pulse pack containing a transformer, capacitor and electronic switch. The pulse pack is sealed in epoxy and bracket-mounted on the lower rear motor cover. **Figure 49** is a schematic of the system. Troubleshooting and test procedures are given in Chapter Three.

Operation

Current provided by the battery is stepped up to 300 volts by a transistorized converter and stored in a capacitor in the pulse pack. When a rotor lobe aligns with the sensor in the distributor, the electronic switch is closed. This sends the capacitor voltage to the pulse transformer, where it is stepped up to 25,000 volts and sent to the spark plugs. As soon as the spark plug fires, the electronic switch opens again and the capacitor is recharged.

Distributor Removal/Installation

See Chapter Eight.

Pulse Pack Replacement

1. Disconnect the positive battery cable.
2. Disconnect all pulse pack electrical leads.
3. Remove the pulse pack mounting screws. Remove the pulse pack.
4. Installation is the reverse of removal.

FLYWHEEL CD BREAKER POINT IGNITION

This ignition system is similar in design and operation to the flywheel CD ignition described in this chapter. It consists of a distributor housing (located under the flywheel) containing 2 breaker point sets. A separate ignition coil and amplifier unit complete the components. The amplifier is sealed in epoxy and bracket-mounted on the lower rear motor cover. **Figure 50** is a schematic of the system.

Some models are equipped with an anti-reverse switch and reverse cut-off spring. This spring is positioned on the crankshaft above the breaker point base and driven against the oiler wick retainer when the engine is running normally. If the crankshaft should run counterclockwise, the spring is driven against the reverse cut-off switch which shorts out the primary breaker point circuit and shuts the engine off.

Troubleshooting and test procedures are given in Chapter Three.

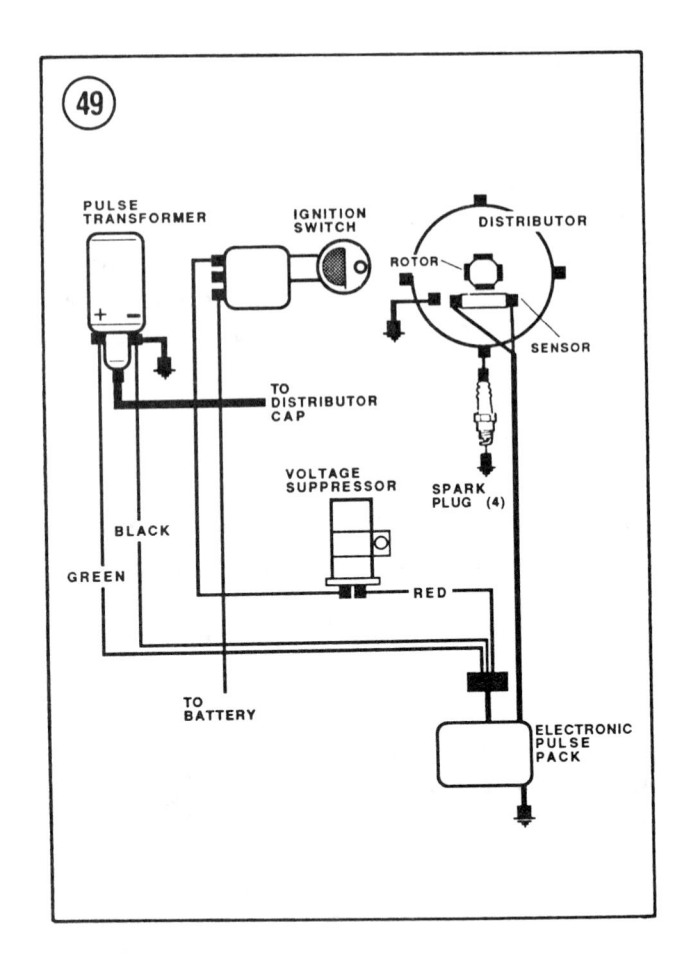

Operation

Current provided by the battery is stepped up to 350 volts by a transistorized converter and stored in a capacitor in the pulse pack. Opening of the breaker points by the distributor cam triggers the amplifier switch, which sends the capacitor voltage to the ignition coil, where it is stepped up to 25,000 volts and sent to the spark plugs. As the crankshaft rotates, the breaker points close and the converter recharges the capacitor.

Distributor Removal/Installation

See Chapter Eight.

Amplifier Replacement

1. Disconnect the negative battery cable.
2. Disconnect all amplifier electrical connections.

ELECTRICAL SYSTEMS

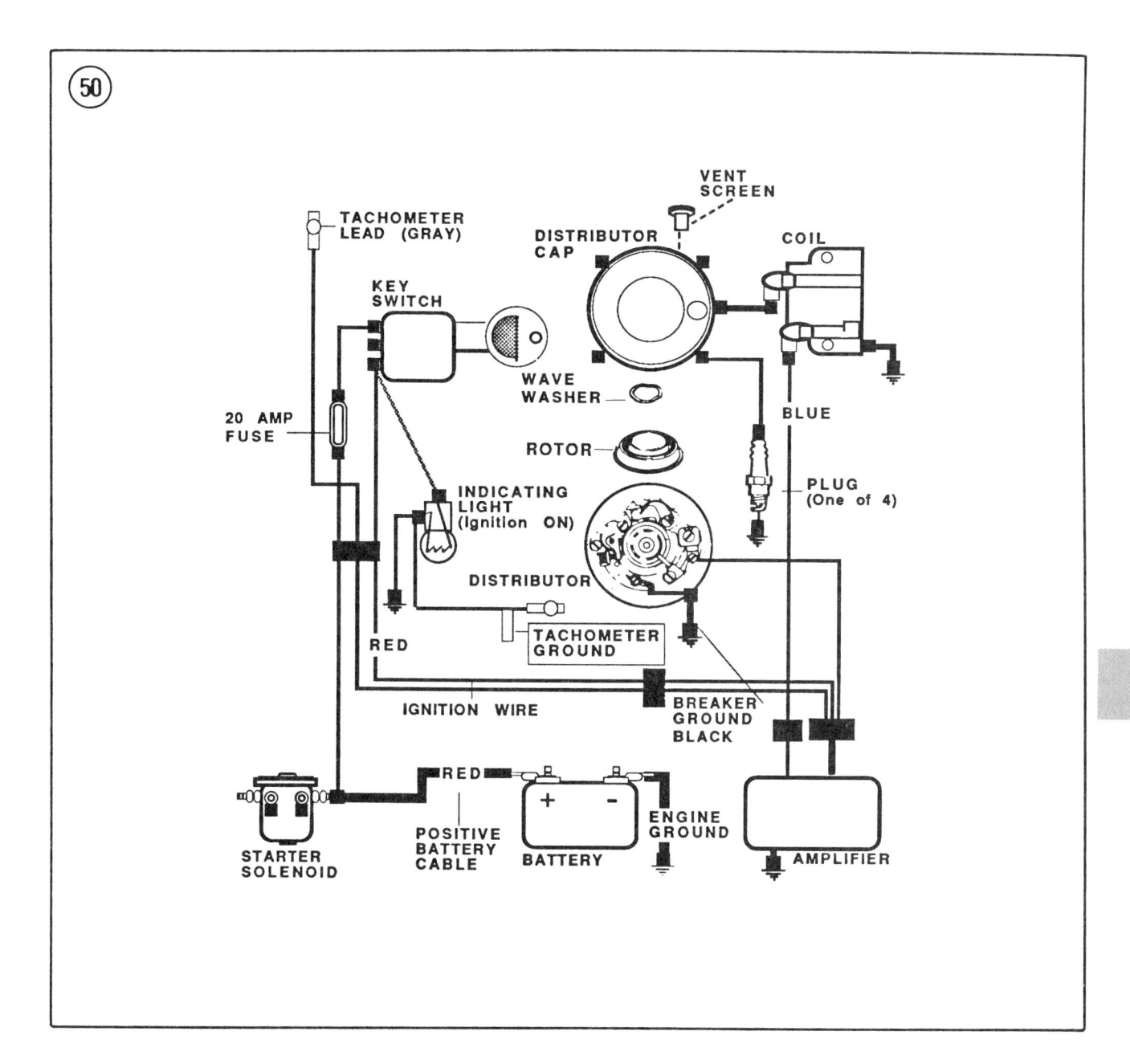

⑤⓪

Figure 50 — Ignition wiring diagram showing tachometer lead (gray), key switch, 20 amp fuse, indicating light (ignition on), distributor, tachometer ground, ignition wire, starter solenoid, positive battery cable, battery, engine ground, distributor cap, vent screen, wave washer, rotor, coil, blue, plug (one of 4), breaker ground black, and amplifier.

3. Remove the amplifier mounting screws. Remove the amplifier.
4. Installation is the reverse of removal.

Ignition Coil Replacement

1. Disconnect the negative battery cable.
2. Disconnect the coil electrical connector.
3. Remove the coil mounting screws. Remove the coil.

NOTE
It may be necessary to remove the flywheel and/or stator on some models for easy access to the coil connection at the distributor cap in Step 4. See Chapter Eight. The lead is an integral part of the coil and cannot be removed at the coil.

4. Unscrew the coil lead at the distributor cap.
5. Installation is the reverse of removal.

Table 1 BATTERY CAPACITY (HOURS)

Accessory draw	80 Amp-hour battery provides continuous power for	Approximate recharge time
5 amps	13.5 hours	16 hours
15 amps	3.5 hours	13 hours
25 amps	1.8 hours	12 hours
Accessory draw	105 Amp-hour battery provides continuous power for	Approximate recharge time
5 amps	15.8 hours	16 hours
15 amps	4.2 hours	13 hours
25 amps	2.4 hours	12 hours

Table 2 SELF-DISCHARGE RATE

Temperature	Approximate allowable self-discharge per day for first 10 days (specific gravity)
100° F (37.8° C)	0.0025 points
80° F (26.7° C)	0.0010 points
50° F (10.0° C)	0.0003 points

Table 3 APPROXIMATE STATE OF CHARGE

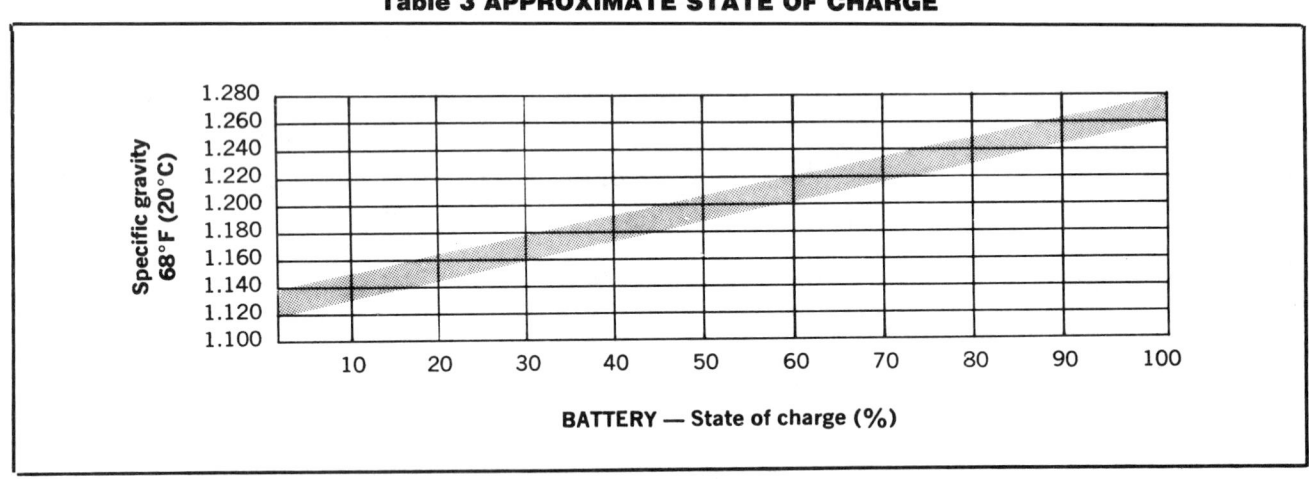

Table 4 TIGHTENING TORQUES

Standard torque values	in.-lb.	ft.-lb.
No. 6	7-10	
No. 8	15-22	
No. 10	25-35	
No. 12	35-40	
1/4 in.	60-80	5-7
5/16 in.	120-140	10-12
3/8 in.	220-240	18-20
7/16 in.	340-360	28-30

Chapter Eight

Power Head

This chapter covers the basic repair of Johnson and Evinrude outboard power heads. The procedures involved are similar from model to model, with minor differences. Some procedures require the use of special tools, which can be purchased from a Johnson or Evinrude dealer. Certain tools may also be fabricated by a machinist, often at substantial savings. Power head stands are available from specialty shops such as Bob Kerr's Marine Tool Co. (P.O. Box 1135, Winter Garden, Florida 32787).

Work on the power head requires considerable mechanical ability. You should carefully consider your own capabilities before attempting any operation involving major disassembly of the engine.

Much of the labor charge for dealer repairs involves the removal and disassembly of other parts to reach the defective component. Even if you decide not to tackle the entire power head overhaul after studying the text and illustrations in this chapter, it can be cheaper to perform the preliminary operations yourself and then take the power head to your dealer. Since many marine dealers have lengthy waiting lists for service (especially during the spring and summer season), this practice can reduce the time your unit is in the shop. If you have done much of the preliminary work, your repairs can be scheduled and performed much quicker.

Repairs go much faster and easier if your motor is clean before you begin work. There are special cleaners for washing the motor and related parts. Just spray or brush on the cleaning solution, let it stand, then rinse it away with a garden hose. Clean all oily or greasy parts with fresh solvent as you remove them.

WARNING
Never use gasoline as a cleaning agent. It presents an extreme fire hazard. Be sure to work in a well-ventilated area when using cleaning solvents. Keep a fire extinguisher rated for gasoline and oil fires nearby in case of emergency.

Once you have decided to do the job yourself, read this chapter thoroughly until you have a good idea of what is involved in completing the overhaul satisfactorily. Make arrangements to buy or rent any special tools necessary and obtain replacement parts before you start. It is frustrating and time-consuming to start an overhaul and then be unable to complete it because the necessary tools or parts are not at hand.

Before beginning the job, re-read Chapter Two of this manual. You will do a better job with this information fresh in your mind.

Remember that new engine break-in procedures should be followed after an engine has been overhauled. Refer to your owner's manual for specific instructions.

CAUTION
Whenever a power head is rebuilt, it should be treated as a new engine. Use a double-strength (twice the normal amount of oil) mixture of gasoline and Johnson or Evinrude 50/1 lubricant during the break-in period.

Since this chapter covers a large range of models over a lengthy time period, the procedures are somewhat generalized to accommodate all models. Where individual differences occur, they are specifically pointed out. Although the power heads shown in the accompanying pictures are representative designs, it is possible that the components shown in the pictures may not be identical with those being serviced. The step-by-step procedures, however, may be used with all models covered in this manual.

Tables 1-3 are at the end of the chapter.

ENGINE SERIAL NUMBER

Johnson and Evinrude outboards are identified by engine serial number. This number is stamped on a plate riveted to the transom clamp (**Figure 1**). It is also stamped on a welch plug installed on the power head. See **Figure 2** (typical). Exact location of the transom clamp plate and welch plug varies according to model. The transom clamp plate is usually easily located; the welch plug may be hidden under some electrical component on larger engines.

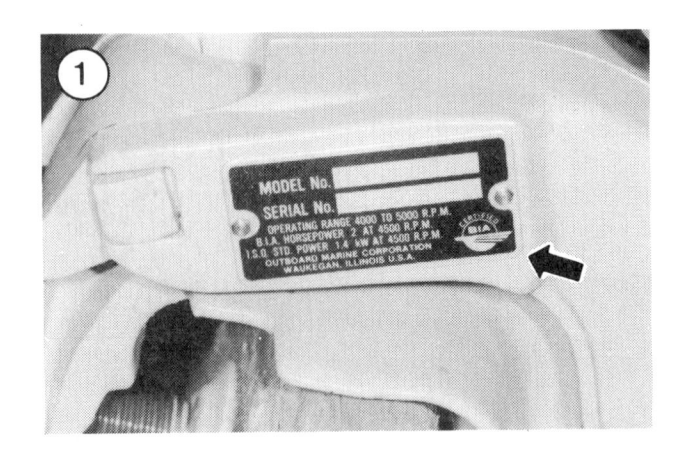

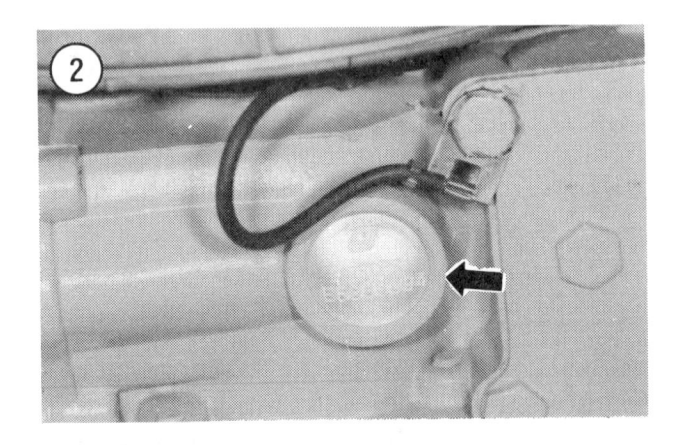

This information identifies the outboard model and indicates if there are unique parts or if internal changes have been made during the model run. The serial number should always be used when ordering any replacement parts for your outboard.

FASTENERS AND TORQUE

Always replace a worn or damaged fastener with one of the same size, type and torque requirement.

Power head tightening torques are given in **Table 1**. Where a specification is not provided

POWER HEAD

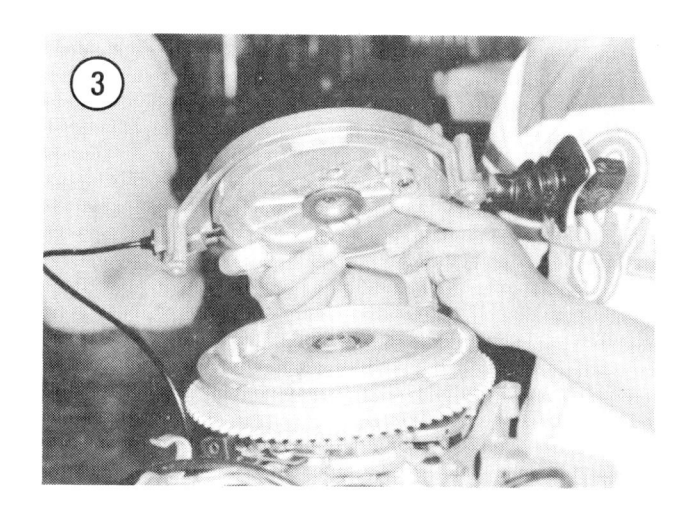

for a given bolt, use the standard bolt and nut torque according to fastener size.

Where specified, clean fastener threads with OMC Locquic Primer and then apply OMC Nut Lock or Screw Lock as required.

To prevent cylinder head warpage, power head fasteners should be tightened in 2 steps. Tighten to 50 percent of the torque value in the first step, then to 100 percent in the second step.

Retighten the cylinder head bolts after the engine has been run for 15 minutes and allowed to cool. It is a good idea to retorque them again after 10 hours of operation.

To retighten the power head mounting fasteners properly, back them out one turn and then tighten to specifications.

When spark plugs are reinstalled after an overhaul, tighten to the specified torque. Warm the engine to normal operating temperature, let it cool down and retorque the plugs.

GASKETS AND SEALANTS

Two types of sealant materials are recommended: OMC Gasket Sealing Compound and Sealer 1000 or Adhesive M. Unless otherwise specified, OMC Gasket Sealing Compound is used with gaskets on older engines. Sealer 1000 or Adhesive M is used primarily with crankcase spaghetti seals (gasket strips). Be sure to use the appropriate sealant specified for your engine.

When sealing the crankcase cover/cylinder block, both mating surfaces must be free of all sealant residue, dirt and oil. Locquic Primer, lacquer thinner, acetone or similar solvents work well when used in conjunction with a broad, flat scraper or a somewhat dull putty knife. Solvents with an oil, wax or petroleum base should not be used. Clean the aluminum surfaces carefully to avoid nicking them with the scraper or putty knife.

FLYWHEEL

Removal/Installation
(All Engines)

A strap wrench is used to hold the flywheel on manual start models. Use a flywheel holding tool on electric start models. The OMC universal puller kit (part No. 378103) is recommended for flywheel removal.

If oil is found under the flywheel, the upper main bearing seal is leaking. The power head should be removed, disassembled and a new upper main bearing seal installed.

1. Disconnect armature plate lead connections or disconnect the spark plug leads to disable the ignition and prevent accidental starting of the engine.
2. Remove the rewind starter assembly (**Figure 3**), if so equipped.
3. Remove the flywheel nut with an appropriate size socket and flywheel holding tool (**Figure 4**).
4. Install puller on flywheel with its flat side facing up.
5. Hold puller body with puller handle and tighten center screw. See **Figure 5**. If flywheel does not pop from the crankshaft taper, pry up on the rim of the flywheel with a large screwdriver while tapping the puller center screw with a brass hammer.
6. Remove puller from flywheel. Remove flywheel from crankshaft (**Figure 6**).

7. Remove the Woodruff key from the crankshaft key slot. If power head is to be disassembled, remove the cam, cam drive pin and retaining ring, if so equipped. See **Figure 7**.
8. Clean the crankshaft and flywheel tapers with OMC Cleaning Solvent.

NOTE
If the Woodruff key is installed incorrectly, cam position and ignition timing will be affected on magneto ignition models.

9. Install Woodruff key with its outer edge parallel to the crankshaft centerline. If key has a single mark on its side, the mark must face downward. See **Figure 8**.
10. If cam was removed, reinstall cam drive pin, then install cam with side marked "TOP" facing up. Install retaining ring with taper facing down.
11. Install the flywheel and flywheel nut. Hold flywheel with the holding tool and tighten flywheel nut to specifications (**Table 2**).
12. Reinstall rewind starter on manual start models.
13. Reconnect the wiring disconnected in Step 1.

ARMATURE PLATE (FLYWHEEL MAGNETO IGNITION)

Removal/Installation

1. Remove the flywheel as described in this chapter.
2. If equipped with integral fuel tank, make sure the fuel shut-off valve is closed, then disconnect the fuel line at the valve and remove the tank from its mounting plate.
3. Disconnect the armature link and control lever.
4. Disconnect the magneto armature plate leads. Disconnect the ground lead, stop

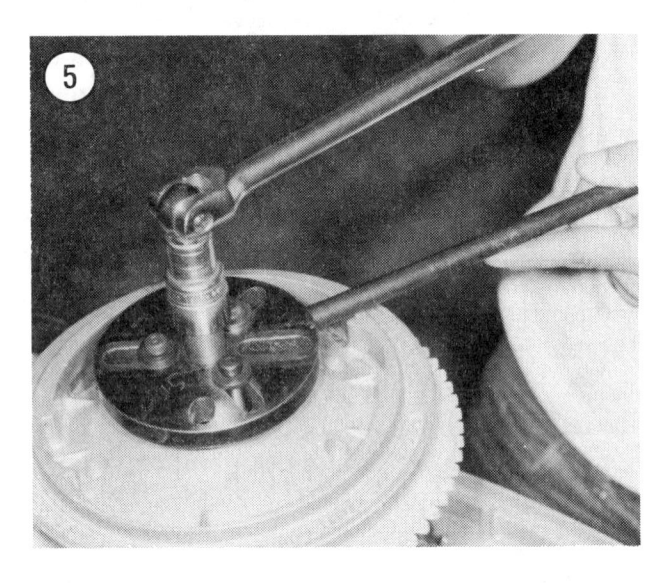

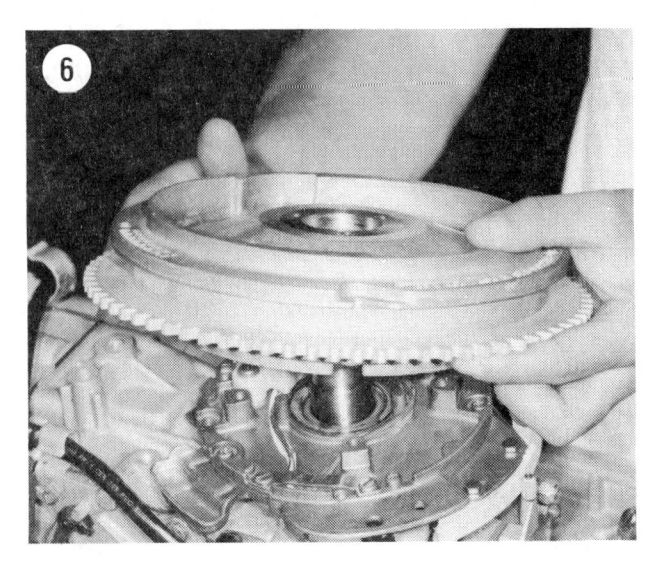

Power Head

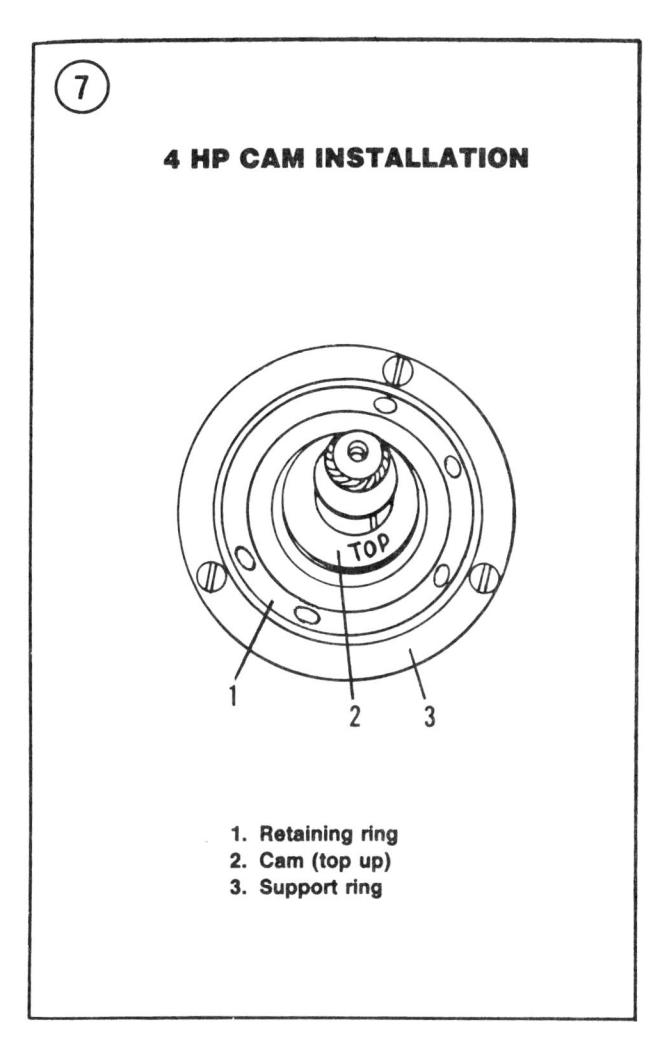

switch connector and vacuum cut-out switch, if used.

5. Disconnect the spark plug leads.
6. On electric start models, disconnect the armature plate leads at the terminal board. See wiring diagram for correct wire color.

NOTE
*A single clamp screw located under the armature plate secures the 1.5 and 2 hp magneto in place (**Figure 9**). Loosen the clamp screw, remove the armature plate and then remove the tongued bushing from the crankcase groove.*

7. Remove the screws holding the magneto armature plate to retainer plate or power head.
8. Remove the magneto armature plate and cable assembly from the power head.
9. Remove the armature plate bearing (Delrin ring).
10. Disconnect any support plate linkage (varies with model). Note exact sequence of washers and bushings used for reassembly.
11. Remove the screws holding the armature support and retaining ring to the power head. Remove the support and retaining ring.

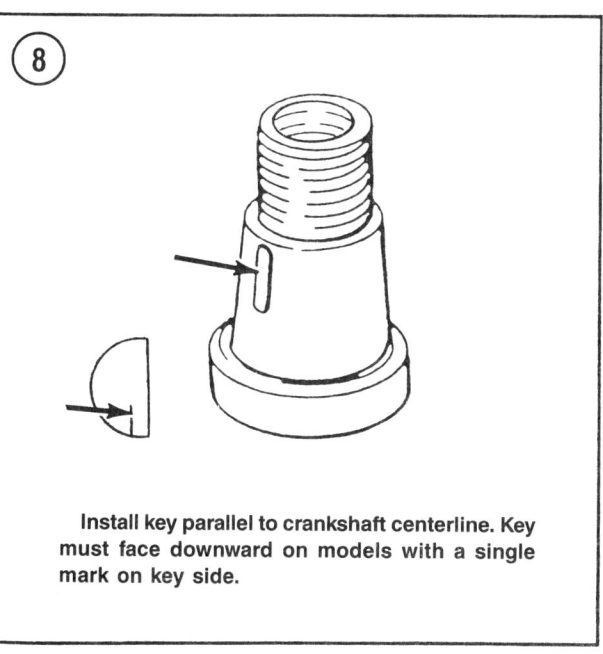

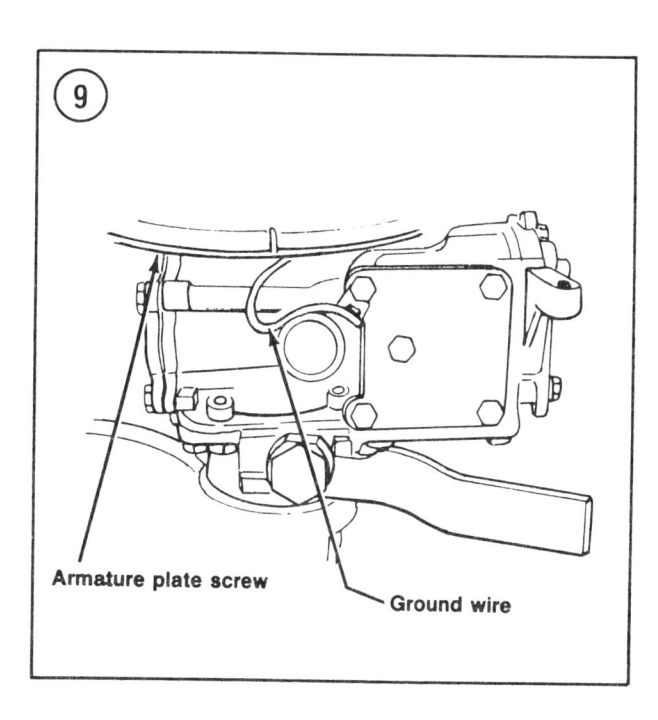

⑦ 4 HP CAM INSTALLATION

1. Retaining ring
2. Cam (top up)
3. Support ring

⑧ Install key parallel to crankshaft centerline. Key must face downward on models with a single mark on key side.

⑨
- Armature plate screw
- Ground wire

12. Installation is the reverse of removal. Coat the crankshaft boss with OMC Moly Lube and the Delrin ring with Johnson/Evinrude 50/1 outboard lubricant. Squeeze ends of Delrin ring together with needlenose pliers and make sure it fits properly into armature plate boss. Check breaker point gap (Chapter Four). Complete engine synchronization and linkage adjustments. See Chapter Five.

BREAKER POINT DISTRIBUTOR (FLYWHEEL CD IGNITION)

Removal/Installation

Refer to **Figure 10** for this procedure.

1. Remove the flywheel as described in this chapter.
2. Disconnect the yellow stator leads at the connector, remove the stator attaching screws and remove the stator from the distributor cap.
3. Disconnect the coil and spark plug leads from the distributor cap.
4. Remove the distributor cap assembly from the base plate.
5. Remove the wave washer from inside the distributor rotor. Remove the rotor.
6. Remove the anti-reverse spring. See **Figure 11**.
7. Disconnect the base plate ground lead. Disconnect the primary lead to the amplifier.
8. Remove the retaining clips and screws holding the base plate in position on the power head. Remove the base plate with retainer ring.
9. Reposition the base plate on the power head. Lubricate the nylon base plate retainer ring with Shell EP-2 grease (or equivalent). Compress the ring and work it into the power head upper bearing recess as the base plate is seated. Install the base plate retaining clips and screws.
10. Install the anti-reverse spring. Lightly lubricate the area on the crankshaft where the

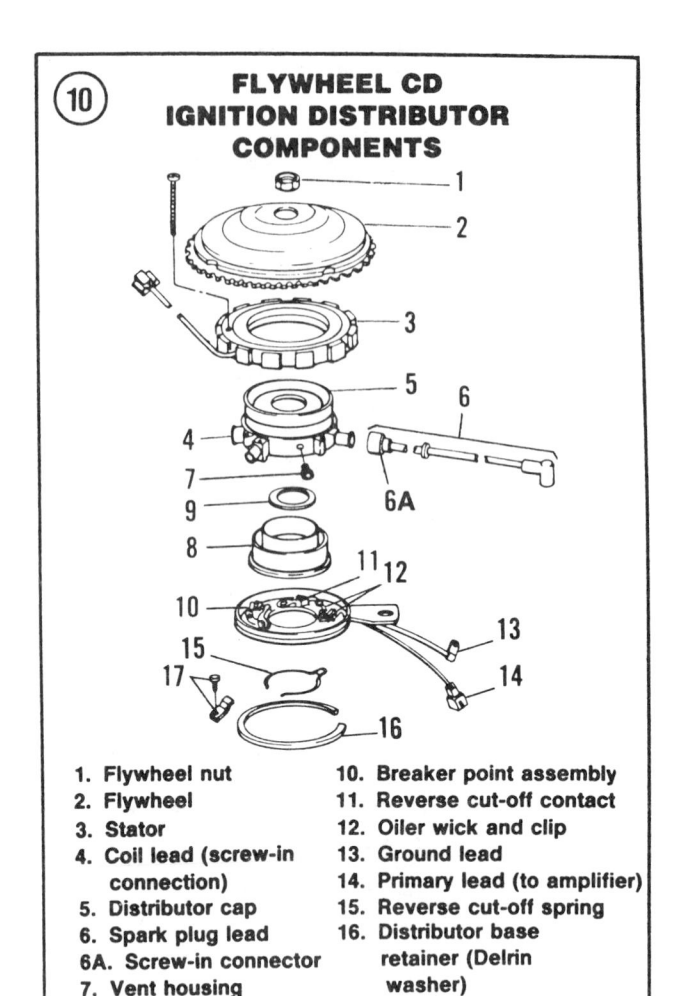

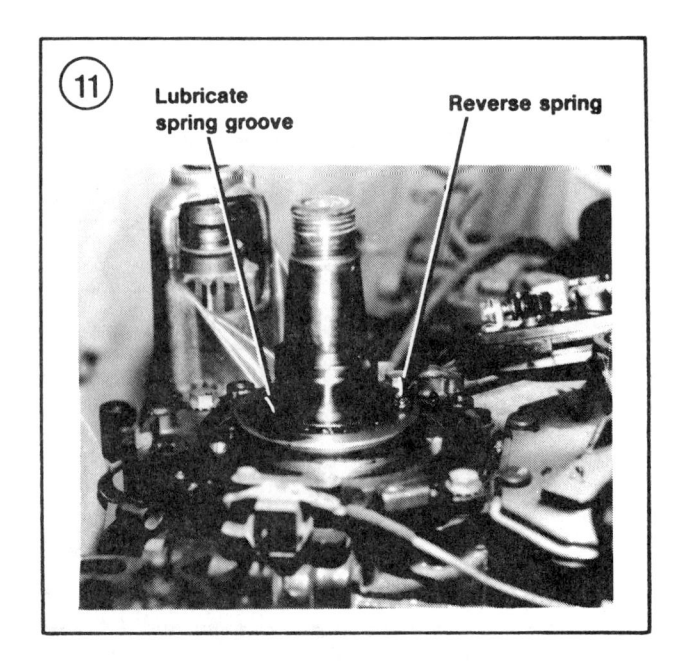

FLYWHEEL CD IGNITION DISTRIBUTOR COMPONENTS

1. Flywheel nut
2. Flywheel
3. Stator
4. Coil lead (screw-in connection)
5. Distributor cap
6. Spark plug lead
6A. Screw-in connector
7. Vent housing
8. Rotor
9. Rotor spring washer
10. Breaker point assembly
11. Reverse cut-off contact
12. Oiler wick and clip
13. Ground lead
14. Primary lead (to amplifier)
15. Reverse cut-off spring
16. Distributor base retainer (Delrin washer)
17. Base plate clamp

Figure 11: Lubricate spring groove / Reverse spring

POWER HEAD

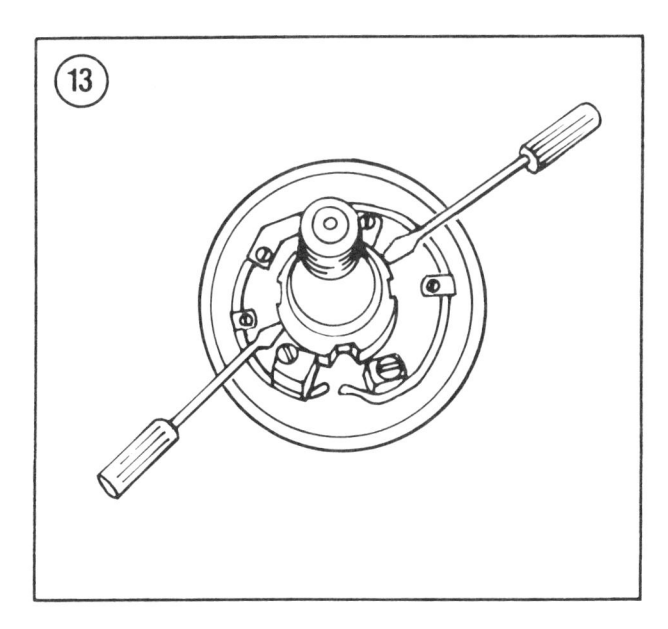

(12) *Wave washer*

(13)

spring rides with OMC Extreme Pressure Grease. See **Figure 11**.

11. Reconnect the distributor base ground lead and primary lead to the amplifier.
12. Check and adjust breaker point gap as required. See Chapter Four.
13. Index the distributor rotor tab with the crankshaft recess and install rotor. Make sure rotor is fully seated, then install the wave washer (**Figure 12**).
14. Install the distributor cap. Make sure it is properly seated on the upper bearing housing or it will be damaged when the stator screws are installed.

15. Reconnect the coil and spark plug leads to the distributor cap.
16. Reinstall the stator. Wipe the stator screw threads with OMC Screw Lock and tighten to 48-60 in.-lb. Connect the stator leads.
17. Reinstall the flywheel as described in this chapter.
18. Check and adjust engine timing. See Chapter Five.

BREAKERLESS DISTRIBUTOR (FLYWHEEL CD IGNITION)

Removal/Installation

1. Remove the flywheel as described in this chapter.
2. Disconnect the yellow stator leads at the connector, remove the stator attaching screws and remove the stator from the distributor cap.
3. Disconnect the coil and spark plug leads from the distributor cap.
4. Remove the distributor cap assembly from the base plate.
5. Remove the wave washer from inside the distributor rotor. See **Figure 12**. Remove the rotor.
6. Carefully pry sensor rotor from crankshaft as shown in **Figure 13**.
7. Unsnap the spark advance link from the nylon ball-joint on the control arm.
8. Remove the anti-reverse spring (**Figure 14**).
9. Remove the retaining clips and screws holding the base plate in position on the power head. Remove the base plate with nylon retainer.
10. Install the anti-reverse spring (**Figure 14**). Lightly lubricate the area on the crankshaft where the spring rides with OMC Extreme Pressure Grease.
11. Reposition the base plate on the power head. Lubricate the nylon base plate retainer ring with Shell EP-2 grease (or equivalent). If

ring was removed from base, reinstall with its flat face against the base. Compress the ring and work it into the power head upper bearing recess as the base plate is seated. Install the base plate retaining clips and screws.

12. Reinstall sensor rotor drive pin, if removed from crankshaft. Install sensor to engage the drive pin. Reconnect sensor leads, if disconnected.
13. Check and adjust sensor gap. See Chapter Four.
14. Index the distributor rotor tab with the crankshaft recess and install rotor. Make sure rotor is fully seated, then install the wave washer (**Figure 12**).
15. Install the distributor cap. Make sure it is properly seated on the upper bearing housing or it will be damaged when the stator screws are installed.
16. Reinstall the stator. Wipe the stator screw threads with OMC Screw Lock and tighten to 48-60 in.-lb. Connect the stator leads.
17. Reinstall the flywheel as described in this chapter.
18. Check and adjust engine timing. See Chapter Five.

STATOR
(FLYWHEEL CD IGNITION)

Removal/Installation

1. Remove the flywheel as described in this chapter.
2. Disconnect the yellow stator leads at the connector, remove the stator attaching screws and remove the stator from the power head.
3. Installation is the reverse of removal.

POWER HEAD

When removing any power head, it is a good idea to make a sketch or take an instant picture of the locating, routing and positioning of wires and J-clamps for reassembly reference. Take notes as you remove wires, washers and engine grounds so they may be reinstalled in their correct positions. Unless otherwise specified, install lockwashers on the engine side of the electrical lead to assure a good ground.

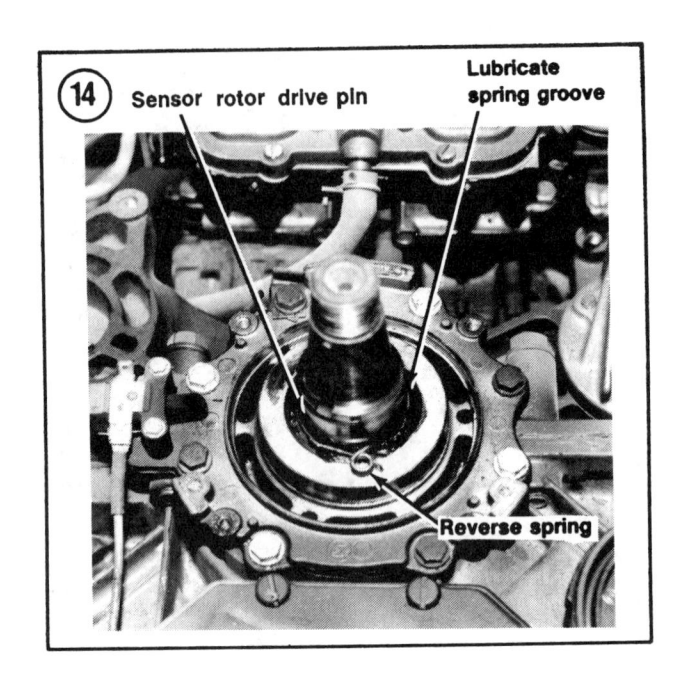

Removal/Installation
(1.5 and 2 hp)

1. Disconnect the spark plug lead and remove the spark plug.
2. Make sure the fuel shut-off valve is closed, then disconnect the fuel line at the valve.
3. Remove the screws holding the fuel tank to the mounting plate. Remove the fuel tank.
4. Remove the carburetor low-speed knob.
5. Remove the screws holding the port and starboard motor covers. Remove the 2 control panel screws. Remove the motor covers.
6. Remove the carburetor. See Chapter Six.
7. Remove the 4 screws holding the intake manifold to the crankcase. Remove the manifold and reed valve assembly.
8. Remove the flywheel as described in this chapter.

POWER HEAD

9. Remove the magneto armature plate as described in this chapter.
10. Remove the 6 bolts holding the power head to the exhaust housing. Carefully lift the power head from the exhaust housing. Place on a clean workbench for disassembly. Discard the gasket.
11. Clean all gasket residue from the exhaust housing mating surfaces.
12. Installation is the reverse of removal. Lubricate drive shaft splines with OMC Moly Lube. Coat a new power head-to-exhaust housing gasket with OMC Gasket Sealing Compound. Tighten fasteners to specifications (**Table 1**). Connect fuel line, open fuel valve and check for leakage. Complete engine synchronization and linkage adjustments. See Chapter Five.

Removal/Installation
(3 hp with Integral Fuel Tank)

1. Remove the lower engine cover, choke and low-speed knobs and the control panel.
2. Remove the air silencer.
3. Make sure the fuel shut-off valve is closed. Disconnect the fuel line at the carburetor.
4. Disconnect the cam follower spring. Remove the carburetor. See Chapter Six.
5. Remove the intake manifold and reed valve assembly. Discard the gasket.
6. Remove the manual starter.
7. Remove the fuel tank mounting fasteners. Remove the tank.
8. Remove the flywheel as described in this chapter.
9. Remove the magneto armature plate as described in this chapter.
10. Remove the fuel tank mounting plate.
11. Remove the fasteners holding the power head to the lower unit. Carefully lift the power head from the lower unit. Place on a clean workbench for disassembly. Discard the gasket.

12. Clean all gasket residue from the lower unit mating surfaces.
13. Installation is the reverse of removal. Lubricate drive shaft splines with OMC Moly Lube. Coat a new power head-to-exhaust housing gasket with OMC Gasket Sealing Compound. Tighten fasteners to specifications (**Table 1**). Connect fuel line, open fuel valve and check for leakage. Complete engine synchronization and linkage adjustments. See Chapter Five.

Removal/Installation
(3 hp Without Integral Fuel Tank, 4, 5, 5.5, 6, 7.5, 9.5, 10 and 15 hp)

1. Remove the engine cover.
2. Remove the choke and low-speed knobs.
3. Remove the manual starter.
4. Disconnect the fuel line at the fuel pump. Remove the fuel pump.
5. Disconnect the cam follower spring. Remove the carburetor. See Chapter Six.
6. Remove the intake manifold and reed valve assembly. Discard the gasket.
7. Remove the flywheel as described in this chapter.
8. Remove the magneto armature plate as described in this chapter.
9. Remove the fasteners holding the power head to the exhaust housing. Remove the power head and discard the gasket. Place on a clean workbench for disassembly.
10. Clean all gasket residue from the exhaust housing mating surfaces.
11. Installation is the reverse of removal. Lubricate drive shaft splines with OMC Moly Lube. Coat a new power head-to-exhaust housing gasket with OMC Gasket Sealing Compound. Tighten fasteners to specifications (**Table 1**). Connect fuel line, open fuel valve and check for leakage. Complete engine synchronization and linkage adjustments. See Chapter Five.

Removal/Installation
(18, 20, 25, 28, 33, 35 hp)

1. Remove the engine cover.
2. Remove the manual starter.
3. Electric start—Remove the starter motor. Remove the generator, if so equipped. See Chapter Seven.
4. Remove the choke and low-speed knobs, if so equipped.
5. Remove the low-speed valve arm and linkage support, if so equipped.
6. Disconnect the fuel line at the fuel pump. Remove the fuel pump.
7. Remove the throttle lever link and disconnect the cam follower spring.
8. Remove the carburetor. See Chapter Six.
9. Remove the cut-out switch, if so equipped.
10. Remove the intake manifold and reed valve assembly. Discard the gasket.
11. Remove the flywheel as described in this chapter.
12. Remove the magneto armature plate as described in this chapter.
13. Remove the port and starboard starter mounting brackets.

NOTE
At this point, there should be no hoses, wires or linkage connecting the power head to the exhaust housing. Recheck this to be sure nothing will hamper removal.

14. Remove the fasteners holding the power head to the exhaust housing. Carefully lift the power head from the exhaust housing and adapter assembly. Place on a clean workbench for disassembly. Discard the gasket.
15. Clean all gasket residue from the exhaust housing mating surfaces.
16. Installation is the reverse of removal. Lubricate drive shaft splines with OMC Moly Lube. Coat a new power head-to-exhaust housing gasket with OMC Gasket Sealing Compound. Tighten fasteners to specifications (**Table 1**). Connect fuel line, open fuel valve and check for leakage. Complete engine synchronization and linkage adjustments. See Chapter Five.

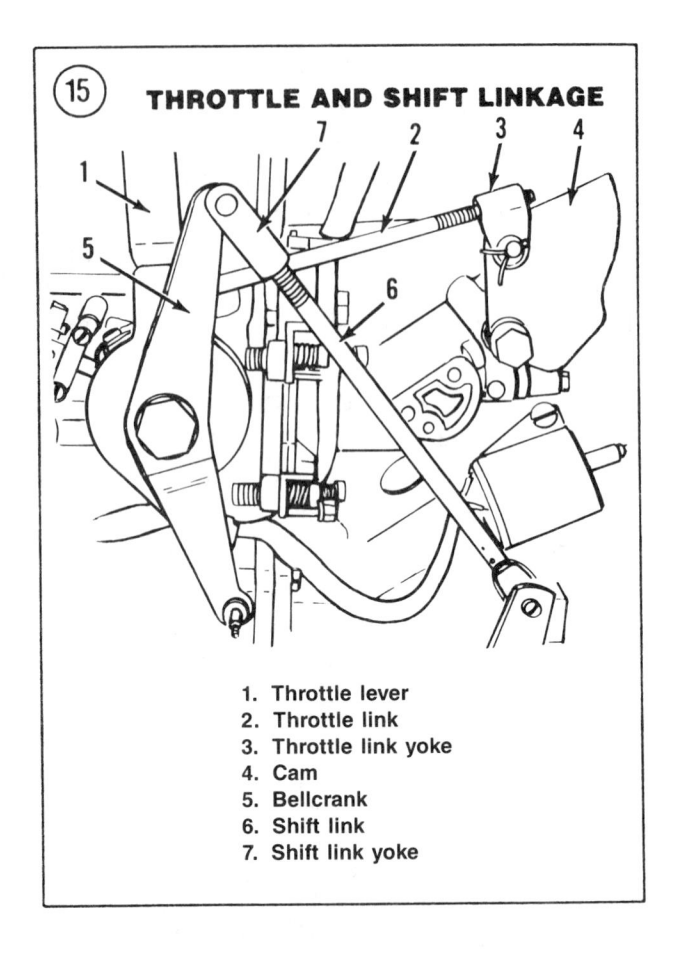

Removal/Installation
(40 hp)

1. Remove the engine cover.
2. Remove the manual starter. Remove the ring gear guard.
3. Remove the heat exchanger tube and shield, if so equipped.
4. Electric start—Remove the starter motor. Remove the generator, if so equipped. See Chapter Seven.
5. Disconnect the fuel line at the fuel pump. Remove the fuel pump.
6. Disconnect the cam follower link.
7. Remove the carburetor. See Chapter Six.

15 THROTTLE AND SHIFT LINKAGE

1. Throttle lever
2. Throttle link
3. Throttle link yoke
4. Cam
5. Bellcrank
6. Shift link
7. Shift link yoke

POWER HEAD

Figure 16. Shift clevis attachment screw

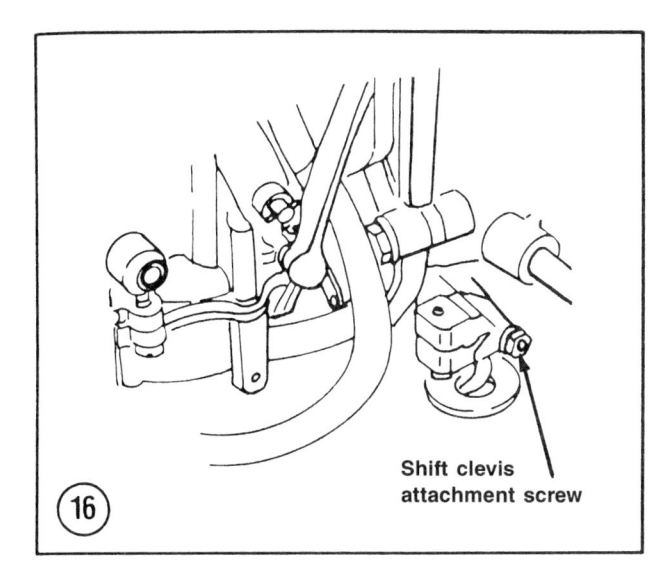

8. Remove the cut-out switch, if so equipped.
9. Remove the intake manifold and reed valve assembly. Discard the gasket.
10. Remove the flywheel as described in this chapter.
11. Remove the magneto armature plate as described in this chapter.
12. Remove the port and starboard starter mounting brackets.
13. Remove the rear exhaust cover.
14. Remove the fasteners holding the power head to the exhaust housing. Remove the power head and discard the gasket. Place on a clean workbench for disassembly.
15. Installation is the reverse of removal. Lubricate drive shaft splines with OMC Moly Lube. Coat a new power head-to-exhaust housing gasket with OMC Gasket Sealing Compound. Tighten fasteners to specifications (**Table 1**). Connect fuel line, open fuel valve and check for leakage. Complete engine synchronization and linkage adjustments. See Chapter Five.

Removal/Installation
(55, 60 and 65 hp Inline)

1. Disconnect the negative battery cable.
2. Remove the engine cover.
3. Remove the flywheel as described in this chapter.
4. Remove the stator as described in this chapter. Remove the distributor. See Chapter Seven.
5. Remove the starter motor. See Chapter Seven.
6. Remove the carburetor and fuel pump. See Chapter Six.
7. Disconnect all wiring connectors and ground leads. Remove wires from J-clamps.
8. Remove the amplifier with wiring intact.
9. Remove the throttle and shift levers. Remove the throttle cam. See **Figure 15** (typical).
10. Remove the screw holding the shift clevis to the shift rod (**Figure 16**).
11. Remove the screws holding the crankcase front bracket to the lower motor cover.
12. Remove the front and rear exhaust cover screws.
13. Remove the nut and washer from the stud at the rear of the power head.
14. Remove the screws on each side holding the power head to the exhaust housing and adapter assembly.

NOTE
At this point, there should be no hoses, wires or linkage connecting the power head to the exhaust housing. Recheck this to be sure nothing will hamper removal.

15. Carefully lift the power head from the exhaust housing and adapter assembly. Place on a clean workbench for disassembly. Discard the gasket.
16. Clean all gasket residue from the adapter assembly mating surfaces.
17. Installation is the reverse of removal. Lubricate drive shaft splines with OMC Moly Lube. Coat both sides of a new power head-to-adapter housing gasket with OMC Gasket Sealing Compound. Rotate power head slightly in a clockwise direction as it is

lowered onto the exhaust housing to engage the gearcase drive shaft splines. Align power head stud with hole in adapter and seat power head. Coat fasteners with OMC Screw Lock and tighten to specifications (**Table 1**). Complete engine synchronization and linkage adjustments. See Chapter Five.

Removal/Installation
(V4)

Carefully identify wiring leads as components are removed and make notes of lead routing for reinstallation reference.

1. Disconnect the negative battery cable.
2. Remove the engine cover.
3. Remove the manual starter, if so equipped.
4. Remove the heat exchanger tube, if so equipped.
5. Remove the flywheel as described in this chapter.
6. Disconnect the distributor linkage at the spark advance lever.
7. Remove the choke control link. Remove the throttle control shaft with linkage, if so equipped.
8. Label and disconnect all electrical connections.
9. Remove the ignition coil. Remove amplifier, rectifier and voltage regulator, if so equipped.
10. Unscrew the high tension lead at the distributor cap.
11. Remove the alternator stator and distributor as described in this chapter. If distributor is not located under flywheel, see Chapter Seven.
12. Electric start—Remove the starter motor and solenoid. Remove the generator, if so equipped. See Chapter Seven.
13. Disconnect the fuel lines at the fuel pump. Remove the fuel pump. See Chapter Six.
14. Remove the air silencer and carburetors. See Chapter Six.
15. Disconnect lower throttle and choke links from throttle and choke arm retainers.
16. Remove the electrical bracket.
17. Remove the rear exhaust housing cover.
18. Remove the port and starboard cover mount screws.
19. Disconnect the thermostat hoses and ground strap.
20. Remove the throttle lever and cam, leaving the link connected.
21. Remove the cylinder heads and bypass covers.
22. Remove the fasteners holding the power head to the exhaust housing.
23. Disconnect the shift linkage.

NOTE
At this point, there should be no hoses, wires or linkage connecting the power head to the exhaust housing. Recheck this to be sure nothing will hamper removal.

24. Temporarily reinstall the lift bracket. Attach a hoist to the lift bracket and remove power head from exhaust housing. Discard the gasket.
25. With power head on hoist, reinstall nuts on studs at power head base until flush with stud ends to protect threads.
26. Lower power head onto a clean workbench. Place in a horizontal position with crankcase side facing up. Remove the hoist from the lift bracket. Remove the lift bracket.
27. Remove any remaining components from outside of power head to provide access to power head assembly fasteners.
28. Clean all gasket residue from the exhaust housing mating surfaces.
29. Installation is the reverse of removal. Lubricate drive shaft splines with OMC Moly Lube. Remove nuts from power head studs. Install a new power head-to-exhaust housing

POWER HEAD

gasket. Install a new drive shaft O-ring. Lower power head in position with hoist. Use a drop of OMC Screw Lock on threads of each power head-to-exhaust housing screw. Complete engine synchronization and linkage adjustments. See Chapter Five.

Overhaul

If a power head has been removed for a normal overhaul, all covers should be removed, inspected and reinstalled with new gaskets. All seals and O-rings should be replaced.

Cover bolts that are corroded may be removed more easily with the use of penetrating oils. If this is not sufficient, heat can be applied. Work slowly and carefully to prevent twisting off a bolt head. If the bolt is broken during removal, it will have to be drilled out and the hole tapped with new threads. It is a good idea to discard corroded bolts and use new ones on reassembly. Such bolts may not withstand the required torque during reassembly.

When removing bolts, note their length and location. The upper and lower main bearing bolts often differ in length. These should be identified and labeled for reinstallation in the same location. It is a good idea to reinsert the bolts in the component holes once the component is removed. This will prevent them from getting lost or mixed up and should make reassembly faster and easier.

Be sure to inspect the inner exhaust plate or intermediate exhaust cover (used on larger engines) carefully. This plate/cover is used to help dissipate the heat from exhaust gases and is cooled by water circulating between the plate/cover and outer exhaust cover. The combination of hot exhaust gases and circulating water make the inner exhaust plate/intermediate exhaust cover especially prone to corrosion. This is particularly true of outboards manufactured into the early Sixties, when the inner plate was manufactured of aluminum. Although inner plates of stainless steel replaced those made from aluminum, even they may corrode if the outboard is used in salt water.

All Johnson and Evinrude engines use taper pins to index and align the block and crankcase cover. Taper pin location varies according to model and model year. Before attempting to separate the block and crankcase cover, inspect the assembly carefully to locate *all* taper pins and determine in which direction they should be removed. Use an appropriate size center punch and hammer to remove the pins. Sharp hammer blows are most effective, as they prevent damage to the pin head.

If engine uses babbitt (non-roller) main and/or rod bearings, omit all bearing installation steps in the following procedures.

Disassembly
(1.5 and 2 hp)

Refer to **Figure 17** for this procedure.
1. Remove the cylinder head screws. Remove the cylinder head and gasket. Discard the gasket.
2. Remove the exhaust cover bolts. Remove the exhaust cover and gasket. Discard the gasket.
3. Remove the intake manifold and reed valve assembly.
4. Straighten the lockplate tabs on each connecting rod cap screw. Remove the connecting rod cap and 30 needle bearings.

NOTE
The lower main bearing and seal housing are serviced as an assembly. If bearing or seal requires replacement, install a new bearing and seal housing.

5. Remove the 4 lower main bearing housing bolts. Remove the bearing housing and 28 needle bearings.

1.5 AND 2 HP POWER HEAD

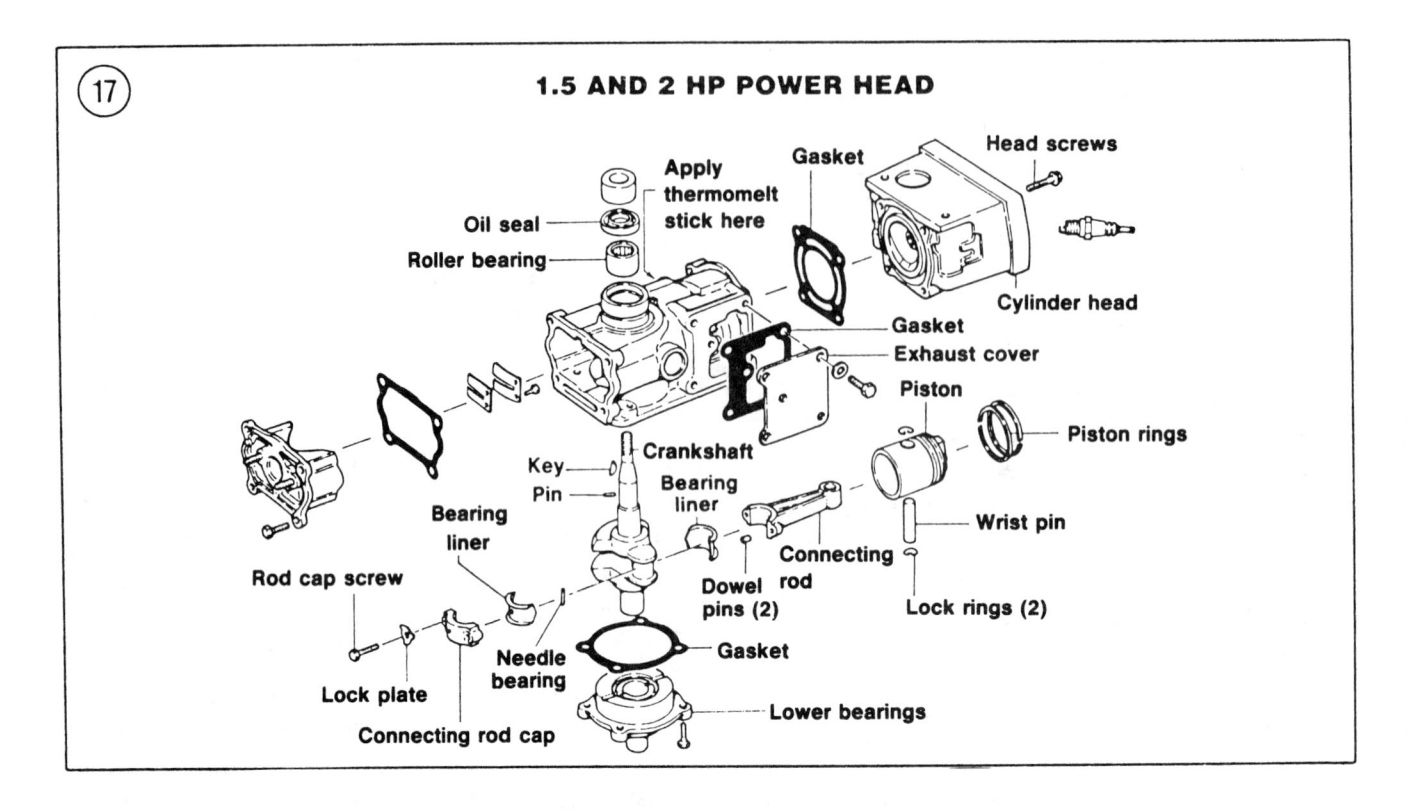

6. Remove the crankshaft through the bottom of the crankcase.

7. Reinstall connecting rod cap on connecting rod. Push the piston toward the cylinder head end of the crankcase until the piston rings can be seen.

8. Remove and discard the piston rings with a ring expander tool.

9. Remove the piston and connecting rod through the carburetor end of the crankcase.

10. Support crankcase and push upper main bearing and seal out with a suitable tool.

11. If piston is to be removed from the connecting rod, remove the piston pin retaining rings with needlenose pliers. See **Figure 18**.

12. Place piston in a suitable cradle with "L" mark on inside of piston boss facing upward. This positions the driver on the loose end of the piston pin. Drive piston pin through piston with a suitable driver. See **Figure 19**.

13. If connecting rod piston pin bearing requires replacement, remove with a suitable driver.

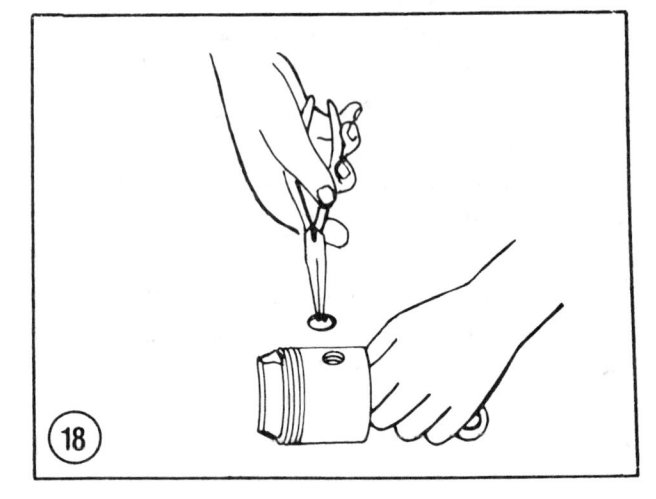

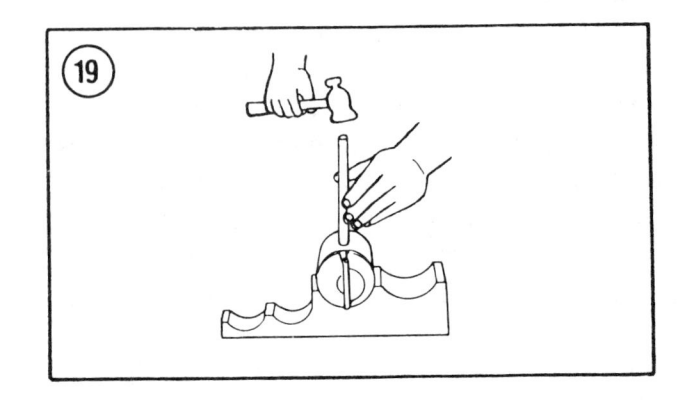

POWER HEAD

POWER HEAD COMPONENTS

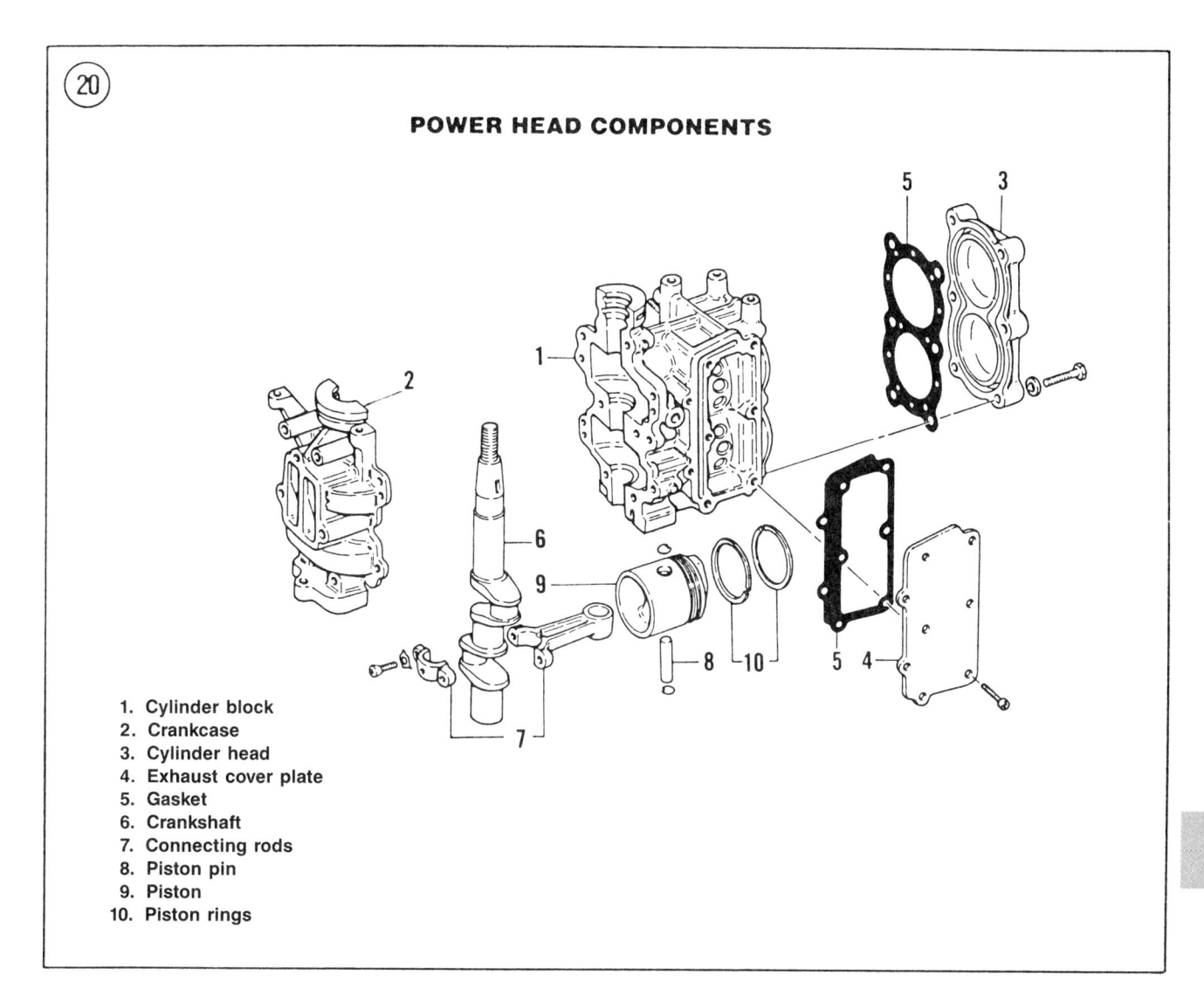

20

1. Cylinder block
2. Crankcase
3. Cylinder head
4. Exhaust cover plate
5. Gasket
6. Crankshaft
7. Connecting rods
8. Piston pin
9. Piston
10. Piston rings

Disassembly
(3-20 hp)

Refer to **Figure 20** (typical 3 hp), **Figure 21** (typical 5-7.5 hp), **Figure 22** (typical 9.5 hp) or **Figure 23** (typical 15-20 hp) for this procedure.

1. Remove the thermostat cap, gasket and components from cylinder head, if so equipped. Discard the seal and gasket.
2. Remove the cylinder head and gasket. Discard the gasket.
3. Remove the cover from the cylinder head, if so equipped. Discard the gasket.
4. Remove the bypass covers and gaskets, if so equipped. Discard the gaskets.

NOTE
Check inner/intermediate exhaust cover for signs of corrosion or pitting. If found, discard the cover.

5. Remove the exhaust cover and gasket. If equipped with an inner or inner and intermediate exhaust cover, remove the cover(s) and gasket(s). Discard the gaskets.
6. Remove the oil drain valve, if so equipped.
7. Remove the inner flange, if so equipped.
8. Remove and discard any crankcase hose clamps. Remove hose from crankcase.

CHAPTER EIGHT

21

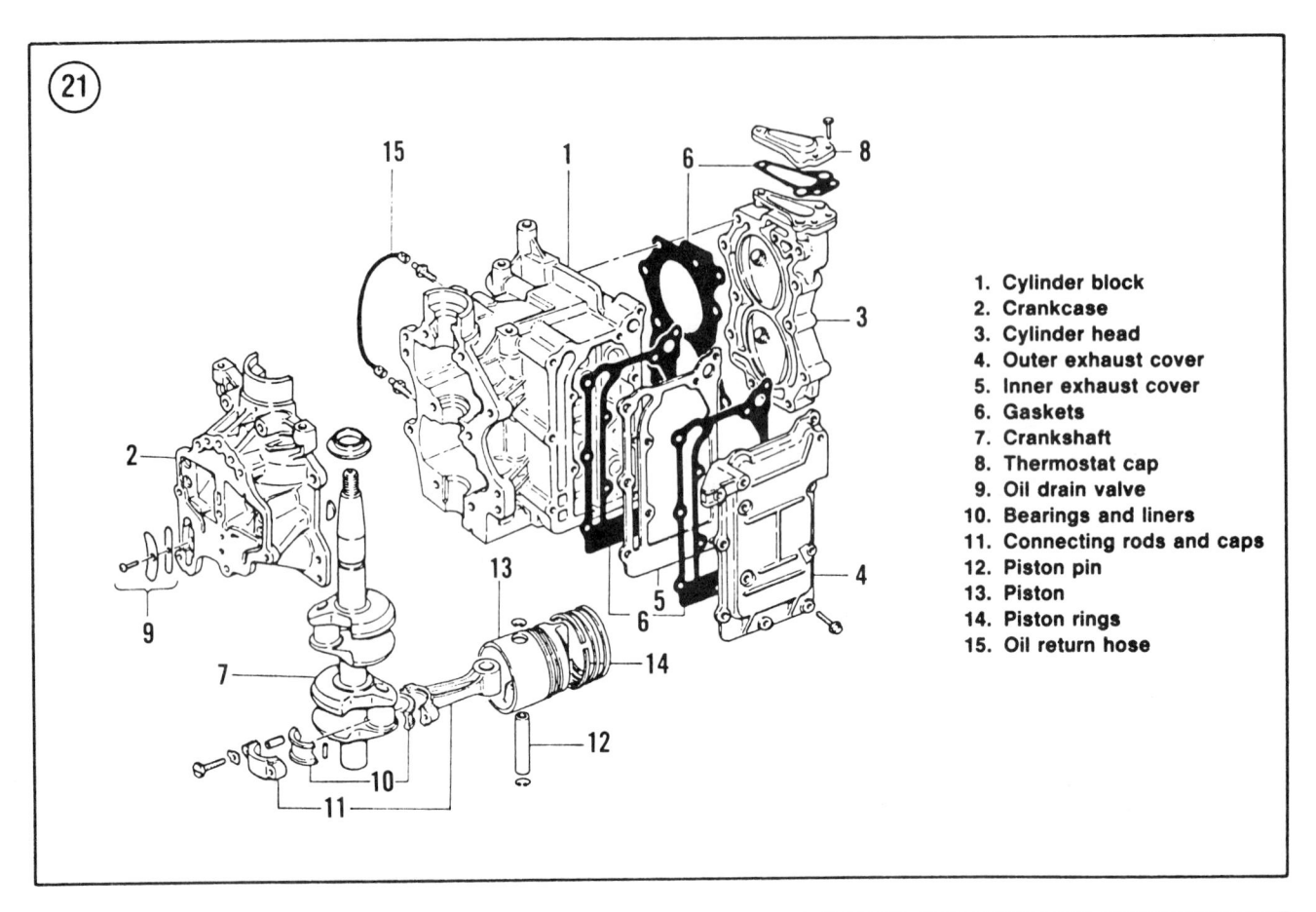

1. Cylinder block
2. Crankcase
3. Cylinder head
4. Outer exhaust cover
5. Inner exhaust cover
6. Gaskets
7. Crankshaft
8. Thermostat cap
9. Oil drain valve
10. Bearings and liners
11. Connecting rods and caps
12. Piston pin
13. Piston
14. Piston rings
15. Oil return hose

23

POWER HEAD COMPONENTS

1. Cylinder block
2. Crankcase
3. Cylinder head
4. Bypass covers
5. Gaskets
6. Outer exhaust cover
7. Inner exhaust cover
8. Oil drain valve
9. Oil line hose
10. Crankshaft
11. Cam
12. Seal
13. Bearing and seal assembly
14. Crankshaft key
15. Bearings
16. Bearings and retainers
17. Connecting rods
18. Pistons
19. Piston rings
20. Piston pin

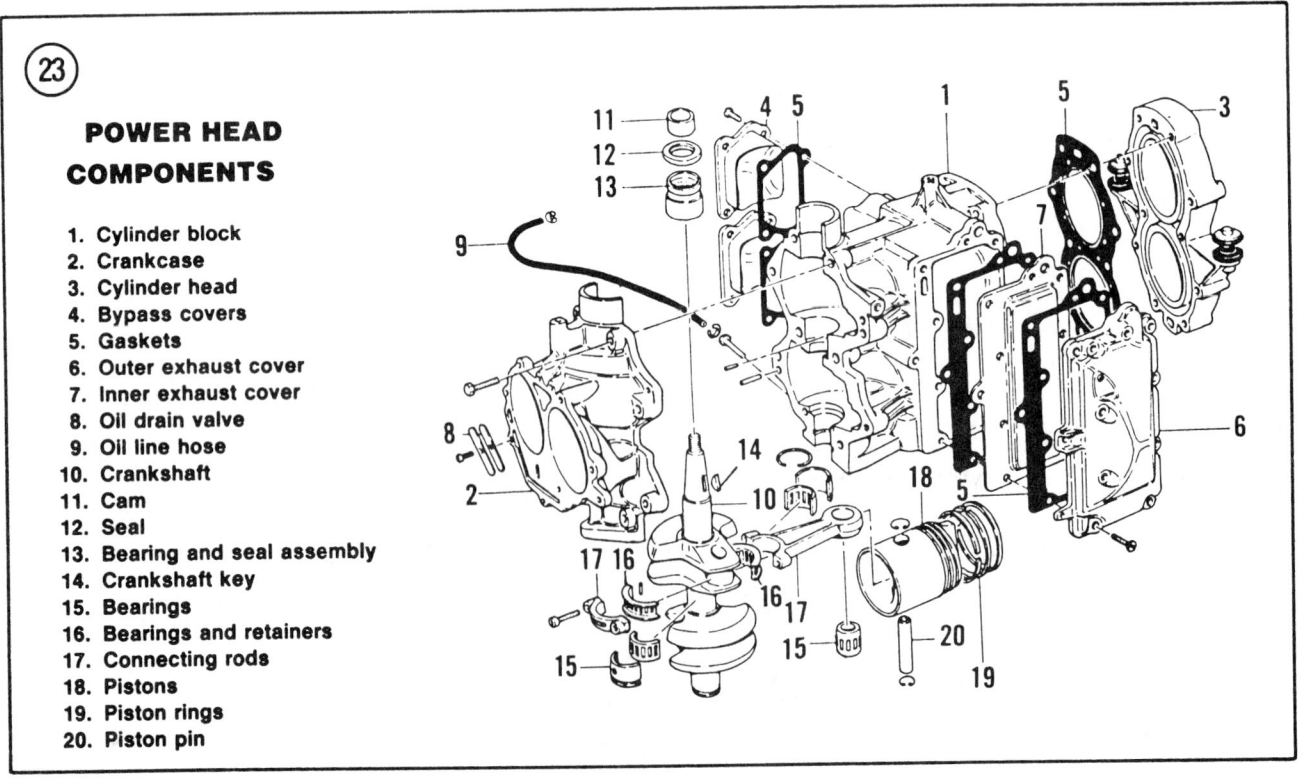

Power Head

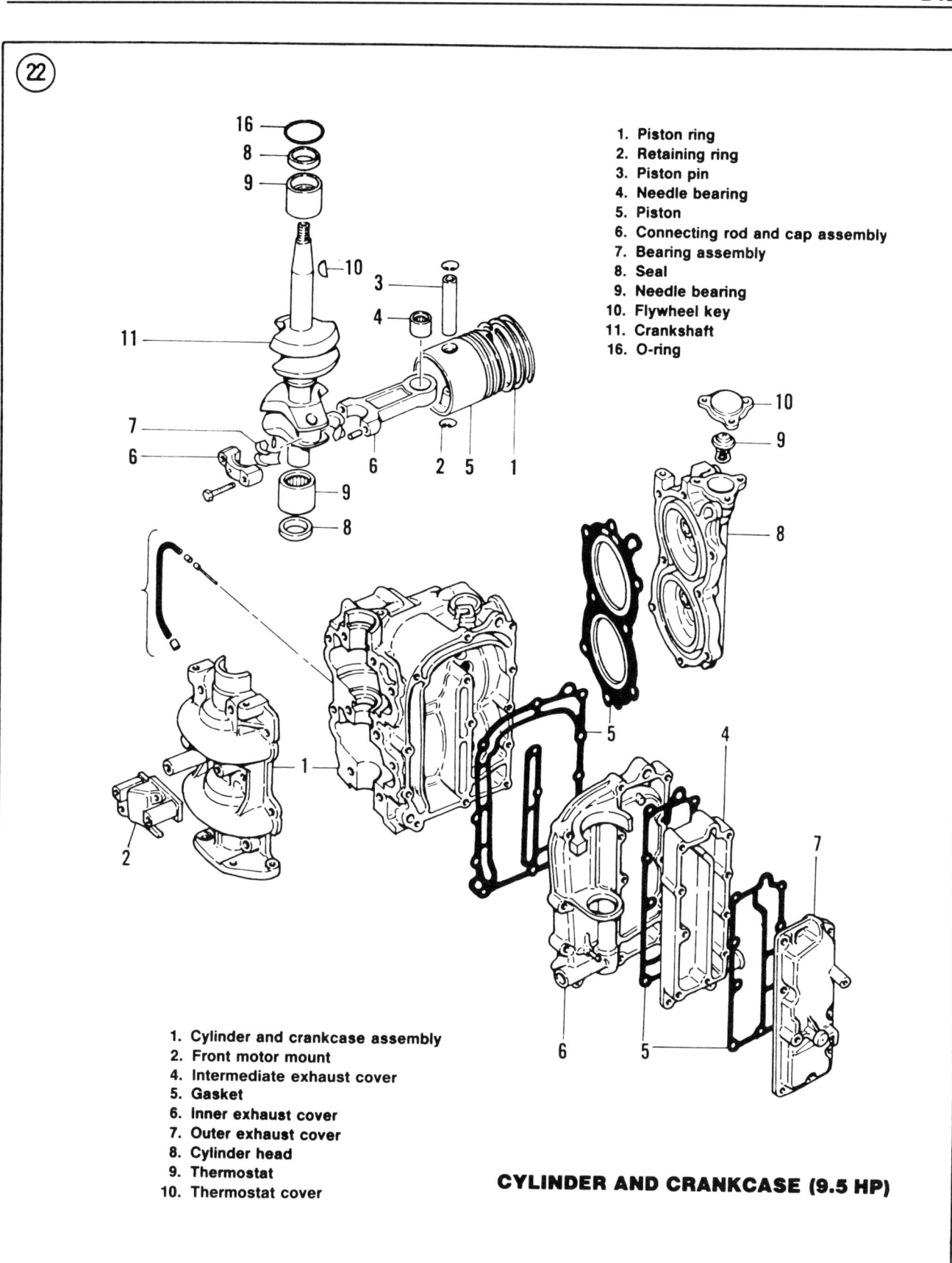

(22)

1. Piston ring
2. Retaining ring
3. Piston pin
4. Needle bearing
5. Piston
6. Connecting rod and cap assembly
7. Bearing assembly
8. Seal
9. Needle bearing
10. Flywheel key
11. Crankshaft
16. O-ring

1. Cylinder and crankcase assembly
2. Front motor mount
4. Intermediate exhaust cover
5. Gasket
6. Inner exhaust cover
7. Outer exhaust cover
8. Cylinder head
9. Thermostat
10. Thermostat cover

CYLINDER AND CRANKCASE (9.5 HP)

CHAPTER EIGHT

NOTE
Most engines use 2 taper pins. Inspect your engine carefully before proceeding with Step 9. Remove both pins, if so fitted, before attempting to separate the crankcase and cylinder in Step 11.

9. With crankcase and cylinder block on a solid surface, drive the taper pin(s) from the crankcase.

CAUTION
Do not use excessive force if pins are difficult to remove. You may be driving the pins the wrong way.

10. Remove the crankcase-to-cylinder block bolts.
11. Tap the top of the crankshaft on one side with a plastic mallet to separate the cylinder and crankcase halves.

NOTE
The main bearing and connecting rod caps must be removed before the crankshaft can be removed from the cylinder block. Omit Step 12 if the main bearings are cast into the cylinder block or secured to the crankshaft with a retaining ring.

12. Remove the center main bearing liner and needle bearings. Place in a clean container.

NOTE
The connecting rod bearings are larger than the center main bearings.

13. Mark the connecting rod and cap. Straighten the lock plate tabs on each connecting rod cap screw. Remove each connecting rod cap and needle bearings. Place in a clean container.

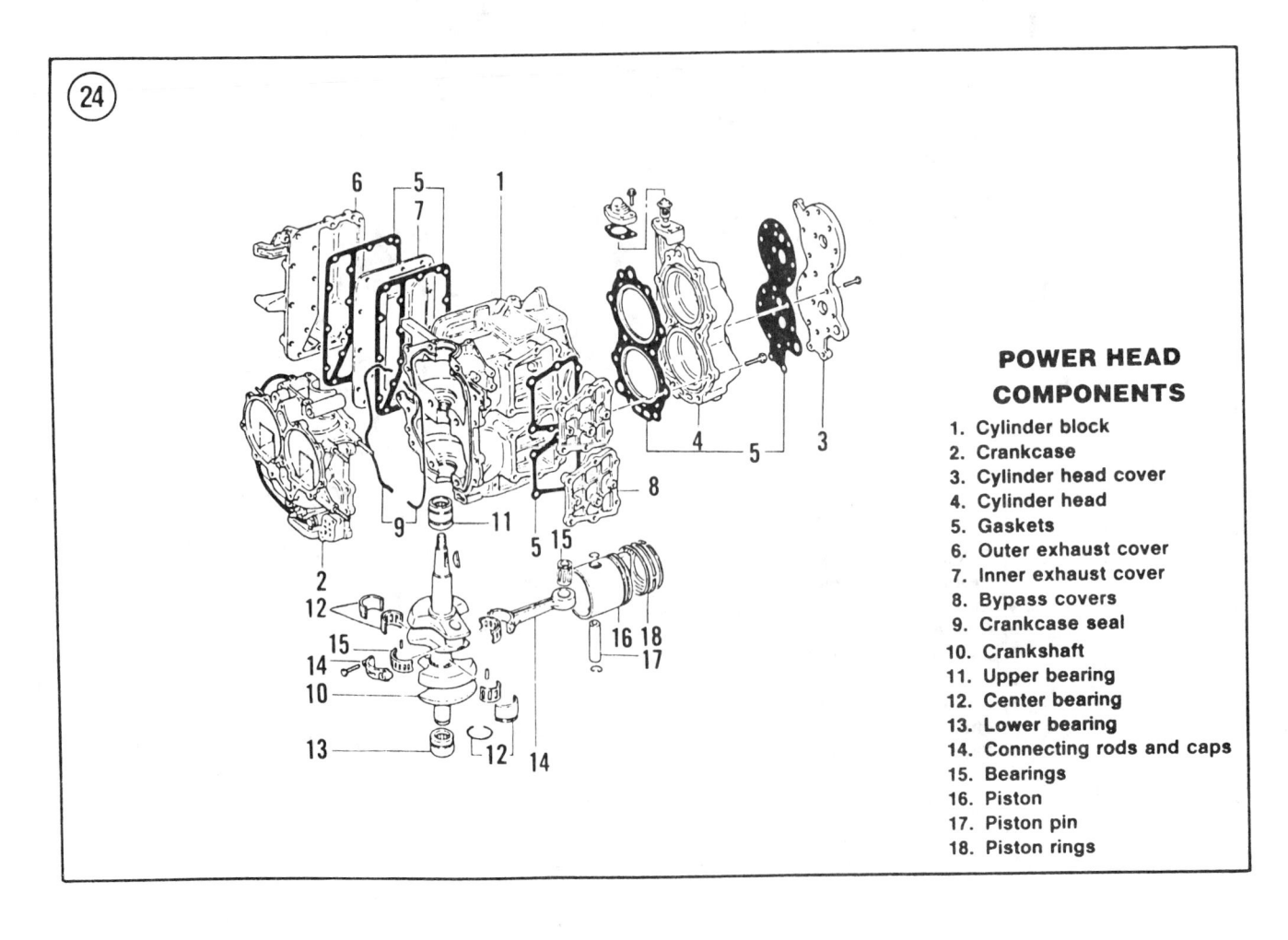

(24)

POWER HEAD COMPONENTS
1. Cylinder block
2. Crankcase
3. Cylinder head cover
4. Cylinder head
5. Gaskets
6. Outer exhaust cover
7. Inner exhaust cover
8. Bypass covers
9. Crankcase seal
10. Crankshaft
11. Upper bearing
12. Center bearing
13. Lower bearing
14. Connecting rods and caps
15. Bearings
16. Piston
17. Piston pin
18. Piston rings

POWER HEAD

14. If lower main bearing or carbon seal (on crankshafts so equipped) requires removal, remove snap ring and remove bearing or seal.
15. Remove the crankshaft from the cylinder block.
16. Remove the remaining center main and connecting rod needle bearings from the crankcase and place in their respective containers.
17. If main bearings are secured to the crankshaft with a retaining ring, carefully pry the ring from its groove. Slide ring to one side and remove the bearing assembly. Place in a clean container.
18. Remove the flywheel Woodruff key and magneto cam, if not removed when the flywheel was removed.
19. Remove the oil seal or slinger, if so equipped.
20. Slide the upper and lower main bearings (if so equipped) off the crankshaft. Discard the O-ring, if used.
21. Reinstall each rod cap to its connecting rod. Remove each piston and connecting rod assembly from its cylinder. Mark the cylinder number on the top of the piston with a felt-tipped pen.
22. Pry each ring far enough from the piston to grip it with pliers, then break the rings off the piston and discard.
23. If the piston is to be removed from the connecting rod, remove the piston pin retaining rings with needlenose pliers or snap ring pliers (part No. 303857), as required. See **Figure 18**.
24. Place piston in a suitable cradle with "L" mark on inside of piston boss facing upward. This positions the driver on the loose end of the piston pin. Drive piston pin through piston with a suitable driver. See **Figure 19**.

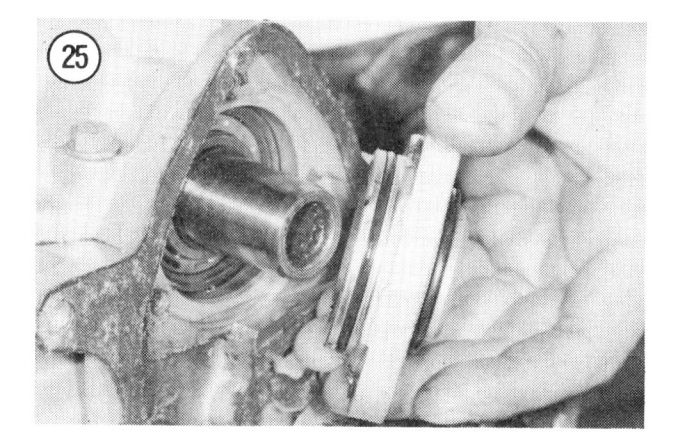

NOTE
Some connecting rod small ends are fitted with an integral bearing liner instead of needle bearings. If this type of piston pin bearing requires replacement, remove with a suitable driver.

25. Remove piston from connecting rod along with needle bearings and washers. Place bearings and washers in a clean container.

Disassembly (28-40 hp)

Refer to **Figure 24** (typical) for this procedure.
1. Remove the lower main bearing seal housing (**Figure 25**). Remove and discard the seal housing O-rings and the O-ring inside the crankshaft. Drive the seal from the housing with an appropriate size punch.
2. Remove the cylinder head cover and gasket (**Figure 26**). Discard the gasket.
3. Remove the thermostat cap, gasket and components (if so equipped) from cylinder head. See **Figure 27** (typical). Discard the seal and gasket.
4. Remove the cylinder head and gasket (**Figure 28**). Discard the gasket.
5. Remove the bypass covers and gaskets, if so equipped. See **Figure 29**. Discard the gaskets.

NOTE
Check inner exhaust cover for signs of corrosion or pitting. If found, discard the cover.

6. Remove the outer exhaust cover screws. Tap cover if necessary to break the seal. Remove the outer cover and gasket (**Figure 30**). Discard the gasket.

7. Remove the inner exhaust cover and gasket (**Figure 31**). Discard the gaskets.

8. Remove and discard any crankcase hose clamps. Remove hose from crankcase.

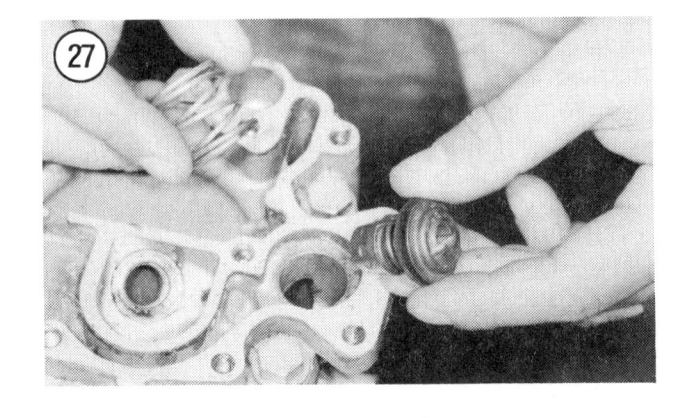

NOTE
Most engines use 2 taper pins. Inspect yours carefully before proceeding with Step 9. Remove both pins, if so fitted, before attempting to separate the crankcase and cylinder in Step 9 and Step 10.

9. With crankcase and cylinder block on a solid surface, drive the taper pin(s) from the back to the front of the crankcase.

10. Remove the crankcase-to-cylinder block bolts. On late models, there may be 2 hex head bolts inside the crankcase which must be removed before it can be separated from the block. See **Figure 32** (typical).

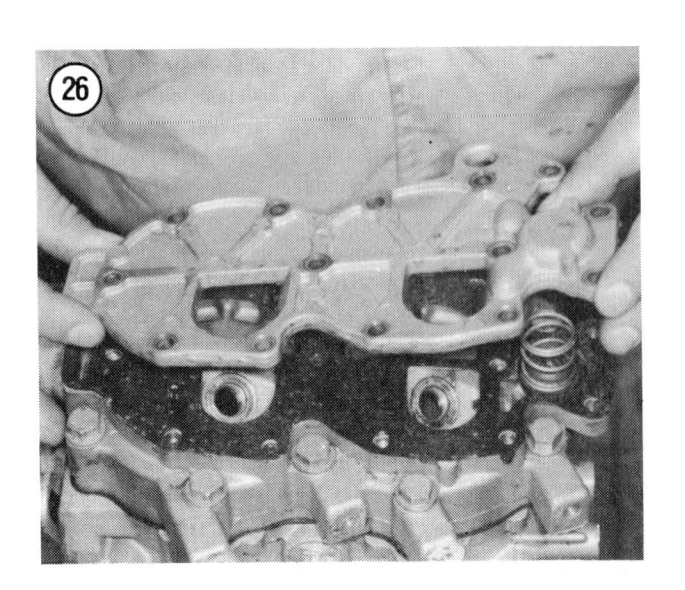

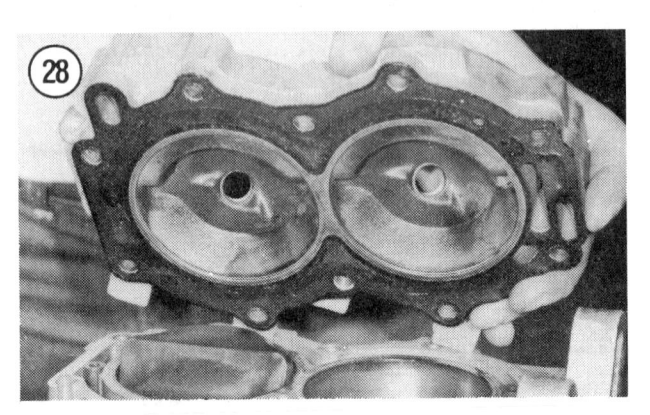

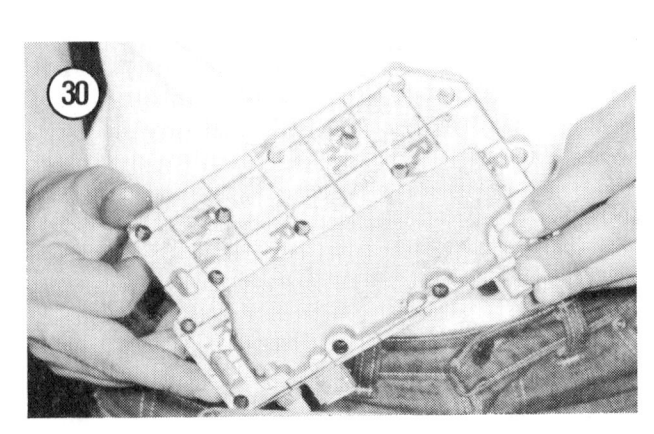

POWER HEAD

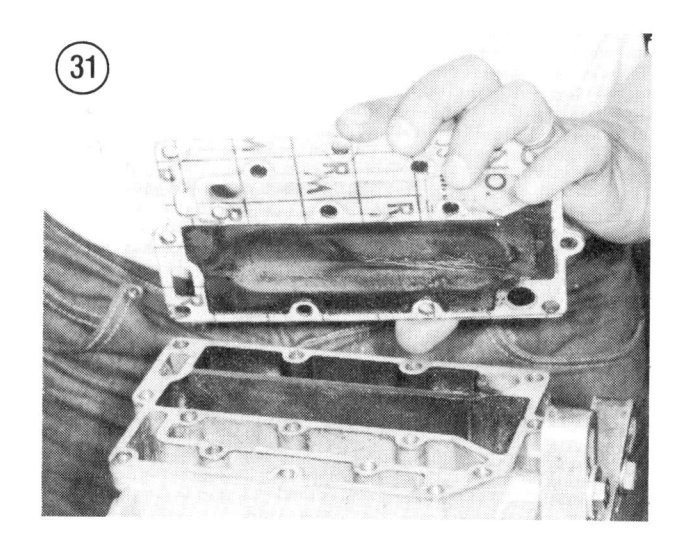

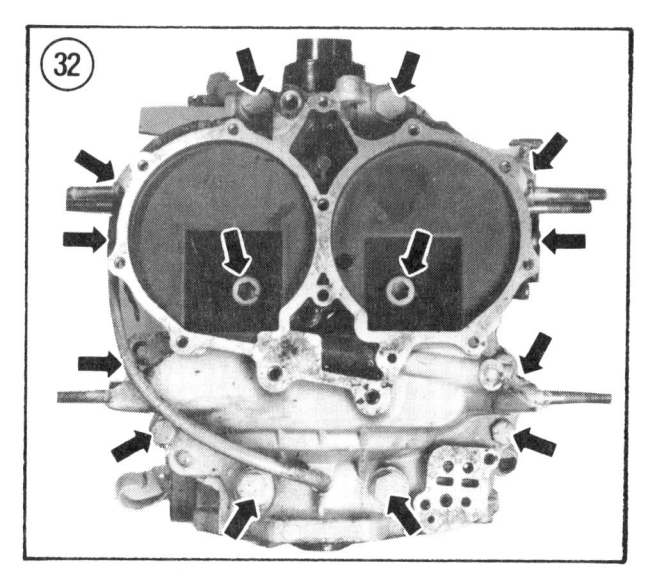

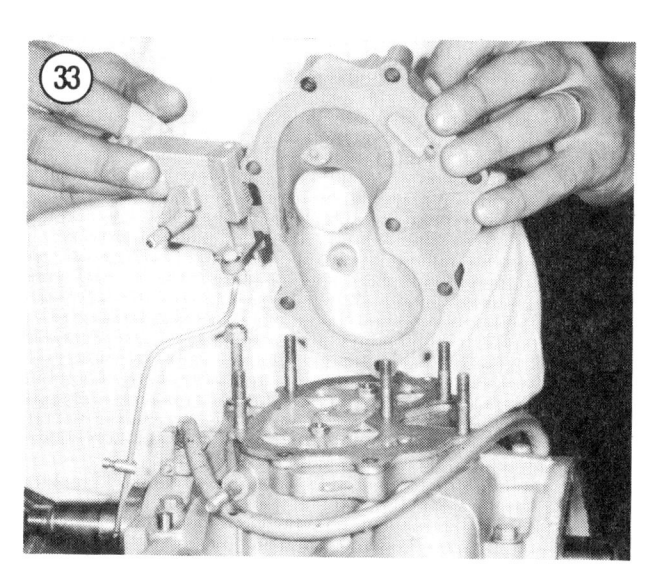

11. Remove the intake manifold and gasket (**Figure 33**). Discard the gasket.
12. Remove the screw holding the reed valve assembly. Remove the reed valve assembly (**Figure 34**).
13. Tap the top of the crankshaft on one side with a plastic mallet to separate the cylinder and crankcase halves.
14. Remove the crankcase oil drain valve, if so equipped.

> *NOTE*
> *The center main bearing (on some models) and connecting rod caps (all models) must be removed before the crankcase can be removed from the cylinder block. Note that one side of rod and cap has raised dots and the corners are chamfered for proper rod/cap alignment. Caps are not interchangeable and cannot be turned.*

15. If center main bearing is not secured with a retaining ring, remove the lower sleeve and the cage/roller assembly. See **Figure 35**.
16. Check connecting rod and cap alignment with a pencil point or dental pick (**Figure 36**). Alignment must be correct at 3 of the 4 corners. Record alignment points of each cap for reassembly reference.

17. Mark both connecting rods and caps. Straighten the lockplate tabs on each connecting rod cap screw. Remove each connecting rod cap and needle bearings or bearing retainer. See **Figure 37** (typical). Place in a clean container.

18. If lower main bearing or carbon seal (on crankshafts so equipped) requires removal, remove snap ring and remove bearing or seal.

19. Remove the crankshaft from the cylinder block (**Figure 38**).

20. Remove the remaining connecting rod bearing and center main bearing retainers and needle bearings (**Figure 39**). Place bearings and retainers in their respective containers.

21. If main bearing halves are secured by a retaining ring, carefully pry the ring from its groove. Slide ring to one side and remove the bearing assembly. Place in a clean container.

22. Remove the crankshaft Woodruff key, if not removed with the flywheel. Slide the upper and lower main bearings off the crankshaft, if so equipped. Discard the O-ring, if used.

23. Reinstall the rod cap to its respective connecting rod. Remove each piston and connecting rod assembly from its cylinder. Mark the cylinder number on the top of the piston with a felt-tipped pen.

24. Pry each ring far enough from the piston to grip it with pliers, then break the rings off the piston and discard.

25. If the piston is to be removed from the connecting rod, remove the piston pin retaining rings with snap ring pliers (part No. 303857).

NOTE
If the pin cannot be driven out easily in Step 26, heat the piston with a heat lamp or submerge it in hot water for approximately 10 minutes.

26. Place piston in a suitable cradle with "L" mark on inside of piston boss facing upward. This positions the driver on the loose end of the piston pin. Drive piston pin through piston with a suitable driver. See **Figure 19**.

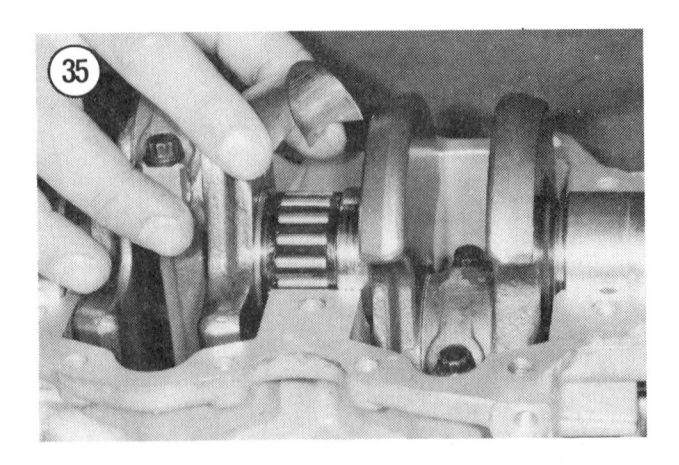

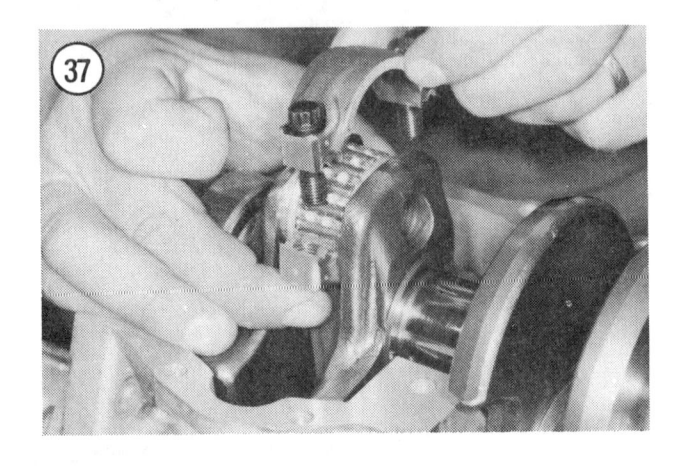

27. Remove piston from connecting rod along with needle bearings and washers or caged bearing retainer (**Figure 40**). Place bearings and washers in a clean container.

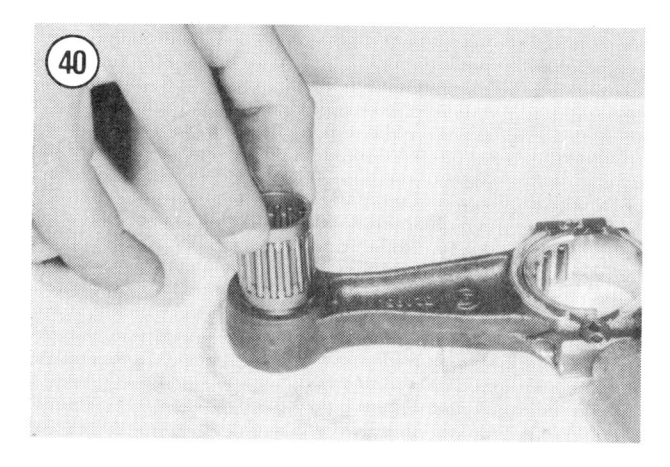

POWER HEAD

Drive the seal from the housing with an appropriate size punch.
2. Remove the intake manifold and reed valve assembly.
3. Remove the thermostat spring, thermostat and seal. Discard the seal.
4. Remove the cylinder head cover and gasket. Discard the gasket.
5. Remove the motor temperature and choke thermal switches.
6. Remove the cylinder head and gasket. Discard the gasket.
7. Remove the exhaust cover screws. Tap cover if necessary to break the seal. Remove the outer cover and gasket. Discard the gasket.
8. Remove the inner exhaust cover, deflector and gasket. Discard the gasket.
9. Remove the crankcase taper pins with a punch. Drive pins from front to rear of crankcase.
10. Remove the crankcase-to-cylinder block fasteners. Tap the side of the crankshaft lightly with a rubber mallet to break the gasket seal, then remove the cylinder half from the crankcase.

NOTE
The connecting rod caps must be removed before the crankshaft can be removed from the cylinder block. Note that one side of rod and cap has raised dots and the corners are chamfered for proper rod/cap alignment. Caps are not interchangeable and cannot be turned.

11. Check connecting rod and cap alignment with a pencil point or dental pick (**Figure 36**). Alignment must be correct at 3 of the 4 corners. Record alignment points of each cap for reassembly reference.
12. Mark both connecting rods and caps. Straighten the lockplate tabs on each connecting rod cap screw, if used. Remove each connecting rod cap and needle bearings or bearing retainer. Place in a clean container.

Disassembly
(55, 60 and 65 hp Inline)

Refer to **Figure 41** (typical) for this procedure.
1. Remove the lower main bearing seal housing. Remove and discard the housing O-rings and the O-ring inside the crankshaft.

CHAPTER EIGHT

POWER HEAD COMPONENTS
(55, 60 AND 65 HP INLINE)

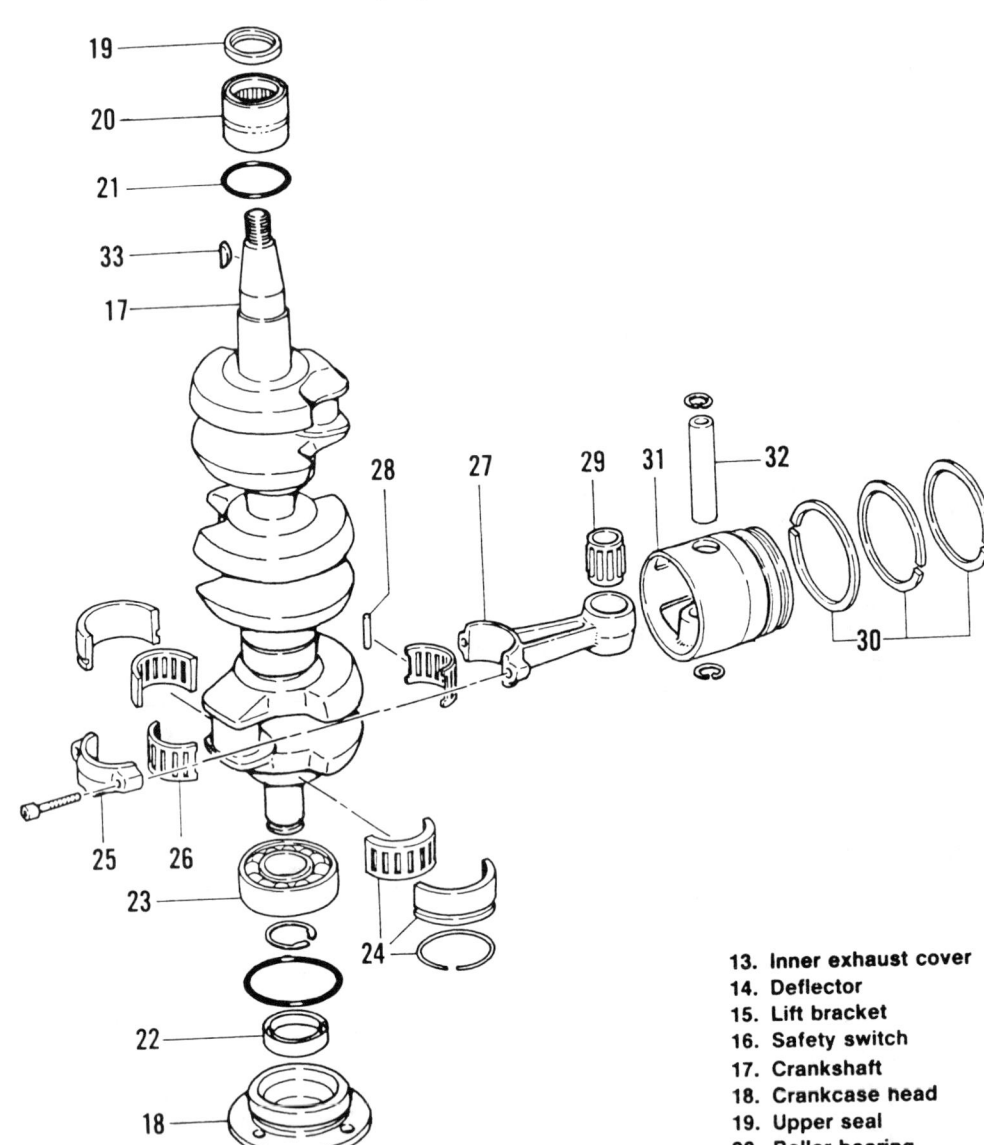

1. Cylinder block
2. Crankcase
3. Taper pin
4. Crankcase seal
5. Cylinder head
6. Gasket
7. Choke thermal switch
8. Cylinder head cover
9. Thermostat cover
10. Thermostat
11. Motor temperature switch
12. Outer exhaust cover
13. Inner exhaust cover
14. Deflector
15. Lift bracket
16. Safety switch
17. Crankshaft
18. Crankcase head
19. Upper seal
20. Roller bearing
21. O-ring
22. Crankcase head seal
23. Bearing assembly
24. Center bearing assembly
25. Connecting rod cap
26. Bearing retainer
27. Connecting rod
28. Connecting rod bearings
29. Connecting rod small end bearing
30. Piston rings
31. Piston
32. Piston pin
33. Woodruff key

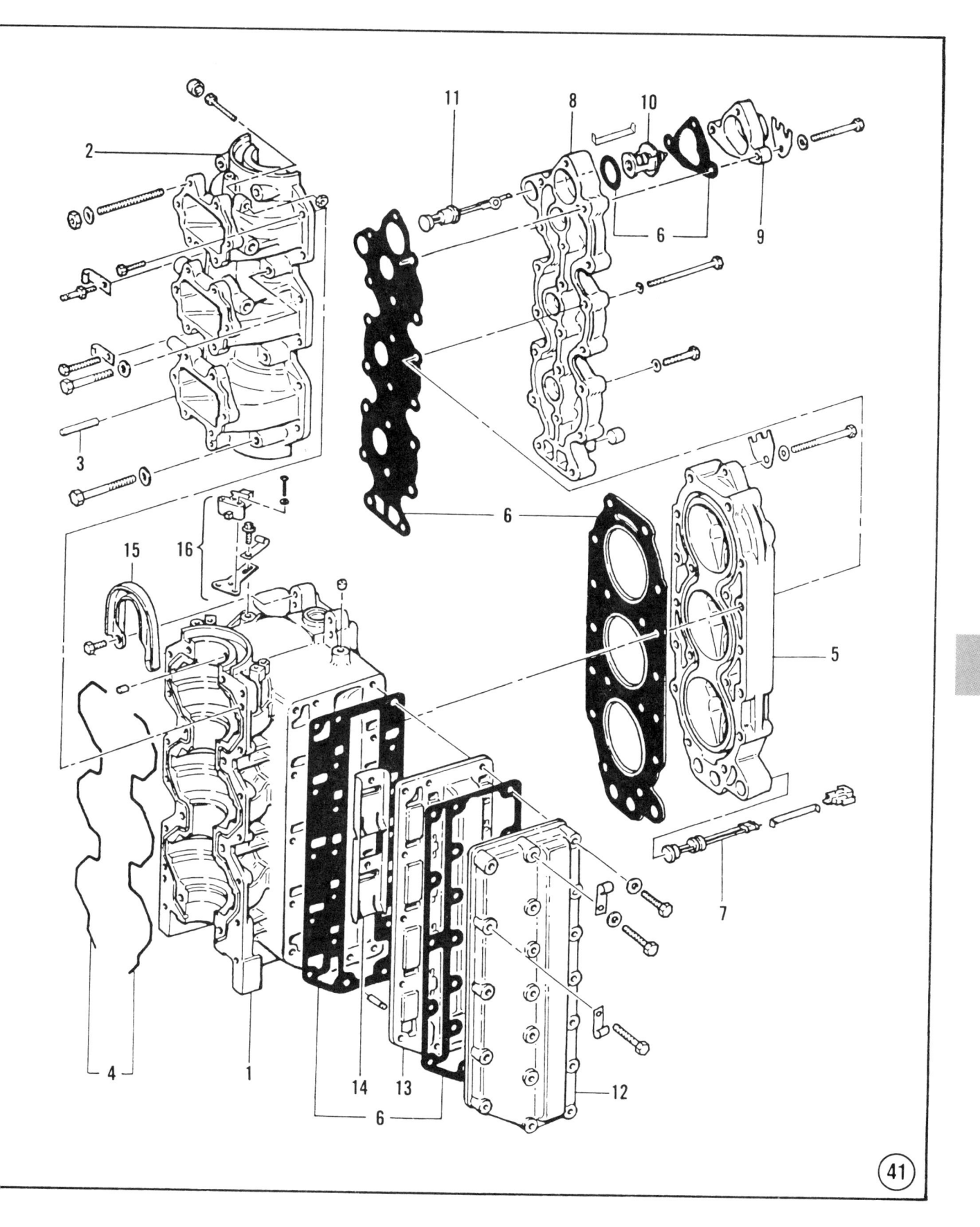

POWER HEAD

253

(41)

13. Remove the crankshaft from the cylinder block.
14. Remove the remaining connecting rod bearing retainers and needle bearings. Place bearings and retainers in their respective containers.
15. Orient each rod cap to its connecting rod and reinstall with cap screws finger-tight.
16. Remove the piston and rod assemblies from their cylinders. Mark the cylinder number on the top of each piston with a felt-tipped pen.
17. Remove the crankshaft Woodruff key, if not removed with the flywheel. Slide the upper seal and main bearing assembly off the crankshaft.
18. If lower main bearing requires removal, remove snap ring and then remove bearing with an appropriate puller.
19. Slide the crankshaft center main bearing retaining ring from its groove. Remove the bearing split sleeves. Remove the bearing cages and roller bearings. Place cages and bearings in a clean container. Repeat this step to remove the other main bearing.
20. Pry each ring far enough from the piston to grip it with pliers, then break the rings off the piston and discard.

NOTE
If piston pin bore has a small cutout facing the top of the pistons, the retaining rings can be removed in Step 21 by inserting a small screwdriver blade or awl in the cutout and prying the ring free.

21. If the piston is to be removed from the connecting rod, remove the piston pin retaining rings with snap ring pliers (part No. 303857).
22. Slide piston pin from piston/connecting rod, then remove piston from connecting rod along with needle bearings and washers or caged bearing retainer. Place bearings and washers in a clean container.

Disassembly
(V4)

Refer to **Figure 42** (V4 power head components) or **Figure 43** (V4 crankshaft assembly) for this procedure.

1. Note location of intake bypass cover fasteners, recirculation hoses, clamps and hose connectors. The cover on which the starter solenoid is mounted must be reinstalled in the same location as removed; the other covers are interchangeable. Remove each cylinder bypass cover and gasket. Discard the gasket.
2. Remove the upper and lower crankcase head screws. See **Figure 44** and outer ring of screws in **Figure 45** (typical).
3. Locate the taper pins at opposite ends of the crankcase and cylinder block assembly. Drive the pins from the back to the front of the crankcase with a suitable drift and hammer.
4. Loosen but do not remove the 4 screws holding the lower bearing retainer plate to the lower crankcase head (**Figure 45**).
5. Tap the side of the crankshaft with a soft mallet to break the gasket seal, then remove the crankcase.

NOTE
The connecting rod caps must be removed before the crankshaft can be removed from the cylinder block. Note that one side of rod and cap has raised dots and the corners are chamfered for proper rod/cap alignment. Caps are not interchangeagle and cannot be turned.

6. Rotate the crankshaft to position the No. 1 and No. 2 connecting rods as shown in **Figure 46**. Remove the connecting rod cap screws with a 5/16 in. 12-point deep socket. Remove the connecting rod caps, retainers and bearing assemblies. Mark each rod cap according to cylinder number. Place retainers and bearings from each rod cap in individual containers marked with the cylinder number.

POWER HEAD

CRANKSHAFT ASSEMBLY (TYPICAL V-4)

㊷

CHAPTER EIGHT

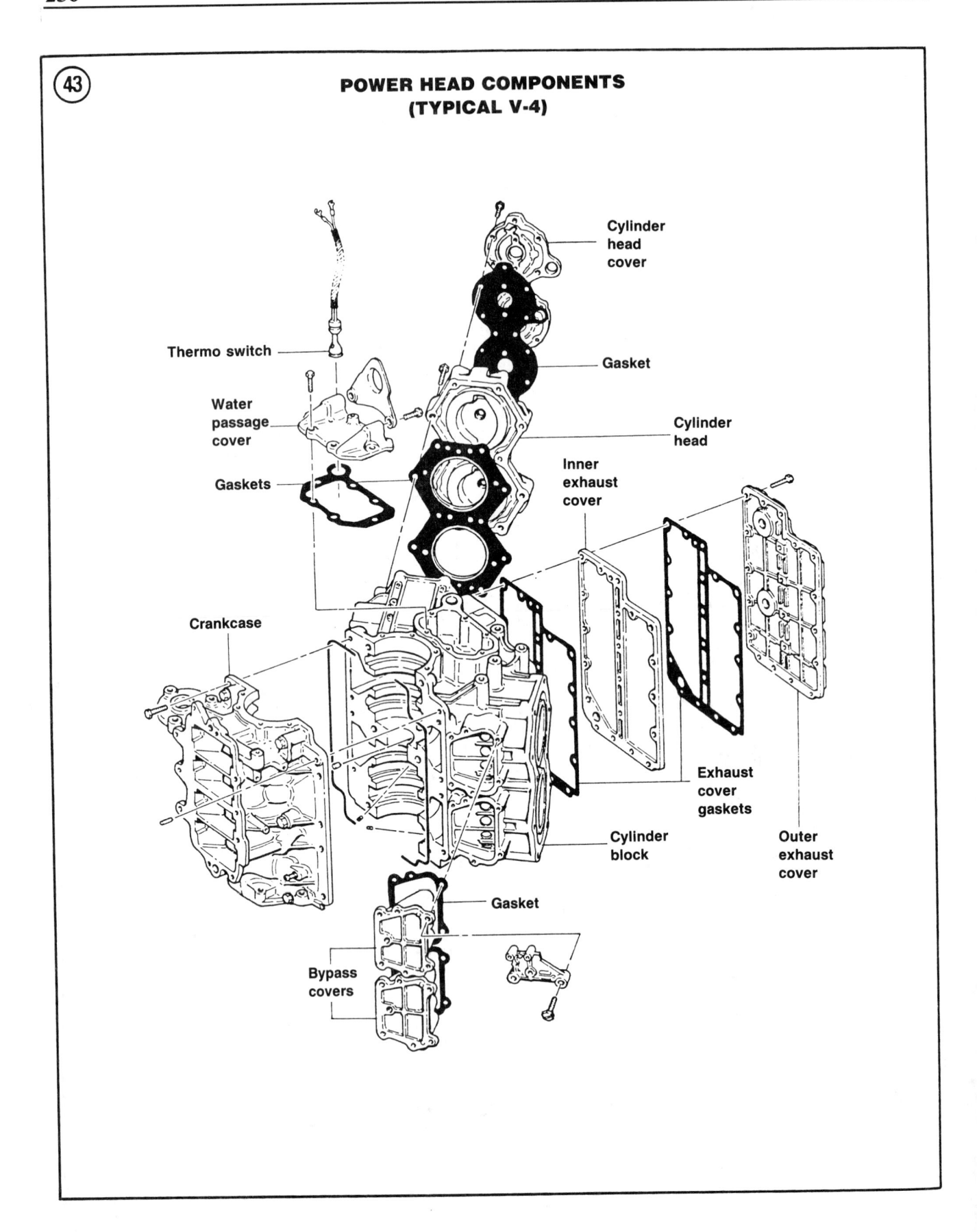

43 POWER HEAD COMPONENTS
(TYPICAL V-4)

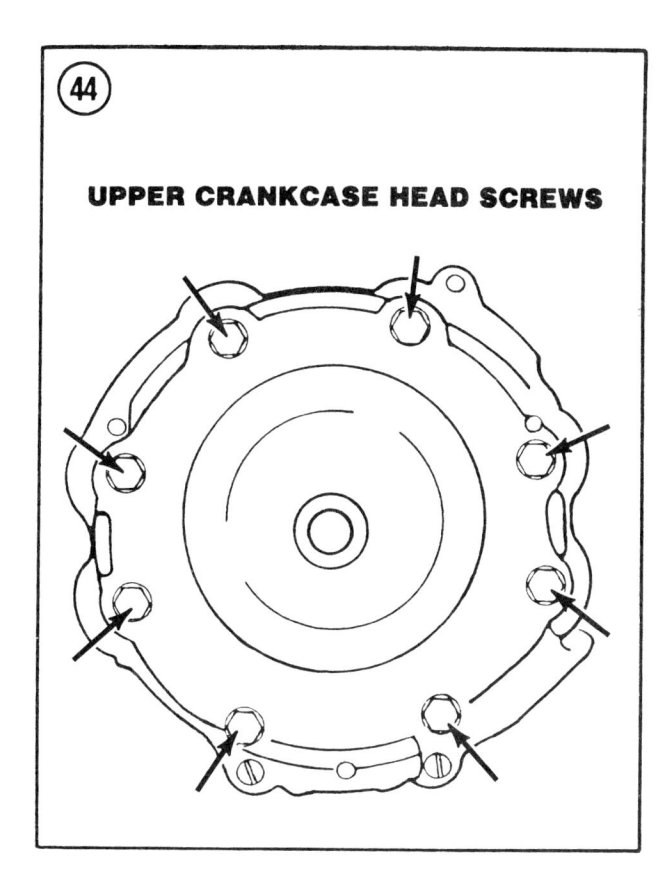

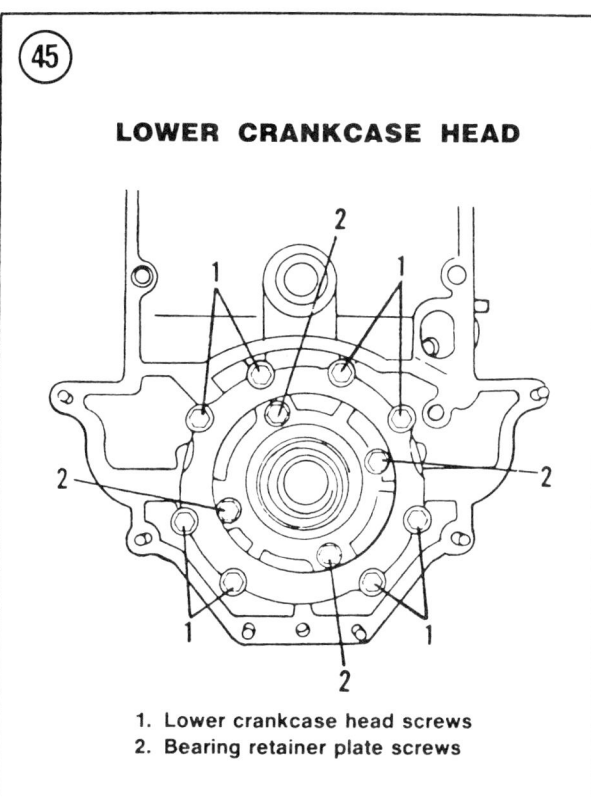

POWER HEAD

44 UPPER CRANKCASE HEAD SCREWS

45 LOWER CRANKCASE HEAD

1. Lower crankcase head screws
2. Bearing retainer plate screws

7. Repeat Step 6 to remove the remaining rod caps, retainers and bearings.

8. Grasp the upper and lower crankcase heads and lift the crankshaft from the cylinder block. Place crankshaft on a clean workbench.

9. Remove the bearings and retainers from the connecting rods. Place in the containers with the rod cap bearings and retainers.

10. Remove the cylinder head covers and gaskets. Discard the gaskets.

11. Remove the cylinder heads and gaskets. Discard the gaskets.

12. Reinstall rod caps to their respective rods, then remove each piston from its cylinder.

13. Remove the flywheel Woodruff key, if not removed with the flywheel. Slide the upper crankcase head from the crankshaft. Remove and discard the O-rings. Carefully drive seal from crankcase head with a punch inserted through the bottom of the bearing to engage the seal lip.

14. Remove and discard the screws loosened in Step 4, then remove the lower crankcase head from the crankshaft. Remove and discard the O-rings. Carefully drive seal from crankcase head with a punch inserted through the bottom of the bearing to engage the seal lip.

46

15. Remove the center main bearing sleeve retaining rings. Note that the retaining ring groove in the bearing sleeve faces toward the bottom of the crankshaft, then separate the bearing sleeve halves and remove from the crankshaft.

16. If lower main bearing requires removal, remove snap ring and then remove bearing with an appropriate puller.

17. Pry each ring far enough from the piston to grip it with pliers, then break the rings off the piston and discard.

NOTE
If piston pin bore has a small cutout facing the top of the pistons, the retaining rings can be removed in Step 18 by inserting a small screwdriver blade or awl in the cutout and prying the ring free.

18. If the piston is to be removed from the connecting rod, remove the piston pin retaining rings with snap ring pliers (part No. 303857).

19. Place piston in an appropriate cradle with the "L" mark on the inside of the piston facing upward. This positions the driver on the loose end of the piston pin.

20. Heat the piston to 200-400° F with a heat lamp, then press piston pin through the piston using an appropriate driver.

21. Let the piston cool, then remove the connecting rod and bearings.

22. Remove bearings or bearing retainer from connecting rod and place in the container with the other bearings from that piston/cylinder assembly.

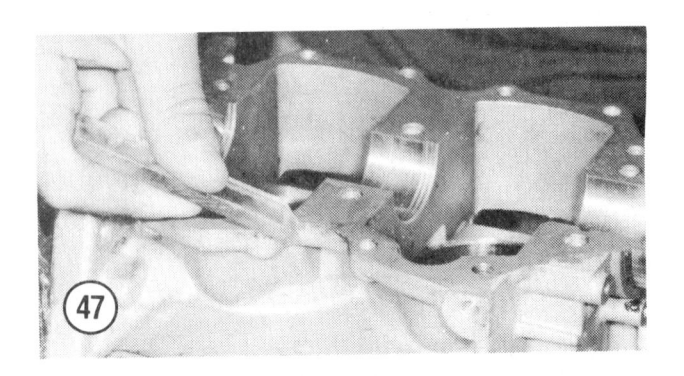

Cylinder Block and Crankcase Cleaning and Inspection (All Engines)

Johnson and Evinrude outboard cylinder blocks and crankcase covers are matched and line-bored assemblies. For this reason, you should not attempt to assemble an engine with parts salvaged from other blocks. If inspection indicates that either the block or crankcase cover requires replacement, replace both as an assembly.

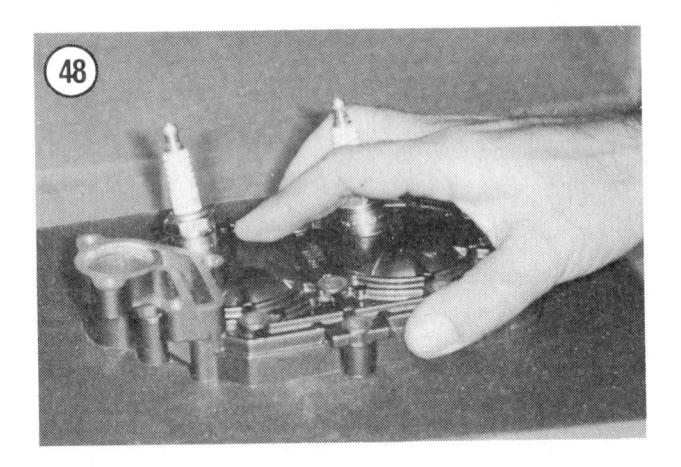

Carefully remove all gasket and sealant residue from the cylinder block and crankcase cover mating surfaces. Clean the aluminum surfaces carefully to avoid nicking them. A dull putty knife can be used but a piece of Lucite with one edge ground to a 45° angle is more efficient and will also reduce the possibility of damage to the sufaces. See **Figure 47**. Once the area is clean, wipe it with OMC Cleaning Solvent. When sealing the crankcase cover and cylinder block, both mating surfaces must be free of all sealant residue, dirt and oil or leaks will develop.

Once the gasket surfaces are clean, place the mating surface of each component on a large pane of glass. Apply uniform downward

POWER HEAD

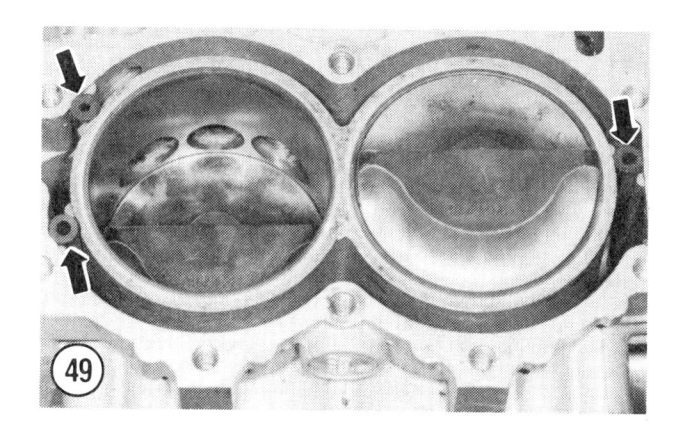

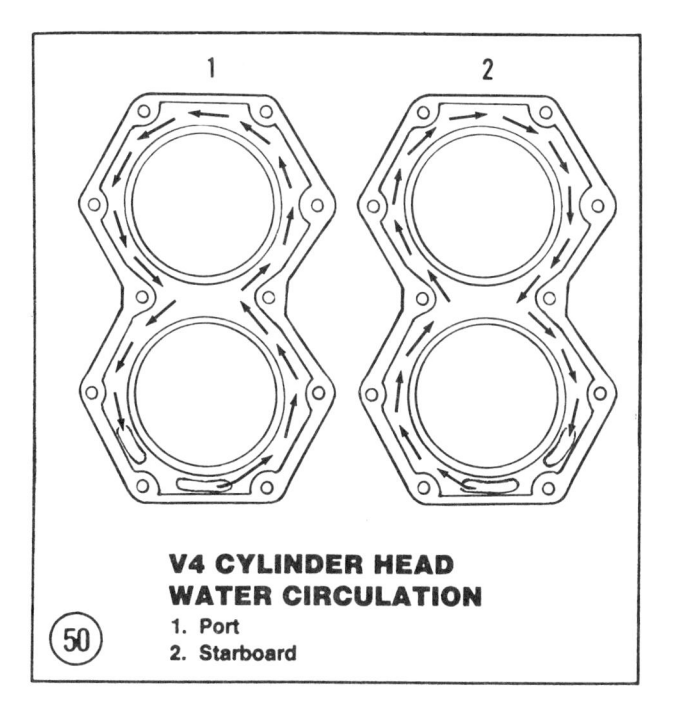

(49)

(50) V4 CYLINDER HEAD WATER CIRCULATION
1. Port
2. Starboard

pressure on the component and check for warpage. Replace any component if more than a slight degree of warpage exists. In cases where there is a slight amount of warpage, it can often be eliminated by placing the mating surface of each component on a large sheet of 120 emery cloth. Apply a slight amount of pressure **(Figure 48)** and move the component in a figure-8 pattern. Remove the component and emery cloth and recheck surface flatness on the pane of glass.

If warpage exists, the high spots will be dull while low areas will remain unchanged in appearance. It may be necessary to repeat this procedure 2-3 times until the entire mating surface has been polished to a dull luster. Do not remove more than a total 0.010 in. from the cylinder block and head. Finish the resurfacing with 180 emery cloth.

1. Clean the cylinder block and crankcase cover thoroughly with solvent and a brush.
2. Carefully remove all gasket and sealant residue from the cylinder block and crankcase cover mating surfaces.
3. Check the cylinder heads and exhaust ports for excessive carbon deposits or varnish. Remove with a scraper or other blunt instrument.
4. Check the block, cylinder head and cover for cracks, fractures, stripped bolt or spark plug holes or other defects.
5. Check the gasket mating surfaces for nicks, grooves, cracks or excessive distortion. Any of these defects will cause compression leakage. Replace as required.
6. Check all oil and water passages in the block and cover for obstructions. Make sure any plugs installed are properly tightened.
7. Make sure all water passage restrictors **(Figure 49)** are in good condition and properly installed. **Figure 50** shows V4 restrictor location and water circulation. Damaged, loose or missing restrictors will interfere with cooling water circulation and result in possible engine overheating.
8. Check the inner and outer exhaust covers for signs of overheating or warpage. Replace as required.
9. Check crankcase recirculation orifice, if so equipped, and clean with tool part No. 326623.

NOTE
If a compression test before disassembling the engine showed a loss of compression and no vacuum leaks were found, check the labyrinth seal condition very carefully in Step 10.

10. If engine uses labyrinth seals (grooves in the block and crankcase cover on either side

of the center main bearing), check their condition. This type of seal fills with oil/gas mixture during engine operation to prevent compression leakage between cylinders. If seal grooves are not clearly defined or otherwise suspect, the block and cover should be replaced.

11. Check condition of V4 cylinder block sealing ring grooves.

NOTE
It is a good idea to have the cylinder walls lightly honed with a medium stone even if they are in good condition. This will break up any glaze that might reduce compression.

12. Check each cylinder bore for signs of aluminum transfer from the pistons to the cylinder walls. If scoring is present but not excessive, have the cylinders honed by a dealer or qualified machine shop.

NOTE
Oversize pistons and rings are no longer available for all engines covered in this book. Before having the cylinders rebored, first make sure that necessary parts are still available from the factory and then wait until they are actually received by your dealer.

CAUTION
If cylinders are rebored for oversize pistons, be sure to allow sufficient clearance between the new bore diameter and the oversize pistons. See your dealer for exact specifications.

13. Check each cylinder bore for size and taper in the port area with an inside micrometer or bore gauge. See **Figure 51** (typical). If bore is tapered, worn or out-of-round by less than 0.002 in. (1.5-7.5 hp), 0.025 in. (9.5 hp), 0.003 in. (all other inline) or 0.004 in. (V4), have the cylinders honed or rebored by a dealer or qualified machine shop. If taper, wear or out-of-round exceeds this dimension, replace the block and cover assembly.

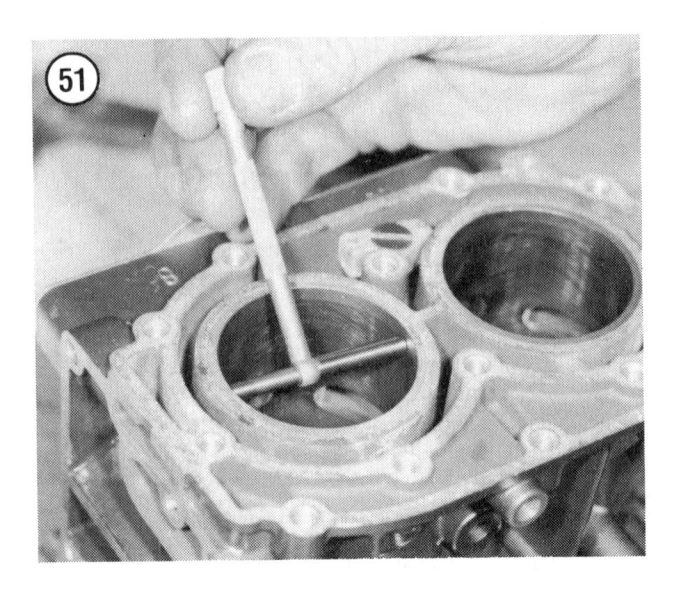

Crankshaft and Connecting Rod Bearings Cleaning and Inspection (All Engines)

Bearings can be reused if they are in good condition. To be on the safe side, however, it is a good idea to discard all bearings and install new ones whenever the engine is disassembled. New bearings are inexpensive compared to the cost of another overhaul caused by the use of marginal bearings.

1. Place ball bearings in a wire basket and submerge in a suitable container of fresh solvent. The bottom of the basket should not touch the bottom of the container.
2. Agitate basket containing bearings to loosen all grease, sludge and other contamination.
3. Dry ball bearings with dry filtered compressed air. Be careful not to spin the bearings.
4. Lubricate the dry bearings with a light coat of Johnson or Evinrude 50/1 oil and inspect for rust, wear, scuffed surfaces, heat discoloration or other defects. Replace as required.

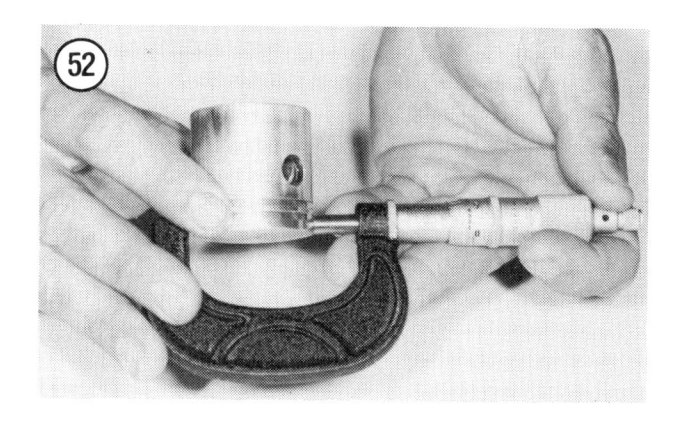

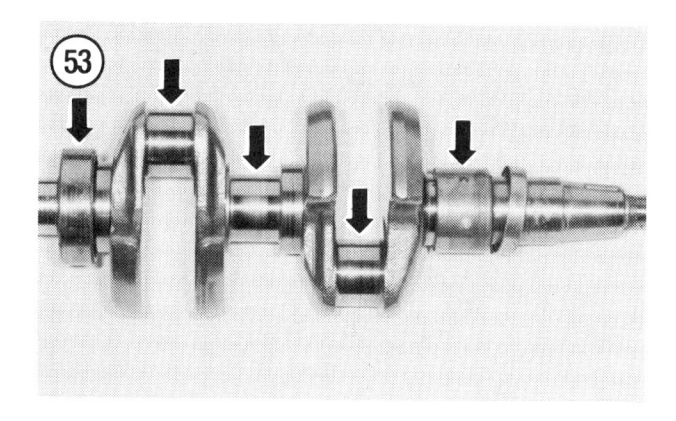

POWER HEAD

Figure 52

Figure 53

5. If roller bearings are to be reused, repeat Steps 1-4, cleaning one set at a time to prevent any possible mixup. Check bearings for flat spots. If one roller bearing is defective, replace all in the set with new bearings and liners.

6. Repeat Step 5 to check caged piston pin bearings. If bearing is defective, replace the bearing and its corresponding piston pin.

Piston Cleaning and Inspection (All Engines)

1. Check the piston for signs of scoring, cracking, cracked or worn piston pin bosses or metal damage. Replace piston and pin as an assembly if any of these defects are noted.

2. Check piston ring grooves for distortion, loose ring locating pins or excessive wear. If the flexing action of the rings has not kept the lower surface of the ring grooves free of carbon, clean with a bristle brush and solvent.

NOTE
Do not use an automotive ring groove cleaning tool in Step 3 as it can damage the piston ring locating pin.

3. Clean the piston skirt, ring grooves and dome with the recessed end of a broken ring to remove any carbon deposits.

4. Immerse pistons in a carbon removal solution to remove any carbon deposits not removed in Step 3. If the solution does not remove all of the carbon, carefully use a fine wire brush and avoid burring or rounding of the machined edges. Clean the piston skirt with crocus cloth.

5. Check all pistons with a micrometer at the top and piston skirt (**Figure 52**). Measure at a 90 degree angle to the piston pin and at a point parallel with the piston pin bosses. Compare the 2 top and skirt measurements to determine if piston is out-of-round. Replace piston and pin as an assembly if the piston is out-of-round by more than 0.0025 in. (1.5-7.5 hp), 0.003 in. (9.5-40 hp) or 0.004 in. (all others).

Crankshaft Cleaning and Inspection (All Engines)

1. Clean the crankshaft thoroughly with solvent and a brush. Blow dry with dry filtered compressed air and lubricate with a light coat of Johnson/Evinrude 50/1 oil.

2. Check the crankshaft journals and crankpins for scratches, heat discoloration or other defects. See **Figure 53** (inline) or **Figure 54** (V4).

3. Using a micrometer, measure the crankshaft journals and crankpins in 4 locations, each 90° apart. The journals and crankpins should be perfectly round; replace the crankshaft if out-of-round or tapered.

4. Check drive shaft splines and flywheel taper threads for wear or damage. Replace crankshaft as required.

5. Check V4 crankshaft seal rings for excessive wear or damage and replace if they

do not seal tightly around the crankshaft web. Measure seal ring clearance with a feeler gauge. If not between 0.0015-0.0025 in., replace the seal ring. Do not remove seal rings unless replacement is required.

6. If a V4 crankshaft seal ring breaks during crankshaft removal, measure the ring thickness near its outer edge with a micrometer and obtain a new seal ring of the same thickness from your dealer (if one is broken, it is a good idea to replace all at the same time). Carefully spread the end gap just enough to slip the ring over the crankshaft journal and complete installation with a piston ring expander.

7. If the lower crankshaft ball bearing has not been removed on crankshafts so equipped, grasp its inner race and try to work it in and out. Replace the bearing if excessive play is noted.

8. Lubricate the ball bearing with Johnson/Evinrude 50/1 oil and rotate its outer race. Replace the bearing if it sounds or feels rough or if it does not rotate smoothly.

Piston and Connecting Rod Assembly (All Engines)

If the pistons were removed from the connecting rods, they must be correctly oriented when reassembling. The exhaust or slanted side of the piston dome must face the exhaust ports when installed. See **Figure 55** (inline) or **Figure 56** (V4). The connecting rod oil hole must face toward the flywheel end of the engine. With V4 engines, remember to consider the difference between port and starboard cylinders. Double-check rod and piston orientation before installing the piston pin.

1A. If a caged needle bearing was removed from the connecting rod piston pin end:
  a. Position connecting rod with oil hole facing up.
  b. Reinstall the connecting rod piston pin bearing with an arbor press.

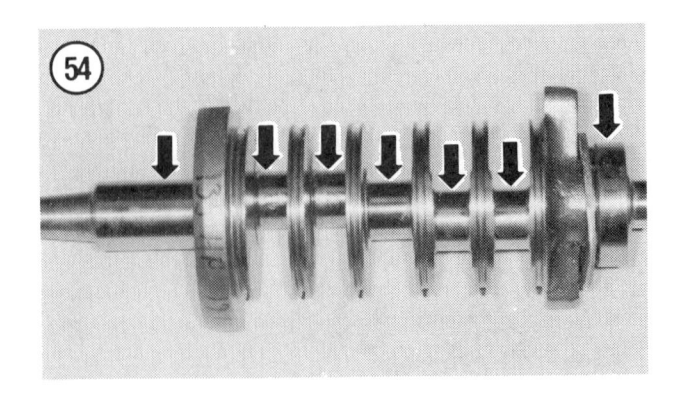

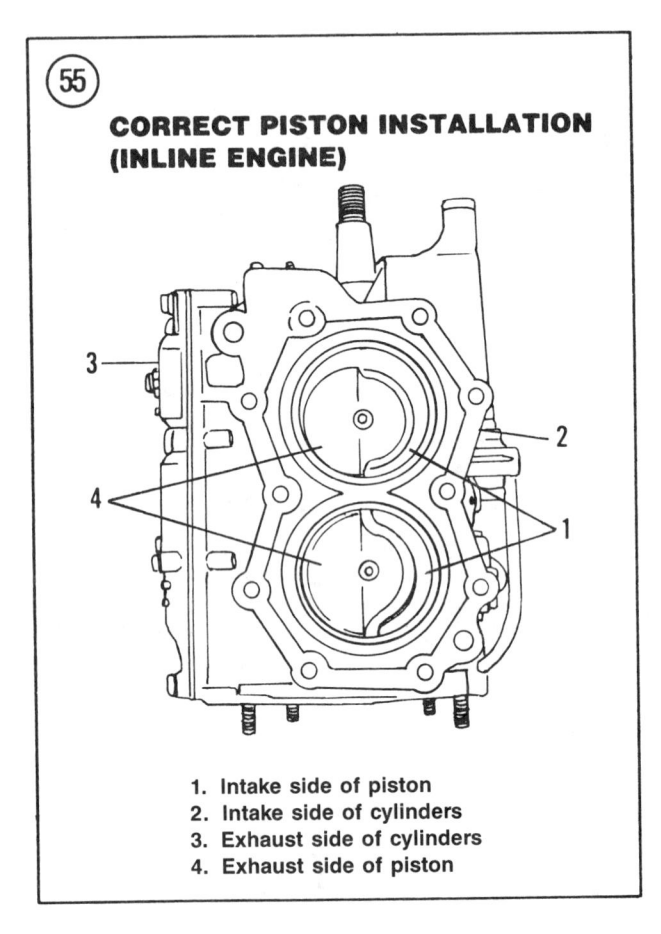

1B. If needle bearings were removed from the connecting rod piston pin end:
  a. Position connecting rod with oil hole facing up.
  b. Wipe inside of connecting rod piston pin bore with OMC Needle Bearing grease.

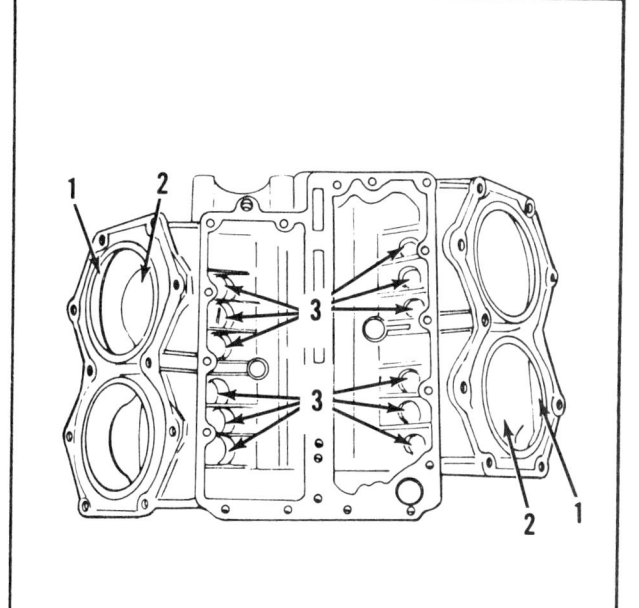

POWER HEAD

CORRECT PISTON INSTALLATION (V4 ENGINE)
1. Intake side of piston
2. Exhaust side of piston
3. Cylinder exhaust ports

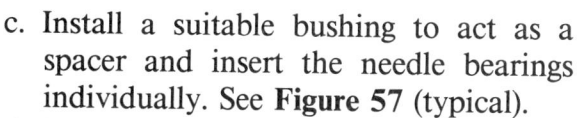

c. Install a suitable bushing to act as a spacer and insert the needle bearings individually. See **Figure 57** (typical).

d. When all bearings are in place, fit washers at top and bottom of bearing assembly.

NOTE
Older engines may use a flat dome piston. If so, the piston will have a cutout or hole in its side. The piston and rod should be assembled so the piston hole will align with the cutout or hole in the cylinder wall.

2. Fit the piston over the connecting rod piston pin end with the exhaust (slanted) side of the dome facing the starboard side of the connecting rod (oil hole facing up). With V4 engines, the exhaust side of the dome will face the port side of the connecting rod on the starboard bank pistons and the starboard side of the connecting rod on the port bank pistons. See **Figure 55** (inline) or **Figure 56** (V4).

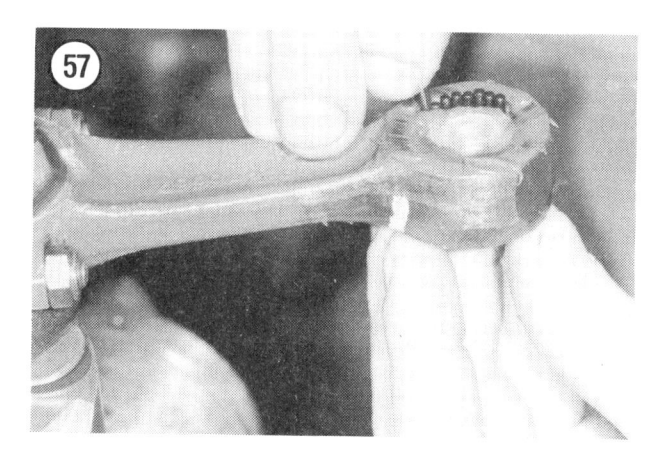

3. Lightly coat piston pin and lubricate each piston pin hole with a drop or two of Johnson/Evinrude 50/1 oil.

NOTE
Position piston in Step 4 to press piston pin in place from the "L" or "LOOSE" side of the piston. See piston pin boss inside piston skirt for marking. If there is no marking, the pin can be installed from either side.

4. Insert piston pin through piston pin hole and engage connecting rod. Make sure piston dome or cutout and connecting rod oil hole are properly oriented. Position piston on the same cradle used to disassemble it and press piston pin in place with the same piston tool used to remove it. If necessary, heat the piston with a heat lamp or submerge it in hot water for approximately 10 minutes to make piston pin installation easier.

5. Install new piston pin retaining rings on each side of the piston. Use needlenose pliers to install wire retaining rings and snap ring pliers to install snap rings. Make sure rings fit into grooves in the piston pin bore.

6. Measure the bottom of each piston skirt at a point parallel with the piston pin and 90°

from the piston pin. Compare the measurements. If measurements vary more than 0.0025 in. (1.5-7.5 hp), 0.003 in. (9.5-40 hp) or 0.004 in. (all others), the piston was distorted during assembly and should be replaced.

7. Check end gap of new rings before installing on piston. Place ring in cylinder bore, then square it up by inserting the bottom of an old piston. Do not push ring into bore more than 3/8-1/2 in. Measure the gap with a feeler gauge (**Figure 58**) and compare to specifications (**Table 3**).

8. If ring gap is excessive in Step 7, repeat the step with the ring in another cylinder. If gap is also excessive in that cylinder, discard and replace with a new ring.

9. If ring gap is insufficient in Step 7, the ends of the ring can be filed slightly. Clean ring thoroughly and recheck gap as in Step 7.

NOTE
The upper ring on some late-model pistons is a pressure-back type and has a tapered groove which cannot be checked in Step 10.

10. Once the ring gaps are correctly established, roll the lower ring around the piston pin groove to check for binding or tightness. See **Figure 59**.

11. Install the lower ring on the piston with a ring expander. Spread the ring just enough to fit it over the piston head and into position. See **Figure 60**.

12. Repeat Step 11 to install the remaining ring on 2-ring pistons; repeat the step twice to install the remaining rings on 3-ring pistons.

13. Position each ring so the piston groove locating pin fits in the ring gap. See **Figure 61**. Proper ring positioning is nessary to minimize compression loss and prevent the ring ends from catching on the cylinder ports.

14. Coat the piston and cylinder bore with Johnson or Evinrude 50/1 oil, then proceed as follows:

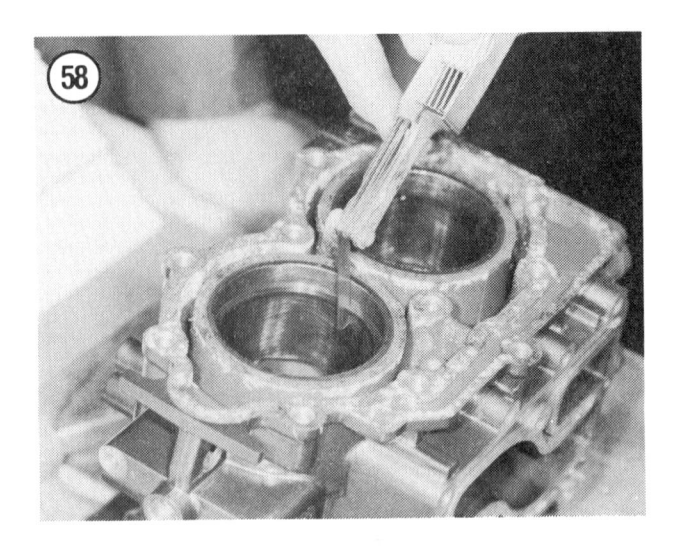

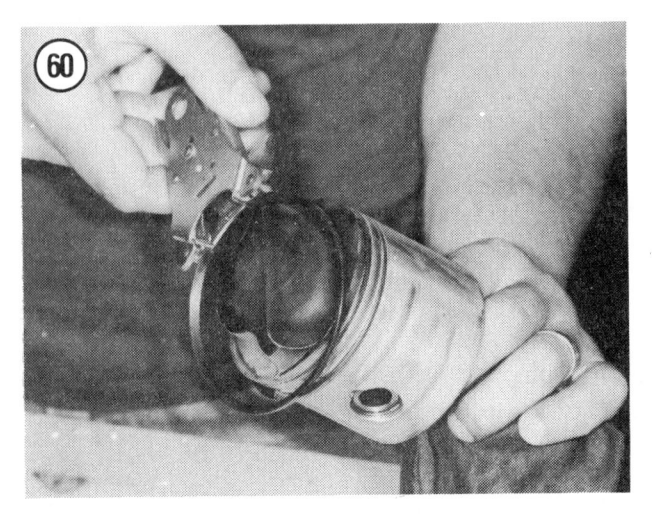

POWER HEAD

Figure 61
a. Ring groove locating pin

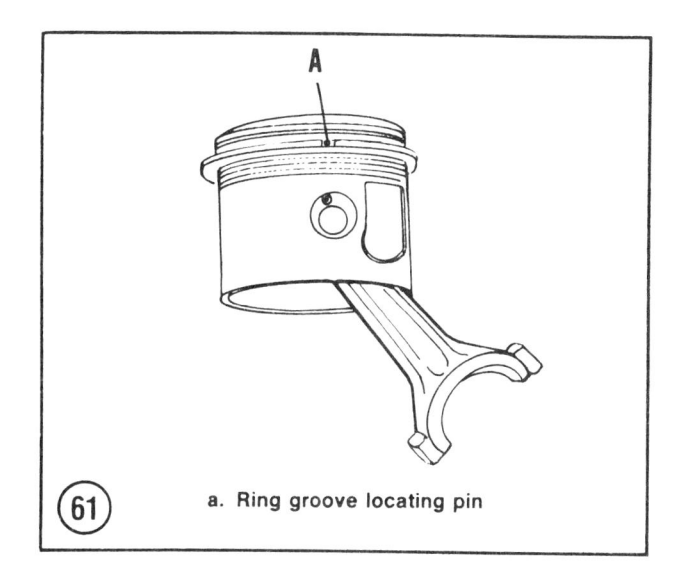

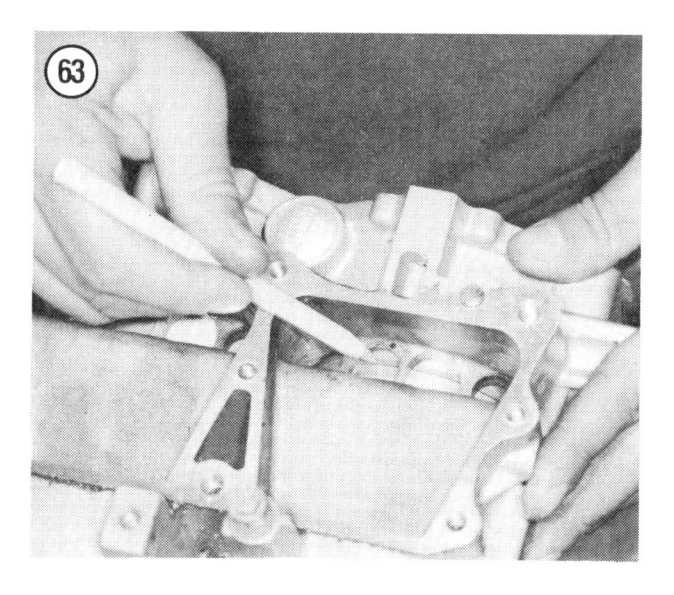

Figure 62

Figure 63

a. Check the piston dome number made during disassembly and match piston with its correct cylinder.
b. Orient exhaust side of piston to exhaust port side of cylinder block.
c. Make sure connecting rod oil hole faces flywheel end of engine.
d. Insert piston into cylinder bore. Recheck ring gap and groove locating pin alignment.
e. Install a suitable ring compressor tool (available from your dealer) over the piston dome and rings (on one-cylinder pistons, it is possible to carefully compress the rings by hand without the use of a ring compressor tool).
f. Hold connecting rod end with one hand to prevent it from scraping or scratching the cylinder bore and slowly push piston into cylinder. See **Figure 62**.

15. Remove the ring installer tool and repeat Step 14 to install the remaining pistons on multi-cylinder engines.

16. Reach through the exhaust port and lightly depress each ring with a pencil point or small screwdriver blade. See **Figure 63** (typical). The ring should snap back when pressure is released. If it does not, the ring was broken during piston installation and will have to be replaced.

17. Temporarily reinstall the cylinder head(s) with 2 screws to prevent the pistons from slipping out while the crankshaft is being installed.

Connecting Rod and Crankshaft Assembly (All Engines)

If engine uses babbitt (non-roller) main and/or rod bearings, omit all bearing installation steps in the following procedure.

1. 1.5-2 hp—Install new upper main bearing (lettered side up) through the bottom of the crankcase. Work carefully to prevent losing

the bearing needles and press the bearing case until it is recessed 1/16 in. below the crankcase finish thrust surface. Install a new oil seal with its lip facing inward until flush with the top of the crankcase.

2. 4-40 hp—Reinstall upper and lower main ball bearings on crankshaft, if removed. Install new upper oil seal with its lip facing inward.

3. V4—If lower crankshaft bearing was removed, install retainer plate and press bearing on crankshaft. Install a new snap ring and lubricate the bearing with Johnson or Evinrude 50/1 oil. See **Figure 64**.

4. V4—Install lower crankcase head with new O-rings. Align holes in retainer plate and crankcase head. Install new retainer plate screws tightly, then back off each screw 2 turns.

5. V4—Install new upper crankcase head seal with appropriate installer. Seal lip should face inward and be flush with top of crankcase head. Install upper crankcase head and bearing assembly on crankshaft.

6. 55-65 hp inline engine—Install new upper main bearing seal with appropriate installer. Seal lip should face inward.

7. Install a new O-ring on the upper bearing, if used.

8. Remove connecting rod caps. Coat connecting rod bearing surfaces with OMC Needle Bearing Grease and install bearing retainer half. Install needle bearings. Repeat this step for each connecting rod.

9A. If crankshaft center main bearing(s) use a sleeve and retainer ring, install bearings, fit sleeves into position with retaining ring groove toward the bottom of the crankshaft and install retainer ring(s) in sleeve groove(s).

9B. If center main bearing does not use a sleeve and retainer ring, install the center main bearing liner in the block with its pointed end facing the intake side. The locating flange should engage the locating pocket. Install the bearing cage and roller assembly on the liner. See **Figure 65**.

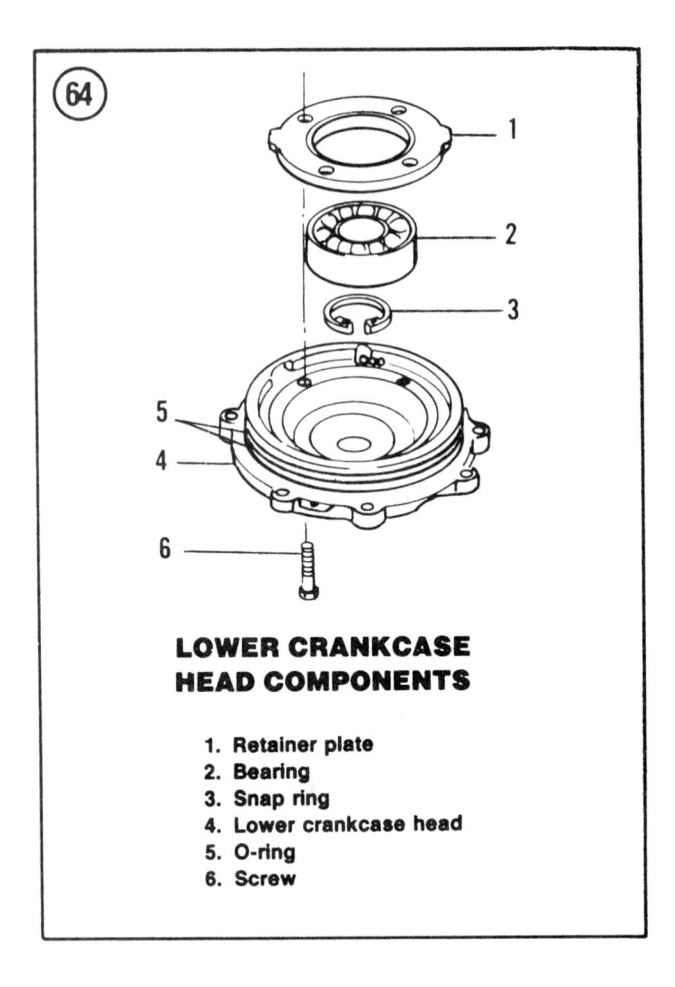

10. Coat outer edge of top crankshaft seal with OMC Gasket Sealing Compound.

NOTE
Locations of upper and lower bearing holes and dowel pins vary according to model. Determine which is in the block and align the bearings accordingly so pin and hole will mate when crankshaft is installed in Step 11.

11. Lubricate the crankshaft assembly with Johnson or Evinrude 50/1 oil and install in cylinder block. Align upper and lower main bearing dowels and pin holes, if used. See **Figure 66** (typical). On crankshafts with a center main bearing sleeve retainer ring, align hole in sleeve with dowel pin in block. Carefully seat crankshaft in place.

64

LOWER CRANKCASE HEAD COMPONENTS

1. Retainer plate
2. Bearing
3. Snap ring
4. Lower crankcase head
5. O-ring
6. Screw

POWER HEAD

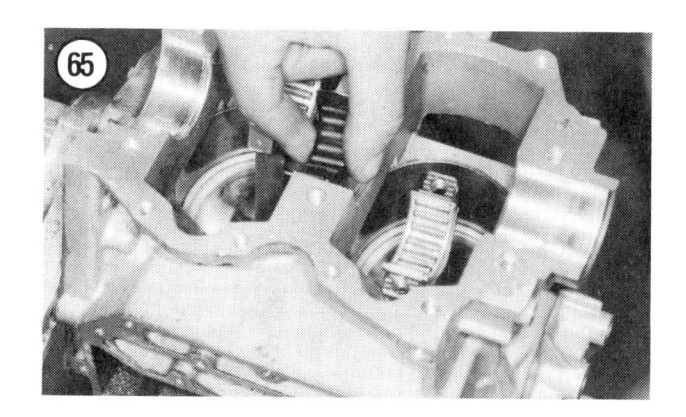

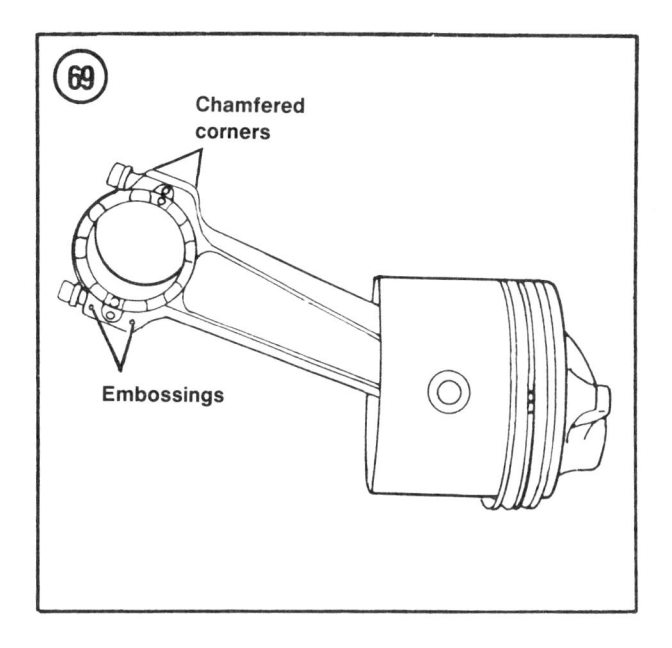

Chamfered corners

Embossings

12. If crankshaft does not use a retainer sleeve ring, coat the main bearing journal with OMC Needle Bearing Grease and install remaining retainer half, needle bearings and sleeve. See **Figure 67** (typical).

13. Draw connecting rod(s) up around crankshaft crankpin journal. Coat crankpins with OMC Needle Bearing Grease and install remaining retainer halves and needle bearings on each crankpin. See **Figure 68** (typical).

14. Orient the connecting rod cap according to the small raised dots and marks made during disassembly. See **Figure 69**. Install the caps with new screws finger-tight.

CAUTION
The procedure detailed in Steps 15-17 is critical to proper engine operation as it affects bearing action. If not done properly, major engine damage can result. It can also be a time-consuming and frustrating process. Work slowly and with patience. If alignment was satisfactory when checked during disassembly, it should be possible to achieve a similar alignment on reassembly.

15. Run a pencil point or dental pick over the chamfers on each rod and cap to check

alignment (**Figure 70**). Refer to notes made during disassembly. Rod and cap must be aligned so that the pencil point or dental pick will pass smoothly across the break line on at least 3 of the 4 corners.

16. If rod and cap alignment is not satisfactory in Step 15, gently tap cap in direction required with a soft mallet and recheck alignment. Repeat this procedure as many times as necessary to achieve alignment of at least 3 corners.

17. If satisfactory alignment cannot be achieved in Step 15 or Step 16, replace the connecting rod and cap.

18. Once rod and cap alignment is correct, carefully torque rod caps to specifications in three stages, repeating Step 15 after each stage to make sure that torque application has not affected rod/cap chamfer alignment. Bend bolt locking tabs upward, if used.

19. 1.5-2 hp—Install lower bearing housing with a new gasket and tighten to specifications (**Table 1**).

20. Rotate the crankshaft to check for binding. If the crankshaft does not float freely over the full length of the crankpin(s), loosen the rod cap(s) and repeat Steps 15-18.

Cylinder Block and Crankcase Assembly (General Procedures)

The cylinder head gasket on some models may be impregnated with sealant during manufacture and requires no additional sealer when installed. Check the gasket package to determine if it is this type.

All gaskets which have not been impregnated with sealant should be lightly coated on both sides with OMC Gasket Sealing Compound. The outer diameter of the crankshaft upper seal should also be coated with OMC Gasket Sealing Compound.

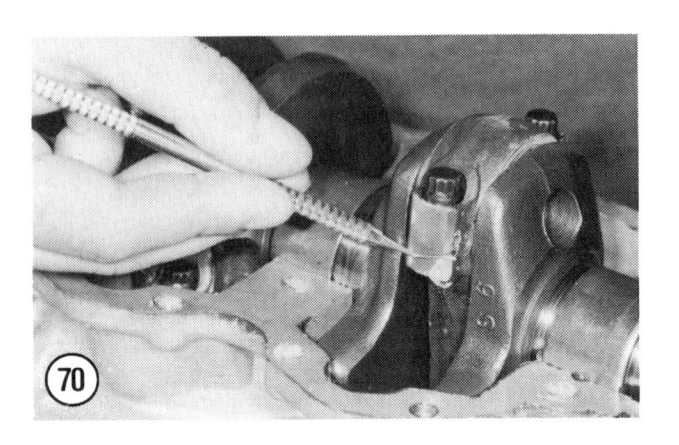

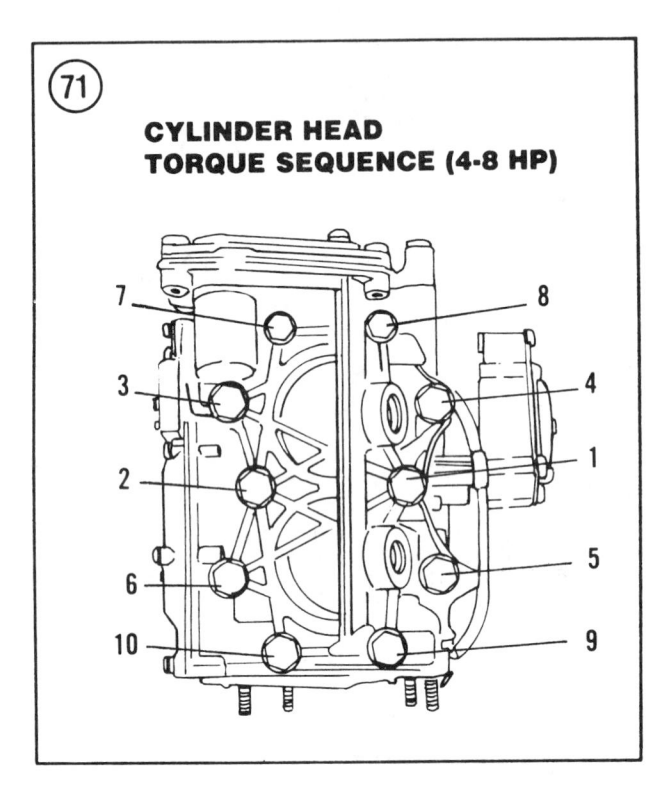

The crankcase face on some models is grooved for the use of a spaghetti or rubber seal. The new seal should be fully seated in the grooves and then cut 1/2 in. longer at each end to assure a good butt seal against both crankcase bearings. Run a thin bead of Sealer 1000 or OMC Adhesive M in the groove before installing the seal. Force the seal into the groove and let it set 15-20 minutes. Trim the ends of the seal with a sharp knife, leaving about 1/32 in. of the seal end to butt against the bearings. Apply

POWER HEAD

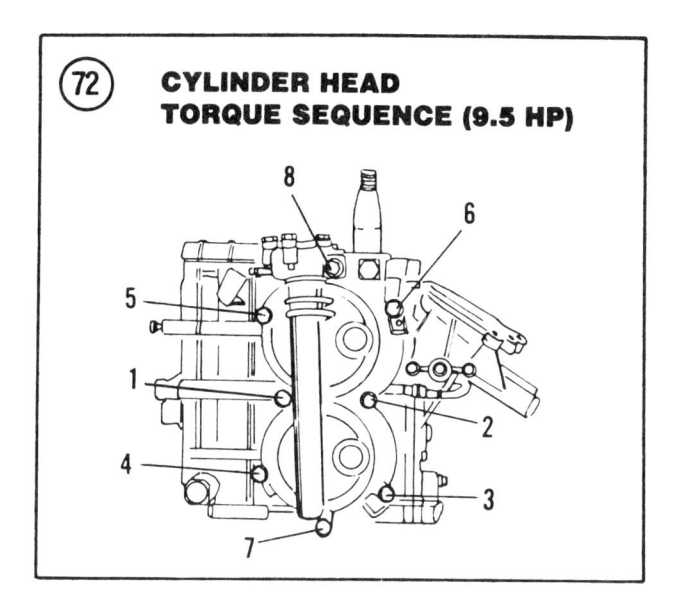

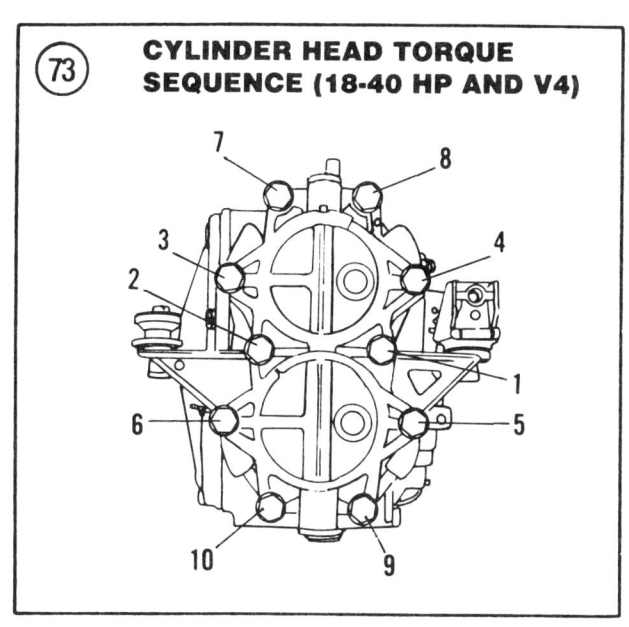

72 CYLINDER HEAD TORQUE SEQUENCE (9.5 HP)

73 CYLINDER HEAD TORQUE SEQUENCE (18-40 HP AND V4)

another thin bead of Sealer 1000 or OMC Adhesive M to the crankcase face. Use care not to apply an excessive amount, as it can squeeze over when the parts are mated and may block oil or water passages.

Cylinder Block and Crankcase Assembly (1.5 and 2 hp)

1. Install the cylinder head with a new gasket.

2. Install the intake manifold and reed valve assembly with a new gasket.
3. Install the exhaust cover with a new gasket.
4. Tighten all fasteners to specifications (**Table 1**).
5. Install the magneto cam drive pin and cam. Cam side marked "TOP" must face the flywheel.
6. Install the power head as described in this chapter.

Cylinder Block and Crankcase Assembly (3-20 hp)

1. Install crankcase cover to cylinder block. Install bolts finger-tight, then install crankcase taper pin(s) with a mallet and punch. Tighten bolts to specifications (**Table 1**).
2. Install the oil drain valve, if so equipped.
3. Install lower bearing snap ring in crankcase, if used, with beveled edge facing out.
4. Install lower crankshaft seal (lip facing out) until it bottoms on the snap ring.
5. Rotate the crankshaft several turns to check for binding. If crankshaft does not turn easily, disassemble and correct the interference.
6. Remove the cylinder head temporarily installed to hold the pistons in place during crankshaft installation. Reinstall with a new gasket. Tighten bolts to specifications (**Table 1**) following the sequence shown in **Figures 71-73** as appropriate.
7. Install the cylinder head cover with a new gasket, if so equipped.
8. If equipped with a thermostat, install the thermostat with a new seal. Install the thermostat cap with a new gasket.
9. Install inner exhaust cover with an new gasket (if so equipped). Install intermediate exhaust cover with a new gasket (if so equipped). Install outer exhaust cover with a

new gasket. Tighten all fasteners finger-tight, then torque to specifications (**Table 1**).
10. Install the bypass covers with new gaskets, if so equipped.
11. Reinstall crankcase hose with new clamps.
12. Install inner flange, if so equipped, and tighten screws to specifications (**Table 1**).
13. Install the power head as described in this chapter.

Cylinder Block and Crankcase Assembly (28-40 hp)

1A. Grooved crankcase flange—Install a new spaghetti seal with Sealer 1000 or OMC Adhesive M as described in this chapter.
1B. Smooth crankcase flange—Install with a new gasket in Step 2.
2. Install crankcase cover to cylinder block. Install bolts finger-tight, then install crankcase taper pins with a mallet and punch.
3. Tap the bottom of the crankshaft with a mallet to seat the lower main bearing. Wipe the threads of all bolts which enter the crankcase cavity through holes with Sealer 1000 or OMC Adhesive M as required, then tighten to specifications (**Table 1**). Start with the center bolts and work outwards in a clockwise direction.
4. If the seal was not removed from the lower crankcase head (**Figure 74**) during disassembly, drive it out with a punch and mallet. Clean the seal bore and wipe the outer diameter of a new seal with OMC Gasket Sealing Compound. Install seal in crankcase head with a suitable installer with lip facing out.
5. Lubricate new O-rings with Johnson or Evinrude 50/1 oil and install on crankcase head.
6. Install the lower crankcase head with OMC Gasket Sealing Compound on the screw threads. See **Figure 75**. Tighten to specifications (**Table 1**).

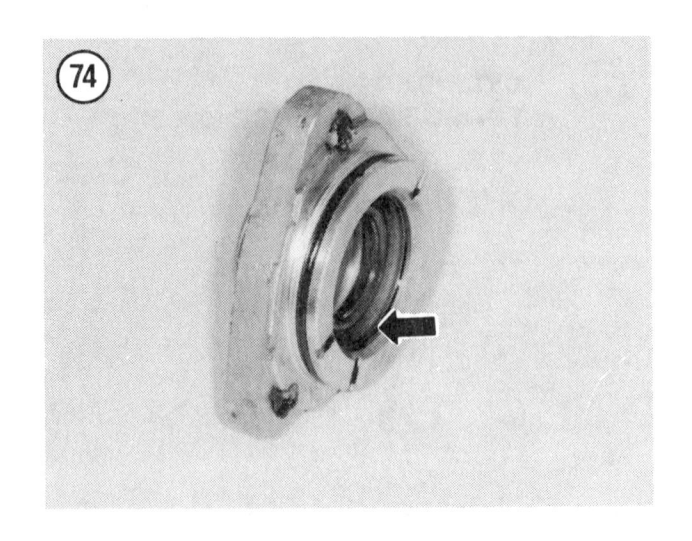

NOTE
If cylinders have been honed, crankshaft will be more difficult to turn by hand in Step 7. In this case, temporarily install flywheel and crankshaft should turn with a minimal effort.

7. Rotate the crankshaft several turns to check for binding. If crankshaft does not turn easily, disassemble and correct the interference.
8. Remove the cylinder head temporarily installed to hold the pistons in place during crankshaft installation. Reinstall with a new gasket. Tighten bolts to specifications (**Table 1**) following the sequence shown in **Figure 73**.
9. If equipped with a thermostat, install with a new seal in the cylinder head cavity. Install the cap with a new gasket.
10. Install the cylinder head cover with a new gasket.
11. Install the inner and outer exhaust covers with new gaskets. Tighten fasteners to specifications (**Table 1**).
12. Install the bypass covers with new gaskets, if so equipped. Tighten fasteners to specifications (**Table 1**).
13. Install the reed valve assembly with a new gasket. Wipe attaching threads with Permatex No. 2 or equivalent and tighten screw securely.

POWER HEAD

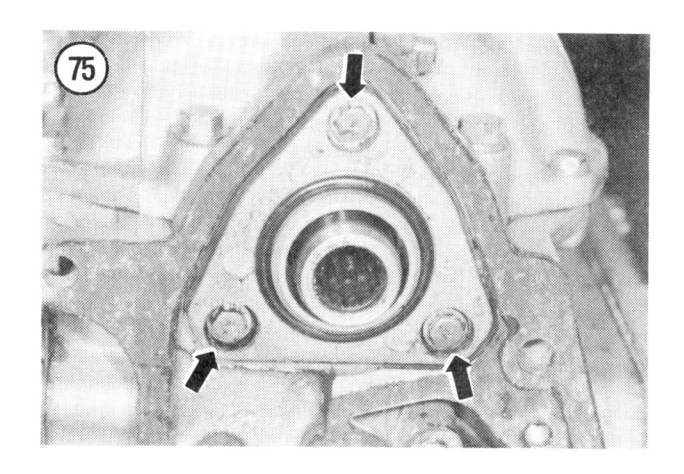

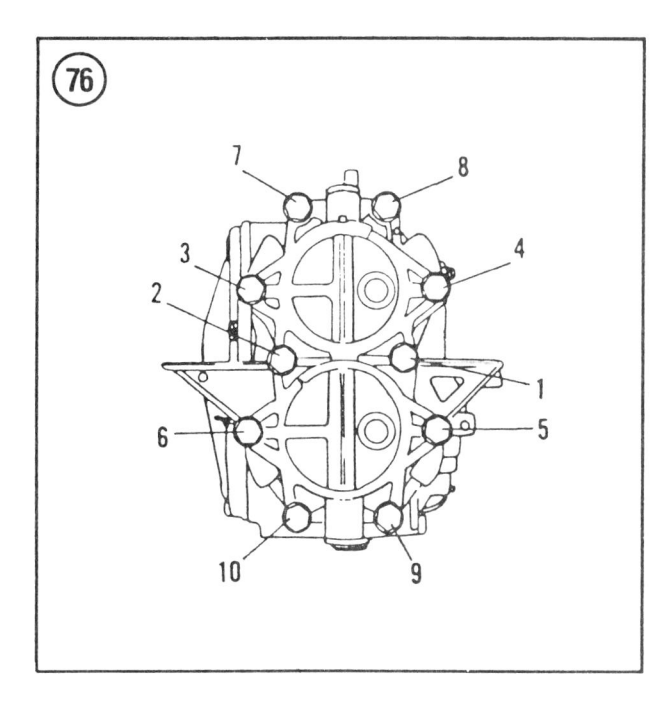

75

76

14. Install the intake manifold with a new gasket. Tighten fasteners to specifications (**Table 1**).

15. Connect intake crankcase oil return or recirculation hoses with new clamps.

16. Adjust the cut-out circuit safety switch and install the power head as described in this chapter.

Cylinder Block and Crankcase Assembly (55, 60 and 65 hp Inline)

1. Install a new spaghetti seal with Sealer 1000 or OMC Adhesive M as described in this chapter. Apply a very thin bead of the sealer to the crankcase flange.

2. Install crankcase cover to cylinder block. Install bolts finger-tight, then install crankcase taper pins with a mallet and punch.

3. Tap the bottom of the crankshaft with a mallet to seat the bearings, then temporarily install flywheel and rotate the crankshaft to check for binding. If crankshaft does not turn easily, disassemble and correct the interference.

4. Tighten all crankcase cover screws to specifications (**Table 1**).

5. Install the intake manifold and reed block assembly with a new gasket.

6. Remove the cylinder head temporarily installed to hold the pistons in place during crankshaft installation. Install a new head gasket.

7. Install the thermostat with a new seal. Install the thermostat spring.

8. Install the cylinder head and tighten head bolts to specifications (**Table 1**) following the sequence shown in **Figure 76**.

9. Install the motor temperature and choke thermal switches.

10. Install the cylinder head cover with a new gasket.

11. Install the inner exhaust cover, deflector and outer exhaust cover with new gaskets. Tighten fasteners to specifications (**Table 1**).

12. If the lower main bearing housing seal was not removed during disassembly, remove it with a punch and mallet. Clean the seal bore and wipe the outer diameter of a new seal with OMC Gasket Sealing Compound. Install seal in crankcase head with a suitable installer with lip facing out.

13. Lubricate new O-rings with Johnson or Evinrude 50/1 oil and install on crankcase head.

14. Install the lower crankcase head with OMC Gasket Sealing Compound on the screw threads. Tighten to specifications (**Table 1**).

15. Adjust the cut-out circuit safety switch and install the power head as described in this chapter.

Cylinder Block and Crankcase Assembly (V4)

1. Install a new spaghetti seal with Sealer 1000 or OMC Adhesive M as described in this chapter. Apply a very thin bead of the sealer to the crankcase flange.
2. Install crankcase cover to cylinder block. Install bolts finger-tight, then install crankcase taper pins with a mallet and punch.
3. Carefully install the crankcase to the cylinder block to avoid damage to the crankcase head seals. Rotate the crankcase heads to align the screw holes.
4. Install the upper and lower crankcase head screws finger-tight.
5. Install the crankcase taper pins with a mallet and punch.
6. Install the main bearing and crankcase screws finger-tight.
7. Temporarily install the flywheel and rotate the crankshaft to check for binding. If crankshaft does not turn easily, disassemble and correct the interference.
8. Tighten all crankcase-to-block screws to specifications (**Table 1**).
9. Tighten the upper and lower crankcase head screws to specifications (**Table 1**).
10. Remove the cylinder heads temporarily installed to hold the pistons in place during crankshaft installation. Install a new head gasket.
11. Install the thermostat with a new seal. Install the thermostat spring.
12. Install the cylinder heads and tighten head bolts to specifications (**Table 1**) following the sequence shown in **Figure 73**.
13. Install the cylinder head cover with a new gasket. Tighten fasteners to specifications (**Table 1**).
14. Install the water cover, exhaust and intake bypass covers with new gaskets. 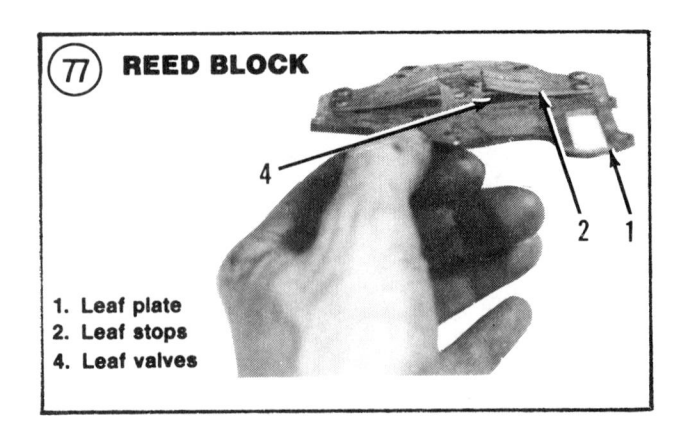 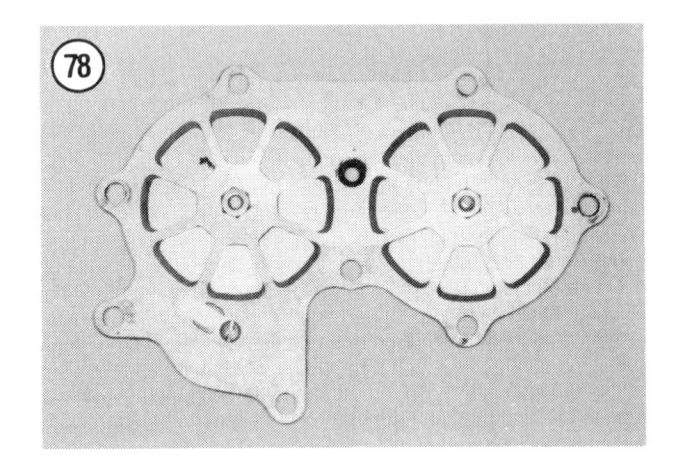
15. Reinstall recirculation hoses.
16. Adjust the cut-out circuit safety switch and install the power head as described in this chapter.

REED BLOCK SERVICE

The reed block or leaf valve assembly is located behind the intake manifold. **Figure 77** and **Figure 78** show typical 3-40 hp reed block assemblies. **Figure 79** shows a typical 55-65 hp inline reed block assembly; those used with the V4 engine are similar.

The reeds remain in constant contact with the leaf plate until a predetermined crankcase pressure is exerted on them. A reed stop limits the amount of travel from the plate. Once the crankcase pressure is removed, the reed returns to contact the plate.

Reeds and reed stops should not be disassembled from the plate for cleaning. Do

POWER HEAD

Figure 79

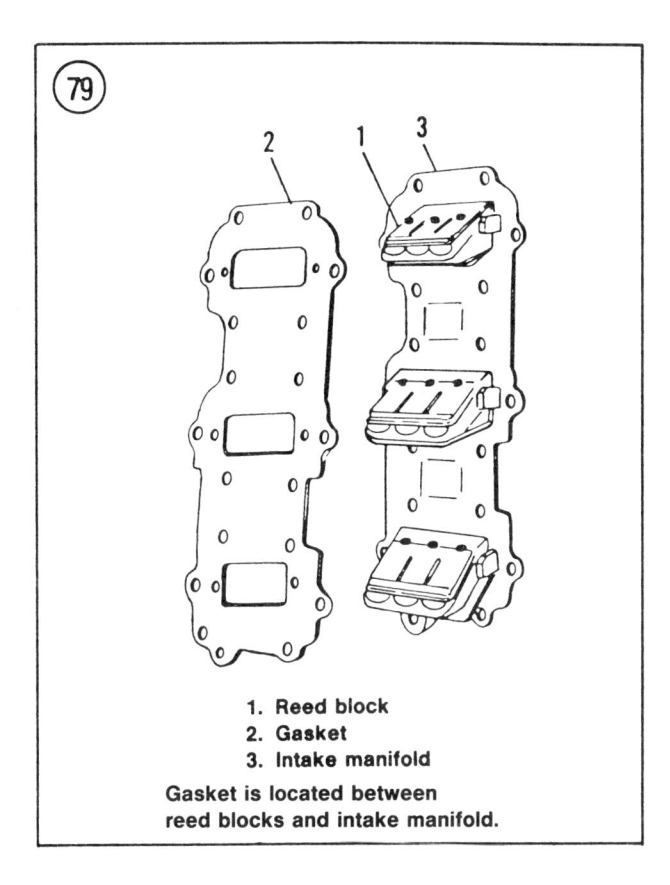

1. Reed block
2. Gasket
3. Intake manifold

Gasket is located between reed blocks and intake manifold.

Figure 80

- Pressure valve
- Pressure valve spring
- Vernatherm control element
- Thermostat valve
- Thermostat spring

the screws holding the reed blocks to the intake manifold. Carefully clean all components in OMC Engine Tuner and reassemble with a new intake manifold gasket.

Some reed blocks contain a recirculation valve hole and reed; others may use a recirculation valve and screen assembly. These require no service beyond an occasional cleaning in OMC Engine Tuner to remove any gum or varnish.

THERMOSTAT SERVICE

V4 thermostats and pressure valves are a part of the exhaust housing adapter. Inline engines have a thermostat in the cylinder head. A temperature switch in the cylinder head (No. 3 cylinder on V4 engines) is connected to a warning horn or lamp in the remote control box. Whenever water jacket temperatures exceed the temperature switch rating, the warning horn will sound or the lamp will light to alert the user to potential engine damage from overheating. The thermostat and pressure valve should be serviced whenever the power head is removed or when engine overheating is indicated.

NOTE
*Inline engine thermostat removal/installation is described under **Power Head Disassembly** and **Cylinder Block and Crankcase Assembly** in this chapter.*

Removal/Installation (V4 Engines)

Refer to **Figure 80** for this procedure.
1. Remove the power head as described in this chapter.
2. Remove the thermostat housing fasteners.
3. Tap the cover with a soft hammer to break the gasket seal, then remove the cover.
4. Remove the pressure valve and spring, thermostat and spring and control element. Remove and discard the gaskets.

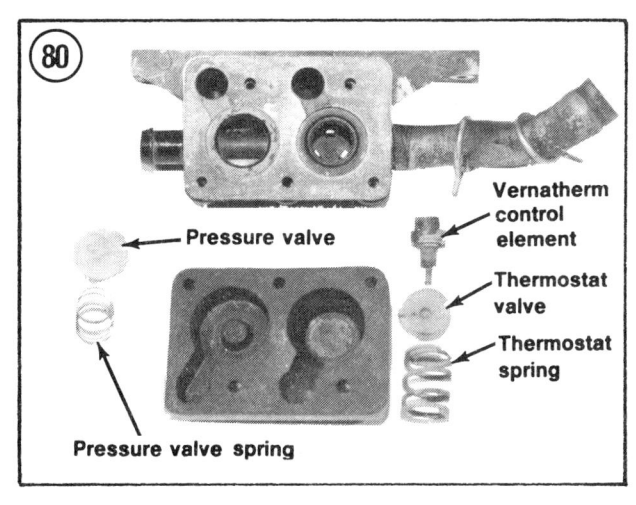

not attempt to bend or flex the reeds if they are distorted and won't contact the plate as designed. If the reeds or reed stops are defective, replace the entire assembly.

Whenever the intake manifold is removed, inspect the reed blocks for signs of gum or varnish and broken, chipped or distorted reeds. If gum or varnish is present, remove

5. Clean all gasket residue from the exhaust housing adapter, valve body and thermostat cover mating surfaces.
6. Clean and inspect the thermostat as described in this chapter.
7. Installation is the reverse of removal. Coat both sides of a new valve body-to-adapter gasket with OMC Gasket Sealing Compound. Start and run the engine in a test tank or in the water and check for leakage.

Cleaning and Inspection

1. Remove the thermostat (A, **Figure 81**) as described in this chapter.
2. Discard the gasket or seal (B, **Figure 81**).
3. Wash thermostat in clean water.
4. Test thermostat if suspected of malfunctioning. See Chapter Three.
5. Check thermostat spring (C, **Figure 81**) for loss of tension, distortion or corrosion. Replace as required.
6. Repeat Step 5 to check pressure valve spring.

SAFETY SWITCH

A cut-out circuit is used to prevent the engine from reaching full throttle under a high crankcase vacuum condition. This circuit consists of a vacuum switch and a safety switch installed on the power head. **Figure 82** shows a typical vacuum switch installation; the safety switch is installed on a bracket under the flywheel on 2-cylinder engines (**Figure 83**) or distributor on V4 engines (**Figure 84**). The safety switch also functions as part of the starting circuit. See Chapter Seven.

Adjustment

The safety switch should be adjusted so that it will open and momentarily short out the lower cylinder breaker point when its plunger reaches the mid-point of the shifter

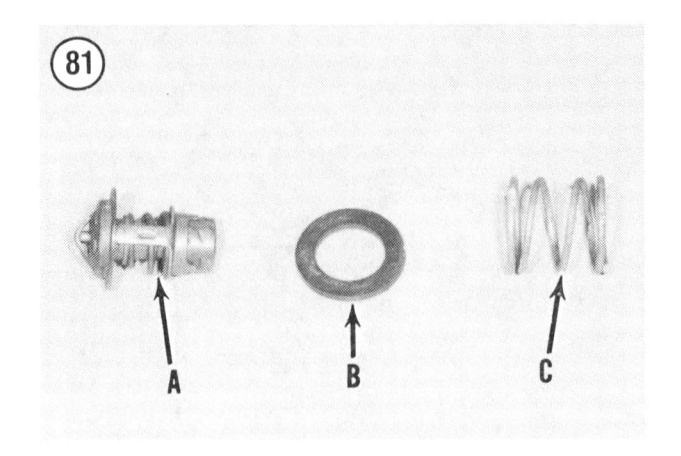

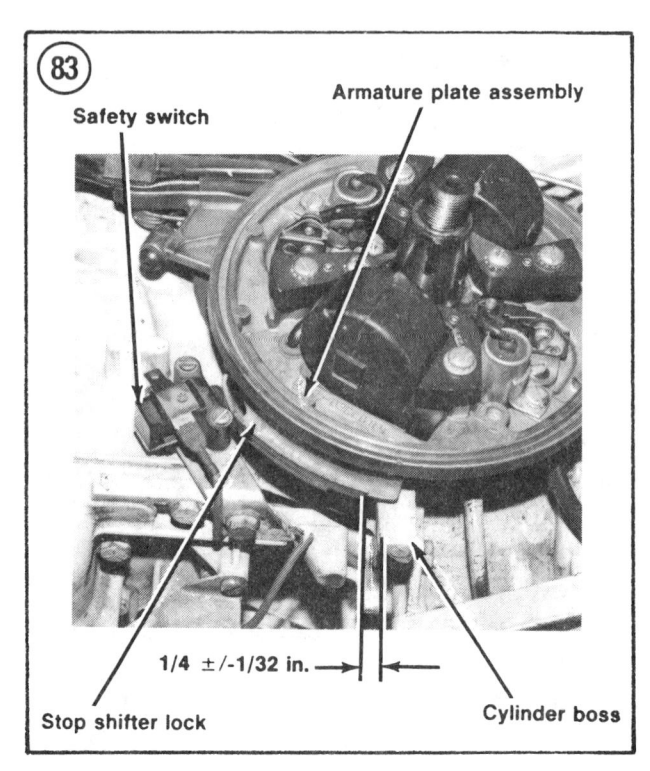

POWER HEAD

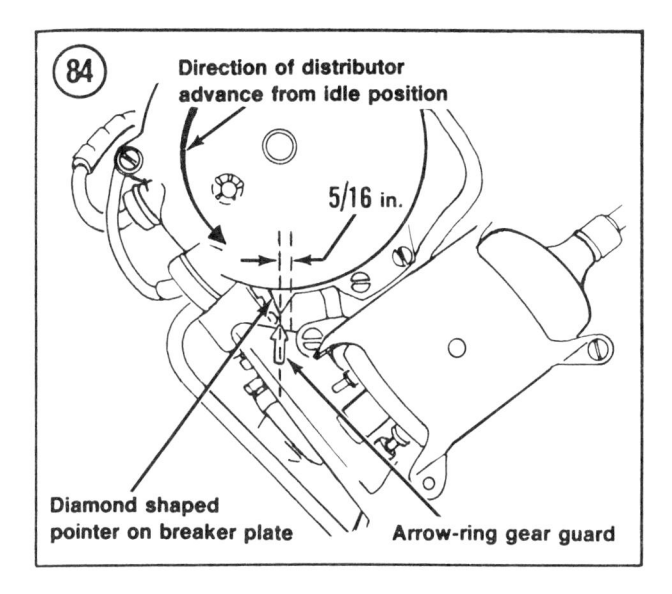

Figure 84 (labeled): Direction of distributor advance from idle position; 5/16 in.; Diamond shaped pointer on breaker plate; Arrow-ring gear guard

lock stop slope (2-cylinder) or distributor cam slope (V4).

1. Connect a test lamp between the switch terminal and ground. The lamp should light.

2A. 2-cylinder—Slowly advance the armature plate from its idle position until the end of the shifter lock stop is 1/4 in. from the cylinder boss. See **Figure 83**. At this point, the test lamp should go out, indicating a break in continuity.

2B. V4 magneto ignition—Slowly advance the distributor from its idle position until the switch plunger reaches the mid-point of the cam slope. At this point, the test lamp should go out, indicating a break in continuity.

2C. V4 battery ignition—Slowly advance the distributor from its idle position until the breaker plate pointer is 5/16 in. beyond the ring gear cover arrow. See **Figure 84**. At this point, the test lamp should go out, indicating a break in continuity.

3. If the switch does not perform as described above, loosen the mounting screws and position the switch as required. Move the switch toward the shifter lock cam (2-cylinder) or distributor (V4) if the switch opens too early. Move the switch away if it opens too late.

Tables are on the following pages.

Table 1 POWER HEAD TIGHTENING TORQUES

Fastener	in.-lb.	ft.-lb.
Connecting rod		
3 hp	60-96	
1.5-7.5 hp	60-66	
9.5 hp	90-100	
10-25 and 30 hp	180-186	
28, 33 and 40 hp		29-31
35 hp		18
50 hp		22
75 hp		
1960-1961		22
1962-1965		30
All others		30
Cylinder head bolts		
3, 5.5 and 7.5 hp	60-84	
1.5, 2, 4, 5 and 6 hp	60-80	
9.5-25 hp	96-120	
28, 33 and 40 hp		14-16
30 and 35 hp		18-20
50-125 hp		15
Crankcase-to-cylinder bolts		
3, 5.5 and 7.5 hp	60-84	
1.5, 2, 4, 5 and 6 hp	60-80	
9.5-15 and 25 hp		10-12
18 hp		
1957-1970		10-12
1971-1972		
Upper/lower		9-11
Lower		10-11
20 hp		
1966-1970		9-11
1971-1972		
Upper/lower		9-11
Center		10-11
28 and 35 hp		13.5-14
30 hp		
Upper/lower		12-14
Center		13.5-14
33 and 40 hp		
Upper/lower		12.5-15
Lower		13.5-14
55 and 60 hp		13
All others		
Upper/lower		13
Center		14
Standard torque values		
No. 6	7-10	
No. 8	15-22	
No. 10	25-35	
No. 12	35-40	
1/4 in.	60-80	5-7
5/16 in.	120-140	10-12
3/8 in.	220-240	18-20
7/16 in.	340-360	28-30

Power Head

Table 2 FLYWHEEL NUT TORQUE

	ft.-lb.
1.5-2 hp	22-25
4 hp	30-40
3, 4-25 hp	40-45
28, 33 and 40 hp	100-105
30 and 35 hp	60-65
50 hp, 1964-1967 60 hp, 75, 80 and 90 hp	80
85 hp	
1968	80
1969-1972	100
100 hp	
1966-1967	80
1968	100
All others	100

Table 3 POWER HEAD SPECIFICATIONS

Model	Stroke	Bore	Piston-to-cylinder clearance (in.)
1.5 hp			
1968	1.37	1.56	0.0013-0.0025
1969-1970	1.37	1.56	0.0043-0.0055
2 hp	1.37	1.56	0.0043-0.0055
3 hp			
1956-1967	1.37	1.56	0.0013-0.0020
1968	1.37	1.56	0.0013-0.0025
4 hp			
1969	1.37	1.56	0.0014-0.0049
1970	1.37	1.56	0.0020-0.008
1971-1972	1.37	1.56	0.0018-0.0030
5 and 6 hp	1.50	1.94	0.0018-0.0030
5.5 hp	1.50	1.94	0.0013-0.0025
7.5 hp	1.75	2.12	0.0015-0.0030
9.5 hp			
1968	1.81	2.31	0.0030-0.0045
1969-1972	1.81	2.31	0.0035-0.0050
10 hp	1.875	2.37	0.0030-0.0035
15 hp	2.50	2.37	0.0030-0.0035
18 hp			
1957-1964	2.25	2.50	0.0035-0.0040
1965-1968	2.25	2.50	0.0030-0.0045
1969-1970	2.25	2.50	0.0032-0.0047
1971-1972	2.25	2.50	0.0033-0.0048
20 hp			
1966-1968	2.25	2.50	0.0030-0.0045
1969-1970	2.25	2.50	0.0032-0.0047
1971-1972	2.25	2.50	0.0033-0.0048
25 hp			
1969-1970	2.25	2.50	0.0033-0.0045
1971-1972	2.25	2.50	0.0033-0.0048

(continued)

Table 3 POWER HEAD SPECIFICATIONS (continued)

Model	Stroke	Bore	Piston-to-cylinder clearance (in.)
28 and 30 hp	2.75	2.875	0.0025-0.0040
33 hp	2.75	3.06	0.0030-0.0045
35 hp	2.75	3.06	0.0035-0.0040
40 hp			
1960-1961	2.75	3.19	0.0035-0.0040
1962-1970	2.75	3.19	0.0030-0.0045
1971-1972	2.82	3.19	0.0030-0.0050
50 hp	2.50	3.00	0.0035-0.0040
55 hp			
1968	2.34	3.00	0.0040-0.0055
1969	2.34	3.00	0.0040-0.0055
60 hp			
1964-1967	2.50	3.00	0.0035-0.0050
1970	2.34	3.00	0.0035-0.0050
1971	2.34	3.00	0.0035-0.0050
65 hp	2.50	3.00	0.0035-0.0050
75 hp			
1960-1961	2.34	3.375	0.0045-0.0060
1962-1965	2.34	3.375	0.0045-0.0060
80 hp			
1966	2.50	3.375	0.0045-0.0060
1967	2.50	3.375	0.0025-0.0040
85 hp			
1968	2.50	3.375	0.0025-0.0040
1969	2.59	3.375	0.0040-0.0055
1970	2.59	3.375	0.0025-0.0040
1971-1972	2.59	3.375	0.0025-0.0040
90 hp	2.50	3.375	0.0045-0.0060
100 hp			
1966-1967	2.50	3.375	0.0045-0.0060
1968	2.50	3.375	0.0025-0.0040
1971	2.59	3.375	0.0025-0.0040
1972	2.59	3.375	0.0025-0.0040
115 hp			
1969	2.59	3.44	0.0040-0.0055
1970	2.59	3.44	0.0035-0.0050
125 hp			
1971	2.59	3.50	0.0030-0.0045
1972	2.59	3.50	0.0025-0.0040

Model	Ring groove (in.)	Ring width (in.)	Ring gap (in.)
1968	0.0010-0.0035	0.0925-0.0935	0.005-0.015
1969-1970	0.0010-0.0035	0.0615-0.0625	0.005-0.015
2 hp	0.0020-0.0040	0.0615-0.0625	0.015-0.025
3 hp			
1956-1967	0.0010-0.0035	(see note 1)	0.005-0.015
1968	0.0010-0.0035	0.0925-0.0935	0.005-0.015

(continued)

POWER HEAD

Table 3 POWER HEAD SPECIFICATIONS (continued)

Model	Ring groove (in.)	Ring width (in.)	Ring gap (in.)
4 hp			
1969	0.0010-0.0035	0.0615-0.0625	0.005-0.015
1970	0.0020-0.0040	0.0615-0.0625	0.005-0.015
1971-1972	0.0020-0.0040	0.0615-0.0625	0.005-0.015
5 and 6 hp	0.0010-0.0035	0.0925-0.0935	0.005-0.015
5.5 hp	0.0010-0.0035	0.0925-0.0935	0.005-0.015
7.5 hp	0.0010-0.0035	(see note 1)	0.005-0.015
9.5 hp			
1968	0.0010-0.0035	0.0925-0.0935	0.007-0.017
1969-1972	0.0010-0.0035	0.0925-0.0935	0.007-0.017
10 hp	0.0015-0.0030	(see note 1)	0.007-0.017
15 hp	0.0015-0.0030	(see note 1)	0.007-0.017
18 hp			
1957-1964	0.0015-0.0030	0.0925-0.0935	0.007-0.017
1965-1968	0.0010-0.0035	0.0925-0.0935	0.007-0.017
1969-1970	0.0020-0.0040	0.0615-0.0625	0.007-0.017
1971-1972	0.0020-0.0040	(see note 2)	0.007-0.017
20 hp			
1966-1968	0.0010-0.0035	0.0615-0.0625	0.007-0.017
1969-1970	0.0020-0.0040	0.0615-0.0625	0.007-0.017
1971-1972	0.0020-0.0040	(see note 2)	0.007-0.017
25 hp			
1969-1970	0.0020-0.0040	0.0615-0.0625	0.007-0.017
1971-1972	0.0020-0.0040	(see note 2)	0.007-0.017
28 and 30 hp	0.0045-0.0070	(see note 1)	0.007-0.017
33 hp	0.0045-0.0070	0.0925-0.0935	0.007-0.017
35 hp	0.0050-0.0065	(see note 1)	0.007-0.017
40 hp			
1960-1961	0.0050-0.0065	(see note 1)	0.007-0.017
1962-1970	0.0020-0.0045	0.0925-0.0935	0.007-0.017
1971-1972	0.0015-0.0040	(see note 2)	0.007-0.017
50 hp	0.0050-0.0065	(see note 1)	0.007-0.017
55 hp			
1968	0.0045-0.0070	0.0925-0.0935	0.007-0.017
1969	0.0010-0.0045	0.0615-0.0625	0.007-0.017
60 hp			
1964-1967	0.0045-0.0070	0.0925-0.0935	0.007-0.017
1970	0.0015-0.0045	0.0615-0.0625	0.007-0.017
1971	0.0015-0.0040	(see note 2)	0.007-0.017
65 hp	0.0045-0.0070	0.0925-0.0935	0.007-0.017
75 hp			
1960-1961	0.0045-0.0070	0.0925-0.0935	0.007-0.017
1962-1965	0.0045-0.0070	0.0925-0.0935	0.007-0.017
80 hp			
1966	0.0045-0.0070	0.0925-0.0935	0.007-0.017
1967	0.0045-0.0070	0.0925-0.0935	0.007-0.017
85 hp			
1968	0.0045-0.0070	0.0925-0.0935	0.007-0.017
1969	0.0045-0.0070	0.0930	0.007-0.017
1970	0.0045-0.0070	0.0930	0.007-0.017
1971-1972	0.0045-0.0070	0.0925-0.0935	0.007-0.017

(continued)

Table 3 POWER HEAD SPECIFICATIONS (continued)

Model	Ring groove (in.)	Ring width (in.)	Ring gap (in.)
90 hp	0.0045-0.0070	0.0925-0.0935	0.007-0.017
100 hp			
1966-1967	0.0045-0.0070	0.0925-0.0935	0.007-0.017
1968	0.0045-0.0070	0.0925-0.0935	0.007-0.017
1971	0.0045-0.0070	0.0925-0.0935	0.007-0.017
1972	0.0045-0.0070	0.0925-0.0935	0.007-0.017
115 hp			
1969	0.0045-0.0070	0.0620	0.007-0.017
1970	0.0015-0.0040	0.0620	0.007-0.017
125 hp			
1971	0.0020-0.0040	(see note 2)	0.007-0.017
1972	0.0020-0.0040	(see note 2)	0.007-0.017

1. Not available.
2. Top or top and center ring, 0.0895-0.0900 in.; bottom ring, 0.0615-0.0625 in.

Chapter Nine

Gearcase

Torque is transferred from the engine crankshaft to the gearcase by a drive shaft. A pinion gear on the drive shaft meshes with a drive gear in the gearcase to change the vertical power flow into a horizontal flow through the propeller shaft. On Johnson and Evinrude outboards with a shift capability, a sliding clutch engages a forward or reverse gear in the gearcase. This creates a direct coupling that transfers the power flow from the pinion to the propeller shaft.

The gearcases covered in this chapter differ primarily in the type of shift mechanisms used. Those used with 1.5-5 hp engines are a direct drive unit and have no shift capability; the engine is rotated 180° to operate the boat in reverse. Two types of mechanical shift gearcases are used: a single enclosed housing and a split lower unit. Electric shift gearcases containing electromagnetic coils are used on late-model 3-cylinder and V4 outboards, as well as a hydro-electrical unit containing an oil pump and selector valve solenoids.

The gearcase can be removed without removing the entire outboard from the boat.

This chapter contains removal, overhaul and installation procedures for the propeller, water pump and gearcase. **Table 1** (tightening torques) is at the end of the chapter.

The gearcases covered in this chapter differ considerably in design and construction over the years covered and thus require different service procedures. The chapter is arranged in a normal disassembly/assembly sequence according to gearcase type. When only a partial repair is required, follow the procedure(s) for your gearcase to the point where the faulty parts can be replaced, then reassemble the unit.

Since this chapter covers a wide range of models over a lengthy time period, the gearcases shown in the accompanying illustrations are the most common ones. While it is possible that the components shown in the pictures may not be identical with those being serviced, the step-by-step procedures may be used with all models covered in this manual.

SERVICE PRECAUTIONS

Whenever you work on an outboard engine, there are several good procedures to keep in mind that will make your work easier, faster and more accurate.

1. Never use self-locking nuts more than twice. It is a good idea to replace such nuts with new ones each time they are removed. Never use worn-out stop nuts or non-locking nuts.
2. Use special tools where noted. In some cases, it may be possible to perform the procedure with makeshift tools, but this procedure is not recommended. The use of makeshift tools can damage the components and may cause serious personal injury.
3. Use a vise with protective jaws to hold housings or parts. If protective jaws are not available, insert wooden blocks on either side of the part(s) before clamping them in the vise.
4. Remove and install pressed-on parts with an appropriate mandrel, support and hydraulic press. Do not try to pry, hammer or otherwise force them on or off.
5. Refer to the table at the end of the chapter for torque values, if not given in the text. Proper torque is essential to assure long life and satisfactory service from outboard components.
6. Apply OMC Gasket Sealing Compound to the outer surfaces of all bearing carrier, retainer and housing mating surfaces during reassembly, unless otherwise stated. Do *not* allow the material to touch O-rings or enter the bearings or gears.
7. Discard all O-rings and oil seals during disassembly. Apply OMC Triple-Guard grease to new O-rings and seal lips to prevent damage when the motor is first started.
8. Keep a record of any shims and where they came from. As soon as the shims are removed, inspect them for damage and write down their thickness and location. Wire the shims together for reassembly and store them in a safe place. Follow shimming instructions closely. If gear backlash is not properly set, the unit will be noisy and suffer premature gear failure. Incorrect bearing preload will result in premature bearing failure.
9. Work in an area where there is good lighting and sufficient space for component storage. Keep an ample number of clean containers available for storing small parts. Cover parts with clean shop cloths when you are not working with them.

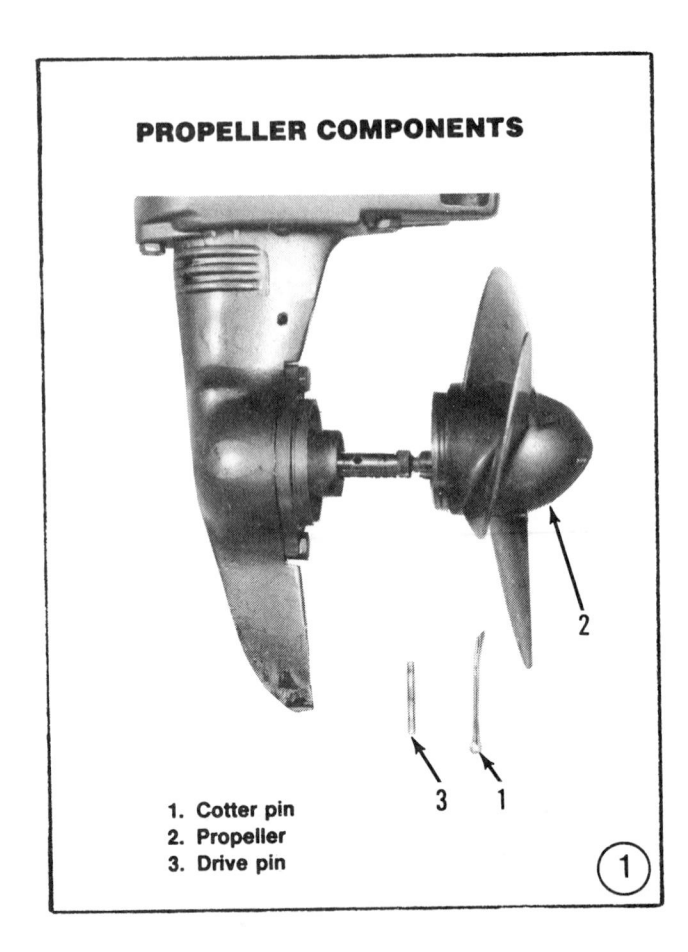

PROPELLER COMPONENTS

1. Cotter pin
2. Propeller
3. Drive pin

PROPELLER

Johnson and Evinrude outboards use variations of 2 propeller attachment designs. Smaller gearcases use a drive pin that engages a slot in the propeller hub, which is retained by a cotter pin (**Figure 1**). On some models, the cotter pin passes through a cone-type nut that is separate from the propeller.

GEARCASE

②

Cotter pin — Thrust washer — Nut — Thrust bushing

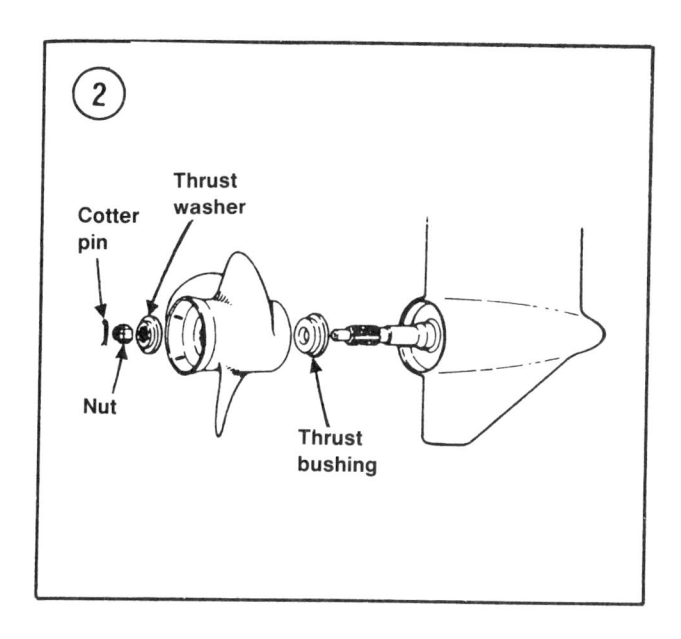

In this design, a metal pin installed in the propeller shaft engages a recessed slot in the propeller hub. As the shaft rotates, the pin rotates the propeller. The drive pin is designed to break if the propeller hits an obstruction in the water. This design has 2 advantages. The pin absorbs the impact to prevent possible propeller damage. It also alerts the user to the fact that something is wrong, since engine speed will increase if the pin breaks.

Propellers used on the larger gearcases ride on thrust bearings and are retained by a castellated nut and cotter pin (**Figure 2**). An underwater impact is absorbed by the propeller hub.

Removal/Installation

1. To remove the propeller on smaller units:
   a. Remove and discard the cotter pin.
   b. Pull the propeller or propeller and nut off the propeller shaft.
   c. Remove and discard the drive pin from the propeller shaft. Inspect the pin engagement slot in the propeller hub for wear or damage.
   d. Installation is the reverse of removal. Lubricate the propeller shaft with OMC Triple-Guard grease. Use a new drive pin and cotter pin.
2. To remove the propeller on larger units:
   a. Remove and discard the cotter pin.
   b. Remove the castellated nut.
   c. Remove the thrust washer, propeller and thrust bearing or bushing assembly from the propeller shaft.
   d. Installation is the reverse of removal. Lubricate the propeller shaft with OMC Triple-Guard grease. Tighten castellated nut finger-tight, then tighten with a wrench to align the cotter pin hole in the nut and shaft. Install a new cotter pin.

WATER PUMP

Johnson and Evinrude outboards use a volume-type or a pressure-type water pump. The 2 can be distinguished by the size and shape of the impeller. Volume-type water pumps use a thin impeller with long vanes; pressure-type pumps have a thick impeller with short vanes. Both types are serviced in essentially the same manner. An optional chrome water pump available for some models is recommended for use in areas where the water contains considerable sand or silt.

The water pump impeller is secured to the drive shaft by a key that fits between a flat area on the drive shaft and a similiar cutout in the impeller hub. As the drive shaft rotates, the impeller rotates with it. Water between the impeller blades and pump housing is pumped up to the power head through the water tube.

All seals and gaskets should be replaced whenever the water pump is removed. Since proper water pump operation is critical to outboard operation, it is also a good idea to install a new impeller at the same time.

Do not turn a used impeller over and reuse it. The impeller rotates clockwise with the drive shaft and the vanes gradually take a "set" in one direction. Turning the impeller over will cause the vanes to move in a direction opposite to that which caused the "set." This will result in premature impeller failure and can damage a power head extensively.

Removal and Disassembly (1.5-40 hp)

1. Secure the gearcase in a holding fixture or a vise with protective jaws. If protective jaws are not available, position the gearcase upright in the vise with the skeg between wooden blocks.
2. Remove the water tube from the pump housing. See **Figure 3**.

NOTE
If only the water pump is to be serviced, hold the drive shaft in place on 1.5-4 hp gearcases during Step 3 to prevent it from moving up enough to dislodge the pinion gear.

3. Remove the impeller housing screws and washers. Insert screwdrivers at the fore and aft ends of the impeller housing and pry it loose.
4. Slide the impeller and impeller housing up and off the drive shaft (**Figure 4**).

NOTE
In extreme cases, the impeller hub may have to be split with a hammer and chisel to remove it in Step 5.

5A. 1.5-2 hp gearcase—Remove the impeller from the gearcase cavity. This completes water pump disassembly on this model.
5B. All others—If the impeller did not come off with the impeller housing, carefully pry it up and off the drive shaft. Remove the drive key.
6. Remove and discard the top impeller plate gasket, if loose. See **Figure 5**. If it is not loose, remove in Step 7 with the impeller plate.

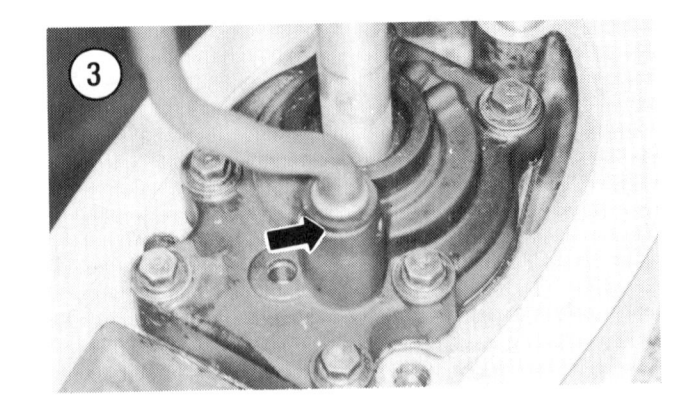

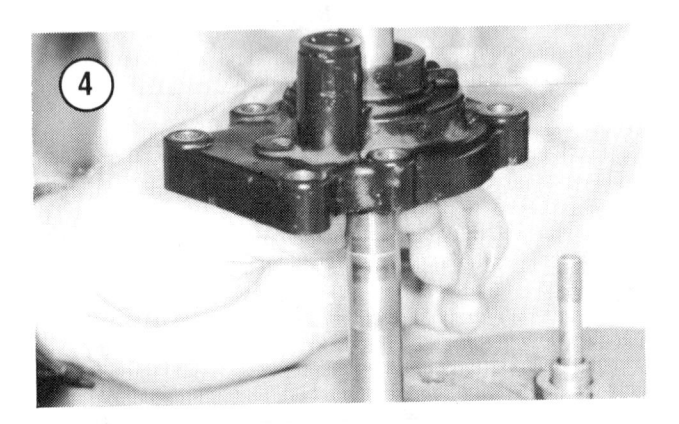

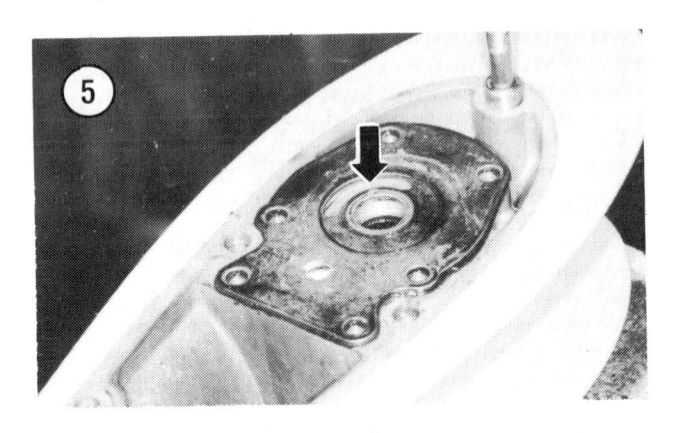

GEARCASE

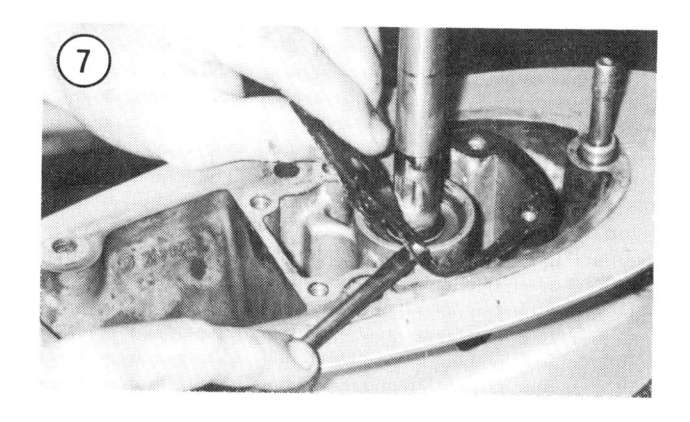

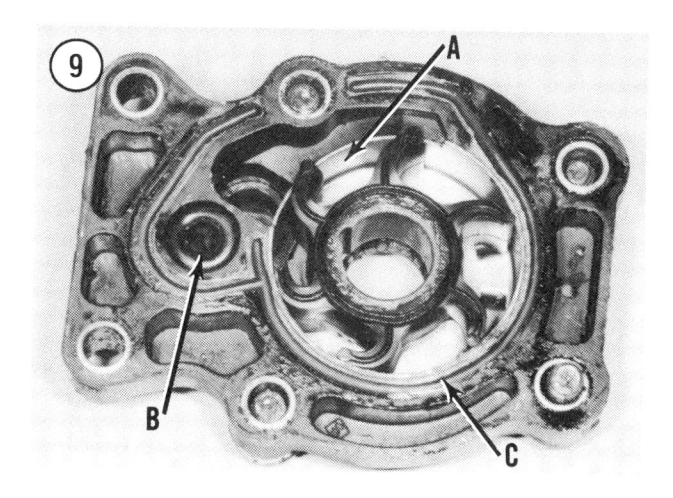

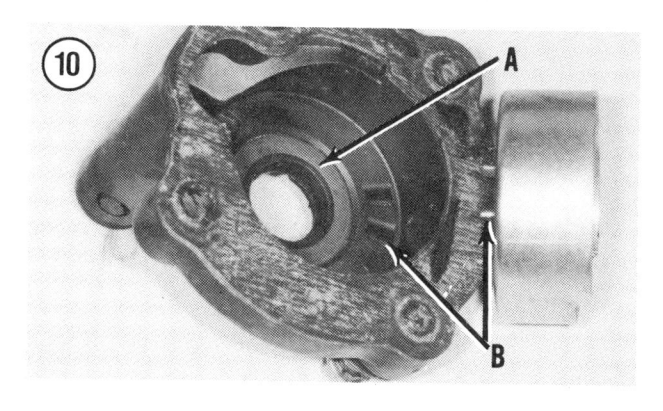

7. Carefully pry the impeller plate loose with a screwdriver (**Figure 6**), then slide the plate and gasket (if used) up and off the drive shaft. Discard the gasket.

8. If the bottom impeller plate gasket did not come free with the impeller plate, carefully loosen with a screwdriver tip and scrape off the housing. See **Figure 7**.

9. Remove the nylon water intake screen from the gearcase cavity, if so equipped. See **Figure 8** (typical).

NOTE
When removing seals from impeller housing, note and record the direction in which each seal lip faces for proper reinstallation.

10. Invert the impeller housing and remove the impeller and impeller cup (A, **Figure 9**).

11. Remove and discard the O-ring or drive shaft seal under the impeller cup, if used. The seal is shown in A, **Figure 10**.

12. Remove and discard the shift rod O-ring and bushing (B, **Figure 9**) and spaghetti seal (C, **Figure 9**), if so equipped.

13. Turn the housing right side up. Remove and discard the water tube grommet (**Figure 11**). Remove and discard the O-ring, if used.

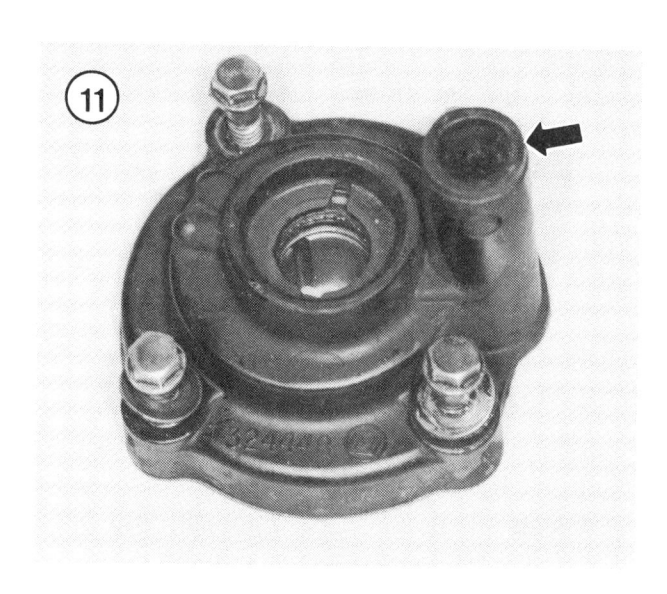

Removal and Disassembly (50-125 hp)

1. Secure the gearcase in a holding fixture or a vise with protective jaws. If protective jaws are not available, position the gearcase upright in the vise with the skeg between wooden blocks.
2. Remove the impeller housing fasteners. Insert screwdrivers at the fore and aft ends of the impeller housing and pry it loose.
3. Slide the impeller housing and impeller up and off the drive shaft. See **Figure 12** (typical).

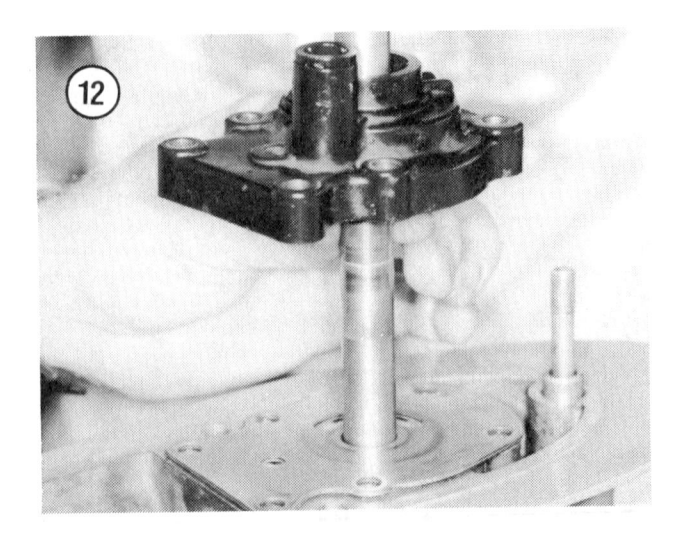

NOTE
In extreme cases, the impeller hub may have to be split with a hammer and chisel to remove it in Step 4.

4. If the impeller did not come off with the impeller housing, carefully pry it up and off the drive shaft. Remove the drive key or pin.
5. Carefully pry the impeller plate gasket loose with a screwdriver, then slide the plate and gasket (if used) up and off the drive shaft. Discard the gasket.
6. Remove the guide bracket from the impeller housing, if so equipped.
7. Remove and discard the impeller housing water tube grommet. See A, **Figure 13** (typical).
8. Remove and discard the impeller housing water tube grommet. See A, **Figure 13** (typical).
9. Remove the impeller from the housing. Remove the impeller cup and insert. See **Figure 14** (typical).

Cleaning and Inspection (All Models)

1. Check the housing for cracks, distortion or melting. Replace as required.
2. Clean all metal parts in solvent and blow dry with compressed air, if available.
3. Carefully remove all gasket residue from the mating surfaces.
4. Check impeller plate and cup for grooving or rough surfaces. Replace if any defects are found.
5. If original impeller must be reused, check bonding to hub. Check side seal surfaces and

GEARCASE

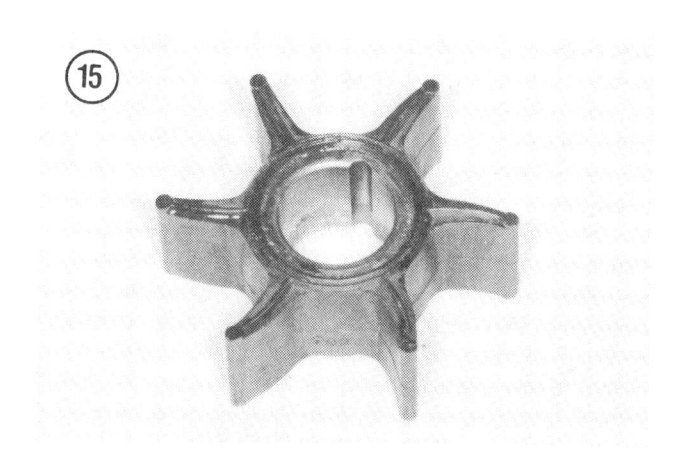

vane ends for cracks, tears, wear or a glazed or melted appearance. See **Figure 15**. If any of these defects are noted, do *not* reuse the impeller.

6. Check nylon water intake screen for blockage, distortion or other defects. Replace as required.

Assembly and Installation (1.5-40 hp)

When a new seal is installed in the impeller housing, its lips should face in the direction recorded during disassembly. After installation, wipe the seal lips with OMC Triple-Guard grease.

1A. If impeller housing uses a drive shaft seal, wipe the seal casing with OMC Gasket Sealing Compound and install with a suitable driver.

1B. If impeller housing uses an O-ring, install a new one in the housing groove and lubricate with OMC Triple-Guard grease.

2. Lubricate a new shift rod bushing and O-ring (if used) with OMC Premium Blend Gearcase Lubricant and install in impeller housing.

3. 1.5-2 hp gearcase—Install a new water tube seal in the impeller housing and proceed to Step 10.

NOTE
Always install a new impeller cup when the impeller is replaced.

4. Align the impeller cup tabs with the housing cutouts (B, **Figure 10**) and install the cup.

CAUTION
*If the original impeller is to be reused, install it in the same rotational direction as removed to avoid premature failure. The curl of the blades should be positioned as shown in **Figure 16**.*

5. Lubricate the inside diameter of the impeller cup with a light coat of OMC Premium Blend Gearcase Lubricant and install the impeller with a downward rotating motion.

6. Coat the outside diameter of a new water tube grommet with Scotch Grip Rubber Adhesive 1300. Install grommet so its bosses will fit into the holes in the impeller housing.

7. If impeller housing uses a spaghetti seal (C, **Figure 9**), apply a thin coat of Sealer 1000 or OMC Adhesive M to seal the groove, then install the new seal.

8. Install nylon water intake screen in gearcase cavity, if used. See **Figure 8**.

9. Coat both sides of a new impeller plate gasket with OMC Gasket Sealing Compound and install on the gearcase. Install impeller plate. Coat both sides of a second gasket and install. Align gasket and impeller plate holes

with those in the gearcase. See **Figure 17** (typical).

10. Wipe the drive shaft key flat with OMC Needle Bearing Grease and install the drive key. See **Figure 18** (typical).

11. 1.5-2 hp gearcase—Coat bottom surface of impeller housing with Sealer 1000 or OMC Adhesive M.

12. Lightly lubricate the drive shaft splines with OMC Premium Blend Gearcase Lubricant and slide the impeller housing and impeller over the drive shaft.

13. Rotate the drive shaft as required to align the drive key with the impeller groove. Press the impeller housing down with a smooth, even motion so impeller hub groove will ride over the drive key. See **Figure 19**.

CAUTION
Housing fastener torque is important in Step 14. Excessive torque can cause the pump to crack during operation; insufficient torque may result in leakage and exhaust induction which will cause overheating.

14. Wipe all impeller housing fastener threads with OMC Gasket Sealing Compound and install with washers (if used). See **Figure 20**. Tighten fasteners to specifications (**Table 1**).

Assembly and Installation (50-125 hp)

When a new seal is installed in the impeller housing, its lips should face in the direction recorded during disassembly. After installation, wipe the seal lips with OMC Triple-Guard grease.

1A. Inline engines—Install a new drive shaft grommet on impeller housing.

1B. V4—Wipe the outer diameter of a new drive shaft seal with OMC Gasket Sealing Compound and install in impeller housing (lip facing gearcase) with a suitable installer. After installation, wipe the seal lips with OMC Triple-Guard grease.

2. Lubricate a new water tube grommet with OMC Premium Blend Gearcase Lubricant and install in impeller housing.

3. If impeller housing uses a guide bracket, install bracket to housing with a new grommet.

4. Install impeller plate on gearcase. If a gasket is used, coat both sides with OMC Gasket Sealing Compound and install on gearcase under the impeller plate.

5. Wipe the drive shaft flat with OMC Needle Bearing Grease and install impeller drive key or pin on the shaft flat.

6. Lubricate the impeller blade tips with OMC Premium Blend Gearcase Lubricant. Install the impeller on the drive shaft and engage its hub cutout over the drive pin. Seat impeller on the impeller plate.

GEARCASE

9. Carefully slide impeller housing on drive shaft to prevent seal or grommet damage, then push housing over impeller while rotating the drive shaft clockwise to correctly position impeller blades in housing.

CAUTION
Housing fastener torque is important in Step 10. Excessive torque can cause the pump to crack during operation; insufficient torque may result in leakage and exhaust induction which will cause overheating.

10. Wipe all impeller housing fastener threads with OMC Gasket Sealing Compound and install with washers (if used). Tighten fasteners to specifications (**Table 1**).

GEARCASE CLEANING AND INSPECTION (ALL MODELS)

1. Clean all parts in fresh solvent. Blow dry with compressed air, if available.
2. Clean all nut and screw threads thoroughly if OMC Screw Lock or OMC Nut Lock has been used. Soak nuts and screws in solvent and use a fine wire brush to remove residue.
3. Remove and discard all O-rings, gaskets and seals. Clean all gasket residue from gasket mating surfaces.
4. Check drive shaft splines for wear or damage. If gearcase has struck a submerged object, the drive shaft and propeller shaft may suffer severe damage. Replace drive shaft as required and check crankshaft splines for similar wear or damage.
5. Check propeller shaft splines and threads for wear, rust or corrosion. See A, **Figure 21**. Replace shaft as required.
6. Install V-blocks under the drive shaft bearing surfaces at each end of the shaft. Slowly rotate the shaft while watching the crankshaft end. Replace the shaft if any signs of wobble are noted.

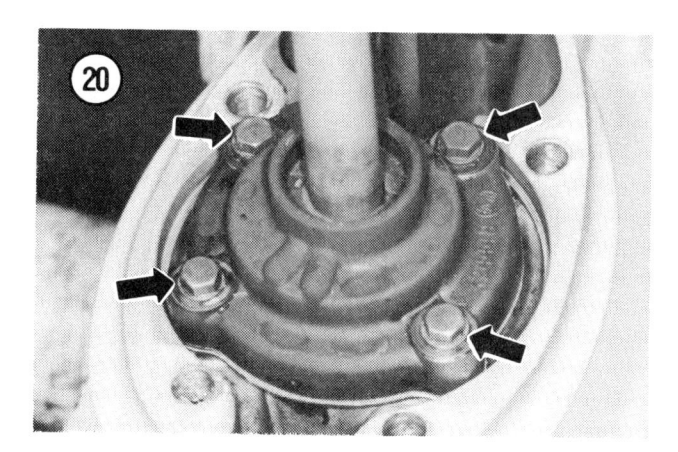

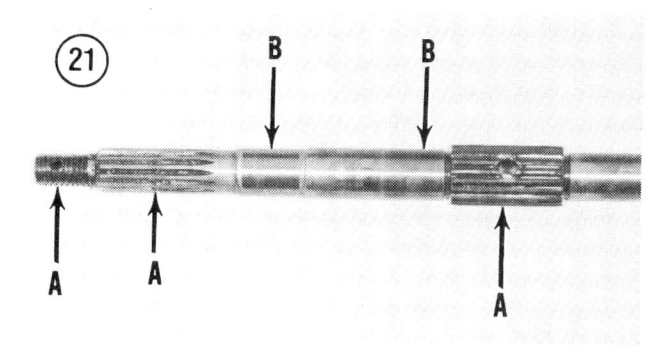

NOTE
Always install a new impeller liner and cup when the impeller is replaced.

7. Install the impeller housing liner, then align the impeller cup tabs with the housing cutouts and install the cup.
8. Install a new O-ring in bottom of impeller housing with Sealer 1000 or OMC Adhesive M.

7. Repeat Step 6 with the propeller shaft. Also check the shaft surfaces where oil seal lips make contact. Replace the shaft as required.

8. Check bearing housing and needle bearing for wear or damage. See **Figure 22**. Replace as required.

9. Check bearing housing contact points on the propeller shaft (B, **Figure 21**). If shaft shows signs of pitting, grooving, scoring, heat discoloration or embedded metallic particles, replace shaft and bearing.

10. Check water pump as described in this chapter. Check and clean water intake screen as required.

11. Check all shift components for wear or damage. Look for excessive wear on the shift lever, cradle (A, **Figure 23**), shifter shaft and clutch dog engagement surfaces (B, **Figure 23**). Replace as required.

12. Clean all roller bearings with solvent and lubricate with OMC Premium Blend Gearcase Lubricant to prevent rusting. Check bearings for rust, corrosion, flat spots or excessive wear. Replace as required.

13. Check pinion gear needle bearing and thrust washers for wear or damage (**Figure 24**). Replace as required.

14. Check the forward, reverse and pinion gears for wear or damage. See A, **Figure 25** (typical). Check clutch engagement dogs on forward and reverse gears (B, **Figure 25**). If clutch dogs or teeth are pitted, chipped, broken or excessively worn, replace the gear.

15. Check gearcase upper drive shaft bearing and pinion bearing for wear or damage. Replace pinion bearing as required. If upper drive shaft bearing requires replacement, replace the bearing and housing as an assembly.

16. Check the propeller for nicks, cracks or damaged blades. Minor nicks can be removed with a file, taking care to retain the shape of the propeller. Replace any propeller with bent, cracked or badly chipped blades.

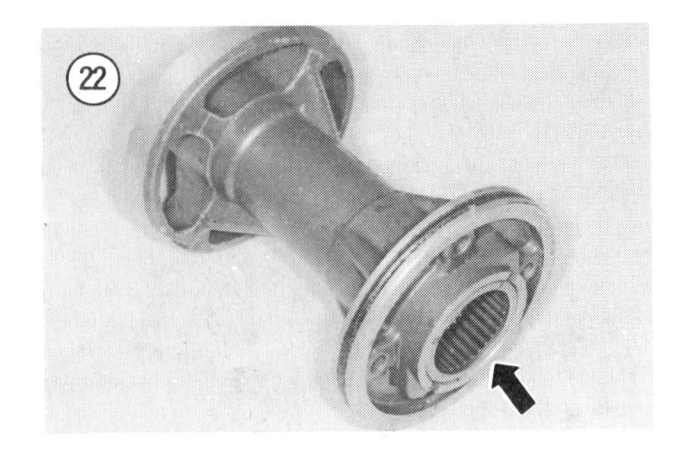

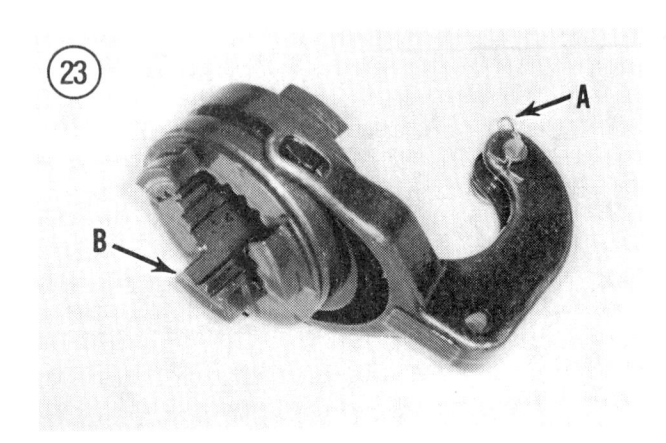

17. Check oil pump pressure relief valve on hydro-mechanical gearcases. If grooved or worn, replace the ball and seat.

18. Check shift rod cover bushing, if so equipped. If worn, remove bushing and O-ring, then install a new set with a suitable driver.

GEARCASE

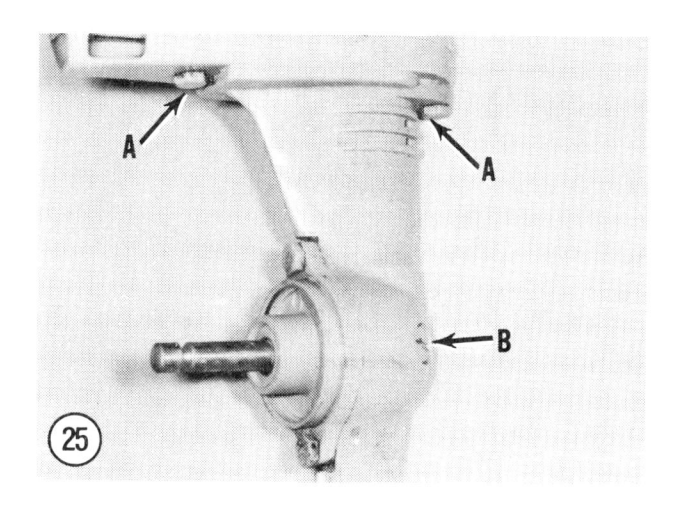

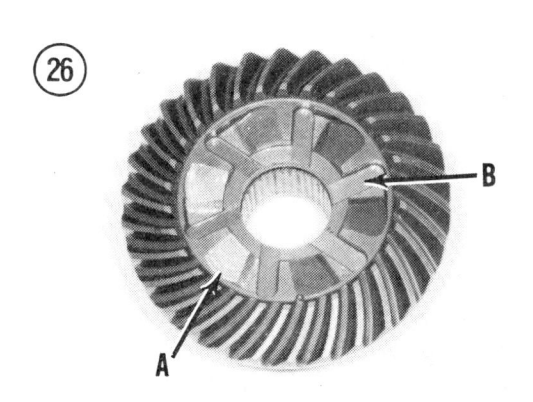

⑤

㉖

DIRECT DRIVE GEARCASE

Removal/Installation

1. Disconnect the spark plug lead(s) as a safety precaution to prevent any accidental starting of the engine during lower unit removal.
2. Remove the propeller as described in this chapter.
3. Remove the screws holding the gearcase to the exhaust housing. See A, **Figure 26** (typical).

NOTE
If the drive shaft does not disconnect from the crankshaft or is pulled upward after disconnecting in Step 4, it will disengage from the pinion gear. This is not serious if the gearcase is to be completely overhauled, but should be avoided if the unit is being removed for water pump or other service.

4. Carefully separate the gearcase from the exhaust housing to prevent damage to the water tube and drive shaft, then hold the drive shaft from moving upward and remove gearcase.
5. Remove the fill/drain plug. See B, **Figure 26** (typical). Hold the gearcase over a container. Drain the lubricant from the unit.

NOTE
If the lubricant is creamy in color or metallic particles are found in Step 6, the gearcase must be completely disassembled to determine and correct the cause of the problem.

6. Wipe a small amount of lubricant on a finger and rub the finger and thumb together. Check for the presence of metallic particles in the lubricant. Note the color of the lubricant. A white or creamy color indicates water in the lubricant. Check the drain container for signs of water separation from the lubricant.
7. If the water tube remained in the exhaust housing, remove it from the grommet.
8. Remove and discard the drive shaft O-ring, if so equipped.
9. Mount the gearcase in a suitable holding fixture.
10. To reinstall the gearcase, lubricate the exhaust housing water tube grommet with liquid soap.
11. Install a new drive shaft O-ring, if used.

CAUTION
Do not grease the top of the drive shaft in Step 12. This may excessively preload the drive shaft and crankshaft when the mounting bolts are tightened and cause a premature failure of the power head or gearcase.

12. Lightly lubricate the drive shaft splines with OMC Moly Lube.

13. Lightly clean the water pump tube with sandpaper to remove any corrosion, then wipe with a clean cloth moistened in solvent to remove any particles. Lubricate the tube and its grommet with OMC Premium Blend Gearcase Lubricant to assist in installation.

CAUTION
Do not rotate the flywheel counterclockwise in Step 14. This can damage the water pump impeller.

14. Position gearcase under exhaust housing and align water tube with grommet and drive shaft splines with crankshaft. Push the gearcase into place, rotating the flywheel clockwise as required to engage the drive shaft and crankshaft.
15. Wipe gearcase screw threads with OMC Gasket Sealing Compound. Install screws and tighten to specifications (**Table 1**).
16. Install the propeller as described in this chapter.
17. Reconnect the spark plug lead(s) and refill the gearcase with the proper type and quantity of lubricant. See Chapter Four.

Disassembly/Assembly

Refer to **Figure 27** (standard gearcase) or **Figure 28** (weedless gearcase) for this procedure.

1. Remove the gearcase as described in this chapter.
2. Secure the gearcase in a holding fixture or a vise with protective jaws. If protective jaws are not available, position the gearcase upright in the vise with the skeg between wooden blocks.

NOTE
If gearcase has been removed to replace the propeller shaft seal in the gearcase head, omit Step 3 and complete Steps 4-6. Further disassembly is unnecessary.

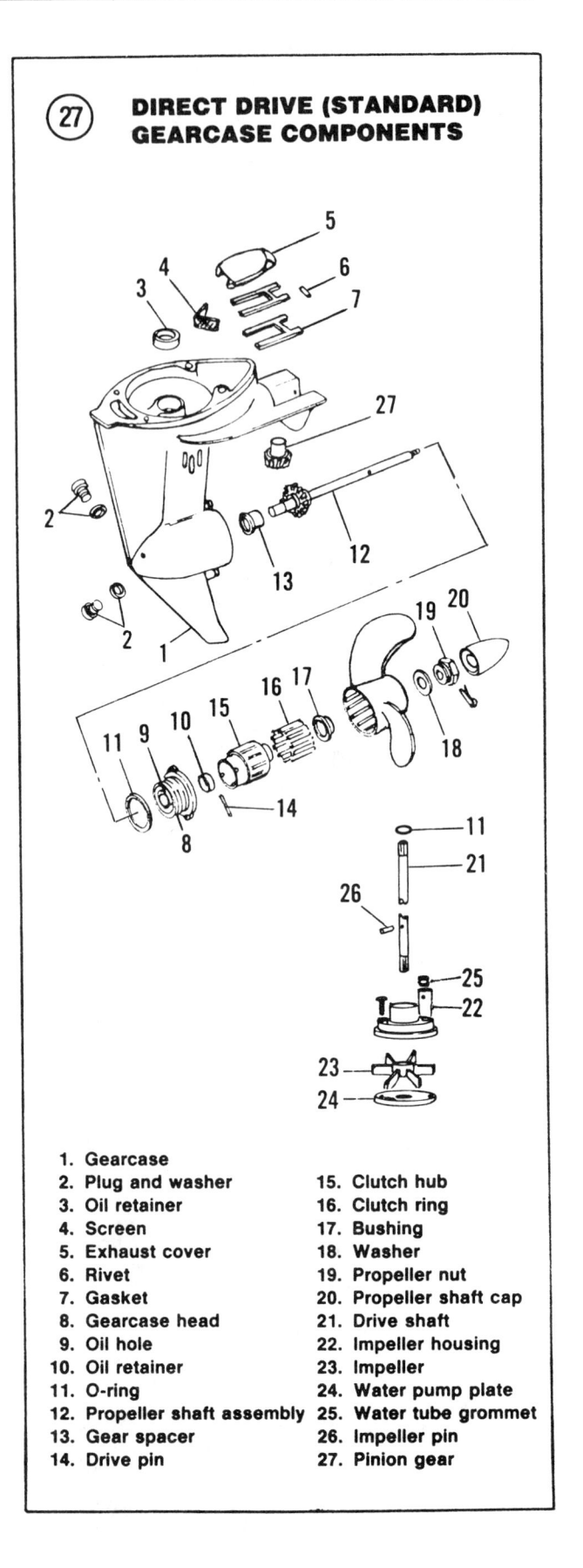

---

27 DIRECT DRIVE (STANDARD) GEARCASE COMPONENTS

1. Gearcase
2. Plug and washer
3. Oil retainer
4. Screen
5. Exhaust cover
6. Rivet
7. Gasket
8. Gearcase head
9. Oil hole
10. Oil retainer
11. O-ring
12. Propeller shaft assembly
13. Gear spacer
14. Drive pin
15. Clutch hub
16. Clutch ring
17. Bushing
18. Washer
19. Propeller nut
20. Propeller shaft cap
21. Drive shaft
22. Impeller housing
23. Impeller
24. Water pump plate
25. Water tube grommet
26. Impeller pin
27. Pinion gear

GEARCASE

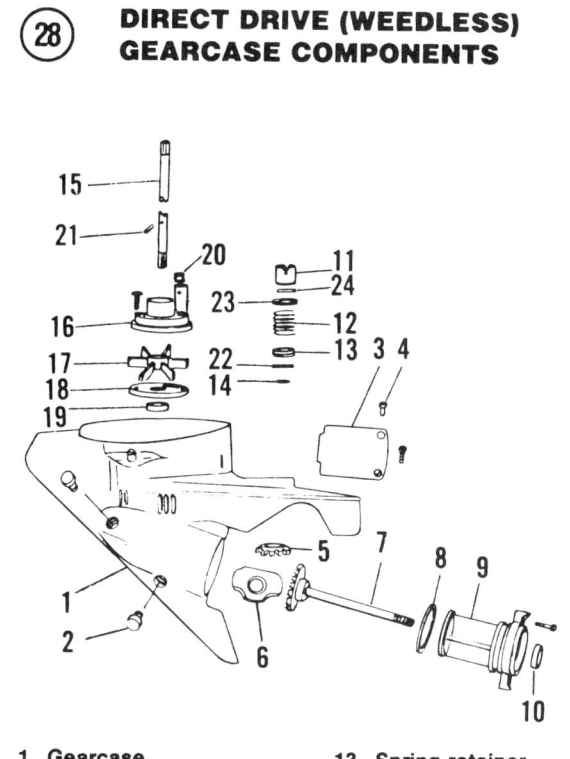

(28) DIRECT DRIVE (WEEDLESS) GEARCASE COMPONENTS

1. Gearcase
2. Plug and washer
3. Exhaust cover
4. Rivet
5. Pinion gear
6. Thrust bearing
7. Propeller shaft assembly
8. Seal
9. Bearing housing assembly
10. Oil retainer
11. Driveshaft coupler
12. Spring
13. Spring retainer
14. O-ring
15. Drive shaft
16. Impeller housing
17. Impeller
18. Water pump plate
19. Oil retainer
20. Water tube grommet
21. Impeller pin
22. Drive shaft pin
23. Retaining ring
24. Pin

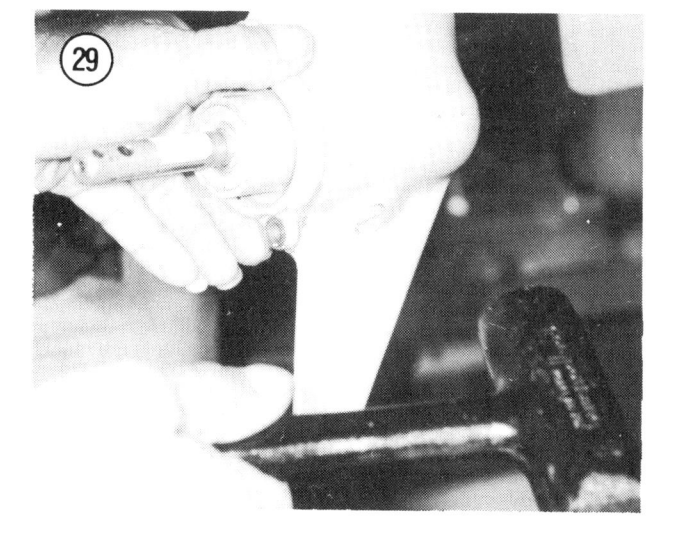

3. Remove the water pump as described in this chapter.

4. Remove the 2 gearcase head screws. Tap the side of the gearcase head ears with a mallet to break the seal (**Figure 29**), then rotate the head off the propeller shaft and gear assembly.

5. Remove and discard the gearcase head O-ring.

6. Remove and discard the gearcase head seal.

7. Remove the propeller shaft and gear assembly.

8A. Standard gearcase—Pull up on the drive shaft, reach inside the gearcase housing and remove the pinion gear.

8B. Weedless gearcase—Reinsert drive shaft and tap on its end to dislodge the thrust bearing holding the pinion gear. Remove the bearing, pinion gear and drive shaft.

9. Remove the drive shaft seal with a suitable seal remover.

10. Clean and inspect all parts as described in this chapter. Check drive shaft bushing in gearcase. If worn or damaged, replace the gearcase housing.

11. Coat the metal case of a new gearcase head seal with OMC Gasket Sealing Compound. Install seal in gearcase head (lip facing inward) with a suitable installer.

12. Repeat Step 11 to install the drive shaft seal (lip facing downward).

13. Lubricate a new gearcase head O-ring with OMC Premium Blend Gearcase Lubricant. Install ring on gearcase head.

14. Slant the gearcase in the holding fixture or vise so the pinion gear will remain in place when installed.
   a. Standard gearcase—Insert pinion gear.
   b. Weedless gearcase—Insert pinion gear with thrust bearing. The boss on the bearing must engage the 2 bosses in the gearcase.

15. Install the propeller shaft and gear assembly to engage the pinion gear.

16. Install the drive shaft in the gearcase. Rotate drive shaft to engage pinion gear, hold propeller gear from turning and rotate drive shaft downward until it is fully seated in the pinion gear.

CAUTION
If screws are not evenly tightened to specifications in Step 17 or if the gear teeth are not properly engaged, the gearcase head will be out of alignment and may be damaged when the unit is operated.

17. Coat the gearcase head screw threads with OMC Gasket Sealing Compound. Make sure the pinion and drive gears are properly engaged. Install standard gearcase head with the flat on the sealing surface facing the upper screw hole in the gearcase. Align gearcase head and gearcase match marks on the weedless model. Tighten screws evenly to specifications (**Table 1**).
18. Pressure and vacuum test the gearcase as described in this chapter.
19. Install the water pump assembly as described in this chapter.
20. Install the gearcase as described in this chapter. Fill with the recommended type and quantity of lubricant. See Chapter Four.
21. Check gearcase lubricant level after engine has been run. Change the lubricant after 10 hours of operation (break-in period). See Chapter Four.

MANUAL SHIFT GEARCASE (SPLIT LOWER HOUSING)

Removal/Installation

1. Disconnect the spark plug lead(s) as a safety precaution to prevent any accidental starting of the engine during lower unit removal.
2. Place a container under the gearcase. Remove the oil level plug, then remove the drain/fill plug. Do *not* remove the Phillips head pivot pin. Drain the lubricant from the unit.

NOTE
If the lubricant is white or creamy in color or metallic particles are found in Step 3, the gearcase must be completely disassembled to determine and correct the cause of the problem.

3. Wipe a small amount of lubricant on a finger and rub the finger and thumb together. Check for the presence of metallic particles in the lubricant. Note the color of the lubricant. A white or creamy color indicates water in the lubricant. Check the drain container for signs of water separation from the lubricant.
4. Remove the propeller as described in this chapter.
5. Move the shift lever into FORWARD. If necessary, rotate the propeller shaft slightly to help unit engage.
6. Remove the fasteners holding the gearcase to the exhaust housing or gearcase extension.

NOTE
On some 1956-1964 5.5 and 7.5 hp models, the power head must be removed and the shift rod disconnected from the shift lever before the gearcase can be removed. See Chapter Eight.

GEARCASE

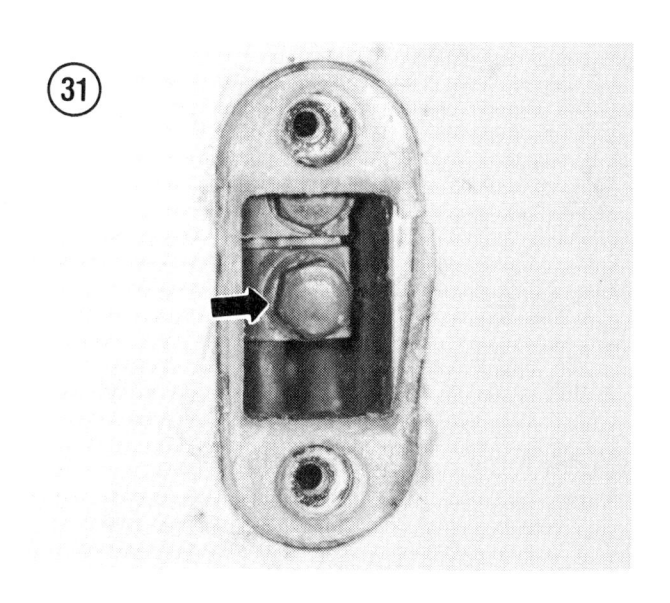

(31)

7A. **5.5, 6 and 7.5 hp**—Rotate the flywheel clockwise to align the upper drive shaft locking pin with corresponding slots in the upper exhaust housing. This is a trial and error procedure; work carefully to avoid damage to the locking pin or housing slots.

7B. **6 and 9.5 hp**—Separate the gearcase or gearcase extension from the exhaust housing enough to expose the shift rod connector. Remove the lower connector screw. See **Figure 30**.

7C. **All others**—Remove the exhaust housing cover plate and gasket to provide access to the shift rod connector screw. See **Figure 31**.

8. Carefully separate the gearcase or gearcase/extension from the exhaust housing to prevent damage to the water tube and drive shaft, then remove gearcase. If impeller housing spacer does not come out with the gearcase on models so equipped, remove it from the extension housing and discard the O-rings.

9. Remove and discard the drive shaft O-ring, if so equipped.

10. Mount the gearcase in a suitable holding fixture.

11. To reinstall the gearcase, install the extension, if so equipped, and make sure the extension exhaust seal is in place.

12. Make sure impeller housing spacer (if used) is properly positioned at the base of the drive shaft and the water tube is installed in the inner exhaust tube.

13. Install a new drive shaft O-ring, if used.

14. Make sure the gearcase shift rod is in FORWARD gear.

CAUTION
Do not grease the top of the drive shaft in Step 14. This may excessively preload the drive shaft and crankshaft when the mounting fasteners are tightened and cause a premature failure of the power head or gearcase.

15. Lightly lubricate the drive shaft splines with OMC Moly Lube.

16. Position gearcase under exhaust housing. Align extension housing water tube with impeller housing grommet, drive shaft with crankshaft splines and shift rod with the shift rod bushing or connector. On 5.5, 6 and 7.5 hp models, align the drive shaft pin with the pin slot in the exhaust housing.

CAUTION
Do not rotate the flywheel counterclockwise in Step 16. This can damage the water pump impeller.

17A. **6 and 9.5 hp**—Push the gearcase into position until the shift rod connector screw can be installed, rotating the flywheel clockwise as required to engage the drive shaft and crankshaft. Install and tighten the shift rod connector screw securely (**Figure 30**). Seat gearcase against exhaust housing.

17B. **All others**—Push the gearcase into place, rotating the flywheel clockwise as required to engage the drive shaft and crankshaft.

18. On models where the shift rod access is through the exhaust housing window (**Figure 31**), align lower shift rod groove with connector screw hole. Install screw with washer and tighten to 10-12 ft.-lb. Install

housing cover plate with a new gasket coated with Sealer 1000 or OMC Adhesive M. Tighten securely.

19. If power head was removed, reconnect shift rod to shift lever and reinstall the power head. See Chapter Eight.

20. Wipe gearcase or extension screw or bolt threads with OMC Gasket Sealing Compound. Install fasteners and tighten to specifications (**Table 1**).

21. Install the propeller as described in this chapter.

22. Move shift lever on motor to NEUTRAL position. The propeller should rotate freely. If not, remove and reinstall gearcase.

23. On models where the shift rod access is through the exhaust housing window, loosen both shift lever screws. Move shift actuator cam until lockout lever detents into cam notch. Tighten shift lever screws to 60-84 in.-lb.

24. Reconnect the spark plug leads and refill the gearcase with the proper type and quantity of lubricant. See Chapter Four.

Disassembly/Assembly

Many design and production changes were made during the years this type of gearcase was manufactured. For this reason, the positioning of components will vary according to engine horsepower and model year. It is also possible that your gearcase may not have all of the bearings, seals and O-rings mentioned. A good practice is to sketch component arrangement prior to removal, keeping notes if necessary and placing components in line on a workbench

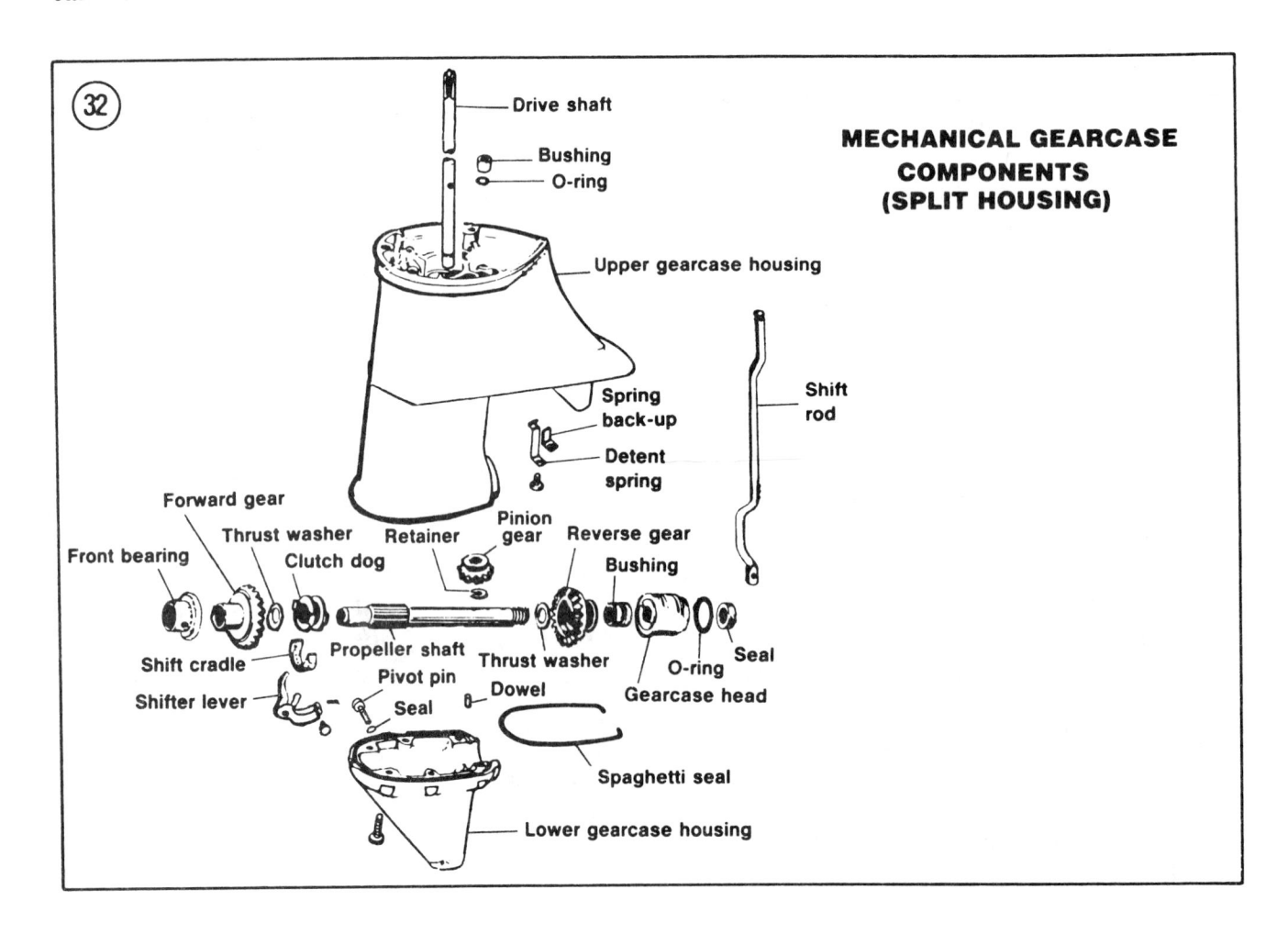

MECHANICAL GEARCASE COMPONENTS (SPLIT HOUSING)

GEARCASE

in the order of removal. If a step is specified that does not seem appropriate for your model, double-check the step and the gearcase, then proceed. Refer to **Figure 32**, **Figure 33** or **Figure 34** (typical).

1. Remove the gearcase as described in this chapter.
2. Secure the gearcase in a holding fixture or a vise with protective jaws. If protective jaws are not available, position the gearcase upright in the vise with the skeg between wooden blocks.
3. Remove the water pump as described in this chapter.
4. Remove the drive shaft from the gearcase.
5. Invert the gearcase in the holding fixture. Remove the Phillips head pivot pin. Remove and discard the O-ring.
6. Remove the fasteners holding the lower half of the gearcase to the upper half. Tap the skeg with a soft hammer to break the seal and remove the lower half (**Figure 35**). Remove and discard the spaghetti seal (**Figure 36**).
7. Pivot the shifter lever to the rear and remove the cradle (**Figure 37**).
8. Slide the propeller shaft assembly straight up and to the side, then remove it from the gearcase. See **Figure 38**.
9. Remove the pinion gear/bearing/washer assembly from the gearcase (**Figure 39**).
10. Examine the upper end of the shift rod for carbon and burrs. Remove with No. 400 grit sandpaper, if found. Slide the shift rod out of the gearcase.
11. To check, clean or replace the water intake screen:

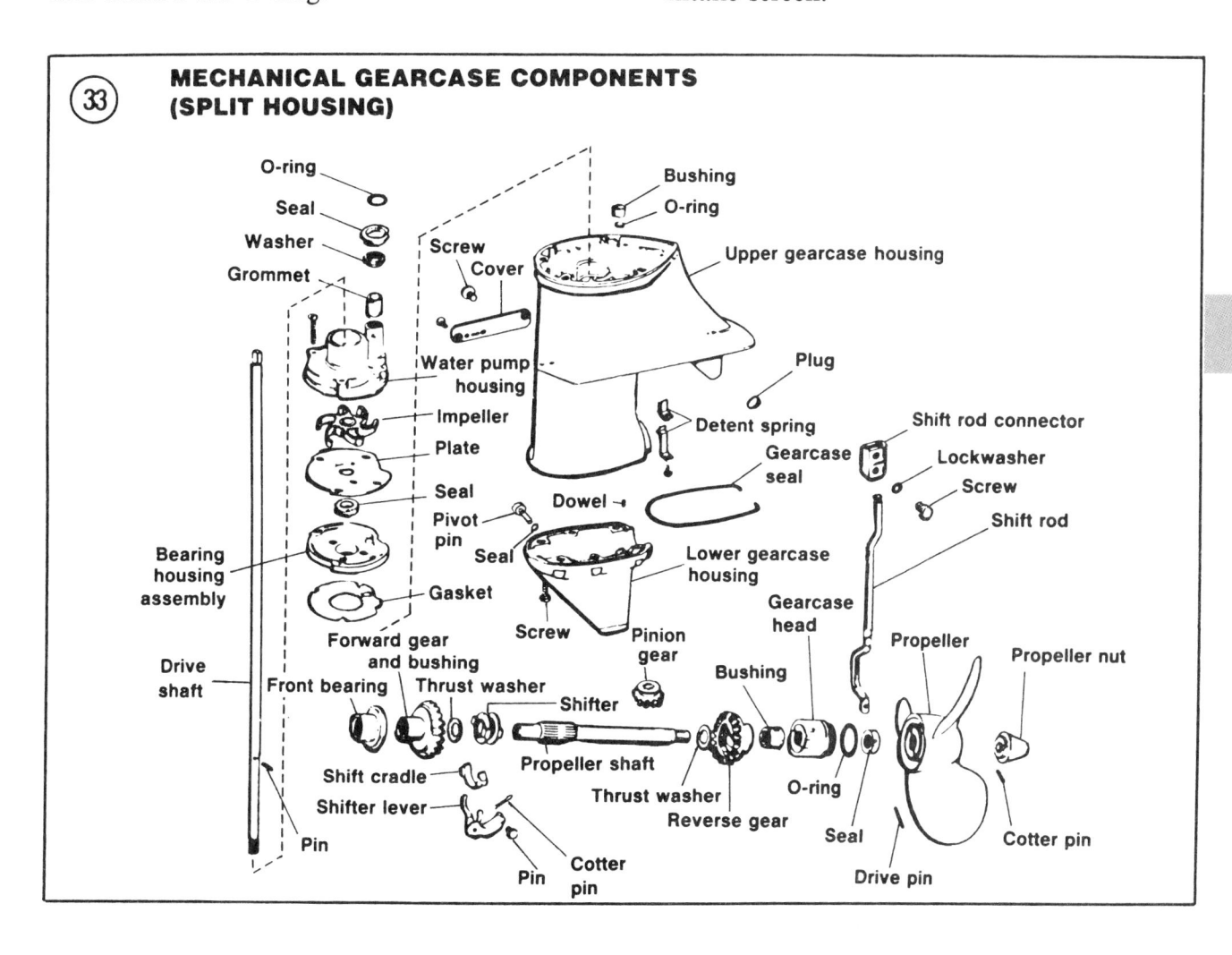

(33) MECHANICAL GEARCASE COMPONENTS (SPLIT HOUSING)

298

CHAPTER NINE

③ MECHANICAL GEARCASE COMPONENTS (SPLIT HOUSING)

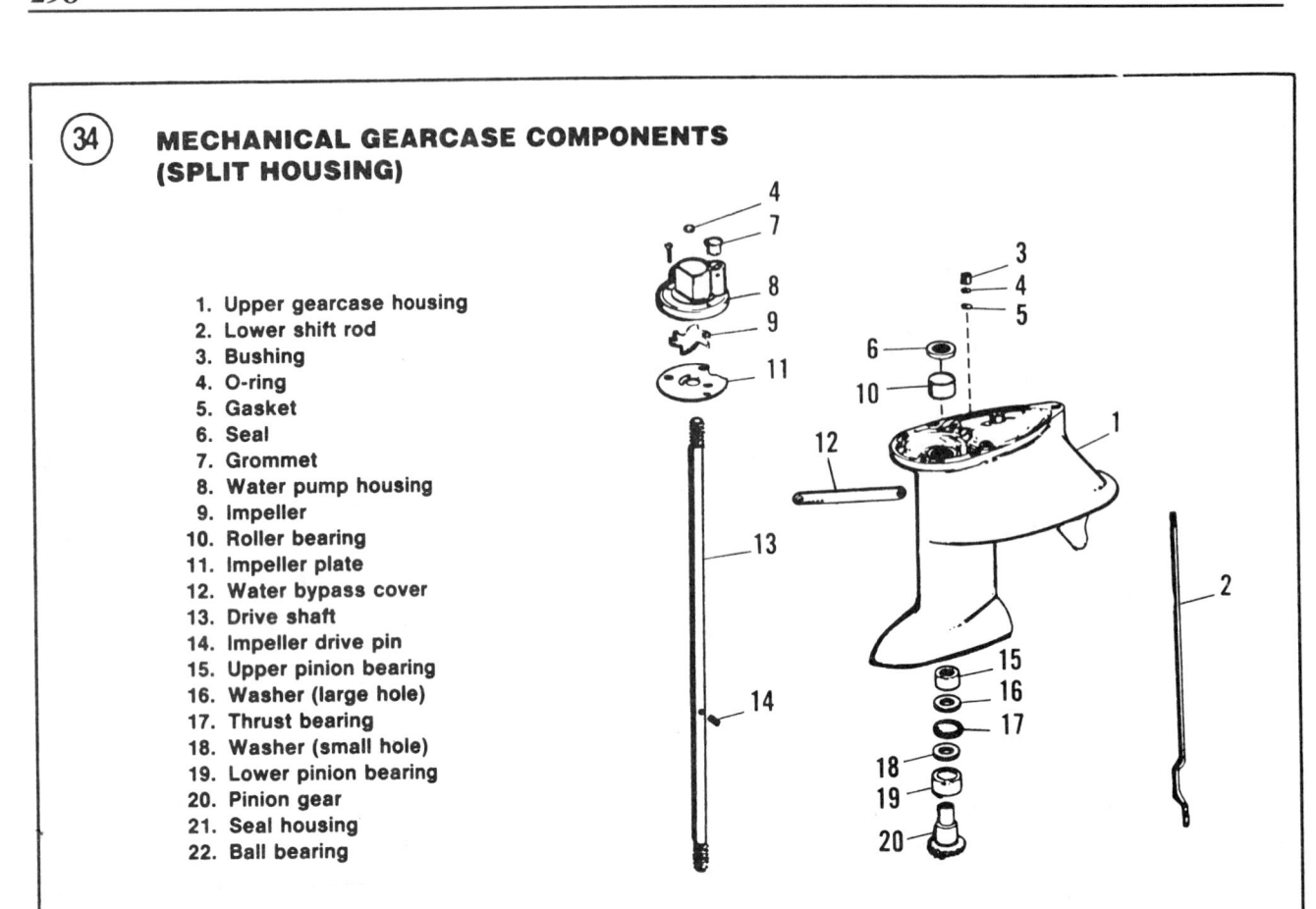

1. Upper gearcase housing
2. Lower shift rod
3. Bushing
4. O-ring
5. Gasket
6. Seal
7. Grommet
8. Water pump housing
9. Impeller
10. Roller bearing
11. Impeller plate
12. Water bypass cover
13. Drive shaft
14. Impeller drive pin
15. Upper pinion bearing
16. Washer (large hole)
17. Thrust bearing
18. Washer (small hole)
19. Lower pinion bearing
20. Pinion gear
21. Seal housing
22. Ball bearing
23. Thrust washer
24. Washer
25. Clutch dog
26. Propeller shaft
27. Forward gear
28. Spring
29. Detent ball
30. Shift cradle
31. Shifter lever
32. Pin
33. Reverse gear
34. Snap ring

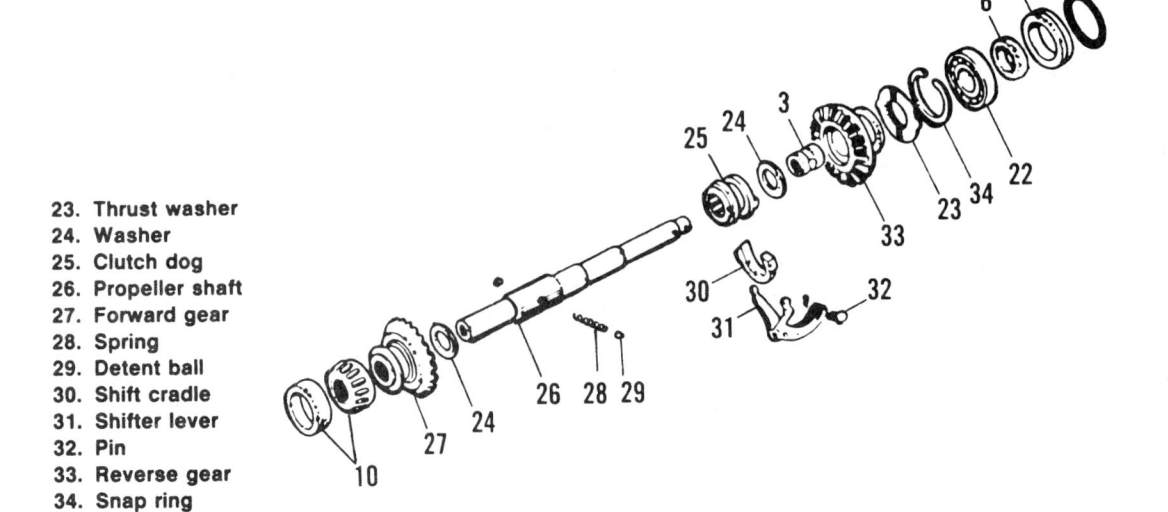

GEARCASE 299

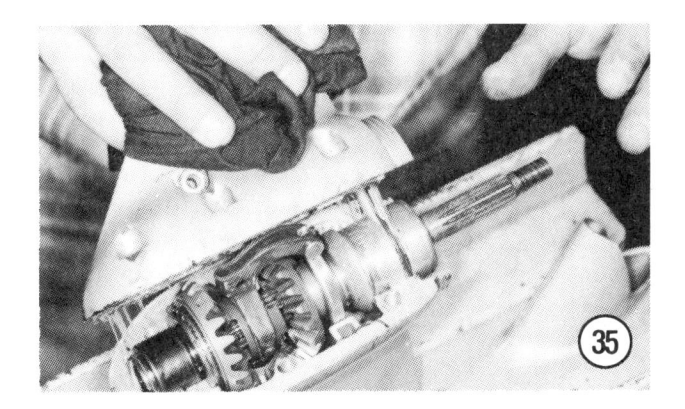

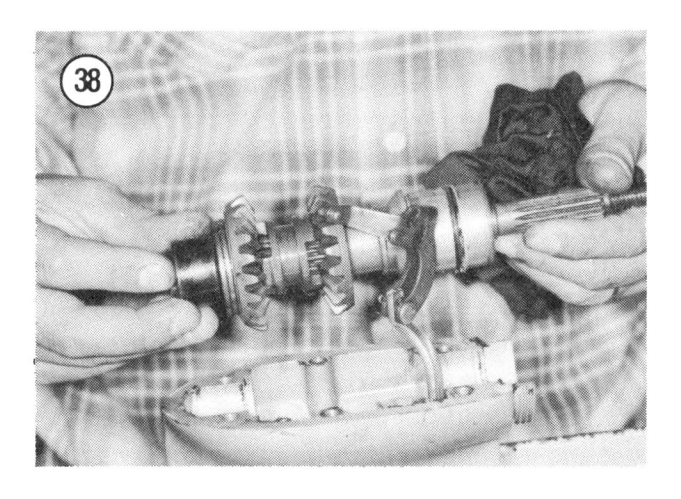

a. Remove the 2 screws holding the cover plate in the side of the gearcase. Remove the cover plate and check for blocked water passages.
b. If the water intake screen requires replacement, drill a 5/32 in. hole in the plug and remove with a No. 3 Easy-out.
c. Slide the screen from the gearcase and check for damage, blockage or metallic chips. Replace as required.
d. Slide the screen back into the gearcase.
e. Coat a new plug with Sealer 1000 or OMC Adhesive M and drive it into the gearcase until it just touches the screen.
f. Reinstall the cover plate and tighten the screws snugly.

12. 50-75 hp—Remove the forward gear snap ring from the propeller shaft. Remove the thrust washers, bearing, another snap ring, the bushing and forward gear. Repeat this step to remove the reverse gear assembly from the rear of the shaft.

13. All others—Slide all components except the clutch dog from the propeller shaft.

NOTE
Not all models use the detent spring and balls mentioned in Step 14.

14. With a hand cupped over the clutch dog, slowly slide it to the front of the propeller

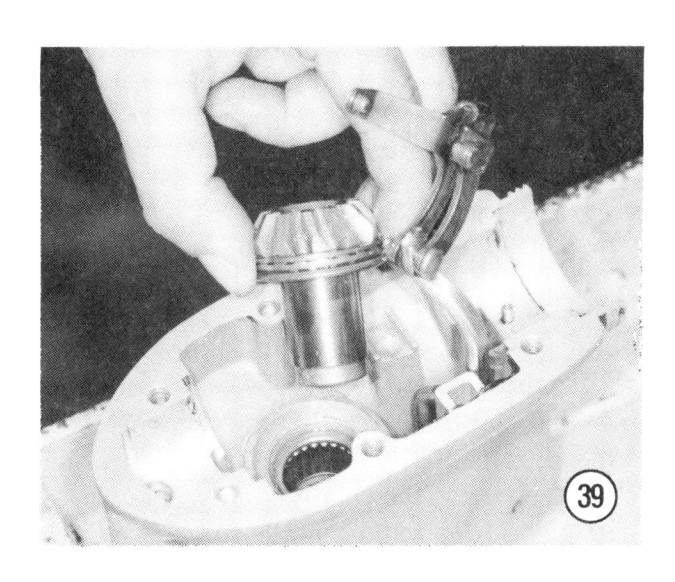

shaft, catching the spring and 2 detent balls as the clutch dog uncovers them.

15. Remove the gearcase head or seal housing seals with an appropriate remover. Remove and discard the O-ring. See **Figure 40** (gearcase head).

16. Soak the gearcase head or seal housing in solvent to remove the dried sealant from the seal bore.

17. Coat the metal case of new gearcase head or seal housing seals with OMC Gasket Sealing Compound. Install the seals in the same direction as those removed. If 2 seals are installed, pack the cavity between them with OMC Triple-Guard grease. Wipe seal lips with the same lubricant.

18. Lubricate a new O-ring with OMC Premium Blend Gearcase Lubricant and install on the gearcase head or seal housing.

19. Drive the upper drive shaft seals and bearing (**Figure 41**) from the gearcase with a suitable mandrel.

20. Lubricate a new bearing with OMC Premium Blend Gearcase Lubricant and install in the gearcase (lettered side up) with a suitable installer.

21. Coat the metal seal of 2 new gearcase head seals with OMC Gasket Sealing Compound. Install the inner seal (lip facing toward gearcase) and the outer seal (lip facing away from gearcase). Pack the cavity between the seals with OMC Triple-Guard grease.

NOTE
The pinion bearing is not serviceable in 5.5-7.5 hp gearcases. Perform Step 22 and Step 23 only if inspection determines that the bearings must be replaced.

22A. 9.5-25 hp—Remove the pinion bearing with remover part No. 326571 and remover part No. 326570. Install remover part No. 326571 with its slide ring behind the bearing cage, then drive the bearing out with remover part No. 326570 and a mallet.

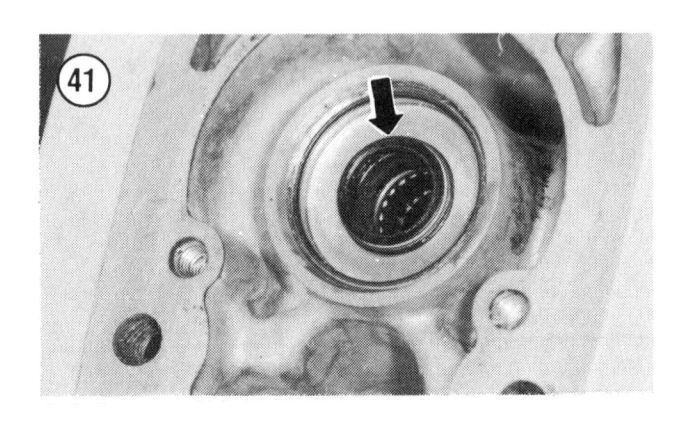

22B. All others—Remove the pinion bearing with puller part No. 378445 and puller jaws part No. 308093.

23A. 9.5-25 hp—Lubricate a new pinion bearing with OMC Premium Blend Gearcase Lubricant and install (lettered side up) in gearcase with tool part No. 326565 until tool seats against the gearcase flange.

23B. All others—Lubricate thrust washers and bearing with Johnson or Evinrude 50/1 oil. Install washer with large hole, bearing and washer with small hole in that order, then install new pinion bearing (lettered side up) in gearcase with a suitable driver and collar.

24. Drive the shift rod bushing, washer and O-ring from the gearcase with bushing punch part No. 304514 and a mallet.

25. Fit a new shift rod bushing on the end of bushing mandrel part No. 304515. Lubricate a new O-ring with OMC Premium Blend Gearcase Lubricant and install on the bushing along with the bushing washer.

GEARCASE

Figure 42
1. Chamfered edge
2. Thrust bearing

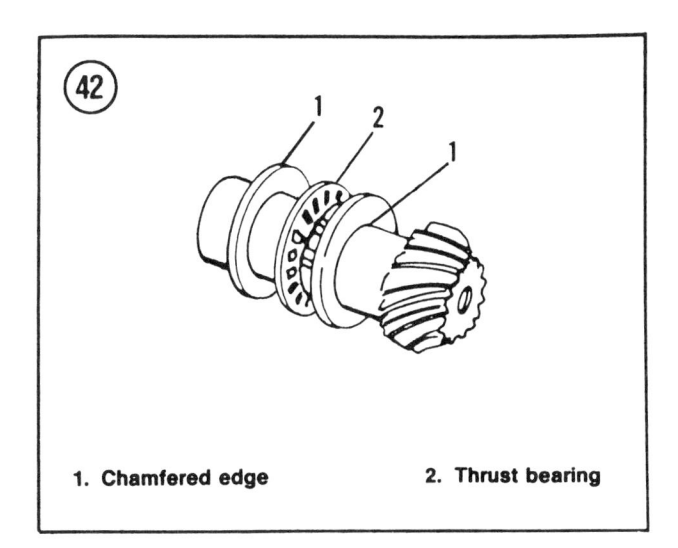

Figure 43

Position the tool and bushing assembly in the gearcase and drive in place until the bushing is fully seated.

26A. If propeller shaft uses a spring and detent balls, insert the spring in the propeller shaft. Position a detent ball on each side of the spring and hold in place while sliding the clutch dog in place until it snaps into NEUTRAL position. Chamfered and grooved lugs of the shift dog should face the front of the shaft.

26B. If propeller shaft does not use a spring and detent balls, slide the clutch dog in place with its chamfered and grooved lugs facing the front of the shaft.

27. Lubricate the remaining propeller shaft components with OMC Premium Blend Gearcase Lubricant.

28A. 50-75 hp—Assemble the forward gear and bushing on the propeller shaft. Install the snap ring and position the babbitt or bronze side of the large thrust washer against the gear. Install a thrust washer, roller bearing and thrust washer, then secure in place with a snap ring.

28B. All others—Install the roller bearing (lettered end facing forward), thrust washer, thrust bearing and gear in that order.

29. Turn the shaft around and install the reverse gear, bushing and gearcase head (if used) in that order.

30. 33-75 hp—Install the thrust washer with its babbitt or bronze side against the reverse gear. Install the ball bearing. Install a new seal and O-ring on the seal housing, then slide the housing on the shaft.

31. Lubricate the end of the shift rod with OMC Premium Blend Gearcase Lubricant. Insert rod through shift rod bushing.

32. Sandwich the pinion gear bearing (if used) between the 2 thrust washers. The washer with the inside chamfer must rest against the pinion shoulder. The chamfered edge of the other washer must face away. See **Figure 42**.

33. Install the pinion gear/bearing/washer assembly in the gearcase (**Figure 43**). If the thrust washers have a tang, position them facing away from the gearcase housing.

34. Run a bead of Sealer 1000 or OMC Adhesive M on the upper gearcase at point A, **Figure 44**.

35. Install the cradle on the shift lever (B, **Figure 44**).

36. Install the propeller shaft assembly in the upper gearcase (**Figure 44**). Make sure the hole in the gearcase head engages the locating pin in the gearcase. Pry the clutch dog forward into gear with a flat-blade screwdriver while rotating the propeller shaft, then position the shift cradle.

NOTE
Spaghetti seal is sold in bulk rolls. Measure the length of the gearcase seal groove on each side, then add 2 in. to your measurement for cutting purposes.

37. Coat the machined surfaces of both gearcase halves and the exposed area of the gearcase head with Sealer 1000 or OMC Adhesive M. Place the spaghetti seal in the lower gearcase groove and cut the ends of the seal flush with the end of the groove using a sharp knife. Apply OMC RTV Sealant on each end of the seal for a distance of 1/2 in.

38. Coat the gearcase screw threads with OMC Gasket Sealing Compound. Install the lower gearcase half with the 2 front and 2 rear screws. Tighten the 4 screws alternately and evenly until finger-tight to draw the halves together.

39. Install he remaining screws finger-tight, then tighten all screws to specifications (**Table 1**), working from side-to-side and front-to-rear.

40. Locate the shift yoke pin hole by probing through the pivot pin hole in the gearcase with an awl. Align the yoke and gearcase holes. Install a new O-ring on the pivot pin. Coat the pin threads and O-ring with OMC Gasket Sealing Compound and tighten the screw to specifications (**Table 1**).

41. Install the drive shaft with a rotating motion to engage the pinion gear splines.

42. Install the water pump as described in this chapter.

43. Pressure and vacuum test the gearcase as described in this chapter.

44. Install the gearcase as described in this chapter. Fill with the recommended type and quantity of lubricant. See Chapter Four.

45. Check gearcase lubricant level after engine has been run. Change the lubricant after 10 hours of operation (break-in period). See Chapter Four.

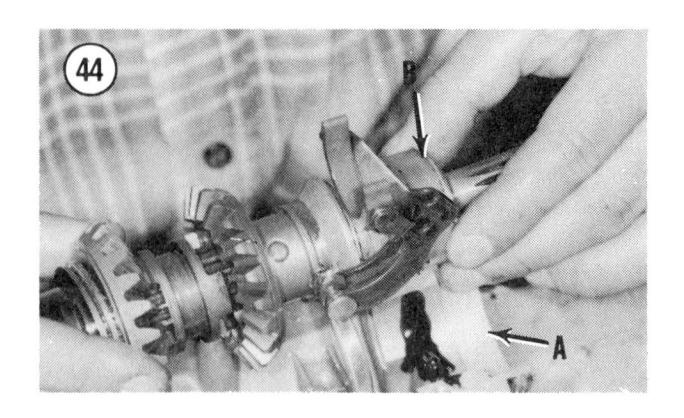

MANUAL SHIFT GEARCASE (SINGLE HOUSING)

Removal/Installation

1. Disconnect the spark plug lead(s) as a safety precaution to prevent any accidental starting of the engine during lower unit removal.

2. Place a container under the gearcase. Remove the oil level plug, then remove the drain/fill plug. Drain the lubricant from the unit.

NOTE
If the lubricant is creamy in color or metallic particles are found in Step 3, the gearcase must be completely disassembled to determine and correct the cause of the problem.

3. Wipe a small amount of lubricant on a finger and rub the finger and thumb together. Check for the presence of metallic particles in the lubricant. Note the color of the lubricant. A white or creamy color indicates water in the lubricant. Check the drain container for signs of water separation from the lubricant.

4. Remove the propeller as described in this chapter.

5. Move the shift lever into FORWARD. If necessary, rotate the propeller shaft slightly to help unit engage.

6. Remove the outer and inner exhaust housing cover plates and gaskets to provide access to the shift rod connector screw. See **Figure 31** (typical).

GEARCASE

7. Remove the fasteners holding the gearcase to the exhaust housing.

8. If trim tab is removable, mark its position relative to the gearcase for reinstallation, then remove the trim tab screw and trim tab. Remove the screw from inside the trim tab cavity (if used).

9. Remove the countersunk screw between the trim tab cavity and gearcase housing with a narrow wall socket.

10. Carefully separate the gearcase or gearcase/extension from the exhaust housing to prevent damage to the water tube and drive shaft, then remove gearcase.

11. Remove and discard the drive shaft O-ring.

12. Mount the gearcase in a suitable holding fixture.

13. To reinstall the gearcase, install a new drive shaft O-ring.

14. Make sure the gearcase shift rod is in FORWARD gear.

CAUTION
Do not grease the top of the drive shaft in Step 15. This may excessively preload the drive shaft and crankshaft when the mounting fasteners are tightened and cause a premature failure of the power head or gearcase.

15. Lightly lubricate the drive shaft splines with OMC Moly Lube.

16. Position gearcase under exhaust housing. Align extension housing water tube with impeller housing grommet, drive shaft with crankshaft splines and shift rod with the shift rod connector.

CAUTION
Do not rotate the flywheel counterclockwise in Step 17. This can damage the water pump impeller.

17. Push the gearcase into place, rotating the flywheel clockwise as required to engage the drive shaft and crankshaft. Align lower shift rod groove with connector screw hole. Install screw with washer and tighten to 10-12 ft.-lb.

Install housing cover plates with a new gasket coated with Sealer 1000 or OMC Adhesive M. Tighten securely.

18. Wipe gearcase bolt threads with OMC Gasket Sealing Compound. Install bolts and tighten to specifications (**Table 1**).

19. Install countersunk screw in anti-ventilation plate and screw in trim tab cavity, if used. Align trim tab and gearcase marks made during removal. Install trim tab and tighten screw securely.

20. Install the propeller as described in this chapter.

21. Move shift lever on motor to NEUTRAL position. The propeller should rotate freely. If not, remove and reinstall gearcase.

22. Reconnect the spark plug leads and refill the gearcase with the proper type and quantity of lubricant. See Chapter Four.

Disassembly/Assembly

Refer to **Figure 45** (typical) for this procedure.

1. Remove the gearcase as described in this chapter.

2. Secure the gearcase in a holding fixture or a vise with protective jaws. If protective jaws are not available, position the gearcase upright in the vise with the skeg between wooden blocks.

3. Remove and discard the drive shaft O-ring.

4. Remove the water pump as described in this chapter.

5. Remove the screws holding the bearing cap to the gearcase. Remove the bearing cap and drive shaft assembly from the gearcase.

NOTE
Some bearing caps may use a gasket. If so, remove and discard in Step 6.

6. Slide the bearing cap off the drive shaft. Remove the bearing cap seals (A, **Figure 46**) with a suitable punch. If bearing cap bearing

MECHANICAL GEARCASE COMPONENTS (SINGLE HOUSING)

(45)

Components shown: Washer, Thrust bearing, Pinion gear, Forward gear, Detent ball, Propeller shaft, Clutch dog, Thrust washer, Retaining plate, Snap ring, Thrust washer, Reverse gear, Bushing, Thrust washer, Spring.

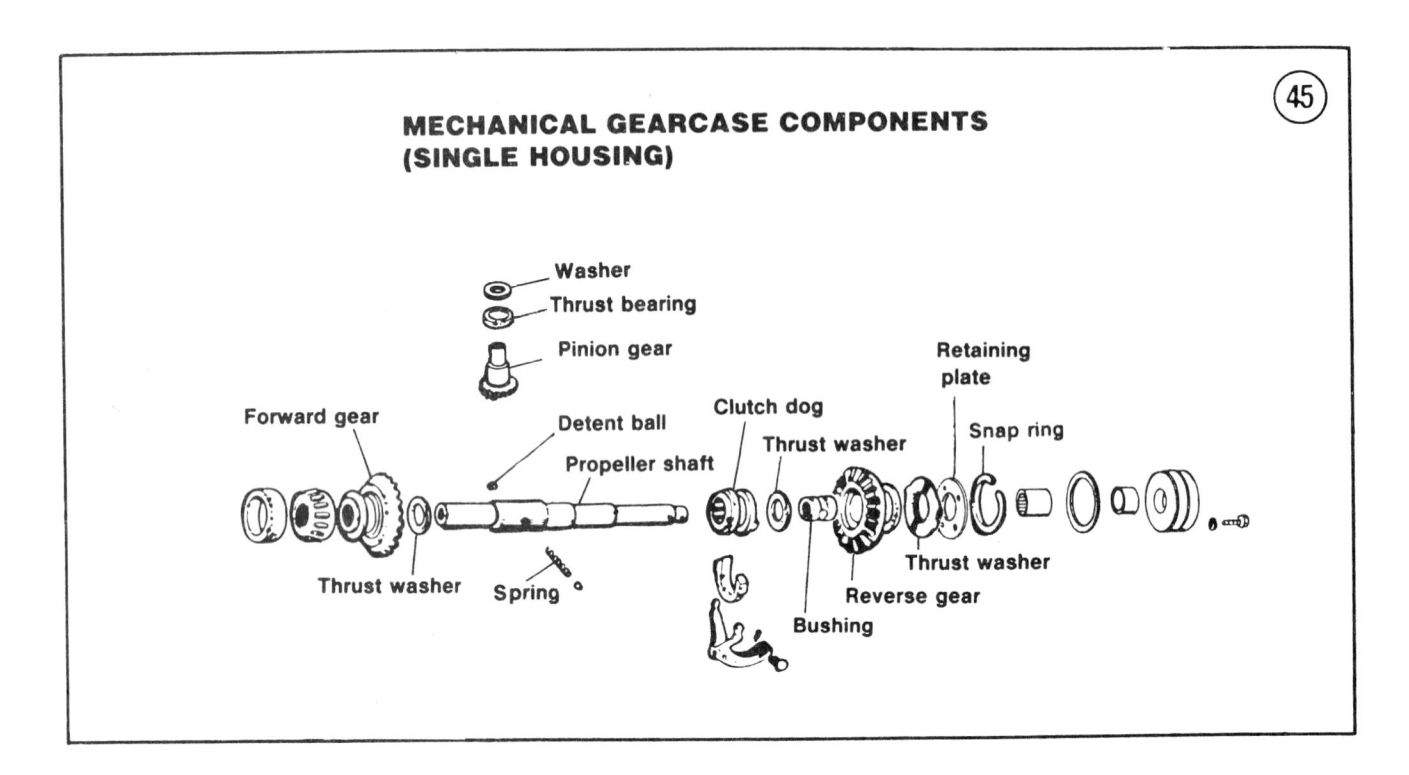

(B, **Figure 46**) requires replacement, remove from cap with an arbor press.

7. Remove and discard the self-locking gearcase stud nuts. See **Figure 47** (typical).

8. Separate the upper and lower gearcase assemblies enough to remove the screw and nut holding the shift rod to the yoke. Remove upper gearcase assembly.

9. Clean all carbon and burrs from the upper end of the shift rod with No. 400 grit sandpaper. Lightly lubricate the shift rod, then remove it from the gearcase with an upward rotating motion.

10. Drive the shift rod bushing, washer and O-ring from the gearcase with a suitable bushing punch and a mallet (drive from bottom to top of gearcase to remove).

11. Remove the shift yokes from the lower gearcase.

12. Remove the gearcase head/bearing housing screws with a thin-wall deep socket. Discard the O-rings on the screws, if used.

13. Install flywheel puller part No. 378103 and two puller bolts (part No. 316982) in gearcase head/bearing housing screw holes. Tighten puller nut until the head/housing comes loose.

14. Carefully remove the snap ring with snap ring pliers. Remove the retaining washer and thrust washer.

15. Remove the propeller shaft and reverse gear assembly. Slide the reverse gear, thrust washer and bushing off the shaft.

16. Remove the shift lever pivot pin (Phillips screw) on the starboard side of the lower gearcase. Remove the cradle, clutch dog and shift lever.

NOTE
The 1960 75 hp lower gearcase does not use a pinion thrust bearing or washer.

17. Tip the pinion gear toward the rear of the housing and remove it with the washer and thrust bearing, then invert the housing and catch the forward gear and bearing assembly as it drops out.

18. Check front bearing race (lower gearcase) and upper/lower pinion bearings (upper gearcase). Use an appropriate bearing/race

GEARCASE

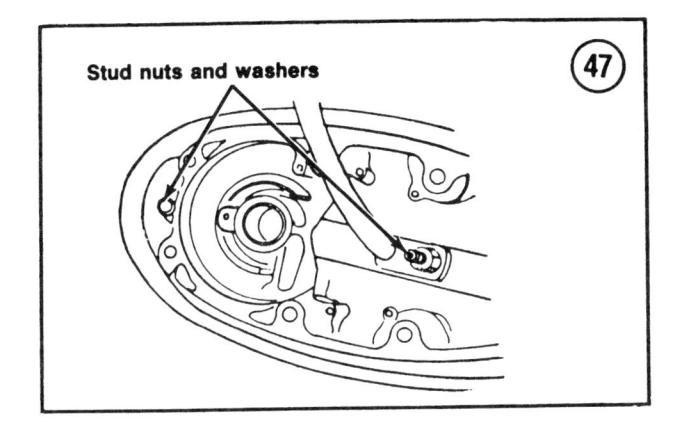

(46) [Image: bearing assembly with labels A and B]

(47) [Image: diagram showing Stud nuts and washers]

puller to remove them *only* if worn, damaged or bearing replacement is necessary. If a suitable bearing race puller is not available, heat the lower gearcase nose and tap it with a plastic or rawhide mallet. This will generally free the race for removal. There are no shims behind it.

NOTE
The gearcase originally had a splined propeller shaft and clutch dog assembly without detent spring and balls. Excessive clutch wear caused Johnson and Evinrude to provide a modification kit which their service centers installed whenever a unit was overhauled. This involves drilling a hole through the propeller shaft and installing the new design clutch dog with detent spring and balls. If your gearcase still has the original shaft/clutch dog design, have it modified by a dealer.

19. With a hand cupped over the clutch dog, slowly slide it to the front of the propeller shaft, catching the spring and 2 detent balls as the clutch dog uncovers them.

20. If forward gear bearing race was removed, position lower gearcase with its nose against a wooden block and drive a new bearing race in place until it bottoms, using a suitable installer tool and plastic or rawhide mallet. Install the roller bearing tapered end first in the race.

21. Make sure the forward gear thrust washer is in position inside the gear. Use a dab of OMC Needle Bearing grease to hold it in place, if necessary. Install the forward gear with thrust washer. Machined surface of washer should face the gear.

22A. Original propeller shaft/clutch dog—Install the clutch dog on the shaft splines.

22B. Modified shaft/clutch dog—Insert the detent spring in the propeller shaft. Position a detent ball on each side of the spring and hold in place with OMC Needle Bearing Grease. Slide the clutch dog onto the shaft until the detent balls slip into the groove inside the clutch dog. Reposition the clutch dog until it snaps into the NEUTRAL position. Chamfered and grooved lugs of the clutch dog should face the front of the shaft.

23. Install shift cradle to clutch dog and insert shifter lever in gearcase housing.

24. Install the pinion gear, washer and bearing assembly.

25. Hold pinion gear in place and insert propeller shaft in gearcase with cradle facing the shifter lever fingers. Use a long screwdriver to move the shifter lever fingers into the cradle.

26. Align the shifter lever pivot pin hole with the hole in the starboard side of the gearcase. Install a new O-ring on the pivot pin screw, coat the threads with Sealer 1000 or OMC Adhesive M and thread the screw into the gearcase to engage the shifter lever. Tighten screw securely.

27. Make sure reverse gear is properly assembled with the bushing and thrust washer installed, then fit the gear assembly on the propeller shaft, indexing its teeth with the pinion gear.

28. Install large thrust washer with its bronze side facing the reverse gear, then install the retaining plate.

29. Install retaining plate snap ring with snap ring pliers. Flat side of snap ring should face retaining plate.

30. Install 2 guide pins in the retaining plate holes. Install thrust washer (babbitt side facing gear) and index its tangs with the retaining plate cutouts.

31. Install a new O-ring on the bearing cap. Coat O-ring with Sealer 1000 or OMC Adhesive M. Fit the bearing cap on the guide pins and work it in position, then tap in place with a soft mallet.

32. Install new O-rings on each of the 4 bearing cap screws, then coat the O-rings with Sealer 1000 or OMC Adhesive M. Install 2 of the cap screws in the retaining plate holes, then remove the guide pins and install the remaining 2 screws. Tighten all screws alternately to specifications (**Table 1**).

33. Insert the 2 shifter yoke arms through top of housing to engage shifter lever pin, then install lower shift rod in yoke so that the bend in the rod faces forward. Install the bolt through the yoke arms and shift rod. Rotate the propeller shaft and pull upward on the shift rod at the same time to shift the unit into FORWARD gear and lift the bolt enough so it can be tightened.

34. Push the shift rod downward to its NEUTRAL position while rotating the propeller shaft clockwise. The pinion gear should not move in this position. Continue depressing the shift rod and rotating the propeller shaft. When REVERSE gear is reached, the pinion gear should rotate counterclockwise. Return the shift rod to FORWARD gear. The pinion gear should rotate clockwise when the propeller shaft is rotated. If the unit does not function as described, disassemble the gearcase and locate the problem.

35. If the drive shaft bearing was removed, invert the upper housing and install a new one.

36. If lower pinion gear bearing was removed, install a new bearing shell with its lettered side facing up. Wipe the inside of the bearing shell with OMC Needle Bearing Grease and install the needle bearings.

37. Lightly coat the outside of the shell with Sealer 1000 or OMC Adhesive M and install a new O-ring in the recess around the shell. Wipe away any excess sealer to prevent it from entering the bearing.

38. Wipe the shift rod with OMC Premium Blend Gearcase Lubricant. Coat the lower gearcase housing stud threads with Sealer 1000 or OMC Adhesive M. Lower the lower gearcase housing onto the inverted upper gearcase, carefully guiding the shift rod into the shift rod seal to prevent seal damage.

39. Mate the 2 gearcase sections, then install the stud washers and new self-locking nut. Tighten nuts to specifications (**Table 1**).

40. Install the drive shaft in the gearcase with a rotating motion to mesh its splines with those in the pinion gear.

41. Carefully slip bearing cap over drive shaft (with gasket, if used) and position in gearcase. Coat screw threads with OMC Screw Lock and tighten to specifications (**Table 1**).

42. Install the water pump as described in this chapter.

43. Install a new O-ring on the drive shaft groove.

44. Pressure and vacuum test the gearcase as described in this chapter.

45. Install the gearcase as described in this chapter. Fill with the recommended type and quantity of lubricant. See Chapter Four.

GEARCASE

46. Check gearcase lubricant level after engine has been run. Change the lubricant after 10 hours of operation (break-in period). See Chapter Four.

ELECTRIC SHIFT GEARCASE

Removal/Installation

1. Disconnect the spark plug lead(s) as a safety precaution to prevent any accidental starting of the engine during lower unit removal.

2. Place a container under the gearcase. Remove the oil level plug, then remove the drain/fill plug. Drain the lubricant from the unit.

NOTE
If the lubricant is white or creamy in color or metallic paricles are found in Step 3, the gearcase must be completely disassembled to determine and correct the cause of the problem.

3. Wipe a small amount of lubricant on a finger and rub the finger and thumb together. Check for the presence of metallic particles in the lubricant. Note the color of the lubricant. A white or creamy color indicates water in the lubricant. Check the drain container for signs of water separation from the lubricant.

4. Remove the propeller as described in this chapter.

5. Move the shift lever into FORWARD. If necessary, rotate the propeller shaft slightly to help unit engage.

6. Locate the shift cable wire connections next to the exhaust cover. Separate the connections.

7. Remove the outer and inner exhaust housing cover plates and gaskets. Pull the shift cable down and through the outer cover plate opening, then lubricate the cable with liquid soap and remove the inner cover and clamp.

8. Remove the fasteners holding the gearcase to the exhaust housing or gearcase extension.

9. Carefully separate the gearcase from the exhaust housing or extension to prevent damage to the water tube, drive shaft and shift cable, then remove gearcase.

10. Remove and discard the drive shaft O-ring.

11. Mount the gearcase in a suitable holding fixture.

12. To reinstall the gearcase, install a new drive shaft O-ring.

CAUTION
Do not grease the top of the drive shaft in Step 13. This may excessively preload the drive shaft and crankshaft when the mounting fasteners are tightened and cause a premature failure of the power head or gearcase.

13. Lightly lubricate the drive shaft splines with OMC Moly Lube.

14. Position gearcase under exhaust housing. Thread shift cable through exhaust housing opening, a new gasket, the exhaust housing plate and cable clamp. Align extension housing water tube with impeller housing grommet and drive shaft with crankshaft splines.

CAUTION
Do not rotate the flywheel counterclockwise in Step 15. This can damage the water pump impeller.

15. Push the gearcase into place, rotating the flywheel clockwise as required to engage the drive shaft and crankshaft.

16. Slide exhaust housing plate gasket, plate and cable clamp into place. Install inner and outer cover plates. Wipe cover plate screw threads with OMC Screw Lock and install snugly.

17. Wipe gearcase bolt threads with OMC Gasket Sealing Compound. Install bolts and tighten to specifications (**Table 1**).

18. Reconnect the shift cable connections.

19. Install the propeller as described in this chapter.

CHAPTER NINE

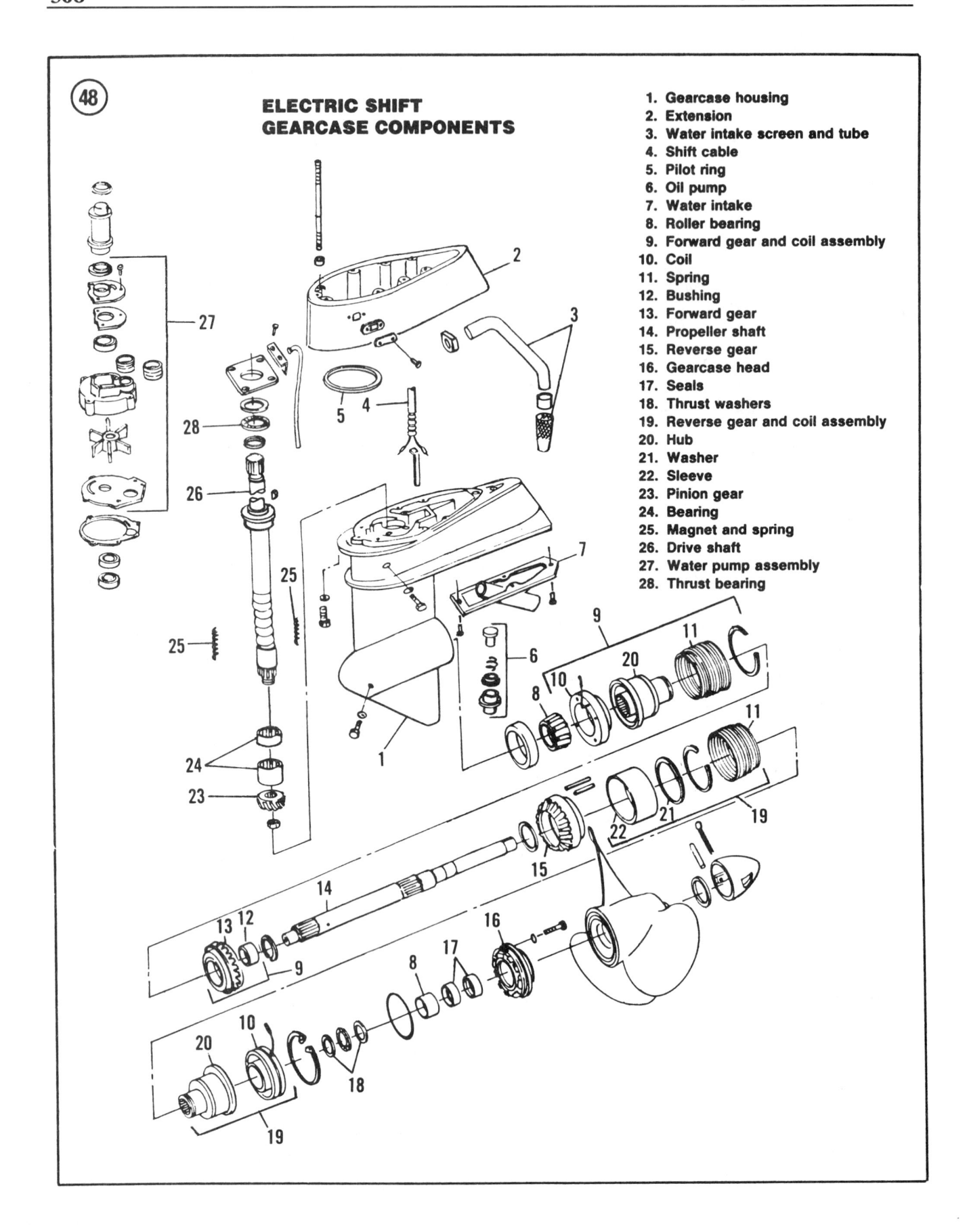

ELECTRIC SHIFT GEARCASE COMPONENTS

1. Gearcase housing
2. Extension
3. Water intake screen and tube
4. Shift cable
5. Pilot ring
6. Oil pump
7. Water intake
8. Roller bearing
9. Forward gear and coil assembly
10. Coil
11. Spring
12. Bushing
13. Forward gear
14. Propeller shaft
15. Reverse gear
16. Gearcase head
17. Seals
18. Thrust washers
19. Reverse gear and coil assembly
20. Hub
21. Washer
22. Sleeve
23. Pinion gear
24. Bearing
25. Magnet and spring
26. Drive shaft
27. Water pump assembly
28. Thrust bearing

GEARCASE

plate, the drive shaft is removed at a later point in the procedure.

5. Remove the screws holding the thrust plate or bearing cap to the gearcase. Remove the thrust plate and bearing assembly or bearing cap and drive shaft assembly from the gearcase.

6. Slide the bearing cap off the drive shaft. Remove the bearing cap seals (A, **Figure 46**) with a suitable punch. If bearing cap bearing (B, **Figure 46**) requires replacement, remove from cap with an arbor press.

7. Remove and discard the self-locking gearcase stud nuts. Remove the stud washers and shift cable retainer. See **Figure 49** (typical).

8. Carefully separate the upper and lower gearcase assemblies enough to slide shift cable insulating sleeve back and disconnect the coil lead terminals. Remove upper gearcase assembly and pilot ring (if used).

9. Remove the shift cable terminal retainer screw and washer (**Figure 50**), then remove the nylon coil lead retainer from the gearcase.

10. Remove the gearcase head/bearing housing screws with a thin-wall deep socket. Discard the O-rings on the screws, if used.

11. Install flywheel puller part No. 378103 and two puller bolts (part No. 309489) in gearcase head/bearing housing screw holes. Tighten puller nut until the head/housing comes loose.

12. Carefully remove the reverse coil snap ring with snap ring pliers. Feed the blue coil wire down through the gearcase opening.

13. Thread 2 gearcase head screws into the reverse coil and gently rock it out of the gearcase housing. See **Figure 51**.

14. Remove the propeller shaft with the reverse gear and hub assembly. If equipped with an oil pump, make sure the cam lobe on the shaft clears the pump plunger.

15. Remove the oil pump plunger, spring and body assembly from the gearcase bore, if so equipped.

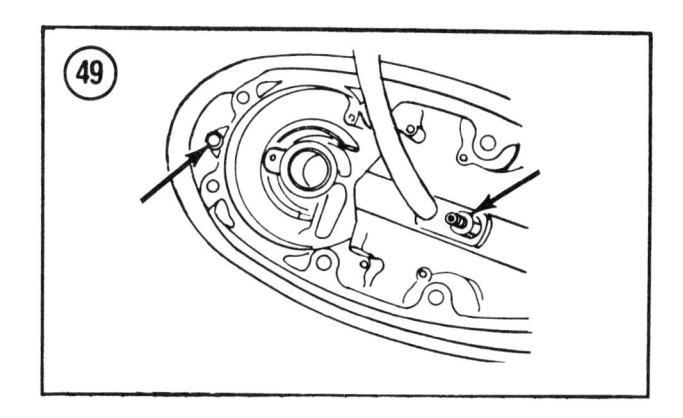

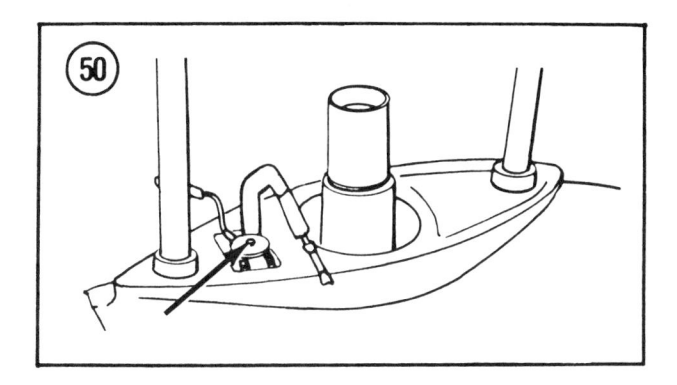

20. Reconnect the spark plug leads and refill the gearcase with the proper type and quantity of lubricant. See Chapter Four.

Disassembly

Refer to **Figure 48** (typical) for this procedure.

1. Remove the gearcase as described in this chapter.
2. Secure the gearcase in a holding fixture or a vise with protective jaws. If protective jaws are not available, position the gearcase upright in the vise with the skeg between wooden blocks.
3. Remove and discard the drive shaft O-ring.
4. Remove the water pump as described in this chapter.

NOTE
The drive shaft on units equipped with a bearing cap is removed with the cap as an assembly. On units with a thrust

16. On units with a drive shaft thrust plate, insert a suitable wrench to hold the pinion nut. Pad the side of the gearcase to prevent housing damage. Install a suitable drive shaft holding socket and rotate the drive shaft counterclockwise to loosen the pinion nut. See **Figure 52**. Once the pinion nut is removed, remove the drive shaft.

17. Tip the pinion gear toward the rear of the housing and remove it, then invert the housing and catch the forward gear/clutch hub/spring assembly as it drops out.

NOTE
After the forward coil comes loose in Step 18, make sure the coil lead is free and that its terminal connector does not become stuck in the gearcase passageway.

18. If forward coil or bearing are to be removed, remove the Phillips head screw holding the metal lead guard in the gearcase and remove the guard, if so equipped. Remove forward coil with a suitable puller.

19. Check front bearing race (lower gearcase) and upper/lower drive shaft bearings (upper gearcase). Use an appropriate bearing/race puller to remove them *only* if worn, damaged or bearing replacement is necessary. If a suitable bearing race puller is not available, heat the lower gearcase nose and tap it with a plastic or rawhide mallet. This will generally free the race for removal. There are no shims behind it.

Forward Gear Disassembly/Assembly

The forward gear assembly should not be disassembled unless parts replacement is required. If clutch has been slipping, replace both the spring and hub.

1. Remove the snap ring and slide the gear, spacer and spring from the hub.
2. Remove the bronze bearing from the gear.
3. Slide the sleeve off the clutch spring.
4. Remove and discard the gear/clutch assembly setscrews.
5. Remove the spring and nylon spacer.
6. To reassemble, install spacer with tang in cutout at back of gear.
7. Position spring in gear with spring tang beside spacer tang. Slide spring tang to side of slot so it will pull against slot when spring is tightened.
8. Clean new setscrews with OMC Locquic Primer and coat with OMC Nut Lock.
9. Install setscrews. Starting with the one nearest the spring tang, tighten setscrews to 30-35 in.-lb. in a clockwise pattern as spring is held in a tightened position.
10. Bake assembly in an oven for 20-30 minutes at 230° F or let the assembly set for 4 hours at room temperature to allow the OMC Nut Lock to cure properly.
11. Install bronze bearing in gear.
12. Install sleeve over the spring with its flanged end facing the coil.
13. Carefully slide gear and spring assembly onto clutch hub. Install snap ring with its lettered side facing out, making sure it fits completely into the hub groove.

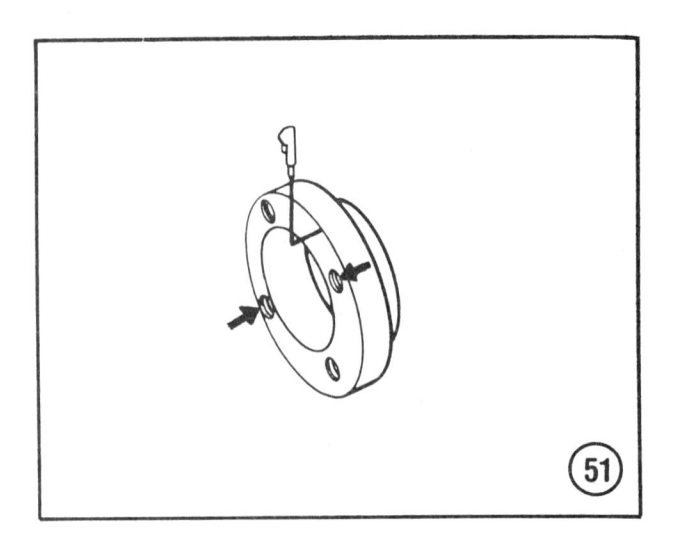

Reverse Gear Disassembly/Assembly

The reverse gear assembly should not be disassembled unless parts replacement is

GEARCASE

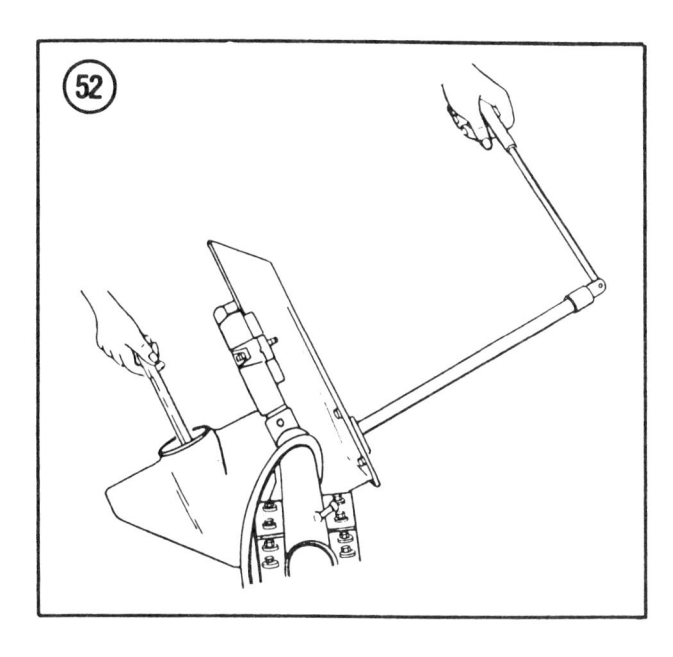

(52)

required. If the clutch has been slipping, replace the spring and hub.

1. Remove the snap ring and slide the gear and spring from the sleeve and clutch hub.
2. Remove and discard the 40 needle bearings around the clutch hub.
3. Remove and discard the gear/clutch assembly setscrews.
4. Remove the spring and nylon spacer.
5. To reassemble, install spacer with tang in cupped end slot of gear.
6. Position spring in gear with spring tang beside spacer tang. Slide spring tang to side of slot so it will pull against slot when spring is tightened.
7. Clean new setscrews with OMC Locquic Primer and coat with OMC Nut Lock.
8. Install setscrews. Starting with the one nearest the spring tang, tighten setscrews to 30-35 in.-lb. in a clockwise pattern as spring is held in a tightened position.
9. Bake assembly in an oven for 20-30 minutes at 230° F or let the assembly set for 4 hours at room temperature to allow the OMC Nut Lock to cure properly.
10. Coat reverse clutch hub with OMC Needle Bearing grease. Install 40 new needle bearings around hub.
11. Fit reverse sleeve over spring with largest end near gear. Slide gear and spring assembly over clutch hub.
12. Install snap ring with its lettered side facing out, making sure it fits completely into the hub groove.

Shift Coil and Cable Check

1. Check shift coil leads for damaged insulation. Repair as required.
2. Connect an ohmmeter between the coil lead and the metal coil case. With the meter set on the low scale, reading should be approximately 6 ohms. If not, replace the coil.
3. Check shift cable for damaged insulation or broken leads. Repair as required.
4. Check cable leads for continuity with an ohmmeter. When meter leads are connected to the same wire, there should be continuity. When meter leads are connected to different wires, there should be no continuity.

Assembly

Refer to **Figure 48** (typical) for this procedure.

1. Note direction of gearcase head seal lips, then remove and discard both seals. Remove needle bearing from gearcase head with a suitable driver.
2. Wipe the outer case of the new gearcase head seals with OMC Gasket Sealing Compound. Install seals back-to-back with a suitable installer, then pack the cavity between the seal lips with OMC Triple-Guard grease.
3. Install a new needle bearing in the gearcase head with a suitable installer.
4. Reinstall front bearing race with a suitable installer, if removed.
5. Connect a length of wire to the forward coil lead. Feed the wire into the propeller shaft bore and up through the forward coil lead opening.

6. Attach the forward coil to the slide hammers used during disassembly and insert the assembly into the propeller shaft bore with the lead wire facing up. As the coil is seated, draw the lead wire through the opening.

7. When forward coil is fully seated, run the coil lead insulating tubing down over the length of wire used to pull the lead in place. Slide the tubing over the coil lead and disconnect the feed wires. Remove the slide hammers.

8. With the forward coil in place, connect an ohmmeter between the coil lead and ground. With the meter on the low scale, the reading should be approximately 6 ohms. If not, the coil or lead was damaged during installation and should be removed for inspection and further testing.

9. Install retaining screw and washer over nylon tubing and install metal lead guard, if used. Tubing should butt against coil for proper installation of lead guard.

10. If drive shaft bearings were removed from gearcase housing, install new bearings with suitable installers.

11. Install the forward gear and clutch assembly in the propeller shaft bore.

12. If fitted with an oil pump, install the pinion gear, then fit the drive shaft into the housing to engage the gear. Install the pinion gear locknut and hold with an open-end wrench. Install a suitable holding socket on the end of the drive shaft and turn the drive shaft clockwise to tighten the locknut to specifications (**Table 1**).

13. Install the oil pump and plunger, if so equipped. Make sure pump cam faces away from pump and shaft engages forward gear hub splines.

14. If not fitted with an oil pump, insert the pinion gear with thrust bearing and washer. Hold pinion gear in place during the next step.

15. Install the propeller shaft and reverse gear assembly.

16. Attach the slide hammers used during disassembly to the reverse coil. Position the coil on the propeller shaft with its lead at the top and work it into the gearcase beyond the lock ring groove.

17. Carefully remove the slide hammers and route the coil lead through the hole at the top of the propeller shaft bore. Reach into the cavity at the top rear of the gearcase and pull the lead through. Make sure lead is not twisted or kinked during installation.

18. Repeat Step 8 to check the reverse coil. Secure coil leads in nylon retainer and install washer and screw (**Figure 50**), if used.

CAUTION
Reverse coil failure will result if the snap ring is installed in Step 19 with its cutout at the bottom of the bore. The cutout is provided to protect the coil lead and if the ring is not properly positioned, it will press against the lead and fray the wire.

19. Install the coil snap ring with its cutout facing upward and lettered side facing out.

20. Install the thrust washer with its bronze side facing inward. If a thrust bearing with washers is used, sandwich the bearing between the washers and install on the propeller shaft with the thin washer (chamfer on inner diameter) facing the reverse coil.

21. Install a new O-ring on the gearcase head. Wipe the O-ring with OMC Triple-Guard grease. Install gearcase head, aligning the countersunk holes in the head assembly with those tapped in the rear coil. Seat the gearcase head in place by tapping with a soft mallet.

22. Install new O-rings on the gearcase head screws. Coat the screw threads with OMC Gasket Sealing Compound. Install and tighten screws securely.

GEARCASE

23. If a drive shaft thrust plate is used, install the thrust bearing, washer, thrust plate, oil line bracket and oil line. Tighten screws securely. Install pilot ring, if used.

24. If lower pinion gear bearing was removed, install a new bearing shell with its lettered side facing up. Wipe the inside of the bearing shell with OMC Needle Bearing Grease and install the needle bearings.

25. Lightly coat the outside of the shell with Sealer 1000 or OMC Adhesive M and install a new O-ring in the recess around the shell. Wipe away any excess sealer to prevent it from entering the bearing.

26. Coat the lower gearcase housing stud threads with Sealer 1000 or OMC Adhesive M. Lower the lower gearcase housing onto the inverted upper gearcase until the assemblies are about 3 inches apart, then connect the coil and shift cable leads. Slide insulators over connections.

27. Make sure the leads are not pinched as the 2 gearcase sections are mated, then install the stud washers and new self-locking nut. Tighten nuts securely.

28. Apply Sealer 1000 or OMC Adhesive M between the shift cable retainer, gearcase and rear stud to prevent exhaust gas from entering the cooling system. See **Figure 49**.

29. Install drive shaft and bearing cap on models so equipped. Wipe bearing cap screw threads with Perfect Seal No. 4 and tighten to specifications (**Table 1**).

30. Install the water intake assembly, if used.

31. Install the water pump as described in this chapter.

32. Install a new O-ring on the drive shaft groove.

33. Pressure and vacuum test the gearcase as described in this chapter.

34. Install the gearcase as described in this chapter. Fill with the recommended type and quantity of lubricant. See Chapter Four.

35. Check gearcase lubricant level after engine has been run. Change the lubricant after 10 hours of operation (break-in period). See Chapter Four.

HYDRO-ELECTRIC SHIFT GEARCASE

Removal/Installation

1. Disconnect the spark plug lead(s) as a safety precaution to prevent any accidental starting of the engine during lower unit removal.

2. Place a container under the gearcase. Remove the oil level plug, then remove the drain/fill plug. Drain the lubricant from the unit.

NOTE
If the lubricant is white or creamy in color or metallic particles are found in Step 3, the gearcase must be completely disassembled to determine and correct the cause of the problem.

3. Wipe a small amount of lubricant on a finger and rub the finger and thumb together. Check for the presence of metallic particles in the lubricant. Note the color of the lubricant. A white or creamy color indicates water in the lubricant. Check the drain container for signs of water separation from the lubricant.

4. Remove the propeller as described in this chapter.

5. Move the shift lever into FORWARD. If necessary, rotate the propeller shaft slightly to help unit engage.

6. Locate the shift cable wire connections on the starboard side of the power head (**Figure 53**). Separate the connections.

7. Lubricate the shift cable sleeve with liquid soap to assure smooth passage through the exhaust housing adapter when gearcase is removed.

8. Remove the fasteners holding the gearcase to the exhaust housing or gearcase extension.

9. Mark the trim tab position relative to the gearcase for reinstallation, then remove the trim tab screw and trim tab (A, **Figure 54**).

10. Remove the countersunk 5/8 in. screw between the trim tab cavity and gearcase housing with a narrow wall socket (B, **Figure 54**).
11. Remove the screw from inside the trim tab cavity with a 1/2 in. socket and extension. See **Figure 55**.
12. Remove the gearcase-to-exhaust housing screws on each side of the gearcase.
13. Carefully separate the gearcase from the exhaust housing or extension to prevent damage to the water tube, drive shaft and shift cable, then remove gearcase. Do not lose plastic water tube guides.
14. Remove and discard the drive shaft O-ring.
15. Mount the gearcase in a suitable holding fixture.
16. To reinstall the gearcase, install a new drive shaft O-ring.

> *CAUTION*
> *Do not grease the top of the drive shaft in Step 17. This may excessively preload the drive shaft and crankshaft when the mounting fasteners are tightened and cause a premature failure of the power head or gearcase.*

17. Lightly lubricate the drive shaft splines with OMC Moly Lube.
18. Position plastic water tube guides in the water pump housing cover.
19. Lubricate the upper end of the shift cable sleeve with liquid soap.
20. Connect a length of wire to the gearcase shift cable terminals. Feed wire through shift cable hole in adapter.
21. Coat gearcase and exhaust housing mating surfaces with Sealer 1000 or OMC Adhesive M.
22. Position gearcase under exhaust housing. Move gearcase upward, aligning drive shaft with crankshaft splines. Make sure the plastic tubes guide the water tubes into the water pump grommets and pull the shift cable into place with the attached wire.

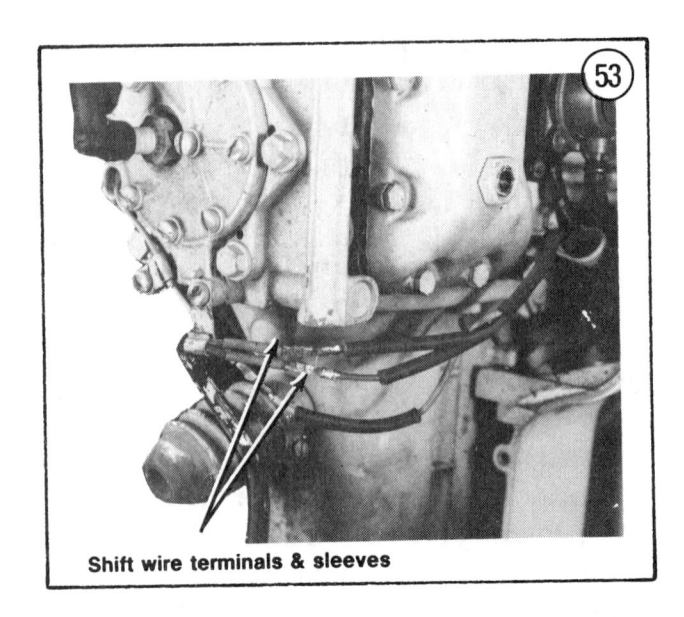

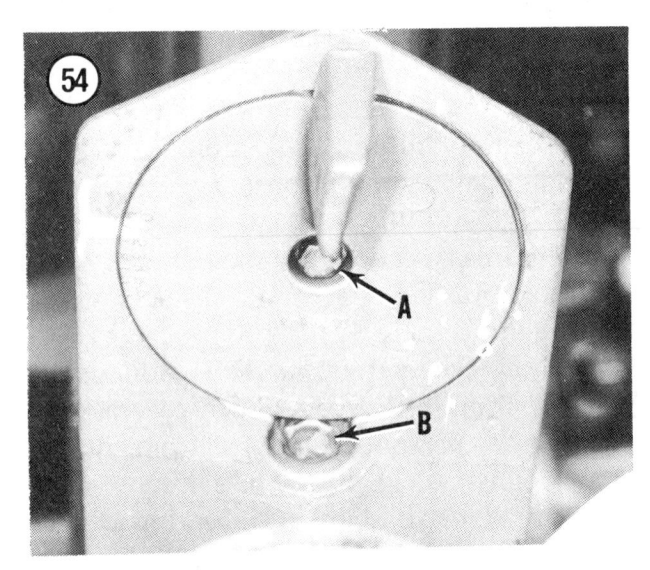

> *CAUTION*
> *Do not rotate the flywheel counterclockwise in Step 23. This can damage the water pump impeller.*

23. Push the gearcase into place, rotating the flywheel clockwise as required to engage the drive shaft and crankshaft.
24. Wipe gearcase bolt threads with OMC Gasket Sealing Compound. Install bolts and tighten to specifications (**Table 1**).

GEARCASE

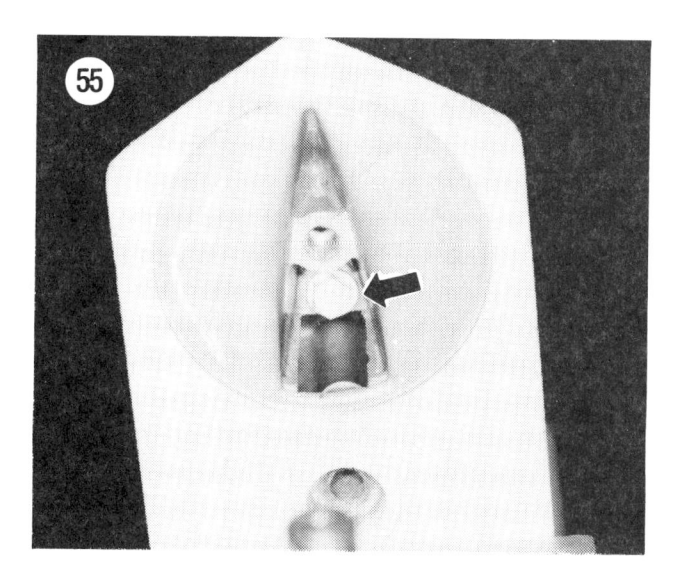

315

55

25. Connect an ohmmeter between ground and each shift cable wire in turn. With the meter on the low scale, both should read 5-7 ohms. If not, the solenoids or leads may have been damaged during installation. Locate and correct the problem before proceeding.
26. Reconnect the shift cable connections.
27. Install the propeller as described in this chapter.
28. Reconnect the spark plug leads and refill the gearcase with the proper type and quantity of lubricant. See Chapter Four.

Disassembly

Refer to **Figure 56** (typical) for this procedure.

1. Remove the gearcase as described in this chapter.
2. Secure the gearcase in a holding fixture or a vise with protective jaws. If protective jaws are not available, position the gearcase upright in the vise with the skeg between wooden blocks.
3. Remove the water pump as described in this chapter.
4. Remove the screws holding the drive shaft upper bearing housing to the gearcase. Carefully pry the bearing housing loose and remove it from the drive shaft.

5. Remove the screws holding the solenoid cover to the gearcase. Remove the cover, gasket and wave washer. Discard the gasket.
6. Remove the solenoids, shift rod and casing assembly from the gearcase. See **Figure 57**.
7. Remove the drive shaft bearing housing seals (A, **Figure 46**) with a suitable punch. If the bearing (B, **Figure 46**) requires replacement, remove from housing with an arbor press.
8. Remove the 4 propeller shaft bearing housing screws with a thin-wall deep socket. Discard the O-rings on the screws, if used. Scribe a mark at the top of the bearing housing for reinstallation reference.

NOTE
If bearing housing does not have threaded holes for use in Step 9, use puller legs (part No. 321631) instead of bolts. Fit legs around bearing housing flange legs and tighten the puller nut to remove housing.

9. Install flywheel puller part No. 378103 and two 8 in. 5/16-20 bolts in bearing housing screw holes. Tighten puller nut until the housing comes loose.
10. Remove the puller assembly from the bearing housing. Remove the bearing housing from the gearcase (**Figure 58**). Remove and discard the bearing housing O-ring.
11. Reach into the gearcase propeller bore and remove the thrust washer and thrust bearing, if used.
12. Use snap ring pliers (part No. 311879) and carefully remove the 2 large snap rings in the gearcase propeller shaft bore (**Figure 59**).
13. Remove the propeller shaft with reverse gear and retainer plate from the gearcase (**Figure 60**).
14. Install drive shaft holding socket (part No. 312752) on the drive shaft splines and connect a breaker bar. Hold the pinion locknut with a socket and flex handle. Pad

9

CHAPTER NINE

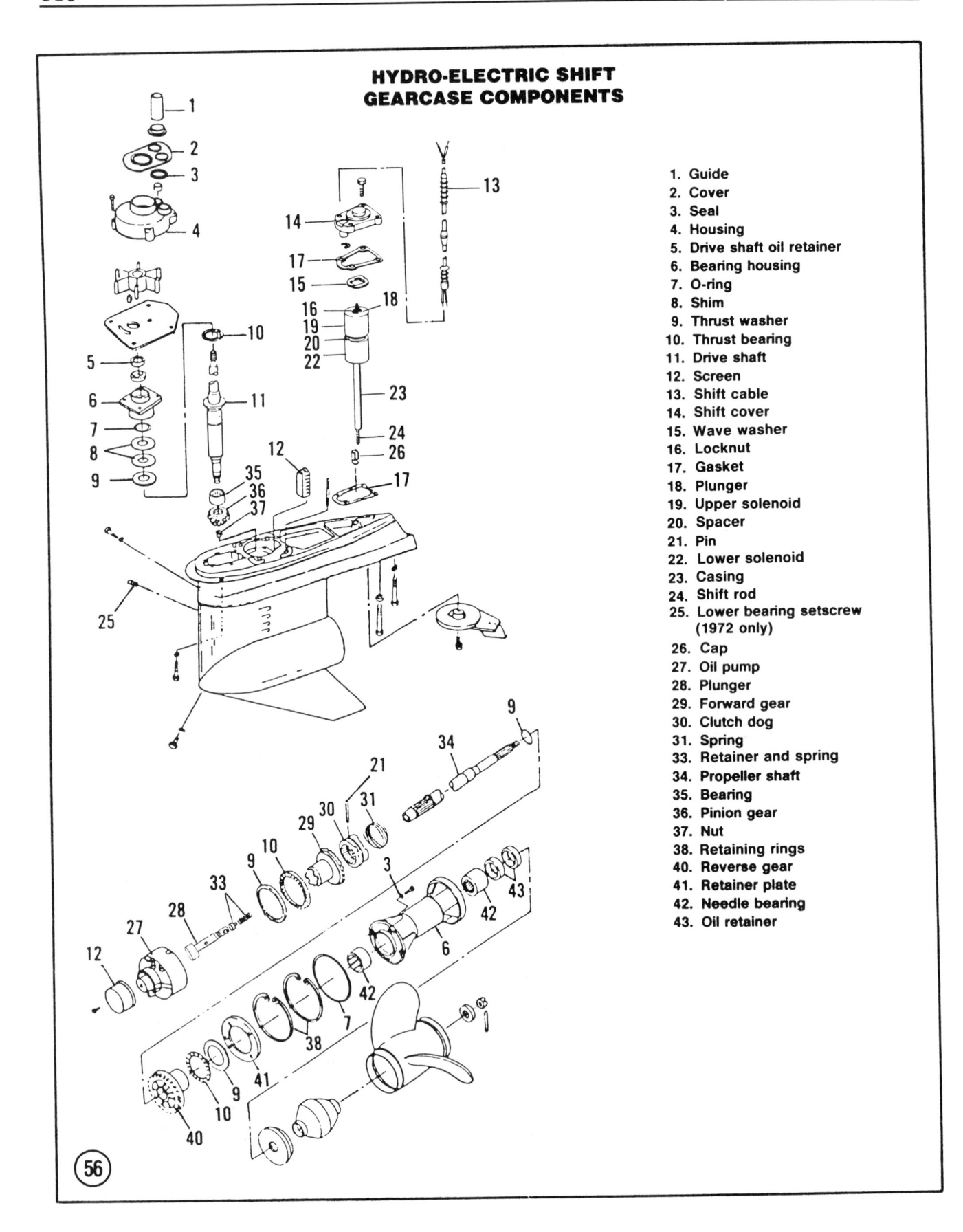

HYDRO-ELECTRIC SHIFT GEARCASE COMPONENTS

1. Guide
2. Cover
3. Seal
4. Housing
5. Drive shaft oil retainer
6. Bearing housing
7. O-ring
8. Shim
9. Thrust washer
10. Thrust bearing
11. Drive shaft
12. Screen
13. Shift cable
14. Shift cover
15. Wave washer
16. Locknut
17. Gasket
18. Plunger
19. Upper solenoid
20. Spacer
21. Pin
22. Lower solenoid
23. Casing
24. Shift rod
25. Lower bearing setscrew (1972 only)
26. Cap
27. Oil pump
28. Plunger
29. Forward gear
30. Clutch dog
31. Spring
33. Retainer and spring
34. Propeller shaft
35. Bearing
36. Pinion gear
37. Nut
38. Retaining rings
40. Reverse gear
41. Retainer plate
42. Needle bearing
43. Oil retainer

GEARCASE

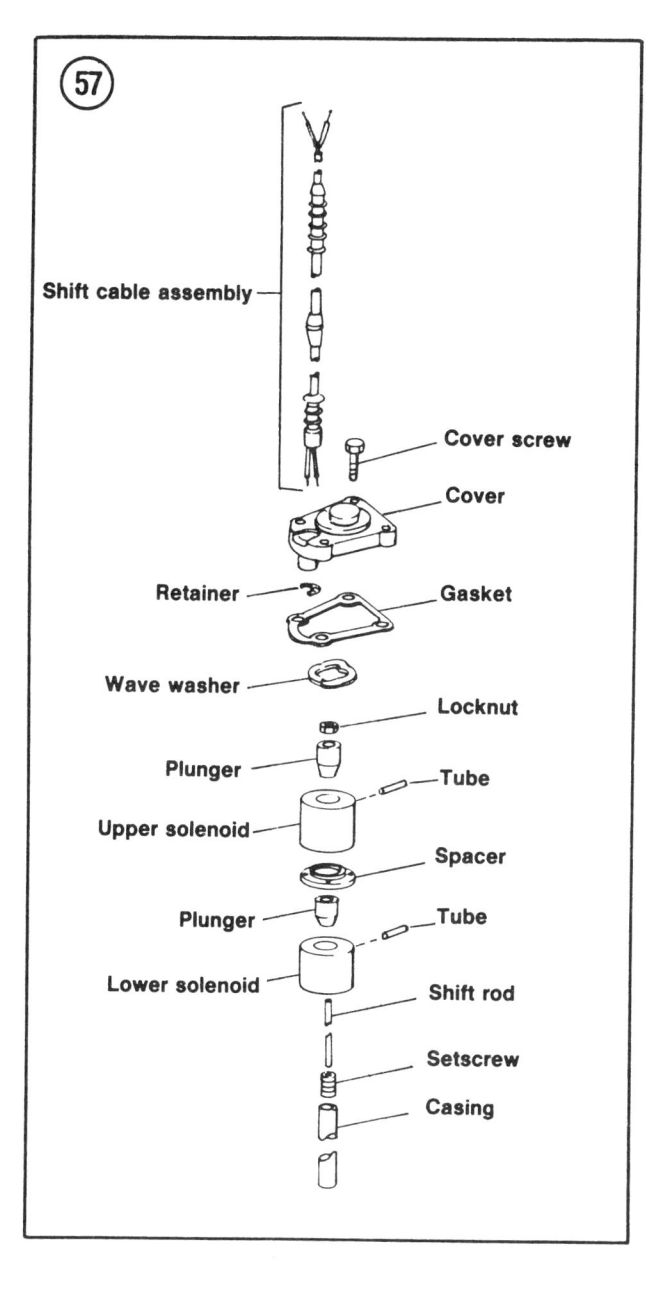

the gearcase where the flex handle will hit with shop cloths to prevent housing damage.

15. Hold the pinion nut from moving and turn the drive shaft counterclockwise to break the pinion nut loose. See **Figure 61**. Remove the pinion locknut and drive shaft holding tools.

16. Remove the pinion locknut from the gearcase. Remove the pinion gear (**Figure 62**) from the gearcase.

17. Remove the drive shaft from the gearcase with shims, thrust washers and bearing.

18. Remove the forward gear, thrust washers and bearing from the gearcase (**Figure 63**).

19. Thread two 12 in. 1/4-20 rods into the oil pump housing. Attach slide hammers to the rods. Make sure the slide hammers are installed evenly and apply a uniform pressure on each to remove the oil pump from the

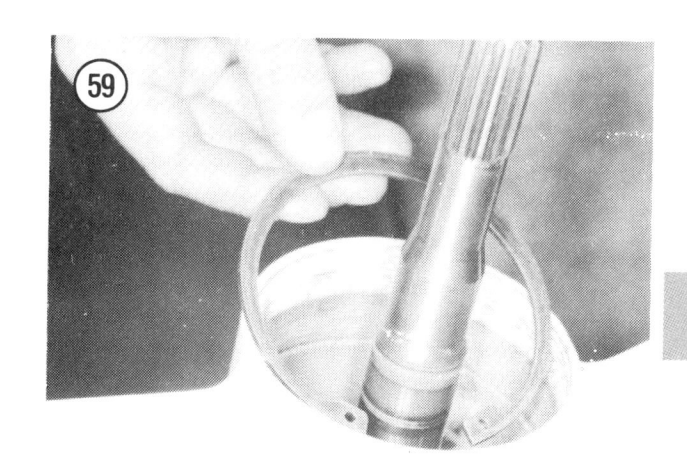

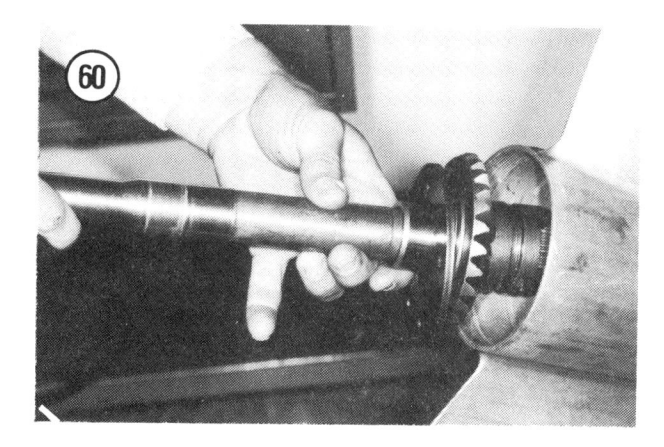

gearcase without cocking the unit. If the unit does cock, reverse the pressure to reseat the pump and start over.

Lower Drive Shaft Bearing Replacement

Do not remove the bearing unless it requires replacement. On all except 1972 models, the bearing can be driven out with a suitable punch. On 1972 models, a setscrew must be removed from the starboard side near the water pickup slot. The bearing can then be pulled from the gearcase with special tool part No. 385546.

A special installation kit is required to install a new bearing. Use part No. 383173 (55 and 60 hp), part No. 385547 (1972 V4) or part No. 384096 (all others). Assemble the tools as shown in **Figure 64** and pull the bearing into place. On 1972 models, coat the setscrew threads with Loctite and install snugly in gearcase.

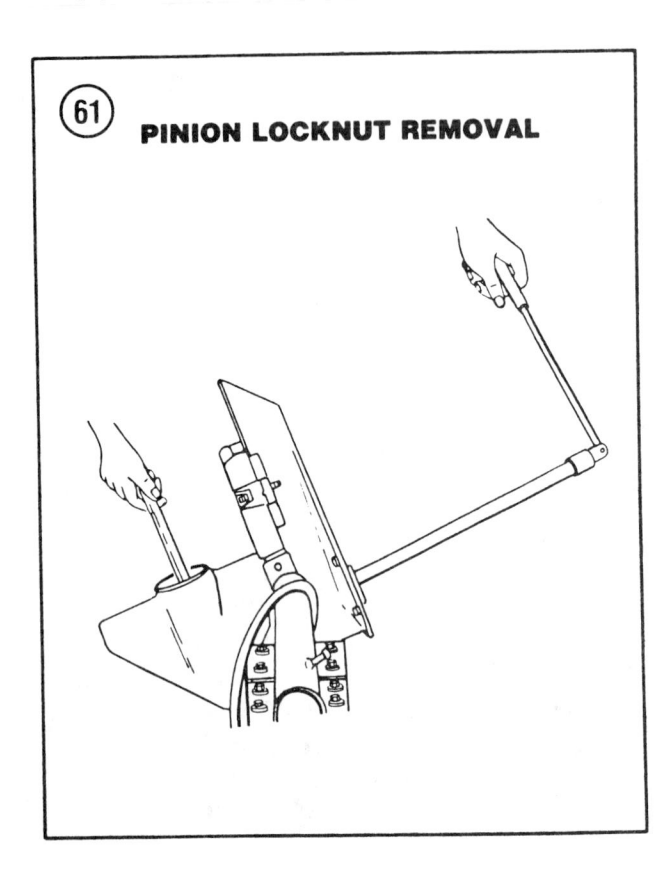

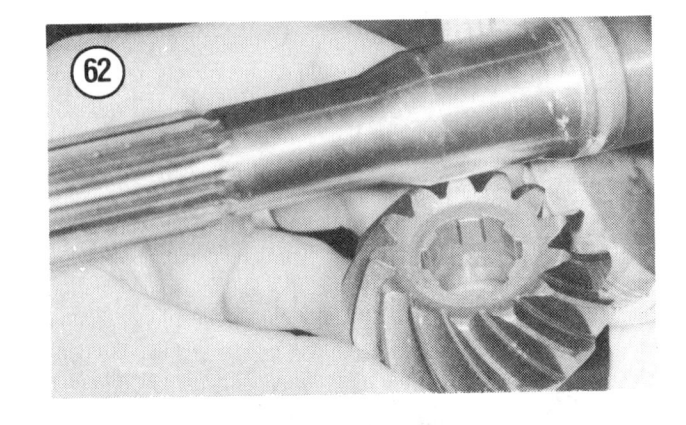

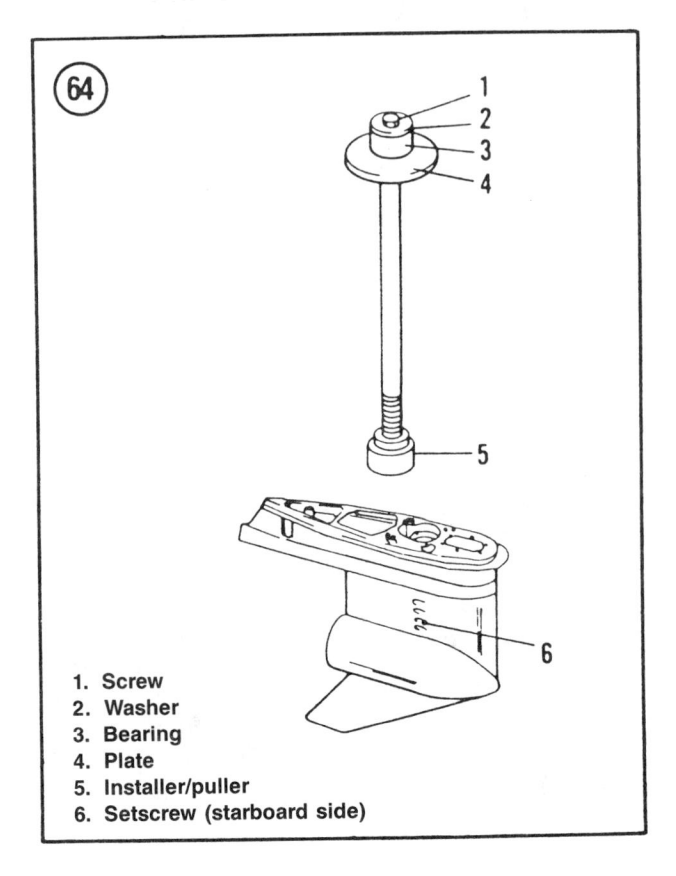

61 PINION LOCKNUT REMOVAL

64
1. Screw
2. Washer
3. Bearing
4. Plate
5. Installer/puller
6. Setscrew (starboard side)

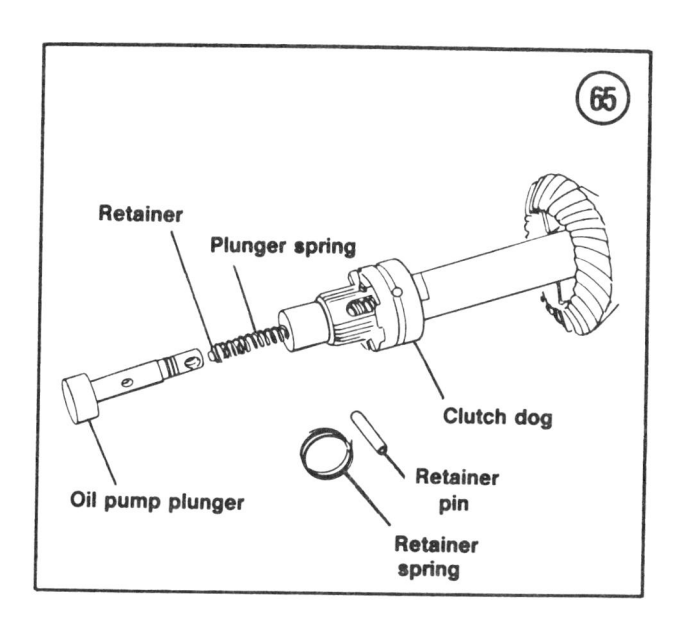

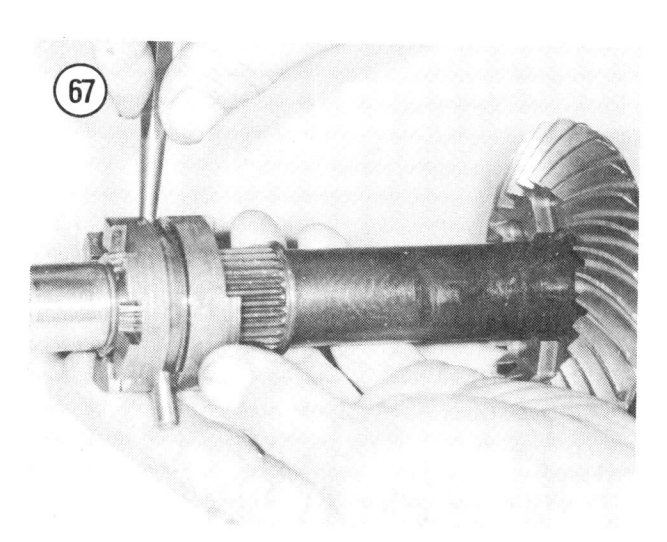

GEARCASE

319

Figure 65 — Retainer, Plunger spring, Oil pump plunger, Clutch dog, Retainer pin, Retainer spring

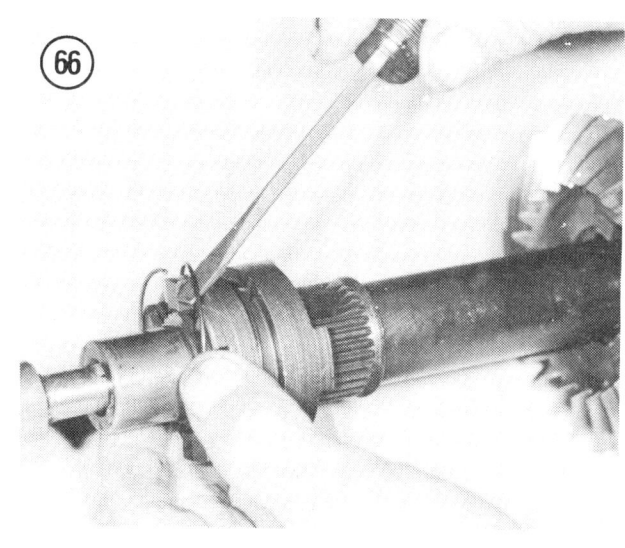

Propeller Shaft Disassembly/Assembly

Refer to **Figure 65** for this procedure.

1. Carefully lift one end of the clutch dog retaining spring and insert a screwdriver blade under it as shown in **Figure 66**. Holding the screwdriver stationary, rotate the propeller shaft to unwind the spring.
2. Remove the retainer pin with an appropriate size punch. See **Figure 67**.
3. Remove the pump plunger, retainer and spring from the propeller shaft. See **Figure 68**.
4. Remove the clutch dog from the propeller shaft.
5. To reassemble, align clutch dog holes with propeller shaft holes, then install on shaft with 3-ramp side facing front of shaft. Some clutch dogs may be marked with the words "PROP END" to indicate proper positioning.
6. Install the retainer in the end of the spring, then insert spring in the end of the shaft followed by the pump plunger.
7. Compress the retainer/spring assembly with the plunger until the retainer hole aligns with the shaft and clutch dog holes, then insert the retainer pin.
8. Reinstall one end of the clutch dog retaining spring over the clutch dog, then rotate the propeller shaft to wind the spring back in place.

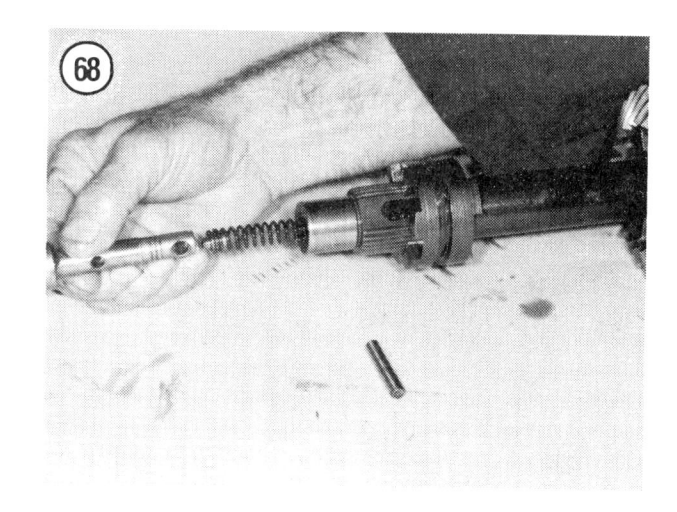

9

Oil Pump Disassembly/Assembly

1. Remove the 4 screws and lockwashers from the oil pump cover. Remove the cover from the housing. See **Figure 69**.
2. Remove the rubber oil seal and band from the pump cover, if used.
3. Remove the screw holding the screen to the cover. See **Figure 70**. Carefully remove the screen (sealed with Sealer 1000 or OMC Adhesive M) from the cover.
4. Drive out the reverse valve lever pin (**Figure 71**).
5. Remove the pin, valve, arm and check valve balls. See **Figure 72**.
6. Note the identification marks on the pump gears if they are to be removed. Gears must be reinstalled in the same relationship.
7. Check balls and seats for nicks, grooves or other defects. Replace if any damage is noted.
8. Check pump bearing. Replace pump if bearing is damaged.
9. To reassemble, insert check valve balls. Reconnect the valve lever with the pin.
10. If pump gears were removed, coat with OMC Premium Blend Gearcase lubricant and reinstall in housing.
11. Align pump cover tang with cutout in housing and install the cover to the housing. Tighten screws to specifications (**Table 1**).
12. Coat mating edge of pump cover screen with Sealer 1000 or OMC Adhesive M. Reinstall screen and tighten screw securely. Install band and oil seal, if used.
13. Install the forward gear to the pump housing. Tangs on gear must fit into the housing slots.

Solenoid/Shift Assembly

Do not disassemble this unit. If defective, it is serviced by replacement only.

Assembly

1. Remove and discard the propeller shaft bearing housing seals. Check the housing

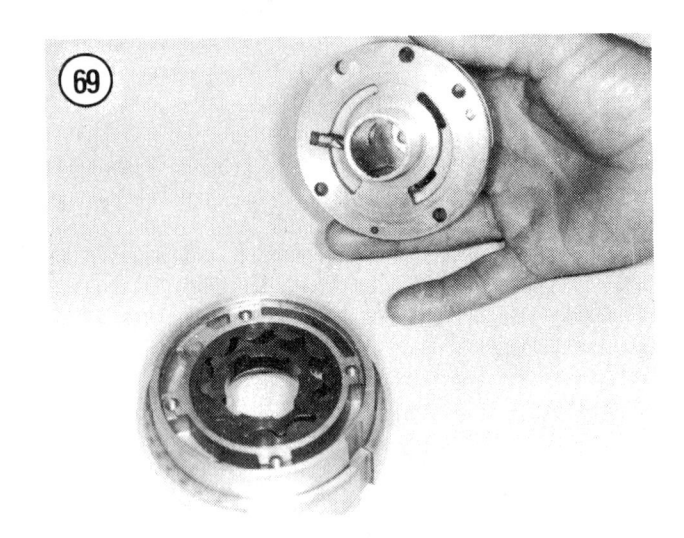

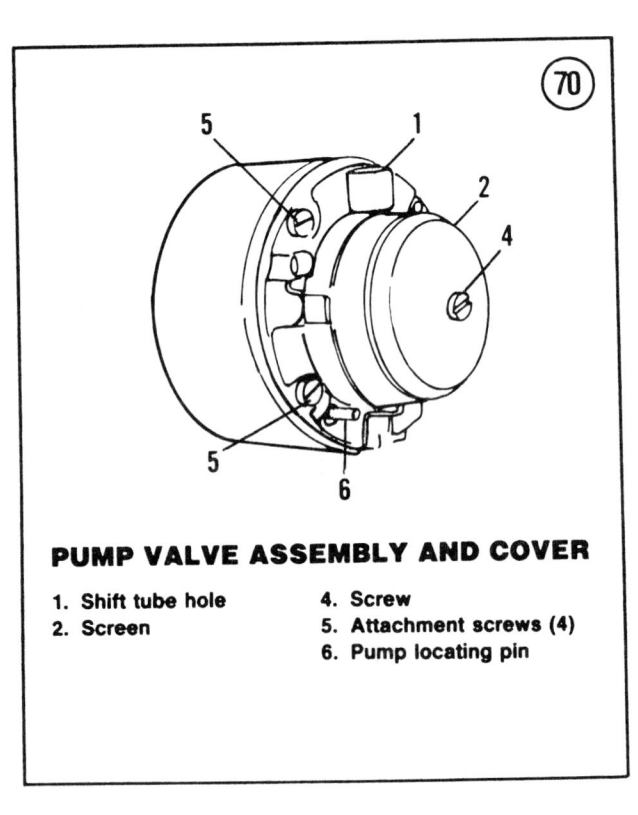

PUMP VALVE ASSEMBLY AND COVER
1. Shift tube hole
2. Screen
4. Screw
5. Attachment screws (4)
6. Pump locating pin

bearings. If replacement is required, drive bearings out with a suitable punch.
2. If bearing housing bearings were removed, install a new bearing at each end of the housing with its lettered side facing out. Use a suitable socket and drive into place.
3. Wipe the outer case of the new bearing housing seals with OMC Gasket Sealing Compound. Install seals back-to-back with a

GEARCASE

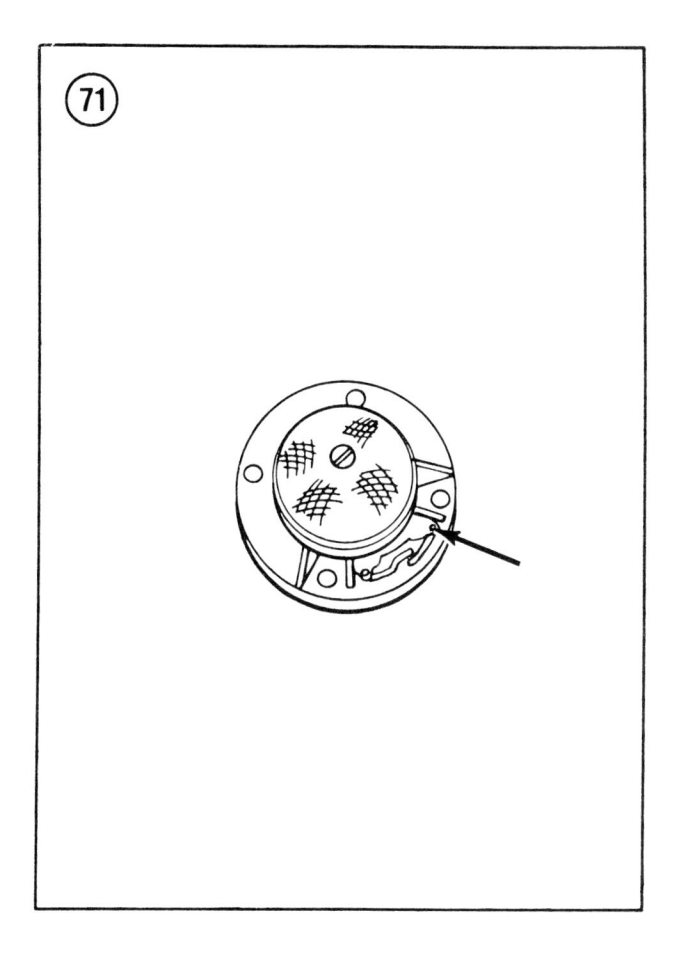

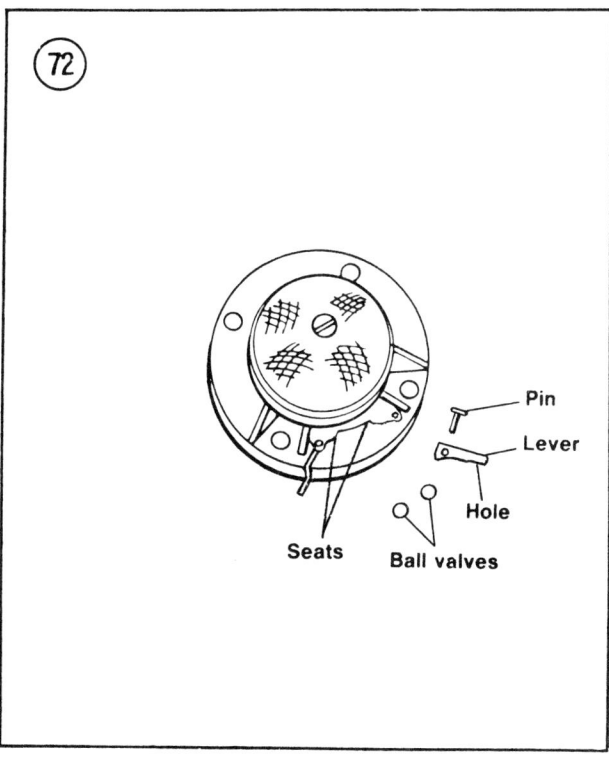

71

suitable installer, then pack the cavity between the seal lips with OMC Triple-Guard grease.

4. Position the gearcase with the propeller shaft bore facing upward.

5. Remove the forward gear from the oil pump. Attach the slide hammers and threaded rods (used during removal) to the pump. Align the tang and pin on the rear of the pump with the top of the gearcase, then lower the assembly into the propeller shaft bore. When properly installed, the pin will engage a hole in the housing and prevent the pump from rotating. It may take a little patience and several tries to accomplish this. When pump is seated, remove slide hammers and rods.

6. Coat the pump plunger with OMC Premium Blend Gearcase Lubricant and install large end of plunger in oil pump.

7. Install the pump snap ring, if used.

8. Install the thrust washer and bearing in the oil pump with flat side of bearing facing out.

NOTE
Step 9 should be relatively easy if the pump gears were not disturbed during pump installation. This was the purpose of reattaching the 2 units earlier. If gears were moved, use a flashlight and long-blade screwdriver to reposition them as required.

9. Reinstall the forward gear in the propeller shaft bore and index the gear tangs with the pump housing slots.

NOTE
Steps 10-13 apply only to V4 gearcases.

72

10. Secure the drive shaft in a vise with protective jaws or between wooden blocks. Install the pinion gear and tighten the locknut to specifications.

11. Install the shims removed during gearcase disassembly on drive shaft shoulder.

Install shim gauge part No. 315767 on drive shaft (**Figure 73**).

12. Hold gauge against shims and measure the clearance between the bottom of the gauge and top of the pinion gear. If the clearance is not 0.000-0.002 in., add or subtract shims as required.

13. Remove the gauge, shims, pinion gear locknut and pinion gear from the drive shaft. Remove the drive shaft from the vise.

14. Install pinion gear in gearcase. Flat side of bearing must face upward in gearcase and gear teeth must mesh with forward gear teeth.

15. Hold the pinion gear in place and install the drive shaft, rotating it as required to index the shaft and gear splines. Install pinion gear locknut.

16. Install drive shaft holding socket (part No. 312752) on the drive shaft splines and connect a breaker bar. Hold the pinion locknut with a socket and flex handle. Pad the gearcase where the flex handle will hit with shop cloths to prevent housing damage.

17. Hold the pinion nut from moving and turn the drive shaft clockwise to tighten the pinion nut. See **Figure 61**. Remove the pinion locknut and drive shaft holding tools.

18. V4—Reinstall the thrust bearing, thrust washer and shims (in that order) on the drive shaft shoulder.

19. Wipe the outer case of new drive shaft bearing housing seals with OMC Gasket Sealing Compound. Install seals back-to-back with a suitable installer, then pack the cavity between the seal lips with OMC Triple-Guard grease. Install a new O-ring on bearing housing and wipe with the same lubricant.

20. Wrap the drive shaft splines with tape to protect the bearing housing seals. Carefully work bearing housing over drive shaft and into position in the gearcase. Install and tighten the screws to specifications (**Table 1**). Remove the tape from the drive shaft splines. Clean any adhesive residue from the splines with solvent. Lubricate drive shaft with OMC Premium Blend Gearcase Lubricant.

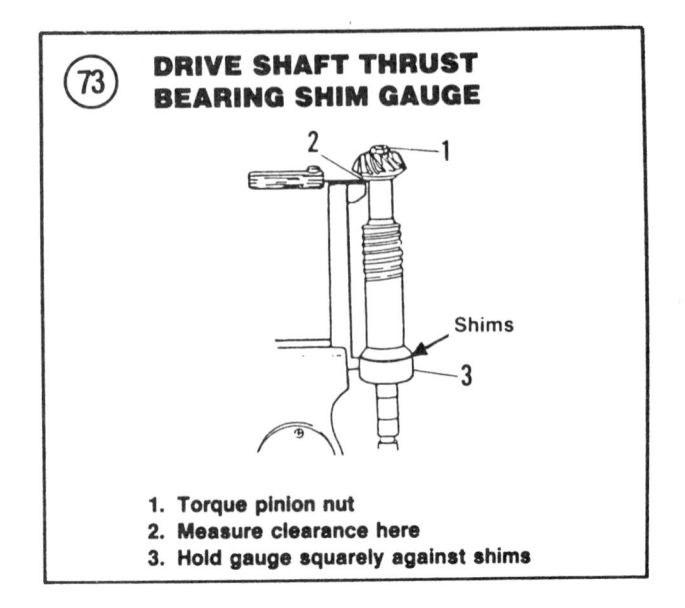

21. Make sure the forward gear thrust washer is still in place, then lower the propeller shaft assembly into the gearcase bore until the shaft indexes over the oil pump plunger.

22. Lightly coat the reverse gear thrust washer with OMC Needle Bearing Grease. Install thrust washer in reverse gear.

23. Install the thrust bearing and thrust washer on the reverse gear shank, then install the gear and retainer plate on the propeller shaft (**Figure 74**) and index its teeth with the pinion gear teeth.

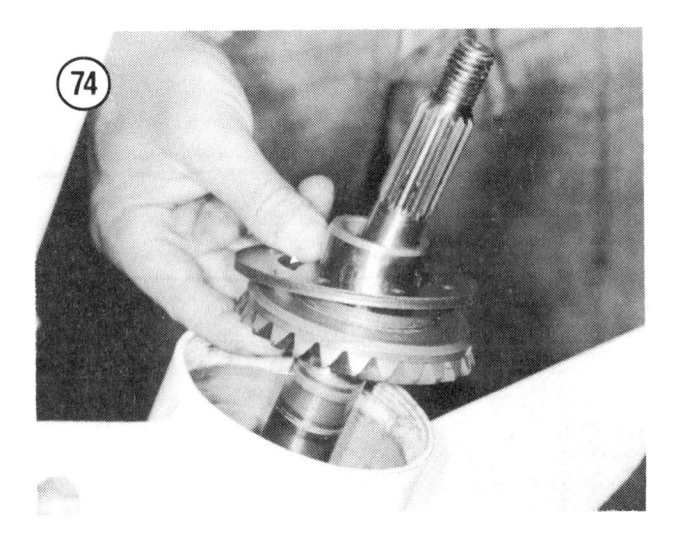

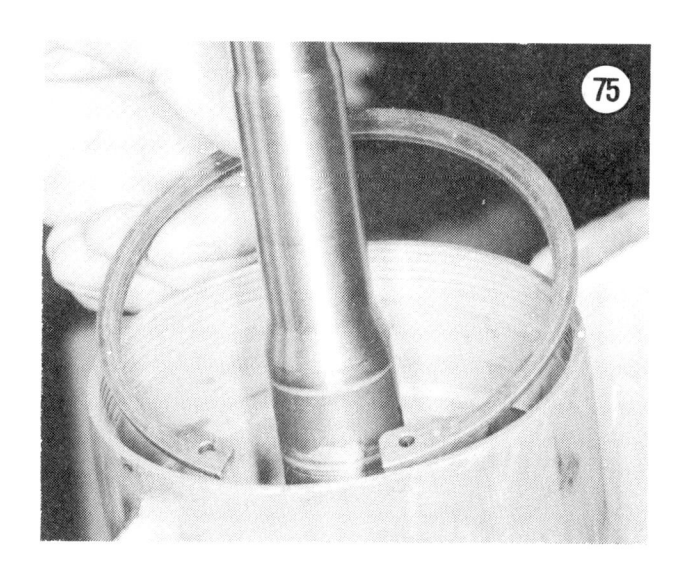

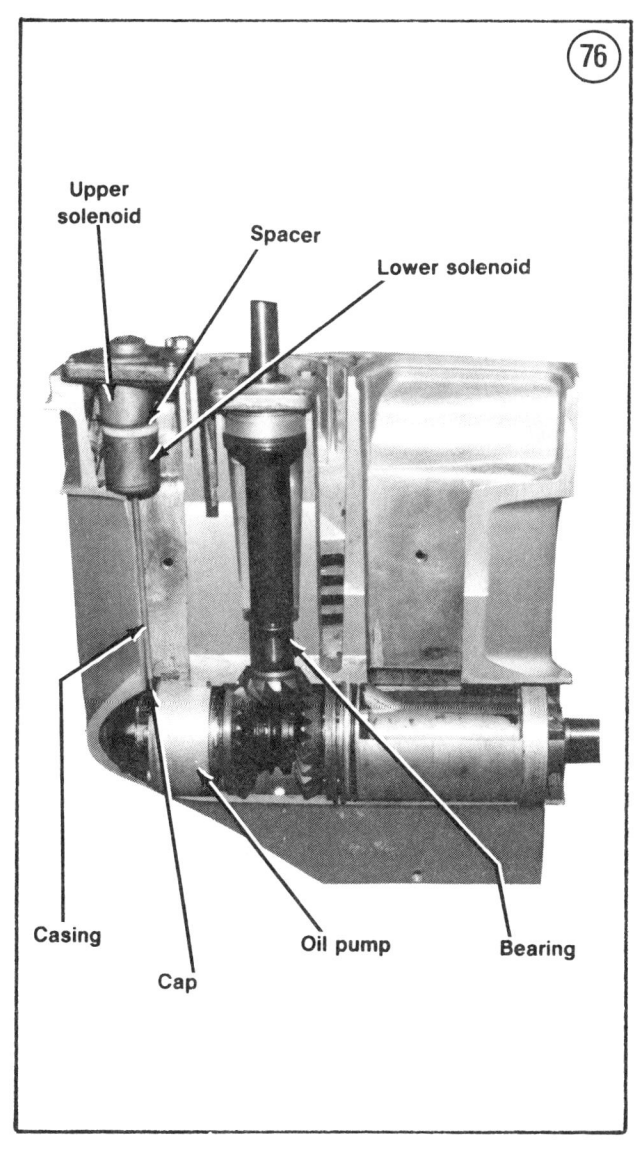

GEARCASE

NOTE
*The snap rings installed in Step 24 fit into **separate** grooves in the gearcase. Make sure the first ring is installed in the bottom groove all the way around before releasing the snap ring pliers.*

24. Slip one snap ring (flat side facing out) over the propeller shaft (**Figure 75**) and install with snap ring pliers part No. 311879. Repeat this step to install the other snap ring.

25. Thread the 2 guide pins used during removal into the retainer plate about 2-3 turns. Position the bearing housing with its drain slot facing down or the mark made during removal facing up. Slide it over the guide pins and into the gearcase.

26. Install new O-rings on the bearing housing screws. Coat screw threads with OMC Gasket Sealing Compound. Install 2 screws with a long screwdriver or a screwdriver tip socket and extension. Remove the guide pins and install the other 2 screws.

NOTE
*Refer to **Figure 76** for Steps 27-32.*

27. Separate the 2 shift solenoids. Insert the lower solenoid (blue wire) into the gearcase cavity until the shift rod casing cap rests on the top of the valve lever/check ball unit.

28. When the solenoid is fully seated, the lower plunger will be flush with the top of the solenoid. If it is not, remove the solenoid and rotate the plunger on the shift rod casing as required, then reinstall the solenoid. Repeat this adjustment as required until correct.

29. Install the spacer with its lip facing up. See **Figure 77**.

30. Insert the upper solenoid (green wire) into the gearcase cavity, then install the shift rod in the shift rod casing.

31. If the upper plunger is not flush with the top of the solenoid, remove the solenoid and loosen the plunger nut. Adjust as required, tighten plunger nut to 3-5 in.-lb. and reinstall

the solenoid. Repeat this adjustment as required until correct.

32. Make sure that the inside plunger indexes into the oil pump hole.

33. Install the wave washer in the gearcase cavity. Position the shift cable wires so they will not be pinched, then install the shift cover with a new gasket. Hold the cover in place and install the screws finger-tight.

34. Connect an ohmmeter between ground and each of the solenoid leads in turn. With the meter set on the low scale, each solenoid should read approximately 5-7 ohms.

35. Install the water pump as described in this chapter.

36. Install a new O-ring on the drive shaft groove.

37. Pressure and vacuum test the gearcase as described in this chapter.

38. Install the gearcase as described in this chapter. Fill with the recommended type and quantity of lubricant. See Chapter Four.

39. Check gearcase lubricant level after engine has been run. Change the lubricant after 10 hours of operation (break-in period). See Chapter Four.

PRESSURE AND VACUUM TEST

Whenever a gearcase is overhauled, it should be pressure and vacuum tested before refilling it with lubricant. If the gearcase fails either the pressure or vacuum test, it must be disassembled and the source of the problem located and corrected. Failure to perform a pressure and vacuum test or ignoring the results and running a gearcase which failed one or both parts of the test will result in major gearcase damage.

1. Install a new seal on the oil level plug.
2. Thread a pressure test gauge into the fill/drain plug hole. See **Figure 78** (typical).
3. Pump the pressure to 3-6 psi. If the pressure does not hold, submerge the gearcase in water and check for the presence of air bubbles to indicate the source of the leak.
4. If pressure holds at 3-6 psi, increase it to 16-18 psi. If the pressure does not hold at this level, submerge the gearcase in water and check for the presence of air bubbles to indicate the source of the leak.
5. If the pressure holds at 16-18 psi, release the pressure and remove the pressure tester.
6. Thread a vacuum test gauge into the fill/drain plug hole. See **Figure 78** (typical).
7. Draw 3-5 in. Hg vacuum. If vacuum does not hold at this level, coat the suspected seal with lubricant to see if the leak stops or if the lubricant is sucked in.
8. If the vacuum holds at 3-5 in. Hg in Step 7, increase it to 15 in. Hg. If vacuum does not hold at this level, coat the suspected seal with lubricant to see if the leak stops or if the lubricant is sucked in.
9. If the vacuum holds at 15 in. Hg, release the vacuum and remove the tester.
10. If the source of a pressure or vacuum leak cannot be determined visually, disassemble the gearcase and locate it.
11. If the gearcase passes the pressure and vacuum test, fill it with the required type and quantity of lubricant. See Chapter Four.

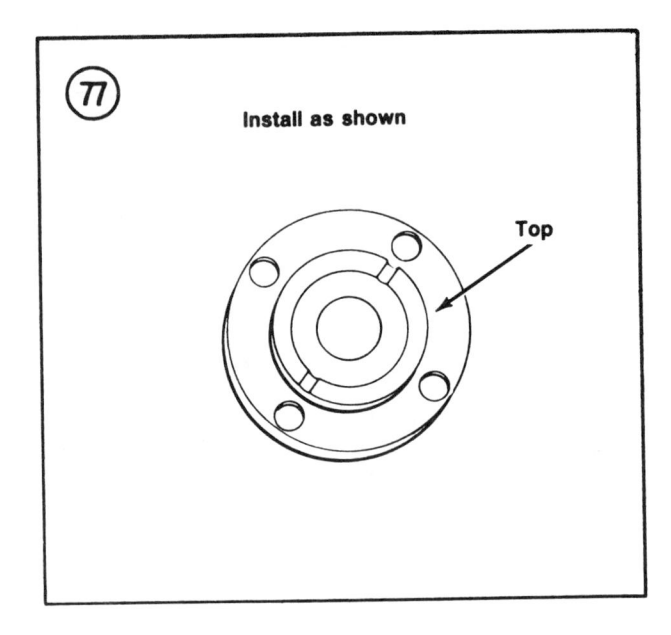

GEARCASE

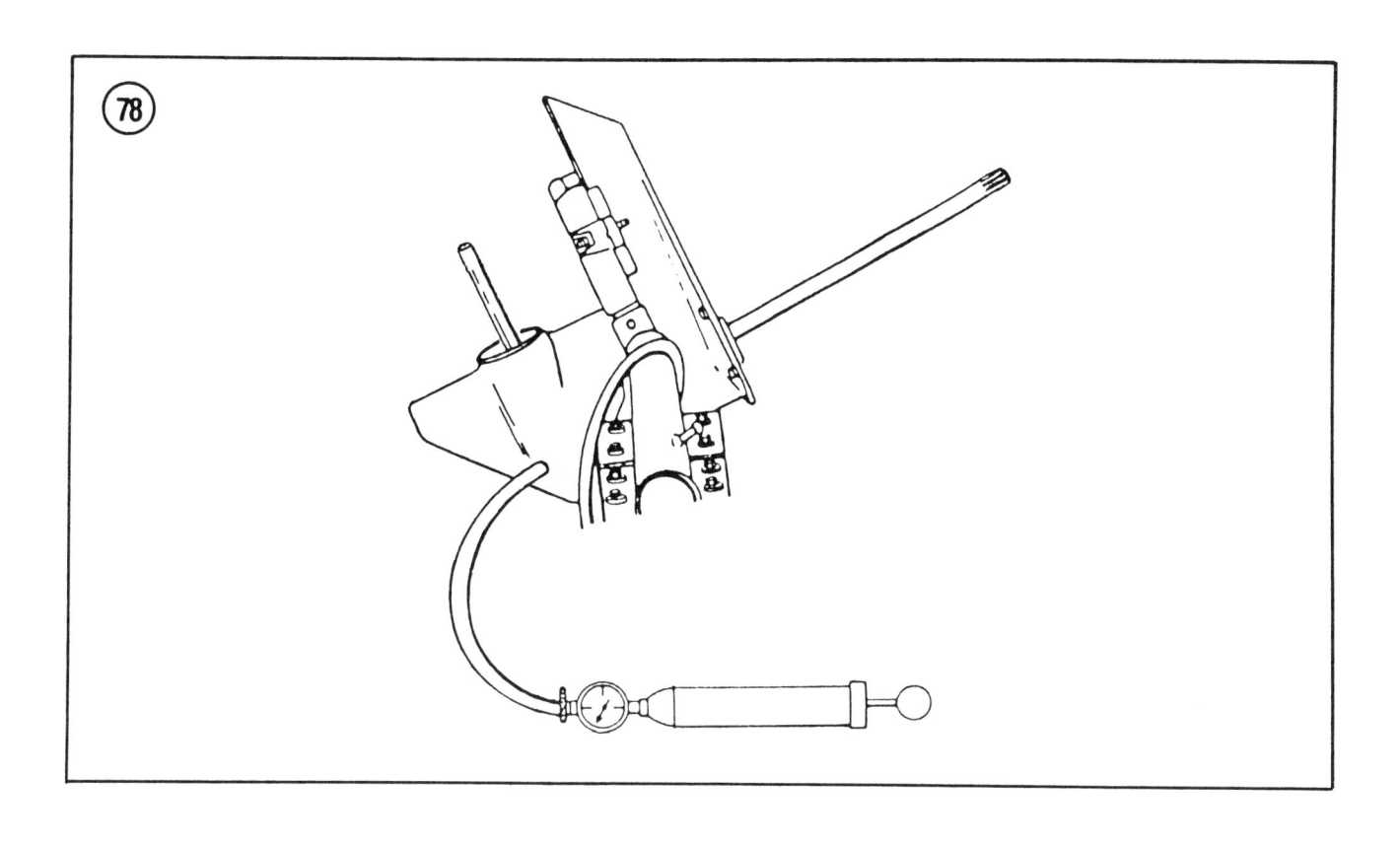

⑦⑧

Table 1 GEARCASE TIGHTENING TORQUES

Fastener	in.-lb.	ft.-lb.
Drain/fill/oil level plugs		5-7
Drive shaft bearing housing/ thrust plate screws		
Inline engine		18-20
V4		22-24
Gearcase		
To extension stud		16-18
Self-locking stud nut		
Electric shift		16-18
Hydro-electric shift		24-26
Pinion locknut		70-80
Propeller shaft bearing housing screws	60-80	
Water passage cover		3-7
Water pump screws	60-80	
Standard torque values		
No. 6	7-10	
No. 8	15-22	
No. 10	25-35	
No. 12	35-40	
1/4 in.	60-80	5-7
5/16 in.	120-140	10-12
3/8 in.	220-240	18-20
7/16 in.	340-360	28-30

9

Chapter Ten

Automatic Rewind Starters

All 1.5-40 hp and 1958-1965 V4 models are equipped with a rope-operated rewind starter. The starter assembly may be mounted in the engine cover (1.5-2 hp), beside the flywheel (1968 3 hp, all 4, 5, 6 and 9.5 hp) or above the flywheel (all others). Pulling the rope handle causes the starter spindle shaft to rotate against spring tension, moving the drive pawl or pinion to engage the flywheel and turn the engine over. When the rope handle is released, the spring inside the assembly reverses direction of the spindle shaft and winds the rope around the pulley.

All 5 hp and larger outboards are equipped with a starter interlock feature. This prevents operation of the rewind starter whenever the throttle is advanced beyond the START position.

Automatic rewind starters are relatively trouble-free, with a broken or frayed rope the most common malfunction. This chapter covers rewind starter and rope/spring service.

ENGINE COVER STARTER

This starter type is used on all 1.5 and 2 hp outboards.

Removal/Installation

1. Disconnect the spark plug lead to prevent the engine from accidentally starting.
2. Remove the fuel tank cap. Remove the engine cover. Reinstall the cap on the fuel tank.
3. Installation is the reverse of removal. Tighten cover screws to 60-80 in.-lb.

Starter Rope Replacement

1. Place the engine cover upright on a flat surface.
2. Pull the starter rope out as far as it will go and tie a slip knot in the rope near the cover.
3. Untie the knot in the handle end of the rope and remove the handle assembly.
4. Invert the engine cover and pull the rope out enough to release the slip knot tied in Step 2.

NOTE
Some models use a pulley plate installed over the pulley. This plate must be removed before the rope can be disconnected from the pulley in Step 6.

AUTOMATIC REWIND STARTERS

1. Link
2. Retaining ring
3. Friction spring
4. Starter pawl

Disassembly

WARNING
Disassembling this starter mechanism without holding the spring in place can result in the spring unwinding violently, causing serious personal injury. Wear safety glasses and gloves during this procedure.

Refer to **Figure 1** for this procedure.
1. Remove the starter rope as described in this chapter.
2. Remove the circlip holding the starter pawl in place. Lift the pawl off its shaft and disengage the friction spring and links. Remove the pawl and spring/link assembly.
3. Place the engine cover on its side. Hold the pulley and spindle in place with one hand and remove the starter spindle screw from the top of the cover.
4. Invert the engine cover and remove the spindle while holding the pulley in place.
5. Slowly lift the pulley straight up and out of the starter housing in the engine cover. The spring should remain in the housing.
6. Position the cover right-side up on the workbench or floor and rap it sharply. The spring will fly out of the engine cover starter housing and be contained inside the cover.

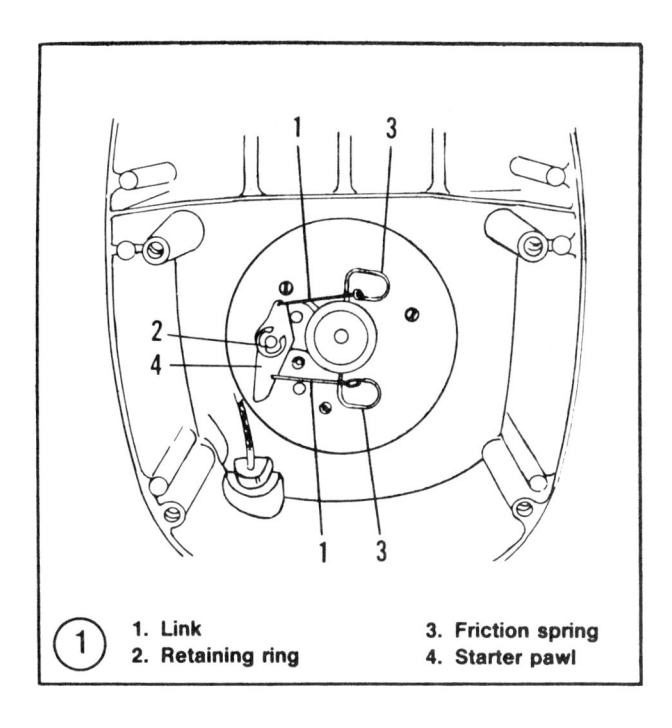

5. If equipped with a pulley plate, remove the plate screws and plate.
6. Hold the pulley firmly and pull knotted end of rope from pulley. Slowly allow pulley to rotate until it is completely unwound.
7. Tie a knot in the end of a new rope.
8. Rotate the pulley 3 1/2 turns counterclockwise to tension the spring and hold in that position.
9. Insert the unknotted end of the rope in the pulley hole. If pulley uses a plate, reinstall plate and tighten screws. Thread the rope around the pulley and out the starter housing hole, then pull the rope until the knot bottoms in the pulley.
10. Holding the free end of the rope, carefully release pressure on the pulley and allow it to slip slowly. Wind all but approximately 12 in. of the rope on the pulley in this manner.
11. Tie a slip knot in the rope to hold it in place and install the handle assembly. Tie a knot in the end of the rope and seat the knot in the handle.
12. Release the slip knot and allow the starter pulley to rewind the remaining rope.

Cleaning and Inspection

1. Wash all metal parts in solvent and blow dry with compressed air.
2. Check spring for wear or broken end loops. Replace as required.
3. Check pawl, friction spring and spindle for wear.
4. Remove any sharp edges or rough surfaces from pulley and housing that might fray the rope.
5. Check rope for fraying. Replace as required.

Assembly
(Models With Pulley Plate)

1. Lubricate the spring and housing spring cavity with Lubriplate 777 or OMC Triple-Guard grease.
2. Loosely coil the spring and insert it in the engine cover. Locate the inside coil in the housing slot with its loop facing the center of the spring cavity.
3. Position rope pulley over the spring and engage the pulley pin in the spring loop. See **Figure 2**.
4. Wipe the outer diameter of the spindle with Lubriplate 777 or OMC Triple-Guard grease. Insert spindle through pulley and engage spindle slot with housing rib.
5. Dip spindle screw threads in OMC Screw Lock and install screw.
6. Rotate pulley counterclockwise to wind spring into housing until the outer spring loop engages the outer face of the spring cavity.
7. Insert knotted end of rope in pulley slot. Wrap the rope counterclockwise around the pulley flange.
8. Install pulley plate with 3 screws and tighten securely. Wind pulley counterclockwise 3 1/2 turns to preload the spring, then insert a punch through the remaining screw hole (**Figure 3**) and engage one of the starter housing ribs to hold the pulley against spring tension.
9. Feed the rope through the starter housing hole and install the rope assembly. Tie a knot in the end of the rope.
10. Remove the punch and install the remaining plate screw.
11. Install the starter pawl and friction spring assembly. Secure the pawl in place with the circlip.
12. Test the starter action by pulling the rope handle. The pawl should extend when the rope is pulled and retract when released.

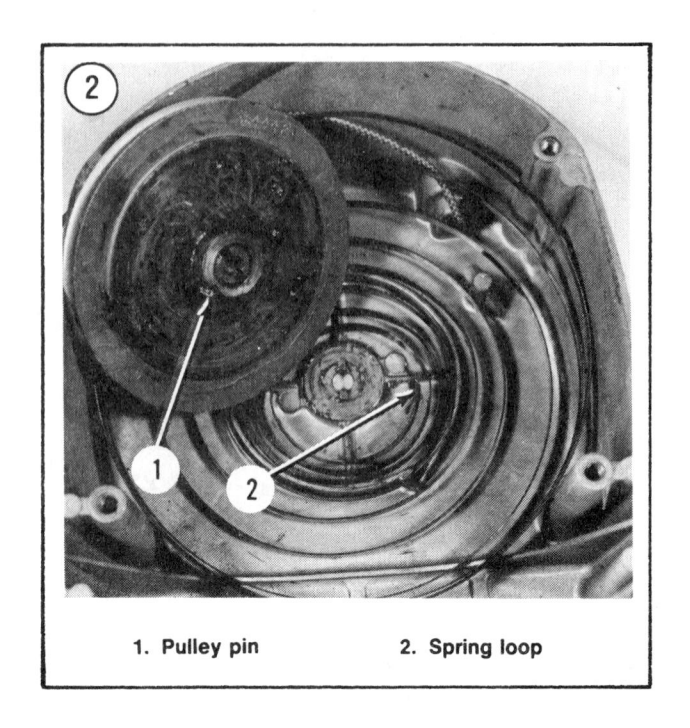

1. Pulley pin   2. Spring loop

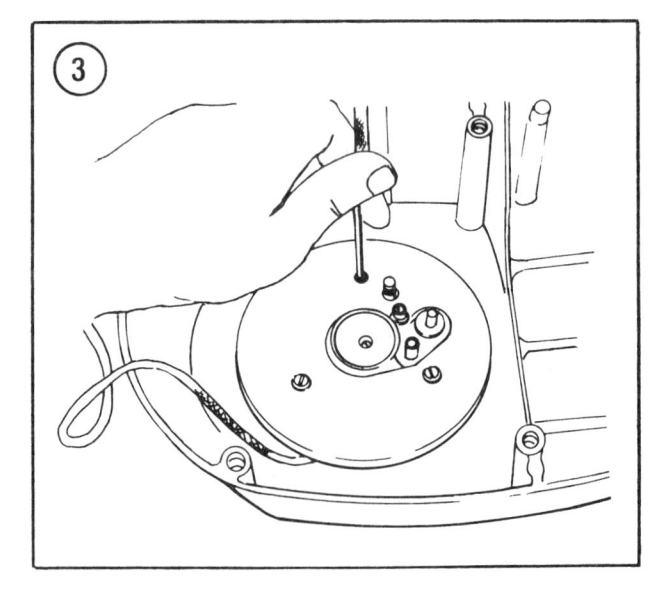

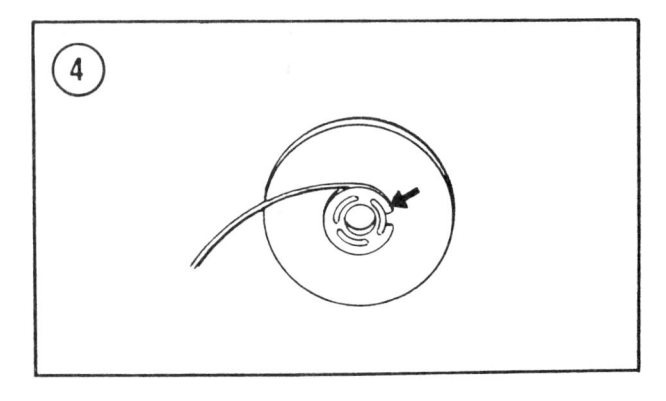

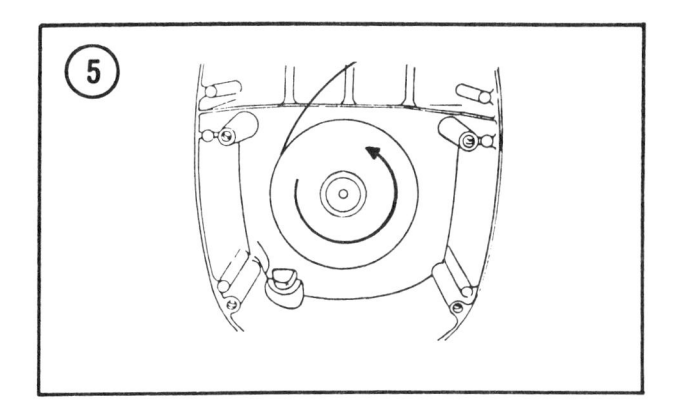

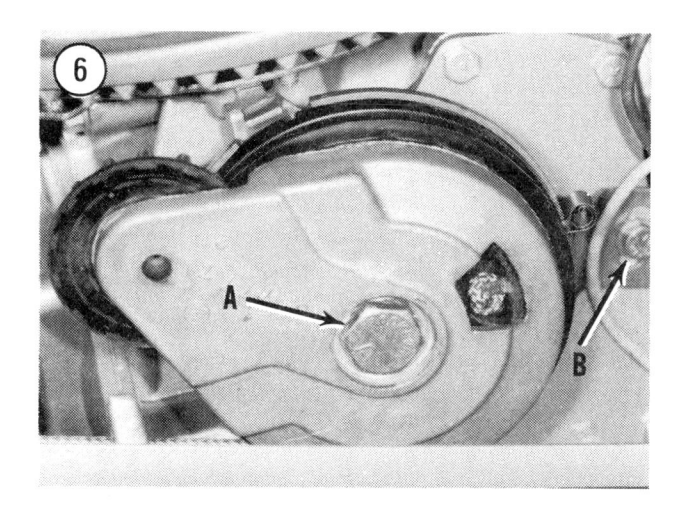

AUTOMATIC REWIND STARTERS

Figure 5

Figure 6 (showing A and B)

6. Rotate pulley counterclockwise until outer spring loop engages outer face of spring cavity (**Figure 5**).
7. Install the starter pawl and friction spring assembly. Secure the pawl in place with the circlip.
8. Install rope as described in this chapter.
9. Test the starter action by pulling the rope handle. The pawl should extend when the rope is pulled and retract when released.

SWING ARM GEAR DRIVE STARTER

This starter type is used on 1968 3 hp and 1969-1972 4 hp outboards. It must be partially disassembled to replace the rope.

Removal/Installation

1. Disconnect the armature plate connection to prevent the engine from accidentally starting.
2. Pull the starter rope out enough to tie a slip knot behind the handle. Untie the knot holding the rope in the handle and remove the handle assembly.
3. Release the slip knot made in Step 2 and gradually allow the starter to unwind while holding the pulley.
4. Disconnect the starter spring at the cup and stop assembly and pull it out as far as possible to relieve spring tension.

NOTE
On some models, removal of the ignition coil will increase access for screw removal and subsequent starter assembly removal.

5. Remove the shoulder screw (A, **Figure 6**) and the adjustment screw (B, **Figure 6**). Remove the starter assembly from the power head.
6. Clean shoulder and adjustment screw threads to remove all old adhesive. Spray threads with OMC Locquic Primer.

Assembly
(Models Without Pulley Plate)

1. Lubricate the spring and housing spring cavity with Lubriplate 777 or OMC Triple-Guard grease.
2. Wipe the outer diameter of the spindle with Lubriplate 777 or OMC Triple-Guard grease.
3. Install spring on pulley as shown in **Figure 4**.
4. Install pulley in housing with spring passing through the spring cavity gate. The rib in the center of the housing should engage the spindle slot.
5. Clean the spindle screw threads of all old adhesive. Spray threads with OMC Locquic Primer. Install lockwasher on screw and wipe screw threads with OMC Screw Lock. Install and tighten screw.

7. Wipe the shoulder screw threads with OMC Screw Lock. Make sure the idler gear arm is located between the 2 tabs of the cup and stop assembly. Position the starter assembly to the power head and install the shoulder and adjustment screws finger-tight.

8. Wipe starter spring with a light coat of Lubriplate 777 or OMC Triple-Guard grease.

9. Install OMC tool part No. 383967 in lower motor cover groove at side of idler arm. Rotate tool thumbscrew as required to position it in the idler arm hole.

10. Make sure idler gear engages flywheel, then turn flywheel clockwise and wind starter spring into cup and stop assembly until the spring loop touches the pulley slot. See **Figure 7**.

11. Hold pulley from turning and remove tool, then let pulley rotate slowly until spring tension is relieved.

12. Reinstall tool part No. 383967 and turn flywheel clockwise enough to rotate starter pulley 1 1/2 turns to preload the spring. Hold pulley and remove tool.

13. Release the end of the rope and feed it through the lower motor cover hole, pulling it out as far as possible. Hold rope fully extended and grasp the spring end loop. Pull spring from cup and stop assembly. See **Figure 8**. If spring can be pulled out 8-18 in., preload is satisfactory. If not, repeat Steps 10-13.

14. Install rope handle assembly and tie a knot in the end of the rope.

15. Hold the idler gear arm stop against the cup stop. Make sure the idler gear teeth engage the flywheel properly, then tighten the adjustment screw.

16. Tighten the shoulder screw to 10-12 ft.-lb.

17. Install the ignition coil, if removed.

18. Reconnect the armature plate connections.

Disassembly

1. Remove the idler gear arm, gear and gear arm spring from the starter assembly. See **Figure 9**.

2. Separate the pulley from the cup and stop assembly. Note spring loop position and disconnect the spring from the pulley roll pin. See **Figure 10**.

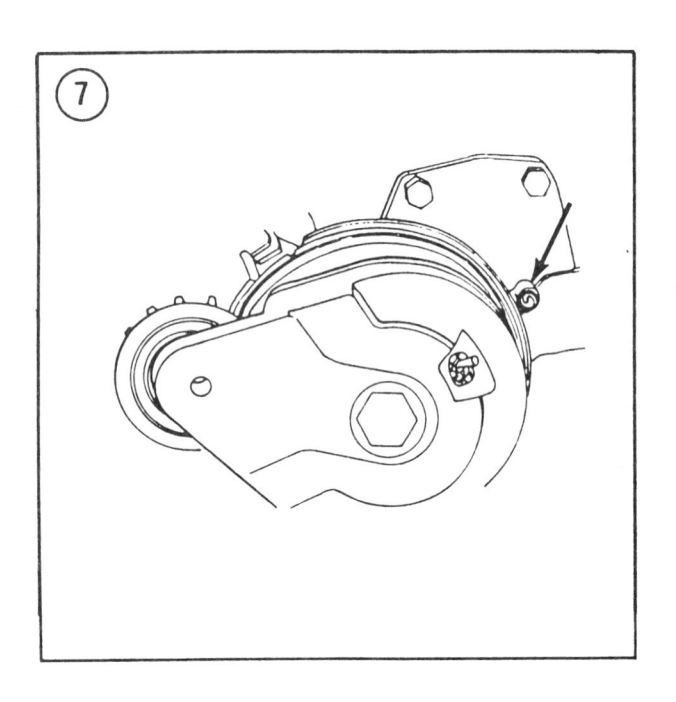

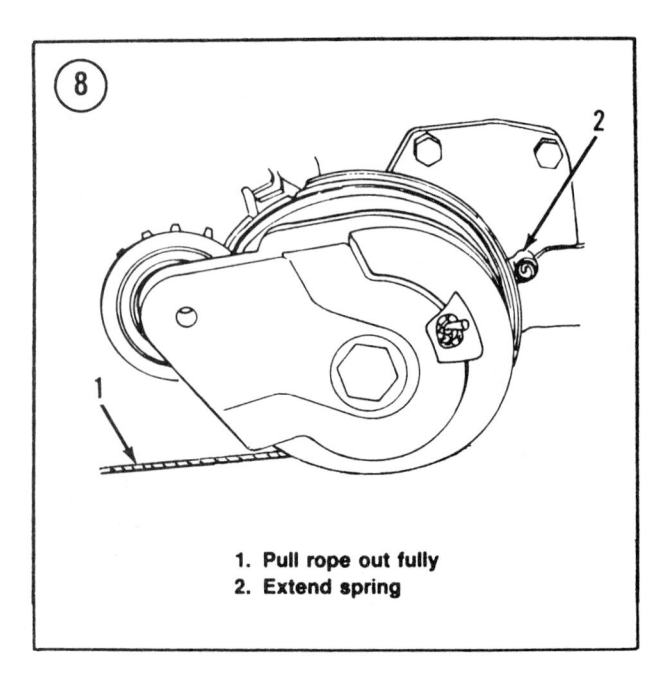

AUTOMATIC REWIND STARTERS

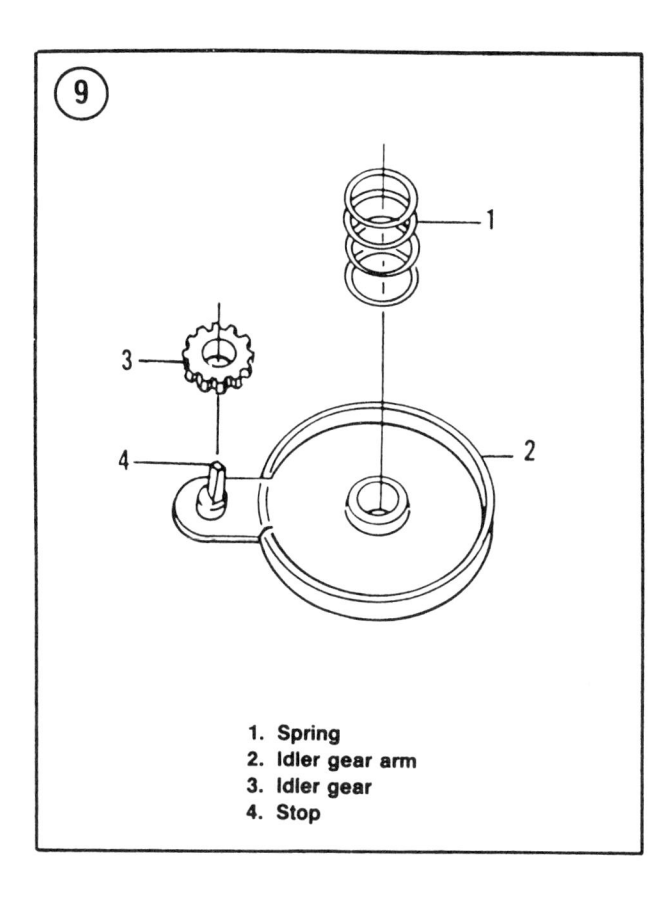

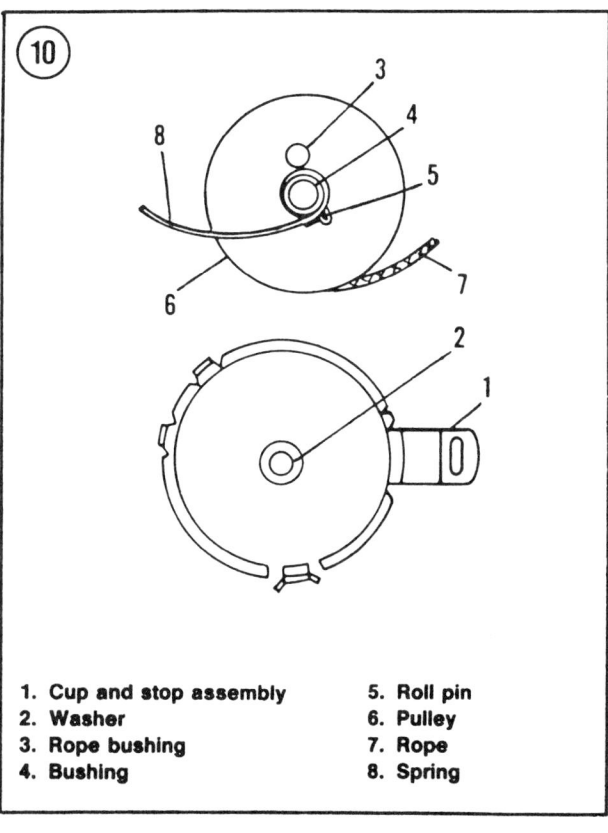

3. Remove the rope from the pulley, then remove the rope bushing.

4. Remove the idler gear arm bushing. Remove the bushing from each side of the pulley.

Cleaning and Inspection

1. Wash all metal parts in solvent and blow dry with compressed air.
2. Check metal parts for corrosion. Remove corrosion, if found, and wipe parts with an oil-dampened cloth.
3. Check spring for wear or broken end loops. Replace as required.
4. Check rope for fraying. Replace as required.

Assembly

1. Insert pulley bushing.
2. Tie a knot in one end of the rope. Insert the other end through the bushing rope hole. See **Figure 11**.
3. Pull the rope through until the knot seats in the pulley bushing. Hold the pulley with the knot facing you, then wind the pulley clockwise. Tape or install a rubber band to hold rope in pulley.

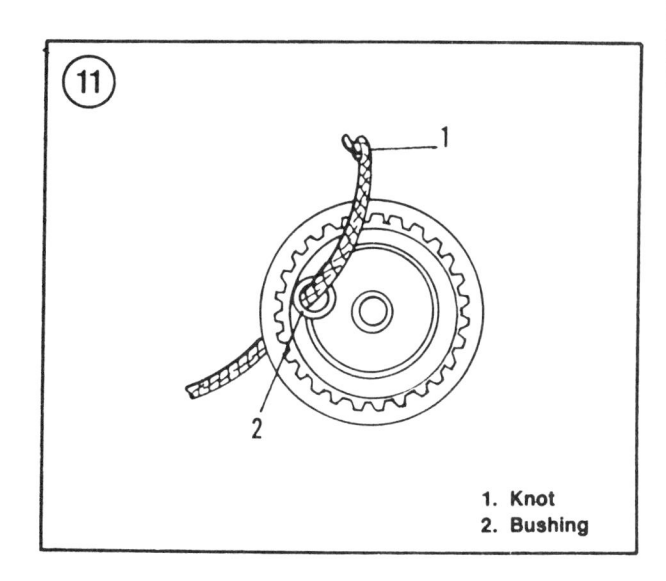

Figure 9
1. Spring
2. Idler gear arm
3. Idler gear
4. Stop

Figure 10
1. Cup and stop assembly
2. Washer
3. Rope bushing
4. Bushing
5. Roll pin
6. Pulley
7. Rope
8. Spring

Figure 11
1. Knot
2. Bushing

4. Wipe bushings with Lubriplate 777 or OMC Triple-Guard grease and insert in pulley and idler gear arm.
5. Install the washer in cup and stop assembly hooking spring end loop to pulley roll pin. See **Figure 10**.
6. Sandwich pulley and spring to cup and stop assembly. The spring should extend through the cup slot. See **Figure 12**.
7. Assemble idler gear with shoulder resting against gear arm, then install arm and spring to pulley and cup. Locate the idler gear shaft stop between the cup and stop assembly tabs without turning pulley and disengaging spring end. See **Figure 13**.
8. Install starter mechanism to power head as described in this chapter.

SIDE-MOUNTED PINION GEAR STARTER

This starter type is used on 5, 6 and 9.5 hp outboards. It operates in a manner similar to an automotive starter. The nylon pinion slides up to engage the flywheel as the rope is pulled, then disengages when the engine starts.

Removal/Installation

1. Disconnect the armature plate connections to prevent the engine from accidentally starting.
2. Pull the starter rope out enough to tie a slip knot behind the handle. Untie the knot holding the rope in the handle and remove the handle assembly.

NOTE
The version used on the 9.5 hp engine has no lower retainer plate fasteners.

3. Remove the 2 top starter screws (A, **Figure 14**). Remove the front spring retainer plate screw (B, **Figure 14**).
4. Loosen the rear retainer plate screw (C, **Figure 14**). Let the plate drop enough to release the starter spring hook.

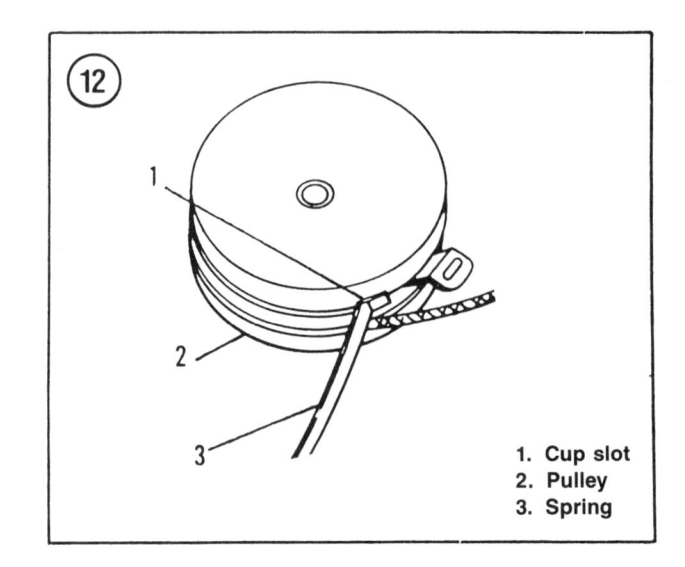

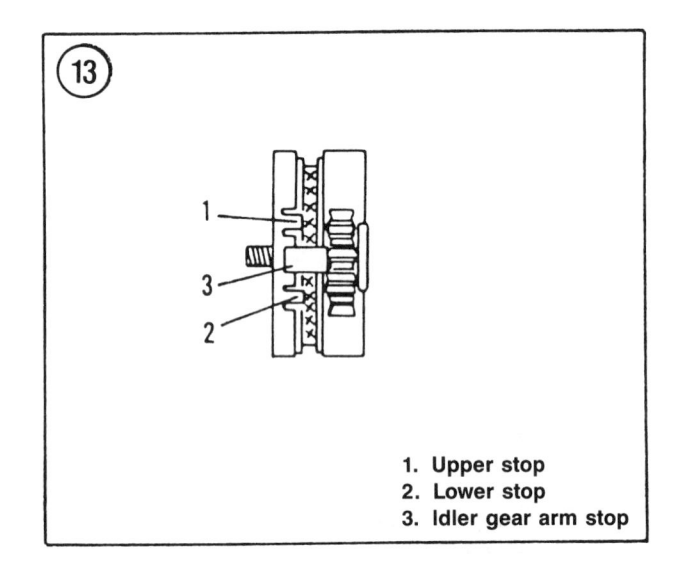

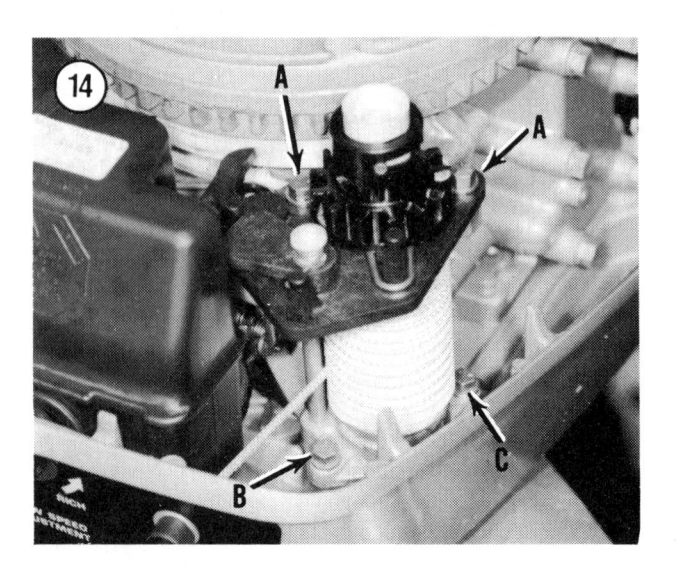

AUTOMATIC REWIND STARTERS

Figure 15

Figure 16

Figure 17
1. Punch
2. Roll pin

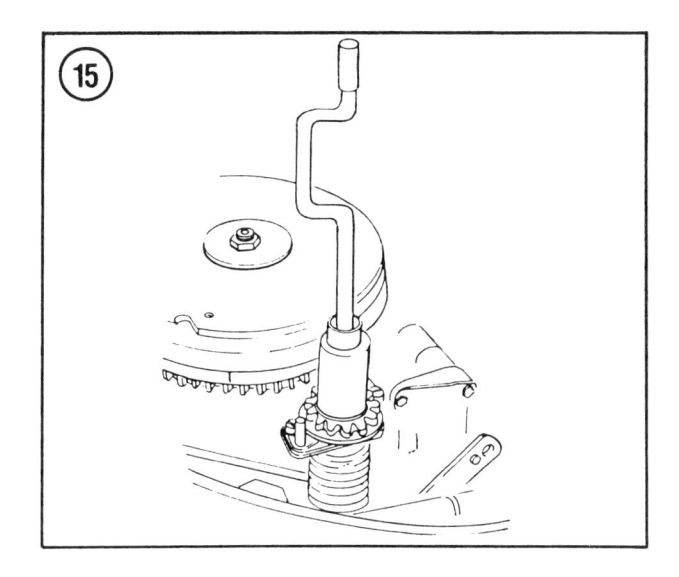

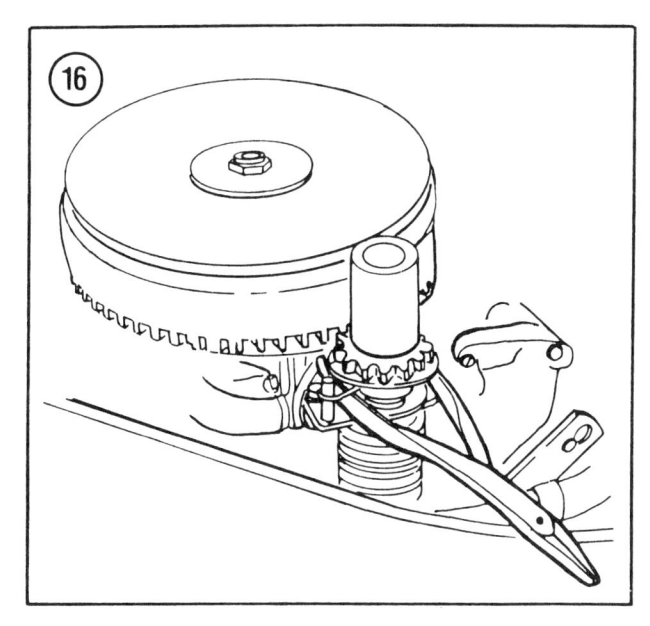

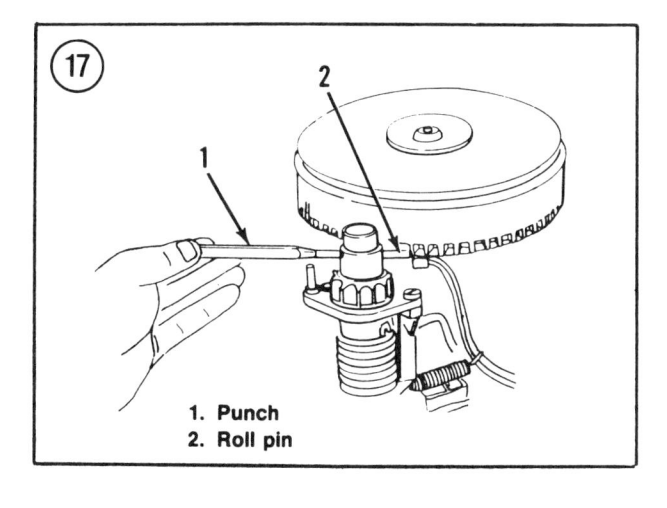

5. Remove the starter and main spring from the power head.

6. Lubricate the lower retainer bushing with several drops of Johnson or Evinrude 50/1 outboard lubricant.

7. Fit the external tang of the starter assembly main spring into the lower retainer plate slot. Tighten both lower retainer plate screws.

8. Install the starter spool assembly so that the spool slot engages the internal rewind spring tang. Install and tighten the top starter screws to 60-84 in.-lb.

9. Disengage the cam follower and insert a flat-blade screwdriver in the lever arm slot. Install an O-ring or rubber band above the pinion teeth to prevent engagement with the flywheel.

10. Rotate the spool counterclockwise 16 1/2 turns (except 9.5 hp) or 20 1/2 turns (9.5 hp) using a speeder or ratchet wrench and a flat tip driver which fits into the inner slot of the spool. See **Figure 15**.

11. With 9.5 hp models, raise the pinion gear to engage the flywheel and lock in place by sliding plier handles under the gear. See **Figure 16**.

12. With all others, insert a pin punch in the pinion gear roll pin hole to prevent the spool from unwinding. See **Figure 17**.

13. Insert the knot end of the starter rope through the spool slot. Hold the rope and remove the pliers or pin punch. Let the starter slowly wind the rope up.

14. Insert the rope through the lower motor cover eyelet and tie a slip knot. Install the handle assemble and tie a knot in the end of the rope to fit into the handle.

15. Release the slip knot and remove the screwdriver and O-ring or rubber band. Pull the starter handle several times to make sure it engages with the flywheel.

16. Make sure the starter interlock functions properly. The starter should lock when the

throttle is opened beyond the START position.

17. Reconnect the armature plate connectors.

Starter Rope Replacement

1. Disconnect the armature plate connections to prevent the engine from accidentally starting.
2. Pull the starter rope out until it is fully extended. On 9.5 hp models, raise the pinion gear to engage the flywheel and lock in place by inserting plier handles under the gear. See **Figure 16**. On all others, insert a small punch in the roll pin hole to lock the starter in the extended position. See **Figure 17**.
3. Untie the knot holding the rope in the handle and remove the handle assembly. Pull the rope from the spool.
4. If the rope has broken while in service, rotate the spool counterclockwise 20 1/2 turns (9.5 hp) or 16 1/2 turns (all others) using a speeder or ratchet wrench and a flat tip driver which fits into the inner slot of the spool. See **Figure 15**.
5. Tie a knot in the new rope about 1/2 in. from the end, then feed the rope through the pulley slot until the knot rests snugly against the pulley.
6. Feed the rope counterclockwise around the pulley once and between the spool and guide.
7. Insert the rope through the lower motor cover and install the handle assembly.
8. Hold rope handle securely and remove pliers or punch holding starter pinion gear. Let starter rope rewind slowly.

Disassembly/Assembly

Starter disassembly should be necessary only if the pinion gear is damaged. Refer to **Figure 18** (9.5 hp) or **Figure 19** (all others) for this procedure.

1. Remove the roll pin with a pin punch.
2. Remove the pinion. Release the cam follower and slide the bearing head off the starter spool.
3. Remove the main spring from the spool assembly.
4. On 9.5 hp models, remove the lower spring retainer setscrew. Remove retainer, bushing and outer bearing.
5. To assemble, install outer bearing, bushing and retainer on 9.5 hp models. Tighten setscrew.

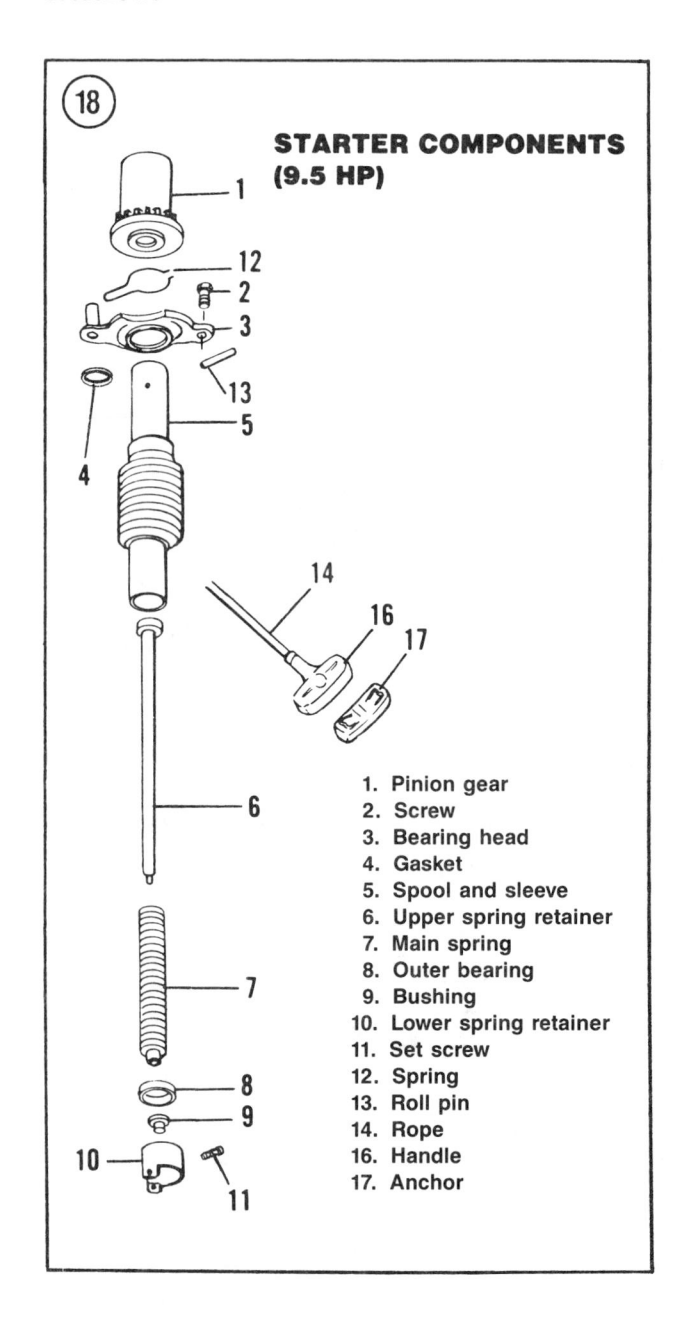

STARTER COMPONENTS (9.5 HP)

1. Pinion gear
2. Screw
3. Bearing head
4. Gasket
5. Spool and sleeve
6. Upper spring retainer
7. Main spring
8. Outer bearing
9. Bushing
10. Lower spring retainer
11. Set screw
12. Spring
13. Roll pin
14. Rope
16. Handle
17. Anchor

AUTOMATIC REWIND STARTERS

Figure 19 STARTER COMPONENTS (ALL MODELS EXCEPT 9.5 HP)

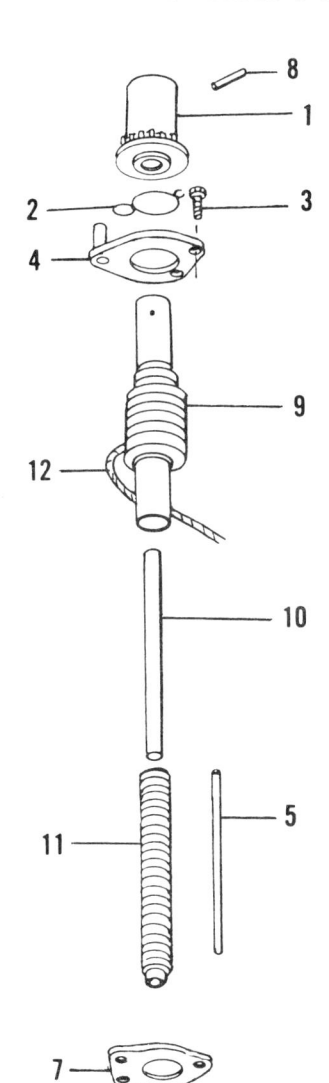

1. Pinion gear
2. Spring
3. Screw
4. Bearing head
5. Guide
7. Spring retainer plate and bushing
8. Roll pin
9. Spool
10. Sleeve
11. Main spring
12. Rope

6. Install the pinion spring. Position bearing head and pinion gear on starter spool. Spring loop must fit over bearing head post.

7. Align pinion slot with spool holes. Install roll pin with split seam facing to the side to prevent dragging against the pinion gear slot.

8. Install main spring in spool assembly.

Cleaning and Inspection

1. Wash all parts in solvent and blow dry with compressed air.
2. Check all parts for excessive wear or damage. Replace as required.
3. Check rope for fraying. Replace as required.

FLYWHEEL MOUNTED STARTER

This starter type is used on 1956-1967 3 hp and all 5.5, 7.5 and 10-75 hp outboards. During the years covered by this manual, 3 variations of the flywheel mounted starter have been used: 3 pawls with return springs, 3 pawls with friction ring and a single pawl design.

A locking plunger connected to the gear shift lockout lever prevents starter engagement if the motor is in gear. See **Figure 20** (typical). The starter must be disassembled to replace the rope.

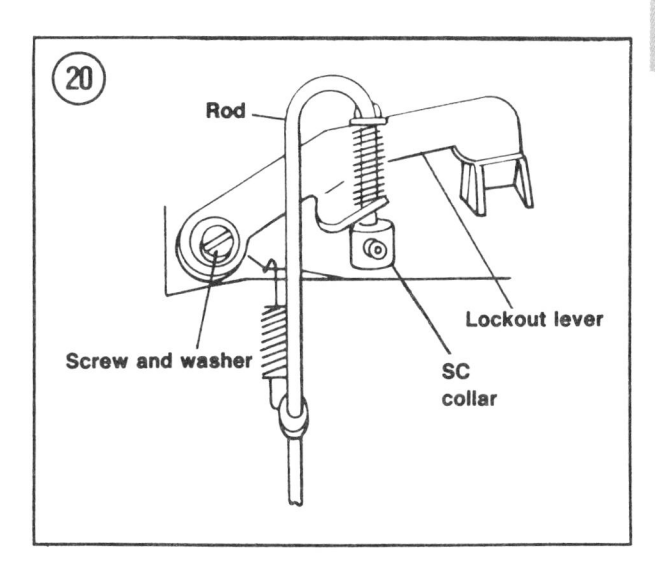

CHAPTER TEN

FLYWHEEL STARTER COMPONENTS (THREE PAWL DESIGN)

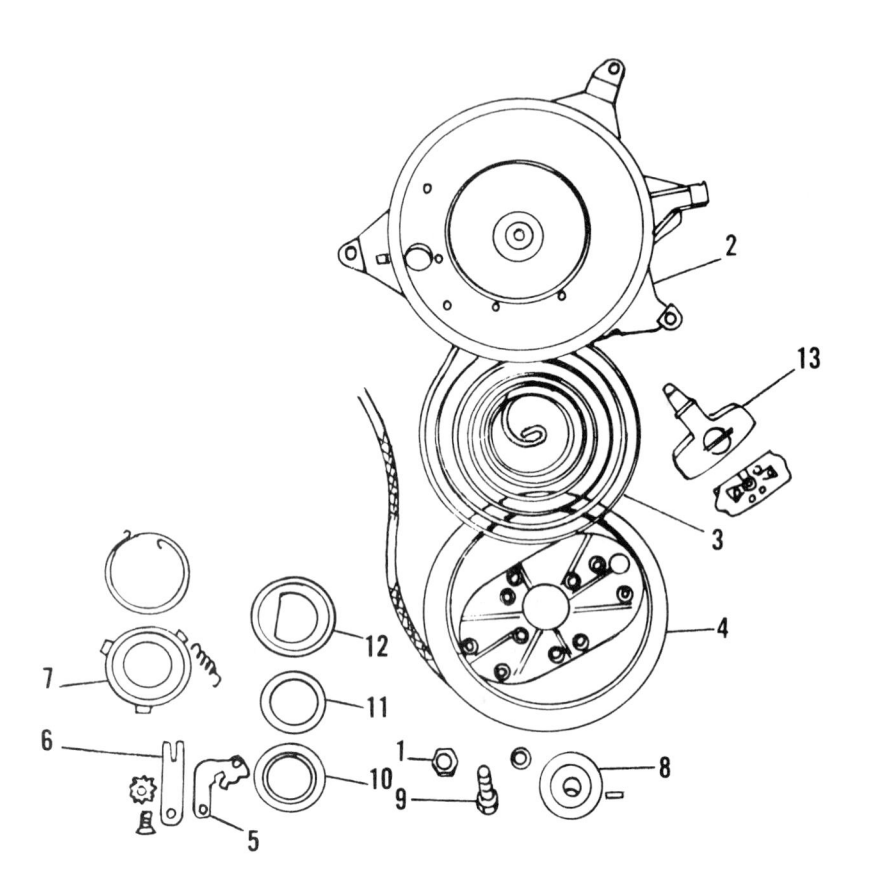

1. Spindle screw nut
2. Rewind starter housing
3. Spring
4. Pulley
5. Pawl
6. Pawl retainer
7. Eccentric cup (early type)
8. Spindle
9. Screw
10. Nylon bushing (late type)
11. Spring washer (late type)
12. Friction ring (late type)
13. Handle

AUTOMATIC REWIND STARTERS

Removal/Installation

1. Remove the engine cover.
2. Remove the screw and washer holding the lockout lever to the starter housing. See **Figure 20** (typical).
3. Remove the 3 screws holding the starter housing to the power head. Remove the starter housing.
4. Installation is the reverse of removal.

Disassembly

WARNING
Disassembling this starter mechanism without holding the spring in place can result in the spring unwinding violently, causing serious personal injury. Wear safety glasses and gloves during this procedure.

Refer to **Figure 21** (3-pawl design) or **Figure 22** (single pawl design) for this procedure.

1. Pull the starter rope out enough to tie a slip knot behind the handle. Unscrew or pry the rope anchor from the handle, as required.

2. Remove the handle, untie the slip knot and gradually allow the starter to unwind while holding the pulley.

3A. 3-pawl design—Remove the 3 pawl springs, if so equipped. See **Figure 23**.

3B. Single pawl design—Remove the circlip holding the starter pawl in place. See **Figure 24** (typical).

4A. 3-pawl design—Remove the screw holding each pawl in place. Remove the pawls. See **Figure 23**.

4B. Single pawl design—Lift the pawl off its shaft and disengage the friction spring and links. Remove the pawl and spring/link assembly. See **Figure 25** (typical).

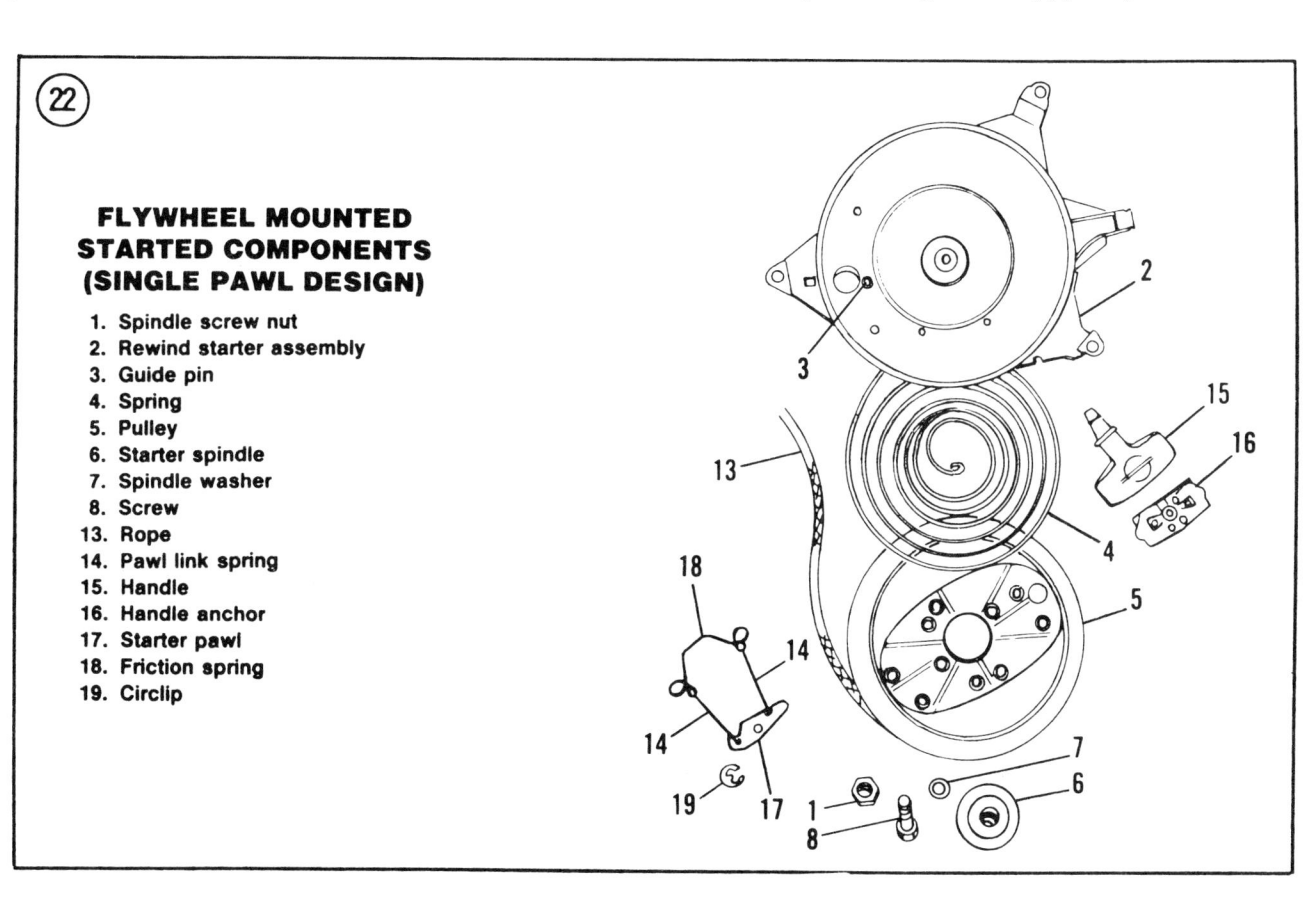

22

FLYWHEEL MOUNTED STARTED COMPONENTS (SINGLE PAWL DESIGN)

1. Spindle screw nut
2. Rewind starter assembly
3. Guide pin
4. Spring
5. Pulley
6. Starter spindle
7. Spindle washer
8. Screw
13. Rope
14. Pawl link spring
15. Handle
16. Handle anchor
17. Starter pawl
18. Friction spring
19. Circlip

CHAPTER TEN

NOTE
Some early starters may not use a nut on the spindle screw or the screw may have backed itself off and become loose. If screw has a threaded end, there should be a nut. If the end is not threaded, a nut is not used.

5. Remove the screw and washer from the spindle (**Figure 26**). It may be necessary to hold the nut on the top of the starter housing with a wrench while loosening the screw.

6. Remove the spindle and washer (**Figure 27**). Remove the equalizer cup and friction spring, if so equipped. Hold pulley in housing and turn it over (legs downward) on the workbench or floor.

7. Release the pulley and rap the housing sharply to dislodge the pulley and spring. The spring should uncoil within the starter housing legs.

8. Lift the housing up and remove the spring and pulley.

Cleaning and Inspection

1. Wash all metal parts in solvent and blow dry with compressed air.
2. Check spring for wear or broken end loops. Replace as required.
3. Check pawl(s), friction spring and spindle for wear.
4. Remove any sharp edges or rough surfaces from pulley and housing that might fray the rope.
5. Check rope for fraying. Replace as required.

Assembly

WARNING
During starter mechanism assembly, the spring may unwind violently, causing serious personal injury. Wear safety glasses and gloves during this procedure.

Refer to **Figure 21** or **Figure 22** for this procedure.

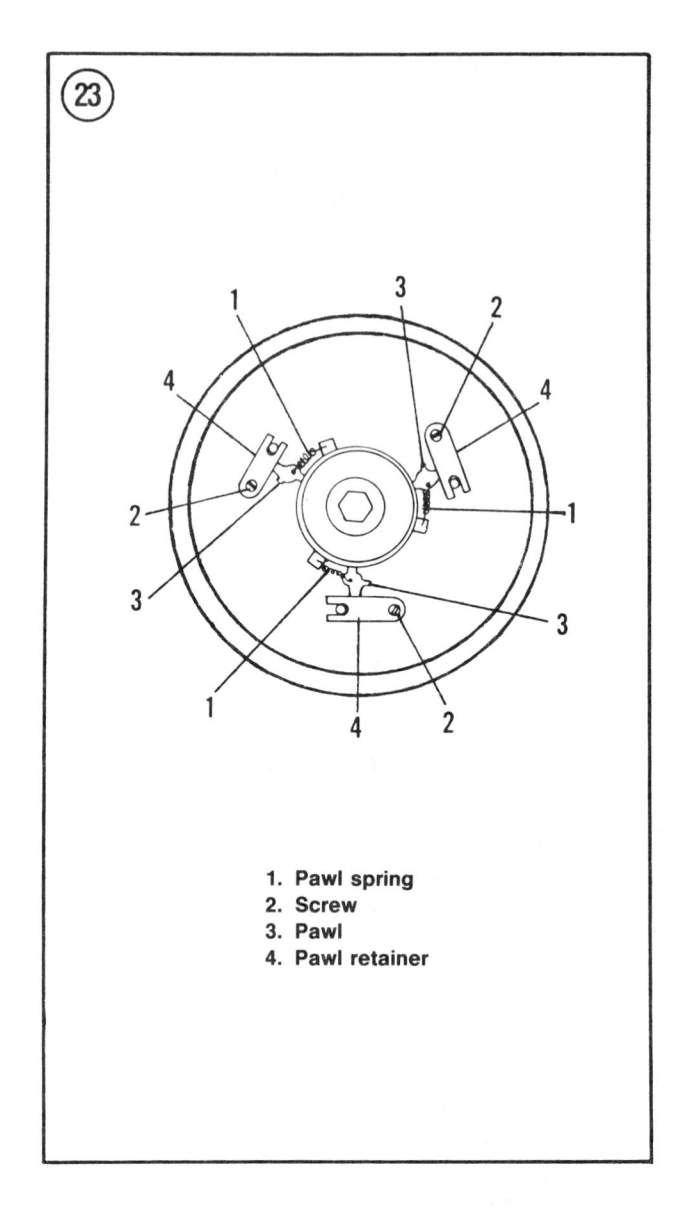

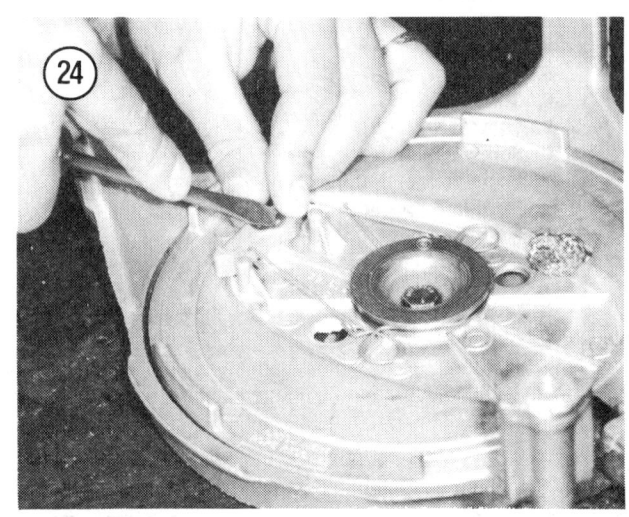

1. Pawl spring
2. Screw
3. Pawl
4. Pawl retainer

AUTOMATIC REWIND STARTERS

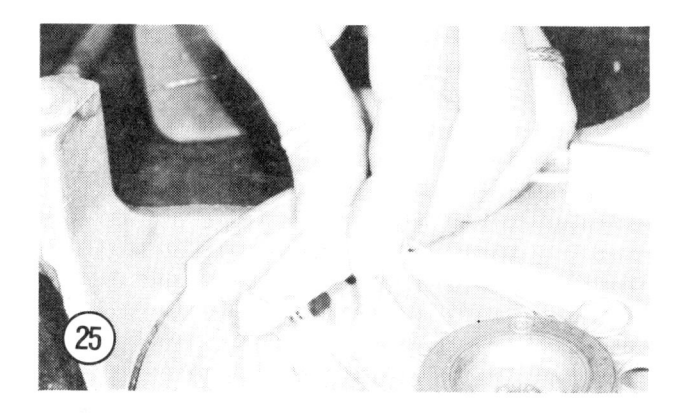

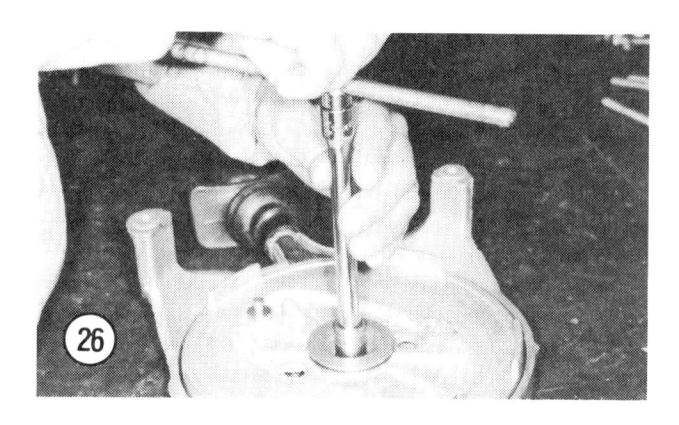

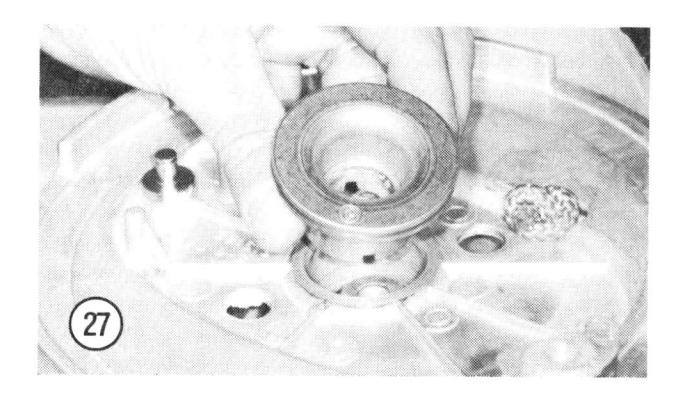

1. Lubricate the spindle and housing spindle area with Lubriplate 777 or OMC Triple-Guard grease.
2. Insert one spring loop over the pin in the housing cutout and carefully coil the spring into the housing. See **Figure 28**.
3. Install pulley in housing, making sure that the pin on the pulley engages the inner spring loop. See **Figure 29**.

NOTE
Some early starters may not use a nut on the spindle screw or the screw may have backed itself off and become loose. If screw has a threaded end, there should be a nut. If the end is not threaded, a nut is not used.

4. Install equalizer cup on spindle, if used. Install spindle in housing, indexing spindle pin with hole in housing. Install spindle screw with washer. Thread nut on screw as it protrudes through the top of the housing. Hold nut with one wrench and tighten the spindle screw with a second wrench.
5. Wind pulley counterclockwise until spring is tight, then back pulley off 1/2-1 turn and align the pulley and housing holes (arrow, **Figure 30**). Insert a nail, punch or drill bit in the holes to lock the pulley in place.

6. Tie a knot in the end of a new rope. Insert the opposite end of the rope in the pulley hole and feed the rope until it comes out the side of the housing. Pull the rope through the pulley until the knot rests against it.

7. Lubricate the handle end of the rope with Lubriplate 777 or OMC Triple-Guard grease. Thread rope through handle using Johnson or Evinrude tool part No. 378774.

8. Press rope into channel in rope anchor with end of rope butted tightly against channel. Install anchor in handle.

9A. 3-pawl design—Install each pawl in its retainer. Tip of pawl should rest over the top of the nylon bushing. Install the pawl retainers and tighten screws securely.

9B. Single pawl design—Lightly lubricate pawl pin with Lubriplate 777 or OMC Triple-Guard grease. Install pawl and link assembly. Install circlip.

10. Pull starter rope out and check pawl operation. Pawl(s) should extend when rope is pulled out and retract when rope is released.

11. Single pawl design—Pull the rope out and release it several times, then check to make sure the housing arrow aligns with the pulley mark. These marks should align when the starter handle is at rest against the housing. If not aligned properly, pull rope out and release several more times. A new rope must lose some of its stiffness and stretch slightly before the marks will align properly.

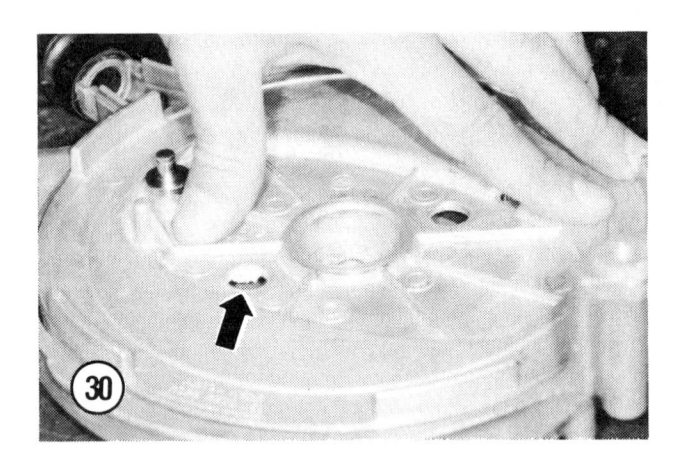

STARTER LOCKOUT ADJUSTMENT

If the lock link collar is improperly adjusted, the starter lock will engage prematurely and result in hard starting. Refer to **Figure 20** for this procedure.

1. Place gear shift lever in NEUTRAL.
2. Loosen collar setscrew.
3. Rotate twist grip until magneto stop rests against shifter lock.
4. Push lock link collar against locking lever until the lever clears the starter pulley lock lugs, then tighten the setscrew.

Chapter Eleven

Power Tilt System

The usual method of raising and lowering the outboard gearcase is a mechanical one, consisting of a series of holes in the transom mounting bracket. To trim the engine, an adjustment stud is removed from the bracket, the outboard is repositioned and the stud reinserted in the proper set of holes to retain the unit in place.

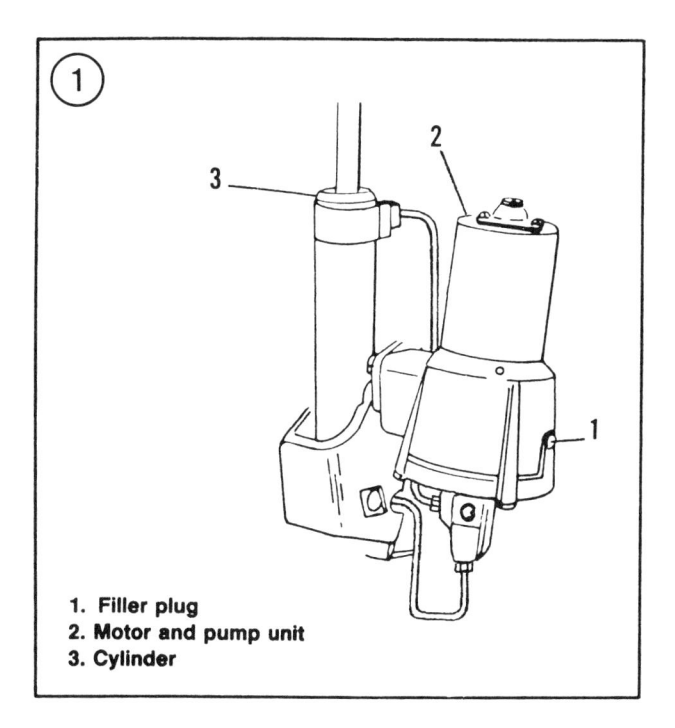

A power tilt system was offered as an accessory for most 60-100 hp engines through 1968 and some 40, 50, 60 and 65 hp engines through 1972. The power tilt system allows the outboard to be raised or lowered a full 70° for beaching, launching or removing the boat from the water. It also permits low-speed operation for passing through shallow water without damage to the propeller or gearcase and makes it possible to change the propeller with the boat in the water.

This chapter includes maintenance, troubleshooting procedures and tilt cylinder replacement.

Components

The power tilt system consists of a hydraulic pump (containing an electric motor, oil reservoir, oil pump and valve body), hydraulic tilt cylinder (replaces starboard shock absorber), tilt switch and the necessary hydraulic and electrical lines. **Figure 1** shows the major components.

1. Filler plug
2. Motor and pump unit
3. Cylinder

Operation

Moving the tilt switch to the UP position closes the pump motor circuit. The motor drives the oil pump, forcing oil into the UP side of the tilt cylinder which functions until it reaches a maximum of 70°.

Moving the tilt switch to the DOWN position also closes the pump motor circuit. The reversible motor runs in the opposite direction, driving the oil pump to force oil into the DOWN side of the tilt cylinder and bringing the engine back to the desired position.

A hydraulically-operated plunger releases the reverse latch catch before the engine is tilted up. This catch is not relocked until the engine returns to a complete vertical position. If the engine is run partially tilted at above low power speeds, a spring-loaded pressure relief valve opens to return the engine to the vertical position.

A release valve with a slotted head permits manual raising and lowering of the engine if the electrical system fails. When electrical power is restored, the valve must be returned to the AUTOMATIC position. See **Figure 2**.

Hydraulic Pump Fluid Check

Perform this check with the engine in its full vertical or upright position.

1. Clean area around pump fill plug. See **Figure 1** or **Figure 2**. Remove the plug and visually check the fluid level in the pump reservoir. It should be at the bottom of the fill hole threads.
2. Top up if necessary with SAE 30W engine oil.
3. Reinstall plug and tighten securely.

Hydraulic Pump Fluid Refill

Follow this procedure when a large amount of fluid has been lost due to an overhaul of the system or leakage that has been corrected, or when system bleeding is required. See **Figure 1** or **Figure 2**.

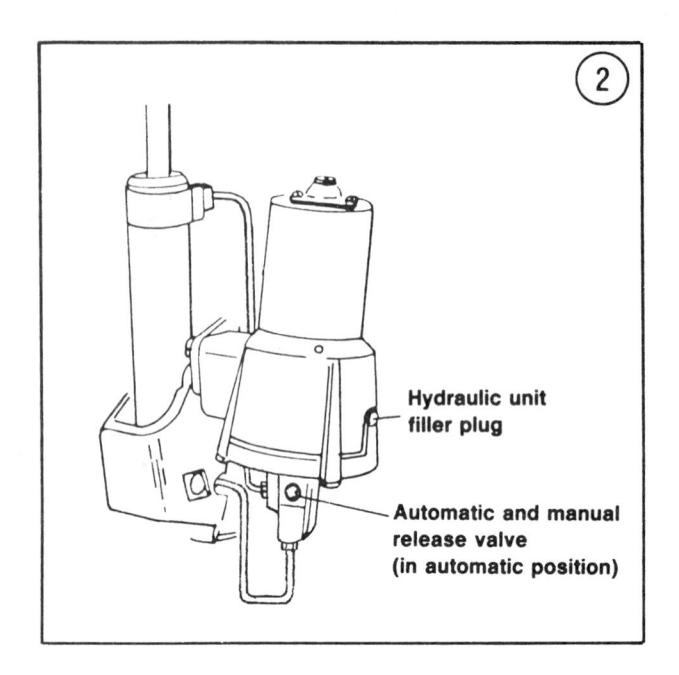

1. Make sure the release valve is in the AUTOMATIC position.
2. Remove the fill plug and top off the reservoir with SAE 30W engine oil. Reinstall the plug.
3. Manually tilt the engine and return it to a vertical position several times. Each time this is done, it should be more difficult to move it the following time.
4. Remove the fill plug and recheck the reservoir level. It should be at the bottom of the fill hole threads.
5. If the fluid level is not correct, add more SAE 30W engine oil and repeat Step 3 and Step 4 as required.
6. When fluid level is correct, reinstall fill plug and tighten securely.

Preliminary Check Procedure

1. Make sure the battery is fully charged with a specific gravity reading of 1.260-1.280. Charge or replace as required.
2. Operate the tilt switch toggle lever. Make sure it returns to the center position.

POWER TILT SYSTEM

3 To reverse latch catch release / Automatic and manual release valve / Location 1

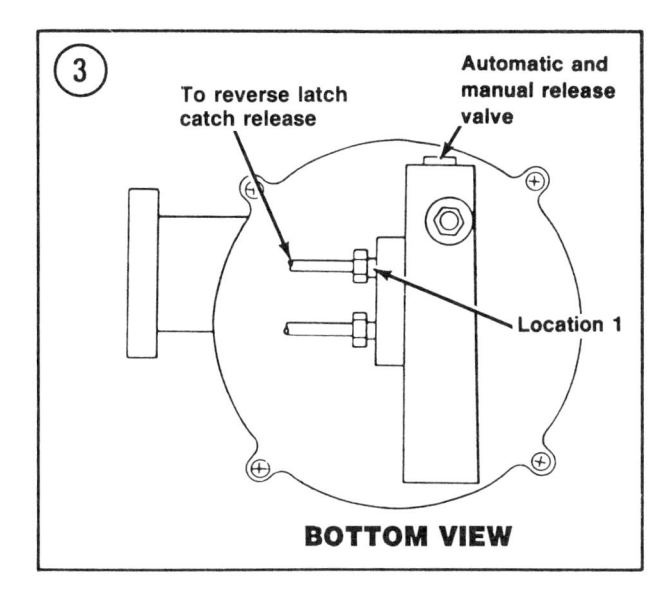

BOTTOM VIEW

3. Make sure the connector at the rear of the tilt switch is fully plugged in and that all terminals and wires are free of corrosion. Tighten and clean as required.
4. Check the 20 amp fuse located in the line between the ignition switch and tilt switch near the switch connector.
5. Make sure the manual release valve is in the AUTOMATIC position.
6. Check the hydraulic system for leakage, poor connections and damaged or kinked lines.
7. Move the tilt switch to the UP position, hold until the tilt cylinder piston has extended to its full limit, then release the switch.
8. Move the tilt switch to the DOWN position, hold until the tilt cylinder piston has retracted completely, then release the switch and make sure the reverse latch catch has fully engaged.
9. Repeat Step 7 and allow the outboard to remain in the fully tilted position for several minutes to check for downward creep.
10. If the outboard creeps downward during Step 9, check the manual release valve position. If it is in AUTOMATIC, bleed the system as described under *Hydraulic Pump Fluid Refill* in this chapter.

Troubleshooting

Whenever a problem develops in the power tilt system, determine whether the problem is in the electrical or hydraulic system. If the problem appears to be in the hydraulic system, refer it to a dealer or qualified specialist for the necessary service.

A hydraulic pressure gauge capable of reading up to 2,000 psi (in increments of 100 psi) is required for the following hydraulic procedures. It should have a flexible tube approximately 18 inches long with a short length of 3/16 in. OD flared copper tubing fitted with a 3/8×24 inverted gland nut to fit the power tilt pump fitting.

To determine whether the problem is in the electrical or hydraulic system, proceed as follows:

Outboard will not raise, but lowers under power when raised manually

Refer to **Figure 3** for this procedure.
1. Disconnect the hydraulic line at location 1, **Figure 3**.
2. Connect a suitable pressure gauge to the pump fitting.
3. Move the tilt switch to the UP position. The gauge should show at least 500 psi. If the pressure is above this minimum, the pump and motor are satisfactory but the tilt cylinder is defective. If the pressure is below the minimum, test the electric motor as described in this chapter. If the motor is satisfactory, the pump is malfunctioning and should be repaired or replaced.

Outboard will not lower, but raises under power when lowered manually

Refer to **Figure 4** for this procedure.
1. Disconnect the hydraulic line at location 2, **Figure 4**.
2. Connect a suitable pressure gauge to the pump fitting.

3. Move the tilt switch to the DOWN position. The gauge should show at least 265 psi. If the pressure is above this minimum, the pump and motor are satisfactory but the tilt cylinder is defective. If the pressure is below the minimum, test the electric motor as described in this chapter. If the motor is satisfactory, the pump is malfunctioning and should be repaired or replaced.

Outboard will not tilt in either direction

Test the electric motor as described in this chapter. If the motor is satisfactory, repeat the hydraulic tests above.

Electric Motor Test

Refer to **Figure 5** for this procedure.
1. Remove the 4 screws holding the pump base to the motor housing.
2. Disconnect and remove the 3 metal hydraulic lines and hose line clamp.
3. Place a suitable container under the pump housing to catch the oil.
4. Carefully remove the pump body with even pressure applied around the entire flange.
5. Clean the reservoir with a lint-free cloth or paper towel.
6. Modify a 3/16 in. hex socket as shown in **Figure 6** and connect it to an in.-lb. torque wrench.
7. Fit the torque wrench over the end of the motor shaft and rotate the shaft through 360°, taking torque readings at each 30°. If the readings are less than 7-10 in.-lb., replace the motor.
8. Reverse Steps 1-4 to return the pump to service.

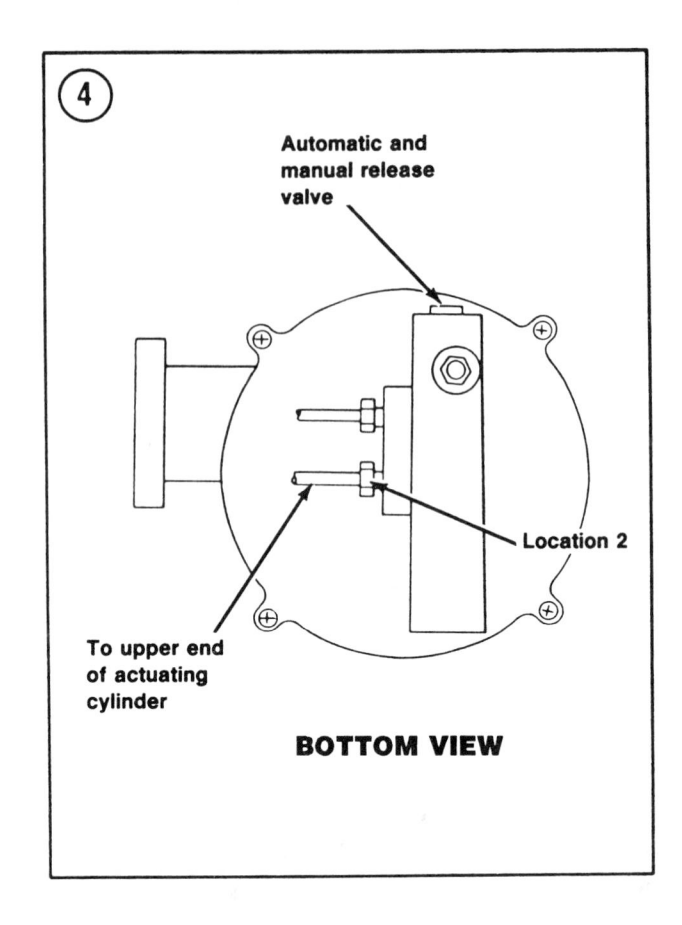

Tilt Cylinder Check

The tilt cylinder is serviced as an assembly if defective. However, it is possible to correct a malfunction caused by a dislodged check valve in the piston.
1. Remove the tilt cylinder from the stern bracket assembly.
2. Slide the piston rod rubber boot upward.
3. Use a spanner wrench to unscrew the top of the cylinder.
4. Remove the piston and rod assembly from the cylinder.
5. Locate the 2 piston check valves and make sure they seat properly. If either check valve is open, the unit will not raise or stay in the UP position.
6. If the spring-loaded check valve is off its seat, reposition it with a length of stiff wire such as a straightened paper clip.
7. Reverse Steps 1-4 to reassemble the tilt cylinder.

POWER TILT SYSTEM

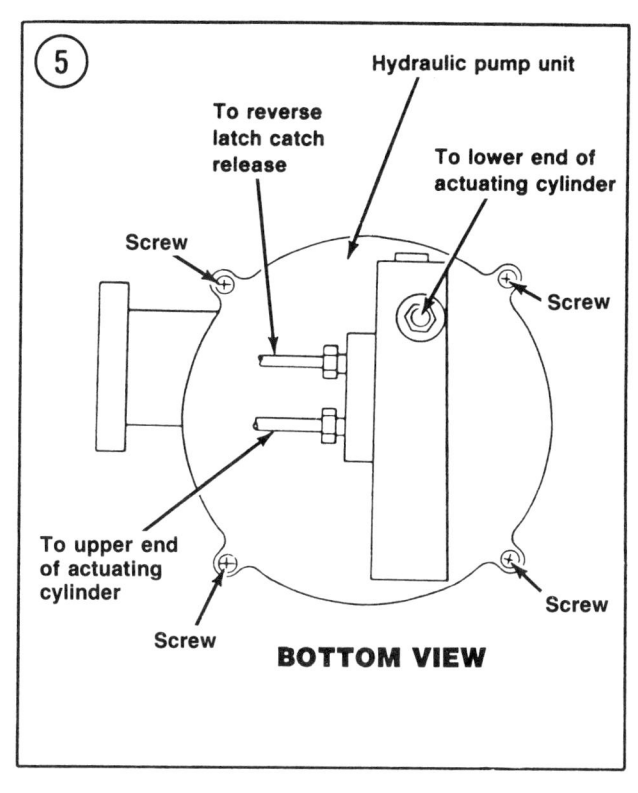

Tilt Cylinder Removal/Installation

The entire system must be removed from the outboard in order to service the tilt cylinder.

1. Remove the engine cover.
2. Remove the outboard from the boat transom. Carefully place it on its port side and block the engine to prevent it from moving.
3. Release the reverse lock and pull the stern brackets out to the tilt position.
4. Remove the starboard stern bracket, tilt cylinder and thrust rod.
5. Disconnect the hydraulic lines at the tilt cylinder and remove the cylinder from the pump motor unit.
6. Reverse Steps 1-5 to reinstall the tilt cylinder. Make sure the reverse lock engages properly, then perform the *Hydraulic Fluid Level Refill* procedure in this chapter.

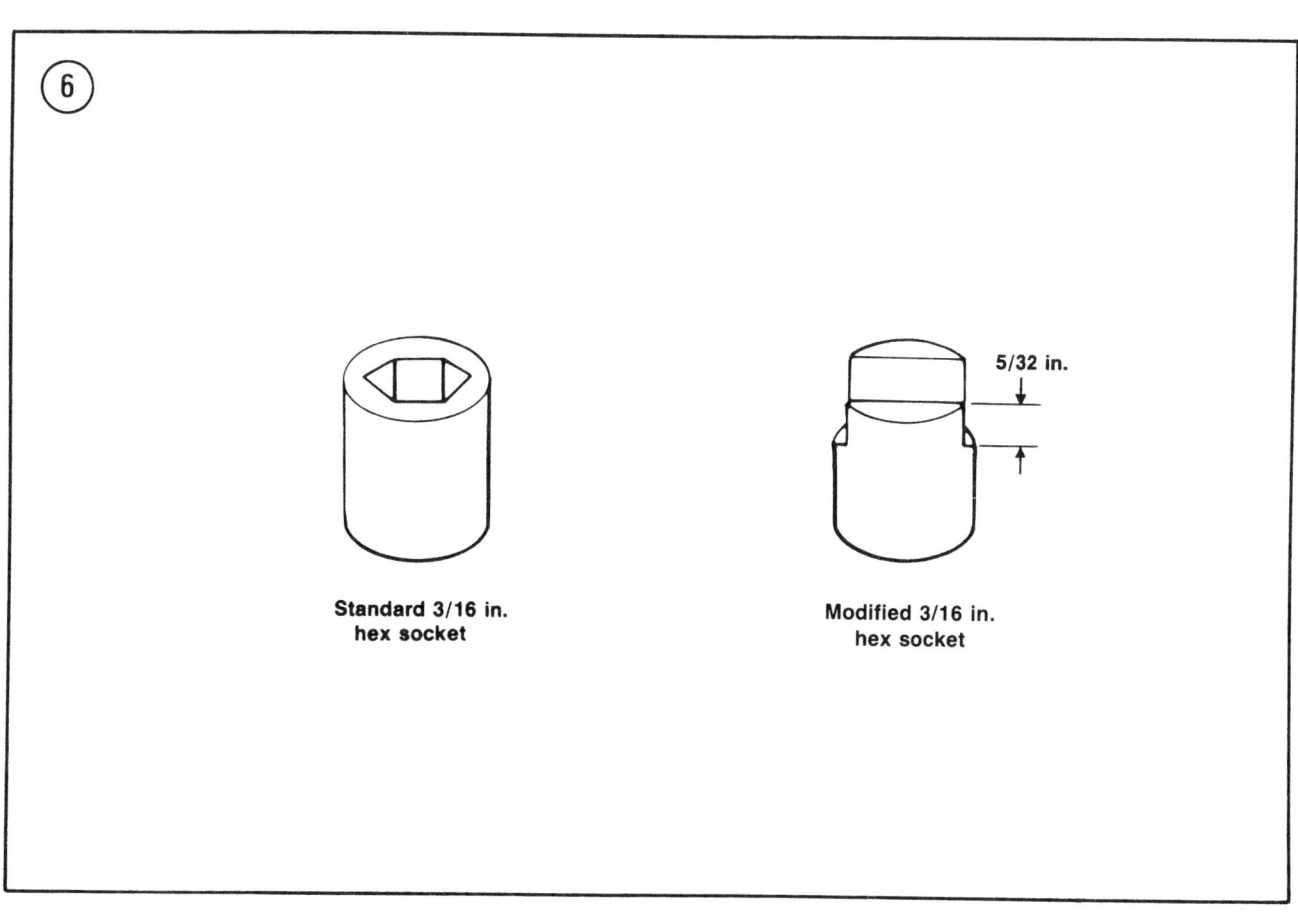

Index

A

Alternator charging system
   Description 206
   External voltage regulator 207-208
   Junction box voltage
      regulator/transistor 206-207
   Stator 206
   Troubleshooting (6-15 amp) 43-45
   Troubleshooting (20 amp) 41-43
Anti-corrosion maintenance 97
Armature plate (flywheel
   magneto ignition) 232-234
Automatic rewind starters
   Engine cover starter 326-329
   Flywheel mounted starter 335-340
   Side-mounted pinion gear
      starter 332-335
   Starter lockout adjustment 340
   Swing arm gear drive
      starter 329-332

B

Battery
   Care and inspection 197-202
   Charging system 203-208
   Installation in aluminum boats 198
   Jump starting 202
   Storage 201
   Testing 200-201

Breakerless distributor (flywheel
   CD ignition) 235-236
Breaker point distributor
   (flywheel CD ignition) 232-234
Breaker point ignition system
   Description 107
   Point replacement (distributor
      battery ignition) 110-111
   Point replacement (distributor
      CD ignition) 111-113
   Point replacement (distributor
      magneto ignition) 109
Breaker points
   Ignition system service 107
   Replacement (distributor
      battery ignition) 110-111
   Replacement (distributor CD
      ignition) 111-113
   Replacement (distributor magneto
      ignition) 109
   Replacement (flywheel magneto
      ignition) 107-108
Brush replacement, starter (see Electric
   starting system)

C

Carburetor
   Adjustments (See Engine synchroni-
      zation and linkage adjustments)
   Choke solenoid service 192-193
   Cleaning and inspection 161-162

Core plug service 162-163
Core plugs and lead shot 162
Lead shot service 163
Model A carburetor 163-166
Model B carburetor 166-168
Model C carburetor 168-175
Model D carburetor 175-178
Model E carburetor 178-182
Model F carburetor 182-188
Model G carburetor 188-192
Charging system (see Alternator charging
   system, Battery or Generator
   charging system)
Choke solenoid 192-193
Compression check 99-100
Corrosion
   Anti-corrosion maintenance 97
   Galvanic 11-12
   Protection from galvanic 12-14
   Salt water 90
Cut-out switch,
   vacuum operated 215-216

D

Distributor
   Breakerless (flywheel CD
      ignition) 235-236
   Breaker point (flywheel CD
      ignition) 232-234
Drive unit, lower (see Gearcase)

INDEX

E

Electric starting system
- Brush replacement (Autolite) 210-211
- Brush replacement (Bosch) 211-212
- Brush replacement (Delco-Remy) 212-213
- Brush replacement (Prestolite) 213-214
- Cut-out switch 215-216
- Safety switch 214, 274-275
- Starter motor description 208-209
- Starter motor removal/installation (2-cylinder) 209-210
- Starter motor removal/installation (except 2-cylinder) 210
- Starter solenoid 214-215

Engine flushing 97-89
Engine operation 2
Engine serial number 230
Engine synchronization and linkage adjustments
- Engine timing 118-119
- Synchronizing 119-120
- 1- and 2-cylinder engines 120-128
- 1958-1959 50 hp V4 128-130
- 1960-1966 60-100 hp V4 130-133
- 1967 80 hp V4 130-133
- 1964-1965 60 hp 133
- 1966-1967 60 hp 133-134
- 1960-1965 75 hp 133-134
- 1966-1967 80 hp 133-134
- 1963-1964 90 hp 134-135
- 1966-1967 100 hp 134-135
- 1967 100 hp V4 135-137
- 1968-1969 55 hp 137-140
- 1970-1971 60 hp 137-140
- 1968 65, 85 and 100 hp 141-143
- 1969-1970 85 and 115 hp 143-145
- 1971-1972 85, 100, 125 hp 145-149
- 1972 65 hp 149-151

F

Fasteners 2-8
Fasteners and torque 230-231
Filter, fuel
- Petcock filter screen 104
- Pump filter screen 105
- Sediment bowl filter 105
- Service 104
Flushing, engine 97-98
Flywheel 231-232
Fuel
- Consistent mixtures 88
- Correct mixing method 87-88
- Gasohol 86
- Recommended mixture 86-87
- Selection 85
- Sour 85-86

Fuel filter service 104
Fuel line and primer bulb 196
Fuel lines 104
Fuel pump 105, 156-161
- Filter screen 105
- Pressure test (inline engines) . 105-106
- Pressure test (V4 engines) 106-107
Fuel system
- Carburetors (see Carburetors)
- Fuel filter service 104
- Fuel line and primer bulb 196
- Fuel lines 104
- Fuel pump 105, 156-161
- Fuel system service 104
- Fuel tank 193-196
- Petcock filter screen 104
- Pump filter screen 105
- Pump pressure test (inline engines) 105-106
- Pump pressure test (V4) 105-106
- Sediment bowl filter 105
Fuel tank 193-196

G

Gaskets and sealants 231
Gearcase
- Cleaning and inspection 289-290
- Direct drive 291-294
- Electric shift
  - Assembly 311-313
  - Disassembly 307-310
  - Forward gear disassembly/assembly 310
  - Removal/installation 306-307
  - Reverse gear disassembly/assembly 310-311
  - Shift coil and cable check 311
- Hydro-electric shift
  - Assembly 320-324
  - Disassembly 315-318
  - Lower drive shaft bearing replacement 318
  - Oil pump disassembly/assembly 320
  - Propeller shaft disassembly/assembly 319
  - Removal/installation 313-315
  - Solenoid/shift assembly 320
- Manual shift (single housing) 302-306
- Manual shift (split lower housing) 294-302
- Pressure and vacuum test 324-325
- Propeller 282-283
- Service precautions 282
- Water pump 283-289
Gearcase and water pump check 104
Generator charging system
- Removal/installation 203-205

I

Ignition systems
- Distributor battery breaker point ignition 220-223
- Distributor CD sensor ignition 223-225
- Distributor magneto breaker point ignition 218-220
- Flywheel CD breaker point ingition 226-227
- Flywheel CD sensor ignition . 225-226
- Flywheel magneto breaker point ignition 216-217
- Troubleshooting 48-50

J

Jump starting 202

L

Lower drive unit (see Gearcase)
Lubricants 8-10
Lubrication 85-90
- Fuel mixing, correct method 87-88
- Fuel mixture, recommended 86-87
- Fuel mixtures, consistent 88
- Fuel selection 85
- Fuel, sour 85-86
- Gasohol 86
- Gearcase bearing carrier/nut, saltwater corrosion of 90
- Lower drive unit 88-89
- Lubrication points (except lower drive unit) 89-90

P

Petcock filter screen 104
Power head
- Connecting rod and crankshaft assembly 265-268
- Crankshaft and connecting rod bearing cleaning and inspection 260-261
- Crankshaft cleaning and inspection 261-262
- Cylinder block and crankcase assembly (general procedures) 268-269
- Cylinder block and crankcase assembly (1.5 and 2 hp) 269
- Cylinder block and crankcase assembly (3-20 hp) 269-270
- Cylinder block and crankcase assembly (28-40 hp) 270-271
- Cylinder block and crankcase assembly (55, 60 and 65 hp inline) ... 271-272
- Cylinder block and crankcase assembly (V4) 272
- Cylinder block and crankcase cleaning and inspection 258-260

INDEX

Disassembly (1.5 and 2 hp) ... 241-242
Disassembly (3-20 hp) 243-247
Disassembly (28-40 hp) 247-250
Disassembly (55, 60 and 65 hp
   inline) 251-254
Disassembly (V4) 254-258
Overhaul 241
Piston and connecting rod
   assembly 262-265
Piston cleaning and inspection 261
Reed block service 272-273
Removal/installation
   (1.5 and 2 hp) 236-237
Removal/installation (3-15 hp) 237
Removal/installation (18-35 hp) .. 238
Removal/installation (40 hp) 238-239
Removal/installation (55, 60
   and 65 hp inline) 251-254
Removal/installation (V4) 240-241
Thermostat service 273-274
Power tilt system
   Components 341
   Electric motor test 344
   Hydraulic pump fluid check 342
   Hydraulic pump fluid refill 342
   Operation 342
   Preliminary check procedure . 342-343
   Tilt cylinder check 344
   Tilt cylinder removal/
     installation 345
   Troubleshooting 343-344
Pressure and vacuum test
   (gearcase) 324-325
Primer bulb and fuel line 196
Propellers 14-20, 282-283
   Shaft disassembly/assembly
     (hydro-electric gearcase) 319
Pump, fuel 105, 156-161

R

Reed block service 272-273

S

Safety first 21
Safety switch, starter 214
Sealants and gaskets 231
Sediment bowl filter 105
Sensor gap check/adjustment (break-
   less distributor CD ignition) 113
Serial number, engine 230
Solenoid, starter 215
Solenoids
   Starter 214-215
   Choke 192-193

Spark plugs
   Description 100
   Gapping 103
   Installation 103-104
   Removal 100-102
Starters, automatic rewind
   Engine cover starter 326-329
   Flywheel mounted starter 335-340
   Side-mounted pinion gear
     starter 332-335
   Starter lockout adjustment 340
   Swing arm gear drive
     starter 329-332
Starting system, electric
   Brush replacement
     (Autolite) 210-211
   Brush replacement (Bosch) 211-212
   Brush replacement
     (Delco-Remy) 212-213
   Brush replacement
     (Prestolite) 213-214
   Cut-out switch 215-216
   Safety switch 214
   Starter motor description 208-209
   Starter motor removal/installation
     (2-cylinder) 209-210
   Starter motor removal/installation
     (except 2-cylinder) 210
   Starter solenoid 214-215
   Stator (flywheel CD ignition) 236
   Storage 90-96
   Submersion 96-97

T

Tank, fuel 193-196
Test equipment 26-28
Thermostat service 273-274
Tilt cylinder
   Check 344
   Removal/Installation 345
Tools, basic hand 21-26
Torque specifications 2
Torque and fasteners 230-231
Troubleshooting
   Alternator charging system 39-45
   CD breakerless ignition system . 59-73
   CD breaker point ignition
     system 51-59
   Clipper circuit 45-46
   Engine 75-77
   Fuel system 73-75
   Generator charging system 37-39
   Ignition 49-51
   Operating requirements 34
   Shift circuit 46-58

Starting system 34-37
Tilt system 343-344
Tune-up
   Battery and starter motor check .. 113
   Breaker point ignition system
     service 107
   Breaker point replacement (distributor
     battery ignition) 110-111
   Breaker point replacement (distributor
     CD ignition) 111-113
   Breaker point replacement (distributor
     magneto ignition) 109
   Breaker point replacement (flywheel
     magneto ignition) 107-108
   Compression check 99-100
   Engine synchronizing and
     adjustment 114
   Fuel filter service 104
   Fuel lines 104
   Fuel pump 105
   Fuel pump filter screen 105
   Fuel pump pressure test
     (inline engines) 105-106
   Fuel pump pressure test
     (V4 engines) 106-107
   Fuel system service 104
   Gearcase and water pump check . 104
   Internal wiring harness check 114
   Performance test (on boat) 114
   Petcock filter screen 104
   Sediment bowl filter 105
   Sensor gap check/adjustment (breaker-
     less distributor CD ignition) 113
   Solenoid check
     (electric start) 113-114
   Spark plugs (description) 100
   Spark plug gapping 103
   Spark plug installation 103-104
   Spark plug removal 100-102

V

Vacuum and pressure test
   (gearcase) 324-325
Voltage regulator
   External (alternator) 207-208
   Generator 205
   Junction box voltage regulator/
     transistor (alternator) 206-207

W

Water pump 104, 283-289
Winterizing (see storage)

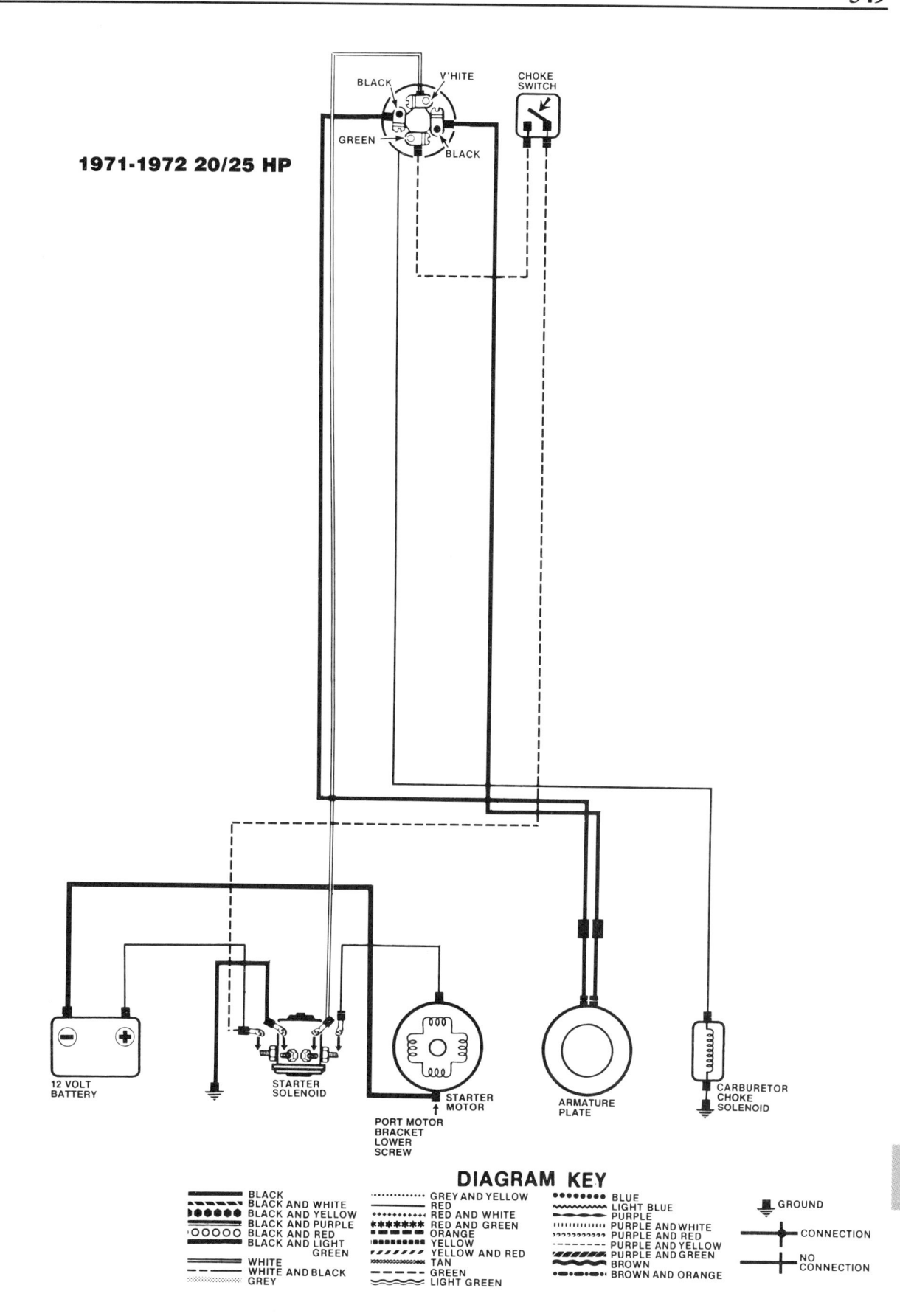

WIRING DIAGRAMS

1971-1972 20/25 HP

BLACK, WHITE, GREEN, BLACK
CHOKE SWITCH

12 VOLT BATTERY — STARTER SOLENOID — STARTER MOTOR (PORT MOTOR BRACKET LOWER SCREW) — ARMATURE PLATE — CARBURETOR CHOKE SOLENOID

DIAGRAM KEY

- BLACK
- BLACK AND WHITE
- BLACK AND YELLOW
- BLACK AND PURPLE
- BLACK AND RED
- BLACK AND LIGHT GREEN
- WHITE
- WHITE AND BLACK
- GREY
- GREY AND YELLOW
- RED
- RED AND WHITE
- RED AND GREEN
- ORANGE
- YELLOW
- YELLOW AND RED
- TAN
- GREEN
- LIGHT GREEN
- BLUE
- LIGHT BLUE
- PURPLE
- PURPLE AND WHITE
- PURPLE AND RED
- PURPLE AND YELLOW
- PURPLE AND GREEN
- BROWN
- BROWN AND ORANGE
- GROUND
- CONNECTION
- NO CONNECTION

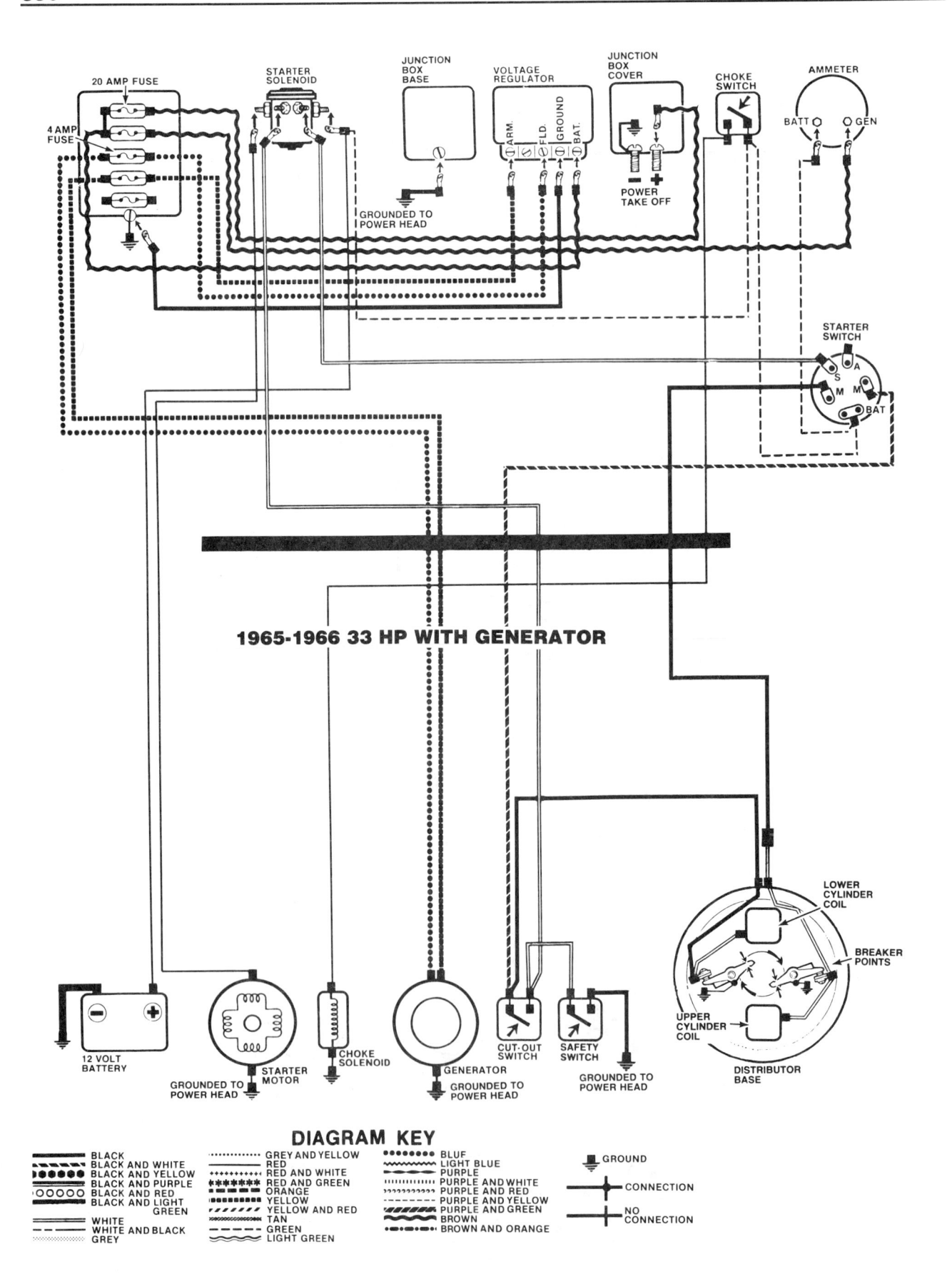

WIRING DIAGRAMS

1965-1966 33 HP WITH GENERATOR

DIAGRAM KEY

- BLACK
- BLACK AND WHITE
- BLACK AND YELLOW
- BLACK AND PURPLE
- BLACK AND RED
- BLACK AND LIGHT GREEN
- WHITE
- WHITE AND BLACK
- GREY
- GREY AND YELLOW
- RED
- RED AND WHITE
- RED AND GREEN
- ORANGE
- YELLOW
- YELLOW AND RED
- TAN
- GREEN
- LIGHT GREEN
- BLUE
- LIGHT BLUE
- PURPLE
- PURPLE AND WHITE
- PURPLE AND RED
- PURPLE AND YELLOW
- PURPLE AND GREEN
- BROWN
- BROWN AND ORANGE
- GROUND
- CONNECTION
- NO CONNECTION

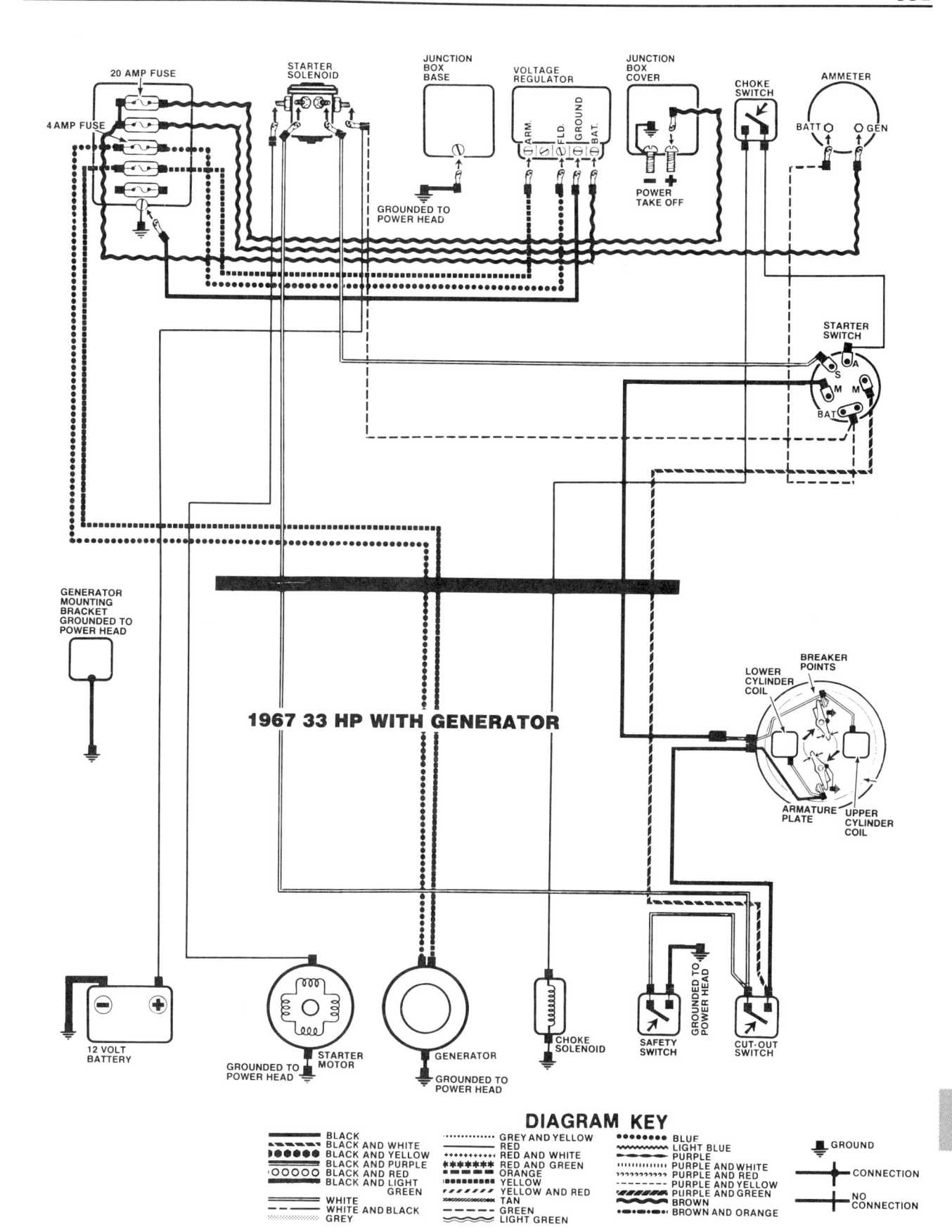

WIRING DIAGRAMS

1967 33 HP WITH GENERATOR

DIAGRAM KEY

- BLACK
- BLACK AND WHITE
- BLACK AND YELLOW
- BLACK AND PURPLE
- BLACK AND RED
- BLACK AND LIGHT GREEN
- WHITE
- WHITE AND BLACK
- GREY
- GREY AND YELLOW
- RED
- RED AND WHITE
- RED AND GREEN
- ORANGE
- YELLOW
- YELLOW AND RED
- TAN
- GREEN
- LIGHT GREEN
- BLUE
- LIGHT BLUE
- PURPLE
- PURPLE AND WHITE
- PURPLE AND YELLOW
- PURPLE AND RED
- PURPLE AND GREEN
- BROWN
- BROWN AND ORANGE
- GROUND
- CONNECTION
- NO CONNECTION

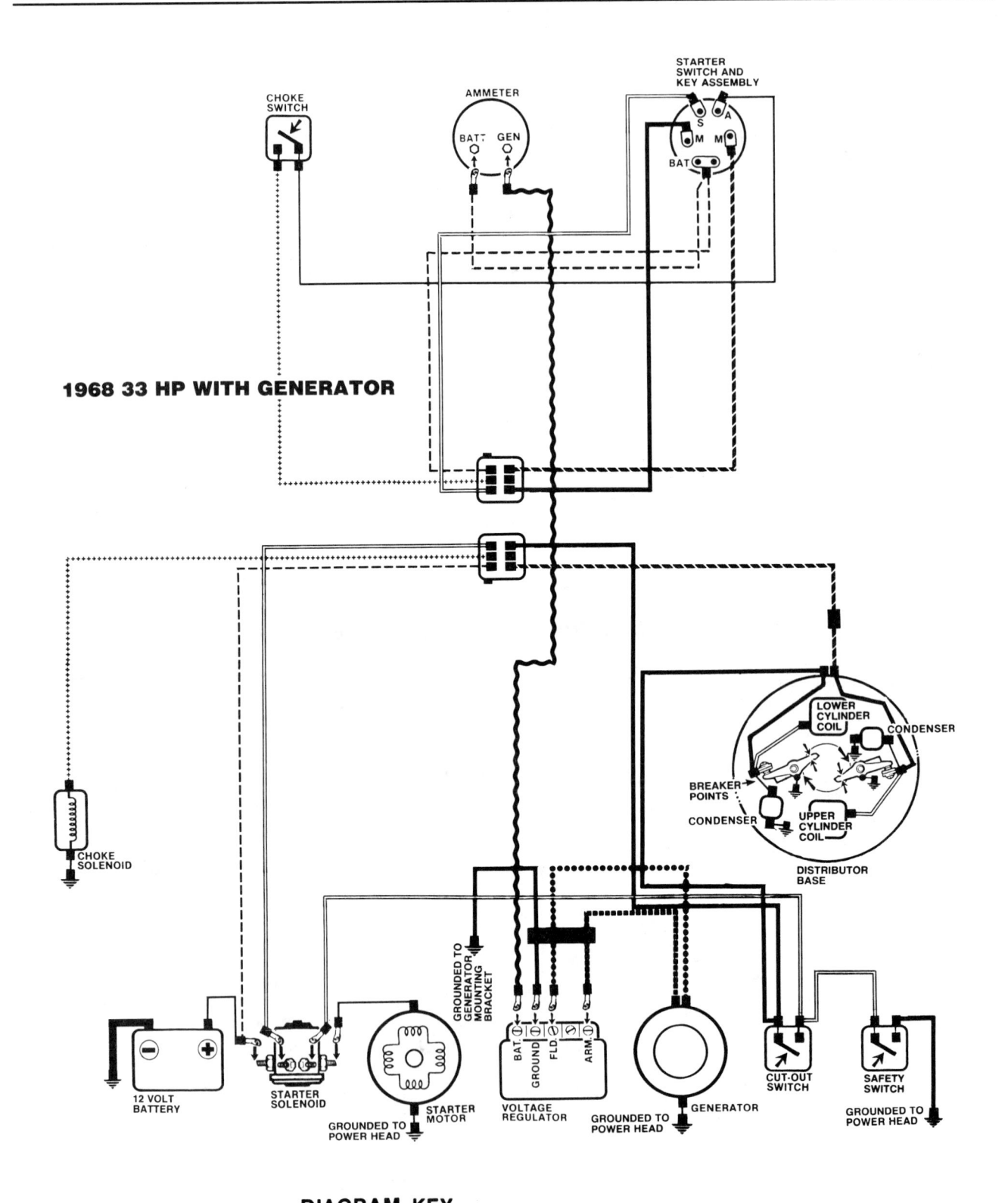

WIRING DIAGRAMS

1968 33 HP WITH GENERATOR

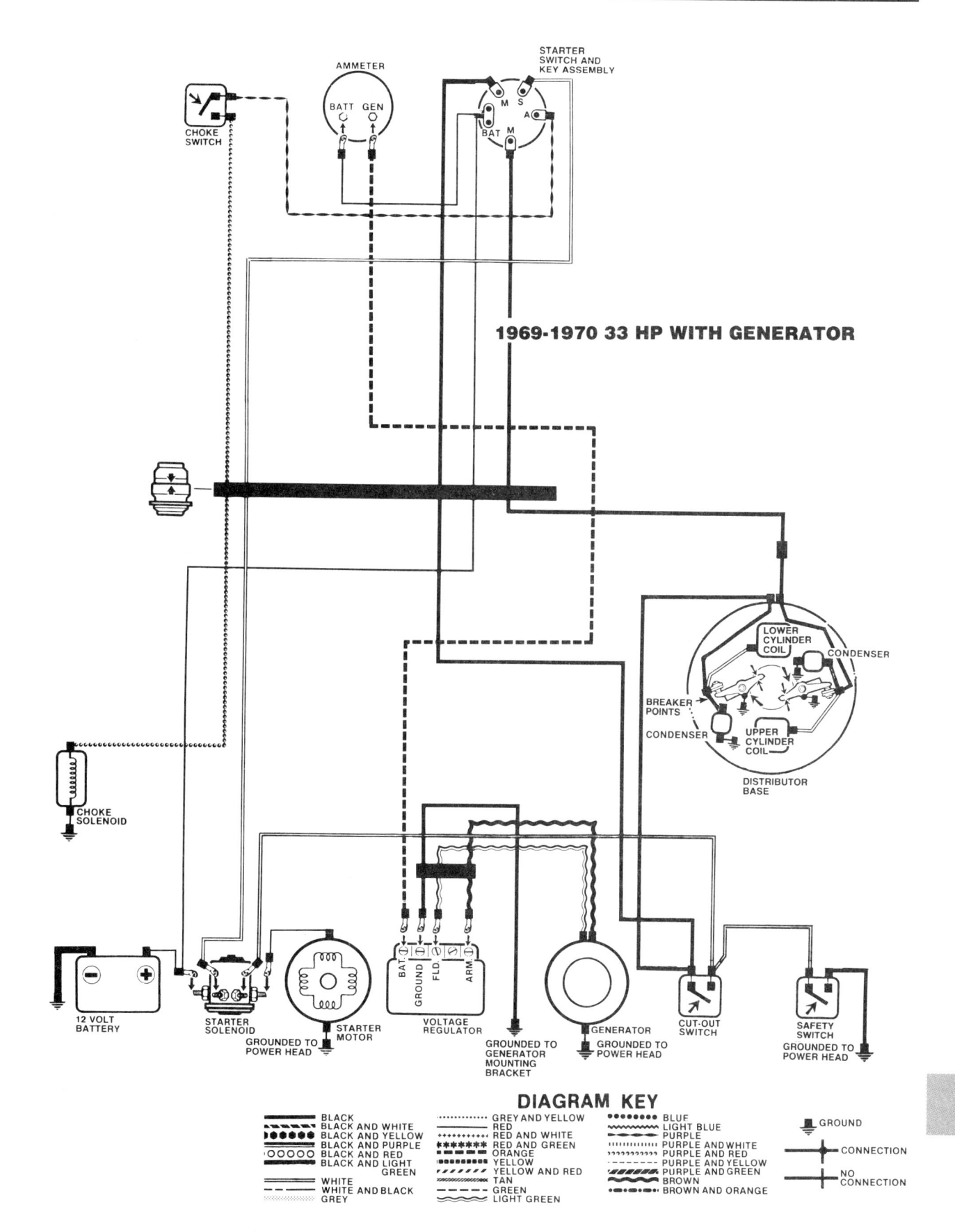

WIRING DIAGRAMS

1969-1970 33 HP WITH GENERATOR

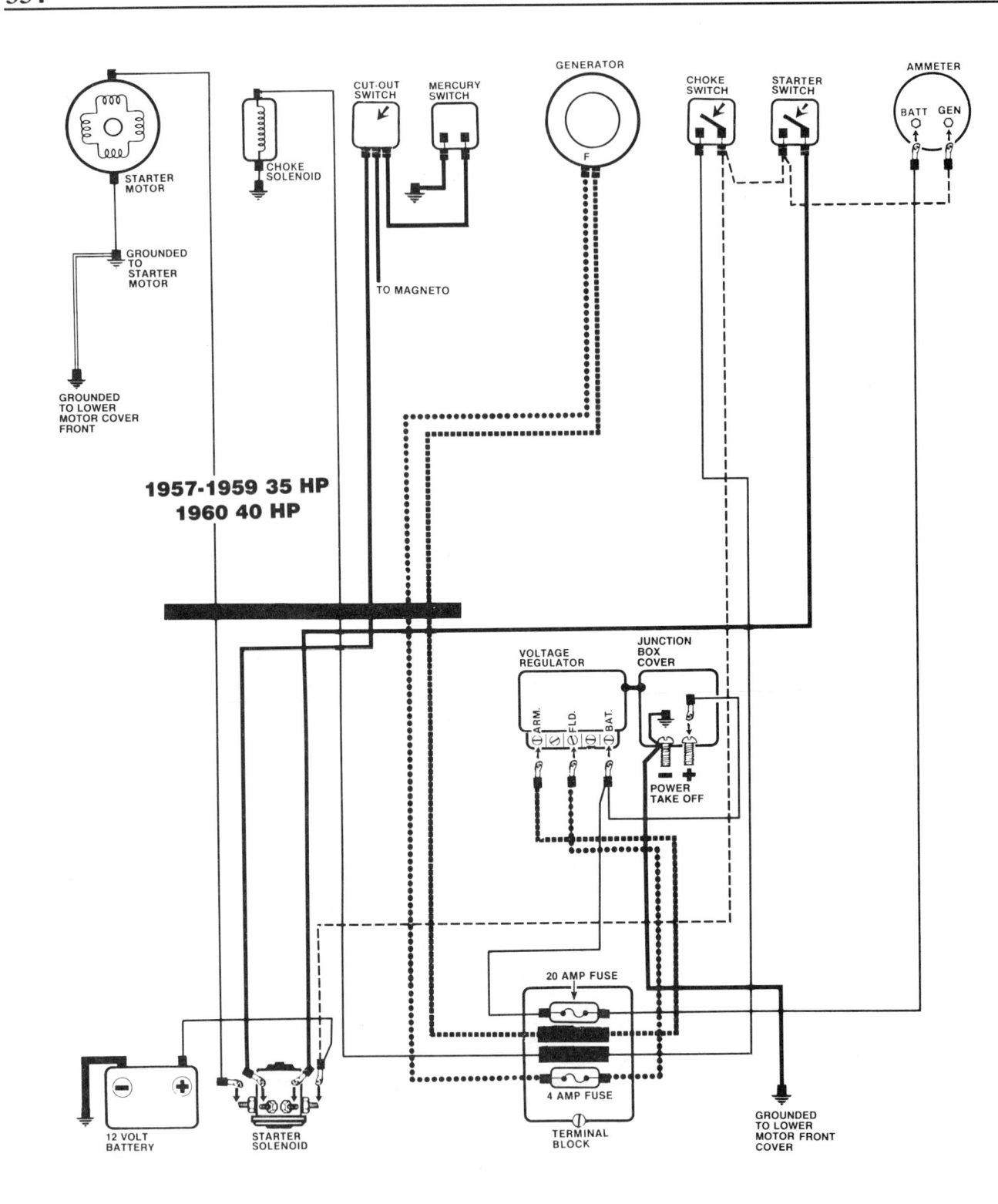

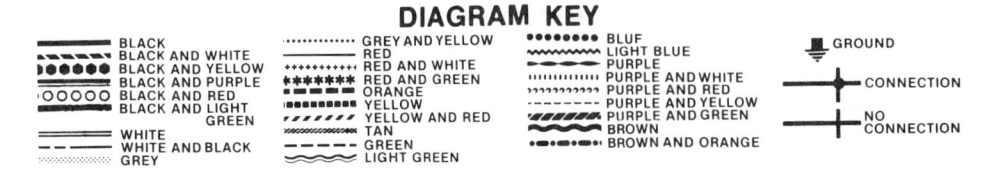

WIRING DIAGRAMS

1957-1959 35 HP
1960 40 HP

DIAGRAM KEY

- BLACK
- BLACK AND WHITE
- BLACK AND YELLOW
- BLACK AND PURPLE
- BLACK AND RED
- BLACK AND LIGHT GREEN
- WHITE
- WHITE AND BLACK
- GREY
- GREY AND YELLOW
- RED
- RED AND WHITE
- RED AND GREEN
- ORANGE
- YELLOW
- YELLOW AND RED
- TAN
- GREEN
- LIGHT GREEN
- BLUE
- LIGHT BLUE
- PURPLE
- PURPLE AND WHITE
- PURPLE AND RED
- PURPLE AND YELLOW
- PURPLE AND GREEN
- BROWN
- BROWN AND ORANGE
- GROUND
- CONNECTION
- NO CONNECTION

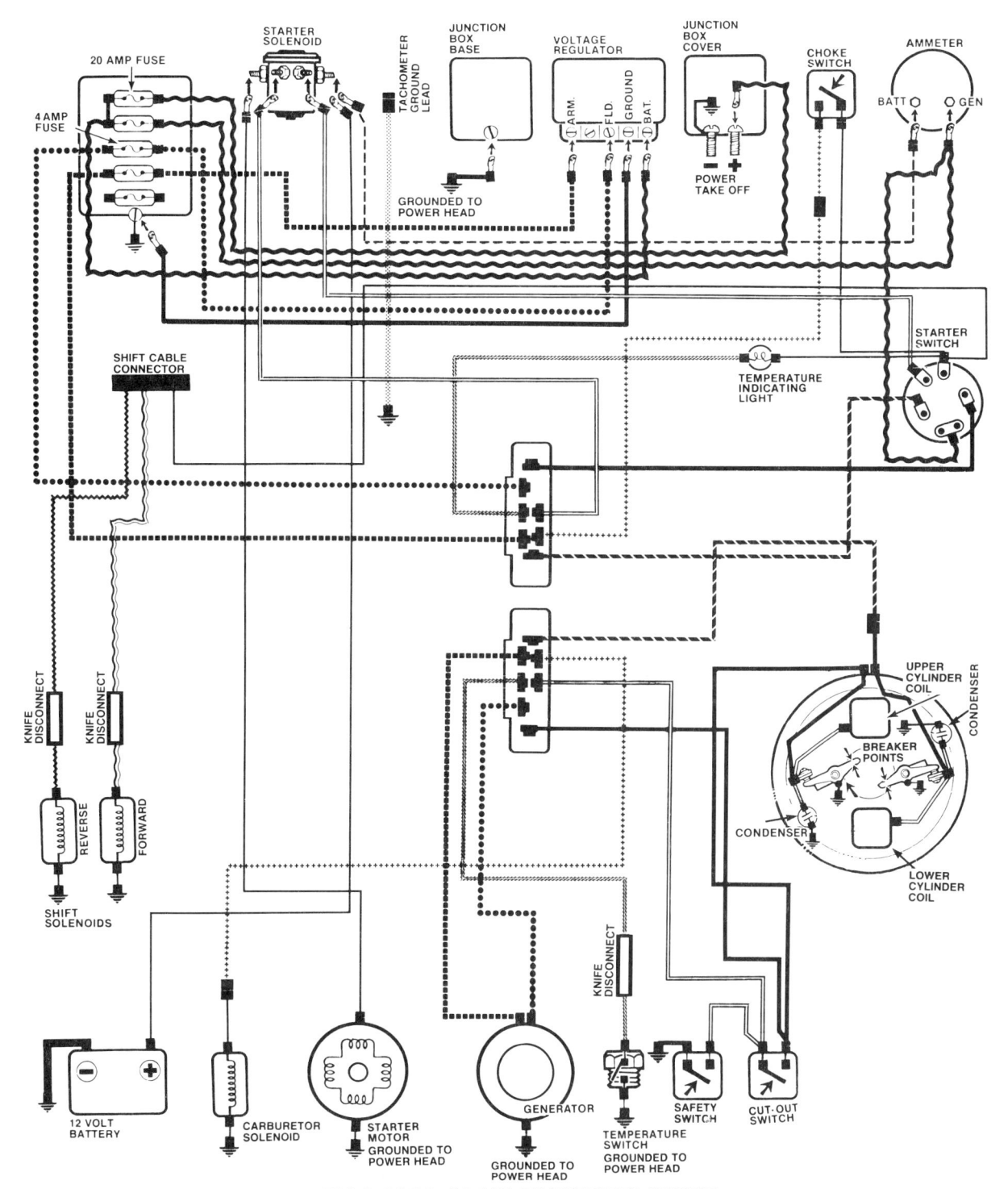

WIRING DIAGRAMS 355

1961-1966 40 HP ELECTRIC SHIFT WITH GENERATOR

DIAGRAM KEY

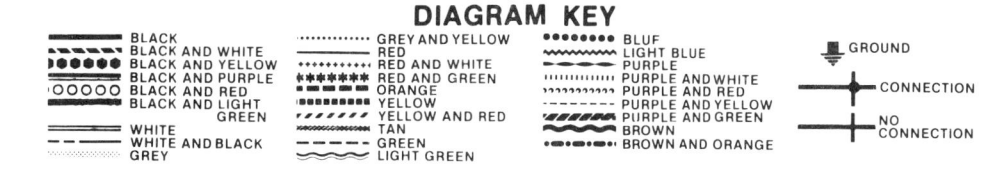

- BLACK
- BLACK AND WHITE
- BLACK AND YELLOW
- BLACK AND PURPLE
- BLACK AND RED
- BLACK AND LIGHT GREEN
- WHITE
- WHITE AND BLACK
- GREY
- GREY AND YELLOW
- RED
- RED AND WHITE
- RED AND GREEN
- ORANGE
- YELLOW
- YELLOW AND RED
- TAN
- GREEN
- LIGHT GREEN
- BLUE
- LIGHT BLUE
- PURPLE
- PURPLE AND WHITE
- PURPLE AND RED
- PURPLE AND YELLOW
- PURPLE AND GREEN
- BROWN
- BROWN AND ORANGE
- GROUND
- CONNECTION
- NO CONNECTION

13

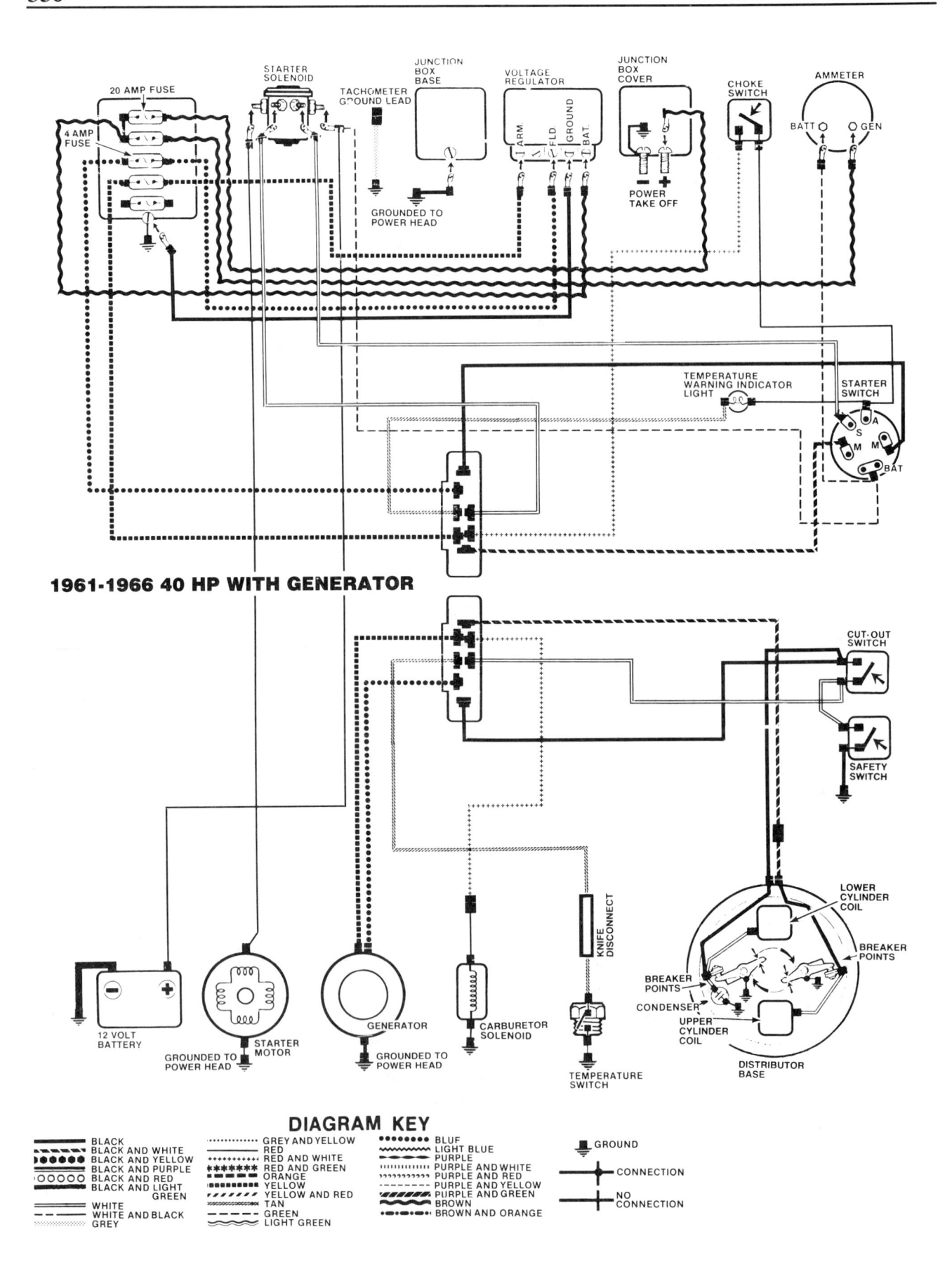

WIRING DIAGRAMS

1961-1966 40 HP WITH GENERATOR

DIAGRAM KEY

- BLACK
- BLACK AND WHITE
- BLACK AND YELLOW
- BLACK AND PURPLE
- BLACK AND RED
- BLACK AND LIGHT GREEN
- WHITE
- WHITE AND BLACK
- GREY
- GREY AND YELLOW
- RED
- RED AND WHITE
- RED AND GREEN
- ORANGE
- YELLOW
- YELLOW AND RED
- TAN
- GREEN
- LIGHT GREEN
- BLUE
- LIGHT BLUE
- PURPLE
- PURPLE AND WHITE
- PURPLE AND RED
- PURPLE AND YELLOW
- PURPLE AND GREEN
- BROWN
- BROWN AND ORANGE
- GROUND
- CONNECTION
- NO CONNECTION

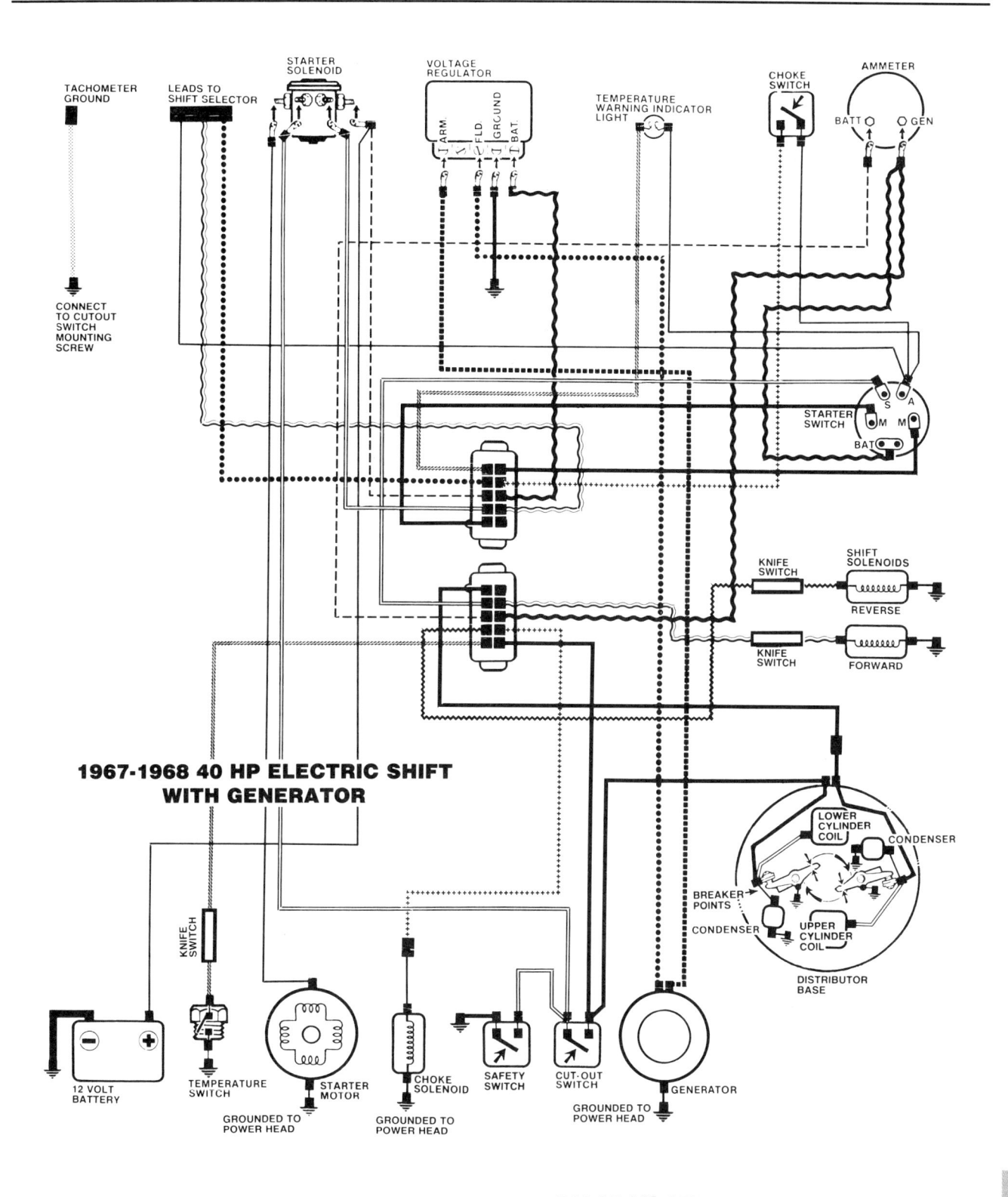

WIRING DIAGRAMS

1967-1968 40 HP ELECTRIC SHIFT WITH GENERATOR

WIRING DIAGRAMS

1967-1968 40 HP WITH GENERATOR

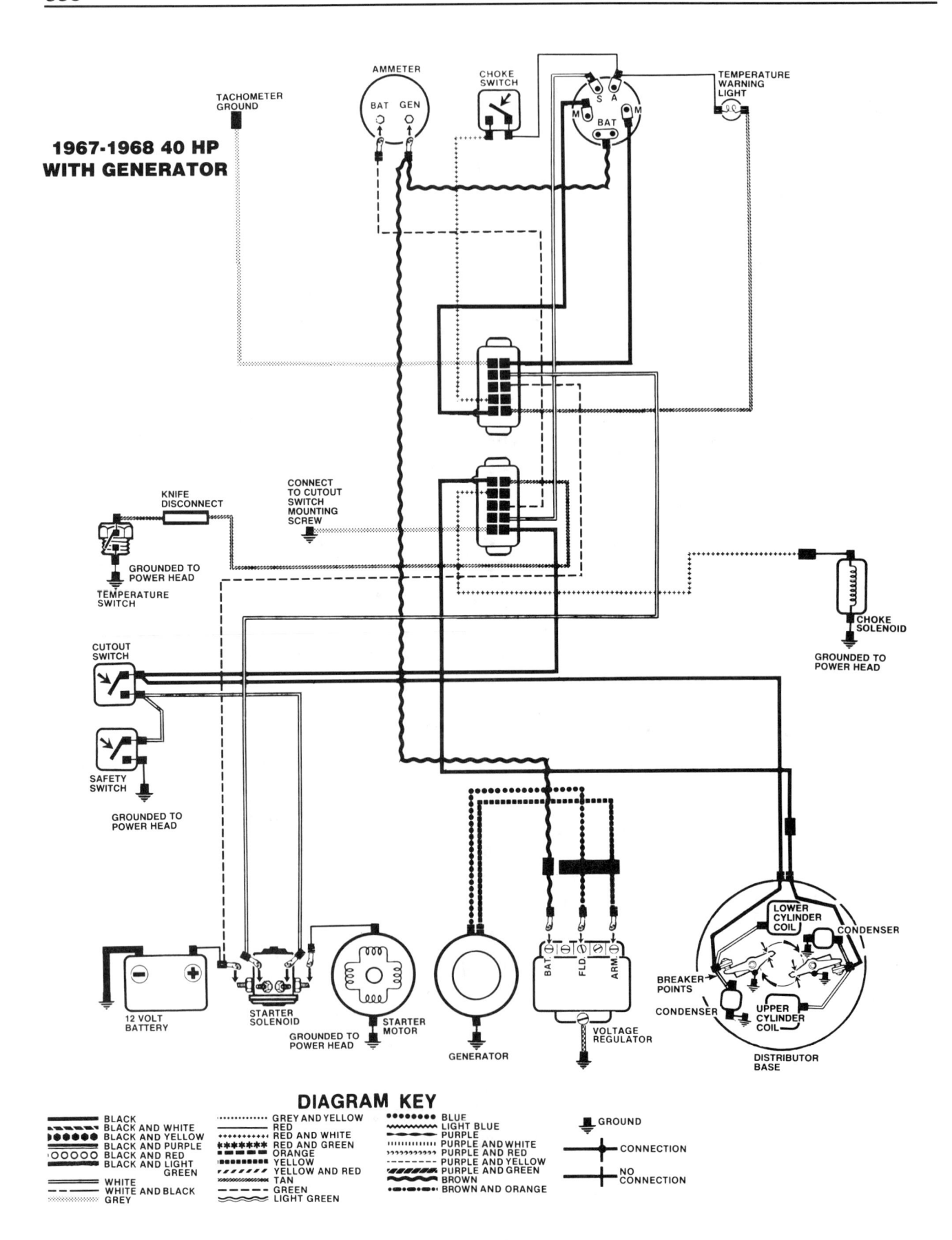

DIAGRAM KEY

BLACK	GREY AND YELLOW	BLUE
BLACK AND WHITE	RED	LIGHT BLUE
BLACK AND YELLOW	RED AND WHITE	PURPLE
BLACK AND PURPLE	RED AND GREEN	PURPLE AND WHITE
BLACK AND RED	ORANGE	PURPLE AND RED
BLACK AND LIGHT GREEN	YELLOW	PURPLE AND YELLOW
WHITE	YELLOW AND RED	PURPLE AND GREEN
WHITE AND BLACK	TAN	BROWN
GREY	GREEN	BROWN AND ORANGE
	LIGHT GREEN	

- GROUND
- CONNECTION
- NO CONNECTION

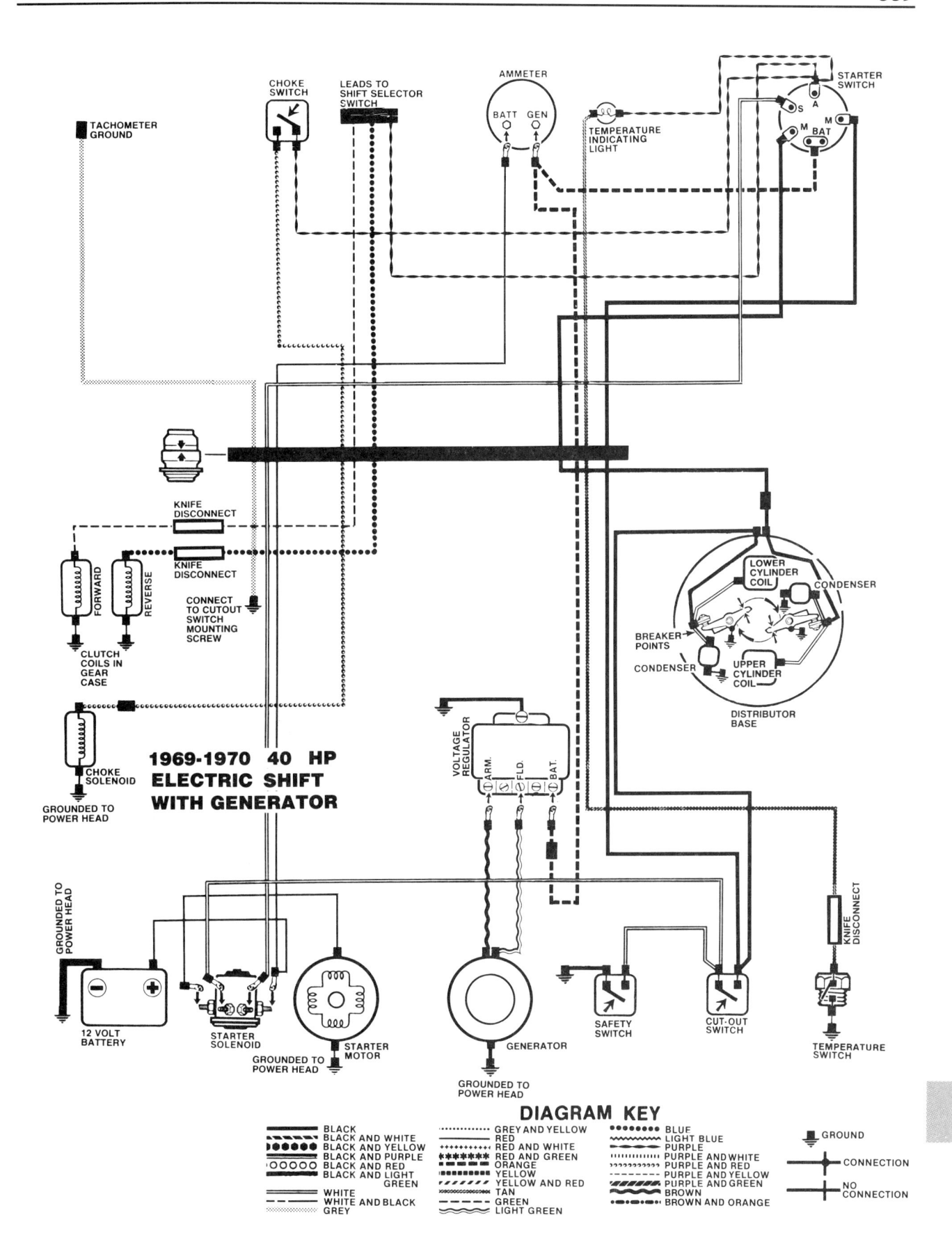

WIRING DIAGRAMS

359

13

WIRING DIAGRAMS

1969-1970 40 HP WITH GENERATOR
1958-1959 50 HP

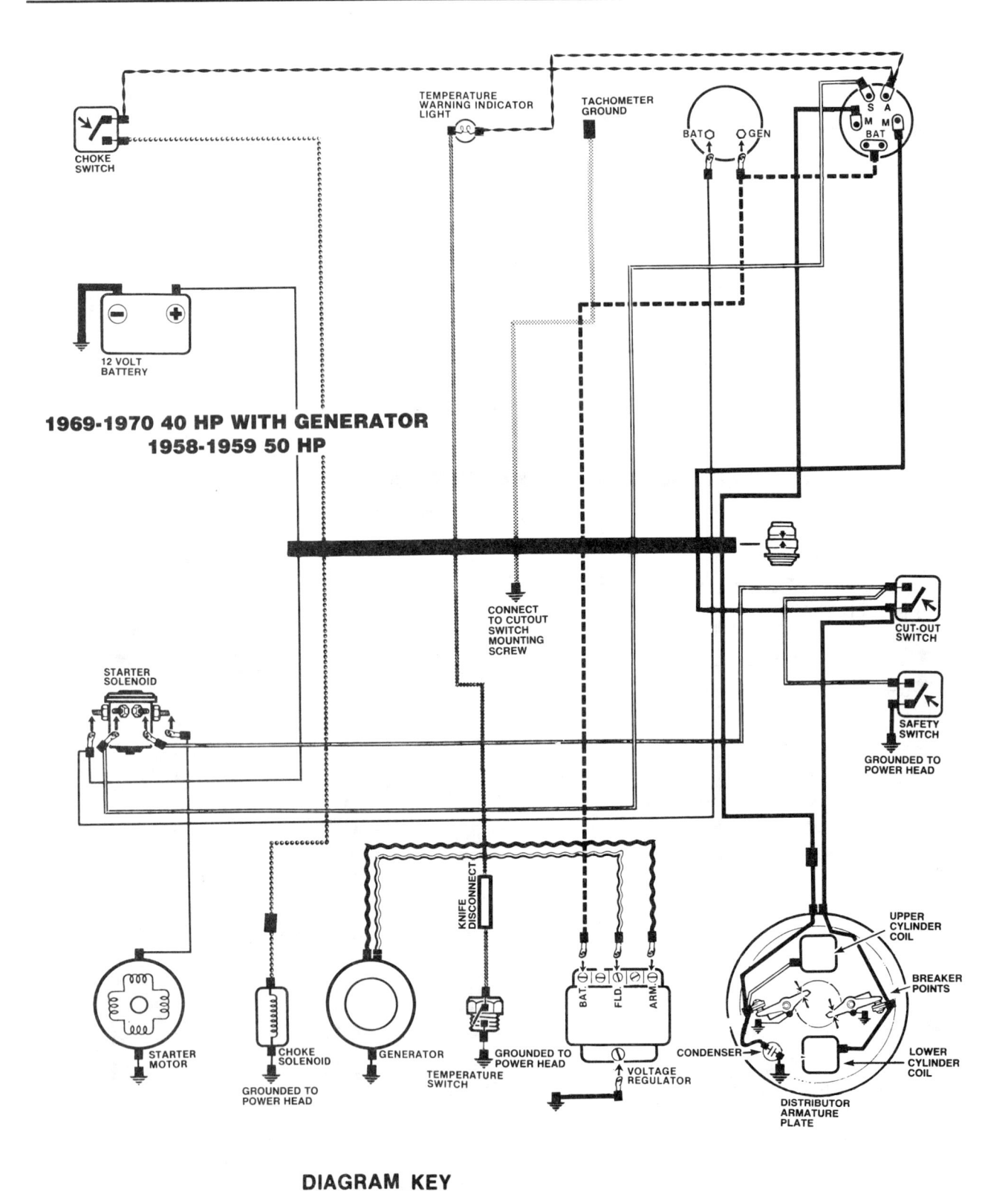

DIAGRAM KEY

- BLACK
- BLACK AND WHITE
- BLACK AND YELLOW
- BLACK AND PURPLE
- BLACK AND RED
- BLACK AND LIGHT GREEN
- WHITE
- WHITE AND BLACK
- GREY
- GREY AND YELLOW
- RED
- RED AND WHITE
- RED AND GREEN
- ORANGE
- YELLOW
- YELLOW AND RED
- TAN
- GREEN
- LIGHT GREEN
- BLUE
- LIGHT BLUE
- PURPLE
- PURPLE AND WHITE
- PURPLE AND RED
- PURPLE AND YELLOW
- PURPLE AND GREEN
- BROWN
- BROWN AND ORANGE
- GROUND
- CONNECTION
- NO CONNECTION

WIRING DIAGRAMS

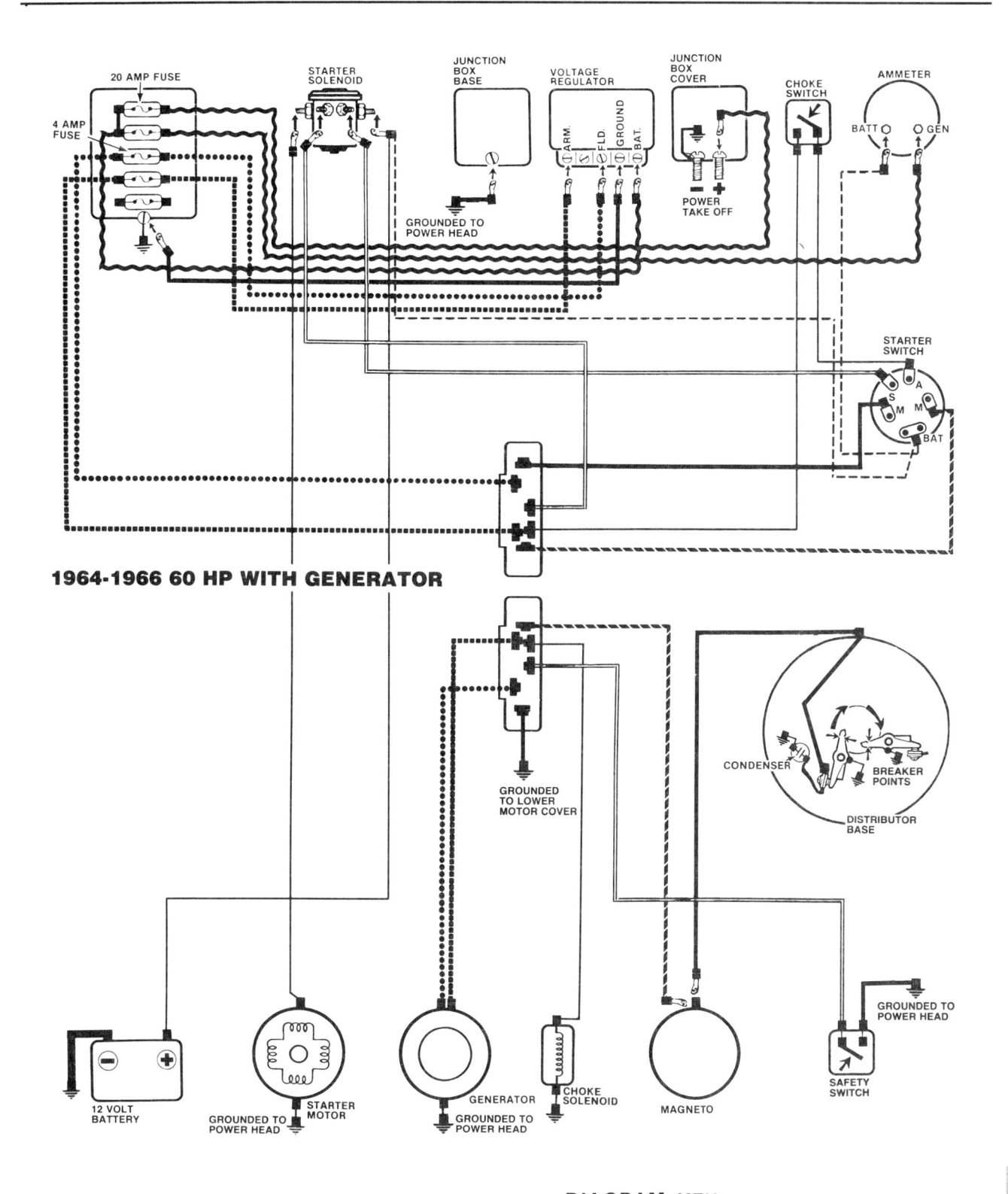

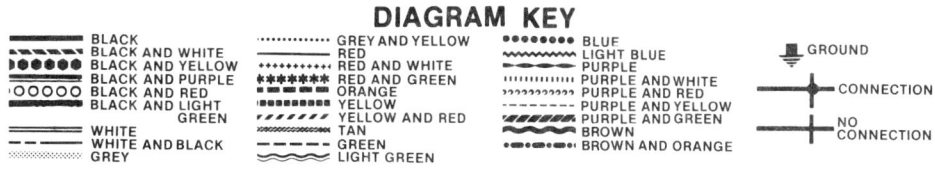

1964-1966 60 HP WITH GENERATOR

DIAGRAM KEY

▬▬	BLACK	········	GREY AND YELLOW	●●●●●●	BLUE	⏚	GROUND
▬▬	BLACK AND WHITE	∼∼∼∼	RED	────	LIGHT BLUE	─┼─	CONNECTION
●●●●●	BLACK AND YELLOW	++++++	RED AND WHITE	─‖─‖─	PURPLE	─┴─	NO CONNECTION
◆◆◆◆	BLACK AND PURPLE	✱✱✱✱	RED AND GREEN	⁞⁞⁞⁞	PURPLE AND WHITE		
○○○○○	BLACK AND RED	▬▬▬	ORANGE	»»»»»	PURPLE AND RED		
▬▬▬	BLACK AND LIGHT GREEN	═══	YELLOW	─ ─ ─	PURPLE AND YELLOW		
────	WHITE	✕✕✕✕	YELLOW AND RED	═══	PURPLE AND GREEN		
··········	WHITE AND BLACK	── ──	TAN	∼∼∼∼	BROWN		
········	GREY	─ ─ ─	GREEN	●─●─●	BROWN AND ORANGE		
		▬ ▬ ▬	LIGHT GREEN				

361

13

WIRING DIAGRAMS

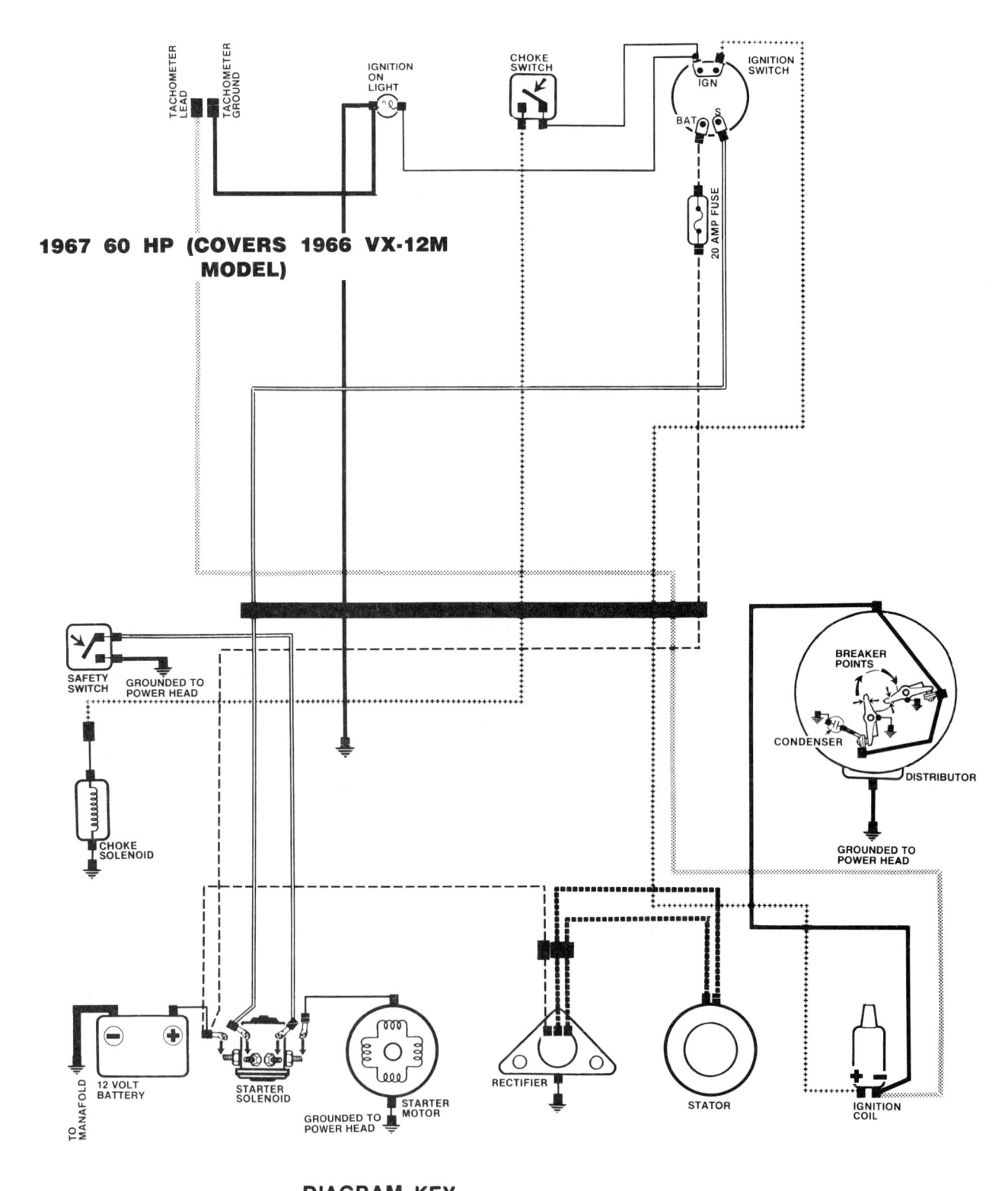

1967 60 HP (COVERS 1966 VX-12M MODEL)

DIAGRAM KEY

BLACK	GREY AND YELLOW	BLUE
BLACK AND WHITE	RED	LIGHT BLUE
BLACK AND YELLOW	RED AND WHITE	PURPLE
BLACK AND PURPLE	RED AND GREEN	PURPLE AND WHITE
BLACK AND RED	ORANGE	PURPLE AND RED
BLACK AND LIGHT GREEN	YELLOW	PURPLE AND YELLOW
WHITE	YELLOW AND RED	PURPLE AND GREEN
WHITE AND BLACK	TAN	BROWN
GREY	GREEN	BROWN AND ORANGE
	LIGHT GREEN	

GROUND
CONNECTION
NO CONNECTION

WIRING DIAGRAMS

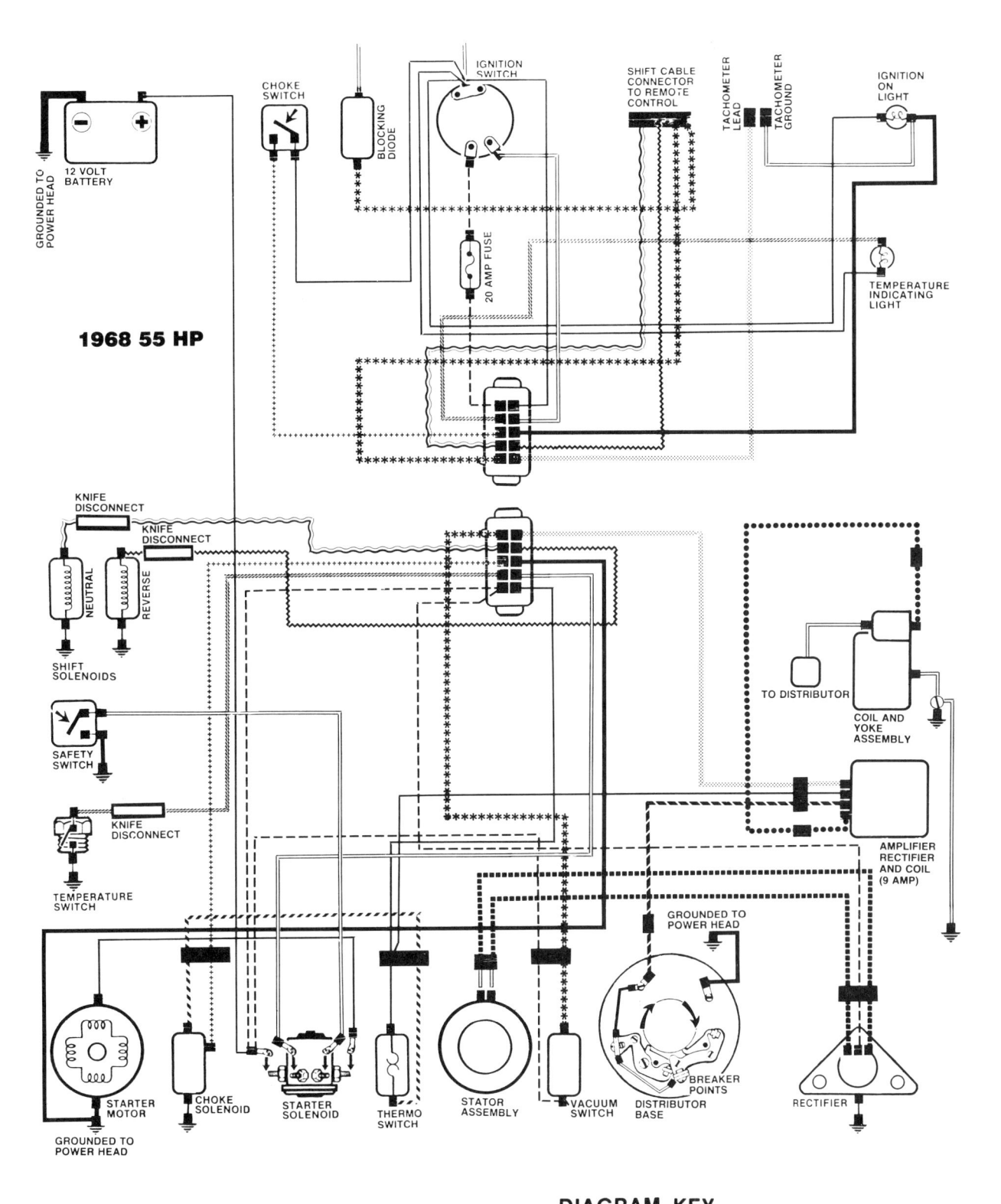

1968 55 HP

DIAGRAM KEY

- BLACK
- BLACK AND WHITE
- BLACK AND YELLOW
- BLACK AND PURPLE
- BLACK AND RED
- BLACK AND LIGHT GREEN
- WHITE
- WHITE AND BLACK
- GREY
- GREY AND YELLOW
- RED
- RED AND WHITE
- RED AND GREEN
- ORANGE
- YELLOW
- YELLOW AND RED
- TAN
- GREEN
- LIGHT GREEN
- BLUE
- LIGHT BLUE
- PURPLE
- PURPLE AND WHITE
- PURPLE AND YELLOW
- PURPLE AND RED
- PURPLE AND GREEN
- BROWN
- BROWN AND ORANGE
- GROUND
- CONNECTION
- NO CONNECTION

WIRING DIAGRAMS

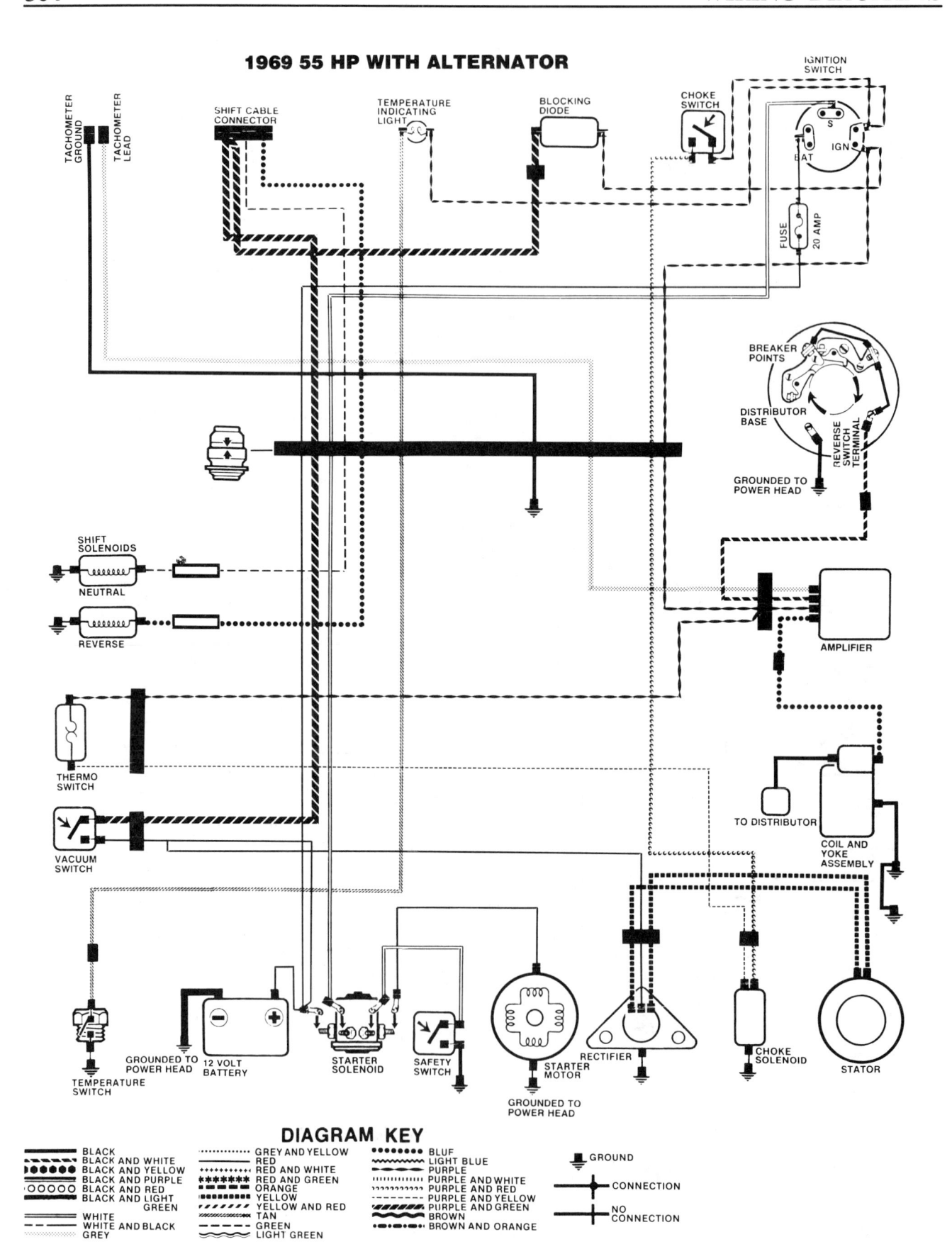

1969 55 HP WITH ALTERNATOR

DIAGRAM KEY

- BLACK
- BLACK AND WHITE
- BLACK AND YELLOW
- BLACK AND PURPLE
- BLACK AND RED
- BLACK AND LIGHT GREEN
- WHITE
- WHITE AND BLACK
- GREY
- GREY AND YELLOW
- RED
- RED AND WHITE
- RED AND GREEN
- ORANGE
- YELLOW
- YELLOW AND RED
- TAN
- GREEN
- LIGHT GREEN
- BLUE
- LIGHT BLUE
- PURPLE
- PURPLE AND WHITE
- PURPLE AND RED
- PURPLE AND YELLOW
- PURPLE AND GREEN
- BROWN
- BROWN AND ORANGE
- GROUND
- CONNECTION
- NO CONNECTION

Wiring Diagrams

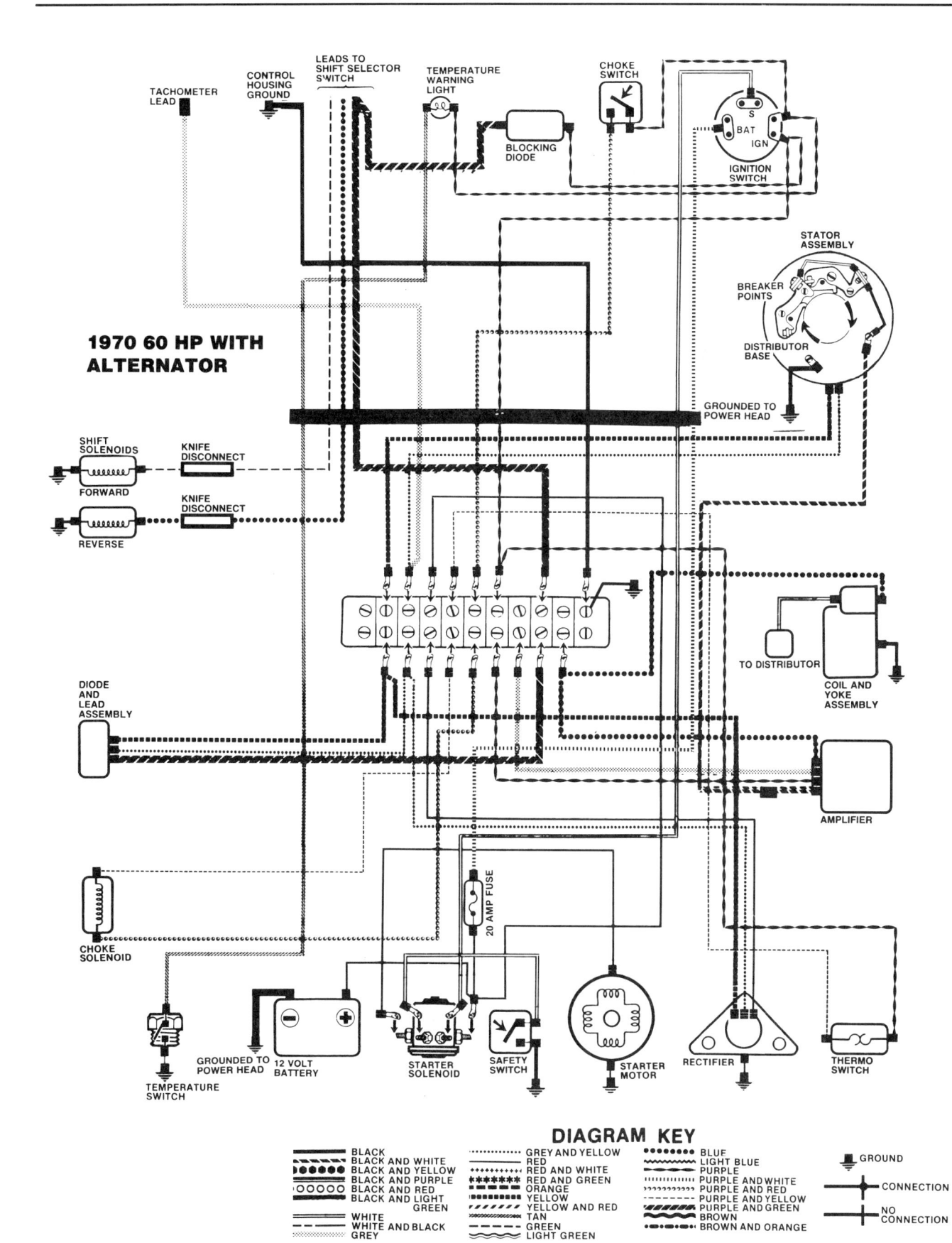

1970 60 HP WITH ALTERNATOR

WIRING DIAGRAMS

1971 60 HP WITH ALTERNATOR

DIAGRAM KEY

- ▬▬▬ BLACK
- ●▬●▬ BLACK AND WHITE
- ●●●●● BLACK AND YELLOW
- BLACK AND PURPLE
- ○○○○○ BLACK AND RED
- BLACK AND LIGHT GREEN
- ▬▬▬ WHITE
- ▬ ▬ ▬ WHITE AND BLACK
- ▓▓▓▓ GREY
- ⋯⋯⋯ GREY AND YELLOW
- ▬▬▬ RED
- ▬+▬+▬ RED AND WHITE
- ✱✱✱✱ RED AND GREEN
- ▬▬▬ ORANGE
- ■■■■ YELLOW
- ▬✕▬✕ YELLOW AND RED
- ─ ─ ─ GREEN
- ░░░░ LIGHT GREEN
- •••••• BLUE
- ∼∼∼ LIGHT BLUE
- ⌇⌇⌇ PURPLE
- ⋮⋮⋮ PURPLE AND WHITE
- ⌇⌇⌇ PURPLE AND RED
- ≈≈≈ PURPLE AND YELLOW
- ─·─·─ PURPLE AND GREEN
- ▬▬▬ BROWN
- ●▬●▬ BROWN AND ORANGE
- ⏚ GROUND
- ┼ CONNECTION
- ─│─ NO CONNECTION

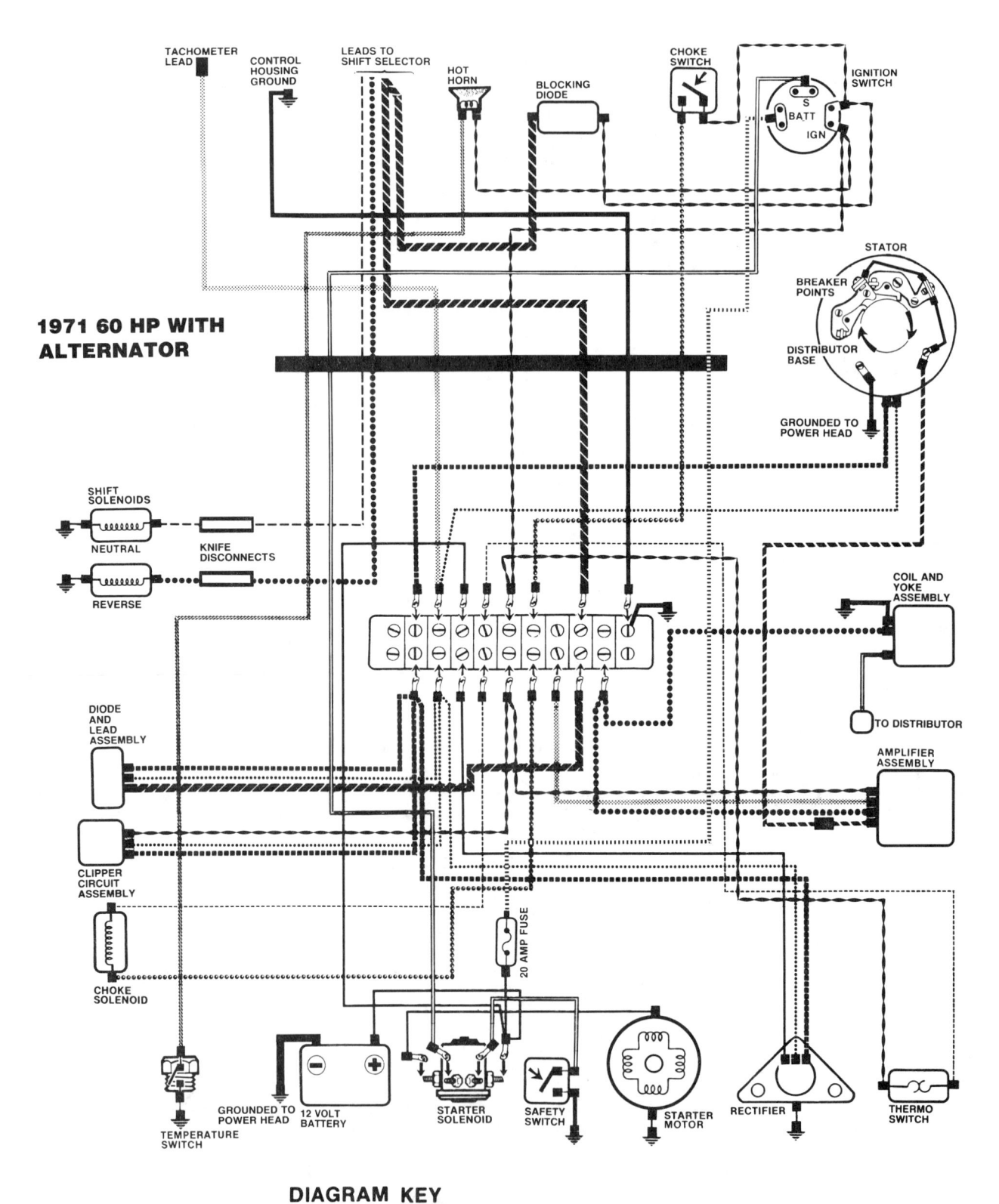

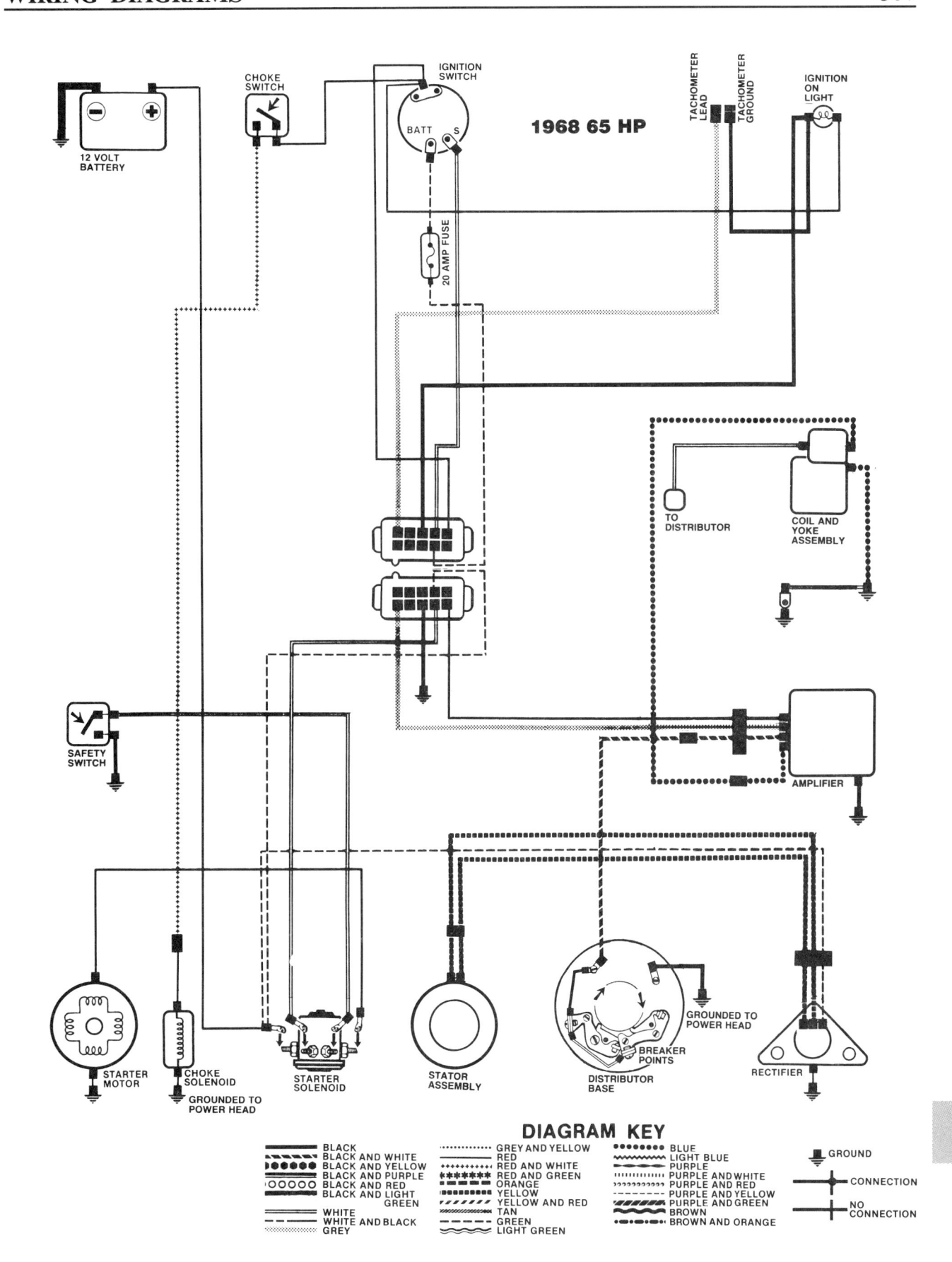

WIRING DIAGRAMS

1968 65 HP

WIRING DIAGRAMS

1972 65 HP WITH ALTERNATOR
1960 75 HP

DIAGRAM KEY

- BLACK
- BLACK AND WHITE
- BLACK AND YELLOW
- BLACK AND PURPLE
- BLACK AND RED
- BLACK AND LIGHT GREEN
- WHITE
- WHITE AND BLACK
- GREY
- GREY AND YELLOW
- RED
- RED AND WHITE
- RED AND GREEN
- ORANGE
- YELLOW
- YELLOW AND RED
- TAN
- GREEN
- LIGHT GREEN
- BLUE
- LIGHT BLUE
- PURPLE
- PURPLE AND WHITE
- PURPLE AND RED
- PURPLE AND YELLOW
- PURPLE AND GREEN
- BROWN
- BROWN AND ORANGE
- GROUND
- CONNECTION
- NO CONNECTION

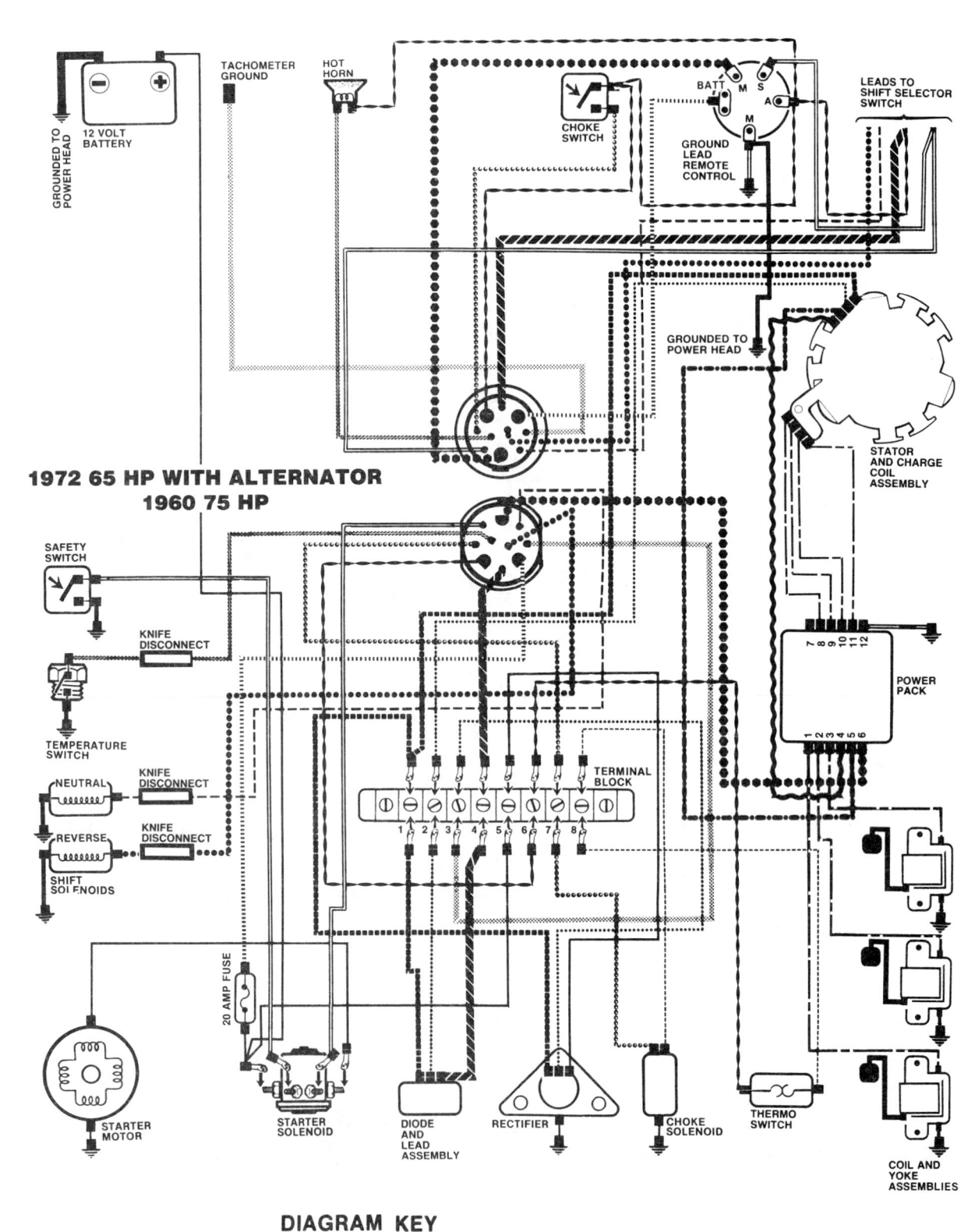

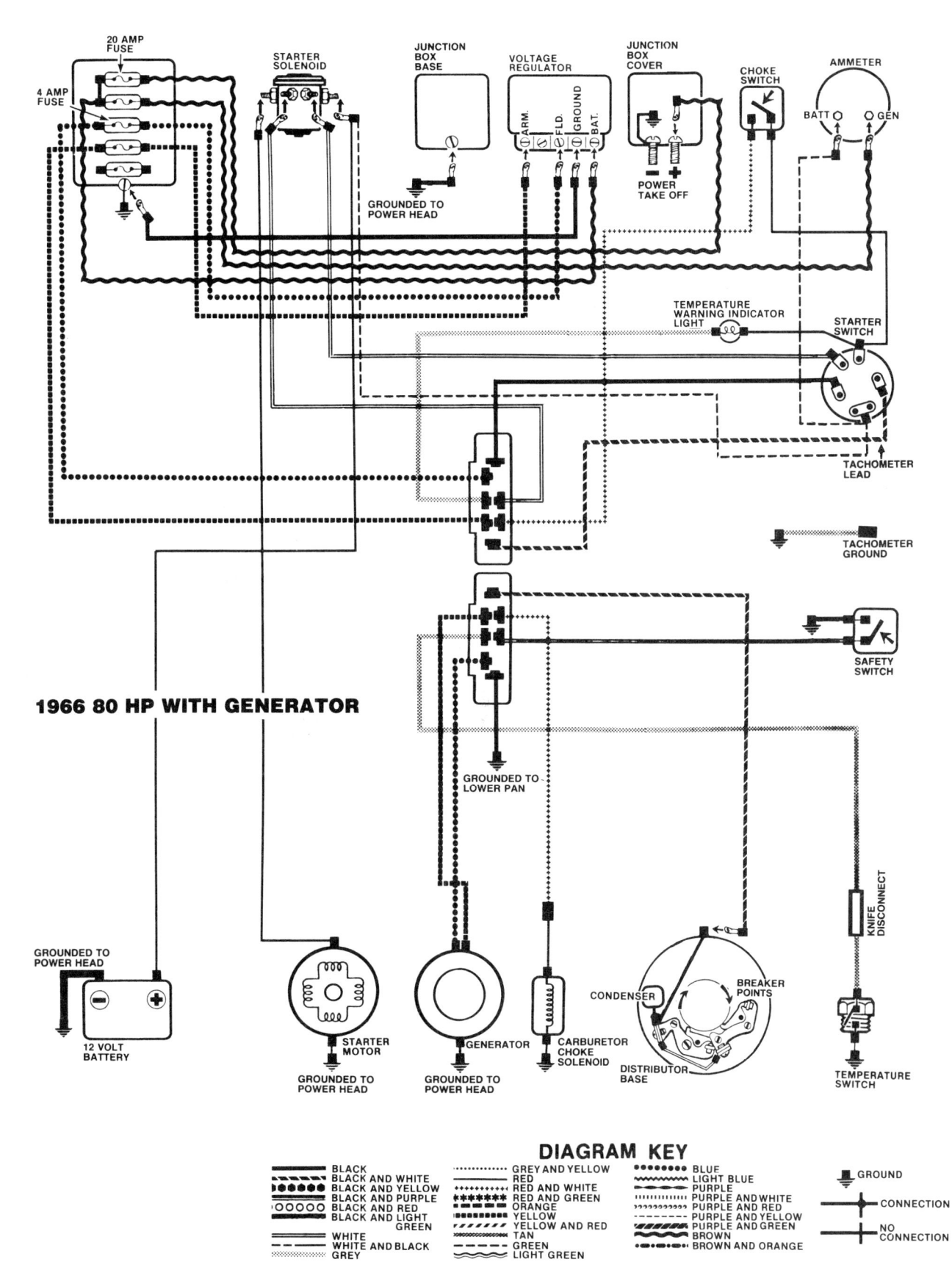

WIRING DIAGRAMS

1966 80 HP WITH GENERATOR

DIAGRAM KEY

- BLACK
- BLACK AND WHITE
- BLACK AND YELLOW
- BLACK AND PURPLE
- BLACK AND RED
- BLACK AND LIGHT GREEN
- WHITE
- WHITE AND BLACK
- GREY
- GREY AND YELLOW
- RED
- RED AND WHITE
- RED AND GREEN
- ORANGE
- YELLOW
- YELLOW AND RED
- TAN
- GREEN
- LIGHT GREEN
- BLUE
- LIGHT BLUE
- PURPLE
- PURPLE AND WHITE
- PURPLE AND RED
- PURPLE AND YELLOW
- PURPLE AND GREEN
- BROWN
- BROWN AND ORANGE
- GROUND
- CONNECTION
- NO CONNECTION

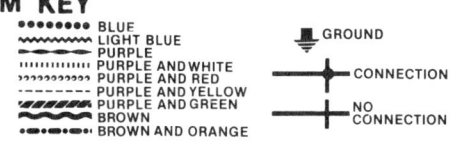

WIRING DIAGRAMS

1966 80 HP & 100 HP ELECTRIC SHIFT

DIAGRAM KEY

- BLACK
- BLACK AND WHITE
- BLACK AND YELLOW
- BLACK AND PURPLE
- BLACK AND RED
- BLACK AND LIGHT GREEN
- WHITE
- WHITE AND BLACK
- GREY
- GREY AND YELLOW
- RED
- RED AND WHITE
- RED AND GREEN
- ORANGE
- YELLOW
- YELLOW AND RED
- TAN
- GREEN
- LIGHT GREEN
- BLUE
- LIGHT BLUE
- PURPLE
- PURPLE AND WHITE
- PURPLE AND RED
- PURPLE AND YELLOW
- PURPLE AND GREEN
- BROWN
- BROWN AND ORANGE
- GROUND
- CONNECTION
- NO CONNECTION

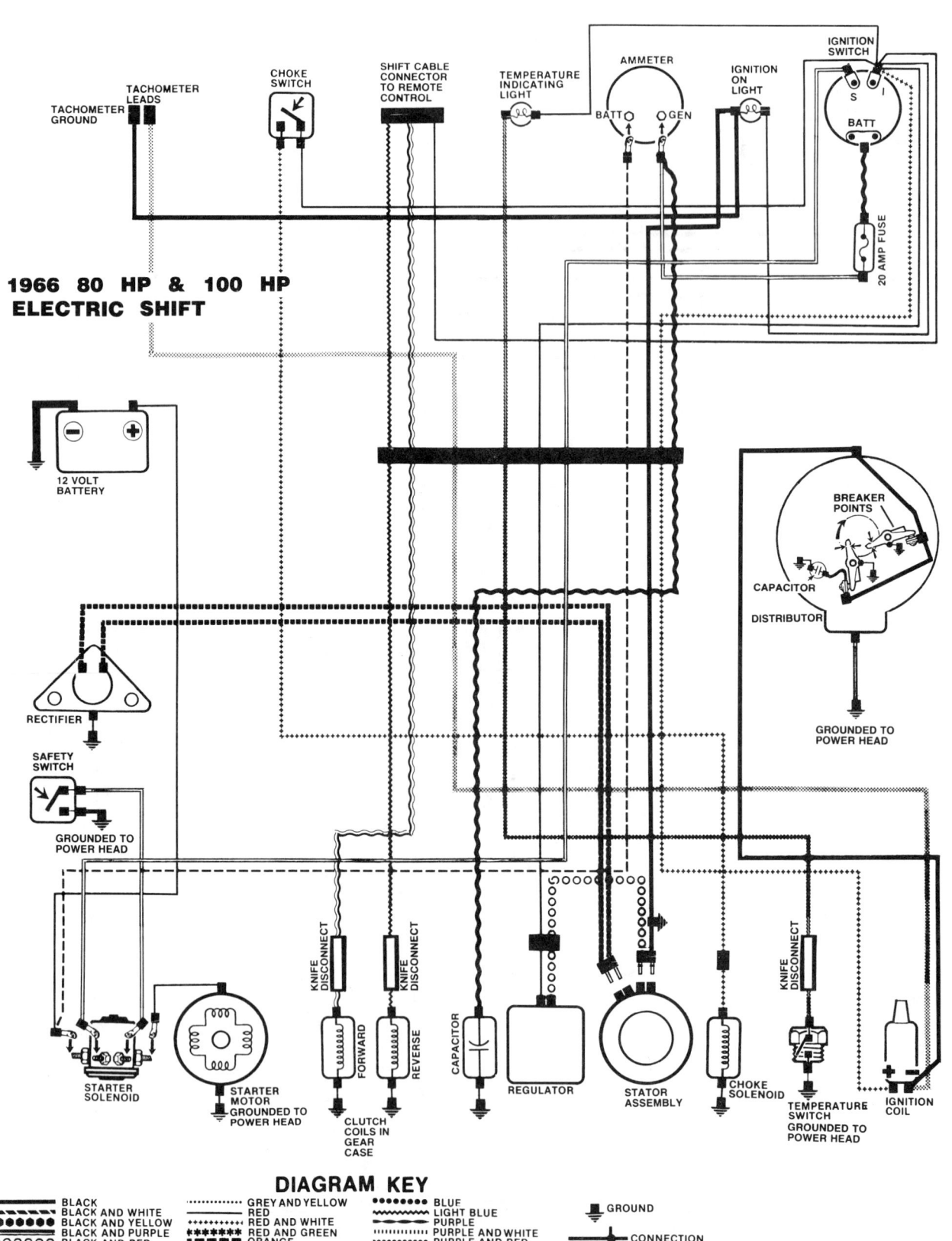

WIRING DIAGRAMS

1967 80 HP

DIAGRAM KEY

- ▬▬▬ BLACK
- ●●●● BLACK AND WHITE
- ◉◉◉◉ BLACK AND YELLOW
- ✱✱✱✱ BLACK AND PURPLE
- ○○○○ BLACK AND RED
- ━ ━ ━ BLACK AND LIGHT GREEN
- ═══ WHITE
- ─── WHITE AND BLACK
- ▓▓▓ GREY
- ⋯⋯⋯ GREY AND YELLOW
- ─── RED
- ✚✚✚ RED AND WHITE
- ✺✺✺✺ RED AND GREEN
- ▬▬▬ ORANGE
- ▬▬▬ YELLOW
- ⁄⁄⁄⁄ YELLOW AND RED
- ─ ─ ─ TAN
- ─── GREEN
- ∼∼∼ LIGHT GREEN
- ●●●●● BLUE
- ∼∼∼ LIGHT BLUE
- ─── PURPLE
- ⟩⟩⟩⟩ PURPLE AND WHITE
- ⟩⟩⟩⟩ PURPLE AND RED
- ⟩⟩⟩⟩ PURPLE AND YELLOW
- ∼∼∼ PURPLE AND GREEN
- ∼∼∼ BROWN
- ─•─• BROWN AND ORANGE
- ⏚ GROUND
- ✛ CONNECTION
- ✢ NO CONNECTION

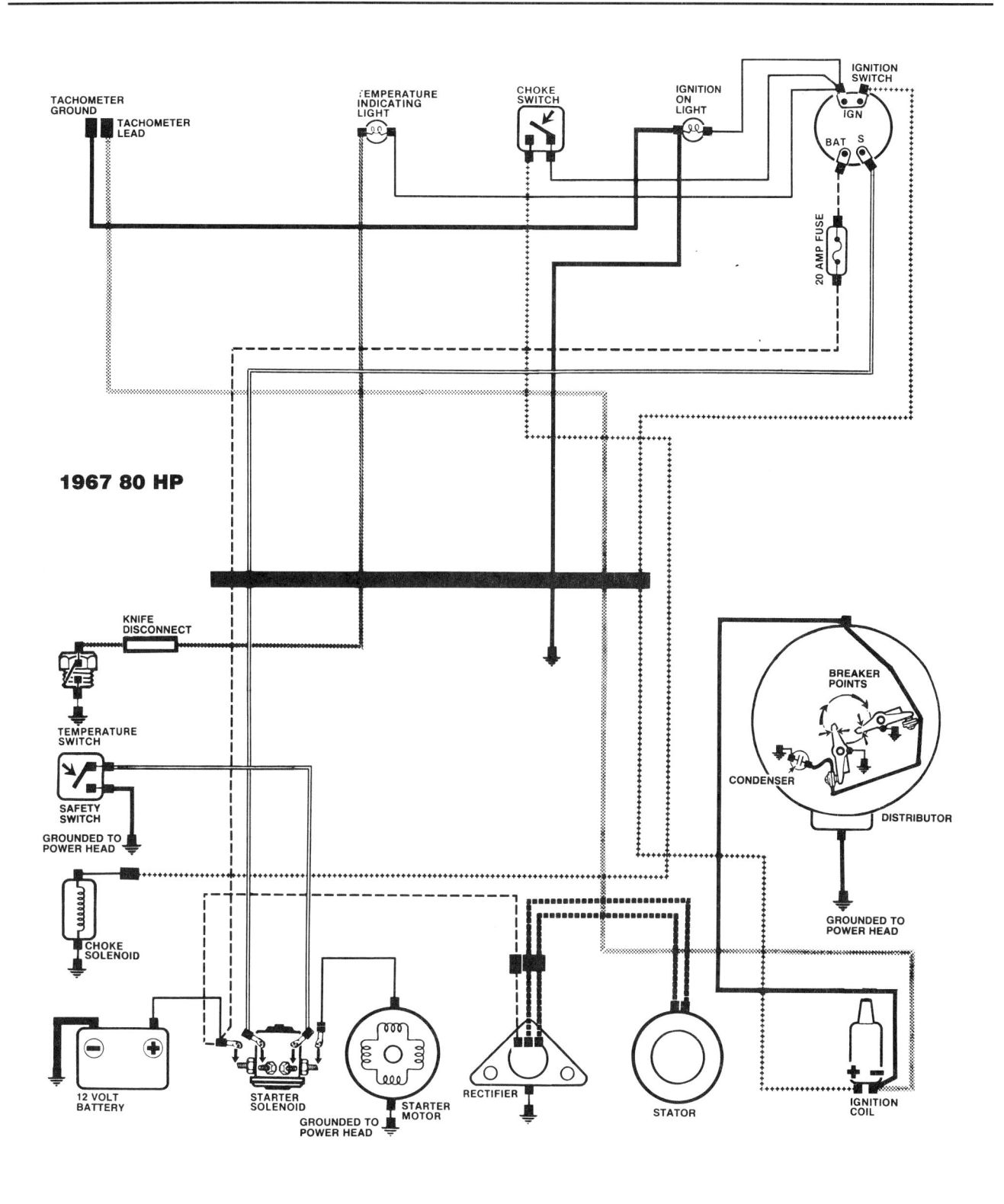

13

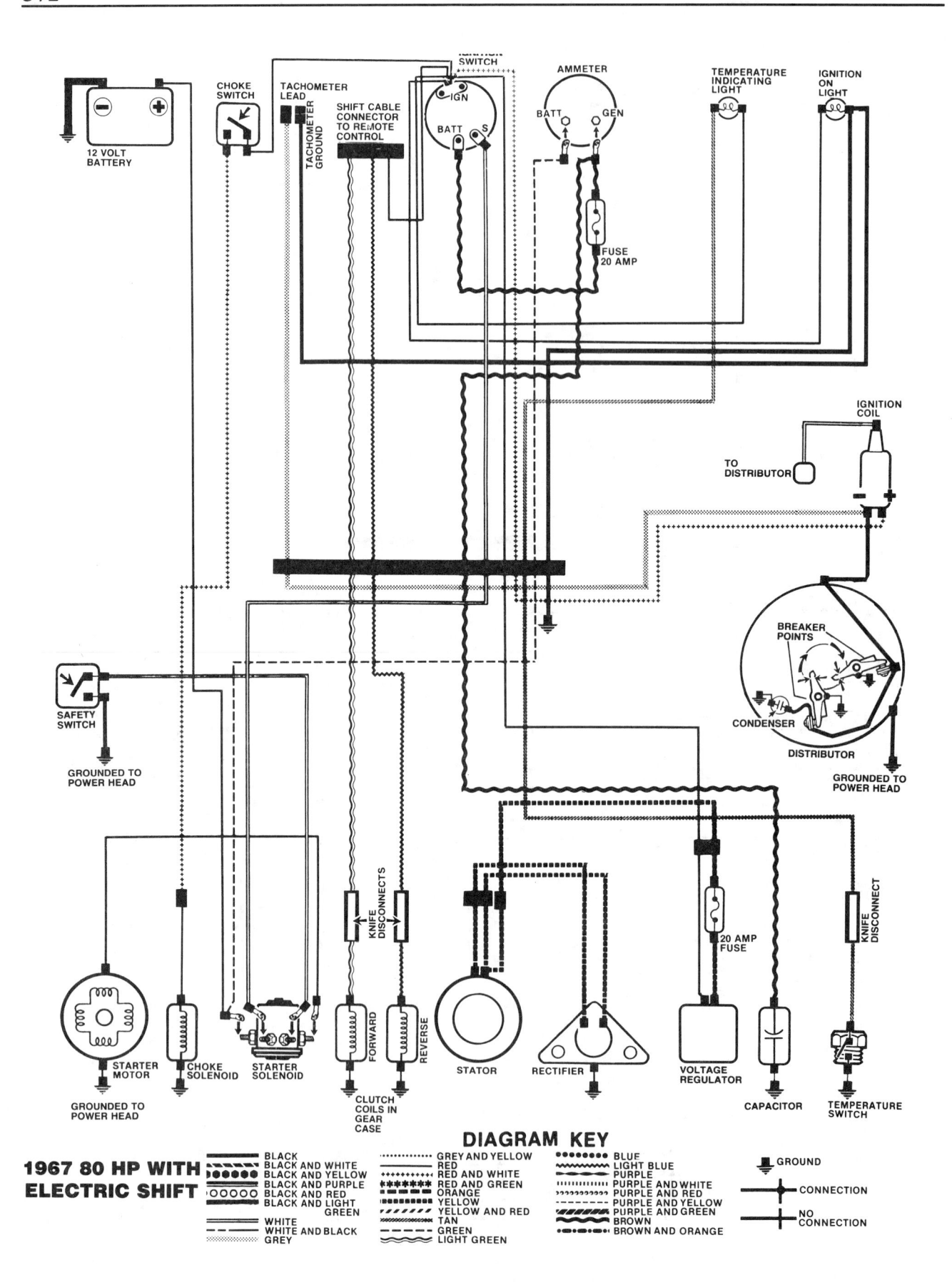

WIRING DIAGRAMS

1967 80 HP WITH ELECTRIC SHIFT

Wiring Diagrams

373

1968 85 HP

DIAGRAM KEY

- BLACK
- BLACK AND WHITE
- BLACK AND YELLOW
- BLACK AND PURPLE
- BLACK AND RED
- BLACK AND LIGHT GREEN
- WHITE
- WHITE AND BLACK
- GREY
- GREY AND YELLOW
- RED
- RED AND WHITE
- RED AND GREEN
- ORANGE
- YELLOW
- YELLOW AND RED
- TAN
- GREEN
- LIGHT GREEN
- BLUE
- LIGHT BLUE
- PURPLE
- PURPLE AND WHITE
- PURPLE AND RED
- PURPLE AND YELLOW
- PURPLE AND GREEN
- BROWN
- BROWN AND ORANGE
- GROUND
- CONNECTION
- NO CONNECTION

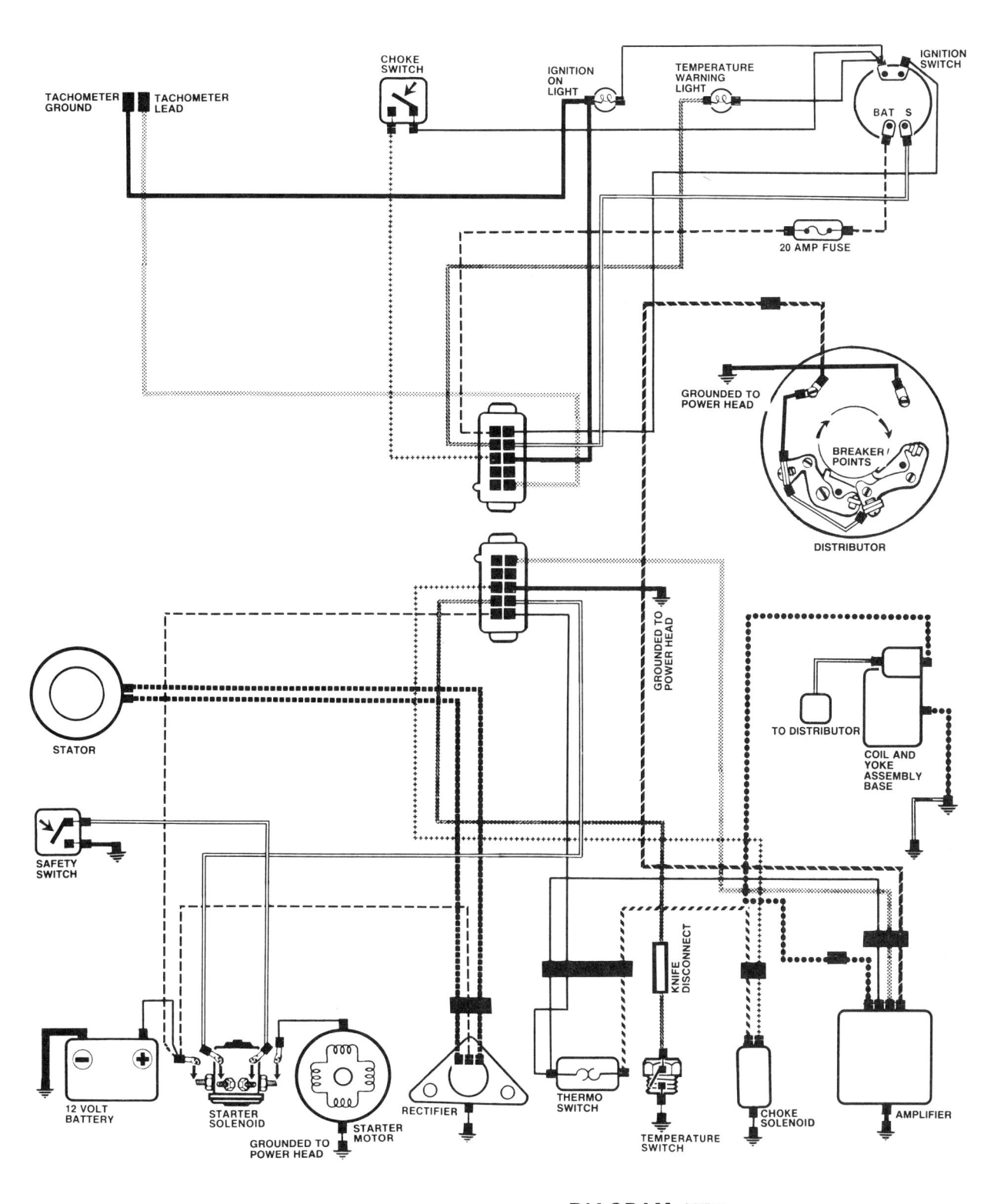

13

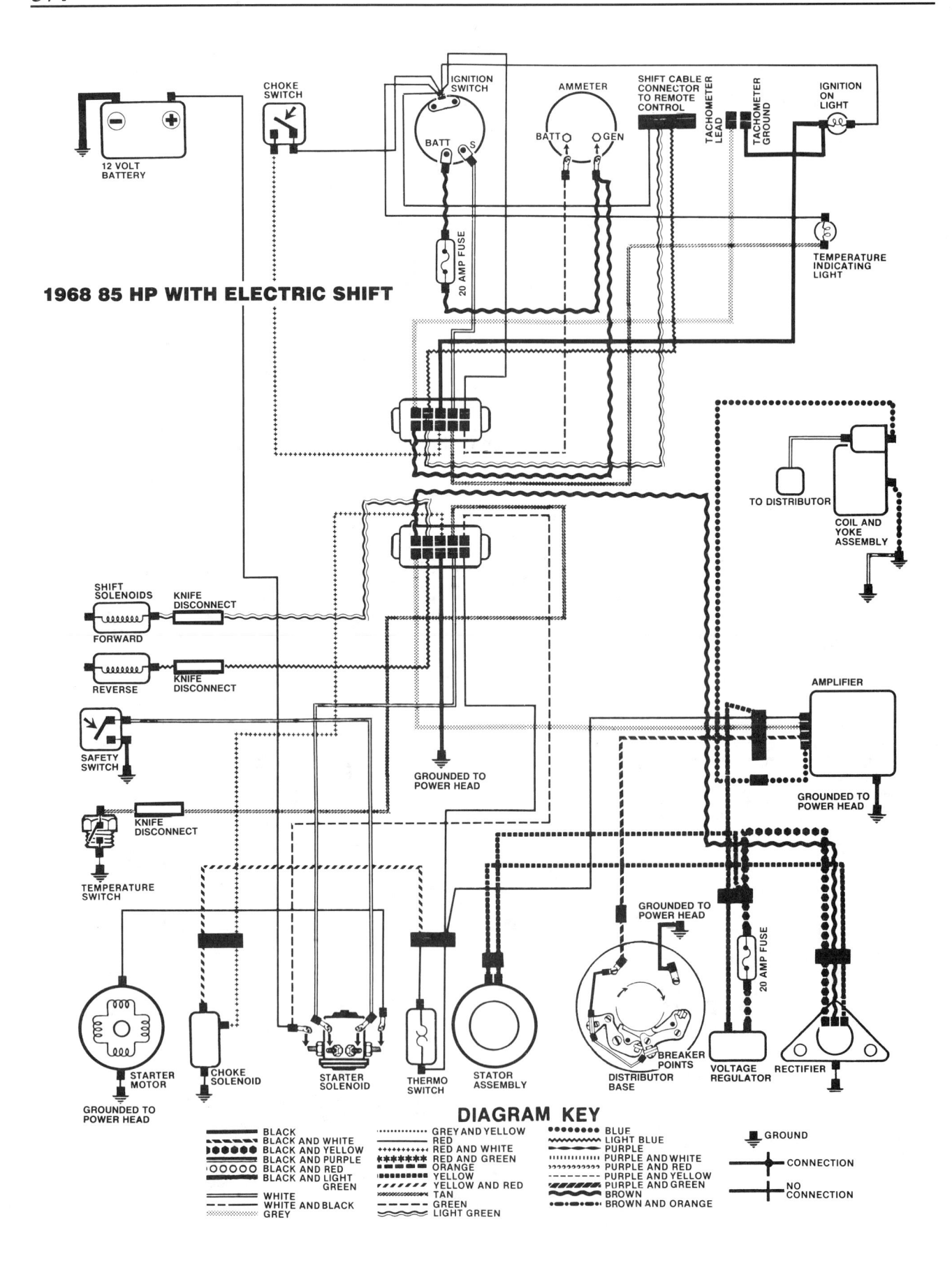

WIRING DIAGRAMS

1968 85 HP WITH ELECTRIC SHIFT

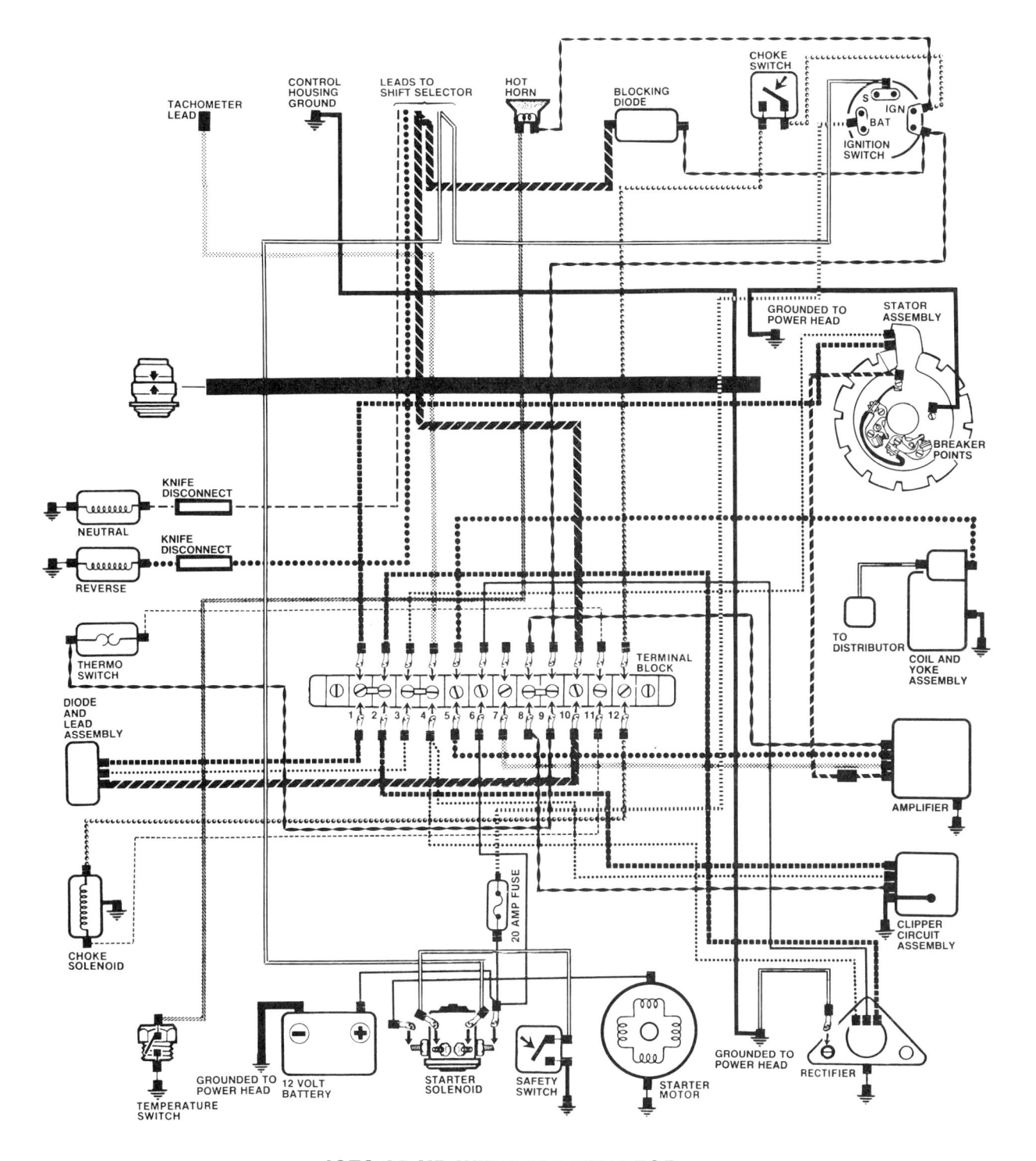

WIRING DIAGRAMS

1972 85 HP WITH ALTERNATOR

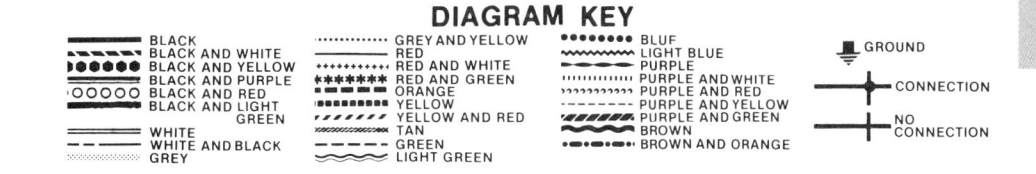

WIRING DIAGRAMS

1969-1970 85 HP WITH ALTERNATOR

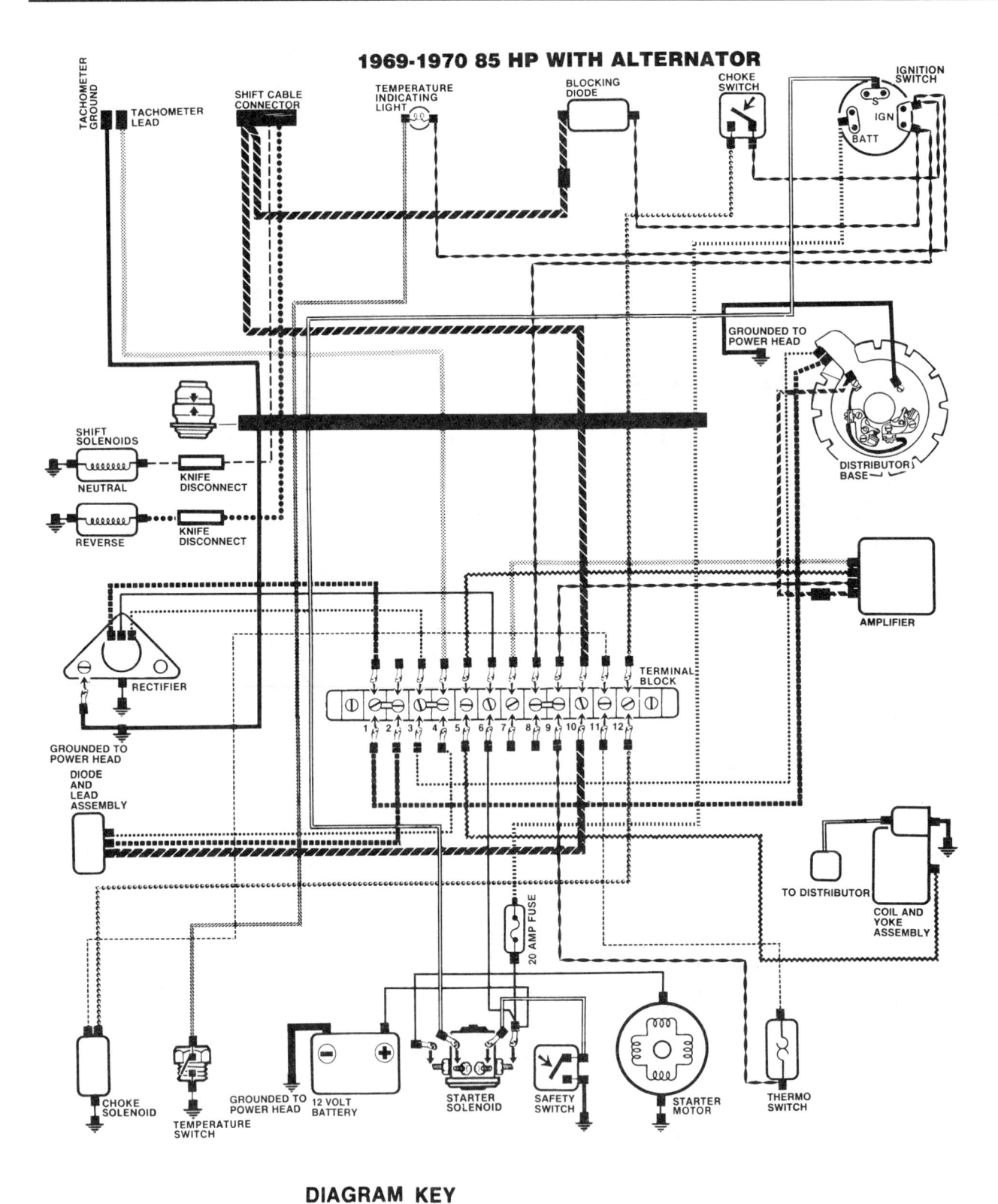

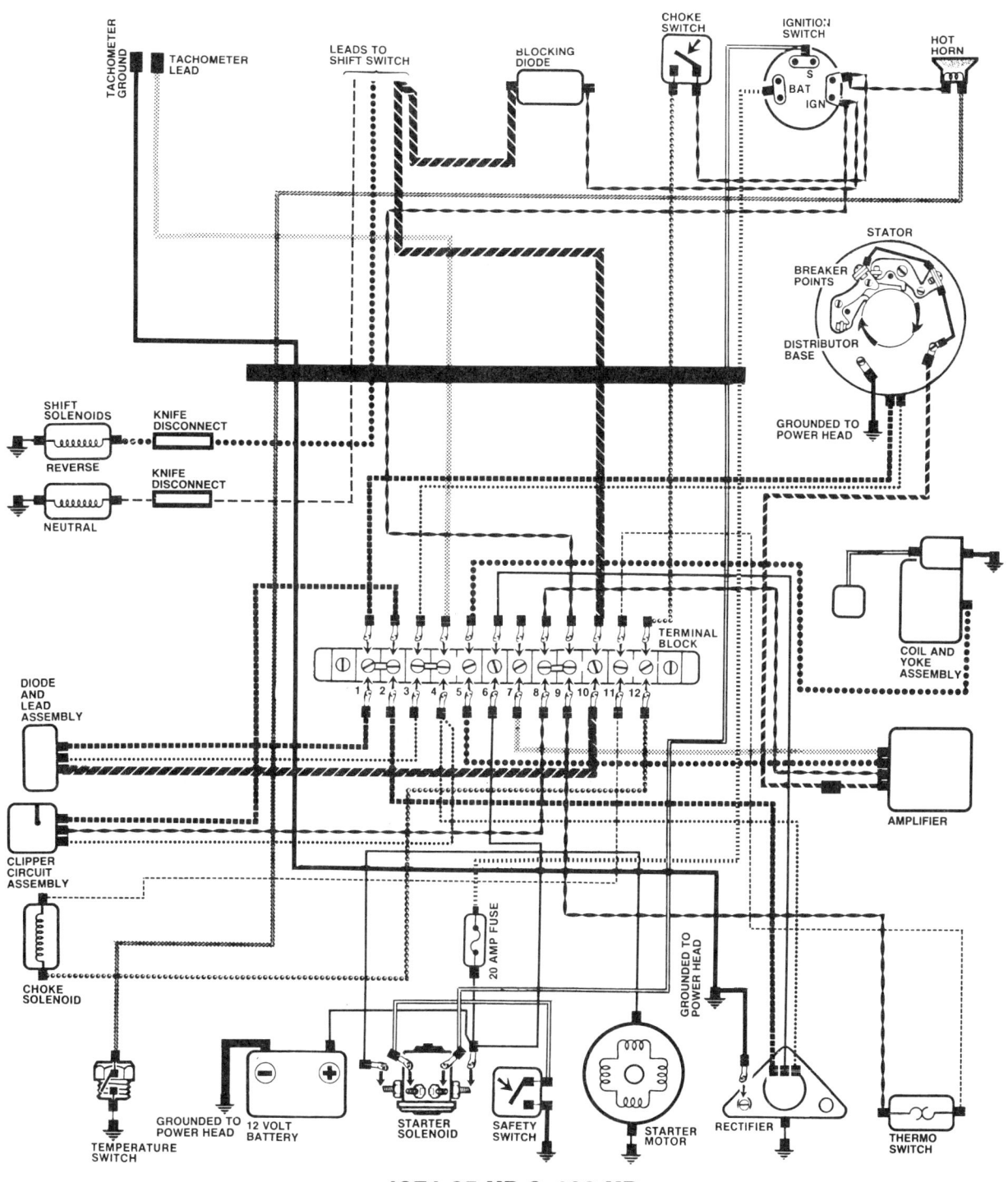

WIRING DIAGRAMS

1971 85 HP & 100 HP WITH ALTERNATOR

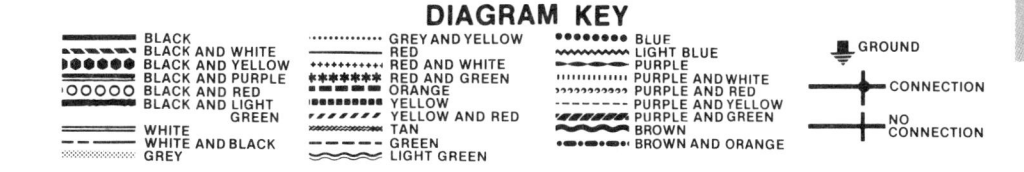

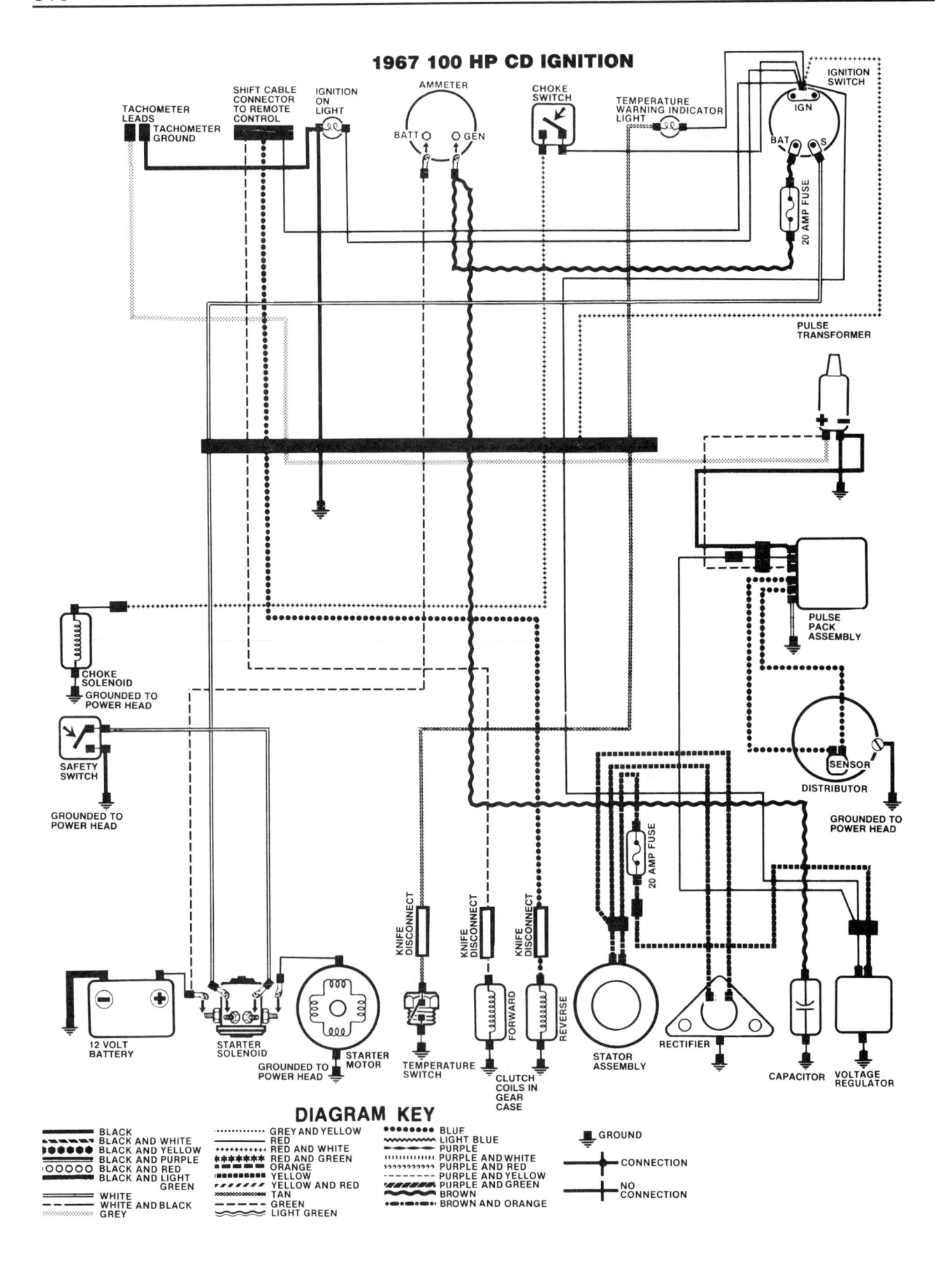

WIRING DIAGRAMS

1967 100 HP CD IGNITION

WIRING DIAGRAMS

1968 100 HP CD IGNITION

DIAGRAM KEY

▬▬▬	BLACK	········	GREY AND YELLOW	●●●●●●	BLUE	⏚	GROUND
▬ ▬ ▬	BLACK AND WHITE	────	RED	∿∿∿	LIGHT BLUE	┼	CONNECTION
●●●●●	BLACK AND YELLOW	++++++	RED AND WHITE	────	PURPLE	┼	NO CONNECTION
▬▬▬	BLACK AND PURPLE	∷∷∷∷	RED AND GREEN	∥∥∥∥	PURPLE AND WHITE		
ooooo	BLACK AND RED	✱✱✱✱	ORANGE	»»»»	PURPLE AND RED		
▬▬▬	BLACK AND LIGHT GREEN	────	YELLOW	────	PURPLE AND YELLOW		
		∼∼∼	YELLOW AND RED	≋≋≋	PURPLE AND GREEN		
────	WHITE	────	TAN	●●●●●	BROWN		
─ ─ ─	WHITE AND BLACK	────	GREEN	▬●▬●▬	BROWN AND ORANGE		
░░░░	GREY	────	LIGHT GREEN				

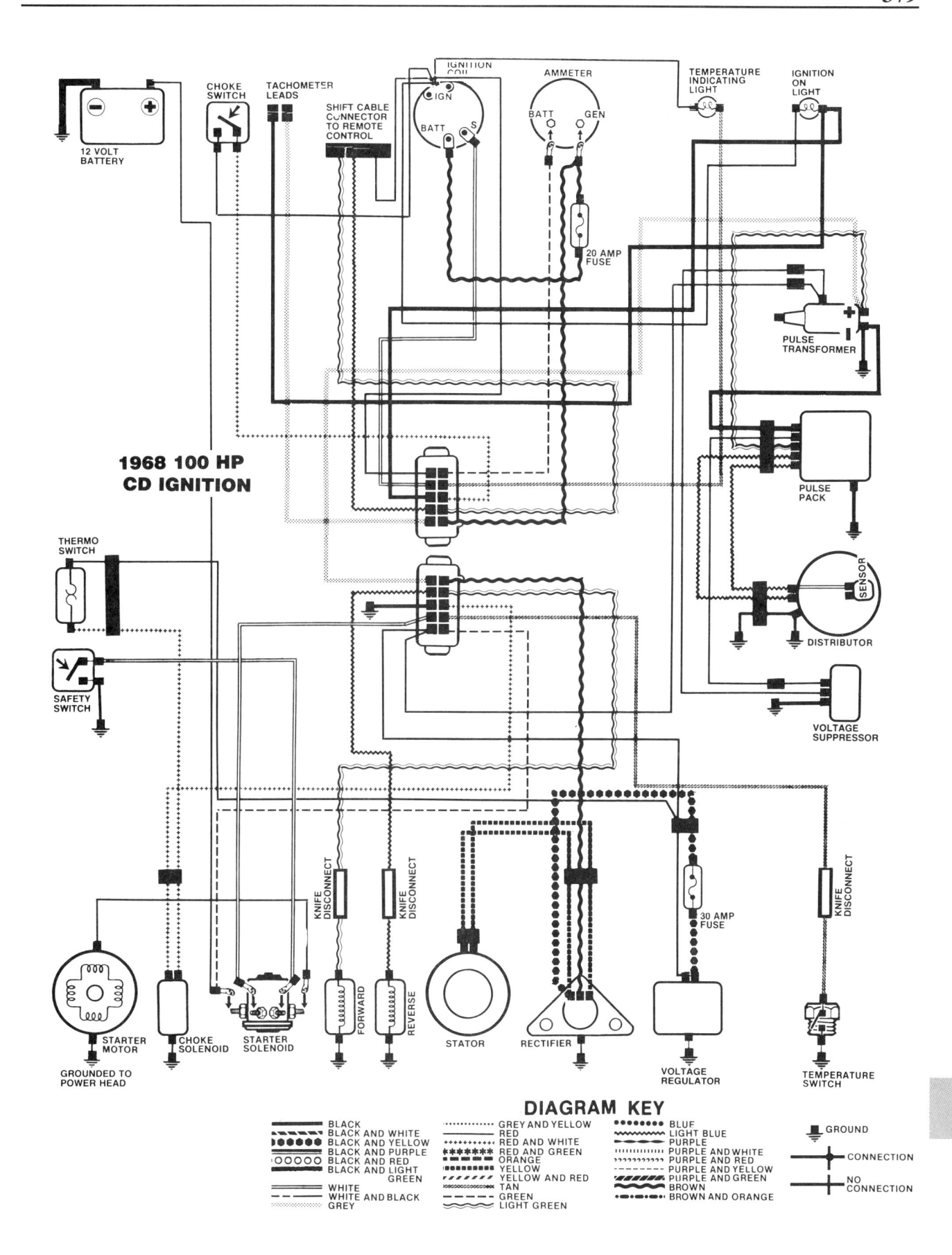

WIRING DIAGRAMS

1969-1970 115 HP WITH ALTERNATOR

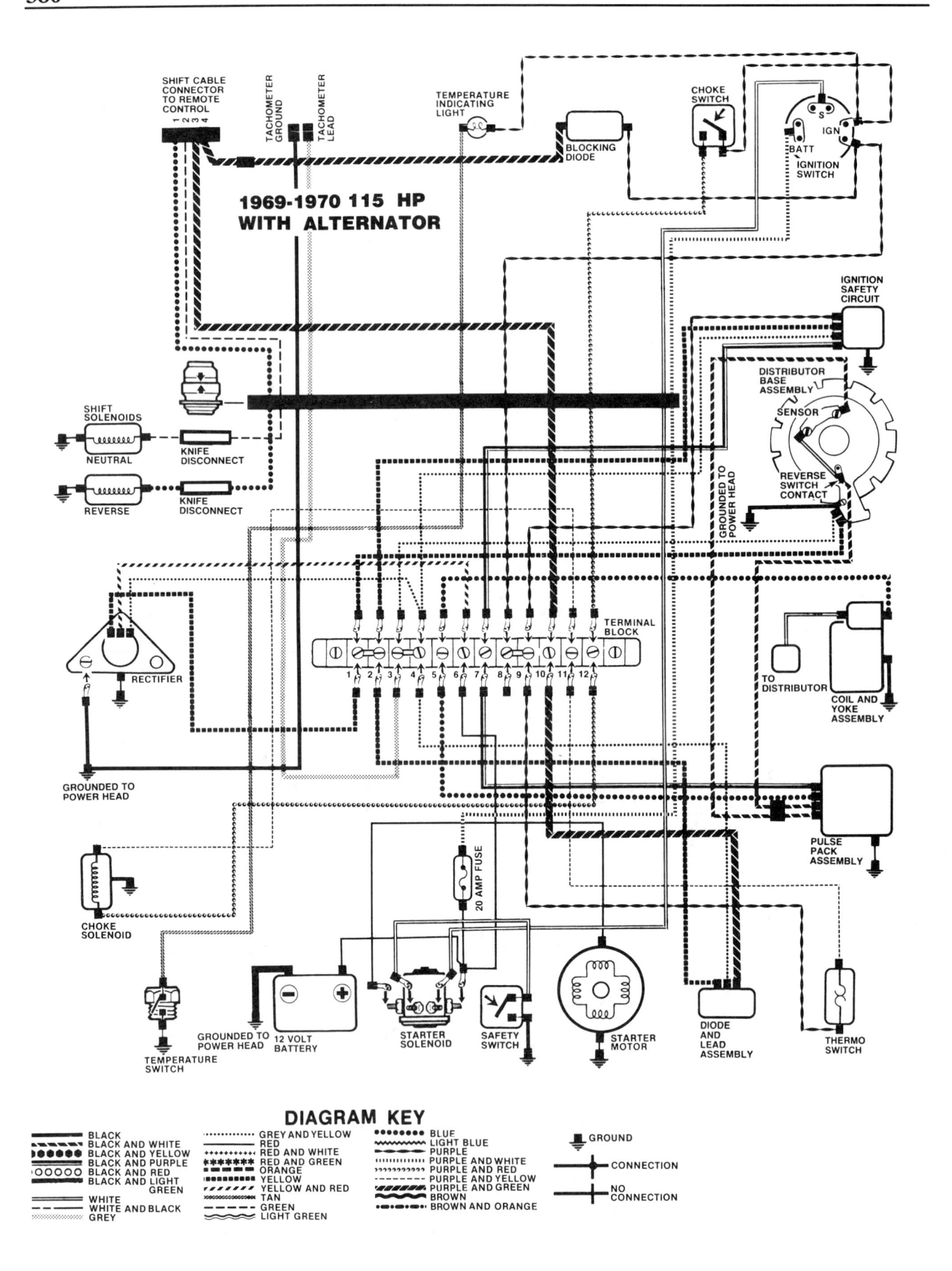

DIAGRAM KEY

- BLACK
- BLACK AND WHITE
- BLACK AND YELLOW
- BLACK AND PURPLE
- BLACK AND RED
- BLACK AND LIGHT GREEN
- WHITE
- WHITE AND BLACK
- GREY
- GREY AND YELLOW
- RED
- RED AND WHITE
- RED AND GREEN
- ORANGE
- YELLOW
- YELLOW AND RED
- TAN
- GREEN
- LIGHT GREEN
- BLUE
- LIGHT BLUE
- PURPLE
- PURPLE AND WHITE
- PURPLE AND RED
- PURPLE AND YELLOW
- PURPLE AND GREEN
- BROWN
- BROWN AND ORANGE
- GROUND
- CONNECTION
- NO CONNECTION

Components labeled:
SHIFT CABLE CONNECTOR TO REMOTE CONTROL, TACHOMETER GROUND, TACHOMETER LEAD, TEMPERATURE INDICATING LIGHT, BLOCKING DIODE, CHOKE SWITCH, IGNITION SWITCH (S, IGN, BATT), SHIFT SOLENOIDS (NEUTRAL, REVERSE), KNIFE DISCONNECT, IGNITION SAFETY CIRCUIT, DISTRIBUTOR BASE ASSEMBLY, SENSOR, REVERSE SWITCH CONTACT, GROUNDED TO POWER HEAD, RECTIFIER, TERMINAL BLOCK (1-12), TO DISTRIBUTOR, COIL AND YOKE ASSEMBLY, GROUNDED TO POWER HEAD, CHOKE SOLENOID, 20 AMP FUSE, TEMPERATURE SWITCH, GROUNDED TO POWER HEAD, 12 VOLT BATTERY, STARTER SOLENOID, SAFETY SWITCH, STARTER MOTOR, DIODE AND LEAD ASSEMBLY, PULSE PACK ASSEMBLY, THERMO SWITCH

WIRING DIAGRAMS

1971 125 HP WITH ALTERNATOR

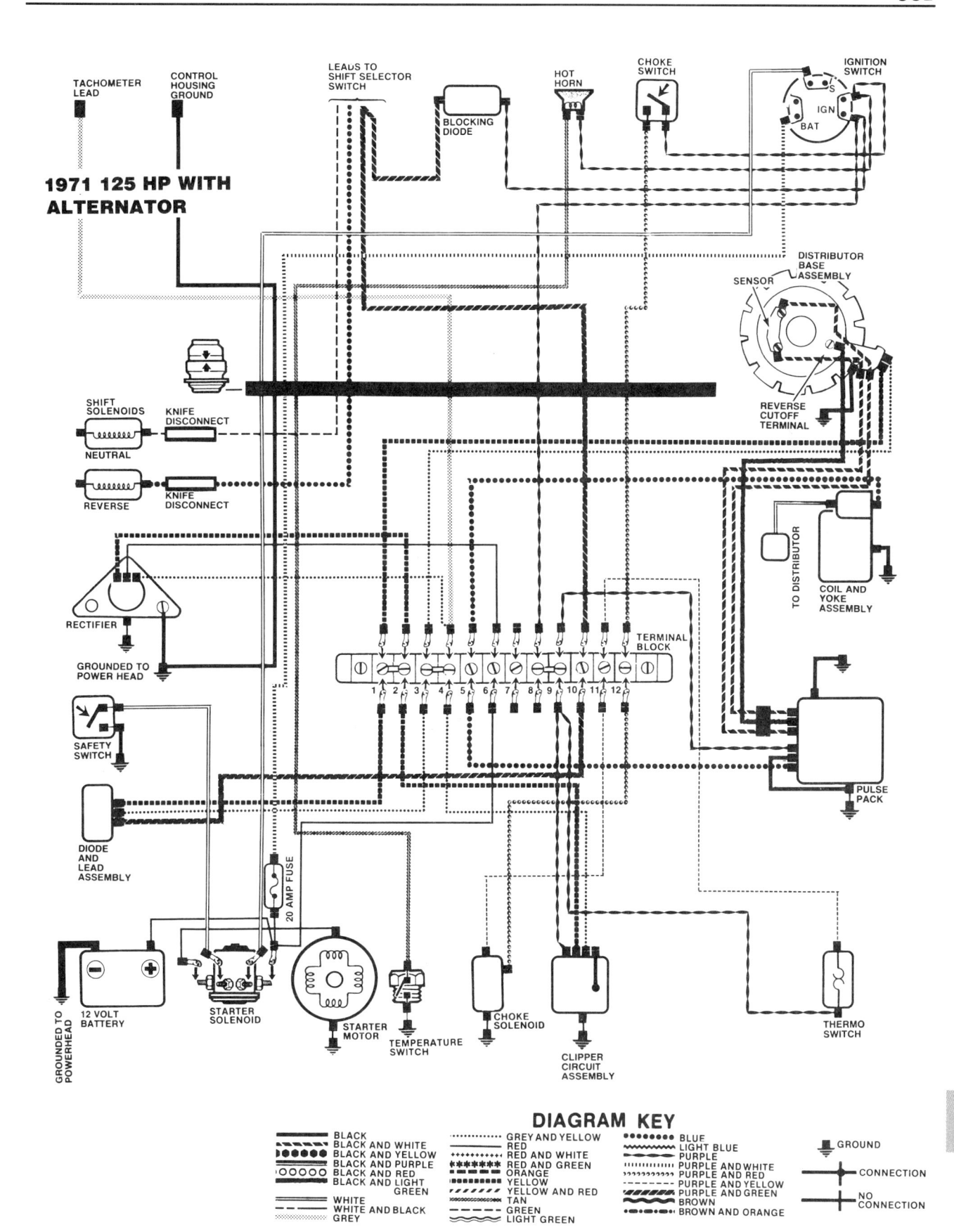

DIAGRAM KEY

BLACK	GREY AND YELLOW	BLUE
BLACK AND WHITE	RED	LIGHT BLUE
BLACK AND YELLOW	RED AND WHITE	PURPLE
BLACK AND PURPLE	RED AND GREEN	PURPLE AND WHITE
BLACK AND RED	ORANGE	PURPLE AND RED
BLACK AND LIGHT GREEN	YELLOW	PURPLE AND YELLOW
WHITE	YELLOW AND RED	PURPLE AND GREEN
WHITE AND BLACK	TAN	BROWN
GREY	GREEN	BROWN AND ORANGE
	LIGHT GREEN	

- GROUND
- CONNECTION
- NO CONNECTION

13

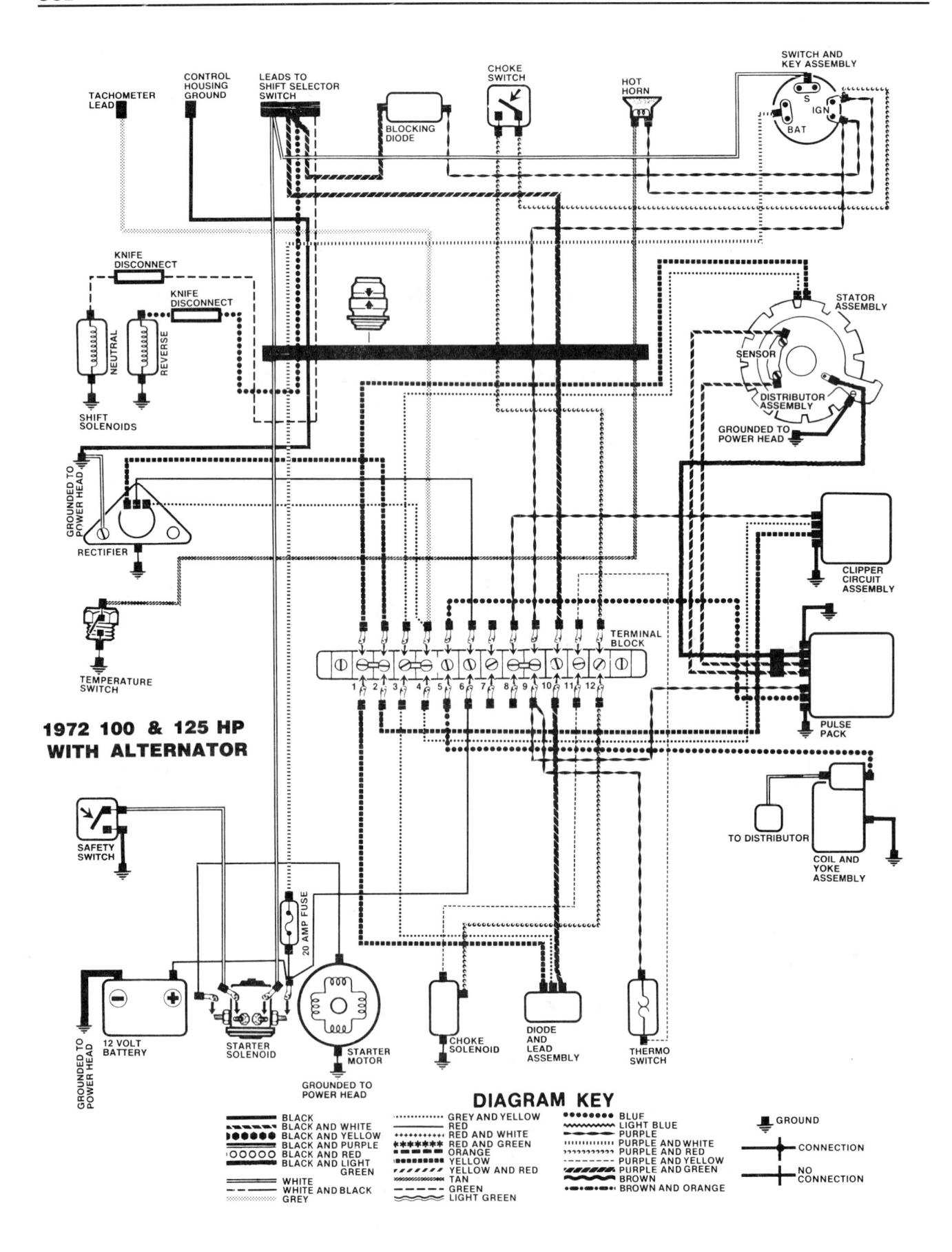

NOTES

MAINTENANCE LOG

Date	Maintenance performed	Engine hours